THE WANING OF THE WEST:
AN INCONVENIENT TRUISM
The Political Philosophy of a Conscientious Dissenter

PETER J. SANDYS

Copyright © 2019 Peter J. Sandys.

All rights reserved. No part of this book may be used or reproduced by any means, graphic, electronic, or mechanical, including photocopying, recording, taping or by any information storage retrieval system without the written permission of the author except in the case of brief quotations embodied in critical articles and reviews.

This book is a work of non-fiction. Unless otherwise noted, the author and the publisher make no explicit guarantees as to the accuracy of the information contained in this book and in some cases, names of people and places have been altered to protect their privacy.

Archway Publishing books may be ordered through booksellers or by contacting:

Archway Publishing
1663 Liberty Drive
Bloomington, IN 47403
www.archwaypublishing.com
1 (888) 242-5904

Because of the dynamic nature of the Internet, any web addresses or links contained in this book may have changed since publication and may no longer be valid. The views expressed in this work are solely those of the author and do not necessarily reflect the views of the publisher, and the publisher hereby disclaims any responsibility for them.

Any people depicted in stock imagery provided by Getty Images are models, and such images are being used for illustrative purposes only.
Certain stock imagery © Getty Images.

ISBN: 978-1-4808-7443-5 (sc)
ISBN: 978-1-4808-7444-2 (e)

Library of Congress Control Number: 2019901379

Print information available on the last page.

Archway Publishing rev. date: 2/11/2019

Nothing lifts up more than humility; nothing repels more than arrogance.

The truth only hampers compromising, but
compromising always conceals the truth.

To Emily and Eva

Contents

Preface XIX

1. The Screenplay of the Velvet Revolution 1
   Why Are the Perpetrators Still among Us? 2
   The Moral Dilemma: The Price of the Peaceful Political Transition 4

2. The Western Political Realignment 9
   The West's Move to the Left 10
   The New American Reality: Hesitation and Loss of Purpose 11
   Israel's Role in the Reshaping the World: The American–
   Israeli Alliance 13
   The EUtopian Dream 14
   The Specter of Separatism and Disintegration Haunting Europe 18
   The Homogenization of the Totalitarian Liberal Democracies 21
   The Changing Western Intervention Concepts 23

3. European Federalism under German Leadership 30
   The Ever-Present German Question 31
   Binding Germany to Europe: The German Perspective 32
   Europe's Economic Crisis: A New Aspect of the German Problem 33
   The Future Is Fraught with German Political Alternatives 35
   German Leadership: Loss of National Sovereignty, Subjugation to
   the Supranational State 37
   The German Destiny in European Affairs 42

4. Russia's Newly Found Old Identity 45
- Russian National Identity 45
- The Effect of Foreign Elements on the Russian and Soviet Empires 46
- The Bolshevik Retardation of Russian Society 48
- When Did the Soviet Union Truly Disappear? 50
- 1993–99: A Democratic Nightmare 51
- Continuing Down the Once Lost Russian Liberal-Conservative Road .. 53
- The Distortion of Culture and the Russian Conservative Mind 56
- The Fear of the Russian Alternative: The Antagonistic West 65

5. China Rising 71
- Building Socialism with Chinese Characteristics 72
- China's Hybrid Economy 75
- No Big Bang 77
- The Policy of the Central Government 78
- China Rising—America Resisting 79
- The Revisionist Danger 82
- Exploiting the Problem of Taiwan 84
- The Perils of Pluralism: Sugarcoated Threats 86
- The China–Russia Relationship: Not Allies Just Yet 90

6. Political Philosophy 96
- Ethical Foundations 97
- Methodological Issues 98
- Western Political Schools of Thought 100
- Desires and Aspirations 101
- On Difference and Equality 102
- Diversity or Uniformity 105
- The Search for Social Justice and the Rise of the Victim Intimidator ... 107
- Existentialism without Context 112
- The Left–Right Fallacy: A Totalitarian Tactic 114
- The Public Position: Within the Infinite Range of Possibilities 119

  Modern Western Nihilism 123
  False Freedom, Relativism, and Nihilism 126
  The Reformation: The Deformation of a Unifying Western
  Ideology, The Ideology of Revolutions 127

7. A CRITIQUE OF DEMOCRACY 130
  Definition of Democracy and the Democratic Problem 130
  Ethics and Representation 134
  The Applied History of Democracy 138
  Disaffection and Decontextualization 145
  Opinions, Majorities, and Other Inherent Defects 147
  Reproduction of Democracy: The Ultimate Trick 149
  The Election Scam: Voting for the Devil We Know 152
  Democracy Is Only a Single Component of Our Lives 156
  Political Parties: Campaign Financing 157
  Irrational Voters—Inefficient System 160
  Oppression by the Majority: Mob Rule 161
  Anxiety, Greed, Civic Indifference, and the Perils of
  Democratic Dictatorship 163
  Liberty (Freedom) vs. Equality (Democracy) 165
  Democratic Uniformity Leading to Totalitarianism 168
  Conclusion 169

8. A CRITIQUE OF MODERN LIBERALISM 173
  The Definition of Liberalism 175
  Modern Liberalism and the False Idea of Liberty 179
  The Age of Reason: The Birth of Philosophical Liberalism 183
  Rational Liberalism and the Death of Nations 189
  The American Liberal Left: Transformation from Classical
  Centrist to Modern (Leftist) Liberalism 195
  The Liberal Metamorphosis of the West: Transformation from
  Classical Liberalism to Liberal Conservatism 200

The Emergence of Neoliberalism 202
The Struggle of Classical Old-School Liberalism in
the Twentieth Century 204
Economic and Corrupted Neoliberalism 206
Neoliberal Class Project: Globalization.................................208
Opposing Neoliberalism.. 210
Liberal Democracy: The Sum of Hypocrisies........................ 211
Western Liberal Machinations around the World 214
Officially Endorsed Liberal Conspiracy Theories vs. the
Disapproved Truth 220

9. A Critique of Socialism 225
Central Ownership and the Redistribution of Resources 225
The Socialists' Moral Critique of Capitalism........................228
Starting with the French Revolution 229
The Definition of Horror: Totalitarian Socialism.................232
Totalitarian Logic Disguised as Oxymoron 233
The Second Generation of Antisocialist Critics....................236
Nietzsche's Acerbic Critique of Socialism..............................237
    I.   The Forerunners of Socialism 238
    II.   The Grandfather of Socialist Thought: Christianity 238
    III.   The Grandmother of Socialist Thought: Jean-Jacques
        Rousseau and the Eighteenth Century 240
    IV.   The Birth of Socialism 241
    V.   Nietzsche's Critique of Socialist Idealism............................244
    VI.   Nietzsche's Critique of Socialism as a Politics of Revenge 246
    VII.   Categorizing Nietzsche's Critique of Socialism: Where
        Nietzsche's Critique Does Not Fit 251
    VIII.   Joining Nietzsche's View of Human Nature with Freud 252
    IX.   Nietzsche and Oakeshott against Rationalism in Politics 254
    X.   Nietzsche's "Vital Socialism" with Human Rights to
        the Proletariat 255
Socialism and the Proletariat 257

10. A Critique of Modern Conservatism 261
American Intellectual Conservatism 264
The Definition of Conservatism 268
The Perverted Conservatism of America 278
The Dead-End Street of Modern Conservatism 286
Who Still Speaks for Conservatism? 289

11. The German Dream Coming True: The Socialist Transformation of the West 292
Prussian–German Socialism and Anglo-Saxon Liberalism 293
The Path from Authoritative Prussian–German Socialism to National Socialism 305
National Socialism Is a Natural Outgrowth of Socialism 309
Socialist Economy Leading to Terror 320
German Socialist Domination and the European Union 326
Western Political Correctness: Euphemism with Attitude 333

12. Western Economic Changes 339
Capitalism, the Corporate State, and State Capitalism: The First Signs of the Social Market Economy 339
Between Ideologies: The Road toward the Social Market Economy 341
    I.   The Social Market Economy as the Third Way 343
    II.   Christian Social Doctrines 347
    III. Ethical Goals of the Social Market Economy 349
    IV. The Concept and Misuse of Subsidiarity 350
    V.   Rules for the Market: Reversed Social Market 353
    VI. Social Security 360
    VII. Compulsory Insurance 361
The Social Market Economy and Its Future in Eastern Europe 363
Russia and the Market Economy 366
Attempted Reconciliation: Economic Dynamics and the Social Market Economy 370
Globalization and Migration 375

    I.   Globalization and Its Effect on the Home Base 380
    II.   Globalism's Failed Promise and Its War on
          the Nation-State.. 384
Free Trade's Hidden Shackles 385
The Supranational Corporations and Their Ignorance of Society 388
The False Fetish of Economic Growth 392
    I.   Undermining the Foundations... 396
    II.   Confused Thinking... 399
    III. Conclusion.. 402

13. The Crumbling of the American Middle Class and the Proletarianization of Society 403

The Historical Appearance of the Middle Class................................ 404
Middle-Class Ideology: Outlook and Values..................................... 406
The Middle Class under Attack: Trials, Tribulations, and Decline....... 407
The Destruction of the Middle-Class Ideology 418
Petit Bourgeois Rising 431
A New Performing and Achieving Ideology Is Needed 434
The New Proletarianization of the West 435

14. Deteriorating Social Values.. 438

Education... 438
Economic and Social Life without Objective Truth 440
The Decline of Morality in Western Society 445
    I.   Judeo-Christian Values vs. Western Values........................... 445
    II.   Relative Morality or Absolute Moral Standards?................... 448
    III. Right or Wrong? 451
Western Values Imposed on Eastern Europe...................................... 452
The Problems of Immigration: Multiculturalism
Creates Multiple Problems... 456
Principles of Media Criticism 467
What Happened to the West? The False Faith in Progress 472

15. The Decay of Culture, Arts, Sports, and Environment 479

    Internal Cohesion 479
    Patriotism 481
    Fighting Spirit 482
    Repudiation of the Past: The New Culture of Imposed Arts 483
    Cultural Degeneration: A Critique of Contemporary Art 486
        I.   Spirit of the Renaissance 489
        II.   From Impressionism to Expressionism 490
        III. Expressionist Reaction Sets In 491
        IV. Modernism: Schisms in Art 492
        V.   The Placing of Modern Art 495
        VI. Cult of the Ugly 498
            i.   New Standard of Values: Mirroring the
                Rejection of Moral Standards 500
            ii.   Symbols in Art 502
            iii. The Ugliness, Themes, and Death of Modernism 503
            iv. Themes of Postmodernism 506
        VII. The Future of Art: Not Without Moral Renewal 508
    Modern Music: Akin to Modern Art 513
        I.   Perverting Opera 519
        II.   Classical Music Means Beauty 523
    Modern Sport: Professionalism, Entertainment, and Business 524
        I.   Amateurism in Sports 528
    Environment: Climate Change Caused by Population Growth 530

16. The Cultural Abdication and Intellectual Arrogance of the Western Elite 534

    The Persistence of Nationalism 548
    The Western Elite against the Nation-State 553
    The Death of Nations, the Death of Freedom 560
    War on the Middle Class 564
    The War on Terror 566

    Liberal Democracy: The Terror Ideology of the West..........................568
    Man, Men, and Misanthropy 573

17. Western Renewal Philosophy: Conservatism and Subsidiarity 575
    Conservatism as Part of the Western Renewal 584
    The Western Renewer: The New Conservative................................595
    Remembering the Old Liberals..597
    Distributism: The Subsidiarist Alternative to
    Socialism and Plutocracy 600

18. Proposal for the Future: The Essential Option 605
    Exploring Alternative Methods..605
    Duality vs. Absolutes.. 606
    The Essential Option...608
        I.   Elements of the Anglo-American System............................609
        II.   Elements of the Franco-German System 612
        III. Elements of the Russian System 614
    Rebuilding the West Based on the Essential Option..................... 616
        I.   Political Philosophy of the Western Renewal: The
             Sandys Doctrine 617
        II.   Hierarchical System of Government.................................. 619
        III. National-Conservative Ideology 623
        IV. Building on the Principle of Subsidiarity 625
        V.   Real Social Market Economy Based on Incentives 628
        VI. Foreign Policy Based on National Interest, Sovereignty,
             and Self-Determination...635
        VII. Leadership Principles Based on Proven Merit, Not on
             Electioneering 640
        VIII. Supporting Forgiveness, Distinction, Achievement, and
             Aspiration 642
        IX. Overcoming Evil with Grace, Integrity, Morality, and
             Virtue 647
        X.   Overcoming Angry Politics by Rebuilding Trust.................649

XI.	Education: Returning to the Humanities and Recognizing the Individual	651
XII.	Controlled Immigration Based on National Interest, Merit, and Employment Opportunities	656
XIII.	Judiciary: Upholding the National Law	657
XIV.	Environment: Protecting from Uncontrolled Population Growth	658
XV.	Social Policy: Supporting the Return to Meritocracy	658
XVI.	Self-Limitation: Emphasizing Moral Justice Instead of Social Justice	658
XVII.	High Culture Supported by the Meritorious Elite of the Hierarchical System	659

19. Reflecting on the Forms of Government— Ars Politica 661

Good Government, Good Society 662
Russia and Western Europe: Proposal for Eastern Europe 674
The Coming of the Postsecular Age 679
Ars Politica 680
The Politics of Richard Nixon 685
Epilogue 693

Bibliography 703
Endnotes 731

PREFACE

Not unlike many people of my age, I hated growing up in a communist country. Born in Hungary in 1947, my early years were in all likelihood influenced by the trauma of living in a paranoid, closed society. The pathologically evil government and, above all, the omnipresent Communist Party took advantage of their control of the minds, media, and educational institutions and exercised an absolute monopoly over command of the youth.

My parents, born and raised in Hungary around the First World War, came from bourgeois families. After 1945, Hungary's bourgeois middle-class citizens (rather a minority in that country at the time) had their properties confiscated, nationalized, and flatly appropriated without any compensation. Some of them were expelled from their homes and sent to live like peasants in the countryside, following a similar justification to that which the Khmer Rouge used in Cambodia a few decades later.

The situation of the dispossessed and displaced German refugees after 1945 and the hardships they endured while being expelled from their homes in areas that today are the Czech Republic, Poland, and Russia to the parts of Germany occupied by the United States, Great Britain, and France, were horrible. However, I consider them to be the lucky ones; they could at least leave and start new, meaningful, and useful lives. The "natives" had to stay and rot under the Soviet/Bolshevist rule, eking out a living for many lost decades to come while not only being brutalized and oppressed but also having their very lives taken away from them.

I still remember traveling in cattle cars with primitive wooden benches and no toilet facilities. My father could give me only handmade small wooden toys for Christmas that I still have and cherish as treasures. I still remember being sick at home sometime in the 1950s and how happy my parents were when they could get me a lemon (my father was able to obtain the fruit from a good-hearted Soviet officer who probably also had his own children somewhere).

Unlike in Western Europe, there was no Marshall Plan in the socialist countries to rebuild the destroyed infrastructure and ruined cities, towns, and industries to start providing the population with the basic necessities of life again. The bombed-out and completely leveled cities that had been exposed to the vicious fighting and had become the victims of brutal successive occupations by Germans and Soviets were stripped bare of whatever value they once possessed. Everything had to be rebuilt from ground zero, from nothing, with nothing, and without any capital. Then came the punishment: the scraped-together products had to be shipped to the Soviet Union as "war compensation." The people could not even enjoy even real weekends, and Saturday was a full working day. All too often, rationing was a cover-up for shortages, and even coupons did not guarantee a purchase. That was life in Soviet-occupied Hungary in the 1940s and '50s.

An entire population of ten million people was not given proper wages but only small allowances, the kind one gives to children, except for the privileged class who occupied leading positions in the party and administration. Monthly salaries in postwar Hungary were in the range of 400 Hungarian forints. On the black market, one dollar was worth at least one hundred Forints. Thus, monthly earnings were worth about three to ten dollars. My mother made four dollars per month; my father made about eight dollars—and we were the lucky ones.

In Hungary, as in the other Soviet-occupied Eastern European socialist countries, the intimidated, oppressed, and exploited people lived like this for decades.

However, I, as a young, impressionable, and enthusiastic boy, was taken by my country's call at first and wanted to be a good soldier—a real patriot. This unquestioning enthusiasm—one could say blind fanaticism—that is typical of young boys the world over lasted until I reached about fourteen or fifteen years of age. Then, rather inconspicuously, as if I had been touched by a magic wand slowly lifting the veil from my eyes and giving me the light to see, my brain cells connected, and I started to think. I wanted to start asking questions, but whom could I have asked? Could it be that even my parents would not tell me the truth?

The situation was frustrating; I was getting more and more desperate, like a person drowning in a storm. There were more and more questions and more and more confused thoughts. Could it be that I had been lied to?

Finally I ran away—or, rather, tried to run. I was fifteen years old when caught very near the Austrian border and put in jail—in three different prisons, to be exact: first a military prison of the frontier guard troops, followed by a "regular prison" under police surveillance, and then, finally, a juvenile detention camp. The charge was the "attempt of forbidden border crossing," an anathema to the ruling Communists, who would consider any act of trying to leave the "dictatorship of the proletariat" as outright treason. I was released only due to the direct intervention of one of my mother's work colleagues—a woman whose family had been in the communist movement long before the war and who therefore enjoyed all the special privileges of the ruling Communists. Only because of such fortuitously high-level protection obtained by my desperate mother was I released without any further charges. Still, I had to present myself periodically to the Communist authorities for "personal conversation" for years to come.

I quickly learned that I had to play the game—their game—if I wanted to survive. I had no other choice, as I was locked in a prison—a country-size jail this time. Soviet Bloc countries were, in fact, large prison camps disguised as people's republics. As in any prison, inmates of the Bloc could not leave at will. There were only a few ways of crossing the border that did not involve risk of capture, injury, or even death. Nevertheless, I vowed then and there to leave the "workers' paradise," should the opportunity ever arise.

The outlook was not good. The Communist rule seemed assured as long as the Soviet occupation continued and no one harbored realistic hopes about the Soviets leaving voluntarily.

Accordingly, I pretended to be a passive believer just like everybody else—a nominal and silent follower of their socialist system. But my hatred of communism grew with time. Between the ages of fifteen and twenty-five, socialism's vocabulary, words, phrases, definitions, and repertory of tools, procedures, practices, and mannerisms were etched in my brain. Party functionaries spoke as if playing back a tape from a tape deck inside their skull; every wicked deed was done for the sake of "world peace." The source of all virtue was the Soviet man; the source of all evil was the imperialist oppressor. Likewise, good people were "progressive"; bad people were "reactionary."

After graduating from technical high school, I was accepted to engineering college, which automatically meant I needed to serve in the army first. Only after completing army reserve officer school could I begin my studies at the technical university—while keeping one and only one goal in mind: getting away from here, away from this system, away from this life.

Then, after years of careful planning and preparation, I was able to escape in 1972, exactly five days after receiving my engineering diploma. I legally crossed the Hungarian border to Romania and was then illegally able to continue to Yugoslavia and finally to Italy, where, without a valid passport, they put me in one of their refugee camps. The West maintained these camps for those lucky escapees who could get through the Iron Curtain one way or another.

In the 1960s, 1970s, and 1980s, thousands of refugees from the Eastern Bloc communist states called the three Italian towns of Padriciano, Capua, and Latina home for months as they waited to be processed. I was housed in a former World War II prisoner of war camp just outside of Capua, the worst camp of the three. Breakfast consisted of bread and black coffee, and lunch was a plate of spaghetti or *pastasciutta* (a traditional Italian pasta dish) every day. There were occasional incidents with the Italian residents of Capua getting into fights with refugees who illegally visited the town, but nothing too serious. Many of the refugees were a source of cheap manual labor for local farms, where many people picked watermelons for hours and either got the payment that was promised to them or did not. Many times the compensation consisted of a big sandwich and a bottle of Coca-Cola, which was a rare treat after months of eating nothing but spaghetti.

I was free to stay in these facilities under police guard, technically not allowed to work or leave the compound, delivered to the whims and grace of unknown and unseen bureaucrats somewhere who could care less about strange foreigners. We were these strange foreigners—we, the refugees coming from the Eastern European socialist countries. Welcome to the West.

West? What kind of West was this? Was it the enemy of communism? The democratic countries enjoying freedom and offering refuge to the few who could get away from the "dictatorship of the proletariat"? I just had to wait and see.

And so I did. I had to endure eight months of humiliation, living as a stateless person under prison-like conditions while followers of the Italian Socialist and Communist Parties marched and demonstrated under my window. *They* were free to do that in their democratic and open country, but I was not. *They* were free to protest against the "capitalist West," and *they* were free to support the socialist and communist parties from whose "brothers" and criminal accessories I had just escaped. And I had to watch them silently.

While the real West—the "Free World," the "democracies"—ignored us Eastern Europeans fleeing from Soviet-occupied countries, some private citizens, civic organizations, members of the clergy, and even sympathetic police officers and carabinieri tried to help in any way they could. And I will never forget their understanding, sympathy, support, and courage.

Yes, *they* needed courage to help us, fellow Europeans, refugees from the communist East, in the "free, liberal, and democratic" Western European countries in 1972–73. *Their* help was a statement—an unofficial, subtle political protest of the right helping the escapees from socialism.

Therefore, I duly noted that the official "liberal," if not already socialist, West was silent, disinterested, ignorant, and, above all, hypocritical—the characteristic that I find to this day the most distinctive attribute of liberal democracy.

When I finally arrived in the United States in May 1973, I was incredibly thankful, inspired, driven, and thinking that socialism, in both its Eastern and Western European forms, was forever behind me. How little I knew.

The United States was a new country and new world for me, with a new language, new culture, and new life—but that much one could have expected.

Richard Nixon had already been elected to the presidency by a landslide for a second term. The Watergate protests were at their peak. I could not understand it: Wasn't the West, *we*, fighting the most abominably wicked political force on the planet? Communism crippled the lives of my fellows, ruined the lives of my parents, and destroyed the lives of generations. Communism obstructed the private lives and personal development of at least two generations in Central Europe (and perhaps four in Russia) by restricting access to what could be read, listened to, and discussed, and where one could live or travel. Communism subjected the people of Hungary to terror-initiated poverty that required bartering ability and exceptional vigilance (unknown in the West) just to obtain simple household goods. Communism made them live on monthly allowances of ten to fifteen dollars. It moreover impaired them by preventing any chance of advancement in many professions without membership in the Communist Party.

American students did not know or care about any of this, and when I went back to college to study business administration, my liberal professors did not want to know. They not only believed that socialism or communism stood for a new era in the development of humanity and that interference with them was unacceptable, but they also taught their students accordingly.

I remember the protesters in New York chanting that Nixon was worse than Hitler. This ridiculous act was the last straw. To me, a naive newcomer from the East, Nixon was the champion of trying to stop communism in Vietnam, and I considered American intervention to be a heroic act by a great power that I hoped would halt the spread of Bolshevism around the world.

The brainwashing performed by socialist apologists in the United States was universal at the time, and only people on the right were bold enough to say that the pro-Soviet permissiveness was based on idealistic desires rather than fact. As always, the liberals were like drunken ropewalkers on a worn-out cord fastened between two swaying poles.

How could it happen that in the United States, a supposedly free and democratic country, the media, the academia, and a significant part of the intelligentsia had all fallen under the influence of the sly spell of socialism? Their deliberate indifference toward the malevolence, brutality, and deception of the Soviet system made me take a second look at other "generally accepted ideas" (i.e., apologies) of Western liberal thinkers.

I discovered that they praised the French Revolution, which started the change of direction of Western civilization (see my comments later), just as it had been in the textbooks I read in Soviet-occupied Hungary.

I discovered that, just as in the of Hungarian People's Republic, the Spanish Civil War was always described in one-sided, biased, and simplistic terms, Franco being all black, fascist, and revisionist, and the Republicans all white, democratic, and progressive.

I discovered that the rise of communism in Hungary (and in Germany) after the First World War was artfully and purposely smoothed over, as if the Hungarian (or German) Communists were the morally upright heroes opposing the all-bad dark forces of the "fascist" gangs.

I discovered that the Hungarian Soviet Republic of 1919, the second successful communist takeover in the world after the Russian Revolution in 1917, was merely a rather neutral footnote in the history books. The Communist misrule, which caused lawlessness, political anarchy, economic chaos, and enormous suffering in the newly defeated, truncated, and humiliated Hungary, received only some ignorant, apologetic leftist remarks. Although it had a consequential catastrophic aftereffect not only on that country but also on Germany (with the resulting rise of National Socialism there) and, indirectly, the world, this disastrous Communist dictatorship remained hushed up.

I discovered that the Polish-Soviet war of 1920—in which the newly reconstituted, if still quixotic and vengeful, Poland spectacularly stopped and defeated the Red Army, thus blocking the spread of communism westward and arresting Trotsky's goal of "world revolution"—had been erased from America's historical memory.

I discovered that the flimsy articles and airy comments by the American "sovietologists" on the Soviet Union misrepresented the forced and dubious connection between the Soviet Union and the conquered and subjugated nations of Central and Eastern Europe.

I discovered the Left's effort to hush up the fact that were it not for Stalin's "understanding" with Hitler manifested in the Molotov–Ribbentrop Pact of August 23, 1939, possibly the Second World War would not have begun.

I discovered that to get accepted in sophisticated intellectual circles in America, one had to accede to a substantial amount of the politically correct misconceptions that I knew were wrong and profess disinterest in any historical inquiry that did not correspond to an agenda friendly to the Left. Additionally, the power of money combined with the desire to get accepted, societal pressure, and political correctness lured superb authors to concede to the Left. Liberal writers, journalists, and professors stamped in the public's head their doctored version of European history.

I discovered that the West met any anticommunist action with systematic rejection. The media, of course, demonized the Chilean coup d'état by General Pinochet that prevented a second Cuba in Latin America by the Soviet-supported socialist government of the Marxist Salvador Allende. The media deprecated the Argentine military's desperate fight against the Maoist guerillas terrorizing South America in the 1970s or any force fighting Bolshevism and gave lopsided, biased, and manipulated "news" about the facts; it was not unlike the media coverage of the Vietnam War. Who remembers today the Marxist Tupamaros guerrillas or the Montoneros mercilessly gunning down people on the streets of Uruguay, Argentina, Chile, Bolivia, or Brazil? All these terrorists have become martyrs brutally killed by the military dictatorships, while the indiscriminate killings perpetrated by the communist-supported terror brigades to bring about the total collapse of society have been forgotten.

I noted with incredulity and disgust that even Gerald Ford, the Republican president of the United States, claimed that the "People's Republic of Poland" was not "dominated" by the Soviet Union.

I noted when *Time* magazine published a curiously sympathetic article about János Kádár, the Communist ruler of Hungary since the people's uprising there in 1956, claiming that his "goulash communism" was so successful and popular that he could probably even be elected—provided there were free elections there.

The only people who unequivocally proclaimed that the Evil Empire was indeed evil were on the conservative right.

As years went by and my political and philosophical horizons broadened, I also realized that, although it is not exactly what I had expected from it, the most acceptable and persuasive arguments about reality also came from the right. I also discovered, albeit rather slowly, that to be intellectually a liberal in this world, one needed only to ignore facts, logic, and reason.

What I had not expected, however, was an early political awakening, maturing, or "sobering up" after only a relatively short time. This process was a sort of "political enlightenment" that, after the long and painful experience gained in the socialist East and burned indelibly into my brain, seemed rather a surprisingly recognizable revelation to me even then. I was quite aware, sensitive, conditioned, or "well trained" to pick up any suspicious sign of either latent or apparent similarity with the socialist East in the "free and democratic West." Such signs included the use of the media for official propaganda, political double-talk, manipulation of the masses, confusing and misleading reasoning, corruption, hypocrisy, etc.

About thirty-five years ago, I first put together some notes analyzing "the world's most critical political issues" of the time, at least from my perspective. It is striking how much of these matters have changed since my thoughts were first put down on paper in 1982. Not only did the Eastern Bloc disappear in its entirety with the Soviet Union, Warsaw Pact, Council for Mutual Economic Assistance, et al., but also a seemingly complete turnaround took place in the political ideologies of the onetime adversaries, East and West. For someone like me, who rose against the

Soviet system, it was stupefying to see the 180-degree turn the world has taken since the 1980s.

The West has since openly adopted a left-leaning liberal, mainly socialist, philosophy, hoping to stem the tide of the upward-moving, fast-developing, non-Western, and largely nondemocratic nations by "spreading democracy" around the world. At the same time, the West kept westernizing, liberalizing, and democratizing (meaning "socializing") former European dictatorships like Spain, Portugal, and the formerly socialist countries that had not been "progressive leftist" in the Western sense of the term.

However, the previously socialist Eastern European countries are still searching for their national identity, just like Russia, which, after a rather painful and desperate attempt at Western democracy, started down its original Russian-liberal-conservative path, which was interrupted in 1917. Meanwhile, China, having adopted state-controlled capitalism as its chosen economic system while retaining one-party rule Singapore-style, already has the second largest economy in the world and is striving to become the world's leading power—as it had been before. None of these countries, including India, Brazil, and South Africa, is actually left-liberal socialist in the Western sense. Politically they are, to a certain extent, nationalist; economically they are pursuing their very own form of state-controlled capitalism, which is the most important single element they took from the West.

Has the Western world turned on itself? By condemning and even physically attacking countries to promote, spread, or push democracy as a political system around the globe and Jacobin definitions of human rights, the West identifies with the international left today. Russia, after the catastrophic experience with Bolshevism, is slowly reasserting her historic role as leader of the international right. To all outward appearances, this seems to be a historic reversal, but is it really that? Isn't it, in fact, only the latest political, philosophical and historical realignment by the old precepts? After all, the West is the birthplace of liberalism, socialism, leftist movements, and revolutions. And where is the home of morality-based conservatism and religion-supported self-identity if not in the East?

As the above developments show, as soon as the Soviet danger, the "Bolshevik alternative" to the West, was over, the once conservative, anti-Communist, capitalistic West of the Cold War period quickly changed into a left-leaning, modern-liberal, and socialistic bloc both politically and morally. By the same token, the once communist

East became more identity conscious and capitalistic while remaining illiberal and conservative.

Who would have thought this in the middle of the Cold War, thirty-five years ago? Does the seeming unpredictability of these changes tell us it is futile to pretend we can foretell anything real and tangible that could happen in the future?

I wanted to find the reasons and correlations of the systemic changes first in the Soviet Union, then in Central Eastern Europe, and finally in the West. The reader will see that my representation of the events differs in many respects from what the media typically reports on the subject. The significant developments, such as wars, revolutions, and major crises, do not always take place in reality as the newspapers and other media would have readers and viewers believe. What happens backstage is different from what the audience is presented.

The above applies in particular to recent times concerning the upheavals after the end of Communism in Eastern Europe, the so-called Arab Spring in North Africa, the Ukrainian developments, or the War on Terror in the Middle East. Relevant facts do not come to the fore, because the framers of politics, for whatever reasons or interests, do not want them to.

It has been a commonly held and eagerly disseminated opinion of the Western liberal media that the Left is somehow "good" and the Right is "bad." This thread does not allow enough characters to expose the folly of this opinion.

But the sad legacy of two world wars, fascist and communist dictatorships, socialist revolutions, and antirevolutionary uprisings, followed by a left-liberal final assault, is that the Western bourgeoisie has massively weakened and the middle class has practically disintegrated.

The cultural vacuum was filled with mediocre, flighty, and preconceived ideas that pointed almost categorically to the Left in the 1960s. These partly antidemocratic and totalitarian ideologies led to political radicalism. It was not surprising when Oskar Lafontaine, at the time in the leadership of the West German Social Democratic Party (SDP), was against German reunification, arguably less because of the cost than out of sympathy for the former socialist system.

It cannot simply be that every leftist provocation is considered fair and just but any hint of mildly critical centrist ideas is branded "extremist." No one with a modicum of historical consciousness can remain unmoved when cultural cities like Berlin, London, Paris, Athens, Stockholm, Hamburg, or Vienna are ignited, burned, and looted by black-clad thugs today. And this happens in the great cities of the European Union pretending to be the flag bearers of Western civilization.

While cars burn day and night during the demonstrations, there is massive violence against police officers, who are regarded as attempted murderers. Meanwhile, violent leftist criminals do not hesitate to attack police stations. This state of affairs is already close to the sort of civil war that is known only in Afghanistan or Iraq—and some still rant about the extreme danger to the democratic state coming from the right's corner.

The supposedly right-wing and purportedly nationalistic and conservative perpetrators calling themselves skinheads are the work of a handful of bewildered, confused, sad, and disoriented creatures whose violent acts can be counted on the fingers of one hand in comparison with the massive acts of terrorism by the Left.

The leftists, however, with their consistent and successful marching through and taking over the Western state institutions since 1968, have changed the entire political and cultural landscape of the Western world. They made the United States a shadow of its previous self and reduced Europe from a postwar international success story to a sick and socialist "EUtopia." Lo and behold, their helpers and supporters even warn that, by the old cry "Stop, thief!" the danger is coming from the right.

Whoever orchestrated this absurd theater did it at the expense of Western society, which has already lost to a large extent.

I worry about the breakdown of civil society in the West caused by individual rights not being paired with personal responsibility. The growing culture of entitlements has convinced Westerners that failure is not their fault but is rather the fault of the political-economic system. Once charity becomes an entitlement, the stigma of living on charity disappears. As a result, entitlement costs outpace government resources, resulting in enormous debts for future generations. In the meantime, the political leaders of the West kick the can down the road to win elections. Westerners have abandoned an ethical basis for society, believing that all problems are solvable by "good government."

I could not decide for a long time if I should write down some events occurring in my lifetime, the underlying concepts behind them explained with a few of my thoughts. There were many reasons for this hesitation; the main one for going ahead was my ever-strengthening notion that after Europe lost its thousand-year hegemony over the world, the entirety of Western civilization began following in its path.

The "Age of the West" is ever so slowly but inexorably coming to close, and the new world will need new people to replace the enervated ones of the old. Even if a "United States of Europe" would ever come into being (although I see no danger of it ever happening), its role would still be similar to that of Spain's within Europe: old brilliance, past power, and honorary glory, but without any real authority, strength, or influence.

It is like when a senile old man is revered for his age.

Any dissenter today who insists on upholding the prevailing law is a natural enemy in the eyes of the rulers. With all the energy at the rulers' command, he will be denounced and defamed, charged and sued. Thoughts are not free in the West today but are dangerous. Words could become actions; therefore, any arguing is to be avoided. The characteristic signs of a totalitarian state are the persecution of certain tendencies, the harassment of certain attitudes, and the relentless assault on certain philosophies of life. The dehumanization of the opponents appears to be the highest concern; the rivals' motives are represented as illegitimate. The intentions of the antagonist are outrageous, disgraceful, and infamous; the official causes are sacrosanct, perfect, and inviolable. The purpose does not sanctify the means, but the utilized means desecrate the purpose. As soon as any form of inimical act is contemplated, the affair immediately exposes itself as "fascist"—and thus automatically worth the fight. And then ideological ditches will rapidly become genuine graves.

Such is the Western world today.

Peter J. Sandys
Memmingen, Germany
January 2017

1

THE SCREENPLAY OF THE VELVET REVOLUTION

During the Cold War (1948–91), there were two poles of this world: the West, led by a so-called superpower, the United States; and the East, which was one superpower, the Soviet Union.

The United States–led West also included the modern, industrialized, and "most democratic" countries of Western Europe, Australia, Canada, New Zealand, and Japan. The East, other than the Soviet Union itself, nominally included the semi-industrialized Eastern European socialist countries, as well as China, Vietnam, and North Korea.

The so-called "nonaligned nations," such as Yugoslavia, Egypt, India, Indonesia, and Ghana, were, in reality, third-world, nondemocratic, mostly less-developed countries.[1]

With the collapse of the Soviet Union in 1991, the Warsaw Pact, and its member countries, the East, or "left," pole ceased to exist as such. The total economic and political collapse of it was also a significant tectonic shift—a social implosion—that was rapid in its finality. It was not only a moral shock but also a philosophically profound one that the world had not experienced for many years.

The socioeconomic and political breakdown created an ideological vacuum that has been reshaping and reforming our world ever since. This real cataclysm is similar to volcanic eruptions, whereby existing social formations disappear only to reappear a few years later—or at least this was the popular theory during the early 1990s.

Why Are the Perpetrators Still among Us?

What would the people and the media in the West have said if the victors of the Second World War had permitted the political elite of the Nazi regime, the war criminals, to continue functioning unpunished—even to keep their leading positions in postwar German society? Alternatively, what if they had been given the opportunity not only to have and distribute the Jews' confiscated property among themselves but also to declare them openly as their private assets?

The above assumption would have outraged and disgusted everyone indeed. For this reason—and, of course, because of the determination and resoluteness of the wartime allies—it would never have become a reality.

Nevertheless, after the collapse of the Soviet Union and its Eastern European satellites, such absurdities happened in the formerly Communist countries. The evidence that the Soviet system was also based on a monstrous ideology (to which millions of people fell victim) will not diminish the exceptional brutality of the Nazi crimes. Since the collapse of the Soviet Union, and despite the opening of the archives, one can still hardly find any exhaustive and detailed examination of the "Red version" of mass murders committed against innocent people in so many countries. Dealing with the past is evidently a subject not to be tinkered with in Russia, in the Commonwealth of Independent States, or in the former Eastern European satellite countries.

The liquidation of innocent people who had been declared enemies of the (Communist) state, or "enemies of the people," was the natural governing method of the Soviet regimes. The apparent goal was to intimidate and terrorize the population for the sake of keeping it in constant fear. Even members of the ruling Communist Party were not spared from the periodic purges, and thousands of them paid for their illusions with their lives. Power struggles and political infighting at the highest levels of the party hierarchy often ended with the liquidation of the opponent. The number of victims of the Communist terrors amounts to several million. Not many prisoners survived their detention in the penal camps, the gulags, which constituted a network in the entire area of the former Soviet Union and remained in existence in various forms until the collapse of the system.

The perpetrators of the "Red crimes"—many of whom enjoy retirement today—not only are able to live unmolested in the successor states but can also even occupy higher political offices, as if nothing happened or as if all that happened was only a nightmare.

No scrutiny has taken place in any of the countries involved after the supposed political change or transition either to punish the perpetrators and their auxiliaries or even to discover their identities.

Direct outside pressure by the victorious Allies forced the denazification process in Germany after the war, but who could or should have objectively conducted these post-Communist investigations in Eastern Europe? Above all, the Communist powers with their governments, administrations, courts, political police, and intelligence apparatuses carried out the transition from dictatorship to democracy—or at least they did not foil the plot by force in most of the states.

Since the Communist Party secretaries of all political organizations, regional administrations, and even business firms had to work together with the state security services, it becomes quite apparent what a vast circle and what a high percentage of the population comprised the perpetrators in the society. Virtually the entire elite of the inhumane system was involved in the functional machinery of the state. About every tenth worker or employee was an informant of the state security services.

So *this* society, with its tightly meshed security network, organized the transition of the political systems. Given that each country has only one nation, and each population remains almost identical before and after the day of transition, it goes without saying that neither the Russians nor the Czechs nor the Hungarians had a fundamental interest in dealing with the past. One could not expect from them a policy of self-destruction or self-cleaning.

In the Soviet Union, there was no politically unblemished and still-functioning organization, or strong opposition, that could have undertaken the investigation of the Red crimes. Interestingly, such an effort did not take place even in the Eastern European countries where there were some stronger groupings of political dissidents.

All this implies that a backdoor, undisclosed screenplay—a "master plan"—arranged the peaceful political transition in the form of a gently rolling Velvet Revolution, which also stipulated that awkward questions about the political crimes of the past will not be brought up by the "victors."[2]

The above supports the conjecture that there had to be an agreement between East and West (to be precise, between Moscow and Washington) as to the modalities of a peaceful dismantling of the Communist system in the Soviet Union and its Eastern European sphere of control—in fact, a peaceful surrender under certain conditions.

The Moral Dilemma: The Price of the Peaceful Political Transition

The proposal for peaceful political transition must have come from the Soviet rulers, who had concluded that the system, imposed on the population by the most brutal means, was neither politically nor economically viable any longer and could not hope to be competitive against the capitalistic societies of the West.

Without an understanding of the actions about to happen, it would have been unthinkable for the West to enter into a maneuver fraught with risks. However, the West did join the Soviet plan—without any critical comments, meddling, scoffing, or ridicule.

According to "reliable sources," Gorbachev's proposal was supposed to contain the following five points:

1. The Soviet Union would do away with the communist system and open itself up to other political infrastructure and forms through free elections.
2. The communists may not be punished for their criminal acts committed in the past.
3. The Soviet Union would stay clear of the Yalta Agreement of 1945 and the division of Europe; it would grant freedom to its European satellite states.
4. As compensation for the abrogation of power, the communist elite may acquire the productive public property of the Soviet Union through privatization.
5. This form of political and economic transformation was to also apply to the other countries of the Eastern Bloc without any further curtailment.[3]

This Soviet proposal appeared to the Western Allies (the United States, the United Kingdom, and France) as the capitulation of their nemesis after the long years of the Cold War. Under the intoxicating effects of their unexpected victory, they had not considered their decision long. The Soviet proposal offered the West numerous advantages, of course. First of all, the unique perspective of ridding itself of the Communist challenge, and with it the permanent international tension as well as the enormous costs of the nuclear arms race, was attractive. On the whole, Washington, London, and Paris saw no reason to deny their approval, since the

Soviet proposal asked them neither to forgo nor compromise on anything; nor did it ask them to get involved in the process of transition.

Washington considered Gorbachev's plan of doing away with communism as a once-in-a-lifetime political bonanza for which the groundwork had been laid chiefly by Americans, as President Reagan proclaimed: "We are going to outspend the Russians forever."[4]

However, that the end came so quickly to the Soviets still very much surprised the West. They had overestimated the cohesiveness of the Soviet political system while at the same time underestimating the already noticeable power erosion in the 1970s and 1980s. The importance, consequences, and momentousness of Moscow's proposal were so overwhelmingly great that the details of it were apparently not even fully grasped.

The West did not express either moral or political compunction about letting the Communists' political crimes go virtually unnoticed, the living perpetrators stay unpunished, and the politically tired and economically exploited population whose fate had been the product of the Communist system come out from the distribution of the national wealth empty-handed.

The allied powers of the West, combating Nazi Germany, had no compunction about embracing the Soviet Union as their ally (where the murdering of people under Stalin had already reached to the millions). So why would they be entitled to demand from Gorbachev the handling of the wrongdoings committed for decades now? This argument sounds good indeed, but it still tremendously misses the point.

Stalin, ideologically stubborn and unchallenged, became the enemy of the free world after the Second World War. After he had driven the enemy out of his land and then engrossed Eastern Europe as well, he started an expansion policy to stretch further the Soviet sphere of influence. Stalin completely changed the relationship between the Western powers and the Soviet Union after 1945. Since he wanted the complete isolation of the Soviet area of domination, the erection of an Iron Curtain between East and West became a reality. Stalin's struggle to acquire nuclear weapons at any price to solidify the power of the Soviet Union, making it invulnerable and equal to the West, also made it the enemy of the Western world.

The establishment of NATO, the Marshall Plan, the World Bank, the reintegration of West Germany in the West, and the signing of the Treaty of Rome, just to name a few, were all the main Western strategic milestones. They were the pillars of the great effort to stop the spread of communism in Europe and of the building the central front against Stalin's aggressive policies. A similar pacification and reintegration of Japan were taking place in Asia, where, after losing China to the communists, the West had to fight a major war in Korea.

Still, despite the enormous economic successes of the West both in Europe and in Asia, the Soviet Union seemed to be "on the move" in the 1960s. After launching the first Sputnik satellite, putting the first man (and woman) in space, and putting robots on the moon, there was a desperate race for superiority, with the Communist Parties of Italy and France exerting pressure on Western democracy.

Even the Vatican reckoned with the possibility during the 1970s that Western Europe could turn to communism and tried to come to an accommodation with the Eastern European governments, as the sad example of Cardinal Mindszenty of Hungary infamously proves.[5]

There was a real and present danger to Western liberal democracy; it cost tremendous sacrifices regarding lives and wealth, particularly on behalf of the American people, to slowly turn the tide of the Cold War. Therefore, the Western powers did not have to feel obligated to take the onetime friendship with the Soviet Union into consideration at the collapse of communism. It was something entirely different.

Gorbachev had to explain to the Americans that he could guarantee the success of his undertaking only if his conditions were met. Meeting his conditions would be the price of a peaceful political transition; there would be no "total defeat," no capitulation, and not even a conditional surrender, but only the abandonment of the socialist ideology with all of its consequences—under the above conditions.

That the Americans and the Europeans accepted all this without any qualification can be seen in their attitude ever since the political transition. They accepted everything, guided by political expediency and disregarding their basic moral principles and the otherwise so eagerly practiced human rights policy. Not even the United Nations objected to the second expropriation of the populations of those nations that had lived under communist rule.

This chapter of European history indeed cannot yet be regarded as closed. The legitimacy of the new rulers will sooner or later be called into question in their countries, even if the West unreservedly accepted it. The Ukraine, Poland, and Hungary already provide some examples.

The so-called reform socialists led the political transition in Eastern Europe's top-down revolution, and the people did not feel at all that the new system faced up to the old system. To have a real political transition, the political mentality—the political frame of reference—must also change.

Where does Eastern Europe belong, then—the West or the East? A certain feeling of duality lives in the souls of all Eastern European nations; there is no clear, unequivocal answer to the question. There is something that causes the Eastern Europeans to scrutinize their belonging to the West. It could be a reaction of instability, uncertainty, or even malevolence that is not necessarily rooted in the souls of the people because of some grievance. Instead the people of Eastern Europe subconsciously know that to survive and prosper, they *must* belong to the West. They do not necessarily like it, but they do not, in fact, have much choice in the matter.

This is precisely the point the West should understand, which it has failed to do so far, if it ever has the intention to finally integrate Eastern Europe. Some people there know their histories and forget slowly; they cannot, or do not want to, change their culture; it is the culture that rules their minds, rather than only the indelible memory of socialism. They have been looking for Western leadership, guidance, and political and, yes, moral advice—but they have not received them as yet. Moreover, it is doubtful they ever will.

The spirit of Eastern Europe, based on a strong sense of morality, kept on living during the long decades of socialism. The essence of repression was not the idea of communism itself but rather the Soviet military occupation, without which the communists could never have gained power.

For the above reasons, similarly to the thorough investigations conducted regarding the Nazi regime after World War II, the Communist dictatorships should have been, and still should be, scrutinized after the political transition.

If the West considers that liberal democracy is supposedly based on the guarantee of human rights and that the separation of power is essential to the successful political transition from communist dictatorship, then why did it not directly intervene from the outside just like it did after the Second World War? Why have the ever-vigilant Western journalists, the all-observant investigative reporters, and the conscientious upholders of freedom of speech never bothered to ask any relevant questions concerning the fate of the leading men of the collapsed regimes?

Sadly enough, the answers to the above questions are quite evident.

The West allegedly won the Cold War against communism. Did it truly? Were there any big celebrations, military parades or victory marches through New York City? Was this great political and economic success, this tectonic shift, immortalized in any memorable way for the people of the victorious West to remember?

No. In reality, there was not any total or unconditional—even decisive or conditional—victory, and consequently, there was not even a thank-you heard from anyone in power. There was no expression of gratitude to the millions in the West, especially in America, who sacrificed so much of their lives and wealth—not only their own but also those of future generations—to hold the line and prevail against communism. The West seems to or pretends to believe that it won the Cold War, but it has apparently never considered the possibility that the internal contradictions of communism caught up with it before the internal contradictions of the Western liberal democracies will catch up with them.

At the heart of the problem is the festering wound that keeps gnawing on the still living parts and values of the West: the communists were never thoroughly defeated. Perhaps communism as an ideology has no message for the future currently, but unlike Nazism, it prevailed for so long that its leaders could create their culture, which maintained, and still maintains, their power. They upheld envy as a perception of life, making people disagree with the world as it is and try to destroy it. Their ideology and mentality have been allowed to be safely and surreptitiously transferred into the body of the West and accepted there.

Practically no one is a Communist today. It must be one of the most amazing spectacles of history to be flooded with the rhetoric, theory, and practice of communism and yet see not one Communist around. We read and hear daily about class warfare, redistribution of wealth, the "dispossessed" masses, the disadvantaged, universal health care, speech codes, sensitivity training, restrictions on parents' rights, the need to centralize and federalize—the list goes on and on. The political agenda is still with us, only the party, at least directly by its old name, is not.

However, the lessons have been learned by the Left and absorbed into the latest mature and brilliantly reconstituted incarnation of communism, which is busily constructing its bridges to the twenty-first century—and already organically built into the West under its camouflage of social justice.

The moral decline of the West, if it did not start at the moment, certainly accelerated with the "winning" of the Cold War—a "victory" that was nothing but a wily deal struck with the devil. So with that Faustian act, the cold peace has begun.

2

THE WESTERN POLITICAL REALIGNMENT

The victorious West had no problem or difficulty filling in the vacuum economically or militarily. However, the sociopolitical implications of the change have been reverberating around the world ever since the alleged disappearance of the "left pole."

The fact that the countries of all three of the previous blocs found themselves suddenly living in a unipolar world has caused a reevaluation of the situation. The old left temporarily disappeared, only to reemerge, reorganize itself, and reassert its values, ideology, and goals under new names, new political parties, and new alliances.

The remaining sole superpower, the United States of America, could immediately fill the vacuum militarily and assume the role of the world's police. However, its socioeconomic values did not coincide with those of most nations—including those of Western Europe.

Western Europe suddenly found itself in an entirely new age. With its old and traditional enemy, the Soviet Bloc, disappearing, its enduring and latent animosity against the United States needed a new outlet.

The new, heretofore ignored or misapplied question of the real meaning of "superpower" has come to the surface. What is a superpower? It is a country represented by a government that can influence or even annihilate any other country on the face of the earth.

With the removal of the Soviet Union from the world stage, the question arose as to whether the Soviet Union was a real superpower. If it was, what made it one? The answer to the first question is in the affirmative; the Soviet Union could and did influence even the last remaining superpower, the United States, and it could have delivered a devastating attack on America or any other country. Economically speaking, it was not significant as an inefficient, bureaucratic, semi-industrialized socialist command economy. The country could have and should have belonged to the Third World rather than being called a superpower. Its economy, wealth, ideology, and social structure did not make it possible for the Soviet Union to gain the status of a real superpower. What did then?

It was the possession of nuclear, thermonuclear, chemical, and biological weapons. It was the possession of a military machine, based in essence on a war economy and its military industry, that made it possible for the Soviet Union to achieve superpower status. It was the fear and knowledge that the Soviet Union would not hesitate to use its might to prove that point, as it repeatedly did in Korea, Hungary, Cuba, Czechoslovakia, Vietnam, the Middle East, and Afghanistan. Other than the United States, only the Soviet Union possessed weapons of mass destruction that it could deliver from starting points on land, at sea, in the air, and in space against any other country on earth. In short, only its military capability made the Soviet Union a superpower (which is the case with any country).

The Western European powers had feared the Soviet Union and communism during the Cold War. Although they did not necessarily subscribe to the American form of democracy or to the US socioeconomic political system or its values, they needed US protection and support.

The West's Move to the Left

After the collapse of the Soviet Union, and without the "left bloc" behind them, the newly organized leftist socialist parties quickly recognized that their survival and ideology depended on the fusion, alliance, cooperation, or coalition with existing more liberal parties—even those that were nationalistic.

The anti-imperialism of the old socialist and communist parties quickly became the anti-Americanism of the new red and green social-democratic and socialist alliance. Moreover, an ever-expanding Western Europe was ready to welcome the new leftist partners—allies in a broad democratic left-liberal group. The new European society was supposed to be based on respect for human rights, democratic values, and the protection of the environment in any case.

The change in the political direction taken by the Western European countries can be particularly eye-opening in the newly reunified Germany. The old West Germany, before the reunification of the country, was one of the most conservative members of the European Community, with hardly any trace of a radical leftist political party. The trade unions, traditionally strong, always strove for an amicable social contract with the employers, and West Germany, even during the leadership of social-democratic governments, remained a loyal member of the anticommunist Western alliance.

However, the collapse of the Eastern Bloc and the reunification of Germany have quickly changed past attitudes, opinions, and loyalties; the new, unified Germany has in a sense adopted and absorbed the vestiges of the old and once hated East German communist party (SED). That party was first renamed PDS, the German abbreviation for "Partei des Demokratischen Sozialismus," meaning "Party of Democratic Socialism," in 1989. That party was renamed again "The Left Party.PDS" ("Die Linkspartei.PDS") in 2005, then "Die Linke" ("The Left") in 2007. The party performed particularly well in its home ground in and around Berlin, even merging with the far-left wing of the Social Democratic Party (SPD). The anticapitalist statements of the Social Democratic Party leadership, the populist and anti-American attitude of the SPD, German reaction, and public opinion about almost anything American all show one result: the positive attitude toward and willingness to accept US leadership is passé.

The socialist parties also recognized after the demise of the Soviet Union that even a superpower can fail if its economic system cannot keep up with that of the West—namely, capitalism. However, what if, by adopting capitalism, they were to challenge the remaining superpower, their old nemesis? (Notice the direct similarity between this concept and that taken by China.)

THE NEW AMERICAN REALITY: HESITATION AND LOSS OF PURPOSE

The new position of the United States was somewhat frightening. The entire world was looking at it with fear, suspicion, doubt, and envy. With its archenemy, the

Soviet Union, gone, its purported allies in Western Europe, mainly the major industrialized world other than Japan, slowly and surreptitiously but inexorably were shifting to the left. What could be done under these circumstances? What was the future to bring to the sole remaining superpower?

It appeared that the whole world was moving, if ever so slowly, into a bloc ambivalent toward the United States. The old left wanted to survive by reinventing itself, and the old Allies wanted to get rid of the burden they had been forced to assume and live with while the greater enemy was still around the corner. The Third World was just envious, suspicious, and fearful.

America needed any reason, and all the excuses, to save its hegemony over the old alliance (based militarily on NATO), which few countries needed or wanted to put up with anymore. America needed to exhibit leadership and prove its indispensable role to be able to cope with a new world that was, and still is, slowly turning to challenge its authority as the sole remaining superpower. Therefore, the (first European-led and sponsored) disintegration of Yugoslavia came in handy for the United States. The ethnic wars in Croatia, Bosnia, and Kosovo were to show and prove to the Europeans they needed NATO even after the Cold War.

Similarly to the sudden and violent disintegration of Yugoslavia, the Iraqi occupation of Kuwait, brought about under very dubious circumstances, provided the next excellent opportunity for the United States to project its power promptly after the collapse of the Soviet Union. The timing of the war against Iraq in 1991 was also extremely fortuitous for the expansion of strategic interests in the Middle East and beyond.

The United States still spends as much on defense as the military expenses of the rest of the world combined. Why? To maintain unchallenged military and technological superiority; to be able to fight two local wars simultaneously; and to establish a command, control, and communication infrastructure that enables US forces to operate and win against any enemy anywhere, anytime, under any conditions—with impunity. This expenditure, this economic sacrifice on the part of the American people, can limit American losses to a minimum and make the enemy sure of the certainty of a US response to any challenge.

However, how long can an already hopelessly indebted United States afford this kind of military outlay in the face of a looming financial and economic breakdown, not unlike that causing the downfall of the Soviet Union? How long can a country maintain its world hegemony based on financial and military domination, but with an eroding political, economic, social, and moral foundation?

Israel's Role in the Reshaping the World: The American–Israeli Alliance

The State of Israel, since its birth in 1948, has been able to rely only on itself and the United States. The undeniably unjust and unfair circumstances that led to the recognition of the new country by the United Nations (UN) made Israel resistant to considering the approval of the UN again. With an assured US veto in the UN Security Council, with the absolute and unqualified backing of one of the five permanent UN Security Council members, Israel always acts *exclusively in its interest* and is not influenced by world opinion. This policy requires the visible, continuous, and practically unconditional support of the sole remaining superpower, making the United States thereby the *de facto proxy of Israel*. However, Israel is the principal; the United States is merely the proxy holder, acting on Israel's behalf in this relationship.

Based on Israel's development into a modern "Western" country, in addition to its recognized status as an undeclared nuclear power with not only sophisticated but also battle-hardened and experienced armed forces, it could afford the working out of new military doctrines. Unlike its hostile Muslim Arab neighbors, and despite the direct and practically unlimited support of the United States, Israel will always have limited resources available. To survive without UN backing and world assistance, without being able to count on a single country other than the United States for help in war or peace, Israel must have overwhelming technological, military, and industrial superiority in the face of all odds.

This self-reliance on limited resources, and the need to establish and maintain technical and military superiority, puts Israel squarely in the camp of the United States, which faces very similar challenges around the world. Israel has become the "local superpower" on its own account in the Middle East, having very similar problems as the United States does on a global scale. Israel, like the people of the United States, knows sacrifice, can fight for its goals and values, and is willing to forgo idleness, comfort, and peace against all the odds for the seemingly hopeless dream of survival. The American people are apparently also still ready to make tremendous sacrifices to keep the dream of American democracy alive around the world. Israel's conviction to survival through dominance goes very well with America's mindset of freedom through dominance.

The religious and ideological values of the Jews and American Protestant fundamentalist conservatives coincide. They see themselves as natural allies and are ready to reshape the world to their liking.

There are some fascinating and significant changes to consider:

- While Jews in the past have tended to be historically left-leaning and liberal intellectuals sympathizing with socialist or communist parties worldwide, if not founding such parties themselves, present-day Israel has slowly become more right-wing and conservative in its ideological outlook.
- There has been a shift from the trade unionist, democratic, Euro-socialist line toward the pro-American, republican, fundamentalist direction.
- The old-style red liberal leftist Jewish intellectuals standing up to the conservative anti-Semitic aristocracies of Europe have changed into the new-style illiberal capitalist Jewish fundamentalists standing up to the red socialist left-liberal intellectuals in Europe.

"New America" and "New Israel" are, and will remain, close friends, allies, and codominant factors in a politically and economically stratified world. The drive and willingness to sacrifice force both of them to go forward with their dreams, however confusing or nebulous they may be.

THE EUTOPIAN DREAM

What is the European response to all this? What can America's alleged friends and allies in Europe do in case the old alliance crumbles? Do they want to split from the US path? Alternatively, do they want their independent military forces, and are they willing to spend more on the military? Are they ready to sacrifice at all?

They are not at this time; however, things can change. Europe is appalled at the thought of building up its military might again. To the modern European mind, war is not an option. If indeed that were the case, what would be the logic in spending on it?

There is no real European willingness to fight—to become a soldier or to sacrifice lives or resources. Europe would like to see itself as a world economic power and not a military one; it will be hesitant to support the military actions of the United States in the long-term future. In principle, the European Union wants to become not only a world economic power but also *the* socioeconomic political leader of the world.

By offering a new-style socialist left-liberal state-controlled capitalistic parliamentary democracy, Europe directly challenges the old-style American right-wing neoliberal-conservative corporatist capitalistic elitist/aristocratic special-interest-controlled lobbyist democracy.

By allowing itself to be joined by the old left of old Europe after the political transition in Eastern Europe, the European Union has changed its original sociopolitical path and adopted the goal of becoming a left-leaning socialist/liberal "EUtopia."

The European Union, perhaps anticipating an American incursion into the still conservative formerly socialist Eastern European countries, quickly (much too quickly) accepted the most developed ones among them at first, and later the rest, thereby preventing an "American encirclement" from the east. Although this move will inevitably result in very severe existential consequences in the future, Europe did not want to let the Americans fill in the vacuum by themselves.

The New Europe of EUtopia rejects the American way of life and the whole socioeconomic political system that the American form of democracy brings with it. Based on inequality and military might, Europe sees America as a hypocritical, if not schizophrenic, illiberal (in the sense of not being left-liberal), unjust society. Europe sees an America in which special-interest groups support the ruling elite and in which the ruling elite keep the masses down, withholding proper education, health care, and social services, or providing the people only with a modicum of such benefits.

The way New Europe sees it, the social market economy advocated by it is fairer and brings more benefits to the people. The future will belong to this social market economy, while the traditional (free) market economy (based solely on greed and exploitation) will destroy the societies of the countries practicing it.

Europe's prewar political order was based on competition, mistrust, power rivalries, and, ultimately, war among sovereign states. This old order ceased to exist on May 8, 1945, and was replaced by a system based on mutual trust, solidarity, the rule of law, and compromise—however, this new system existed in the context of the Cold War. The European Economic Community was created and made responsible for coordinating the activities of its member nation-states, for this reason. It has a finely tuned and very complex, if not overly bureaucratic, institutional superstructure.

With the political changes in Eastern Europe ending the Cold War, with the shifting of Western Europe to the left, and with the left-liberal takeover of European ideas, the original foundation of the Treaty of Rome started to erode. Trust is giving way to mistrust, solidarity is succumbing to ancient prejudices (and even new animosity between the needy South and the affluent North), and compromise is being overwhelmed by diktat. Left-liberal-led socialism stands once again at the center of the process of disintegration.

The European Union (EU) is in an upheaval, and a lot has changed during the last thirty years. Having been in constant crisis mode since the eurozone disaster started, it has become less and less clear what the union stands for or means. The economic and social decline induced by its austerity policy has eroded the social foundations; and for the unemployed young of today, the EU seems more like a threat rather than a promise for a better future.

It was just a question of time before one of the larger European countries (it turned out it would be Britain) decided that it would no longer accept the diktats from Brussels. Come election time, national governments more or less openly promise to protect their citizens from Europe, because the current European Union has seen to it that austerity and structural reforms take first place in managing the crisis.

Thirty years of constant and relentless shifting of Europe's direction to the left has resulted in the rapid generation of economic contraction, massive unemployment (upward of 50 percent among young people), and fiscal deterioration, owing to rising debt-service costs. Indeed, all eurozone members are now experiencing weak economic growth, if not recession.

What does the European Union want, or indeed, what does its left-liberal leadership want? It has long been clear what needs to be done, but the explanation of it—the rationalization of the consequences if the recommendation—is not followed, is a typical political befuddling.

The European citizens are told that the price of the monetary union's survival, and thus that of the "European project," is more community: a banking union, a fiscal union, and a political union. The people are also threatened with the warning, "Those who oppose this because they fear overall accountability, transfers from rich to poor, and a loss of national sovereignty will have to accept Europe's re-nationalization – and thus its exit from the world stage. No alternative – and certainly not the status quo – will work! It has become common knowledge in Europe that the ongoing crisis will either destroy the EU or bring about a political union and that, without a solidarity-based solution to existing debt and a partial mutualization of new debt, the euro cannot be saved. Such steps will make far-reaching transfers of sovereignty unavoidable."[6]

We are also told that the EU must have a compelling social dimension—a social Europe—instead of merely being a bureaucracy with a reputation that is rapidly deteriorating because it is perceived to inflict undeserved harm.

In other words, in a union characterized by either much faster political integration or creeping renationalization in its eurozone core, coupled with growing skepticism across all member states and economic and social problems unprecedented in modern times, the solution is the first choice. There should be even more integration, a closer union, and the complete federalization of the EU—on socialist terms, of course. The first European Union would have to be redefined (moved further to the left); it needs to become a unified socialist EUtopia or it will disintegrate into its continually feuding national states again, practically ensuring a new world war.

This horror scenario based on fear and intimidation with its artificially created apocalyptic future is supposed to convince the peoples of the twenty-seven remaining member states that they do not have a choice. They must give up their identities and individual sovereignties and turn their countries over to a single, unified, state-controlled EUtopian entity, or they will have to go back to the status quo that existed just before World War II. They must accept the fact that the relatively comfortable lives they have enjoyed under EU guidance (and subsidies) can be maintained only if they give up on the nation-states.

The left-liberal Eurocrats think that the people will not notice that the latent socialization of the past quarter of a century has turned Europe from a flowering economic powerhouse to a basket case of democracy. They think the Eastern European countries that joined the EU mainly for economic reasons, not even dreaming about their future resocialization, will again eagerly and voluntarily give up their remaining independence for another socialist EUtopian experiment.

There is, of course, much to dislike about the EU. The so-called democratic deficit is real. The high-handed manner in which Eurocrats push through sometimes quite misguided policies (the euro, to mention just one) has, rightly, put people's backs up. Moreover, the European Parliament is filled with obscure cranks suffering from the anxieties of modern Western democracy removed from reality, and members of the arrogant and self-appointed liberal elite—the educated mandarins and commentators, the know-it-all writers and ivory-tower academics, the left-of-center internationalists, the cosmopolitans, the social justice seekers and the self-appointed do-gooders. In short, they are the sorts of people whose superior airs and arrogant self-righteousness are supposed to make all others feel inadequate and filled with fear.

How can we define "European integration" then? For example: "A process whereby political actors in several distinct national settings are persuaded to shift their loyalties, expectations, and political activities toward a new center, whose institutions possess or demand jurisdiction over pre-existing national states. The end result of a process of political integration is a new political community, superimposed over the pre-existing ones."[7]

Which sovereign European nation will readily embrace the idea of a left-liberal, socialist-dominated European Union, for which it would be worth giving up national identity, independence, sovereignty, and nationhood? Probably Germany—if all the others will, voluntarily of course, accept its leadership and domination. Anyone who would not, or who would point out the fact that this EUtopia has not only become leftist but is also slowly and surreptitiously spreading its socialist program based on a bureaucratic empire, will immediately be labeled as an anti-European populist and nationalist, if not worse. This smearing makes, of course, a mockery of democracy (let me call it "demockeracy") and practically guarantees the eventual disintegration of the currently twenty-seven-member group of dissension.

THE SPECTER OF SEPARATISM AND DISINTEGRATION HAUNTING EUROPE

In conjunction with the efforts preparing and supporting federalism, the specter of separatism seems to be hovering over Europe. From Belgium, Britain, and the Balkans to Spain, Romania, and the Caucasus, regional independence or autonomy movements are gaining strength everywhere. So unless the European Union comes to grips with its existential crisis, desperately camouflaged by the large, if decreasing, number of its member states, history suggests these independence movements could become even stronger and more successful, transforming Europe as we have known it in the past.

The success of independence and secessionist movements has accompanied major upheavals in the European geopolitical order. Such violent disruptions have taken place every two to three generations during the last two hundred years since the Congress of Vienna.

Thus Bismarck's unification of Germany and the Ottoman Empire's decline set in motion processes that in 1878 allowed small states such as Bulgaria, Montenegro, and Serbia to gain international recognition at the Congress of Berlin.[8]

Then, in 1918, the collapse of the great empires (the Habsburg, Ottoman, and Romanov Empires) at the end of World War I led to another round of redrawing lines on the map. Countries such as Albania, the Kingdom of Serbs, Croats, and Slovenes (later called Yugoslavia), the Baltic republics, Finland, Czechoslovakia, and Poland broke out of the empires they had been attached to and became fully recognized members of the international community.

After 1945, the end of World War II and the process of decolonization ushered in the third wave of nation-building across much of the globe as European colonies in Africa, Asia, Central and South America, and Oceania gained independence.

Next, from 1989 to 1992, the collapse of communism and the downfall of the Soviet Union triggered the fourth and most recent wave of European nation-building. There are twenty-three or twenty-four countries now (depending on who is doing the counting) in the same geographical area that comprised only three states (Czechoslovakia, the Soviet Union, and Yugoslavia) before 1989. Similarly, the numbers tell the global story equally well: there were only 59 independent countries in the world in 1914, on the eve of World War I. By 1950, there were 89. By 1996, there were 192. As of 2016, there were 193 member states of the United Nations, plus some nonmembers (like the Vatican, Kosovo, and Taiwan).

Moreover, the state-proliferation process continues, which makes the Balkans and the Caucasus real nightmares for cartographers and diplomats trying to reconcile the competing ethnic territorial claims. In the Caucasus and eastern Anatolia, Abkhazia, Chechnya, Nagorno-Karabakh, South Ossetia, the Kurds of eastern Turkey and northern Iraq, and the Turks of northern Cyprus have all declared some form of independence or autonomy.[9]

Southeastern Europe, of course, has with good reason given birth to the term "Balkanization." In Bosnia, the Croats harbor dreams of recreating their wartime entity (Herceg-Bosna) or someday joining Croatia proper, and Serbs would not mind making the Republika Srpska independent or joining Serbia itself.[10] Meanwhile, in the Sandžak region between Montenegro and Serbia, a regional Muslim autonomy movement would be happy to unify with coreligionists to the north and create a Greater Bosnia.[11] Serbs in northern Kosovo have declared their independence from Pristina, and Albanians in Serbia's Presevo Valley have likewise in the past stated their desire for unification with Kosovo.[12] Similarly, Albanians in western Macedonia in 1992 declared a Republic of Ilirida and are now pushing for a federal territorialization of that state.[13] A significant number of Bulgarians believes that much of eastern Macedonia rightfully belongs to them, autonomist and irredentist sentiments among Hungarians in Transylvania cause constant anxiety in Romania, and the breakaway region of Transnistria continues to generate problems for Moldova.[14]

The surge of separatism in Western Europe over the past several years has followed similar problems in the East, contradicting the accepted view that democracy and widespread prosperity alleviate nationalist tensions and aspirations. Separatism in Western Europe has taken two forms: rejection of current state arrangements (as in Belgium, Spain, and the UK) and rejection of the European Union itself. In Scotland, nationalism has gained more force than at any other time since William Wallace. Similarly, in Belgium Flemish nationalism has been steadily gaining strength for the past decade. The New Flemish Alliance (N-VA), a center-right Flemish nationalist political party, has become the largest party in Flanders as well as in Belgium as a whole and is leading the 2014–19 Flemish government. In Spain, separatist parties won the absolute majority in Catalonia's regional elections. The European Free Alliance based in Brussels currently boasts some forty nationalist and autonomist parties from across the continent.

Exacerbating the separatist and secessionist pressure on Europe's existing geopolitical order has been the notable rise in public dissatisfaction with the European Union. In Britain, public opinion polls had already consistently shown even before the 2016 "Brexit" election that a near majority of Britons would opt out of the EU. In Germany, a summer 2012 survey revealed that 49 percent of the Germans surveyed believed they would be better off without the EU.[15]

The above data reflect the frequently overlooked degree of Europe's vulnerably delicate stability and imply the possible consequences concerning the EU's and, to a great extent, NATO's future. If the EU were to collapse under the weight of its inherent complications, the resulting reconstitution of Europe's geopolitical arena would provide the opportunity and political breathing space for many of Europe's concealed nationalists to have a go at it. Unfortunately, the historical pattern shows that the creation of new states is usually a tremendously bloody affair; Czechoslovakia's Velvet Divorce was the notable exception to the historical experience, and Yugoslavia's bloody demise is the much more typical case.

Given that the last "final" reordering of Europe's geopolitical structure took place in 1989–91, along with the knowledge that such significant transformations take place in every two to three generations, and Europe's ongoing political quandary, it is reasonable to ponder whether we are near the starting point of another upheaval. Political pundits are eager to see longevity and stability in the world at any given moment, no matter how ephemeral that endurance is in reality. Groundless contentment based on wishful thinking often makes it difficult to see the real problems looming just over the horizon; Ukraine is a primary example of this.

THE HOMOGENIZATION OF THE TOTALITARIAN LIBERAL DEMOCRACIES

Western culture is homogenized. Everything is uniform. Nothing is unique. The homogenization of the West is evidenced in the ubiquitous artificiality of the corporate retail culture; it feeds political correctness, celebrity culture, mass media, and the appeal to the broadest possible audience with the greatest potential spending power. Political correctness eliminates all differences.

Education's value is marked not by excellence but by good grades that will ensure admission to a leading university to allow one to secure a "top job." The danger in cultural homogenization is that the system breaks those who are capable of excellence. Rather than exalting excellence, the outstanding are told to sit down. Peer pressure forces them not to be different or "weird," so they abandon their gifts to fit in. Phony egalitarian ideologues, driven by sentimentality, offer the same rewards to all, making sure that there are no such things as rewards any longer at all. Those who study and strive are accused of being stuck up, while those who do not are admired as "one of us."

The continuous rise of relativism has been one of the underlying drivers for the homogenization of the West. Without knowing the truth, there can be no value judgment. Without value judgment, one thing is not better than another. If one thing cannot be better than another, if one person cannot be better than another, and if one's moral choice cannot be better than another, the only judgment is that there shall be no judgment. Relativism pushes egalitarianism to its logical and absurd limit so that we live in a cultural bewilderment where there is no truth, no reference point to steer by, no values to be held, and no standards to be met.

When all is relativized in such a way, the only ones who rise to the top are those who are the richest and strongest—and this is barbarism, not civilization.

This author stands against the homogenization of culture because he knows that value judgments exist; that there is always, perhaps still undiscovered, truth. He knows that some cultures were better than others, their philosophy was lofty, their literature inspiring, their heroes noble, pure, and daring, their art was dominant, their music was superior, their poetry was sublime, and their architecture inspired awe. Classical education safeguards the best of the past, informs the present, and builds a foundation for the future.

The forms of "liberal democracy are a mere facade—camouflage for the largely unconstrained power of the ruling elite. Thus, what people enjoy in the West today is not democratic liberty but rather the *image* of liberty. We live in a tyranny of tolerance.

Today we live in totalitarian democracies wherein the forms of a commonwealth disguise absolute power. The masters of the Western World surround their authority with darkness, conceal their overwhelming and irresistible strength, and humbly profess themselves the politicians whose supreme decrees must be obeyed. The image of liberty—or the trappings of constitutionalism—is apparently sufficient to keep the people satisfied. The rulers know that the people would submit to slavery, provided they were respectfully assured that they would still enjoy their "freedoms." An enervated people cheerfully acquiesce in the pleasing illusion as long it is supported by the "good life." As long as the government is tolerably efficient, reliably provides the bread and circuses on which the people had come to depend, and maintains the facade of a constitution, the different peoples of the West are content to be supine subjects.

Governance today occurs at the national or even supranational level rather than the local or ground level. At the ground level, much or most of the federal law that regulates the day-to-day affairs is enacted not by Congress or Parliament but rather by unelected administrative agencies whose procedures maintain only a pretense—a pleasing illusion—of conformity to the constitutional separation of powers. The most serious issues are resolved not by elected legislators but rather by unelected judges based on a mere figment of connection to a constitution.

Both at the ground, or local, level and at the higher, or national, level, the realities of governance today deviate substantially from the kind of exercise of authority that free and independent people would require. We might argue on both levels about the law that governs us, whether it is "for the people" or not, but it is surely not of or by the people in a sense contemplated by a historical constitution.

What is to be done?

The peoples of the Western world still enjoy degrees of liberty and prosperity today that would have been envied by most people through most of history. Then why not just be grateful for what we have—the image of liberty?

Because without securely established self-governance, there is no guarantee that such benevolent rule would or could continue. In fact, it will not.

Indeed, the powers and reach of our rulers are in many respects more formidable today than at any prior time in history. Our police forces, our bureaucratic machinery, and our powers of surveillance vastly exceed anything the dictators of the old days could have imagined. As we contemplate the choice between regular or irregular efforts to uphold the constitution and acquiesce to the seemingly irresistible power of the administrative state and the imperial judiciary, we would be wise to keep that fact in mind.

The question then is whether we will demand real liberty—including the authority to govern ourselves—or whether we will be content with "the image of liberty." Time will tell.

The Changing Western Intervention Concepts

Undoubtedly, defense systems will continue to be expensive and complex; this fact means that they will increasingly be the tools of professionalized, if not mercenary, forces. All of history shows that the shift from a mass army of citizen soldiers to a smaller army of professional fighters leads to a decline of democracy in the long run.

There can be no doubt that the specialist weapons of today will continue to dominate the military scenario into the foreseeable future. If so, there is also little reason to doubt that authoritarian rather than democratic political regimes will dominate the world for this foreseeable future. To be sure, traditions and other factors may keep "democratic systems," or at least some pseudodemocratic models, in particular areas, such as the United States or Europe. To the person of today, brought up on the staple of democratic ideology, this may seem very tragic or surprising, but some perhaps redeeming features in this situation may well be considered.

For one, although Western civilization is almost fifteen hundred years old, it has been democratic in political action for less than two hundred of those years. Equally significant is the fact that a period of limited warfare seeking limited political aims may well be coming with a professionalized army, as was also the case in the eighteenth century. The limited wars of our time in Iraq, Afghanistan, and Syria support that theory, if for no other reason than that professionalized forces are less willing to kill and be killed for remote and total objectives.

The relatively simple and cheap amateur weapons used during the two centuries following the French Revolution made possible the mass citizen armies that fought in the Napoleonic wars, the American Civil War, and both world wars. Such mass armies, comprising several million people, could not be offered financial rewards for risking their lives, but they could be presented with ideological, idealistic, extreme, dogmatic, and "total" goals that would convince and inspire them to willingness to die and to kill. Ending slavery, making the world safe for democracy, ending tyranny, and spreading, or at least saving, "our way of life" were some such goals. However, they led to total and unlimited warfare, aiming for total victory and ending in unconditional surrender. As a result, each combatant country felt that not only its way of life but its very existence was at stake—that it would not survive defeat. Thus all combatants felt the compulsion to fight yet more tenaciously. The result was ruthless wars of extermination, such as World War II.

With the continued professionalization of the armed services, caused by the increasing complexity of weapon systems, one can look forward with some assurance to less and less demand for total wars using weapons of mass destruction (WMD) to achieve unconditional surrender and ultimate goals.

The naive, idealistic, and missionary Western idea that war aims must involve the destruction and replacement of the enemy's regime and the imposition on the defeated people of a democratic system with a prosperous economy, such as they have never previously known, will someday become an outmoded concept. Instead what should take its place is the recognition that the enemy regime must survive so that the victors will have some government with whom they can negotiate to obtain more limited aims that brought about the conflict in the first place. Thus, the level of conflict can be lowered as rapidly as possible, consistent with the achievement of the objectives.

The movement toward the professionalization of armed forces, which results in lower intensity of conflict, is part of a much larger process deriving from the nuclear and superpower stalemate between the Soviet Union, later Russia, and the United States. The danger of a nuclear holocaust will remain and become even more horrifying, but for this very reason, it will be a more remote and less likely probability. No country, including the United States, Russia, and China, can win in a nuclear exchange, even if they make the first strike. Thus the mutual veto on the use of missiles, the nuclear stalemate, remains.

This stalemate on the use of nuclear weapons also extends to the use of non-nuclear weapons. The stalemate means that the use of tactical nuclear weapons, and even the use of conventional tactical weapons, is inhibited to an undetermined degree by the presence of strategic nuclear weapons no one wants to see used. The costs of using tactical nuclear weapons are so high that it is very doubtful if they are worth the price. At such a cost, no one would prefer to be defended.

In fact, it appears increasingly likely that fewer and fewer developed countries will regard large-scale war as an efficient method of getting anything. What could a people obtain through a war that they could not get with greater certainty and less effort in some other way? Indeed, the very idea of winning a general war is now almost unthinkable. We do not even know what we mean by "winning." Whatever Germany, Japan, and Italy sought from World War II, they would most likely not have obtained by winning; yet they gained the most significant parts of it by losing.

Glory, power, and wealth may all be achieved with less effort and greater certainty by non-warlike methods. As science and technology advance, making war more horrible, they also make it possible to achieve any aims at which war might be directed by nonviolent methods.

However, none of the above is a call for appeasement or support for any system of tyranny that oppressed, enslaved, and murdered over 180 million people in the twentieth century. Just like the National Socialist regimes have been, the communist system should also be stamped out in this world, not built up in an alternative form with the help of the West.

Superpower neutralization and the corresponding nuclear stalemate will continue into the future. However, from this flows the growing independence of the "neutrals" and nonaligned nations because of their ability to act freely in the troubled waters.

In the Western world, power has been based to a significant extent on brute force, meaning weapons, and to a lesser degree on economic rewards and ideological appeal. Changes in weapons within the Western system have brought about changes in political patterns and organizations that threaten to cause profound changes in politics and probably in the Western system itself.

As a result of all the complex interrelationships of weapons and politics, future international relations will shift from the world we have previously known, in which war was epidemic and total, to a world in which conflict is endemic and controlled. The ending of total warfare means the end of wars for unlimited aims (unconditional surrender, total victory, complete destruction of the opponent's regime and social system) fought with a full mobilization of resources, including men.

Modern warfare means a condition of constant, flexible, and controlled conflict with limited, specific, and shifting aims, sought by limited application of manifold pressures applied against any other state whose behavior the West wishes to influence. Such controlled conflicts involve some changes in Western attitudes and behavior:

- There may be no explicit declarations of war, and perhaps not even the breaking off of diplomatic relations with the adversary, but instead continuous communication with him, whatever level of intensity the conflict may reach.
- There must be acknowledgment that conflict with an adversary regarding some areas, activities, units, or weapons does not necessarily involve conflict in other areas, activities, units, or weapons.
- Military applications and the use of force are to be employed in political considerations and are to operate as one part of the whole policy context.

- Armed forces will be trained and fully prepared to do any task to the degree and level the established political authorities order them. These tasks will be accomplished without any desire or independent effort to carry combat to a level of intensity that does not comply with existing policy and political considerations.
- There must be the full ability at all times to escalate or de-escalate the degree of warfare as seems necessary concerning the policy context and to signal this decision to the adversary as a guide to his responses.
- The ability to de-escalate to the level of termination of violence and warfare must be possible, both in psychological and procedural terms, even under the continuing conflict on lower, non-force levels, such as economic or ideological clashes.
- There must exist a full panoply of military, economic, political, social, and intellectual pressures that can be used in conflict with any diverse states to secure the specific and limited goals that would become the real aims of international policy in a period of controlled conflict.
- Among the methods that the West will be prepared to use in such a period must be diplomatic or tacit agreement with any other state, including Russia or China, to seek parallel or common aims in the world. This understanding will be possible if all objectives are limited to specific goals that each state will recognize are not fatal to its general position and regime, and can be traded even tacitly against another. Also, limited specific goals will be possible for the dual reason that professionalization of the fighting forces and the growing productiveness of the superpower economies will not require either the total psychological mobilization or the almost total economic mobilization that were necessary in World War II.
- All this means a blurring of the distinction between war and peace, with the situation being at all times one of tightly controlled conflict. In this way, regional conflict is accepted for the sake of avoiding, if possible, widespread total war. The change will become possible because the overall policy of all great powers will become the preservation of their way of life and existing regime, with the broadest possible freedom of action. This policy goal is realistic only under controlled conflict but will vanish to all concerned in total war.

Directly supporting surrogate governments and getting involved in the internal affairs of foreign countries by using clandestine methods have been the traditional American approaches. The more modern way of changing regimes and turning public opinion around has been indirect and covert interventions favored by the US government since the 1980s and the EU since the 1990s.

Instigating internal disorder, undermining foreign powers from within, and organizing restlessness with false pretenses are all part of the recognizable new style of the "spreading of democracy." The list of precedents is long: the Polish uprisings in the early 1980s; the sudden toppling of the Romanian dictator Ceausescu in 1989; the dismantling of Yugoslavia, including the Serbo-Croatian-Bosnian-Kosovo wars; the Lebanon crisis; the Ukrainian elections and spontaneous revolution; the Kyrgyz rebellion; the "saving of the Iraqi people" from Saddam Hussein; and the Arab Spring in Tunisia, Egypt, Libya, and Syria.

However, one distinct pattern is recognizable: one particular segment of society, an ethnic or religious minority, claims wrongdoing against it, precipitating change to the advantage of the United States or causing an international crisis that will bring about the support of the West (NATO) in the name of democracy.

The Western liberal elite has a tried and tested playbook for removing foreign leaders and regimes they do not like, and it seems to vary precious little from country to country:

- Through their agents in the mainstream media, they blacken the name of the leader in question with all kinds of ambiguous, blurry, and unsubstantiated allegations of abuse of power or fabricated accusations of wrongdoing.
- They massively fund genuine or puppet opposition movements and use them to foment general discontent.
- If this fails to garner the required electoral gains, they use the media, such as CNN, the BBC, the *New York Times*, the *Washington Post* or similarly experienced news-fabricators to accuse the incumbent regime of rigging the elections.
- They make sure these media outlets always depict antigovernment rallies as the voice of the people; by the same token, they always explain away any pro-government rallies as the result of bribery or intimidation by stooges, even when such rallies are much larger than the opposition protests.

- They fund, organize, and direct the military movements of the favored opposition, and when the government's forces are compelled to take on these Western-backed rebel—if not outright mercenary—movements, they also make sure that the media mouthpieces focus solely on the atrocities, be they real or imaginary, on the government side.
- They call upon their media mouthpieces to depict the opposition activists and fighters as living saints while completely ignoring the representatives of the wished-to-be-toppled government, thereby preventing them from explaining anything contrary to the officially approved and stage-managed reports fed to the public.
- They manufacture a wave of media hysteria about the leader butchering his people and engaging in other human rights violations, and they use this as a pretext for military intervention.
- They make sure the media ignores the many civilian casualties that result from this intervention.
- When the sitting regime has been overthrown, they make sure the Western media leaves the scene and ignores the corruption, thuggery, lawlessness, and breakdown of civil society that has resulted as a consequence of the overthrow. That way the public can be convinced that the whole operation was a great triumph of Western values and arms, and the episode can be used to justify the next "humanitarian intervention."

The above ingeniously sophisticated process is exceedingly difficult, if not impossible, to counter by any government or state without the direct support of at least one friendly great power—especially one of the five permanent members of the UN Security Council. Moreover, the process is apparently designed to deceive the peoples of the West into believing in their "just cause" based on "humanitarian principles."

3

European Federalism under German Leadership

One development in political life during the next generation or so that will be difficult to document concerns the very nature of the modern sovereign state. Like so much of our cultural heritage from the seventeenth century, such as international law and Puritanism, this may now be in the process of change so profound as to modify its very nature. As understood in Western Europe for almost four centuries, the state was the organization of sovereign power on a territorial basis.[16]

"Sovereign" once meant that the state, or ruler, had the supreme legal authority to do just about anything regarded as public, and this power impinged directly on the subject, or citizen, without any intermediaries or buffer entities.

The once almost universal equivalence between residence and citizenship is weakening today. If the state continues to develop its likely characteristics, persons of different ideologies and thus of different allegiances may become intermingled on the same territory. The number of refugees and resident aliens is now increasing in most countries.

The idea of an independent German national strategy contradicts everything that Germany has wanted since World War II and everything the world has required from Germany. To a certain extent, the entire structure of postwar Europe was created to capitalize on Germany's economic dynamism while preventing the threat of German domination.

In writing about German strategy, this author is raising the possibility that the core structure of Western Europe since World War II is slowly disintegrating. If so, the question then arises whether the historical pattern of German strategy will emerge or whether something new is coming to replace it. Of course, it is even possible that the old postwar model can endure in some form at the end. Whatever it is, the future of German strategy is undoubtedly the most critical question in Europe and quite decisive for the world.

THE EVER-PRESENT GERMAN QUESTION

The German question is not, in fact, one problem but a complex of geostrategic, ideological, and cultural dilemmas that have haunted Europe for centuries. The German question before the reunification of Germany had never been considered solved, though it was at least no longer pressing. However, it is back now, rephrased by what is called the EU crisis. It is a question that the entire European Union must answer.

The question, over the centuries, has always had two premises. The first is Germany's geographical centrality. Even today, Germany has more neighbors than any other country in the EU. The second is Germany's "awkward scale," as Kurt Georg Kiesinger, chancellor of West Germany at the time, called it in 1967. It is neither huge like America nor tiny like Luxembourg. It is too small either to dominate Europe outright or to exist independently next to the company of US-, Russia-, China-, or India-sized powers. Even so, it is too big simply to get in line as just another member of the system. Thus Germany may have one vote, equal to Malta's, on the governing council of the European Central Bank (ECB). Nevertheless, as the supplier of almost 20 percent of the ECB's capital, its interests and sway cannot be considered equal to those of Malta (which provides less than 1 percent of the bank's capital).

Henry Kissinger once phrased this dilemma as "too big for Europe, too small for the world."[17] The great German writer Thomas Mann expressed essentially the same idea in a famous speech in 1953 as a tension between "a German Europe" and "a European Germany."[18] The European monetary union forged during and after German unification was not a German project to dominate Europe but a European project to constrain Germany.[19] Hence it is ironic that this same monetary union has, for Greeks or Cypriots or Portuguese, led instead to a Europe made German.

The issue was to prevent Germany from returning to the pursuit of an independent national strategy because the West could not tolerate the reemergence of divisive and dangerous power politics in Europe. The key was binding Germany to the rest of Europe politically, economically, and militarily. This idea meant that German and French interests coincided—taking into account that constant anxiety between France and Germany had been one of the triggers of previous wars. Naturally, this also included other Western European countries, but it was Germany's relationship with France that was most important.

Militarily, German and French interests were tied together under the NATO alliance even after France withdrew from the NATO Military Committee under Charles de Gaulle. Economically, Germany was bound to Europe through the emergence of more sophisticated multilateral economic organizations that ultimately evolved into the European Union.

As Europe now decides whether to submit to "German rules" about fiscal and economic management or forced immigration under the cloak of "refugee crisis," the EU as a whole decides where its political center of gravity should sit. In fact, they are all asking the same perennial question over and over again.

BINDING GERMANY TO EUROPE: THE GERMAN PERSPECTIVE

Following World War II, West Germany had to defend itself against the Soviet Union in concert with an alliance that would in effect command its military through NATO. This strategy limited German sovereignty but eliminated the perception of Germany as a threat.

West Germany also aligned its economy with that of the rest of Europe, pursuing prosperity, based on the social market economy, without undermining the prosperity of other countries. The founding of the European Economic Community based on free trade was an essential element strengthening the export-based German economy.

Then West Germany started exercising its internal political sovereignty, recovering its rights as a nation without presenting an apparent geopolitical threat to Western Europe. This projection of power, carefully veiled as mere enjoyment of national sovereignty, was extended to also include the Eastern European countries after the fall of the Soviet Union.

The European economy, in general, and the German economy, in particular, surged once East Germany had reintegrated with West Germany. With reintegration, internal German sovereignty was ensured. Most importantly, France remained linked to Germany via the European Union and NATO. Russia was relatively secure so long as Germany continued to be a part of the European structure. The strategic and historical problem Germany had faced before appeared to be solved.

EUROPE'S ECONOMIC CRISIS: A NEW ASPECT OF THE GERMAN PROBLEM

The German strategy became more involved after 2008 than it had been before. Germany's formal relationship with NATO remained intact, but without the common threat of the Soviet Union, the alliance was fracturing over the divergent national interests of its members. The European Union, which had become Germany's primary focus, came under intense pressure that made the previous alignment of all European countries more dubious.

Germany needs the European Union. It needs it firstly for the same reasons that have existed since World War II: the EU is the foundation of Germany's relationship with France and is the means to ensure that national interests will not generate the kinds of conflicts that existed in the past.

Germany needs the European Union for another reason as well: Germany is the largest (or sometimes second-largest, depending on the year) exporter in the world. While Germany exports to many countries, Europe is an essential customer. The free-trade zone, which was the foundation of the European Union, was also one of the pillars of the German economy. Protectionism, in general, but certainly protectionism in Europe, threatens Germany, whose industrial capacity substantially outstrips its domestic consumption. The pricing of the euro (vis-à-vis the old West German mark, or DM) was tailored to German needs and has aided German exports to a significant degree. Similarly, the EU regulations in Brussels provided Germany with much other leverage over the competition. Undoubtedly the European Union, as it existed between 1991 and 2008, was critically important for Germany.

However, the European Union no longer functions as it once did when it contained the six founding members, all of them highly industrialized countries. The economic dynamics of New Europe, with its twenty-eight (twenty-seven after Brexit) member states, have placed many countries—especially some of the newer and poorer ones, at a substantial disadvantage. Moreover, the economic crisis of 2008 triggered a very severe sovereign debt and banking crisis in Europe.

In the broadest sense, there were two possible solutions. The first one was that the countries in crisis impose austerity measures to find the resources to solve their problem. The other was that the wealthier part of Europe underwrites the debts, sparing these countries the burden of austerity. The solution chosen has been a combination of the two, but the precise design of that combination remains a complicated and sensitive matter for future negotiations.

Again, Germany needs the European Union for both political and economic reasons. The question is whether a stable economic solution can emerge that the European political systems will support.

Germany is prepared to help relieve other European countries only if they impose severe austerity measures and make sure that they are implemented and the crisis is not repeated. From Germany's point of view, the roots of the crisis lie in the fiscal policies of the troubled countries. Therefore, the German price for underwriting part of the debt is that European bureaucrats, heavily oriented toward German policies, be effectively put in charge of the finances of countries receiving aid against default.

This German condition would mean, of course, that the countries involved would not control either taxes or budgets through their political system; it would be an assault on their national sovereignty. Apparently there has been lots of opposition from potential recipients of aid and from some countries that see it as something that would vastly increase the power of Germany.

If one accepts the German view, which is that the debt crisis was the result of reckless spending, then Germany's proposal seems quite reasonable. If one subscribes to the view of southern Europe, which is that the crisis was the result of the European Union's design (favorable to German interests), then what Germany is proposing is the imposition of German power via economics.

It is hard to imagine a massive surrender of sovereignty to a German-dominated EU bureaucracy, whatever the economic cost might be. It is equally difficult to imagine Germany underwriting the debt without some controls beyond empty promises. Even if the European Union is of vital importance to the Germans, German public opinion will not permit throwing good money after bad. Finally, it is hard to see how, in the long term, the Europeans can reconcile their differences concerning this problem. The issue will come to a climax sooner or later, and there is always going to be the next crisis.

All European institutions exist because the design of both the EU and the euro was supposed to be such that nobody could ever be a hegemon over it—neither Germany nor France or any combination of them. The whole point was that no single country could dominate.

In this context, then, complaints about German hegemony, power, and influence in the current systems of the EU amount to demands for German money without any other form of German influence—euros without strings. This requirement is what Germans fear—another transfer union. They already have two transfer unions at home and like neither. The first is the German system of equalizing revenues among the sixteen German federal states, so that wealthy Bavaria, say, gives money to poor Berlin. The second is a solidarity tax (set to end in 2019) that all Germans have been paying since the reunification so as to send money to eastern Germany. They would rather not add a third layer for the eurozone.

THE FUTURE IS FRAUGHT WITH GERMAN POLITICAL ALTERNATIVES

In the meantime, the basic framework of Europe has changed since 1991. Russia remains a major exporter of natural gas, and Germany depends on that natural gas even as it searches for alternatives. Russia is in need of modern technology and know-how, a considerable amount of which Germany possesses in abundance. Germany, apparently, does not want to invite in any more immigrants out of fear of political instability. However, because of its aging and declining population, Germany must do something.

Russia also has a declining population, but even so, it has a surplus of workers, both unemployed and underemployed. If the workers cannot come to the factories, the factories can come to the workers. In short, there could be substantial synergy between the Russian and German economies. Alas, the Germans feel under heavy pressure from the United States to engage in actions the Germans instead want to be left out of, while the Russians see the Americans as a threat to their interests.

All of the above is pointing to distinct political and economic interests that Germany and Russia have in common—as has happened so many times in their history.

Germany is not an outwardly aggressive power today. The basis of its longstanding strategy is its relationship with France in the context of the European Union, and the French governments have indeed committed to this relationship. However, the French political system, like those of other European countries, is coming under ever more intense pressure. Nevertheless, the willingness of France to engage with Germany, which has a massive trade imbalance with France, cannot be doubted—for now.

Germany's current strategy is still to preserve the European Union and its relationship with France. The difficulty of this approach is that Germany's trade policies are more and more difficult for other European countries, including France, to manage. If Germany faces an impossible situation within the European Union, the second strategic option would be a three-way alliance, with a modified European Union or perhaps outside of the EU structure. If for whatever reason France ever decided it has other interests, such as its idea of a "Mediterranean Union," then even a German–Russian relationship could become a possibility.[20]

A close German–Russian alliance would have the potential to tilt the balance of power in the world; the combination of German technology and Russian resources—an idea dreamed of by many in the past, most notably by Bismarck—would become a challenge on a global basis. Admittedly, the Western powers will and must never submit to that.

All Western strategies concerning Russia depend on the often forgotten fact that Russia has its national interests, be they political, social, economic, or otherwise. As will be pointed out in the corresponding chapter, Russia is not likely, and cannot realistically be expected, to compromise on these owing to mostly economic interests, because the German interests would be based primarily on economics—at least at first. However, a conservative Russia vigilantly guarding its newly rediscovered values that are alien to the Western (e.g., German) socialist-liberal system has no reason to trust such a system—and it does not have to. It can already get technology for resources and markets—just like the Chinese did.

The West tends to forget that economics is not the sole deciding factor in determining strategy.

Germany's strategy, therefore, together with the slowly reappearing "German Problem," is still locked in the EU paradigm. Nevertheless, if this EU paradigm becomes unsupportable, then other strategies will have to be found, and Germany will also have to think about political, instead of only economic, alternatives.[21]

GERMAN LEADERSHIP: LOSS OF NATIONAL SOVEREIGNTY, SUBJUGATION TO THE SUPRANATIONAL STATE

Many experts believe that Germany's austerity plan proposal implies a significant loss of sovereignty for some countries forming the eurozone. It is noteworthy that the German plan to repair Europe does not require much sacrifice from Germany. The German government does not want to pay for the rescuing of other European countries and is staunchly against the creation of Eurobonds, which would help spread the risk of default among all states of the eurozone. Europe is losing its democratic face while Germany is increasingly expanding its leadership.

The process of the EU enlargement has been taking place without any carefully thought-out long-term concept, which resulted in a crisis. The enlarged EU is now an entirely different league than it had previously been. The Franco-German engine is no longer a two-stroke one; it is only Germany dominating today.

At the beginning of the current globalization cycle, mainly during the administration of Chancellor Gerhard Schröder, Germany was able to reach a strategic compromise within the country, which in many ways explains Germany's unique position within the eurozone today. By the rules of the social market economy, workers agreed to a freeze and reduction of income, and businesspeople pledged not to take their production abroad.[22]

Since 1995, business and government have been adhering to specific policies aimed at improving the competitiveness of the German national economy. This approach led to the fact that the competitiveness of German goods has increased by

25 percent compared to other countries in the eurozone over the last ten to twelve years. Between 1996 and 2008, the volume of German exports increased twofold. The increase in the efficiency of the German economy led to a rise in the cost of production in other countries of the eurozone. As a result, other members of the eurozone, especially Italy and France, found themselves in a situation where they could not manage a positive foreign trade balance.[23]

Simply put, the highly competitive German goods displace national products in the other countries of the eurozone. At the same time, the eurozone countries are unable to devalue their local currencies—the most efficient way to improve the competitiveness of their goods. After the introduction of the euro, they do not have such authority.

The modern, reunified Germany is not only the EU's largest economy but also a country that sets the rules for the domestic macroeconomics of the eurozone. The most likely scenario for the further development of the eurozone might be the following: the countries unable to get out of the budget crisis will have to transfer some of their sovereign powers to Germany or will have to leave the eurozone. The eurozone will either be transformed into a "Greater Germany" or fall apart. Fear that the state might have to deal with a banking collapse makes government bonds riskier. At the same time, the fear that the state could not cope makes a banking collapse more likely.

So the regrettable conclusion is that the nations in the eurozone will eventually have to share their burdens. The eurozone's problem is not the debt's size but its fragmented structure; the banks are not too big for Europe as a whole, just for the individual governments. To the happy, socialist-leaning left-liberal EUrocrats, there is an obvious solution: Europe will have to become more federal, more centralized, and more united.

Accordingly, as one would expect, the European voters will eventually be scared into grudging acquiescence precisely because a euro collapse is so terrifying. To see the eurozone crisis as an opportunity to centralize the EU would be to misread the people's appetite for integration. The wartime generation, which saw the EU as a bulwark against strife, is fading. For most Europeans, the outcome of the EU's most ambitious project, the euro, feels like misery. Also, there is no evidence that voters feel close to the EU. The Lisbon treaty and its precursor, the EU's once-aborted constitution, were together rejected in three out of six referendums; ten governments reneged on promises to put constitutional reform to the vote.[24] The European Parliament is hopelessly remote.

An alternative to the supranational state is to accept that politics remains stubbornly national—and to increase the power of governments to police their neighbors. However, that, too, has problems. As the euro crisis has shown, governments struggle to make collective decisions. The small countries of the eurozone fear that the big ones would hold too much sway. If Berlin pays the bills and tells the rest of Europe how to behave, it risks fostering destructive nationalist resentment against Germany. Moreover, it would strengthen the Eurosceptic camp arguing for an exit.

Centralization would introduce massive changes. Politicians would no longer be able to force their banks to support national firms or buy their government bonds. Banks would no longer be Spanish or German, but increasingly European. Make no mistake: this is integration. However, this integration could be and should be limited to finance—a part of the economy where the monetary union has already swept away national boundaries.

The peoples of Europe passed through that first stage of development when the biological similarity was the most important bond between them; the organic element was relegated to the background a long time ago and superseded by the spiritual component; the tribes and peoples were rarefied into nations. The nation is not the work of nature; it is the work of history. It is a spiritual community held together by common ideals based on shared historical experiences, by shared values manifested in the common ideals, by a universal vocation resulting from the shared values and the corresponding readiness for joint action. Nationhood is the central motif of the state, and this is what the EUtopistic European Union would like to destroy, already claiming that the nation-state is in decline and that only a supranational body can save Europe, denying everything that history has taught us.

What are otherwise the unifying features between, for example, the Estonian and Portuguese nations? Are they common historical experiences, shared ideals, or common values? No, of course not. Are we ready to go back merely to the common biological bond? According to official EUtopia, the answer is no; the common European values should be the bond among all European nations.

So what are these, real or imagined, common European values?

The most frequently proclaimed fundamental values of the EU are democracy, the rule of law, and the tolerance of minorities, gender equality, and other human rights. To claim, however, that by subscribing to these values Estonia and Portugal should and must give up their national sovereignty or that their nation-states should surrender their power to the EU is just absurd.

The European Union's attempts to style itself as the flag bearer of a long tradition of "European values" of tolerance, democracy, and the rule of law contradict both European history and Western policies.

What the author wants to critique here is the EU's claim that democracy, the rule of law, free speech, and tolerance are indeed European values in any meaningful sense. In fact, these values have never been sincerely practiced by either European or indeed Western governments.

Let us take democracy, for example. Even the mainstream textbooks do not claim that democracy necessarily originated in Europe; although Athens is supposed to be its birthplace, there is increasing evidence that the Athenians based it on systems already in place in Africa.[25] The West is fond of saying that freedom does not come from thin air; its roots are in the parliamentary democracy. What is not mentioned, of course, is that this particular version of democracy is based on a total lack of trust of the people and was consciously and openly designed to keep them out of decision-making as far as possible. If democracy means that those who are the subjects of power have some influence over who wields it, Europe is still sorely lacking in this regard.

What about that rule of law? Once again, despite the eight-hundred-year existence of the Magna Carta continually trumpeted by Anglo-American propaganda, when it comes to, let us say, international affairs, the same two countries have treated this apparently sacrosanct English principle with absolute contempt. Only in the author's lifetime, from their support for the destruction of Yugoslavia, Iraq, and Syria to their blitzkrieg against Libya in 2011, Europe, the United States, and the West have been the "proud defenders" of unprovoked wars of aggression. Moreover, an unprovoked war of aggression, as defined by the Nuremberg tribunal, is "not only an international crime; it is the supreme international crime, differing only from other war crimes in that it contains within itself the accumulated evil of the whole."[26]

On the domestic front, too, Europe, the United States, and the entire West have been violating the rule of law whenever and wherever it suits them. At any hint of civil unrest, Western governments will instruct magistrates to ignore their sentencing guidelines and imprison everyone involved in the insurrection. It does not matter how slight or serious the offense, the demands for the security of the people and for law and order will throw judicial independence into the wind in the process. The rule of law may well be valued in Europe, but it indeed is not applied to the higher echelons of the Western elite.

Europe may seem to fare a little better on tolerance and freedom of speech, but only if we ignore history, foreign policy, and legislation. Historically, Europe has hardly been a model of toleration. We need not go back to King Edward I's, King Ferdinand's and Queen Isabella's expulsion of the Jews or the anti-Catholic laws to find institutionalized discrimination.[27] Many of the expelled Jews sought refuge in the historically much more tolerant Islamic empires; the anti-Catholic laws remained in place in Britain until 1829 and were repealed only in response to the threat of civil war in Ireland.[28] This injustice is perhaps not surprising given that the West itself was built on intolerance and discrimination worldwide, stripping people of their political rights, often reducing them to a legal status hardly any different from animals or property. Concerning this, the 2012 laws passed by the NATO-installed Libyan "government" are in line with actual historical European practice abroad—but not with some mythical commitment to tolerance and free speech. These laws threaten the supporters of the previous government with life in prison and grant impunity for anyone who kills them.[29]

Perhaps most insidious of all, however, is the claim that the Western model of combining vibrant democracy with free enterprise has delivered significant progress and prosperity to all. In reality, the Western model has not at all been based on vibrant democracy. On the contrary, it has been based on the deprivation of those subjected to its malfeasant might, from the slaves of time not long past to the countless millions subject to IMF structural adjustment, austerity measures, or NATO bombardments today. In any case, neither has it been based on free enterprise. Every Western nation used massive protectionism during its rise to prosperity. Even today, the most robust industries in the West—from agribusiness and pharmaceuticals to finance—are entirely dependent on massive government subsidies. This was demonstrated most clearly in the $16 trillion global bankers' bailout following the financial crash of 2008.[30]

Protectionism, colonialism or neocolonialism, and political, economic, and military interventions are the real foundations and continuing basis of Western prosperity. To ascribe this success to a set of values that have never been taken seriously by the West's governing elite is not only hypocrisy and a deliberate falsification of history but a slander on those whose own dispossession and impoverishment was the flip side of this prosperity. Only by being honest about the real means of creating Western prosperity can we hope to build a genuinely better, fairer, and more responsible society based on mutual respect and understanding.

The West's governing elite, then, has consistently undermined the very values they hypocritically, and typically, claim to espouse. The purpose of their false claim is not at all that we, as Europeans and Westerners, are supposed to practice these values ourselves. It is about providing solid grounds for hating so-called nondemocratic, illiberal, and national-conservative political systems, which are always presented as the most dangerous transgressors of these values.

However, this duplicitous language not only reinforces ignorant prejudices about others' aversion to democracy, the rule of law, and tolerance, but it also justifies the rejection of such values by non-Western groups not willing to subscribe to them. It is no wonder they feel duty-bound to reject the values the West deceitfully espouses but practices only when it suits it. The more the Western elite claims democracy, tolerance, and the rule of law to be distinctly Western phenomena, the more angry people join the orbit of non-Western, nondemocratic groups. The more the elite insinuates that these "Western values" are not indigenous to other cultures, the more extremists, who have seen their homelands torn apart by the West, fight in militant groups that reject these values.

Why does this author vehemently oppose any further European federalization and political integration? Because he fears that it is nothing else, in its current form, but another project to reconstitute socialism (disguised as liberal democracy) at the supranational level.

THE GERMAN DESTINY IN EUROPEAN AFFAIRS

Today it has become commonplace to consider postwar Germany as a thriving democracy and a Western country—the two concepts being synonymous with common usage. However, Germany is *not* and has *never* been a genuine Western country, let alone a democracy. What we consider to be modern Germany today is little more than the remnants of a Germany forged at the behest of Konrad Adenauer, the first chancellor of West Germany after World War II. Adenauer's West Germany began to dissolve with the reunification of the country after the Cold War and is now on its way toward extinction. The question of what will replace it is a predominant problem of modern German politics, though it remains a question whispered—perhaps even unasked.

By purging the German soul of Prussian militarism, the Catholic Adenauer accomplished a great thing. However, he delayed the possible unification of Europe in peace and reconciliation at least until the time of Chancellor Willy Brandt. Brandt was attuned to the yearning of the new generation to cast off the entire burden of German national history. In a sense, this generation was the German variation of a popular movement sweeping all parts of the world—for good and ill.

The idealists of the 1960s appeared throughout the world, from the United States through Western and Eastern Europe to the Soviet Union and China. The political contexts in which they labored were different, but what united this New Left was a desire to withdraw from the *danse macabre* (dance of death, referring to nuclear annihilation for the '68 generation) of history itself, to forge a common understanding between cultures, and to end all wars. Like all bourgeois revolutionaries, many of them only extended the tensions and flared the conflicts they had set out to tame.

In Germany, however, Brandt's overtures toward Poland and Eastern Europe began the German movement toward reconciliation with her age-old enemies. The fact that Brandt's policies were aided by Nixon's détente only strengthened the German hand in this regard. Historians of the Cold War often misunderstand its nature and fail to recognize that the victory was shared by all of Europe, including Russia, which was finally liberated from the yoke of Bolshevism, the burden of internationalism, and the prospect of atomic war.

That brings us to the Germany of today. The twenty-first century is beginning to take forms and shapes ominously reminiscent of the nineteenth, when the international order was maintained by an intricate balance of power concerning multiple countries. Whether or not one finds it desirable, Germany is now again the critical component of European continental power. This power is a function of two key elements: first, German economic strength, and second, Franco-German union. France is today the military arm of Germany. French economic interests are so tightly intertwined with those of Germany that French nuclear potency always shadows German diplomacy.

Germany finds itself, like Goethe's Faust, confronted by the political Mephistopheles in the form of the eternal temptation of the East, of socialism, of idealistic "save the world from itself" causes and other quixotic tenets, all based on pathological German self-hatred. Today our age is blinded to this fact by the idiocy of modern liberal democracy. We still do not recognize the devil tempting Germany to pursue ruin yet again; in our times, it seems impossible that calls to pursue democracy, gay rights, reproductive rights, human rights, and women's rights could be siren songs meant to destroy Odysseus.

The content of German imperialism has *always* been idealistic. No German imperial enterprise was ever undertaken for any but the high-minded goals of its contemporary spirit of the times. The Teutonic Order slaughtered Polish and Lithuanian Catholics and Russian Eastern Orthodox Christians for the higher cause of Catholicism. The German Empire fought against the four Great Powers to secure its right to "peaceful expansion." The democratic Weimar Republic fought against Polish claims to Silesia and the right to self-determination. Nazi Germany fought to liberate Ukraine and the Baltic States from communism and create a thousand-year peace in the name of Western Civilization. All of the ideologies that animated past German imperialism are now in disrepute.

Nevertheless, we are still oblivious to the fact that this new religion of liberal democracy will, in the same way, become a stigma one day. Unfortunately, we are very similar to previous generations who thought they had freed themselves from human transgression and were in possession of an idea worth risking anything for.

Thus the German destiny once again lies before the German people to decide. Will they keep their sense of reality and order? Alternatively, will they seek to cast off the burden of German character in pursuit of the folly of German idealism, which manifests itself in socialistic liberal democracy today? The fate of Europe rests in German hands again. So this feckless and reckless Europe is turning to dust and slipping through German fingers now because Germans have relapsed into their habitually romantic state of mind and selected to pay for their past sins by becoming liberal democratic idealists. They do not realize that by naively putting the deceptive principles of modern liberal democracy above the simple political duty of maintaining a tolerable European order, they are indeed sinning yet again. Repentance is not just to turn from the wrong idealism to the right one; German repentance should be the rejection of false idealism for sound realism.

4

Russia's Newly Found Old Identity

Russia has always been and still is a fundamentally conservative, traditional, and militarily disposed nation. Russia's entire history teaches one lesson: that Russia's existence, survival, and rise rest on and are closely tied to the military and centralization. The list is correspondingly long: from the fight against the Khazars to the Mongol invasion; from the intruding Teutonic Order to the many Polish, Swedish, and Turkish wars; from the conquest of the East to the struggle against Napoleon; from the two world wars to the post-Soviet present.

Russian National Identity

Russia, as a nation, has always developed according to the principles of an aristocracy. As such, Russia's negative predispositions have always been toward oligarchy because, in the Aristotelian scheme of things, the corrosion of aristocratic institutions is called oligarchy.

The Russian state will always be governed by such elites who oversee a populace for whom a democratic form of self-government, which has been widely accepted in Britain or America, will remain alien. It should not be assumed, however, that Russia is condemned to some eternal despotism. To believe this would be the same as thinking that America is forever doomed to the soft or democratic despotism of which Tocqueville wrote.[31] However, in whatever form human liberty and virtue are manifest in Russia, it will not be along the same lines that freedom and virtue have manifested themselves in other nations. In dealing with Russia, one should not lament the fact that the Russian people do not necessarily follow a liberal democratic Utopia. Russia must be understood as she is; only then is it possible to formulate policy. This statement is not a preference for "realpolitik" over ethics but rather a recognition that to be ethical in the practical sense, politics must be realistic.

The creation of the Bolshevist Soviet Union did not alter the foundation of Russian national identity, and any politics that fails to understand this will fail to deal judiciously with Russia. What Westerners often cannot comprehend is that Stalin used Russian nationalism to advance the causes of internationalist socialism. Russian nationalism served international socialism, at least for a while, because Stalin recognized and associated with the historic moment in 1917, as the Russian nation was believed to be the vanguard of a world revolution.[32]

THE EFFECT OF FOREIGN ELEMENTS ON THE RUSSIAN AND SOVIET EMPIRES

The contradiction of Russian imperialism (in full accordance with what I call "imperial paradox") was that whenever the Russian Empire, just like all other empires in world history, expanded to encompass other nations, it introduced foreign organisms into its body politic. This development paradoxically diluted the Russian identity and compelled Russian statecraft to become preoccupied with managing a multitude of nations within that Empire, rather than nurturing Russian national interests.

The above explanation is the same paradox that eventually led to the Russian Revolution, the collapse of the czar, and ultimately the collapse of the Soviet Union on account of the influx of non-Russian ideas, such as Marxism, liberalism, socialism, democracy, and the whole host of political movements that had originated in Europe. Taking these into account, it is no surprise then that a leaner Russia, divorced not only from the "people's republics" but also many of its component Soviets, would restore a distinctly Russian identity and nationalist policy. No longer being burdened by the imperial tasks of managing conflicting national interests in its provinces, Russia would be free to focus on its own progress at last.

Thus, when contemporary observers bemoan Russian nationalism as the cause of the presently alleged Russian endeavor to rebuild the Soviet empire, they only demonstrate their utter historical ignorance. It was the empire under both the czars and the Soviets that did the most to make the execution of Russian nationalist policies impossible. The nature of an empire is internationalist, and the dominant imperial nation is forever preoccupied with maintaining order among the constituent parts, instead of focusing on the far more organic and comprehensible task of self-government.

The fact that Western thinking fails to grasp this critical point is a function of the Enlightenment. Metternich, a child of the Enlightenment, saw only states and statecraft—but never nations. Modern Western political thought erroneously qualifies Metternich as a conservative statesman, and Metternich's realpolitik is thought of as the antithesis of abstract reasoning.[33] Metternich was, in fact, the Austrian embodiment of the vices of Lord Bertrand Russell.[34] Though ostensibly different (the one embodying conservatism, the other liberalism), they both were mostly reflections of the Enlightenment. Metternich's failure to sustain his empire was mainly a result of his inability to understand the peculiar nature of *nations* as opposed to *states*. Nations are artifices, but they are artifices that spring forth from shared experience, language, history, tradition, and culture as opposed to originating from the mind of an enlightened statesman wanting to construct a state. The organic and intangible nature of *nations* makes their management by state administration uniquely problematic.

The same flaws in Western thinking that infected Metternich, making him unable to preserve what was good in his empire because he did not see the good of the nations he ruled, also infect Western thinking today on, among others, any subject concerning Russia.

A symptom of this fatal flaw in Western understanding is the fear of Russian imperialism as a result of Russian nationalism, for Russian nationalism is anti-imperial. Otherwise, it will only invite the incongruous elements into its organism that created the sorry plight of Russian collapse or, at least, degradation—both under the czars and following the Soviets. Vice versa, Russian nationalism is the natural result of the breaking down of Russian imperialism; *nationalism and imperialism are political adversaries.*

Stalin is still remembered by Russians today as both a nationalist and a

Communist. This fact reflects a moment in Soviet history when, following the Bolshevik Revolution, the internationalist aspect of communism was abandoned. The traditional nationalist (I would openly say "national socialist") Stalin forsook it, turning against the internationalist revolutionary Trotsky when it became necessary to conduct actual policy in post-czarist Russia, which retained imperial structures and lorded over subject nations. Contrary to Marxist historiography, none of those subject nations was particularly enthusiastic about the socialist revolution. Thus, adroitly, Stalin used Russian nationalism to consolidate power domestically. Then, claiming that the Russian nation was the "historical vanguard of the Communist Revolution," he merged Russian nationalism with theories of Marxist socialism. Thereby Stalin justified Soviet–Russian imperial rule over subject nations as having nothing to do with imperialism and everything to do with the Bolshevik Revolution.

This merging of nationalism and socialism explains the phenomenon that often baffles Western observers of Russian politics: How can Russians harbor sentiments toward both Bolshevism and nationalism at the same time? However, that should not confound any Western thinker either; after all, Germans, and many other Europeans harbored similar sentiments under the National Socialist Hitler. Just as the national socialist Stalin removed his rival, the international socialist Leon Trotsky, from power in the Soviet Union, so did the National Socialist Hitler rid himself of his nemesis, the international socialist Ernst Röhm, in Germany.[35]

The system that Stalin built, reaching its apex in Yalta, was untenable because no amount of terror or ideology could stop the continuation of the natural, organic growth of national consciousness in the Soviet Union—particularly among the Russian people who stood at its core and sacrificed the most. Following Stalin's death, all nations of the Soviet sphere breathed a sigh of relief. With the war and Stalin fading away in the past, it was inevitable that a return to the usual and regular relationship between the nations would eventually reemerge—albeit veiled under ahistorical Communist orthodoxy.

The Bolshevik Retardation of Russian Society

What is so tragic about the Russian Revolution is that the triumph of Bolshevism in October 1917 aborted the embryo of a developing and more enlightened modern and indigenous Russian society. The full scope of freedom in czarist Russia before the revolution in the early part of the twentieth century has always been concealed in the West. The country enjoyed full freedom of the press. Censorship had been abolished; even Bolshevik publications appeared without restrictions. There was complete freedom of foreign travel; there were independent trade unions, independent courts, and trial by jury; there was a legislative assembly (or duma) with representatives from parties of every political shade, including the Bolsheviks.[36]

All of that had been swept away by the early 1920s. To quote Solzhenitsyn's summary of the first period of communist rule under Lenin, "It dispersed the [democratically elected] Constituent Assembly … It introduced execution without trial. It crushed workers' strikes. It plundered the villagers to such an unbelievable extent that the peasants revolted, and when this happened, it crushed the peasants in the bloodiest possible way. It shattered the Church. It reduced 20 provinces of our country to a condition of famine."[37]

Democratic socialists may object at this point that prerevolutionary Russia was not as free and democratic as Britain or the United States and that the cause of socialism was compromised by the Bolsheviks' violent seizure of power. Nevertheless, even if Lenin had triumphed in a peaceful election, his subsequent takeover of the economy and nationalization of all previously independent institutions would eventually have produced the same totalitarian outcome.

The Soviet Union vigorously suppressed the leading Russian conservative thinkers for most of the last century, and the liberal West is continuing to ignore them today.

There is a reason for this. Everyone wanted to understand what communism was and why it had succeeded in taking power in Russia. Studies of Russian intellectual leftist history have concentrated on the development of liberal and socialist thought. Russian conservatism, by contrast, was considered a historical dead end unworthy of study.

As a result, Western commentators nowadays, lacking any in-depth knowledge of Russia's conservative heritage, are both unable and unwilling to place any contemporary Russian government within the correct intellectual context. The barrage of anti-Russian propaganda campaigns continues unabated solely because this seems to have become a form of psychotherapy for a panicked and incompetent but forbidding and woeful Western plutocracy.

Western corporate media have apparently been engaged in a sustained strategic campaign to identify and exploit any possible and perceived weaknesses in the Russian political armor and to paint Russia as an undemocratic, illiberal, and authoritarian country—in other words, a threat to the West.

The new Russia of today, at least during President Putin's terms in office, will not become the close ally of either Europe or America but would stand alone, trying to remain an independent, nonaligned, but proudly nationalistic and conservative country. Russia will not sell itself for money to the West or do the fighting for it. Russia will not let the West prevent it from developing an independent economy. Based on its national identity internally (as opposed to the socialist internationalism of the Soviet Union) and capitalism externally (in economic terms), Russia will eventually have to "Russianize" the Chinese model that has been working rather well and efficiently for the Chinese "communists."

When Did the Soviet Union Truly Disappear?

The Soviet Union officially expired on December 26, 1991. On that day, the Supreme Soviet of the Soviet Union adopted Declaration No. 142-H, which officially recognized the dissolution of the Soviet Union as a state subject to international law.

However, although having banned the Communist Party and dismantled the KGB, Yeltsin's liberals still faced the Supreme Soviet of the Russian Federation, which was the parliament of the Russian Soviet Federative Socialist Republic and elected by the Congress of People's Deputies of the Russian Federation. Nobody had abolished this very Soviet institution, which rapidly became the center of almost all of the anti-Yeltsin and pro-Soviet forces in the country. One could say that the new Russia (Yeltsin) and the old USSR (the Supreme Soviet) were fighting with each other for the future of the country.

The two sides presented what appeared to be a stark contrast to most Russians:

- The Russian President Boris Yeltsin: Officially he represented Russia as opposed to the Soviet Union; he presented himself as "anticommunist" and a "Democrat" (never mind that he had been a high-ranking member of the Communist Party and even a nonvoting member of the Politburo). Yeltsin

was without any doubt the darling of the West and promised to integrate Russia into the Western world.
- The Supreme Soviet: Headed by Ruslan Khasbulatov with the support of the vice president of Russia, Alexander Rutskoi, the Supreme Soviet became the rallying point of all those who believed that the Soviet Union had been dissolved illegally and against the will of the majority of its people. Most supporters of the Supreme Soviet were either communists, socialists or, at least, anti-capitalists. A good part of the somewhat muddled Russian nationalist movement also supported the Supreme Soviet.

We all know what eventually happened: Yeltsin crushed the opposition in the so-called "constitutional crisis of 1993," which was a small-scale civil war for the future destiny of the Soviet Union; only with the end of *this* crisis did the Soviet Union finally disappear.

However, both sides were primarily composed of former or current communists, both sides claimed they were defending democracy, and both sides accused the other of being fascists. In reality, both sides were very much alike, and most Russian people felt deeply disgusted with all of the politicians involved. Also, this shows something critical: by 1993, the vast majority of Russians were disappointed with *both* parties, had had enough of the crisis, and were desperately waiting for a third force to appear on the political scene.[38]

1993–99: A Democratic Nightmare

After the crushing of Yeltsin's opposition, the entire country was taken over and pillaged by various mafia organizations and oligarchs. The so-called privatization of the Russian economy created both a new class of multimillionaires and many tens of millions of impoverished people who could barely survive. A massive crime wave overtook the country, the entire infrastructure collapsed, and many regions of Russia began actively planning their secession from the Russian Federation.[39]

Throughout these turbulent and terrible years, the Western elite gave their fullest support to Yeltsin and his oligarchs. Eventually what had to happen did happen: Russia declared bankruptcy in 1998 by devaluing the ruble and defaulting on its debt. By 1999 the country was indeed on the brink of completely disappearing as a unified nation.[40]

Having crushed the opposition in 1993, Yeltsin's (and the West's) liberal accomplices got a free hand to write themselves a new constitution, which would ideally suit their purpose, giving immense powers to the president and minuscule powers to the new parliament, the Russian duma.

Then, after the contentious 1996 presidential elections dubiously won by Yeltsin, it slowly became apparent that he would not last very long.[41] His liberal cronies panicked and, utterly confused, allowed a little-known bureaucrat from Saint Petersburg to replace Yeltsin as acting president: Vladimir Putin.

Putin was a quiet, low-key, but competent functionary whose only quality appeared to be his lack of a strong personality—or so did the liberals think and hope. Alas, that turned out to be one big miscalculation.

As soon as he was appointed, Putin acted with lightning speed, surprising everybody by personally becoming involved in the Second Chechen War. Unlike his predecessor, Putin gave a free hand to the military commanders to wage war. Then Putin surprised everybody again when he made a historic deal with Akhmad Kadyrov even though he had been a leader of the insurgency during the first Chechen War.[42]

Putin's popularity soared, and he immediately used that to his advantage.

In an incredible twist of history, Putin used the very same constitution that had been developed and adopted by the Russian liberals to implement a very rapid series of crucial reforms and to eliminate the power base of the Yeltsin liberals—the oligarchs (such as Berezovsky, Khodorkovsky, and Gusinsky). He also passed new laws destined to "strengthen the vertical power," which gave the Federal Center direct control over the local administrations.[43] This change in turn not only crushed many of the local Mafias who had managed to infiltrate and corrupt the local authorities but also quickly stopped the various secessionist movements inside Russia. Finally Putin used what is called the "administrative resource" to create his United Russia party and to give it the full support of the state.

The irony is that Putin would never have succeeded in these efforts had the Russian liberals not created a hyper-presidential constitution that gave Putin the means to achieve his goals. To paraphrase Lenin, the Russian liberals gave Putin the rope to hang them.

The West, of course, rapidly understood what was going on, but it was too late: the liberals had lost power, and Russia was taken over by a third, previously unseen, force: Vladimir Vladimirovich Putin.

Analyses of President Putin tend to emphasize his KGB past and portray him as bent on suppressing democratic freedoms. As the murdered journalist Anna Politkovskaya put it, Putin "has failed to transcend his origin and stop behaving like a lieutenant colonel in the Soviet KGB. He is still busy sorting out his freedom-loving fellow countrymen; he persists in crushing liberty just as he did earlier in his career."[44] For many in the West, that is the end of the story.

Continuing Down the Once Lost Russian Liberal-Conservative Road

In fact, Contrary to the above view, President Putin fits into the long-standing Russian tradition of liberal conservatism, which could be summed up in the statement that a strong and centralized Russian state is needed not *instead of* liberal reform, but *for* reform. Without a strong state, liberal reforms are impossible in Russia; this is the basis of a uniquely Russian synthesis of liberalism and conservatism embodied in President Putin's rule.

Boris Chicherin (1828–1904) was one of the founding fathers of this ideology. He upheld liberalism and civil rights while at the same time supporting autocracy. "The Russian liberal," Chicherin wrote, "travels on a few high-sounding words: freedom, openness, public opinion … which he interprets as having no limits … Hence, he regards as products of outrageous despotism the most elementary concepts, such as obedience to law or the need for police and bureaucracy … The extreme development of liberty, inherent in democracy inevitably leads to the breakdown of the state organism. To counter this, it is necessary to have strong authority."[45]

This kind of reasoning—or rather interpreting of Western liberalism—is not specifically Russian; it is rooted not only in the conservative Eastern European thought process but also in the general criticism of Western liberalism.

According, however, to the Russian way of thinking, Christian love, embodied in the church, is the *supreme political value*, expressed through political and economic arrangements supported by a close connection between church and state, which respects the dignity and rights of individuals. This philosophy could even be called "liberal theocracy."[46]

Perhaps the most important work in the Russian liberal-conservative canon is a 1909 volume entitled *Vekhi* ("Landmarks"). It contains a series of sharp condemnations of Russia's intelligentsia by prominent liberals such as Pyotr Struve, Nikolai Berdyaev, and Sergei Bulgakov, who had been horrified by the anarchy of the 1905 revolution. *Vekhi* alleged that the intelligentsia had cut itself off from the Russian people by slavishly copying Western ideas while ignoring Russian ones. Also, the authors accused the Russian intelligentsia of having no respect for the law and concluded that a robust legal system must be the foundation of government.[47]

President Putin himself seems to most admire two contemporaries of the *Vekhi* authors: Pyotr Stolypin, who was prime minister of Russia from 1906 to 1911, and the philosopher Ivan Ilyin.

Stolypin became prime minister during the turmoil of revolution and did not recoil from exercising force to suppress it. The many hangings of radicals resulted in the noose being called "Stolypin's necktie." However, at the same time, he pursued liberal reforms in the social and economic spheres, most famously enacting changes to give peasants ownership of their land with the aim of creating a society based on private property.[48]

President Putin chaired a committee organizing the creation of a monument to Stolypin in Moscow. He has called Stolypin "a true patriot and a wise politician." Stolypin "saw that both all kinds of radical sentiment and procrastination, a refusal to launch the necessary reform, were dangerous to the country and that only a strong and efficient government, relying on business and the civil initiative of millions, could ensure progressive development."[49]

President Putin regularly quotes Ivan Ilyin in his writings and speeches. Like Stolypin and the *Vekhi* contributors, Ilyin believed that the source of Russia's problems was an insufficiently developed legal consciousness. Given this, democracy was not a suitable form of government. He wrote, "At the head of the state there must be a single will." Russia needed a "united and strong state power, dictatorial in the scope of its powers." At the same time, however, there must be clear limits to these powers. The ruler must have widespread support, the state organs must be responsible and accountable, and the principles of legality, equal protection under the law, and freedom of conscience, speech, and assembly must be guaranteed. Private property must be sacrosanct.

Ilyin believed that the state must have supreme authority in those areas in which it had competence but should stay out of those areas, such as private life and religion, in which it did not. Totalitarianism, he said, was "godless."[50]

The reality of President Putin's Russia fits this liberal-conservative model reasonably closely. For instance, President Putin, like Stolypin, has made significant efforts to entrench property rights, as well as to liberalize the economy. He and Dmitry Medvedev have installed several liberal-minded finance ministers who have worked to reduce the burden of regulation on small businesses. Progress has been patchy but real, as reflected in Russia's admission into the World Trade Organization. Western observers tend to dismiss this and focus instead on the negative aspects, such as steps taken to bring key actors in the energy sector back under state control.

Like the liberal conservatives, President Putin has emphasized what he calls "the dictatorship of law."[51] Although Western commentators have denounced the blatant and continuing abuses of the legal process, President Putin has pursued legal reforms with far more vigor than his predecessor. He has made considerable progress not only toward updating the inconsistent Russian legal system but also implementing human rights norms from the European Convention on Human Rights in the Russian courts.

Under the Putin doctrine of "sovereign democracy," the state is limited; it does not seek to control every aspect of life.[52] Indeed, it regards freedom as essential for social and economic progress. However, where the state does operate, it should be sovereign—powerful, unified, and free from the influence of foreign powers. In the eyes of Western critics, President Putin's first-term move to rein in the powers of regional leaders was a direct assault on democracy. However, to President Putin, this was an essential step to eliminate the practice of regions disobeying the federal law and to restore legal unity in the nation.

Liberal conservatism also underpins President Putin's attitude toward civil society. The Putin administration was a more steadfast advocate of civil society than the Kremlin under Yeltsin, although it sometimes tried to bend the concept to its purposes. Since 2004, the Russian government has set up public chambers at all levels of government, designed to serve as a forum through which public organizations and state bodies can work together. Participants have received generous federal funding. Nevertheless, because the expectation is that the chambers will help civil society to cooperate with the state and not challenge it, some in the West doubt their value.[53]

Russian liberal conservatives were never "democrats" as the term is understood in the West, and it is not surprising that many here reject their ideology. Some consider that Chicherin's philosophy was an abstract and unrealistic doctrine and the idea that the powerful state could respect civil rights was idealistic. Similarly, Ilyin's vision of a limited, law-based, and accountable dictatorship seems "naïvely impractical" to Western critics.[54]

However, the point here is not whether liberal conservatism is the right choice for Russia; this is for Russia to decide. The real issue is that the West fails, or refuses, to recognize this ideology for what it is. President Putin has a clear vision of a stable, centralized, law-based government with defined and limited competencies, consistent with Russian national schools of thought. Western relations with Russia would be significantly improved if the West would finally acknowledge this reality instead of tilting at irrelevant caricatures of a police state.

Lee Kuan Yew said, on Mikhail Gorbachev's failure to control reform in the Soviet Union, "He had jumped into the deep end of the pool without learning how to swim."[55] Well, President Putin knows how to swim.

THE DISTORTION OF CULTURE AND THE RUSSIAN CONSERVATIVE MIND

The distinctions between the Russian and Western spirit cannot be drawn too sharply. As deep a cleavage as there still exists between the mindset, politics, economics, and religion of England, Germany, France, and America when compared with Russia, these nations suddenly appear as a unified world. The Russians, for the West rather incomprehensible people, have been confused, wounded, tortured, and poisoned by having forced upon them the patterns of a foreign, imperious, masculine, and mature European culture. Western-style urban centers have pierced Russia's flesh with European ambitions; decadent attitudes, philosophies, political ideas, and scientific principles infected its indigenous national consciousness.

Russian conservative thought, like Russian liberal thought, began as a frame of reference imported from the West but soon became something altogether new and uniquely Russian—namely, slavophilism.[56] This development is a natural phenomenon, since any Western worldview, when planted on the non-Western ground, will metamorphose into something uniquely non-Western; otherwise, it would become an abstraction not associated with real men and real places.

Russian conservatism, like British conservatism, grew out of a reaction to the French Revolution on the part of thoughtful men. Insofar as the pillars of British conservatism were built on the British experience from at least the times of the Magna Carta, Russian conservatism began as a rather weak gag reflex experienced by Russian liberalism as it attempted to absorb European culture.

Both liberalism and conservatism are products of a particular time in the history of humanity's development generally referred to as "modernity." For Russia, a consciously forced modernity commenced with Peter the Great; albeit, it was modernity unrecognizable to Westerners because of its peculiarly Russian character. Within this particular implementation of modernity in Russia, the Russian conservative mind was born.

In 1700, Czar Peter the Great forced upon his people the Baroque style of politics, which brought with it cabinet diplomacy, dynastic influence, administration, and a Western-style navy. In 1800, English ideas, fundamentally incomprehensible to the Russian people, made their entrance in the guise of French writers, who succeeded in confusing the minds of a small intellectual minority. Even before 1900, the bookish Russian intelligentsia introduced Marxism to their country, a complex product of Western European dialectics of whose origin they were utterly ignorant.[57]

It was under Peter the Great that Russia was forced to love Europe and become "modern." The West tends to regard the implementation of universal notions of European liberalism as a liberating experience. Westerners think of men and women becoming emancipated from compulsions that had kept them in bondage. If this were so, then it would have been enough for Peter the Great to abolish laws, not pass them. Instead Peter the Great instituted a table of ranks to supplant honors rooted in a hereditary aristocracy; he compelled humble Christian women who entered cities to cut their long skirts so that they were knee-length, and he taxed beards to force men to shave. He wanted to force the Russians to look and act European—to transform by way of fiat. At their height, Peter's reforms ensnared a Russia whose upper class spoke only French to escape any suspicion of being provincial, dated, or primitive.

Peter the Great transformed the czarist state into a major power within the Western system, thus perverting its natural development. The intelligentsia became the product of the Russian spirit corrupted by foreign-style cities. They entered the scene with their melancholic longing for indigenous institutions that must arise in some far-distant future, thereby distorting the truly original thought of their country into a kind of barren, childish theorizing after the manner of professional French revolutionaries. Owing to the Russians' infinite humility and willingness to sacrifice, both what Oswald Spengler calls "Petrinism" and Bolshevism have accomplished some authentic things in senseless and disastrous imitation of such Western creations as the Court of Versailles and the Paris Commune.[58] However, these institutions have affected only the surface of Russian existence; each of them can disappear and reappear with unpredictable swiftness.

Peter's reforms elicited some degree of anxiety among conservative thinkers like Mikhail Shcherbatov, who defended the traditional ways of old Russia, where moral virtue was the product of a world of religion, prayer, and boredom. Nevertheless, Peter's critics, the first Russian conservatives, did not scoff at the czar's aims so much as at some of his methods. At the time, Russian conservatism was still a voice of guarded liberalism. The Russian elites' high regard for liberalism and enlightenment came to a crushing blow when the French Revolution took a turn for the worse.

Nikolai Karamzin, who was one of Russia's first conservative thinkers, revealed this sentiment well: "A bolt of lightning had struck France … we saw the horror of its fire from afar, and each of us returned home to thank Heaven for the totality of our lot and to become reasonable."[59]

"Becoming reasonable" meant accepting the czar as a necessary good and reconsidering the extent to which Russia had bettered itself by adopting enlightened European modes and orders that appeared to lead to terror and tyranny. The horrifying terror of the French Revolution and the possibility of comparable "political reforms" brought to Russia by Napoleon's invading armies convinced Karamzin not only to accept the czar but also to reconsider the desirability of European liberalism for the country.

What had been obvious signs of barbarism and regression inherent in the old Russian ways requiring reform under Peter started to appear in a new light. If the modern European virtues of the Enlightenment carried the face of Robespierre, then perhaps the vices of old Russia were not vices at all? As Shcherbatov had noted under Peter, cleansing the peasantry of superstition was a virtue, but what if it also cleansed them of a genuine and heartfelt love of God?[60]

Until 1917, the French Revolution was the most significant shock to the Russian status quo since the Westernizing reforms of Peter the Great. Count Sergei Uvarov, Czar Nicholas I's minister for national enlightenment, worked out a way of dealing with that fear; he formulated his tripartite slogan of 1833: "Orthodoxy, autocracy, and nationality."[61] This ideology was conservative Russia's answer to the "Liberté, egalité, fraternité" of the 1789 French Revolution. It meant, in something closer to today's terms, autocracy, religious authority, and managed democracy.

Uvarov never intended Russia to be free in a Western sense; Russia's path to nineteenth-century industrialization and mass literacy had to be managed. His formula still underpins Russian conservatism today: state authoritarianism, coupled with the authority of a church that is far from unpopular, as well as managed ways of individual self-expression. Many Russians seem to find that very much acceptable.

In its infancy, Russian conservative thinking became preoccupied with the dreaded vice of *сластолюбие*, or slastolyubiye, the flaunting of a combination of hedonism and libertinism. The Russian expression "slastolyubiye" can be defined as the free and limitless satisfying of the desires of all senses, artificial needs, and sick ambitions combined with the desire to make an impression or to flout oneself.

However, the Russian conservatives' constant preoccupation with slastolubiye was not necessarily or merely a smart approach concerning hedonism, which was a vice natural to certain social classes and age categories. Slastolyubiye was something that, like Western individualism, seemed to arise *alongside* liberal enlightenment. It began innocently enough, as with Peter's reform making it socially acceptable for a man and woman who were betrothed to see one another before their wedding. However, as with all things concerning enlightenment, the impulse to make something better was predicated on the assumption that the reasoning faculties of humanity were up to the task. Although doubtful on that point, the Russian conservatives still accepted a slow and cautious progression in the process of Russian liberalization. Now, however, they were so shocked by the horrors of the French Revolution and the brutality of Napoleonic aggression that a concerted effort was undertaken to cease any further "progress" and make way for a return.

Part of this return originated in the reopening of the question of Russia's origins as a state. Where exactly was this old Russia from, away from which it was supposedly necessary to progress?

Slavic tribes had their *knyaz*—nobles and dukes who submitted to the rule of the great prince. The common ideal accepted by all was that of *mir*, which connotes a community but also refers to unity, harmony, and peace. Slavic states had grown organically; they were not created on account of outside force. For the Western mind, it is challenging to grasp the essence of this world, as it is a total inversion of everything that the Western Enlightenment accepts unquestioningly.

There is perhaps no better example to demonstrate this conceptual reversal than the idea of the rule of law as perceived in the Russian world. In short, the Western concept of the rule of law (whereby everyone obeys the laws) is utter anathema to the *Русский мир* (*Russkiy mir*, or Russian world). It is an abomination not on account of some primitive barbarism, nor on account of tyranny, but rather as the result of the Russian Orthodox heritage that placed the burden of responsibility and duty directly on the shoulders of men. Men rule and not laws; to be governed by laws is to be unworthy of man.

In the Russkiy mir, only a person who *cannot rule* himself requires laws by which to be ruled. The "best men," the nobility, the aristocracy, rule by the laws that make them great. The best man, the czar, rules by the best law, which is *within himself*.

What Westerners call self-government is understood to mean the people governing themselves through representatives who pass laws. In Russia, however, self-government means a government *of the self,* and the czar is the supreme self; this is the self who governs. This principle was plainly illustrated by Karamzin, who saw politics as not the creation of systems or regimes but as a struggle for moral self-discipline:

"If Alexander were suddenly inspired by a noble hatred of the excesses of self-government and took a pen with which he signed a law that was contrary to the laws of God and conscience, then a truly virtuous Russian citizen would boldly grip the Czar by the hand and proclaim: Caesar! You have exceeded the boundaries of your rule. Russia, having been taught by long suffering and failure, came to the Holy Altar and placed the power of self-government in the hands of your forefather and demanded to be governed by a sovereign, indivisible rule. This heritage is the basis of your power; no other e*xists. You may do everything Caesar, but you cannot limit your power.*"[62]

Karamzin concluded that the czarist idea of self-rule was the only way to rescue the Slavic world from the modern vices of slastolyubiye. Karamzin, although a republican at heart and an admirer of French republicanism, ultimately renounced the Western model for the first authentic expression of self-conscious Russian conservative thought. "Not liberty, through which so much is so often lost, but order, justice, and security—these are the pillars of happiness in society."

Karamzin was not blind to the prospect of the abuse of power by czars, but he claimed that such abuses could be opposed only in the moral sense, but never through open rebellion. He differentiated between the low and the high in politics. In the practical realm, he was an admirer of Machiavelli's teachings regarding the virtues of the prince, who ruled alone. In the theoretical domain of politics, he appreciated a Platonic republicanism. He arranged these two contrary interests and fascinations in accordance with Montesquieu's teaching: "When a ruler wishes to undertake a great reform in his state, he must change through law that which exists by law, but change through mores that which exists through mores: it is a bad politics indeed that attempts to change by law that which can only be changed through mores."[63] Karamzin was not an advocate of slavery or of tyranny. He did not expect the people to be either servile, or docile, but *faithful* to the czar.

Russian conservatism later departed from Karamzin's Machiavellian realism and its common roots in British reaction toward the French Revolution. It would instead embark upon a romantic, anti-capitalist, and anti-Western, or anti-modern, path in the person of Vladimir Fyodorovich Odoyevsky, whose romantic and passionate prose saw the birth of a unique conservatism that could almost no longer be called conservative as it moved in the direction of explicit slavophilism. Odoyevsky did not only reject the French philosophers of the Enlightenment; he rejected British ideas as well. Just as Karamzin came to associate French liberalism with an inevitable downward spiral toward revolutionary Jacobinism, Odoyevsky dismissed the idea of British thought because he felt that Great Britain had embarked on the creation of the utilitarian Benthamite man, who was no less a danger to the Russian soul than the Jacobin. No better example of Odoyevsky's critique of British political economy exists than his dystopia "The City without a Name."[64] This text forms a part of his philosophical dialogues contained within *Russian Nights*.[65]

Odoyevsky's work was no longer a mere conservative reaction to Western liberalism, French philosophy, and the Enlightenment; it was something uniquely Russian. It was one of the final steps toward the birth of Slavophilism.[66] His romantic conservatism posed some big questions to Russians: Who are we? What kind of people do we want to be?

Odoyevsky is genuinely the conservative mind of the East. The West must understand this Russian conservative mind if it ever wants to understand the vast chasm that separates Russian and Western civilizations while at the same time also recognizing how Russian culture, having grown out of a constant confrontation with Western thought, allows us to see ourselves in a whole new light.

Based on the above, to all of those in the West who would endeavor to "enlighten" modern Russia, this author can only caution against such ventures. Western modes and orders were adopted in Russia only to the extent that Russian culture did not find them abhorrent, and then only in ways that Western culture often found odd. For example, while parliamentary democracy was a form of government long rooted in the European background and development, the spiritual heritage of the Russian world finds Western modes and orders alien; it either internalizes or plainly rejects them.

Russia's greatest thinkers knew and understood the Western soul well. Do Western scholars know the Russian soul? Have they ever considered what the West might gain in wisdom if it expanded its heritage not only to include Jerusalem, Athens, and Rome but the East as well?

Now, it is true; Russia has never developed either a tradition of partnership between state and society or the traditions of private property necessary for the formation of civil society. In medieval Muscovy, privately owned estates became fiefs held on condition of service to the crown. During the Mongol rule, which lasted from the thirteenth to the fifteenth centuries, the Mongol rulers governed Russia through vassals, who considered the peoples and lands under their control as part of their individual patrimony, and when Mongol rule came to an end, the patrimonial system continued. Roman law, Catholic theology, feudalism, and the commercial culture of cities, which helped to shape Western political theory, were absent in Russia. The sense that Russia was a private possession of its rulers continued right up until 1917; the Russian state failed to evolve from a private to a public institution.

All the above led to the emergence of a particularly radical form of absolutism, which was defended on various grounds over the centuries. At first it was advocated that since the czar was accountable only to God, discussion of his role was not necessary. Later, especially from the era of Peter the Great onward, the argument was not so much about autocracy being the best form of government in general, but rather it being the one most suitable for Russia. According to this view, the country was geographically too large and economically underdeveloped, with a large population too backward for Russia to survive with any other political system; what mattered were not political institutions but enlightenment and virtue of the citizenry. Personal morality was more vital than political reform, and autocracy was Russia's time-honored and proven form of government. Only the autocracy could lead Russia toward enlightenment, and representative government would result in aristocracy rather than democracy. Only the autocracy could save Russia from bourgeois philistinism and nihilism; and autocracy, unlike democracy, rose above class interests.[67]

Mikhail Speransky (1772–1839), Czar Alexander I's chief minister between 1807 and 1812 and a profound and original thinker, sought to create an autocracy that was accountable to the law. He was the first Russian political thinker to emphasize the importance of public opinion, once stating that "no government at odds with the spirit of the times can stand up to its all-powerful action."

Great power status could be obtained only from the strength, vitality, and aspiration of society. Unlike in the Western world, where change, in whatever form, was consistently driven, demanded, or fought for "from below," Russian development was always shaped by the state "from above."

Boris Chicherin, the leader of the conservative-liberal school, distinguished his conservative liberalism from what he called "oppositional liberalism," or the tendency to identify government with oppression. His backing of a synthesis of autocracy, civil rights, laissez-faire economics, and law estranged most of the political spectrum, and he remained an isolated figure.

Alexander Gradovsky believed that autocracy and civil rights were compatible. In practice, it was hard to combine a commitment to autocracy with a belief in liberal ideas in nineteenth-century Russia.

A later conservative liberal, Peter Struve (1870–1944), came to believe that the individual took precedence over the state and that liberalism was a precondition of national greatness. It was Struve who said in 1895 that if autocracy identified with the bureaucracy and not with society, then it would eventually "fall under the pressure of live social forces."[68] Russia could not take the happy medium; its alternatives rested between the black and red extremes.

However, autocracy is not exclusively to blame for the fact that state and society never developed an acceptable partnership in Russian history. Liberal rulers like Catherine II and Alexander I feared to surrender their authority because of their conviction that the empire would otherwise collapse. Alas, they also received no support from society at large. If the state was too powerful, society was itself too weak. The weakness of Russian society inevitably led to the growth and assertiveness of strict principles; autocracy triumphed because there was no stable and fully developed society to act as a counterweight.

The critique by Mikhail Speransky expressed it so well in 1802 when he noted that the only free people in Russia were the paupers and the philosophers; all the rest were slaves, slaves of the czar and slaves of the landlords. This statement is metaphorically true of today's Western liberal society, too—with the ruling elite and their lackeys replacing the czar.

Russia had only religious experiences before 1917, no social or political ones. Dostoyevsky is misunderstood if his social "problems" are considered apart from his novelistic form. His revolutionary politics originated within an insignificantly small metropolitan coterie, which no longer possessed distinctly Russian sentiments and can hardly be called Russian at all. As a consequence, Dostoyevsky's political thought was caught between the extremes of forced dogmatism and instinctive rejection.

Hence Russia's deep, fierce, atavistic hatred of the West, of the poison in its body. It can be felt in the inner suffering of Dostoyevsky, in the violent outbursts of Tolstoy, and in the silent brooding of the common man. It is an irrepressible hatred, often unconscious and often concealed beneath a natural inclination to love and understanding. It is a fundamental hatred of all symbols of the Faustian will: the cities, the arts and sciences, Western thought and emotion, the state, jurisprudence, administrative structure, money, industry, education, society—in fact, everything. It is the old apocalyptic hatred that distinguishes the culture of antiquity.

Bolshevism's rigid dogmatism alone could never have supplied the impetus that sustained that movement for so long. The innate anti-Western instincts of Russia, first directed against Petrinism, have lent strength to Bolshevism. The Russian intelligentsia wishes by instinct, if not always consciously, to destroy its own civilization; that is the meaning of Eastern nihilism (and modern Western liberal democracy). Moreover, Bolshevism's unconscious mission for awakening Russia was nothing else but nihilism. The ideological elements that made Bolshevism work were not significant, and the Bolshevist Soviet experiment imposed on Russia was not and has never become part of Russian culture, mentality, or disposition. In the end, since Bolshevism was itself an outgrowth of Petrinism, it had to be in time destroyed to complete Russia's liberation from the West.

One could say that no other people suffered more or longer under the communist yoke—based on a transplanted alien Western ideology—than the Russian.

In most Western countries, there is a working alliance between state and society based on private property and the rule of law. In the medieval era, Russia failed to develop the political and social institutions needed to sustain that kind of alliance. Following this unpromising beginning, Russian history after 1500 was the story of the consolidation and expansion of autocracy. However, there were also some critical moments, taking place at times of social upheaval or with the appearance of certain brilliant personalities, when breakthroughs of social evolution might have occurred. For a variety of reasons, history has denied the Russian people and state the opportunity to take advantage of these fleeting occasions. If, however, this could be remedied and overcome in the future, and Russia would endorse concepts of limited government or moderate forms of patriotism, there are plenty of liberal currents in Russian history on which to build a healthy and robust Russian society.

THE FEAR OF THE RUSSIAN ALTERNATIVE: THE ANTAGONISTIC WEST

Most cultural differences between the West and Russia are based on outlook. The more ambiguous Western perspective relies on diversity, relativism, pluralism, and social consensus, while the more explicit Russian vision rests on a narrower range of competing opinions and greater uniformity of knowledge, while concurrently being imposing, assertive, unified, complete, and strict.

This difference in outlook proves to be a Russian hindrance when dealing with not only the "real West" but also with the Eastern European countries that were once part of the Soviet orbit. If Russia were more forthright and decisive about genuine reconciliation with those states, the outcome would also significantly improve its strategic position vis-à-vis the West. Russia would need to do more, however, than just uttering a few conceding words, since the nations of Eastern Europe were the victims of Soviet rule for many decades and several generations and suffered irreparable political, economic, social, cultural and, one can safely ascertain, psychological damage as a result. It would take a significant amount of Russian magnanimity to understand, accept, forgive, and get over the ill feelings that accumulated in Eastern Europe during the twentieth century. History is cruel; it is never easy to reconcile with the past, but great nations can overcome even the limits set by their culture. If Russia can do just that, it will, in all likelihood, realign the world again to its benefit.

Time and again in 2013–14, many said, "Thank God for Russia," often adding, "though I never thought I would say this." They were referring to many issues, among them the Russian child protection law forbidding the spread of gay and lesbian propaganda among minors, the Russian stand on Syria, and the Russian response to the Ukrainian crisis. The Western elites misleadingly proclaim they represent "the international community" also on these issues, but they have earned the hostility of Western peoples instead. One of the very few voices still standing up to these dangerous and destructive political and media elites today is coming from Russia. That voice is representing values forgotten in the West—values that are being persecuted by Islamist fanatics in Syria, by nationalist fanatics in Ukraine, and by liberal fanatics in the Western world.

It is notable that the positions above taken by Russia are immensely popular both inside and, it seems, outside of the country. Once again it proves how presumptuous the West has become, in that the policies of its arrogant elite do not reflect the will of its peoples. Thus, regarding attacks against war-torn Syria, it appears that the majority of the American people were against another unprovoked attack against a foreign country in 2013; the figures were only slightly lower in France and Britain.[69]

Similarly, the people in many countries of the Western world would support the introduction of child protection laws just as they did in Russia. Such a gap between elite and people can exist only because the rulers, backed by massive PR spending and voted into power only by minorities of the electorate, are cut off from and entirely ignorant of the people whom they supposedly represent. This state of affairs is the result of Western cultural Marxism, called political correctness in conjunction with modern liberal democracy, which the elite professes. It is no wonder, then, that vast numbers boycott the democratic elections owing to the lack of any relevant subject matter to vote for or any credible candidate.

The Soviet-style, left-liberal, decivilizing Western elite, their heads turned to and by political power and "banksters'" gold, has not only lost contact with but also deliberately ignores the roots of Western civilization. This ignorance is why that part of the Western world, which is still faithful to the origins of its culture, is increasingly becoming reliant on Russia to speak on its behalf.

Russia is the only country today that, once having fallen into the delusion of Western political Marxism, rejected it. Having done this, it has not only returned to its ethnic roots but is emerging once more as the leading conservative power. Moscow appears to understand better than the West that the driving foreign-policy requirement of the twenty-first century is the preservation of the national state in the face of the wars waged by non-state entities around the world, such as those fighting on the rebels' side in Syria. Russia has rightly upbraided the West for destroying states, including Iraq and Libya.

When President Putin came to office following the chaotic Yeltsin years, there was a real possibility the Russian state itself would disintegrate. Putin's greatest achievement is that he saved and strengthened the Russian Federation instead. Blinded by their worship of the fleeting God known as liberal democracy, the Western elite cannot perceive the importance of what Putin did—but others should.

Vladimir Putin has reunited Crimea with Russia as a clear answer to the decade-long abuse, provocation, and humiliation of Russia by the West, culminating in the Ukraine crisis. Had Western policy preserved a neutral or "Finlandized" Ukraine, the issue of Crimea's status might never have reached the boiling point. Instead, almost from the beginning, Western strategists put Ukraine's integration into NATO pointedly on the table—a deliberately provocative act that was perceived by Russia as an extremely aggressive and threatening move designed to cross the red line.

Several US senators and US Secretary of State John Kerry, among others, have lectured President Putin about being stuck in a nineteenth-century mindset while condescendingly offering him an "off-ramp"—a face-saving way to allow the Western alliance to move right up to Russia's borders. The EU foreign policy chief acting at the time, Catherine Ashton, told reporters that she was "trying to send the strongest possible signals to Russia … trying to ensure that they understand the seriousness of the situation."[70]

Who was it really who failed to "understand the seriousness" of the matter—the senators who parachuted into Kiev for a frisson of media coverage or the Russians who gag when the United States tries to push NATO down their throats, contradicting assurances given to Moscow when the Soviet Union broke up? Washington played a decisive role in triggering this dangerous situation, and President Putin's behavior was motivated by the same political realism and geopolitical considerations that influence all great powers, including the United States. Yes, it is true that President Putin has described the collapse of the Soviet Union as "the greatest geopolitical catastrophe of the century" (deliberately misrepresented in the Western media innumerable times) precisely because of those who mismanaged that political process.[71]

What was the goal of the West in Ukraine? It was to provoke Maidan-type demonstrations in Moscow in order to overturn Putin. "Dear Vlad," Senator McCain tweeted on December 5, 2011, "The Arab Spring is coming to a neighborhood near you." Arab Spring? One can just look at Egypt, Libya, Tunisia, and Syria today. The Beltway hawks, the neoconservatives, the neoliberals, and the Western elite all want to defeat Putin, who was depicted as a new Hitler by Hillary Clinton, to punish the Russian leader who put a stop to the oligarchs' looting spree of the 1990s that had sent Russia into a death spiral.[72] Their dream is to humiliate Putin, setting off freedom demonstrations in Moscow, and perhaps a civil war, to bring Putin down. The Ukrainian coup they had orchestrated, which brought Moscow's enemies to power in Kiev, overthrew a democratically elected leader, and even the mob-influenced vote to impeach him fell short of the constitutionally required supermajority.[73] John Kerry was lecturing the Russians about democracy and the rule of law on behalf of a regime that came to power in violation of the most critical of democratic norms, which is that elections count more than crowds that can be mobilized in the streets.[74]

Why would the Western elite want to stir up problems and create chaos in Russia? Because they are concerned about the effects of a national-conservative Russian alternative on their home countries, which could endanger their left-liberal and socialist systems. They are terrified of any prospective new cultural, political, and ideological alternative to their worldwide hegemony, which is slowly withering away. The elite know they can better unite against an adversary; indeed, they need an enemy abroad to keep their intimidated, misled, and confused peoples in line, to take the people's eyes away not only from their condition at home and the elite causing it but also from any potential alternative.

Historical analogies may be inaccurate, but Americans may need to look at their own civil war and compare it to what has happened in Ukraine. Today the United States supports a murderous criminal adventure that has little to do with unifying the country.

Abraham Lincoln never called the rebels of the Confederacy "terrorists." He always said that no matter how bad the civil war was, he wanted his fellow citizens to come back to the Union. The regime in Kiev calls its citizens "terrorists." They are rebels. They are protesters. They have a political agenda. Their demands are not excessive: they want to elect their governors—Americans elect their governors too. They want to have a say on where their taxes go—"no taxation without representation." There are some extremists among them, but there are also people who wish only to live in a Ukraine that is for everybody.

Russia is a potential and essential ally Washington pushes away. The principal partner concerning American national security should be Russia. From Georgia to Azerbaijan, from Iran to Syria, from Afghanistan to Ukraine, from the North Pole to Southern and Eastern Europe, it is the Kremlin, currently occupied by President Putin, whose cooperation, partnership, and active participation required finding solutions in the struggle to achieve lasting peace.

Instead, the way the United States has been treating Russia, President Putin, and his administration, is a direct betrayal of American foreign policy interests. In 1994, George Kennan called the expansion of NATO into the old Soviet bloc "a strategic blunder of potentially epic proportions."[75]

The geopolitical framework of a Western alliance next to or against a diminished Russia is an unsustainable dream of messianic hegemony rooted in the American manifest destiny while also recognizing a definite pattern that manifests itself as a dilemma.[76]

The Russian dilemma is that, on the one hand, the American elite is forced to engage in an ideological struggle based on wishful exceptionalism, a desired worldwide hegemony, and, most importantly, the fear of "losing it all" (or there being "no turning back"). As a consequence, the elite can neither tolerate nor accept any opposing or alternative ideology; ideally, the elite would be satisfied with a world shaped after its image and kept under its total control.

Then again, there is Russia. A reconstituted, stable and secure, semi-modern, and semi-strong Russia, with its cautious predisposition (based on experience) toward the West, can provide the convenient adversary needed by the Western elite to wage the ideological war (or "Cold Peace") against the alternative doctrine. That makes Russia strategically important, but certainly no partner, while kept economically engaged (meaning "down," thus posing no real danger to the West).

The term "Catch-22," to use the title of Joseph Heller's satirical novel, may be applied to the Russian dilemma that best describes the Western strategy: Russia could be accepted as a partner only if it submitted to the West unconditionally, but that would result in its certain demise. Otherwise, the West will provoke and antagonize Russia, forcing it to struggle and sacrifice its resources for an uncertain future. Faced with these alternatives of either an inevitable demise or an uncertain future, the Russians must choose the second option and will try to keep their independence at any cost. The West knows that, of course, and will attempt to raise that cost to Russia to unsustainable levels, whatever the consequences may be.

Russia and the United States should be allies complementing each other in many ways. However, after missing out on the great opportunity of finally becoming strategic partners following the collapse of the Soviet Union, they will just keep staring at each other suspiciously across the ocean. Although they secretly admire one another, sometimes even using the vague euphemism of "partners," both will keep their options open. After the West committing the truly strategic blunder of not wanting to understand, comprehend, accept, and respect Russia, thereby totally alienating her again, Russia will remain an implicit adversary of the United States and the West in the foreseeable future—and that is what the Western elite precisely wants. For the resulting situation, there is no real solution, and it will only be further complicated by the rise of the new and independent great power on the Eurasian landmass: China.

5

CHINA RISING

China already dominates Asia, intends to become the world's leading power, and expects to be accepted on its terms, not as an honorary member of the West. Despite China's progress over the past thirty to forty years, it still has multiple obstacles to overcome, chief among them an absence of the rule of law and the presence of widespread corruption. The biggest fear of China's leaders is widespread revulsion at the corrosive effects of the graft. The Chinese language itself is another obstacle to China's great-power aspirations. So is a culture that does not "permit a free exchange and contest of ideas."[77]

Nevertheless, China is a fast-developing economic and military power. Its space program symbolically shows its ambition, the desperate eagerness to hold the Olympic games proved the same point, and its strategic reach for the South China Sea demonstrates its urge to be recognized and accepted by the world in its own right. But is China the future superpower of the world? This assumption is still not necessarily the case at all.

While competition between the United States and China is inevitable, confrontation need not occur. The West should not expect a democratic China for the simple reason that if China became a liberal democracy, it would collapse. That is, of course, precisely why the West is trying so hard to push China in that direction.

However, the insatiable greed inherent in the American-style corporate-capitalistic economic system makes it possible for China to draw an enormous amount of money from the United States: China became the second largest trading partner of America, after Japan, in 2003. American capitalism sees more immediate gains (profits from cheap Chinese imports) and even more significant market potential in the future by engaging an opportunistic but "socialist" China now rather than becoming a real ally of a nationalistic, conservative, struggling, hesitant, and reluctant Russia.

The United States and the industrialized world recognize that the Chinese "communists" not only allow but also actively encourage and practice capitalism while maintaining one-party rule in China. This policy has proved to be more efficient and far more successful than the Mafia-controlled pseudodemocracy practiced by the Russian oligarchy. The People's Republic of China has been following the example set by Lee Kuan Yew of Singapore, who, after turning away from communism, introduced a centrally controlled political order that thrived on the back of one of the most business-friendly social and economic systems in the world. The consequences of another world power emerging in the center of Asia cannot yet be estimated; however, one thing is sure: the power balance among the leading nations will be changed.

Building Socialism with Chinese Characteristics

In the 1970s and early 1980s, the Chinese Communist Party formulated new ideological and political lines, improved organizational structures, and a series of original principles and policies.

What was the ideological line? To adhere to Marxism and to integrate it with Chinese realities—in other words, it was deemed to be crucial for China to adhere to Marxism and socialism. Why?

For more than a hundred years after the Second Opium War in the nineteenth century, China was subjected to aggression and humiliation. Then the Chinese people were told that only by embracing Marxism and remaining on the road leading from new democracy to socialism could their revolution (actually meaning *national liberation*) become victorious. Just like in Vietnam during the Vietnamese War, the socialist path was chosen to lead to national liberation and to the unification of the country.

Deng Xiaoping asked in the early 1980s, what if the Chinese people had taken the capitalist road instead? Could they have liberated themselves, and could they have finally stood up? According to Deng, the Kuomintang (also known as KMT, or the Chinese Nationalist Party, founded by Song Jiaoren and Sun Yat-sen and later led by Chiang Kai-shek) followed the capitalist road for more than twenty years, but China remained a semicolonial, semifeudal society, which proved that this path led nowhere. In contrast, the communists, integrating Marxism with nationalism (just like Stalin did) succeeded in the revolution by encircling the cities from the countryside. Consequently, Deng reasoned, if the Chinese communists had not integrated Marxism with "Chinese conditions" (Chinese nationalism), the revolution would not have succeeded and China would have remained fractured, weak, and vulnerable. Faith in Marxism was the motivating political force that enabled China to achieve victory (national liberation) in the revolution.[78] This reasoning is very similar to that of Ho Chi Minh's concerning the Vietnamese struggle for the liberation and unification of that country.

However, the West has never been able to grasp the real meaning of "integrating Marxism with local conditions" in non-Western lands—plainly meaning national liberation, since Marxism and nationalism (both purely Western concepts) are mutually exclusive to the dogmatic Western mind.

The Chinese communists inherited from old China a ruined economy with virtually no industry in 1949. There was a food shortage, inflation was acute, and the entire economy was in chaos. The communists solved the problems of feeding and employing the population by stabilizing the commodity prices and centralizing finance. As a result, the economy rapidly recovered. Building on this necessary foundation, they started large-scale reconstruction—relying, again, on Marxism and socialism. Deng's rationale was that if China had taken the capitalist (democratic) road, there would have been no end to the chaos, poverty, and backwardness in the country. Deng repeated that by "Marxism" he meant Marxism integrated with "Chinese conditions," and by "socialism" he meant socialism tailored to "Chinese conditions" and having a specifically "Chinese character." This political decision was Deng's first big decision.[79]

What is Marxism and what is socialism for the Chinese? Chinese Marxism attaches utmost importance to developing the productive forces. Socialism is supposed to be the first stage of communism, and at that advanced stage, the

Marxist principle of "each according to his ability" and "to each according to his needs" will be used.[80]

The Chinese understand that this calls for highly developed productive forces and an overwhelming abundance of material wealth.

Therefore, said Deng, the fundamental task for the socialist stage is to develop the productive forces. As these productive forces form, the people's material and cultural lives will steadily improve. Deng considered that one of the shortcomings after the founding of the People's Republic of China was that not enough attention was paid to the developing of the productive forces. That was Deng's second big decision; it was primarily a political decision but had an economic undertone.

Deng Xiaoping gave the word: Socialism means the elimination of poverty; pauperism is not socialism, still less communism. So how was China supposed to go forward, given that the country was still backward? What road could it take to develop the essential productive forces and raise the people's standard of living? Should it continue the socialist way or stop and turn onto the capitalist road?

Deng argued again that capitalism could enrich less than 10 percent of the Chinese population; it could never enrich the remaining more than 90 percent. Therefore, he stated, if they adhere to socialism but apply the principle of "distribution to each according to his work" (a rather capitalistic way of thinking), there would not be extreme disparities in wealth. Consequently, no polarization would occur as the Chinese productive forces became developed over the next twenty to thirty years. This socioeconomic decision was Deng's third major decision.

The political line of China was to focus on the modernization program and continue development of the productive forces. The minimum target of the Chinese modernization program was to achieve a relatively comfortable standard of living by the end of the twentieth century. By a "relatively comfortable standard," Deng meant a per capita GNP of US$800. If China were to apply the capitalist principle of distribution, said Deng, the majority of the people would remain exposed to poverty, misery, and underdevelopment. However, the "socialist principle of distribution" could enable all the people to lead relatively comfortable lives and was the reason China wanted to uphold socialism.[81]

Deng realized that a critical reason for China's backwardness after the Industrial Revolution in Western countries was its closed-door policy. China's experience had demonstrated that a closed-door policy in the modern world would inhibit development. Deng suggested that China should develop rapidly, and to do that, they needed to invigorate the national economy and open it to the outside world. This political decision was Deng's fourth major decision.

He did not forget that they must, first of all, solve the problem of the countryside. At that time, 80 percent of the population lived on the land, and China's peace still depends on the stability of the rural areas. No matter how successful the work is in the cities, it will not mean much without a stable base in the countryside. Still, the Chinese Communist Party decided in 1983 to shift the focus of reform from rural areas to the cities. The urban change would not only include industry and commerce but science and technology, education, and all other fields of endeavor as well. This purely political decision was Deng's fifth hugely important one.

China opened fourteen large- and medium-sized coastal cities where foreign investment and advanced management techniques were welcome. Deng was not afraid they would undermine Chinese socialism, because the socialist economic base was so huge that it could easily absorb tens and hundreds of billions of dollars' worth of foreign funds without getting damaged. Deng also realized that foreign investment would not only serve as an excellent supplement in the "building of socialism in China" but that this "supplement" was even indispensable.

Deng believed that the course he had chosen, which he called "building socialism with Chinese characteristics," was the right one. China has been following this road for many years and has achieved satisfactory results; indeed, the pace of development has so far exceeded the original projections and has made the Chinese even more confident now.[82]

CHINA'S HYBRID ECONOMY

Notwithstanding the rapid growth of the private capitalist sector and the strengthening of centrifugal market forces, the Chinese state still exercises considerable economic power.

China no longer has a planned economy, but it is not an entirely capitalist economy either. The state exerts power through the allocation of enormous resources and direct control of large SOEs (state-owned enterprises), which continue to overshadow critical sectors of the economy. Even though formally transformed into joint-stock companies (their shares sold to private investors), the largest banks are still actually controlled by the state. Presently in China, state-owned and state holding enterprises account for roughly half of all (non-property) public investment in fixed assets.

What portion of the Chinese economy remains under the direct control of the state? It is not easy to ascertain the state vs. private balance of ownership. Different studies give different figures, but in practice the state has retained control of former SOEs that have become joint-stock companies. With many seemingly privatized companies, the shareholder and accounting structure is such that the party can regain control if necessary at any time.

Conceivably one of the essential characteristics of the Chinese political system is that the Communist Party retains its traditional *nomenklatura* role, in which party committees make all the key personnel appointments in the state sector. The Communist Party holds on to its appointing power and thereby continues to shape the career paths and incentives for enterprise managers.

According to Chinese political line, state ownership is appropriate in four sectors: national security, natural monopoly, essential public goods or services, and vital national resources. Also, a few critical enterprises in "strategic" industries and hi-tech sectors should be maintained under state ownership.[83] Consequently, the continued existence of the large, heavily capitalized, and centrally controlled state sector brings a significant element of stability in the Chinese industrial ownership structure.

While China is still completing its transition away from bureaucratic socialism and toward a market economy, it is in the middle of the industrialization process—the continuing transformation from a rural to an urban society. China is still in the midst of Deng's "economic development"—the process that transforms every aspect of an economy, society, and culture. These two transitions are both far from complete, and so China today carries within it parts of the traditional and modern society, the socialist and the market economy, all mixed up in a jumble of mind-boggling complexity.

China is, therefore, a mixed, or hybrid, society, with neither a socialist nor a capitalist economy. The Chinese economy, and indeed society, is run by a party that is neither revolutionary nor subject to the usual constitutional checks and balances of the Western style.

No Big Bang

The continued function of the state sector reflects the Chinese character of the transition in China. Contrary to the former Soviet Union, there was no (Western-inspired) "big bang" implosion of the centrally planned economy or shattering of the old state apparatus. The Chinese party-state has done everything to prevent an economic meltdown, and this is reflected in the relatively limited extent of privatization of state firms—as opposed to corporatization, which is the running of the SOEs by the rules of the market.

During the first phase of economic reform from 1978–93, privatization, in fact, played almost no role at all. Changes in the agricultural sector, based on the family responsibility system (small family businesses), produced a mushrooming of private firms. Concurrently, the regime encouraged the development of new enterprises with foreign participation, especially in the coastal exclusive economic zones. That is, the private sector developed alongside and around the state sector without destroying and replacing the state-owned companies.

During the second phase of economic reform, from 1996 on, there was a massive downsizing of the SOEs, with a 40 percent reduction in the workforce and the corporatization of SOEs, which were, again, supposedly run according to purely profit-seeking market criteria.

There are millions of small businesses, many of them minuscule and poorly capitalized, accounting for only about one-fourth of industrial sales. There is recent evidence of differentiation within the small-scale private sector, with the growth of the most successful, more technologically advanced firms accompanied by the collapse and disappearance of many unsuccessful businesses.[84]

As the experience of privatization in the former Soviet Union and Eastern Europe has demonstrated, most of the privatized assets would end up in the hands of a small minority of wealthy businesspeople or would-be entrepreneurs. The Chinese leadership fears that a similar sweeping privatization would undermine its strategic control of the economy and, through the growth of inequalities in income and wealth, fan the flames of social protest.

The majority of state-owned or state-controlled firms are no longer operating under a plan, since the regime directed them to function as independent corporations according to market criteria. However, such corporatized, or marketed, state firms are still not identical to private capitalist companies. Undoubtedly they exploit their workers just as ruthlessly as private capitalists do, and many state-owned companies, just like private enterprises, have pursued a zero-profit strategy as well.

Manufacturers can successfully enter into business arrangements in which they earn zero profit, and this approach somehow proves to be economically efficient. How? By increasing capacity and raising output rates, often by soft or nonrepayable loans from the state banks, businesses obtain government approval. They can sell their goods on the official market at a loss—for example, to overseas corporate customers—but at the same time sell similar or identical products on the unofficial market at a handsome profit.

The Policy of the Central Government

The weight of the state-controlled sector has undoubtedly been reduced, and the growth of private enterprises combined with the ambitions of local bureaucrats has stimulated powerful diffusive forces in the Chinese economy. As a consequence, the regime has attempted to strengthen its levers of control through macroeconomic policy and strategic objectives in recent years.

As previously mentioned, during the first period of economic reforms between 1978–93, the trend was overwhelmingly toward decentralization; both the central and the regional governments encouraged the mushrooming of private businesses and the growth of foreign-owned firms. After 1993, however, there was a policy of recentralization again.

No sizeable foreign enterprise, be it in the steel, chemical or pharmaceutical, banking, or insurance industry, can take a direction in China with which the government is not in agreement. Moreover, the crisis of the global economy, including China, is now causing Chinese leaders to reassess their policy approach. Any recurrence of the world's financial crisis coupled with a slide into a global economic recession will increase the likelihood of further shifts in the economic policies of the regime both at home and internationally. The continuing economic power of the Chinese state will be a critical factor in the situation.

However, the perception of China as an aggressive, expansionist power is mistaken. Although China's relative strength has grown substantially in recent decades, the main Chinese foreign policy aims are primarily defensive and have not changed much since the Cold War period. These goals are intended to blunt destabilizing influences from abroad, to avoid territorial losses and lessen strategic susceptibility, to reduce the neighboring countries' suspicions, and to sustain economic growth. China is now so tightly integrated into the world economy that its priorities have become part of a broader pursuit: to define a global role that serves Chinese interests but also wins acceptance from other powers.[85]

Chief among those powers, of course, is the United States, and managing the fraught US-Chinese relationship is Beijing's primary foreign policy challenge. Also, just as Americans wonder whether China's rise is good for US interests or represents a looming threat, Chinese policymakers must puzzle over whether the United States intends to use its power to help or hurt China.

Americans sometimes view the Chinese state as impenetrable. However, given the way power is divided in the US political system and the frequent turnovers between the two main political parties there, the Chinese also have a hard time determining American intentions. Nevertheless, over recent decades, a long-term US strategy seems to have emerged out of a series of American actions toward China, so it is not a hopeless exercise for the Chinese to try to analyze the United States. Accordingly, the Chinese, not unlike the Europeans or South Americans, would most likely believe that the United States is a revisionist power seeking to curtail China's political and economic influence while harming China's interests. This probable view would be very similar to the Russian assessment of US intentions and shaped not only by Beijing's understanding of Washington but also by the broader Chinese view of the international system and China's place in it—a view determined in large part by China's acute sense of its own strategic vulnerability.

China Rising—America Resisting

The world as seen from Beijing must be a terrain of hazards from the streets outside the policymaker's window to land borders and sea lanes thousands of miles away, and on to the mines and oil fields of distant continents. These perceived threats could be described in four strategic spheres.

Beijing believes that foreign actors and forces threaten China's political stability and territorial integrity in the entire area that China administers or claims. Compared with other large countries, China must deal with an unprecedented number of foreign players trying to influence its development, often in ways that the regime considers detrimental to its survival. Foreign investors, businesspeople, development advisers, tourists, and students swarm the country, all with their ideas about how China should change. International foundations and foreign governments give financial and technical support to Chinese groups promoting civil society. Dissidents in Tibet and Xinjiang receive moral and diplomatic support and sometimes even material assistance from ethnic diasporas, sympathetic supporters, and foreign governments. All along the Chinese coast, neighboring countries dispute maritime regions that Beijing also claims. Taiwan has its own government, which is still recognized by twenty-three states and enjoys a security guarantee from the United States.

No other country except Russia has as many adjacent neighbors, fourteen to be exact, as China. They include five countries with which China has been involved in various military conflicts during the past seventy-five years (India, Japan, Russia, South Korea, and Vietnam) and some states ruled by unstable regimes. None of China's neighbors perceives its core national interests as congruent with Beijing's, and China rarely deals with any of its neighbors in a purely bilateral context.

In each of China's security spheres, the United States is ubiquitous. The United States is the most meddlesome outside actor in China's internal affairs while being the guarantor of the status quo in Taiwan. It has a massive naval presence in the East and South China Seas and is the official or unofficial military ally of many of China's neighbors. Moreover, the United States is the primary architect and defender of existing international legal systems. This omnipresence means that China's understanding of American motives determines how the Chinese deal with most of their security issues.

Beginning with President Richard Nixon, who visited China in 1972, successions of American leaders have assured China of their goodwill. Every US administration claims that China's stability, tranquility, and welfare are in the interest of the United States. Indeed, the United States has done more than any other power to contribute to China's modernization. It has drawn China into the global economy and given the Chinese access to markets, capital, and technology. It has trained Chinese experts in science, technology, and international law. It has prevented, at least until recently, the full remilitarization of Japan, maintained the peace on the Korean Peninsula, and helped avoid a war over Taiwan.

Nevertheless, Chinese policymakers are probably more impressed by policies and behaviors they perceive as less benevolent. The American military is deployed all around China's periphery, and the United States maintains a vast network of defense relationships with China's neighbors. Washington continues to frustrate Beijing's efforts to gain control over Taiwan. The United States regularly hectors China concerning its economic policies and maintains an array of government and nongovernmental programs that seek to influence Chinese civil society and politics.

Beijing could view this seemingly contradictory set of American actions through three reinforcing perspectives.

First, Chinese see their country as heir to an agrarian Eastern tradition that is pacifist, defense-minded, non-expansionist, and ethical. In contrast, they see Western strategic culture—especially that of the United States—as militaristic, offensive, expansionist, and selfish. The Chinese could rightly believe that the United States possesses potent ideological weapons and the willingness to use them.

Second, although China has embraced state capitalism with vigor, the Chinese view of the United States is probably still influenced by Marxist political thought, which postulates that capitalist powers attempt to exploit and dominate the rest of the world. China anticipates that Western powers will resist Chinese contest for resources and high-value-added markets. Although China runs enormous annual trade surpluses with the United States and holds a very significant amount of US debt, its leaders probably believe that the Americans get the most out of the deal by employing cheap Chinese labor and credit to help them live beyond their means.

Third, it is safe to assume that China follows the theory of offensive realism, which is the most important lens in international relations and holds that a country will try to control its security environment to the full extent its capabilities permit. According to this theory, the United States cannot be satisfied with the existence of a powerful China and therefore seeks to make the ruling regime there weaker and more pro-American. The Chinese must see evidence of this US intention in Washington's repeated calling for democracy and human rights in China, in addition to American support of what China considers separatist movements in Taiwan, Tibet, and Xinjiang.

Whether they see the United States primarily through a Marxist, realist, or "culturalist" lens, the Chinese leaders must assume that a great power such as the United States will use its might to defend and augment its privileges. Moreover, such a great power will treat efforts by other nations protecting their interests as threats to its own security. The American actions and reactions concerning the Russian–Ukrainian events should undoubtedly reinforce their views.

This assumption leads to a sad conclusion: with China rising, the United States will resist. For the Chinese, the United States uses comforting words; it disguises its actions as a quest for peace, human rights, democracy, and equality, sometimes even offering honest assistance. However, the United States, being a Western power, is two-faced, if not schizophrenic. It is resolved to remain the global hegemon and will prevent China from growing strong enough to challenge it by using any means at its disposal. Although the United States realizes it needs China's help on many regional and global issues, it is also worried about a more powerful rival and will use multiple measures to delay its development and make it follow American values.

Nevertheless, Chinese and American interests are not entirely at odds. The two countries are adequately remote from each other, their core security interests need not clash, and they can gain mutual benefit from trade and other shared interests.

All the same, there are many on both the American and Chinese sides with more confrontational ideas about Sino-American relations whose views are usually kept out of sight to avoid frightening both rivals and friends.

The Revisionist Danger

To look into the logic of the United States' China strategy more deeply, we must look at capabilities and intentions. Although US plans might be subject to interpretation, the American military, economic, ideological, and diplomatic potentials must look devastating from the Chinese point of view.

US military forces are technologically advanced and globally deployed, with massive concentrations of firepower all around the Chinese rim. Regarding its geographic scope and nonwartime human resources, the US Pacific Command (USPACOM) is the largest of the United States' six regional combatant commands. USPACOM's assets include about 325,000 military and civilian personnel, together with some 180 ships and 1,900 aircraft. To the west, USPACOM adjoins the US Central Command (CENTCOM), which is responsible for an area stretching from Central Asia to Egypt. Before September 11, 2001, CENTCOM had no forces stationed directly on China's borders except for its training and supply missions in Pakistan. However, with the beginning of the War on Terror, CENTCOM placed tens of thousands of troops in Afghanistan and gained extended access to the Manas Air Base in Kyrgyzstan (from 2001 through 2014).

Bilateral defense treaties with Australia, New Zealand, Japan, Philippines, and South Korea, in addition to cooperative arrangements with other partners, magnify the operational capabilities of US forces in the Asia-Pacific area. Moreover, the United States possesses some fifty-two hundred nuclear warheads deployed on an invulnerable sea, land, and air triad. This US defense posture, taken together, could rightly create the appearance of a strategic ring of encirclement, from the Chinese point of view.

One must pay attention to the United States' extensive capability to damage Chinese economic interests as well. The US is still China's single largest market, except for the European Union as a single entity. The United States is still one of China's leading sources of foreign direct investment (FDI) and advanced technology. Periodically, Washington has considered wielding its economic power coercively. After the 1989 Tiananmen Square crackdown, the US imposed some limited diplomatic and economic sanctions on China. These included an embargo, which is still in effect, on the sale of advanced weapon systems. For several years afterward, Congress debated whether to punish China further for human rights violations by canceling the low most favored nation (MFN) tariff rates enjoyed by US imports from China, although proponents of the plan could never muster a majority. More recently, US legislators have proposed sanctioning China for artificially keeping the value of the renminbi low, to the benefit of Chinese exporters. The onetime Republican presidential candidate Mitt Romney promised that if elected he would classify China a "currency manipulator" on "day one" in government.

China believes that the United States and its allies would deny, among others, supplies of oil, metal ores, and other raw materials to China during a military or economic crisis. The US Navy could block China's access to strategically crucial sea lanes; one should look at the conflict concerning the South China Sea in this context. The ubiquity of the dollar in international trade and finance also gives the United States the ability to damage Chinese interests. That could happen either on purpose or as a result of the US government printing dollars to address its fiscal problems and increased borrowing. These acts drive down the value of China's dollar-denominated exports and foreign exchange reserves.

China must also consider that the United States possesses potent ideological weapons and the willingness to use them. After World War II, the United States took advantage of its position as the dominant power to enshrine American principles in the Universal Declaration of Human Rights and other international human rights instruments and to install what China sees as Western-style democracies in Japan and, eventually, South Korea, Taiwan, and other countries. China believes that the United States uses the ideas of democracy and human rights to delegitimize and destabilize regimes that espouse alternative values, such as socialism and Asian-style developmental authoritarianism. The Chinese maintain that the Americans' real purpose is not the protection of so-called human rights. Instead, they believe that The United States only uses this pretext to influence and limit China's economic growth and to prevent China's wealth and power from threatening US world hegemony.[86]

The way the Chinese see it, the United States has revealed itself to be a revisionist power that has been trying to reshape the global environment in its favor even further since the end of the Cold War. They see evidence of this everywhere: in the rapid expansion of NATO; the US interventions in Panama, Haiti, Bosnia, and Kosovo; the Gulf Wars; the war in Afghanistan; the invasion of Iraq; the attacks on Libya and Syria; and the Ukrainian crisis. In the economic sphere, the United States has tried to enhance its advantages by pushing for free trade and devaluing the dollar while forcing other countries to use it as a reserve currency. Perhaps most disturbingly to the Chinese, the United States has shown its aggressive designs by promoting so-called color revolutions in Georgia, Ukraine, and Kyrgyzstan. Although the United States has always opposed communist revolutions, it has also supported other revolutions if they served its "democracy promotion strategy."[87]

Exploiting the Problem of Taiwan

The United States tried to contain and isolate China between 1950 and 1972. Among other actions, it prevailed on most of its allies to withhold diplomatic recognition of "mainland China." The US also organized a trade embargo against the mainland, assisted in building up the Japanese military, intervened in the Korean War, propped up the rival regime in Taiwan, supported Tibetan guerillas fighting Chinese control, and even threatened to use nuclear weapons during both the Korean War and the 1958 Taiwan Strait crisis.

Chinese observers concede that the United States' China policy changed after 1972. However, they assert that the change was solely the result of an effort to counter the Soviet Union and, later, to gain economic benefits by doing business in China. Even then, the United States continued to hedge against China's rise by maintaining Taiwan as a strategic distraction, aiding the growth of Japan's military, modernizing its naval forces, and pressuring China on human rights.

The Chinese consistently saw the Americans as demanding and unyielding during ambassadorial talks in the 1950s and 1960s, negotiations over arms control in the 1980s and 1990s, discussions over China's accession to the World Trade Organization (WTO) in the 1990s, and talks over climate change during the decade that followed.

However, most decisive for Chinese understandings of US policy were the three rounds of negotiations that took place regarding Taiwan in 1971–72, 1978–79, and 1982, which created the communiqué framework that governs America's Taiwan policy to this day. When the US–Chinese rapprochement began, Chinese policymakers allegedly assumed that Washington would give up its support for Taipei in exchange for the benefits of standard state-to-state relations with Beijing. According to the Chinese, at each stage of the negotiations, the Americans seemed willing to do so. However, even decades later the United States remains, in Beijing's view, the chief obstacle to reunification.

In the course of President Nixon's trip to China in 1972, he apparently told the Chinese that although he was willing to eschew Taiwan because it was no longer strategically valuable to the United States, he could not follow through with that until his second term. Based on this understanding, the Chinese consented to the 1972 Shanghai Communiqué, even though it included a unilateral proclamation by the United States that "reaffirmed its interest in a peaceful settlement of the Taiwan question."[88] This statement was diplomatic code for a US commitment to block any attempt by the mainland to take Taiwan by force. As it happened, Nixon resigned before he was able to normalize relations with Beijing, and his successor, Gerald Ford, was politically too weak and drained to fulfill Nixon's pledge.

When the next US president, Jimmy Carter, wished to normalize relations with China, the Chinese demanded a clean break with Taiwan. Although the United

States ended its defense treaty with the island in 1979, it again issued a statement rehashing its commitment to a "peaceful resolution of the Taiwan issue."[89] Congress then surprised both the Chinese and the administration by adopting the Taiwan Relations Act, which mandated the United States to "maintain [its] capacity to resist any resort to force or other forms of coercion that would jeopardize the security of the people of Taiwan."[90] Once again, the deterrent intent was clear.

In 1982, when President Ronald Reagan sought closer relations with Beijing to ramp up pressure on Moscow, China prevailed upon the United States to sign another communiqué, which committed Washington to gradually reducing its weapons sales to Taiwan.[91] However, once the agreement was in place, the American side set the reference point at 1979, the year when arms sales had reached their highest level. The United States calculated annual reductions at a small marginal rate, generously adjusting for inflation so that they were actually increases, and claimed that the more advanced weapons systems they sold Taiwan were the qualitative equivalents of older systems. Also, the Americans allowed commercial firms to cooperate with the Taiwanese armaments industry under the rubric of technology transfers rather than arms sales.[92] By the time President George W. Bush approved a broad package of advanced weapons to Taiwan in April 2001, the 1982 communiqué was a dead letter.[93] Meanwhile, as the United States prolonged its involvement with Taiwan, a democratic transition took place there, putting unification even further out of Beijing's reach.

Reviewing this history, Chinese leaders may ask themselves why the United States remains so committed to Taiwan. Although Americans often argue that they are just defending a loyal and democratic friend, most Chinese suspect strategic motives at the root of Washington's conduct. They believe that keeping the Taiwan problem going helps the United States tie China down. In the words of Luo Yuan, a retired general and deputy secretary-general of the Chinese Society of Military Science, the United States has long used Taiwan "as a chess piece to check China's rise."[94]

The Perils of Pluralism: Sugarcoated Threats

Ever since the Tiananmen demonstrations, China has attracted the attention of more American interest groups than any other country. China's political system elicits opposition from human rights organizations, its population-control policies anger the antiabortion movement, and its repression of churches offends American Christians. China's cheap exports trigger demands for protection from organized labor; its reliance on coal and massive hydroelectric dams for energy upsets environmental groups; and its ignoring of intellectual property laws infuriate the film, software, and pharmaceutical industries. These and similar complaints reinforce the anxiety about a China threat, which spread through American political rhetoric—an apprehension that, in Chinese eyes, not only denies or at least questions the validity and justice of Chinese aspirations but itself makes up, to some extent, a threat to China.

Of course, there are also those in the US Congress, think tanks, the media, and academia who support positions favorable to China. This support is on the basis that cooperation is necessary for American farmers, exporters, banks, and Wall Street, or that issues such as North Korea and climate change are more consequential than disputes over rights or religion. Those advocates may be more influential in the long run than those critical of China, but they tend to work behind the scenes. To the observer trying to make any sense of the cacophony of views expressed in US political circles, the loudest voices are the easiest to hear, and the signals are alarming.

In trying to ascertain US intentions, it is worth looking at policy statements made by senior figures in the American executive branch, since one could consider such statements reliable guides to US strategy. These comments often do two things: they seek to reassure Beijing that Washington's intentions are benign, and at the same time they aim to encourage the American public that the United States will never allow China's rise to threaten US interests. One could perceive this combination of themes as sugarcoated threats.

For example, in 2005, Robert Zoellick, the US deputy secretary of state at the time, delivered a China policy address on behalf of the George W. Bush administration. He encouraged his American audience that the United States would "attempt to dissuade any military competitor from developing disruptive or other capabilities that could enable regional hegemony or hostile action against the United States or other friendly countries." However, he also explained that China's rise was not a threat, because China "does not seek to spread radical, anti-American ideologies," "does not see itself in a death struggle with capitalism" and "does not believe that its future depends on overturning the fundamental order of the international system." On that premise, Zoellick said, the two sides could have "a cooperative relationship." Nevertheless, cooperation would depend on certain conditions. China should calm what he called a "cauldron of anxiety" in the United States about its rise. It should "explain its defense spending, intentions, doctrine, and military exercises"; reduce its trade surplus with the United States; and cooperate with Washington on Iran and North Korea. Above all, Zoellick advised, China should give up "closed politics." In the US view, he said, "China needs a peaceful political transition to make its government responsible and accountable to its people."[95]

The Obama administration has repeated the same ideas in slightly gentler language. James Steinberg, then deputy secretary of state, submitted the concept of "strategic reassurance" in the government's first major policy address concerning China in September 2009. He defined the principle in the following way: "Just as we and our allies must make clear that we are prepared to welcome China's 'arrival' … as a prosperous and successful power, China must reassure the rest of the world that its development and growing global role will not come at the expense of security and well-being of others." China would need to "reassure others that this buildup does not present a threat"; it would need to "increase its military transparency to reassure all the countries in the rest of Asia and globally about its intentions" and demonstrate that it "respects the rule of law and universal norms."[96]

Such statements send China the message that Washington wants only one-sided cooperation according to its wishes and, not surprisingly, it attempts to check Beijing from developing such military capability that would compensate for China's strategically vulnerable position. Also, these messages keep strengthening the Chinese belief that the ultimate American intention is to change the Chinese political system.

Admittedly, Beijing's suspicion of Washington would have to confront the fact that the US has done so much to promote China's rise. However, for the Chinese, history provides an answer to this puzzle: as they must see it, the United States contained China for as long as it could. When the Soviet Union's rising strength made doing so necessary, the United States was forced to engage China to reinforce its hand against Moscow and split the two great socialist allies. With that political opening, the US came to believe that collaboration would shift China in the direction of democracy and eventually would win back for the United States the strategic base on the Asian mainland that Washington lost in 1949 when the Communists triumphed in the Chinese Civil War.

Undoubtedly, Washington's gradual rapprochement with Beijing was not born out of idealism and generosity. Instead it was pursued so that the United States could gain from China's economic opening by maximizing profits from US investments, consuming cheap Chinese goods, and borrowing money to support the US trade and fiscal deficits. While busy feasting at the Chinese table, US strategists underestimated the risk of China's rise until the late 1990s. Now when the United States perceives China as a threat, it no longer can prevent it from continuing to develop. In this context, the US strategy of engagement failed, confirming the advice of Chinese leader Deng Xiaoping in 1991, who then advocated a policy of "hiding our light and nurturing our strength."[97] Faced with a prosperous China that has risen too far and too fast to be stopped, the United States can only try to urge cooperation on US terms; intimidate, surround, and confine militarily; and continue to work to change the regime.

Realistically, China cannot challenge the United States in the foreseeable future. The Chinese should expect the United States to remain the global hegemon for several decades, despite what they may perceive as initial signs of decline. For the time being, as described by Wang Jisi, dean of Peking University's School of International Studies, "the superpower is more super, and the many great powers are less great."[98] Meanwhile, both the US and China are increasingly interdependent economically and have the military capability to cause each other harm. It is this mutual vulnerability that carries the best medium-term hope for cooperation. Mutual fear of each other keeps alive the imperative to work together.

Even after it becomes the world's biggest economy in absolute terms, China's prosperity will remain dependent on the welfare of its global challengers (and vice versa), including the United States and Japan. The more prosperous China becomes, the higher will be its stake in the security of sea lanes, the stability of the world trade and financial systems, the nonproliferation of nuclear weapons, the control of the global environment, and cooperation on public health. China will not advance if its competitors do not also prosper.

The United States should encourage China by drawing clear policy lines that meet American security needs without threatening China's. As China rises, it will push against US power to find the boundaries of American will. Washington must push back to establish limits for the growth of Chinese power. However, hawkish campaign talks about trade wars and strategic competition play into Beijing's fears while undercutting the necessary effort to agree on common interests. Putting such rhetoric into action would require a break in mutually beneficial economic ties and would force China into hostile reactions.

For the United States, the right China strategy begins at home. Washington must nurture its relationships with its allies and other cooperating powers, support a peerless higher-education sector, protect US intellectual property from espionage and theft, and, most of all, regain the admiration, respect, and friendship of people the world over. So long as the United States addresses its real problems at home and holds tight to its practical as opposed to idealistic, missionary, or hypocritical values, it can manage China's rise. If it cannot do that, China will assuredly not constitute its most significant problem in any event.

THE CHINA–RUSSIA RELATIONSHIP: NOT ALLIES JUST YET

China and Russia have the longest shared land border in the world, and trade between the two nations is booming, at around $90 billion annually in 2014 but targeted to reach $200 billion by 2020.[99] Russian and Chinese bilateral relations have vastly improved since the fall of the Soviet Union.

Both countries would like to eject what they call US "hegemony," especially near their borders. As an example of that, Russia repeatedly demanded that the US pull out of the Manas Air Base in Bishkek, Kyrgyzstan, and insists on Moscow's consent before any US military deployment occurs in Central Asia, regardless of whether these forces are needed to fight Islamist terrorism. Similarly, China would like to keep the US naval presence in the Western Pacific in check.[100]

Russia's assertive foreign policy, with its anti-American overtones, seeks to establish a Russian "pole" in the global world order. In this context, the Chinese are expected to continue the further development of the Sino-Russian comprehensive strategic partnership.

Russian Foreign Minister Sergey Lavrov stated, "Russia and China have united positions, and promote these united positions in negotiations, on the situation in the Middle East and North Africa, including the Syrian crisis, Afghanistan, the Iranian nuclear program and other crises ... On all these cases, we and our Chinese friends are led by one and the same principle – the necessity to observe international law, respect UN procedures and not allow interference from outside in domestic conflicts and all the more the use of force."[101]

The Shanghai Cooperation Organization, which Moscow and Beijing founded, aims to fight "the three evils: separatism, extremism, and terrorism."[102] Indeed, there are enough territories beset by such evils: Chechnya, Tibet, Xinjiang, Taiwan.

Sino-Russian cooperation is not just geopolitical but also, most importantly, ideological: both Russia and China want to halt the spread of liberal democracy. That means keeping the United States, as well as those regimes friendly to it, out of their internal affairs. They both believe that any government has a sovereign right to deal with its domestic issues and handle its internal problems without outside interference. They both reject the currently politically correct Western notion that foreign governments and nongovernmental organizations have a moral right to meddle in the internal affairs of other countries using as justification human rights or environmental reasons, among others.

With these principles kept in mind, they have worked in agreement to check Western efforts in the Middle East and protect their interests, such as legitimizing regimes that are inimical to the West. They vetoed and stifled sanctions and Western-supported plans for Syria. China, which is the principal auxiliary to North Korea, condemns even the possibility of military action against Pyongyang—and so does Russia. They increasingly present an alternative to Western-style democracy and are two stalwarts of the anti-US front, which tentatively also includes Iran and Venezuela.

China and Russia are expanding their economic ties; they have already moved to trade with each other using their own national currencies—thus excluding the dollar. Moscow and Beijing have promised to increase trade dramatically over the next decade and already finalized a deal concerning the most critical sector of their bilateral trade: energy. A new natural gas pipeline will connect Russia's abundant gas reserves with China's ever-growing need for energy.

Theoretically, the United States should work to prevent the Beijing–Moscow axis from taking root; after all, this was the primary goal of the Nixon–Kissinger effort forty-five years ago. China is making inroads in the Middle East and East

Asia—two regions pivotal to US interests. China is expanding its influence along the Indian Ocean rim and in Africa, its state-owned businesses are investing heavily in Afghan natural resources, and Beijing wields a tremendous amount of weight in Pakistan.

Russia is executing its own pivot to Asia—something Moscow already highlighted when hosting the twenty-fourth APEC (Asia-Pacific Economic Cooperation) summit in Vladivostok during the fall of 2013. Like China with its maritime neighbors, Russia also has an island dispute of its own with Japan over the Kuril Islands. The two could join forces, exert pressure on Japan, and lend international credibility to each other's territorial claims. Nevertheless, Russia is pursuing a rapprochement with Japan, Korea, and Vietnam, indicating that it may be wary of the rising giant of China.

A China–Russia partnership is advocating a discriminative pledge to noninterference in internal affairs, which plays well with the other regimes around the world that do not want to follow the Western liberal-democratic line. They seek arms contracts and economic ties while encouraging their partners to stand up to Western political and economic pressure.

However, as a fast-growing China continues to expand its sphere of influence through military, economic, smart, and soft power, Russia may become its junior partner in international affairs. China's rapid economic rise, including in Central Asia and Beijing, any possible future desire for an extended global position could cause subsequent problems for the Sino-Russian relationship.

Russia's economy is moving very slowly compared to China's, and Moscow could quickly turn into a natural resource adjunct for Beijing. Additionally, the densely populated Chinese provinces bordering the sparsely populated Russian Far East provoke alarm in Moscow that Chinese migrants will settle in and eventually control sizeable parts of Siberia.

Today Russia blames the West for its time of troubles in the 1990s, when a weak and corrupt central government presided over the economic slump and inflation. Moreover, Moscow is increasingly rejecting Western values, such as same-sex marriages. Russia also blames the United States (and the EU) for meddling in its "near abroad," most of all in Ukraine; fomenting the orange revolutions, such as those in Georgia (2003) and Ukraine (2004); and pushing for NATO enlargement along its borders. Operation Enduring Freedom, the official name used by the

US government to refer to the Global War on Terrorism in Afghanistan, while supported by Russia, troubled both Moscow and Beijing. China sees the pivot to Asia as containment policy.

For now, mutual geopolitical, economic, and even ideological interests keep drawing Russia and China together into a partnership of necessity. China's leadership sends the clear message that China seeks to cement closer ties with its neighbors—and not with the United States.

Washington's policy stands in direct conflict with Henry Kissinger's postulate that a Russia–China axis is not in US national security interests. Alas, Washington has never followed Kissinger's prudent advice concerning Iran either.

Russia and China share a border running forty-three hundred kilometers but have long been divided by mistrust. Nevertheless, if the past few years are any indication, the two neighbors are enjoying a distinct warming in relations. A historic oil deal and joint military exercises are the most evident signs of a deepening partnership. Suspicions are likely to linger, along with direct competition in Central Asia, but economic and geopolitical considerations—including the urge to counterbalance the United States—are bringing the two countries more and more in line.

In March 2013, just eight days after he entered office as China's new president, Xi Jinping arrived in Moscow. Russian President Vladimir Putin, who has increasingly steered his land and people away from the West since returning to the Kremlin in 2012, signed on to multiple bilateral agreements with China. He declared that relations between Russia and China were "the best in their history."[103] The Russian leader used the strategic opportunity to align his nation with an economically flourishing, up-and-coming, prosperous, and stable great power.

However, it was the deal sealed in June 2013 that immediately caught the observers' eyes. Rosneft, Russia's state-controlled energy company, signed a $270 billion contract doubling Russian oil deliveries to China.[104] The most striking point about the new deal was not that there was a new agreement, but that the agreed-upon price was much lower than average world prices at the time. In this way, Russia tries to keep China as a valuable associate while signaling that it is ready to compromise in the interest of gaining a new partner. With Russia being aware of both European efforts to become less dependent on its oil and natural gas, as well as the anticipated energy boom in the United States, strategic energy links with

Beijing have become even more urgently important than before. China, in turn, is expected to remain energy hungry for decades to come.

China has its reasons for cozying up to Russia, and they increasingly extend beyond energy and trade. The Chinese navy conducted its largest-ever military exercise with a foreign country as warships from Beijing and Moscow joined forces in the Sea of Japan. By expanding the military maneuvers, the latest war games included fleet air defense, antisubmarine warfare, and surface warfare.

Many read the display of force in part as a signal to the United States, which had repositioned military assets eastward and made new overtures to Pacific allies. China claims the drills were not aimed at a specific threat but acknowledges their importance for the bilateral relationship. Trust between China and Russia is getting deeper and deeper with time.

Does the relationship mean more than just standing up to the superpower? While Chinese and Russian interests in the West will prevent the formation of a full-fledged anti-Western axis, both have been comfortable with playing the foil. Both have seen eye-to-eye at the UN in recent years, citing a policy of noninterference in blocking or weakening the international body's action in Syria, Iran, and North Korea. The two countries' UN records, their recent display of military unity, and their coordination on the travel of accused US leaker Edward Snowden together suggest that they have collaborated to let the wind out of the West's sails.

Both are suspicious about the deployment of US missile interceptors in Alaska and have suggested the founding of a new international lending institution to rival the Western-led International Monetary Fund and World Bank.

As mentioned earlier, there is a Russian search for new self-identity coupled with the country positioning itself in the world—even having perhaps China as a strategic partner. While neither side ever speaks about creating an anti-Western alliance, one can detect many steps taken by both China and Russia that could be regarded as anti-Western or, more precisely, anti-US measures.

Skeptics say energy and arms deals could fall apart before being implemented. Moscow fears Chinese demographic pressure on the sparsely populated Russian Far East. Despite the bold show of military cooperation in July 2013, Moscow is also wary of Beijing's might, and it has not backed Chinese claims to territory in the South China Sea. China, in turn, has refused to recognize the pro-Moscow breakaway Georgian regions of Abkhazia and South Ossetia.

The most critical point of divergence seems to be in Central Asia—a region that Russia continues to consider her near abroad, but one that China is fast integrating into its economic orbit. By 2012, all Central Asian states except for Uzbekistan traded more with Beijing than with Moscow. Analysts say President Putin's efforts to establish the Eurasian Economic Union is mostly an attempt to limit Chinese economic dominance of the region.

The current Sino-Russian relationship is, for the time being, more tactical cooperation than a real strategic partnership. Nevertheless, this could quickly change in the future—with all the consequences that would entail. Just how strong the ties can become between Russia and China remains to be seen, and to a large extent, it also depends on the schizophrenic and hypocritical actions taken by the West.

6

Political Philosophy

Political philosophy begins with the question, what ought to be a person's relationship to society? The subject, on the one hand, explores the use of moral ideas in the social arena and thus deals with the various types of government and social forms according to which people could live. On the other hand, in so doing, it also provides a standard by which to analyze and judge existing institutions and relationships.

Political philosophy is distinguishable from political science, although a range of philosophical issues and methods intimately links the two.

Political science predominantly deals with existing states of affairs, and insofar as it is possible to be amoral in its descriptions, it seeks a thorough analysis of social relations—for example, constitutional issues, voting behavior, the balance of power, the effect of judicial review, and so forth.

Political philosophy generates visions of the good social life: of what ought to be the guiding moral principles and institutions that connect people. The subject matter is extensive and relates readily to various branches and subdisciplines of philosophy, including philosophy of law and economics.

The most important political theories assume the ethical and hence political primacy of humanity and accordingly press on to define what they consider the most appropriate institutions for human survival, development, morality, and happiness.

All political theories are governed by and are dependent on ethical principles of human nature as it relates to the world and others. Because political theory predominantly deals with human social life, it must also deal with human individuality as well as human relationships within groups—with one's sense of self as a political and ethical entity as well as one's need and reason to belong to overarching identities.[105]

Ethical Foundations

Political philosophy has its beginnings in ethics—in questions such as, what kind of life is the good, or proper, life for human beings? Since people are by nature sociable, the inquiry follows as to what kind of life is appropriate for a person among people. The philosophical discourses concerning politics thus develop, broaden, and flow from their ethical underpinnings.

The most crucial and insistent ethical-political point in question that divides philosophers into a multitude of schools of thought is that having to do with the status of the individual: the ethical "person."

Scholars are divided between those who deem the *person* as ethically and politically sacred and those who regard the individual to be a member of a *group* and for whom the group accordingly takes on a sacred status.

There could be other notions. For example, some consider political institutions sacred in their right, but this is not a tenable position; if humanity did not exist, such institutions would be meaningless, and hence they can gain their meaning only from our existence. However, the fundamental question that divides political philosophers always comes back to either the group or the individual being the entity of analysis.

The tone of language used by the contending intellects to define the political primacy of their entity (individual or group) historically changes depending on other opposing or supplementing concepts, but the division is best characterized today by the "rights of the individual" against the "rights of the group."

Other pertinent terms include "the dignity of the individual," "the duties and obligations owing to the group," and "the autonomy or self-determination of the group or individual." These terms in turn resolve into particular and related issues concerning the roles of cultural, racial, religious, and sexual orientations. The debate proceeds today between communitarians and liberals who argue about rights and obligations as they spread across groups and individuals.

This caricature of extremes allows us to examine the differences and the points of agreement among the various schools of political philosophy in a better light. However, as with all generalizations made of historical events, the devil is in the details, and they are much more complicated and subtle because the application of theory in the political realm necessarily deals with social institutions. People are sociable; indeed, we could hardly be said to be human if we possessed no society or culture. Therefore, both extremes must examine and evaluate the social-ethical realms of selfhood, friendship, family, property, exchange, money (that is, indirect exchange), community, tribe, race, association, and the state (and its various branches)—and, accordingly, the individual's relationship with each.

Methodological Issues

Engaging in a philosophical analysis of political activity, philosophers also divide between those who are methodological individualists and those who are methodological holists. Methodological individualists seek to explain social actions and behavior regarding *individual* deed, and politically are known as individualists; whereas holists strive to explain behavior by considering the nature of the group.

The bifurcation results from a theoretical division concerning the appropriate unit of study. In contrast to methodological individualists claiming that society (culture, people or nation) is no more than the sum of its living members, holists argue that the whole is greater than the sum of the parts. This holistic argument in the political realm translates into the notion that the state, nation, race, folk, or people are greater, more, or higher than the individual. Politically, methodological holism leads into the doctrine of collectivism, and all collectivist theories deny or lessen the value and authority of the individual to the higher status accorded a collective entity. Methodological individualism translates into political individualism, in which the individual's social or group membership is either rejected altogether as not worthy of study or its causal or exact relationship is deemed too amorphous, pluralistic, and changing to provide anything by qualitative assessments of social affairs.

It must be mentioned here that there are theological-political philosophies that deny any primacy to the individual or the group for the sovereign status of the divine realm. Nonetheless, once theologians admit to having to have some government or rule for the living on earth, the general debate of political philosophy can be accepted and expounded upon to define the "good life" for people among people.

A second crucial methodological issue that relates to both epistemology and ethics is the role reason plays in social affairs. The extreme positions may be termed as rationalism and irrationalism, but these are not necessarily logical opposites. A rationalist may declare his belief in logic to be conclusively irrational (e.g., Karl Popper) or an irrationalist may function rationally.

Political rationalism accentuates the exercise of reason in social affairs, meaning that individuals ought to submit to the logic and universality of reason rather than their subjective or cultural preconceptions. Rationalists argue that reason unifies humanity politically and hence is conducive to peace.

Irrationalists, on the other hand, downplay the efficacy of reason in our human affairs or, more particularly, in our social relationships. Instead a broad range of alternatives are put forward in reason's place: emotions; cultural, religious, or class expectations; atavistic symbols; and mystical forms of intuition or knowledge. Irrationalists of all hues can also criticize rationalists for ignoring the subtle wisdom of intellectual and social heritage that often lies beneath contemporary society. Politically, they regard the demands of reason to be rationalizations of a particular culture (usually a Western modus operandi) rather than applications that are universal, and they claim that political solutions that appear rational to one group cannot necessarily be translated into solutions for another group.

Some irrationalists uphold the theory that there is (or ought to be) more than one mode of logic, which ultimately collapses into an epistemological subjectivism. This way of thinking leads to the conclusion that "tribal logic" is predicated on the separateness or distinctiveness of particular groups' logic, methods of discourse, and thinking.

Other irrationalists, however, with this author among them, dispute that the human mind develops alternative logic around the world. Instead they maintain that human action develops alternative methods of living both *in* different places and *from* different historical circumstances. Politically, this stance translates into conservatism, a philosophical position that is suspicious of rationalist designs, such as, say, to overthrow all political institutions and to begin "afresh" according to some utopian blueprint.

Conservatism emphasizes the continuity of wisdom—as contained in institutions and the language of politics—over the generations and in particular localities.

Between individualists emphasizing the sacred status of the individual and collectivists emphasizing the sacred status of the group exist a panoply of schools of thought that derive their impetus from the philosophical spectrum—the overlapping gray areas, which are today found in the endless disputes between individualists and communitarians.

Western Political Schools of Thought

From the earliest beginnings, essential differences could be observed between English-American and French-German concepts of liberty, equality, and government. We can duly speak of Franco-German and Anglo-American political ideas today.

The Franco-German or Continental European (or what this author considers fundamentally socialist) philosophical position may be characterized as attributing to human reason an unlimited capacity to comprehend, evaluate, organize, and arrange the affairs of our world. According to this understanding, the proper sequence in charting the future course of humanity is to develop the theory first, and then people and events are to adapt and comply with it.

By contrast, the Anglo-American position considers human reason as confined by limitations and wanting moral guidance as it attempts to provide for the future. In this way of thinking, it is observation, experience, and lessons learned (by trial and error) that form the basis of society's choices in organizing its institutions. The only attainable goal is to improve continuously the conditions that enable individuals to achieve their personal best.[106]

It seems that no area of human activity, no form of human interchange, is unaffected by these two fundamentally different concepts. Accordingly, on the Franco-German side, we find the political theory and corresponding prescriptions that, it is claimed, will necessarily lead to a good society. In that ideal society, all will achieve contentment. The Franco-German-led European Union could be considered as the upside potential of this doctrine, while the Soviet Union and Germany's Third Reich have demonstrated the downside—all three stemming from socialist ideology. This theory can also be examined in the context of Brexit—Britain's decision to leave the European Union.

By contrast, Anglo-American thinkers have settled for more limited goals, one of which was simply to extend the blessings of liberty to more people than was possible in other forms of society. Liberty, in turn, produced an unprecedented accumulation of wealth and increased access to it by a steadily growing number of people. We all know the upside: it was the old Anglo-Saxon world before World War II, later extending to the so-called Western World. The faults and failures of the same players have also demonstrated the downside.

Current political parlance refers to the first, Franco-German, side as "utopian," "statist," and "collectivist"—or even "totalitarian" and "socialist" in the more aggressive form. "Big government" is also often used to characterize this doctrine, but one could rightly name its operational method as "socialism" or the "search for social justice."

The other, Anglo-American, side is often called capitalism or classical liberalism.

All the major conflicts, though colored by additional participants and causes, have been clashes between these two leading schools of Western political thought—with periodically alternating success.

Since the late 1960s, progressives, post-New Dealers, and socialists, not to mention outright communists and later modern-day left-liberals, have all propagated the Franco-German ideas that have been gaining ground everywhere in the West.

Desires and Aspirations

Similarly, there are two major guiding influences in the lives of humans: desires and aspirations. However, the two are entirely different from one another; desire seeks to be satisfied and fulfilled, while aspirations (or goals) must be achieved.

Desire tends to be fundamental and physical: the love of an attractive mate, an opulent home, or an expensive car. Aspiration aims at the intangible, often at the spiritual. Fulfillment of a person's desire, in most cases, will affect the person only; achievement of aspiration is likely to affect others. As an example, to produce a superb meal is the achievement of aspiration, but to eat it is the fulfillment of desire. Desire is by nature passive, while aspiration is active.

The initial activity takes the form of thinking. However, as desire surfaces through the senses and provokes feelings of various sorts, the thought process that gives birth to aspirations develops independently of sensory needs. Aspirations reflect the thought processes of countless generations and deeply embed in the consciousness of people. As the origins go back a long way, so the achievement requires vast expanses of time.

Before the deed, there must be thought. Before the achievement, there must be an aspiration. The realization of equality before the law depends upon a rule of law that grants precedence to no one and which all must obey. Giving the very same rights to every other person under the same jurisdiction best secures a person's rights.

It is because people's appearances, abilities, and station in life are so different that the aspirations for equality welled up in the souls of old. It is because people's appearances, abilities, and stations in life are so different that, of all aspirations, this is the most elusive—and the most exalted.

Among the attributes that render one person distinct from another, aspiration is decisive. One who is possessed by it will act differently from the one who is not. A group, society, or nation in which a critical mass of its members is possessed by it will behave differently from, though not necessarily better than, those who are not.[107]

Equality is the elimination of differences. Since people are different, only force can cover up the differences, and then it can do so only temporarily. Once the force is not present any longer, the differences reappear as the result of different attributes and different aspirations. Entire nations, too, can be compelled to exist on a level of another civilization.

However, it is precisely because we are uniquely unequal in every respect that we may become equal on earth only in the eyes of the law. Equality is achievable in the sense that every person can rise to the highest level that that person's talent, industry, and aspiration allow. The legal framework has to be fair and constant, and it must permit no exceptions to secure such conditions.[108]

ON DIFFERENCE AND EQUALITY

Theodore Roosevelt stated the following on the topic of immigrants and being an American:

> In the first place, we should insist that if the immigrant who comes here in good faith becomes an American and assimilates himself to us, he shall be treated on an exact equality with everyone else,

for it is an outrage to discriminate against any such man because of creed, or birthplace, or origin. But this is predicated upon the person's becoming in every facet an American, and nothing but an American … There can be no divided allegiance here. Any man who says he is an American, but something else also, isn't an American at all. We have room for but one flag, the American flag … we have room for but one language here and that is the English language for we intend to see that the crucible turns our people out as Americans, of American nationality, and not as dwellers in a polyglot boardinghouse; and we have room for but one sole loyalty and that is a loyalty to the American people.[109]

To twenty-first-century ears, aspects of President Theodore Roosevelt's statement sound shockingly direct and refreshingly politically incorrect. It is remarkable in its open-handedness and its recognition of the immigrants' shared humanity. Nevertheless, his generosity and promise entirely depended on the new arrivals' giving up and rejecting their old distinct way of life and living instead under the foreign laws and customs of the American republic. And that promise is predicated on assimilation.

President Roosevelt's letter, in other words, implicitly assumes an antagonistic relationship between difference and equality. In so doing he reveals an unspoken premise that has often annoyed many of the various movements that have, over the past centuries, sought equality for the unequal and voices for the voiceless. This standpoint suggests there cannot be a difference if one is to have equality; indeed, sameness and equality become indistinguishable. Consequently, the burden of assuring equality transforms into the task of erasing difference.

This assumption dominated the thinking and actions of European colonists and American settlers who sought a place for immigrants both before and after President Roosevelt. The same attitude was also present in another example—namely, among those fighting for the equality of Jews in nineteenth-century Germany. Moreover, despite an abundance of multicultural language embracing diversity, it constitutes the unspoken premise of advocates for equal rights in the debates raging today or in the attempts of the European Union to rein in its nation-state members.

A few decades before Theodore Roosevelt's above statement, German liberals in the Lower Chamber of the Grand Duchy of Baden voted for Jewish emancipation for the first time in history. The law, which ultimately stalled in the Upper Chamber, would have given Jews in Baden full equality with Christians, eliminating restrictions on political offices and military positions and granting complete freedom to move from town to town.

However, the Lower Chamber's sudden embrace of Jewish emancipation had less to do with a commitment to universal equality in 1846 than with the liberals' hatred of conservative Catholicism and dread of its rise as a political force in Baden. Conservative Catholics asserted the immutable differences and essential inferiority of Jews, upholding the necessity of barriers between Jews and Catholics. However, significant figures within Badenese liberalism developed remarkably pro-Jewish attitudes at the time. Radical liberals even formed a social club uniquely inclusive of Jews and women, and at least for the leading figures of the club, full political equality merely represented a necessary interim step toward the final goal: they wished, radically at the time, to bring about real "social justice."[110]

As with President Roosevelt's attitude toward immigrants, the pro-Jewish sentiments of German liberals should not be underestimated or scorned because of its limits. Here, as with President Roosevelt, assimilation formed the underlying premise of equality. In rejecting the prejudicial barriers established by conservative Catholics, liberals also dismissed the idea of any difference. Equality and difference became at this moment irreconcilable.

Advocates for Jewish equality disagreed about whether assimilation should precede emancipation or whether emancipation would by itself bring about assimilation—but, one way or another, assimilation was expected and assumed. Pro-Jewish liberals saw a place for Jews in German society, but it depended entirely on the elimination of group differences. Specifically, Jews had the right to participate as equals in German society so long as they stopped doing anything that made them distinctly Jewish.

At first glance, the idea that equality and sameness must go hand in hand seems to have Christian origins, and most progressive measures are intended to bring about equality through the elimination of difference. Indeed, many of the debates raging today show the widespread influence of that premise.

For example, a similar mindset is at work in how churches and society consider differences between the sexes and the meaning of marriage. The above logic suggests that difference and inequality are more or less synonymous, so the drive to get rid of gender difference leading to gender inequality has now shifted to the human body. In present-day debates, the physical reality of the body is rejected as an irrelevance that only disguises the actual reality that we are all the same. Any suggestion to the contrary—that perhaps we are, in fact, not all the same at all—is condemned as rank intolerance. To acknowledge difference is to create inequality, and so in the name of equality, we must phase out, eliminate, or at least ignore differences—together with those who claim the reality of difference.

Now here comes, however, the mutual exclusivity—the dichotomy of this progressive liberal logic: In the past half-century, left-leaning liberals have lauded diversity and celebrated difference. They congratulate themselves on their commitment to diversity, on their embracing of liberal values and multicultural society. However, if "multicultural" is to mean anything at all—that is, if they do cherish difference—they can hardly desire to erase the "bias" that comes with belonging to, say, a particular religious or cultural community.

If the liberal celebration of difference has been partial, the conservative response to difference has been anything but laudable, often marked by fear of difference and xenophobia or by contempt for otherness. In other words, many conservatives have poorly served the strangers sojourning among them.

Ancient Christianity's meteoric rise and broad appeal had mostly to do with its original message, if not deed, of universal human dignity. Whether because of liberal preoccupation with equality in sameness or conservative fears of difference, the West has forgotten the enormous significance of its moral history. No matter how unappealing or even horrifying to some, the West must relearn and practice its long-ignored obligation to respect, hold dear, embrace, and defend each unique human being belonging to its moral community—a very conservative idea indeed.

Diversity or Uniformity

The dilemma of whether society should be organized according to the principle of either diversity or uniformity has a long history in the realm of political philosophy. Its roots reach back to Aristotle, who advocated the guiding principle of variety to build a society, quite unlike his teacher Plato, who recommended the idea of unity as the principle structure of society. The conflict between these two concepts of society runs through the history of political beliefs. Particularly impressively, Karl Popper analyzed this in his 1945 book *The Open Society and Its Enemies*.[111]

On the one side, Aristotle, Locke, and Kant emphasized that the fundamental purpose of the state is to guarantee diversity. Their instruction was to provide as much freedom as possible and as much unity as necessary.

On the other side, for Plato, Rousseau, and Karl Marx, variety appeared disturbing; they described the ideal state as one that places unity over everything else.

It was Jean-Jacques Rousseau (1712–78) who advocated "Du contrat social ou Principes du droit politique" ("The social contract or principles of political right") and a mysterious "volonté générale" ("general will").[112] For him, no society could exist without all of its interests agreeing; he understands the individual *only* as part of the community. Rousseau's ideal was the homogeneity of the people, and he considered diversity to be an indication of crisis: "The nearer opinion comes to unanimity, the greater is the dominance of the general will; whereas long debates, dissensions and tumult proclaim the domination by particular interests and the decline of the state." By belittling differences of opinion as "quarrel," Rousseau justifies his struggle for homogeneity through the general will.[113]

Rousseau's concept, seen as one of the roots of modern totalitarianism, stands in sharp contrast to the ideas of John Locke (1632–1704). In his influential 1690 paper "The Second Treatise of Government," Locke declared that all humans are free as a result of nature (!) and that they disclose this fact through an agreement with members of political society; consequently, he believed that the state must ensure diversity.[114] The origin of modern-day pluralism can be found in this concept of "agreeing to disagree."

In his 1793 essay "On the Old Saw: That may be right in theory, but it won't work in practice," Immanuel Kant (1724–1804) adhered to this line of reasoning. He stated that public welfare could not be used against everyone's "undeniable right to find his blessedness in each way that suits him if he does not harm the freedom of others."[115]

Abraham Lincoln (1809–65) himself translated into a political concept such philosophical thoughts. Lincoln, six years before he was elected as the sixteenth president of the United States, in 1854, wrote his "Fragment on Government." In it he stated that "the legitimate object of government is to do for a community of people whatever they need to have done but cannot do at all, or cannot so well do for themselves in their separate and individual capacities. In all that the people can do as well for themselves, government ought not to interfere."[116]

Even so, the idea has been around long enough to develop its full strength as a grand theory and to be labeled with the brand "subsidiarity" in the Christian social doctrine of the nineteenth century.

THE SEARCH FOR SOCIAL JUSTICE AND THE RISE OF THE VICTIM INTIMIDATOR

The ultimate nonsense is the quest for social justice. This declaration is not intended to insult the millions of well-meaning persons who have been duped into pursuing social justice as their purpose in life. However, the naked truth is that, if subjected to honest scrutiny, the very concept flies in the face of both reason and experience.

Worse still is the presumptuous implication that if social justice *were* possible, some people are better able to judge what it is than others. Moreover, how does such an implication square with the doctrine that we are all the same?

"Social justice" generally means that justice must prevail in society. Alas, society is in constant flux; its state undergoes never-ending change. How do we monitor performance? What are the measurements? Who judges the data? Also, what about the choice between a static and dynamic society? Most would favor a vibrant society, but such a society will produce variable states of social justice.

Therefore, to attain a satisfactory state of social justice, social tensions—the source of dynamism—are to be eliminated. Once that is achieved, society will, of course, be static. We will have to work very diligently indeed to attain a state without any social tensions.

This perfect state, so characterized, is known, of course, as communism.

In many cases, unwittingly perhaps, persons who advocate social justice also support communism. Taking social justice to its logical conclusion, nothing less will or can suffice. The essence of communism is social justice: the elimination of poverty, suffering, and all differences and inequalities that separate people. The essence of communism is an interdependent and socially conscious world where everyone benefits equally. The essence of communism is the global village, therefore globalization.

Once we reach the actual state of communism, there will be no poverty, no suffering, no differences in the living standards of people, no bonuses for corporate executives, no homeless, no persons who are disadvantaged.

Nor will there be any people who can do as they please.

There will be social justice, for there must be an end state; otherwise, the pursuit of social justice is nothing more than an excuse for a permanent state of social warfare.

Since social justice presumes that certain people know best what is in the interest of certain other people, it is informative to remind the reader of the comments from John Locke in his work *Essays on the Law of Nature*: "No one can be a fair and impartial judge of someone else's benefit; and you mock him by merely pretending to recognize his interest if you tell him that he can do anything that is in his interest to do, but at the same time insist that someone else should have the authority to determine what it is that is in his interest."[117]

Those who search for social justice look characteristically upon themselves as having just such authority.

Those who believe that socialism has any merit and is intellectually acceptable but communism is abhorrent and unthinkable are only fooling themselves. It is all one package, because all of it is predicated on the same perspective. One either signs on to the package or does not; partial consent is an illusion.

The package is the idea of social justice or socialism, which has gone through countless transformations and as many versions. It has been Bolshevism in Russia, Fascism in Italy, National Socialism in Germany, Democratic Socialism in Sweden, and the Long March and Cultural Revolution in China.

The battle between the Franco-German and Anglo-American sides has raged for centuries, and it reflects as much an assertion of national identities as a divergence in thinking. The last three centuries produced only two directions of serious thought.

One is the Idea—a compendium of Continental European—essentially Franco-German—theories; the other is based on Anglo-American aspirations and experience.

Under a variety of labels, the former is more concerned with social justice and analytically seeks only those outcomes it considers desirable. The latter has always tried to create such an environment that, based on competitive human nature, experimentation, observation, and trial and error, will offer the best chances for individual success. While the latter holds that successful individuals will constitute a successful society, the former believes that a good theory will produce a good society.

Two world wars and a cold war have now been fought between the two schools of thought. Anglo-American victory in all three demonstrated to the losing side that only with a thoroughly infiltrated West safely in the ranks could the ultimate success of the Idea be assured. Owing to the success of a different approach, the Idea has been installed in the schools, academia, news media, information and entertainment media, environmental movement, and legal system in the West. Using such methods of transforming the West has been far more effective than relying on any political party.

The search for social justice is the current version of the Franco-German line known as the Idea. Unlike communism, social justice sounds wonderfully warm and humane, but if we were to face the fact that the Idea was responsible for the horrors of the twentieth century, we would realize where it is likely to take us. The search for social justice has spawned group rights, redistribution, entitlements, and multiculturalism. None has a basis in law; none has legitimacy—but they beget one another.

What is multiculturalism if not the redistribution of cultural property? What are redistribution and entitlements if not group rights? What is the rationale for group rights if not social justice?

Social justice is communism's new lease on life. Its proponents zeroed in on the West's Achilles' heel—its *conscience*.

Tell the people of the West they did something wrong and you will command their attention. Whole armies of the Western media, academia, and the intellectual elite have been telling the story, spreading the news that everything the West has done is wrong. A civilization whose resolve proved more than a match in the face of history's challenges seems to have lost its footing at last. It has been infected with fear (loss of its invincibility) and self-hate (of its nations, which used to be the source of pride and spirit).

Individual rights make up the bedrock of liberty. Individual rights set the boundaries of power. Therefore, individual rights had to be the first targets of the new tactic of conscience. The dismantling of individual rights occurred through the establishment of group rights.

From the beginning of time, primitive tribes directed their bitterness, hatred, and vengeance on the oddball, loner, or eccentric in their midst. There were the aliens, the poor, and the weak who most often had to answer for the social problems. The mob turned on them as the origin and cause of their troubles; they had to take the blame and became the scapegoat. They were ostracized, excluded, persecuted, and killed, and thereby the source of the tribe's problems was eliminated, and the tribe felt relieved. That held true until, of course, another crisis developed—and at that point, other victims would be needed. Because of the regularity of the crises, religions developed the ritual of regular sacrifice. Victims were found, throats were cut, blood was shed, and if animals were substituted, it did not mitigate the truth that the society still ran on the blood-fuel of the victim.

This practice may seem primitive in a modern age until one sees videos of ISIS soldiers ritually beheading their victims. When crazed and enraged young men—be they Islamist or racist extremists—open fire on their innocent victims, are we so far from the theory of the scapegoat?

Jesus of Nazareth turned the above primitive model on its head by valuing the victim. The poor, outcast, disabled, diseased, blind, and demon-possessed are his prizes. He treasures children and magnifies women. He turns the sacrificial system upside down not only by valuing the victim but also by becoming the victim. He accepts the victim role and willingly becomes the Lamb of God, who takes away the sin of the world. He defeats the sacrificial system by embracing it. He breaks it from the inside. One of Christianity's contributions to civilization has been startling compassion for the victim.

For the last two thousand years, Christianity has been teaching that being the victim is a heroic act.

Today the problem is that everyone is jumping on the bandwagon. Being a victim has become smart, sophisticated, and, yes, liberal; ironically, to be bullied is the best way to intimidate others. To get ahead in the world, to make progress for oneself and one's tribe, to further ambitions, to justify immoral actions, to grab a bigger piece of the pie, or to elbow others away from the trough, the individual, group, or nation must be presented as victims. Once they are successfully portrayed themselves as a downtrodden and persecuted minority, they will instantly gain the sympathy and support of all.

The first key to success in this cunning crusade is to be portrayed in a victim condition over which there is no control. This self-proclaimed helplessness is evident when the victim group is a racial or ethnic minority. The same sense of unjust destiny has to be produced for other groups. So the feminists have exploited the technique to portray all women as downtrodden. Homosexual campaigners have likewise insisted that their condition is something they were born with, and now anyone with a sexual proclivity that is other than heterosexual can be portrayed as a misunderstood and persecuted victim.

People suffering from any illness, disability, or misfortune are always victims of some form of unfairness, injustice, or neglect. Those suffering from poverty, addiction, dysfunctional families, psychological problems, emotional distress, or just simple unhappiness are victims too. The victim mentality immediately connects with an entitlement culture: someone should be responsible for making the victims happy since someone must be culpable for the victims' unhappiness in the first place.

The next step in effective "victim campaigning" is to accumulate, organize, and disseminate the propaganda. Academic papers must be written, sociological studies must be undertaken, groundbreaking books must be published, and articles about the particular minority group being persecuted must make front-page news. The whimpers of the persecuted must rise to heaven, and the shocked response to their victimhood must be expressed as grief, anxiety, and anguish.

If one is not sympathetic, if one is reticent to pour balm into the victim's wounds, then the bullying begins. The victim must be recognized; one must be unconditionally sympathetic and tolerant. Joining the campaign must help the victim, the victim's problems must be solved, and the victim must be made happy at last. Not doing all of that makes one not only coldhearted, remorseless, and indifferent but also part of, if not the source of, the problem.

The final stage of the devious crusade is the expression of outrage. Once the victim is identified and the hype is widespread, the rage can be released. The anger must be expressed because, without it being evident, a new cycle of tribal scapegoating has developed. As the tribe gathers around the victim in sympathy, they must find the culprit, and their search for the culprit (whether he is guilty or not; it does not matter) sends them on the same frantic scapegoating quest that created their victim in the first place. The supposed persecutors have now become the persecuted. The unhappiness of the tribe (which presents itself as sympathy for the victim) is now focused on violence against the new victim—and so the cycle of sin and irrational rage continues.

Observe Western society today. Everywhere one looks, the members of that group are apportioning blame and seeking scapegoats. The blacks blame the whites. The whites blame the blacks. The West blames the Muslims. The Muslims blame the Jews. The homosexuals blame the Christians. The Christians blame the homosexuals. The West blames the Serbs. The Serbs blame everyone else. The national-conservatives blame the immigrants. The immigrants blame the natives. The workers blame the wealthy. The wealthy blame the politicians. However, as the common thread, they all blame the Russians.

Why has Western society descended into the violence of scapegoating and blame? Because it pays; therefore, it is inevitable. The victimhood cycle will continue through cycles of revenge and further victimhood unless there is an outlet.

Existentialism without Context

Existentialism represents the belief that philosophical thinking begins with the human subject—not merely the thinking subject but the acting, feeling, living human individual. In existentialism, the individual experiences a sense of disorientation and confusion in the face of an apparently meaningless or absurd world.

Søren Kierkegaard is considered to have been the first existentialist philosopher. He proposed that *each*—not society or religion—has sole responsibility for bestowing meaningful purpose on life and living it passionately and sincerely ("authentically").

Existentialists oppose definitions of human beings as primarily being rational, and therefore they oppose positivism and rationalism. Existentialism asserts that human beings make decisions based on subjective judgment rather than pure rationality. The rejection of reason as the source of meaning is a common theme in existentialist thought, as is the focus on the awareness of anxiety and dread that we feel when confronted with our fundamental freedom and our consciousness of death.

Kierkegaard advocated rationality only as an instrument to be used to interact with the objective world (e.g., in the natural sciences), but in relation to existential problems, reason in itself is insufficient: "Human reason has boundaries."[118]

Like Kierkegaard, Jean-Paul Sartre recognized the difficulties with rationality, calling it a form of "bad faith"—an effort by the self to impose structure on the world of phenomena, "the Other," which is essentially irrational, random, and conditional. According to Sartre, rationality, logic, and other forms of bad faith prevent people from finding meaning in freedom. He asserts that by trying to suppress their feelings of anxiety and dread, people confine themselves to everyday experience. They thereby relinquish their freedom and acquiesce to being possessed in some way by "the Look" of "the Other" (i.e., possessed by another person—or at least one's idea of that other person).[119]

The outlook of the rising generation is fundamentally existentialist in its emphasis on direct, momentary personal experience, especially with other people. It emphasizes people and finds the highest ideal of life in interpersonal relations, generally handled with compassion and irony. The two chief concerns of life are caring and helping. Caring, which they usually call "love," means a general acceptance of the fact that people matter and are subjects of concern. This love is diffuse and often quite impersonal, not aimed at a particular individual or friend but anyone in general and especially at persons one does not know at all, as an act of recognition, almost of expiation, that we are all helpless children together. The whole idea is very close to Christ's message to "love one another" and has given rise to the younger generation's passionate concern for oppressed peoples, the African or Afro-American people, minorities, and the outcast poor. This concern is reflected in the tremendous enthusiasm among the young for civil rights, racial equality, and the attack on poverty, all of which have more support among middle-class young people than what can be measured even by the surprisingly large numbers who do something, anything, for the cause.

The desire to actively participate in taking care of others is what can be called "helping" or "activism." It is a strange and largely symbolic help since there comes with it a relatively widespread feeling that nothing the helper can do will make any notable dent in the enormous problem. Nonetheless, there is an apparent obligation felt by some members of the rising generation to do something, not only as a symbolic act but also as an almost masochistic rejection of the bourgeois past. The younger generation who support the fight against poverty and the drive for minority rights have an almost irresistible compulsion to do these things as a demonstration of their rejection of their parents' value system, and as some restitution for the adults' neglect of these urgent problems. However, the real motivation behind the urge to help is closely related to the call to care; it consists merely of a desire to show another human being that he is not alone. There is little concern for human perfectibility or social progress, such as that which accompanied middle-class humanitarianism in the nineteenth century.

These urges are existentialist. They give rise to isolated acts that have no meaningful context. Thus, an act of loving or helping has no sequence of causes leading up to it or of consequences flowing from it. It stands alone as an isolated experience of togetherness and brief personal sharing. This failure or lack of context for each experience means a failure or lack of meaning, for meaning and significance arise from context—that is, from the relationship of the particular experience to the whole picture. Alas, the youth has no concern for the whole picture; they have rejected the past and have little faith in the future. Their rejection of intellect and their lack of confidence in human reason give them no hope that any meaning can be found for any experience, so each experience becomes an end in itself, isolated from every other experience.

This skepticism about meaning, closely allied with their rejection of organizations and abstractions, is also closely related to a failure, or rejection, of responsibility. Since consequences are divorced from the act or experience itself, the youth is not bound by any relationship between the two. The result is general irresponsibility.

THE LEFT–RIGHT FALLACY: A TOTALITARIAN TACTIC

It is quite evident today that we are facing the prospect of a return to barbarism. The ancient tradition of Western Civilization (Christendom) that was founded on three pillars of faith, freedom, and law is fading away before our eyes, and in its place there is the spreading of an enormously influential, ferocious, and utterly inhuman system of social organization called democratic totalitarianism.

This system is destroying all forms of civilized life and moral behavior that have been developed for more than a thousand years of continuous, strenuous effort. It is not only bringing back the old evils of barbarism in the modern rendition of slavery, massacre, and torture but is also introducing new forms of organized evil and injustice that the barbarisms of old could never have imagined or devised.

Now, I hope, if we can maintain even some islands of Western Civilization, there is perhaps a chance to turn the tide and the heretofore drowning forces of Western culture will be able to reemerge. This task far transcends politics, but it has its political side, because if we surrender our political judgment and allow ourselves to be hoodwinked and blinded by the dirty tactics of democratic totalitarianism, we lessen our powers of resistance on still more critical issues.

On the one hand, the traditional Western political order was founded on law and liberty. On the other hand, the common bond of loyalty to the state did not exclude all kinds of lesser loyalties and rights through which the rich diversity of Western culture developed. This twofold tradition has been inherited by Western democracy, which is not an abstract ideology but merely the epochal system of self-government. This system, which has been worked out in Western countries in modern times, is supposed to represent institutions, governmental responsibility, free elections, and free discussion.

However, this system, like the older system from which it derives, cannot work unless, despite all disagreements and divergences of interest, there is a common bond of loyalty and will to cooperate. This accord is vital to the existence of a free society, and consequently it is the key point against which the totalitarian attack on Western culture is directed.

The tactics of democratic totalitarianism are to weld every difference of opinion and tradition, as well as every conflict of economic interests, into an absolute ideological opposite, which disintegrates society into hostile factions bent on destroying one another.

In this campaign of disintegration, the right–left mythology is a perfect godsend to the destructive forces. It provides them with a simple but highly effective instrument by which any number of different issues can be merged into a mass of confusion and ideological claptrap in any situation.[120]

Then there are liberals and conservatives, republicans and monarchists, anticlericals and clericals, communists and fascists, socialists and individualists, and Semites and anti-Semites. All of these are different pairs of opposites that have no particular connection with one another, yet all are brought under the headings of "Left" and "Right" and thus artificially fused into ideological mergers, which may be inappropriate and absurd. When the opponents are all neatly ticketed, the same process can be repeated on any section of them. So the socialists can be then divided into socialists of the center left and socialists of the extreme left, and the liberals into moderates and progressives, and by that means submitting them to the same process of distraction and disintegration.

The fault or, depending on the viewpoint, the advantage of the method of division is that it has no rational basis. It grades people and ideas according to their relation to a supposedly central point that, as a rule, does not exist.

Despite the unfounded aspect, left and right become the center of fierce ideological loyalties and enmities that overpower people's reason and sense of judgment and drive them to acts of violence and inhumanity that would rebuke a clan of cannibals.

The process of social disintegration into political factions has been spreading like an epidemic in modern society. It is transforming the West, the guardian of Christian culture, into an inferno of hatred, suspicion, and immorality that can be checked only by those who have not yet been dragged down into this cesspool of decay.

The remedy can be found only in the old political virtues that have been denied and discarded by the new barbarians. They are the virtues of justice, goodwill, truth, patience, and, above all, prudence, which Aristotle defines as the truly rational and practical state of mind in the field of human good and evil.[121] It is only through the exercise of these virtues that society can be saved from the political disintegration that threatens it, and that an island of culture in the midst of the rival barbarians known as the Left and the Right might be sustained.

What we are confronted with is not only a false ideology, which can be met with a rational argument, but a kind of contagious social malady, which is in itself thoroughly irrational and firmly sustained by leftist political culture. Therefore, it would be worth thinking through on what basis this particular right–left double structure is resting from the historical point of view.

In the Western political systems that have existed roughly since the time of the French Revolution, the conservative political parties are delegated to be on the Right, while the Left represents the various forms of socialist parties.

The first immediate dilemma with this political structure is that the third major Western political grouping, namely the liberal parties, apparently cannot be fitted into this right–left dichotomy. The tension that exists between the contemporary right and left was present in one form or another for centuries even before the appearance of the modern Western political systems.

Indeed, what might be called Left in the ontological sense is no other than the emergence of those spontaneous social "immune reactions" with which the closed and traditional peasant society responded to the harsh consequences of Western modernity. These were the peasants' uprisings and revolts that occurred mostly in the fourteenth and fifteenth centuries, sometimes developing into civil wars. The cause of these violent and desperate social movements was that the slowly emerging infant capitalism, from pure business considerations, destroyed the ancient systems of farming with ruthless brutality.

For obvious reasons, this had a very significant impact on the peasant society. So the actual appearance of the Left can be attributed to those first strategic social movements that, to *restore* the traditional and enshrined structure of old, *turned against modernity.*

All this is important to stress because, in the political sense, it leads to the fundamental contradiction of the modern left. While the contemporary left still identifies with these reactionary peasant movements (at least in its original mythology), it remains unexplored how and why the historical left turned into its ontological opposite between the sixteenth and nineteenth centuries.

It is probable that while the old peasant movements were the genuinely spontaneous reactions to the tectonic changes occurring in the society of the time, today's political left, in the modern sense of the word, has been a deliberately and artificially designed construct. Whose and what consciousness created it is certainly difficult to name in a politically correct way. However, it can discreetly be assumed that it was the same calamitous global entity whose firebrand influence has been instrumental in the development of modern Western leftist liberal democracy, but the mere supposition of this is already considered to be a heretical conspiracy theory.

Moreover, this "designer-destroyer" entity has placed the liberals, of all things, in the center of the modern Western political system to be the political representatives of the capital structure determining modernity. In conjunction with that, it also created the modern political left, which is thus the exact ontological opposite of its historical foundation.

However, this historic pedestal is only the original myth, serving as a handy reference explaining a false ideology. Therefore, the political constructs of the existing socialism have been then the utterly confused hodgepodge ideas and practices of the historical left and the modern political left. Since today's liberal left, enthusiastically representing the interests of global capital establishments, enters into coalition alliances almost exclusively with liberal parties representing ex officio those same interests, it is not only betraying the historically leftist values but is going against the very principles and practices of the modern left as well.

This historical perversion of the Left has its effect on the entire Western political system, of course, including those who consider themselves to be on the right of the political spectrum. In some strategic issues concerning Western society, either in the traditional or the modern political sense, today's political parties of the Right represent the values of the Left, rather than those who consider themselves leftists.

The above multidimensional historical confusion has made, and still makes, the Left–Right dichotomy utterly useless and unfit to be considered a valid topic; therefore, using this false and misleading terminology to identify political positions should be abandoned.

Admittedly, the Left–Right separation existed long before the rise of modern totalitarianism, but from the very beginning, it was infected with fittingly similar evils. It was born in the French Revolution under the shadow of the guillotine during the reign of terror, at a time when politics was submerged in civil war and when the totalitarian techniques of purges, liquidations, and single-party dictatorships first evolved. Where such conditions exist, the irrational dualism of Left and Right is natural enough, since every person is forced to take sides by staking one's neck on the success of the victorious party.

Today the whole act has become even more dangerous owing to the breakdown of civilization and social disintegration in the West. However, this circumstance makes it all the more vital that we keep our heads and refuse to allow our political vendetta of Left and Right to take shape; that leads only to destruction. The way of civilization is the way of integrity, which turns neither to the right nor to the left.

The political order of the Western state was founded first on the Roman, then Christian, concept of law and justice—which, however, did not depend on the right of the stronger or the will of the majority. It relied instead on the natural law, to which kings and peoples alike were subject. According to this belief, injustice still exists today, its spiritual foundations forgotten, with "law and order" meaning no more than a tiresome accommodation that we take for granted.

Nevertheless, it is the most precious thing we have, and only so long as there are people who stand for justice and truth against the evils of political passions and propaganda is there still a flicker of hope for Western Civilization.

THE PUBLIC POSITION: WITHIN THE INFINITE RANGE OF POSSIBILITIES

This author is an advocate of the public position as expressed through the majority. Being a member of a community, the individual consents beforehand to the acceptance of obligations of which he does not necessarily approve. It is right the person should do so, because such commitments are implicit in the essence of community life. One can be deeply skeptical about constructing an ongoing political system solely on the foundations of abstract natural-rights individualism; any attempt to do so is contrary to the realities of human nature and the human condition.

In fact, the public position is a way of life and is identical to the Greek *politeia*, which refers to the character or tone of a community. Public position is that matrix of convictions, usually enshrined in custom and folkways, that makes a society what it is and that differentiates it from other societies, as in human thought one thing is always distinguished from another. That is the reason why we may and do speak intelligibly of a Greek, a Roman, or an American way of life.

No society can avoid having a public position. Even when it rejects an old orthodoxy in the name of enlightenment, progress, pluralist society, open society, and the like, it invents, however subtly, a new orthodoxy with which to replace the old one. Man, by nature, is not only a social but also a political animal whose very political life demands politeia. That involves an at least implicit code of manners and a tacit agreement on the meaning of man within the total economy of existence. Without this political position, the state withers, contracts lose their efficacy, the moral bond between citizens is loosened, the state opens itself to enemies from abroad, and the politeia sheds the sacral character, without which it cannot long endure. If the public position upon which the state is founded decays and disintegrates, the state itself will inevitably falter. It is a hard reality: the order and health of the political state rely upon the vitality and character of the public position. Not only is the public position inescapably rooted in the order of being, but it is also a positive "good." Without it, there is no society and no state; civilization, as we have traditionally known it, is destroyed.

This author is firmly against the dogmatic proponents of the absolute open society, who seem to be contending that all public orthodoxies, or public positions, are evil.

John Stuart Mill, for one, was leading the attack of the open society proponents upon the concept of the "public orthodoxy, or public position. Mill assumed, in fact, an absolutist and dogmatic posture on the question of freedom of expression. He wrote,

> Protection, therefore, against the tyranny of the magistrate is not enough; there needs protection also against the tyranny of the prevailing opinion and feeling, against the tendency of society to impose, by other means than civil penalties, its own ideas and practices as rules of conduct on those who dissent from them. [In short, the prevailing public orthodoxy is by definition tyranny and must be displaced.]
>
> This, then, is the appropriate region of human liberty. It comprises, first, the inward domain of consciousness, demanding liberty of conscience in the most comprehensive sense, liberty of thought and feeling, absolute freedom of opinion and sentiment on all subjects, practical or speculative, scientific, moral, or theological … No society … is completely free in which [these liberties] do not exist absolute and unqualified.
>
> There ought to exist the fullest liberty of professing and discussing, as a matter of ethical conviction, any doctrine, however immoral it may be considered.
>
> If the teachers of mankind are to be cognizant of all that they ought to know, everything must be free to be written and published without restraint.
>
> Human beings should be free to form opinions and to express their opinions without reserve.

Mill was unequivocal that his call for "absolute freedom of opinion" included freedom of thought, speaking, and writing.[122] Moreover, in his passionate outburst against public orthodoxy, Mill asserted that the presence of any orthodoxy harmed human happiness and obstructed progress. He wrote, "Where not the person's own character but the traditions or customs of other people are the rule of conduct, there is wanting one of the principal ingredients of human happiness, and quite the chief ingredient of individual and social progress."[123] Finally, Mill lamented, "In politics, it is almost a triviality to say that public opinion now rules the world."[124] It was Mill's relentless aversion to public orthodoxy—or, as he called it, "the despotism of custom"—that made him remark, "If all mankind were of one opinion, and only one person were of the contrary opinion, mankind would be no more justified in silencing that one person, than he, if he had the power, would be justified in silencing all mankind."[125]

Mill's position is at odds with elementary facts of the human condition. It is unnatural and perverse to ask mortal men to accept a posture of absolute relativism, for men do have values; they do think, in fact, that some questions are settled; and they do not take the position that all points of view are relative and equal in value. Mill erred in proposing that any society should make absolute freedom of expression its supreme value. Mill's proposals have a false conception of the nature of society and are, therefore, unrealistic on their face. They assume that society is a debate club devoted above all to the pursuit of truth and capable, therefore, of subordinating itself to that quest.

Except that we know only too well that society is not a debate club—all our experience of society drives the point home—and that even if it were one, the chances of its adopting the pursuit of truth as its supreme good would be negligible. Societies cherish a whole series of goods—among others, their very own self-preservation. They believe they embody in themselves not only the living of the truth already but also the communication of that truth to future generations. These they ought to value as much as, or more than, the pursuit of truth, because these are the very preconditions of the quest for truth.

It is only within the context of and consensus established by politeia that debate or discussion can take place in society. To deny politeia and to ask for an endless abstract debate as Mill does is to request something that is not only impossible to achieve but also indeed, even if it were possible, undesirable. It would be unacceptable for the essence of Mill's freedom of speech to divorce the *right* to speak from the *duties* correlative to that right. Mill's right to speak is a right to speak ad nauseam and with impunity. It is shot through and through with the egalitarian overtones of the French Revolution, which are as different from the measured aristocratic connotations of the pursuit of truth by discussion, as understood by the tradition Mill was attacking, as philosophy is different from phosphorus.

If Mill's doctrine is the right to speak ad nauseam without any correlative duties or obligations, we are installing the cult of individual eccentricity as our supreme value; if this is followed to its logical conclusion, society will be brought to the brink of collapse. Mill was an advocate of the peculiarity of individual eccentricity. He wrote, "In this age, the mere example of nonconformity, the mere refusal to bend the knee to custom, is itself a service. Precisely because the tyranny of opinion is such as to make eccentricity a reproach, it is desirable, in order to break through that tyranny, that people should be eccentric. That so few now dare to be eccentric marks the chief danger of the time."[126]

In Mill's ideal open society, the individual who is blessed with the absolute right of expression is then enlightened that eccentricity is a positive good, and there is a duty to pursue it. That is, there emerges a public orthodoxy of eccentricity, and this will drive individuals to the making of excessive and impossible demands upon society. This requirement, in turn, will lead to confrontation and the disintegration of society itself, for there is no center and, more importantly, no obligation or duty on anyone to hold, for all things political are conceived entirely in terms of individual rights and demands.

Into the vacuum created by disintegration will move force and coercion—in a word, tyranny. Such a society as Mill prescribed will descend inevitably into ever-deepening differences of opinion and the gradual disintegration of those common premises upon which alone a society can manage its affairs by discourse. In the end, Mill's society will disappear into the abandonment of the discussion process and the arbitration of public questions for violence and civil war.

Mill's position of dogmatic relativism leads to the emergence of the coercive state. The proposition that all opinions are equally (hence infinitely) valuable is only one of the two inescapable inferences from the proposition that all opinions are equal. The other deduction is that all opinions are equally (and hence infinitely) without value and that it consequently does not matter if one—particularly not one of our own—gets suppressed.

The open society proponents, such as John Stuart Mill and Karl Popper, present us with the wrong choices; they attempt to force us to choose between closed and open societies. As Karl Popper stated it, "We can return to the beasts [meaning the closed society]. But if we wish to remain human, then there is only one way, the way into the open society."[127] One can only challenge that assumption.

Both Mill and Popper would have us believe that just as a woman cannot be a little bit pregnant, a society cannot be a little bit closed either. All our knowledge of politics bids us not to fall into that trap. Nobody wants all-out thought control or a shut and sealed society, just as nobody has any right to pretend that somebody else wants those things. However, the real question is, how open can a society be and yet remain open?

The choices between and open society and a closed society are false choices, for in fact they are by no means the only alternatives. Fortunately, in the real world, there is an infinite range of possibilities. Indeed, the great irony is that by offering these false choices, the open-society proponents would nudge us closer to the closed society. As the attainment of an entirely open society is impossible and undesirable even to initiate, the promoters of an open society, by their admission and by process of elimination, would leave no alternative other than a closed society, which unfortunately is a reachable goal. Political philosophers would do well to seek realistic and moderate solutions in that infinite range of possibilities lying between those purist concepts of open and closed societies, which political ideologists have been wrongly informing us are our only options.

Modern Western Nihilism

The conclusion from Kant's philosophy is that a life dedicated to the pursuit of truth is meaningless. None can penetrate the veil of phenomena; all attempts to grasp the meaning of the world and human existence are futile. The impossibility of attaining truth renders human life pointless. By the mid-twentieth century, all but a handful of philosophers had ceded truth to the sciences.

In the 1960s, American academicians embraced nihilism, the philosophy of skepticism or the denial of the possibility of an objective basis for truth. Since the life of the mind did not focus on the universality of human experience (or so they thought), intellectual discourse eventually degenerated into an endless labyrinth of opinions. They proclaimed, "All thought inevitably derives from particular standpoints, perspectives, and interests."[128] Music, poetry, philosophy, religion, and ethics were believed to be mere expressions of personal opinions, individual perceptions, or particular cultural viewpoints.

Under the sway of the wise academicians, high school and college students today learn that different cultures believe and teach different moral precepts, and thus that morality is merely a cultural consensus at a particular point in time. To show that certain moral principles are natural, universal, or objective and apply to every person is treated as indoctrination—the violation of a student's right to choose his or her lifestyle. In a national survey, almost half of the young Americans polled agreed that morals are relative and that there are no definite rights and wrongs for everyone.[129] For these young adults, morality is the obligation to accede to parental teaching, the prevailing culture, or the political state, and therefore is a disguised form of coercion.

The narrative of nihilism, while arguably true, is misleading, for the source of nihilism in the modern world is not philosophical reflection but democratic equality and personal freedom. In a modern democratic society, the links connecting generations are broken, and hence people cannot base their beliefs on tradition or class. Democratic equality produces a "general distaste for accepting any man's word as proof of anything."[130]

Western culture teaches that all individuals are equal and that each one can recognize the truth just as well as the next person. Consequently, in the Western world no masters are appreciated, and if anyone holds up someone as a master to follow, most people will intentionally ignore or dismiss that person, since it smacks of inequality.

The American spirit holds that only an autonomous individual can know liberty; the Western hero has no family, no last name, and belongs nowhere. No one can tell him what to do, and moreover, he owes nothing to anyone except what he incurs on his own free will. This hero embodies the American idea of freedom: he does what he wants, provided his actions do not injure others.[131] The American hero has his code of honor, which is self-chosen, independent of others and human nature (for it would only limit his freedom).

All ethical systems, then, are arbitrary social conventions or personal idiosyncrasies.

According to physicists, engineers, and other natural scientists, material things can be known thoroughly, while beauty, human values, and the purpose of life are unverifiable opinions, which are perhaps right for the individual but not necessarily for the rest of humanity. Their scientific minds readily accept scientific truths—say, results of electrodynamics, thermodynamics, fluid dynamics, or electro-optics—because these disciplines do not challenge how they live.

In one of the notorious opinions of US Supreme Court justice Anthony Kennedy, "At the heart of freedom is the right to define one's own concept of existence, of meaning, of the universe, and of the mystery of life."[132] It was a ruling keeping with the widespread opinion that everyone has his or her personal belief system—even the right to one's own concept of the universe.

The outcome of Western nihilism is that democracy will become demagoguery. With tradition, a mere curiosity touched upon in grade school, public discourse cannot be restrained, modified, and directed by reason. In the market of ideas, however, rational debate disappears, replaced by passions and prejudices, a phenomenon most evident on the internet. Anyone, anywhere, anytime can instantly post an opinion on anything now. Not constrained by historical facts or scientific truths, the postings on the internet constitute an ocean of opinions, one comment washing over another, quickly submerging whatever truth tries to surface. Political discourse becomes personal and emotional; opposing viewpoints remain irresolvable. "My" passions are "my" truths; "my" sole interest is "me."

Today's Western "moderns" secretly rejoice over the "advent of nihilism."[133] In the absence of truth, we are entirely free. We do not have to submit to anyone or anything beyond ourselves. We are our own creator, commander, executor, and judge. Each one of us knows what is right, wrong, good, and beautiful; as king of the castle and master of the house, we are demigods, inventing ourselves, devising our own ends, and accepting or rejecting whatever we wish. Our present culture has harnessed the forces of fear, contempt, frustration, craving, and the worship of self in ways that have yielded extraordinary wealth and comfort and personal freedom—the freedom to be lords of our tiny skull-sized kingdoms, alone at the center of all creation.[134]

From the perspective of the Western tradition amassed in Athens, Jerusalem, and Rome, moderns have embraced the above and mistaken notion of freedom. For Socrates, Plato, and Aristotle, the *truth* comes first, not freedom. Moreover, one inherent hazard in human life is to abandon reason and become a prisoner of the passions. Aristotle said that the good life consists of the "active exercise of the soul's faculties in conformity to rational principle," which was his way of saying that the passions must be directed by reason for a person to be happy.[135] Courage frees from the prison of fear, generosity from the prison of avarice, temperance from the prison of addiction. Devoid of freedom, one could not change the self and, therefore, would be condemned to a life in prison. Self-control and discipline are the marks of a free person, not the "license to do whatever one wants."[136]

Based on the ancient wisdom, the only way out of the prison of modern nihilism is to make truth primary and to adopt the mantra that freedom is obedience to truth.

Truth matters. A lie is still a lie even though everyone believes it. The truth is always the truth even though no one believes it.

False Freedom, Relativism, and Nihilism

This author has become increasingly cynical about the Western praise of freedom. "Freedom," it seems, has become a meaningless jingoistic slogan that is used to excuse almost anything. "Our boys died defending our freedom!" they cry as yet another flag-draped coffin is unloaded from the plane bringing it back from a faraway corner of the world. Did that boy die defending our freedom? Really? Exactly which one of our freedoms was threatened by turmoil in Afghanistan or Iraq or Syria or Africa? Which foreign autocrat threatened to attack us or invade our country to take away our freedoms?

The word "freedom" has also been misused and exploited by leftist ideologues to condone every combination of vulgarity, perversion, pornography, and sexual choice; no one is allowed to be dismayed by, much less disapproving or critical of, anyone else's choices or deeds. Without any (often difficult to define) explicit harm caused, everything must be tolerated in the name of freedom.

Increasingly what people mean by "freedom" is a full license, and this license is rooted in relativism. We do not believe restrictive rules are necessary because we do not believe restrictive rules are possible; we do not believe restrictive rules are possible because we do not believe in absolute moral truth. Relativism is another name for nihilism.

However, as has happened so often in history, this sort of relativistic freedom eventually leads to some restraining measures. When a society tolerates anything and everything to be done in the name of liberty, boundaries break, tolerance tires, restraint runs out, and moral chaos and anarchy soon prevail. When there is lawlessness, political corruption, financial and economic theft on a grand scale, unemployment, family breakdown, personal despair, and loss of trust, the final result is violence: violence in the home, violence in the workplace, violence in the streets, and violence even in politics. (Oh, it is so easy and convenient to call this violence "acts of terrorism.")

When violence and pure anarchy threaten, ordinary people will cry out for security, which is supposed to be the first duty of the state. "We have had enough! We demand security in the streets! We want law and order, we want protection, and we will accept any strongman who can promise to get things done once again!" The problem is that we elect the leaders we deserve, and a corrupt, distrusting, immoral, and lawless society cannot produce a just, pure, noble, and honorable leadership.

However, a strongman may well bring law and order. Strongmen do get things done; they do restore law and order by always applying some restraint.

Nevertheless, the prior anarchy had been caused not by freedom but rather by false freedom. False freedom pertains to the idea that everyone may do what one likes. Real freedom is the freedom of the human will to be engaged and come to terms with its fate for the person (or by extension the human society) to achieve his or her full potential. Real freedom is essentially the gift of human free will, which chooses to submit to some higher order of truth to gain inner peace and become the fullest human being possible.

Now, such devotion to freedom requires discipline, hard work, and self-sacrifice—the work of a lifetime. The achievement is the result of a lifetime of study, work, training, and dedication. When we see an example of genuine human achievement, we see both the action and the result of real freedom.

Paradoxically, it is false freedom that results in restraining measures, while it is discipline, hard work, self-restraint, and self-sacrifice that lead to the "perfect freedom."

THE REFORMATION: THE DEFORMATION OF A UNIFYING WESTERN IDEOLOGY, THE IDEOLOGY OF REVOLUTIONS

The year 2017 commemorates the five-hundredth anniversary of the beginning of the Protestant Reformation. It is right, therefore, to look again at the events and their consequences and assess our terminology, for what historians benignly call the Reformation was indeed not only a revolution but also the mother of all revolutions.

Can the Protestant Reformation be considered the deformation of the hitherto unifying Western ideology?

Before the Protestant Revolution, Europeans were united by a shared loyalty and dedication that went beyond individuals and nation-states; to be European was to be Catholic. Whether one was Scottish or Spanish, Swiss or Swedish, the spiritual, intellectual, and cultural origins were first and foremost in the Catholic faith. Similarly, whether one was a prince or a peasant, a monk or a milkmaid, one ascribed to a higher loyalty that transcended national, ethnic, financial, class, and linguistic boundaries. Through the diocesan system of administration, the monastic infrastructure, and the shared Latin language, a genuinely trans-European culture existed. City-states and petty princes might go to war with one another, but there was a higher unity rooted in a shared spiritual and cultural patrimony.

The Protestant Revolution broke all that. As nation-states emerged, canny kings and prehensile princes adopted the Protestant revolutionaries and used their spirit of religious independence to power the temporal ambitions, which led to rapacious vandalism, social chaos, and ultimately persecution, bloodshed, and war. Henry VIII and Elizabeth I's tyranny in England is the prime example. However, the German princes lining up with Martin Luther and the Protestants sparked first the Schmalkaldic War, after which various conflicts simmered for decades, finally breaking out into the Eighty Years' War (the tail end of which was the Thirty Years' War), which tore Christendom into shreds for good. Despite the diplomatic success of the Peace of Westphalia finally ending the devastating wars in Europe, shattered Christendom was then plunged into a series of seemingly endless conflicts, culminating in the American and French Revolutions, the Russian Revolution, and the two world wars of the twentieth century.

Did Protestantism directly cause all these wars and revolutions? The causes are very involved, of course, but it cannot be denied that the Protestant Revolution broached the dam, which allowed the supplying of the consequential flood.

Moreover, the Protestant Revolution set a precedent in providing the spiritual justification for what hitherto had been anathema: rebellion and armed revolution. Suddenly it became a noble and courageous endeavor to rebel against the established powers. The Protestant Revolution cast insurgents as brave pioneers, prophetic voices, and banner-bearing crusaders for the common man. The Protestant Revolution set a new standard: the social dynamic of progress through conflict. Friedrich Hegel would summarize it in the age of revolution with his dialectic: thesis, antithesis, and resolution. Karl Marx exalted it as the class struggle. From then on, the progressive way forward would always be accomplished through revolution.

The Protestant Revolution was about mindset and belief as well as a clash. While uprising was always a possibility, it was the view of "*progress through revolution*" that was most fundamental at the time. Even today, political, religious, and cultural trials are interpreted as conflicts between the revolutionary forces of progress and the conservative forces of tradition. While the fight takes place in back rooms rather than on battlegrounds, the atmosphere and attitude of revolution are still the default setting for peerless progressives who view the world as one ongoing battle against the evil forces of conservatism.

Needs it to be so? Conservatives should always be enthusiastic about genuine renewal. There should be nothing hidebound, legalistic, or defensive about conservatism. In the face of the revolution, conservatives should put forward the principles of proper renewal. Renewal, whether in religion or politics, is a return and refreshment of founding principles. Renewal recharges the original charisma and calling while avoiding the natural temptation of iconoclasm and violent revolution. The renewal repairs and repaints; it does not revolt, and it does not violate. It weeds the garden and prunes the vine if necessary, but it does not uproot and destroy.

While revolution is to be eschewed, and renewal espoused, real unity and lasting peace can be had only when people are united in a higher and nobler belief that transcends nationalism, ethnic loyalties, or individualism. Christianity, the once unifying Western ideology, is broken, and with it, the chance for real peace (instead of a cold one) is also wrecked.

7

A Critique of Democracy

The author decided to compile this chapter because he recognized an inherent tension between democracy and the freedom of individuals to create their lives as they see fit. Defenders of democracy have also acknowledged some of the apparent problems with democracy as well, but they have only contributed to the proposition of amended types of democracies as various advocates tried to shape the concept into an acceptable form.

By contrast, this author proposes to abandon the concept altogether, because he finds some fundamental faults with the idea of democracy itself, whether representative or direct, that new modifications or reforms cannot reconcile. Instead of echoing confused cries for still more democracy, it should be categorically denied that democracy must always be the best political system for everybody everywhere.

Definition of Democracy and the Democratic Problem

Criticism of democracy has always existed in democratic societies, with much of the blame claiming that democracy is economically inefficient, politically idealistic, or morally corrupt.

There is democracy wherever the people effectively participate in resolving their destiny. Democracy is a theory of government wherein the law reflects the will of the majority as determined by direct vote or elected representatives. Typically, the legitimacy of democracy begins with the adoption of a constitution, which establishes the fundamental rules, principles, duties, and powers of the government and some set of rights for individuals against those of the state. The enumeration of rights attempts to protect individuals from the whims of a democratic majority—a concept developed as republicanism during the overthrow of monarchism. However, we should all remember Fisher Ames's words: "Constitutions are but paper; society is the substratum of government."[137]

Any sound parliamentary democracy rests on two pillars: a common framework of reference and a system consisting of more than one party.

Without a common political language and underlying common political philosophy, a real parliament—dialogue between the parties—and constructive discussions are impossible. Under these circumstances, the parties cease to be mere ins and outs, and elections become minor social and political earthquakes.

The presence of more than two parties, on the other hand, leads quickly to minority rule. A small party, being essential to and, for all practical purposes, in control of the absolute parliamentary majority, can quite effectively run the country; and thus the democratic principle of majority rule is eliminated.

However, the establishment and survival of both above conditions fall into the domain of society: the *free* state can decree no common ideological denominator; nor can it prevent the rise of additional parties. The *totalitarian* state, with its "annexation" of society, is in a very different position and desires the number of political parties reduced to a single one. In these societal aspects, we can immediately get a hint as to the intrinsic connections between state and society. Also, they help us realize that constitutions are empty frames in which all sorts of pictures may be hung.

One may conceivably argue, as does this author, that the United States (and some other Western countries as well) has a one-party political system and that the elections merely determine the strength of the wings. The vote often becomes not an ideological manifestation but just a protest against persons in power.

A vital part of the achievements of the democratic and parliamentary regimes in the English-speaking countries can be attributed to the fact that the societies of these countries have tried wisely and jealously to preserve the ideological common denominator in the past. The new democracies set up after World War II subscribe to the same formula.

The majority of the population in the United States believes in republicanism and democracy, and one can safely state that democracy is an essential attribute of American nationalism. Republicanism and democracy, with all their implications, are taught and extolled in schools and theaters, in daily papers and periodicals, in commencement speeches and films, in novels and textbooks, in radio and TV commentaries, and in sermons and at cocktail parties.

Moreover, this is in a country made up mainly of variegated immigrants. However, isn't this precisely the point? In any state with a common ideological denominator, with a common framework of reference, even the plurality of parties could be permitted, since all parties would merely but automatically represent various shades of the same beliefs held in common by most members of society.

This common denominator is the fundamental idea behind the spreading of democracy. If the Americanization of the Western World is complete, what is the next step?

The common framework of reference is, of course, necessary not just for productive parliamentary debate but also for the very steadiness of the country during elections. The two-party system *alone* would never do without the common denominator.

Here is the problem of modern-day America: What happens if the Democratic Party carries out a very far-reaching program of socialization (for example, "Obamacare") and is defeated in the next elections? Will the Republicans be able to reverse the course as they had presumably promised to take before the elections?

Admittedly, the actions of ruling political parties have a certain finality, which creates historically irredeemable and irreparable circumstances. Moreover, if the difference between the parties were considerable, every election would mean a bloodless revolution; thus, the ship of state would soon be on the rocks.

The preservation of the tenet "unity in necessary things" presupposes something like an ideologically totalitarian society, which condemns real dissent and persecutes the nonconformist.[138] Now, however, on the one hand, the politicized individual is a postulate of political democracy since the preservation of well-functioning parliamentary democracy demands a politically alert and informed society—but the first steps toward totalitarianism have already taken place. On the other hand, a society consciously and collectively safeguarding a common political ideology is automatically pledged to universal cultural values, resulting in a rigorous homogeneity as to its way of life.

The establishment and preservation of such conformity involve an extraordinary discipline and solidarity, which rather adversely affect political, religious, racial, and ethnic dissenters; legislation is apparently helpless in the face of social disdain, pressure, or persecution.[139]

From the preceding, it also becomes evident that any analysis of democracy has to use two separate vantage points: one with the existence of a common denominator, the other one in the case of its absence.

The famous remark by Clausewitz that wars are nothing but continuations of diplomacy by other means may or should be adapted to read that revolutions and civil wars are merely the extensions of Democratic Party politics by other methods.

The agreement of parties on a given constitution only indicates the fact that none of them has an absolute majority and the showdown resulting in a one-party dictatorship would be premature. The elections thus receive the character of public manifestations demonstrating numerical strength. If one party gets an overwhelming majority, the transition to dictatorship can be made through bloodless and constitutional means; this change often does not even need the expediency of amendments.

Even in the United States, with its (once functioning) common denominator, the in-power perpetuation of one single political party does not favor the preservation of parliamentary democracy. If for any reason one party were reelected with an overwhelming majority several consecutive times, most checks and balances (together with the composition of the Supreme Court) would get skewed and break down or become obsolete. The safeguards against a tyranny of the fairest constitution are relative and not absolute.

The higher percentage of permanently democratic, socialist, leftist voters in Western democracies is not a consequence of a miracle; leftist parties cater nationwide to the lower—and this means to the bigger—part of the social pyramid. The socialist idea has, by and large, conquered the lower classes—but socialism is capable of far worse blunders than the ideology of a mere lower-class party out only to "soak the rich" but not to "kill the goose that lays the golden eggs." Socialism in the West has already created something of an irredeemable situation, since pseudoconservative or Christian democratic parties, if ever victorious, would lack the courage to undo all the vestiges of socialism. (Woe to Hungarian prime minister Viktor Orbán's party, the FIDESZ, for trying to do just that.) Western socialism is here to stay, since its opponents are prone to sell the soul of their parties and ideologies by repeating socialist slogans (the right becoming left) in a frantic effort to gain lower-class support.

It has been said before, and this author indeed claims no originality for it, that a monarchy might become inefficient, unjust, corrupt or even absolutistic, but, unlike democracy, it cannot peacefully and legally *evolve* into its very contrary.

In a modern democratic state, the individual voice at national elections is not heard; it hardly makes any difference whether one votes or not. The person is only *counted* but not *weighed* and is thus treated by number but not by importance.

Thus, "nobody is indispensable" is a highly democratic, one could say "leftist," slogan. The conservative would say, "Everybody is unique. Everybody is indispensable. Nobody can be replaced."

The intensity of a vote cannot be calculated either; if 51 percent of a nation vaguely approves of a party or a particular measure, the ardent, fervent, and desperate opposition of 49 percent is of no avail.

Ethics and Representation

One critical characteristic of the democratic scene must be evident to all: lack of responsibility.

Irresponsibility was the standard charge against monarchs, who were considered to be responsible to God only. The onset of democracy has hardly increased the sense of responsibility since a composite democratic government has resulted in a division of responsibility (itself anathema to the concept of responsibility), which makes it ubiquitous and at the same time—through the process of atomization—illusory.

The electors who have dropped their ballots in unmarked envelopes can deny their misdeeds with a straight face, and the deputies, who after an initial failure were not reelected, can claim that their tenure was too short to complete their plans.

There is also a widespread tendency to restrict the tenure of chief executives ("Power corrupts!"). As a result, the amateur incumbents of any high office are not only prevented from utilizing their limited experience acquired at a significant cost; the bar against reelection or reappointment outright discourages and alienates them while exhibiting frivolous indifference.

What is the duty of the victorious political candidate—to speak and vote according to his lights, or to become the mouthpiece of his constituency, thus merely voicing the public opinion?

Republicanism will favor the first theory; democracy the latter. The republican aspect of popular representation is one of *transferring* the "possession" of popular sovereignty to electees, while the democratic deputy remains the representative of the "voice of the people."

The implementation or enforcement of the common framework of reference in a democracy is not only dangerous but also produces a kind of uniformity that can and will have adverse effects on the intellectual scene. The result is a lack of distance between the person and society; the secret police are conspicuously absent, but there are ostracism and boycott, which are the typical forms of persecution sanctioned by democratic society and directed against the nonconformist. There is something inherently inhumane in the masses and the "this-worldly" aspects of society that cannot necessarily be found in the individual.

We hear the exclamation everywhere: "There is nothing wrong about it; *everybody* does it!" So the result is that harmful actions and immoral motions invade under an elaborate camouflage in order not to challenge openly the powerful forces of social pressure, which can be far more potent than the state Leviathan. Thus we see socialism in the democratic orbit proclaiming itself not as absolute totalitarianism but as "progressive democracy."

In a democracy with several political parties, the parties will have to compromise not only among themselves but also with reality, the facts, and the oscillations of public opinion. This frenzy of compromise differs curiously from the great scheme: "Sooner die than compromise," and it is the most destructive moral and psychological preparation of the masses for facing oppression and enslavement. One should remember the fact that the most heroic and stubborn resistance against the Nazi invaders came from less-developed nations with a minimum of democratic experience. The resistance of the French, Belgians, Dutch, and Danes cannot in the least be compared with that of the Poles, Serbs, Russians, Greeks, or even the Italians.

It can be expected that the compromising liberal heresy provides a much better soil and lubricant for the smooth functioning of democracy than does philosophy or theology insisting on absolutes. Once we reject either the existence of absolute truth or its human attainability—and this is the essence of liberalism—there can be no virtue attached to a stubborn defense of convictions of verities.

If and when we walk away from the truth, we shift in our predicament from liberal doubt to the compromising democratic procedure—shall the majority decide about the truth?

Is indirect democracy still a full democracy? Just as no constitutional injunction can prevent a republic from becoming—partly or wholly—democracy, the reverse process can also happen, but such a development is less likely because the price for the capital sin of disregarding public opinion is removal by the ballot. Nevertheless, the fact remains that *actual power*, albeit for a limited time, *is invested in a few*.

Viewed from this angle, either a republic or democracy is an oligarchical monarchy with a time limit. Under these circumstances, the differences between oligarchy and democracy (between aristocracy and republic) are gradual rather than fundamental.

Direct democracy is not feasible on any larger scale. The practicality of any democracy begins only when we inject the aristocratic (parliamentary) or monarchical (presidential) element. Either of these is perfectly able to work by itself—as we know from historical experience. Therefore, the ethical defender of the democratic dogma is in the curious position of having to admit a total independence of reality from philosophy. Thus we seem to be confronted with the question of whether government as such is not *in its very essence* an activity emanating from one or only a few.

The law of democracy is the law of numbers. However, every government regulated by the law of numbers becomes a mortal phenomenon subject to its fatality. This fatality consists in the fact that a moment will come when it breaks loose from human control, from the lessons of experience, from the influence of reason.

Accordingly, democracy arrived at what one calls today the government of the masses.

Accordingly, after having been the regime of the bourgeoisie, democracy is becoming the rule of the proletariat.

Accordingly, having been the postulate of liberalism, it becomes that of socialism.

Accordingly, after having turned into its opposite, it preserves nothing of its proper self other than the name—nothing but the label.

The people's loyalty to their nation has nothing to do with democracy. The people are not oblivious to the fact that if conditions are ever to get better, this can occur only if individual leaders will show the masses the way to better things.

Although it is not politically correct even to imply it today, once the people feel they have found a real political leader in the country, they will joyfully accept his leadership and send to the devil all the democratically elected party leaders whose impotence and selfishness they have long suspected. So far, however, the peoples of the modern West have been looking for these individual political leaders in vain. They feel deserted, leaderless, and almost hopeless. They slowly realize and admit that the path they entered has proved to be a cul-de-sac. Meanwhile they continue to try the so-called democratic road. Democracy appears to be the only chance that remains; it seems to promise at least a possibility of attaining political freedom at home.

The people of Western Europe considered the European Union as a framework that could be filled in later—perhaps with some entirely different content. Meanwhile, since no other structure seems possible for the time being, the people must make the best of the one they call "Europe." This supposition, however, does not alter the fact that someday the people may demand measures—Western measures, meaning American or European measures—that will be wholly undemocratic.

Democracy is not contingent on the form of the state but on the people's contribution to the working of the state.

Alas, the peoples of the formerly socialist Eastern European countries feel today they have been cheated of this share. They are beginning to distinguish between the European Union and democracy. The individuals who avow themselves as democrats are the political exploiters of the collapse of socialism in Eastern Europe. These types exist in all parties that have admitted liberal elements. They are the people whom the Velvet Revolution brought to the top: the newly wealthy, the opportunistic parliamentarians, the party leaders, and the publicists. These are the people who acquiesce in the present state of affairs in Eastern Europe. They upheld the state not because they honored what it stood for but because they wanted to keep their wealth and privileges.

Everywhere else in the world, in conservative circles and among the masses, anger is beginning to rise against democracy. However daring the idea of starting all over again, and however dark and unresolved the issue, the people are beginning to clamor for a fresh start and an end to this whitewashing of democracy. They never think of the democracy they have; they are dreaming of another, new, distant, future, and perhaps impossible democracy.

In every stratum of the people, a reaction against democracy begins to set in; it is similar to the sensation a man feels when in the cold light of day he contemplates what acts he committed overnight.

The Applied History of Democracy

There is no use comparing what things were in Eastern Europe before 1914 with what they have been since 1989. These retrospective comparisons are prompted to a large extent by economic rather than political reflections. However, beyond these practical preoccupations, retrospective thought poses other questions about the meaning of this great historical experience we have lived through, and about the honor, conduct, and destiny of nations. The Eastern Europeans learned at last, although very slowly, to grasp the causes and effects of the fate that had overtaken them. They learned to despise political and business leaders who had posed as democrats and had betrayed Eastern European democracy. The point of view thus arrived at ultimately led the people to take stock of the democracy that had become their form of government.

Who were the people who constituted this democracy? They were the liberals. Of course they were not so rash to always call themselves liberals; in the West, they have also deemed themselves "progressives." Liberalism had promised both freedom and progress. Eastern Europe has neither now, but it has democracy. There exists a new stratum of persons there between the people and the state—not the bureaucrats of the old system (though these remained) but a new layer of individuals who now constitute the state and who man the government and staff the offices, the press, and the organizations. They are persons who profess to act for the people but who keep the people at arm's length. It is true that since 1988 the people themselves have elected these individuals in a both revolutionary and supposedly very democratic process, of course.

Again, democracy exists where the people take a share in determining their fate and the future of the people is the people's affair—at least, one would imagine so.

The question is now, how is it possible for the people to take a share and participate in resolving their destiny?

Nations, like individuals, make their own fate. However, in the case of minors, someone else must either make some decisions for them or at least guide their decision-making process. There is a significant difference between nations; some attain maturity early, some late, and some never attain it at all. Some achieve only an apparent maturity and allow themselves to be lured into democracy—not for sound political reasons but by their literati, their theorists, and their demagogues—and find in the democracy their undoing.[140]

Several European and many non-European nations lack the basis of democracy. No inner craving for democracy has run like a guiding thread through the course of their history. We cannot contend that only in a democracy can history find its fulfillment. However, there has not been a single non-Western nation successfully achieving lasting economic development based on a Western-style democratic political system.

Some would mention at this point Japan as an exception, but they should be reminded of the extraordinary interplay between that country's unique culture and the forced introduction of Western democratic elements. This interaction brought about not only enormous changes but also military aggressions, several foreign wars, nuclear strikes, immeasurable suffering, total defeat, and lasting foreign occupation—many of them being first-time events in Japanese history. Yes, Japan's economic achievements have been spectacular in the last seventy plus years, but one must not forget the previous ninety years of violent changes ending in cataclysm and annihilating democracy through direct foreign military occupation and total control. No, the Japanese model has not been a positive example of how to go about spreading democracy in the non-Western world.

All humankind was initially democratic. When the first humans stepped out of the twilight of prehistory, they had already solved the question of how people can take a share in their government. The answer had nothing to do with the general rights of man; it was utterly simple: democracy *was* the people.

There was no social contract; the unit of society was the family. On this rested the constitution of the tribes, and on the tribes rested the community of the people. Confederations of the tribes held the people together; they enjoyed the closeness of their fields in peace and their tents in war. The democracy of those days meant the sovereignty of the people suitable for the conditions of their lives. The rights and duties, according to the law of the confederations, were based on the rules of self-government. This law recognized the right of the people to assert their power inside or outside the tribe, as might seem necessary to them for their self-preservation.

Nature was the origin of leadership: the free choice of free men who chose themselves a "lord" to conduct their forces to victory. As the various tribes and races distributed themselves over a larger and larger area, the next step was to elect themselves kings to secure a consistent and stable policy, and for that purpose it was natural that the office of the king should be vested in one particular family of a well-tried lineage.

All this was pure and primitive democracy. The people established the law in their confederations, and their leader put the law into effect as executor of the people's will. The state was the commonwealth of the people, and its unwritten constitution was the sum of their habits, morals, and customs, which were traditionally expressed in the popular assemblies in which every member of the nation appeared in person and took his share in the decisions that determined his fate.

The unity of the newer state was organized according to the first divisions of races and tribes and the subdivisions of clan and family—in contrast to the states of antiquity that were based on power, law, and state right. This "unity in diversity" gave the state the firm foundation it preserved into historical times until the idea of the empire arose and the broader field of international relations replaced the narrow domain of national policy.

Danger, of course, was inherent in this diversity. As the various members became geographically more widely divided, they tended to become less and less conscious of their essential unity, and more and more inclined to seek independence. The tribal constitution had all along been one centrifugal, dispersing factor. Another was added when the knightly order began to claim precedence over the other estates. In the original feudal organization, the leader and the led were bound together in mutual loyalty, but gradually the greater nobility began to differentiate itself from the lesser nobility, and both left out of their calculations the peasant population, who had formerly constituted the democratic power of the nation. The peasantry was despised, ill treated, impoverished, weak, and powerless. This abuse, disregard, and indifference led to the violent reactions of the peasants' wars of the sixteenth century.

These domestic dissensions would have had no more than internal importance if they had not resulted in external weakness. As early as the Middle Ages, the people showed how unpolitically minded they were when they transferred power into the hands of the king but gave him no means of supporting that power. The kings had no alternative but to build up personal might and private estates of their own.

The development of these private lands and possessions also led to disastrous rivalries among the princes, resulting in the birth of territorial states, and, finally, during the period of absolutism, even in the establishment of new and independent kingdoms. Nevertheless, all through these developments, the idea of national unity was never lost. The towns, becoming more and more the centers of culture, owed their splendid medieval achievements to the influence of national unity. This idea led to associations among the towns by which the citizens assured for themselves the power, wealth, safety, and security that the weakness of a strong central authority denied them.

Even under the emperors of the absolutist period, the idea of national unity did not die. For example, the Kingdom of Prussia was much more democratic than the reputation of its rulers would imply. With sword and scaffold, the Prussian kings put an end to the feudal system; the only duty of the nobility was to the crown, but through the crown also to the people. The royal motto "Ich diene" (I serve) indicates the attitude of these Prussian monarchs toward their subjects, in striking contrast to the divine pretensions of the kings of France: it represents an attempt to restore through a human intermediary the vital bond between state and people that absolutism had severed.[141]

Most states, however, failed to make the foundation of the state at once conservative *and* democratic, unified by a comprehensive system of self-government. Bismarck had to fight against the consequences of this deficiency during his entire political life, and his work finally wrecked on the same rock. Why? Because Germany failed to bring its most original thoughts to their conclusion; instead it welcomed other peoples' most foreign ideas. Instead of a state built on estates, the German state was constructed on a parliament, which was a modern, progressive, and very foreign conception imported from the West.

The Russian example, from Peter the Great to the collapse of the Soviet Union, is a copy of the German recipe—with similar results.

Parliamentary rule in England had always remained a state built on the three estates; it was an aristocratic creation of the great families, who had devised it in a period when their monarchs were ineffective to protect their power and, in addition to that, the power of the people. Montesquieu, who somewhat indiscriminately admired this tyrannical, autocratic, corrupt, and dishonest institution, said that this "beautiful system," as he labeled it, had "been evolved in the forests." He shrewdly grasped the idea of "representation" and accepted as the chief advantage of the system that the representatives were "qualified to discuss affairs of state" while the main drawback of democracy was that the people were wholly unqualified to do so.[142]

Rousseau was the first to declare that all power stemmed from the people. Nevertheless, he strove unsuccessfully to distinguish between "the general will" and "the will of all." The idea of the state as the result of a *Contrat Social* was characteristic of the age when the state was to depend on a mere counting of heads among an electorate that had lost all roots, and that such a state should be called a democracy.[143]

The English conceived the cabinet with the prime minister, whom they gave precedence over their lower house and equipped with almost sovereign powers. The French invented the political clique that manipulated the chambers for its own ends—which were, however, also the aims of France.

It was reserved for the hapless Germans, and typically for non-Western nations, to interpret parliamentarianism literally and to endow parliament with real powers of control, which it then exercised only negatively and obstructively. The political parties assumed the function of the estates, but they suffered, as did the parliaments, from a complete lack of inspiration. The subdivision of a nation into political parties had become a system, and the legislatures merely became institutions for the public dissemination of political platitudes. Party programs, despite all the care given to formulating them, never contained an ideal capable of inspiring the people. Whenever the course of world history looks most ominous, matters of foreign politics receive consideration only to the extent that they might affect internal party politics.

Parliamentarianism concerning democracy had to be discussed not because the two are identical but because they are, erroneously, supposed to be so. Mommsen's observation about ancient Rome appears to be justified: "Democracy has always brought about its own destruction, by pursuing its principle to extremes."[144]

Throughout the land, we see the West stirring. People want to preserve their old nations; they want it more consciously, more passionately, than ever before, but they cannot believe that unity will be secured by the few million atoms of the population. They instead think this integration must be based on the independence of the individual nations, united in their feelings of mutual loyalty and of loyalty to the whole—but not through some centralization or federalization.

The Velvet Revolution gave Russia and Eastern Europe what legally and technically was supposed to be a democracy, but the people lack the democratic spirit—the devotion to and the interest in the state that is the essence of real democracy. Why?

The answer is rather obvious: because an English-style parliamentary system in the Western sense has no tradition in these countries! The left-liberals and social democrats betray how inadequate and how politically uneducated they are by the way they shy off at the mere sound of the word "tradition." "Tradition" for them means "reaction," the old system, and the accursed past: everything from which they want to break for good and all. However, tradition, or indigenous culture, is, in fact, the security guaranteed by the past political experience of the people.

France and England began as national states; they progressed as monarchies, and after they had, by their revolutions, gotten rid of or limited their monarchies, they established the parliamentary system, which they called democracy, and which served as a cover for their nationalism.

The Russian, German, and Eastern European peoples historically took the opposite course from the people of the "real" West. They maintained themselves by their monarchies and finally broke their history off with wars and revolutions, which were not so much of national revolutions as world wars and international revolutions supposedly aimed at universal brotherhood and eternal peace.

Alas, both the national and international hopes of Eastern Europe have been deceived. The democrats of the West have failed to show any understanding, still less justice, to the young democracies of Europe: the republics of the former socialist countries have been thrown back on their resources. However, if they want to maintain themselves in Europe and vis-à-vis the outside world, they must follow the same path as all Western democracies had trodden: they must become nations first. They, just as all nations everywhere in the world, must find their systems, both political and economic, based on their culture, history, and tradition. This process cannot be, and should not be, dictated, managed, or conducted by others from the outside to succeed; it must be homegrown, indigenous, and genuine.

Democracy is the political self-consciousness of a people and its self-assertion as a nation. Democracy is the expression of a nation's self-respect—or it is no democracy at all. Democracy is embodied not in the form of government but in the spirit of the citizens; its foundation is the people.

The conservative thinker studies the relation of cause and effect; he is not afraid to state that the old system itself, the status quo ante, was the cause of its downfall. This phenomenon must be explained using the unique history of Germany as an example because it is not only characteristic of the problem in its clarity but is also distinctive of the culture finding itself to be on the center stage of Europe as the most significant continental nation between East and West.

On the one hand, the old German monarchy always acted for the people. It took over this duty when the German nation lost its medieval maturity. Nothing but the absolute monarchy saved the German people from the extreme weakness that resulted from the Thirty Years' War in the seventeenth century. Without the absolute monarchy, there would have been no power to represent the Holy Roman Empire in the eyes of Europe; the empire would have fallen to pieces. The monarchy saved the nation; it worked and lived for the people, and the people loyally followed their dynasties in Austria and Prussia. A patriarchal relationship existed between princes and their peoples. The great princes of the seventeenth and eighteenth centuries lived for the German nation; they had the strength of the people behind them, and thus the conducting of foreign policy was possible for them.

On the other hand, these advantages were counterbalanced by a disadvantage that became more evident as time went on. The monarchy took care of the people and taught them to look to the state for support, and the people became unaccustomed to acting for themselves. In time, monarchy and nation ceased to form a unity, and in moments of danger and years of trials, this unity had to be restored by the people's initiative. This need for solidarity was evident during the wars of liberation fought against Napoleon during 1813–15. And when the Second German Empire was being founded, Bismarck had to act as intermediary—sometimes on behalf of the monarchy, and at other times in the name of the people. In the days of Kaiser Wilhelm II, the bonds between ruler and ruled grew looser and looser, though the pretense of unity was still kept up by tradition, by convention, and by a disciplined patriotism, until the total collapse with the end of World War I.

As the examples of the British, Americans, French, Germans, or Russians also show, there have been peoples who flourished under democracy, and there have been nations who perished under it (with the Greeks more than once). Democracy may imply stoicism, republicanism, and inexorable severity; or it may mean liberalism, political chatter, and self-indulgence.

One can only wonder whether the democrats have ever been seized by a paralyzing fear that liberal democracy might be the fateful instrument of a nation's ruin.

Disaffection and Decontextualization

We will now investigate the concept of alienation and how democracy promotes it; question the logic of decontextualized decision-making, the reduction of ideas to opinions; and question the near-universal acceptance of majority rule. We will also examine democracy's propensity to demagoguery, lobbying, and corruption, which are readily accepted even by defenders of the system, and then we will discuss why democracy is so good at maintaining and reproducing itself.

It is worth considering the causes of disaffection or alienation in society, since the opinion is clear and logical and estrangement is such a significant problem.

Anarchists distinguish themselves by asserting a direct and unobstructed link between thought and action, between desires and their fulfillment. They reject all social processes that break that connection, such as private property, exchange relations, the division of labor, and democracy. They call that fractured link "disaffection" or "alienation."

Passions and aspirations can lead to happiness only when they are real and definite forces in our lives. In the present *state of disaffection,* however, they are inevitably subdued by the knowledge that the terms of our existence are not under our control.

In that vein, dreams are only for dreamers, because our desires are always faced with the impossibility of action (see the previous comments on desires and aspirations). When we lose our link to the aspirations, passions, and expectations that drive us forward, it is impossible to wrest back control over our lives again, and we are left to linger in a condition of passivity and apathy. Even the desires to change the material and societal conditions that cause alienation are met with this lethargy and hopelessness, permanently leaving these conditions intact.

Society thus winds up split in two: the *alienated*, from whom the ability to manage their lives as they choose has been taken away, and the *elite enjoyers*—those in control of these management processes. The elite enjoyers benefit from this separation by accumulating, utilizing, and managing alienated energy to reproduce and perpetuate the current society and their role in it as its rulers. Most individuals fall into the former category, while people such as the political and business elites or their agents compose the latter.

Therefore, one should be against democracy because its very existence, its very purpose, maintains the division that it is allegedly and hypocritically seeking to abolish. Democracy does nothing but assure the survival of disaffected, alienated power since it requires that our desires (or aspirations) be separate from our ability (or authority) to act, and any attempt to get actively engaged in that system will only help to reproduce it.

Democracies function and reproduce via elections—the very instruments that expertly transfer one's will, thoughts, autonomy, and freedom to an outside power. It is the same whether one transfers that power to an elected representative or an elusive majority; the point is that the power is no longer one's own. The people have been alienated from their capacity to determine the conditions of their existence in free cooperation with those around them.

Political parties are political in their claim to represent the interests of others. This representation is a claim to alienated (i.e., appropriated) power because when this ability is taken with the proclamation to represent someone, the person represented is separated from his freedom to act and, in this sense, has become nonpolitical.

Therefore, the person represented is not interested in a different claim to alienated power under different leadership, in another *form* of representation, in a regime change, or in anything that merely shuffles around the makeup of alienated power. Anytime someone claims to represent him or to act on his behalf or to be the force liberating him—that is a definite red flag.

The inherent hypocrisy of democracy as it represents itself makes it questionable that it can universally be applied a priori as the "best of all options," as the Western rulers like to say.

The critique of disaffection is connected to problems with decontextualization because, in democracies, decisions are also disaffected from the contexts in which they arise.

Democracies require that laws, rules, and decisions be made separate from the circumstances that people find themselves in, thus forcing individuals into predetermined and reactive roles rather than allowing for freethinking persons or groups of individuals to make decisions in various contexts at different times as they see fit.

For example, to organize for a vote, the complexities of an issue, its causes and effects, and its possible resolutions get reduced to yes-or-no, either-or, or for-or-against choices. The questions are meaningless if the method is false; the process of reducing the issue at hand to that of dichotomy is not democratic, and how could it be—by a preelection vote? That has been tried in some places, such as the party primaries in the United States or runoff elections in many areas, but even then the process functions to narrow the range of choices incrementally, as each round eliminates another candidate or option.

OPINIONS, MAJORITIES, AND OTHER INHERENT DEFECTS

Voters are mere spectators in a sham process where they are presented with opinions to choose from, while in reality those who create the agendas—the opinion-makers, the expert elite enjoyers—are really in control. We have all seen the sloganeering and reductionism that occur when representatives or speakers reduce ideas to sound-bite opinions from which to select.

The reduction, simplification, and stratification of ideas to opinions for selection have a polarizing effect on those involved. When studied selection is the only method available and there is nothing to do but choose from *A* or *B*, the parties on either side of an issue push themselves apart. They only strengthen their mutual certainty of rightness; they would rather become caricatures of themselves than to acknowledge the complexity of the issues. Indeed, precisely this is what the opinion-makers want to circumvent.

Some form of capitalism and democratic elections always accompany democracy. There are producers (the expert elite) who dictate the agenda, and there are consumers (the alienated) who are relegated to the role of the spectator customer and allowed to select from the opinion-makers' (producers') ideas. These choices also become a competitive game, and every decision will end with winners and losers.

The concept of the majority winners is particularly troubling. By always accepting the will of the majority winners, democracy allows them to have an absolute tyranny over everyone else. This sad fact means that in the winner-take-all context of democracy, minorities do not influence decisions that are made. This result is much worse than it first seems because the majority in any given situation is usually not even the majority of the people—just the largest group of many minorities. For a stable and consistent outnumbered group, this usual scenario means that democracies bring no more freedom than dictatorships would.

By slyly providing the illusion of participation for everyone, devious democracy allows majorities to justify their actions, no matter how oppressive they may be. Since deceitful democracy claims that everyone can participate in the political process, there is no harm in providing suffrage for groups with minority opinions, since their losing votes will only legitimize the actions of the majority. Likewise, if people wish not to participate in an election, this is still interpreted for all practical purposes as the consent of the majority opinion, since they *could* have voted against it if they had wanted to. There is no escape.

Also, the one-person-one-vote model of democracy cannot account for either the strength of individual preference or the truth of the matter. Two voters who are barely interested in the topic or doing anything about it but cast a supporting vote will still win against a voter strongly opposed to it based on expert knowledge.

In this way, majorities do not offer much, if any, opportunity to give up the status quo. In the words of Errico Malatesta, a nineteenth-century Italian anarchist: "The fact of having the majority on one's side does not in any way prove that one must be right. Indeed, humanity has always advanced through the initiative and efforts of individuals and minorities, whereas the majority, by its very nature, is slow, conservative, submissive to superior force and established privileges."[145]

Admittedly, the Founding Fathers of the United States intended to address this criticism by combining democracy with republicanism. A constitution would limit the powers of what a simple majority could accomplish. However, the machinations of modern parliamentarianism can easily neutralize the good intentions.

There are a few more widely acknowledged inherent defects of democracy as well. These include the susceptibility of democracies to demagoguery, lobbying, and corruption.

"Demagoguery" refers to a political strategy of obtaining the desired result by using rhetoric, agitation, and propaganda in provoking the coveted impulses of the population. All forms of democracy fall prey to demagogues eager to seize any opportunity to advance their aims by manufacturing consent from the momentary fear, hope, anger, and confusion of the general public.

On top of this, representational democracy has a particular vulnerability to lobbying. Special-interest groups send very well-paid people after elected representatives to persuade, threaten, barter, or bribe them into delivering legislation, government funding, or other favors for their organization. Because elected officials frequently come from industries, business sectors, and the upper classes, they already have many vested interests when they take office other than the people's requests. Not forgetting that, lobbyists can be quite resourceful in obtaining what they demand.

Corruption is a pure and straightforward form of appeal to the short-term interests of the voters. One type of corruption is commonly called "pork barrel" when local areas or political sectors are given specific benefits the costs of which are then spread among all taxpayers.

These are also symptoms of problems that arise when individuals are turned into passive spectators in a decision-making process or when personal involvement in creating one's environment is reduced to mere opinion selection. Unlike others who have identified problems with demagoguery, lobbying, and corruption in democracies, this author does not advocate such changes and "improvements" to this political system that would allow us to become still better demagogues, lobbyists, or moral transgressors. Issues such as campaign finance reform, subsidized media, and the like are not appealing to me, because in recognizing the tyranny of political manipulation, one should not seek to refine further and strengthen this ingeniously wicked machinery.

Regrettably, democracy offers only one choice of relieving oneself of oppression: becoming the oppressor. Freedom lies outside of this entire institution.

Reproduction of Democracy: The Ultimate Trick

Democracy is considered the only legitimate form of a political system in the West today, with little clarification of how or why that came to be—except, of course, for

Churchill's illogical wisdom of "It has been said that democracy is the worst form of government except all the others that have been tried." It is hardly ever mentioned that democracies have been tried and failed around the world and under different circumstances over the millennia, just like any other political systems.

Among the many previous versions of "democracy, one can name the Greek democracies and the Roman Republic (an improvement over the Greek system and the model for the American republic). In modern times, the failed Russian Provisional Government (the Kerensky government after Czar Nicholas II abdicated in February 1917) and the Weimar Republic in Germany come to mind. As a non-European example, the Kuomintang government of China can be mentioned.

All peoples live either in democracies today or in countries under the economic and military dominion of these democracies. Given these two options, it would seem reasonable to conclude that democracy means freedom and happiness.

However, the reality of one current status quo does not contradict or invalidate the past or future existence of other conditions. Critical thinking must be applied to the arrogant ways democracy posits itself as the necessary first condition of freedom.

When democracy frames our discussion and forces us to argue in its terms, all actions to change the sociopolitical environment must happen via its means and achieve only those ends it will sanction. For these reasons, democracy reproduces itself with considerable special effort from the ruling class, the expert elite.

A democratic system of majority rule only encourages the alienated and exploited people to *feel* as though they have political control. Real and absolute control (meaning total power), however, safely and securely remains in the hands of the alienating and exploiting class, the expert elite. Even the most obvious contradictions get overlooked because the system has equated its existence with freedom and so places its existence outside the realm of contestable ideas. By claiming itself as the first principle of individual and social liberty, democracy appears to be a tolerant and adaptable source of the public good beyond all scrutiny.

Meanwhile, the very notions of democratic elections, one man—one vote, and majority rule all indicate that "We the People" have the power over our destiny—contrary to all the evidence. It logically follows, then, that when "the People" do not affect changes in our system, we must not want to change it.

Hypothetically, we believe in justice and freedom, or we would not have formed a democracy. Since we freedom-loving, democratic people would naturally act to end oppression as soon as we find out about it, it follows that if a policy, law, or practice does not change, then it must not oppress people at all. Alas, this rationale will never bring us to a genuinely free and virtuous society.

However, rejecting this logic without adopting a more general critique of democracy leads us to another dubious conclusion often voiced by progressive and liberal factions. It sounds something like this: "Our state, our government, and our institutions fail us because we, the people, are too apathetic, too unaware, or too irresponsible to apply our immense power as we ought to. If we progressives could only mobilize, inform, or educate the public, then everything would work out beautifully."

So one sees presumably intelligent people anxiously trying to reform a system that in its best and most functional form can only hope to oppress everyone equally. Again, the ruling elite can rest comfortably as long as we place the blame on ourselves and not on them for our alienated position in modern society. This condition will continue until we realize the inherent flaws in the concept of democracy itself and refuse to reproduce it.

We reproduce and perpetuate democracy by supporting it with our vote and our daily subservience to the outcome of elections. If one understands that democracy will never let someone act outside its narrow parameters and accepts the critique of majority rule, then voting and elections merely serve to reaffirm and legitimize the system and its elite no matter how someone votes. In voting, one might initiate or overrule any policy, practice, or person—except the system itself.

For that reason, the ruling masters, the expert elite enjoyers, of a democratic system as a whole find no real threat in suffrage, even though individual politicians might sustain public disfavor.

Many political historians have pointed out that government extended suffrage to disenfranchised groups during periods when it needed mass support to accomplish some end, often militaristic, rather than during periods when the public demanded it most vocally. Furthermore, providing suffrage enabled the state to channel the energies of mass movements that might have posed a real challenge to the ruling elite into a safe form of action, namely voting, which reduced the speed and magnitude of the desired changes while simultaneously reproducing democracy.

The first suffrage movements in the United States and Europe merely succeeded in making races and women free from official marginalization, only to engage in a system of marginalization. As a result of their efforts, all Western citizens have an equal right to participate in a command system and hope it works out in their favor.

In fact, an astute observer would see any public debate about who can or cannot vote as a misleading deception. The state uses voting to mitigate minority demands and sap the energy building around the direct action. Where there is smoke, there is fire, and where there is suffrage, there is motivated marginalization.

When we swallow the democratic system's bait by voting, we give it the power to take away our potential of being able to control our lives. Elections tend to put people in a passive mode, offering salvation in the wisdom of the majority rather than through self-directed, independent action. A split between leaders and followers develops, whereby voters stand aside as spectators of their government rather than agents in their own right.

Political systems of all types exclude the opportunity for direct action, but democracy's insidious ability to reproduce itself as a restrictive system while continuously incorporating more people into its "let freedom ring" rhetoric makes it uniquely sophisticated, sneaky, and slippery.

THE ELECTION SCAM: VOTING FOR THE DEVIL WE KNOW

In every election in a democratic country, the citizen is bombarded with propaganda about how "your vote makes a difference." According to the official doctrine, ordinary citizens control the state by voting for candidates in elections. The politicians are presumed to be the servants of the people, and the government an instrument of the public. This drill is a fiction.

It makes no difference who is elected, because the way the democratic system is set up, all elected representatives, directly or indirectly, must deliver what big business and the state bureaucracy want, not what the people wish. Elected officials are merely figureheads, although they are genuine representatives—the only question is whose. Politicians' rhetoric may change, depending on the individual elected, but they all have to implement the same policies given the same situation. Their voices may be different, but all members of the same choir must sing the music with one accord.

Elections are a scam, and their function is to create the illusion that the people control the government and not the elite, and to neutralize any real resistance movements. All the voting does is strengthen the ruling class, the governing elite; it is not an effective means to change government policy.

If a political party wins the elections but implements policies contrary to the interests of big business, then corporate profits will go down and investors will flee; the capital flight will crash the economy. The ruling party will either change its policies to appease big business or lose the next elections owing to the weak economy. In practice, most parties change their policies to satisfy the corporate elite in order to avoid losing power. Their rhetoric is different, but the policy is fundamentally the same. Usually the mere threat of capital flight is enough to keep potentially recalcitrant politicians in line (although most politicians never even consider policies that conflict with the corporate elite or state bureaucracy).

In the mid-twentieth century, welfare states expanded in most Western societies as a way of preventing the then powerful socialist movements and communist parties from overthrowing the governments. Popular welfare programs not only make the poor feel better off and less rebellious but also make the state appear more benevolent. The expansion of the welfare state was in the interest of the ruling elite because it was a measure to counteract revolution and decrease unrest, thereby helping them gain and keep power and profit.

Although elections do not secure public control over the state, they do assist in ensuring state control over the populace. Voting is a democratic ritual that reinforces obedience to state authority and maintains the *myth* that the people are in control of the state, thereby masking elite rule. That deception makes rebellion against the state less likely because it is seen as a legitimate institution and an instrument of the popular rule rather than the oligarchy it is. This illusion is why even totalitarian states like the Soviet Union under Stalin had elections. Embedded within all electoral campaigns is the myth that the people control the state through voting. This fiction is implied and assumed by the perverse logic of all election campaigns, because if it were not true, then the campaign for that candidate would be pointless, wouldn't it?

For the above reasons, governments, corporations, and their governing elite are all supportive of elections or at least do not question them today. Public schools usually promote the importance of voting, teaching the official view that citizens control the state via elections, and some corporations even run commercials encouraging people to vote. It is in the interests of the elite, their governments, and large companies to promote voting because elections serve to legitimize the system and reduce unrest.

Also, elections can help neutralize resistance movements by getting disgruntled individuals to channel their efforts into the election instead of any more efficient means of resisting. Since electoral campaigns are ineffective ways of changing policy, all the labor and resources put into election campaigns are wasted. Potential rebellion is thus diverted and channeled into a dead end, where it will not hurt the system. The boycotting of elections does not necessarily change anything, but taking part in elections changes things for the worse by legitimizing the continued reign of the elite.

Any vote is a vote for democracy and the strengthening of the political system. The referenda have always been manipulated by the ruling elite's machinery of business, banks, government, and media. These forces invariably unite in bombarding the bemused public with propaganda predicting disaster should the people not vote for the devil they already know. This propaganda, based on fear of the unknown, suggests that the status quo is better than any unknown alternative. It is better to grin and plow through the hell we know than to nurture belief in anything better.

There is no mentioning of subsidiarity in the vocabulary of globalism. There is no room for political sovereignty, national independence, or local autonomy. It is all about doing what we are told. Those with the power play the tune to which the rest of us, like real puppets, are required to dance.

According to globalism, the political freedom of nations must be sacrificed so that the financial freedom of investors can be protected from obstacles. It is not just that freedom is not free but also that it is simply too expensive for the globalists to tolerate.

Many had always thought that Scotland would not be brave enough to grasp the thistle of freedom because of the fear of the unknown future that freedom might bring. That fear had been instilled into the Scottish voters by the welfare state. Sure enough, the Scots chose to remain shackled to their big brother south of the border, just as they would rather stay in the protective hug of their European comrades rather than risk being free but out in the cold.

Similarly, many had thought that Britain would also lack the courage to pluck the rose of freedom, which the referendum on EU membership placed within its grasp on June 23, 2016. However, lo and behold, although bombarded into submission by the big guns of globalism, the English and Welsh people did not kowtow before the European Empire and did not accept their slavery. They did *not* choose the devil they knew in fear of the devil they did not know.

Voting for the devil is *never* the right choice, and voting for the devil we know is downright foolhardy. As for the devil we do not know, he might not be the devil at all.

Bona fide people's power (called "populism" by its enemies) in the West is under attack from those who most loudly claim to be liberals and democrats. As an example, in 2014 the world saw the *unelected* EU foreign policy chief, Catherine Ashton, meeting the new *unelected* Ukrainian president, Aleksandr Turchynov, who had just come to power following the violent overthrow of that country's democratically elected president with a rebellion backed by the European Union. The Western hailing of a foreign-backed coup d'état in a country where fresh elections were only twelve months away as a "victory for democracy" was truly Orwellian.

The era of neoliberalism has finally seen political power shifting from ordinary people to the 1 percent ruling them. Today, even in those European countries with much-heralded democratic elections, governments follow policies aimed to suit and please the all-powerful global financial and political elite. The elected government officials know only too well that if they upset the expert enjoyers, the real rulers of the system, they are likely to be forced from power.

Then note the attacks on democratic and non-EU member Switzerland for having a referendum on immigration and voting for putting a curb on it. The European elite was furious: How dare a country in the middle of Europe directly ask its people what to do? "The Swiss have damaged themselves with this result. The fair cooperation we have had in the past with Switzerland also includes observing the central, fundamental decisions taken by the EU," warned German foreign minister Frank-Walter Steinmeier.[146] French foreign minister Laurent Fabius warned that the EU would have to review its relationship with Switzerland.[147]

The point here about the Swiss referendum is not whether one agrees with immigration curbs but whether countries have the right to make their decisions on this and other issues. However, today's Western elite hates separate and individual countries, nation-states, and the peoples of those countries deciding for themselves.

In February 2014, EU Commission vice president Viviane Reding insolently questioned the British people's competence in making an "informed decision" on EU membership.[148]

The strange paradox is that as Europe has become less democratic, so the European elite has become more vocal in lecturing others on democracy. Democracy promotion has become big business at a time when people power has been snuffed out at home.

Only a radical reform of the EU, or its total abolition, together with the ditching of the neoliberal model, which transfers political power from the ballot box to the wallet, can reverse the damaging trends. For if the organization that dominates Europe and the economic system under which the continent operates is fundamentally undemocratic, how could one even think of the existence of genuine democracy there?

Democracy Is Only a Single Component of Our Lives

A formal political system addresses only certain aspects of material reality, and so democracy does not wholly determine our right to self-determination.

For instance, whatever freedom one feels under a democratic government on the street does not extend into the workplace. Minimum wages, maximum working hours, safety, and other regulatory conditions enacted by the state under pressure from the people might improve working conditions and prevent specific abuses. Nevertheless, employer and employee do not interact as two democratic equals. One has the role of boss, the other of a worker, and in a sense both pay with their lives for those roles—but another election will not change that.

Consequently, democracy exists only as a part of our total experience. Moreover, when accompanied by capitalism as an economic system, as no other economic system could make democracy work, we come face-to-face with another set of difficulties as well.

In reality, the ruling elite controls the processes of democracy with specific methods that are certainly undemocratic. These manipulations make so-called progressive legislation difficult because progressive actions are usually hostile to the capitalist class and will provoke particular responses in the economic sector.

Nevertheless, precisely this has happened time and time again in all of the leading liberal-democratic states.

Mere elections are just one aspect of the democratic process. Other tenets of democracy, such as relative equality and freedom, are frequently absent in ostensibly democratic countries. Moreover, in many such countries, democratic participation is less than 50 per cent at times, and it can be argued that the election of individuals instead of ideas even disrupts democracy.

This author hopes it was made clear that majority rule of any sort means the repression of individual liberties and the curtailment of direct action in favor of deferred decision-making. However, this does not necessarily lead to any desire for direct democracy either.

Theoretically, one should prefer unmediated relations between free individuals, the absence of any coercive or alienating forces in societies, and an unquestionable universal right to self-determination. Those beliefs can lead to many different visions of the world, but when genuinely held, they would never result in democracy. Even direct democracy demands surrender to the status quo that produces a hierarchy of groups above the individual, thus separating us from our desires and our desires from their unfettered realization through direct action.

POLITICAL PARTIES: CAMPAIGN FINANCING

In most liberal democracies, various political parties often espouse various opinions on many issues and, at least theoretically, provide voters with choices on a variety of matters. However, in standard voting practice, it can be safely assumed that the parties strive to converge on a median (center) stance. One could even argue that having several political parties makes little difference because, irrespective of their original political stand, in most cases all political parties will identify the same electoral issues and often adopt similar measures in response.[149]

In response to recurring problems and issues, modern political parties have embarked on sweeping reforms aimed at creating more transparent and democratic mechanisms. In the United States, many states feature primary elections and party caucuses that are better regulated. Therefore, most often, the winning candidate for the democratic or republican nomination emerges quite clearly and early in the process. As a result, national conventions ceased to be events in which parties would choose candidates and became mere formalities in which the nomination of a candidate is officially announced and celebrated.

In the United Kingdom, the Labor party began to select its party leader through an electoral college, which consisted of a third of the votes of party legislators, a third of the votes of members associated with the trade unions, and a third of the votes of individual party members. These changes were indeed welcome, as they seemed to address many of the flaws of the existing systems through more democratic and transparent mechanisms. However, the reforms have subjected modern political parties to a new series of issues.

One of the main problems is that modern political parties no longer fulfill the role of being independent organizations that feature their unique character and the ability to bring together contrasting social interests to the political process. Furthermore, the reforms have transformed the election of party leadership into a spectacle that is comparable to a general election. This election spectacle has allowed other forces—such as the media, interest groups, and business syndicates—to assume a more compelling function in the internal election process of a political party. The expanding clout of these influence peddlers has come at the cost of the control held by traditional party groupings. As a consequence, the capability of political parties to function efficiently in advancing policy ideas and leadership candidates has dropped substantially.

Around the early twentieth century, it was vital for political parties to develop a network that could rapidly recruit members, supporters, and election workers from among the voters. In this way, parties were strong organizations that could mobilize thousands of election workers during the election cycle. Failure to organize on a larger scale often meant losing the election. However, by the 1970s parties began to evolve into a catchall model. This development required party leaders to run a more direct campaign, and winning candidates had to appeal successfully to the electorate and the media.

Consequently, political finance became crucial to fund media coverage, opinion polls, focus groups, and other essential components of a political campaign. The change transformed political parties into more flexible organizations that could quickly evolve around new leadership while the significance of the party bureaucracy declined. More importantly, these transformations also coincided with dwindling levels of party membership.

Just as campaign financing became the most valuable resource in any election, the main political parties began losing their principal sources of revenue, such as party subscription fees and individual donations. Therefore, party leaders had to depend on generous donors to gain the necessary funds for election campaigns that have become increasingly expensive. This dependence has exposed political parties to the vast financial influence of wealthy individuals and corporate donors. As a consequence, influential contributors can decide on the plan of an entire political campaign or fund candidates who champion policies that are favorable to the donors' interests. This lobbying has even caused some critics to argue that party leaders are now becoming more focused on designing strategies to attract wealthy entities—the special-interest groups.

Accordingly, voters are tasked with electing representatives who are more inclined to serve the interests of their major donors than their constituents. This farce then has initiated a vicious cycle whereby the influence of big donors deters ordinary voters from making anything more than symbolic donations, because they feel that their leverage will always be little in comparison. This in turn forces party leaders to depend on such prominent and influential donors even more. The broad range of campaign-finance-related scandals that have vexed democratic elections in the past few decades have not helped to improve things either.

The idea that Western political parties are parts of the people at large is trustingly amateurish nonsense. Only some hopelessly liberal Germans still cling to this notion. In all places where English political systems have penetrated, the government lies in the hands of very few individuals who, with dictatorial arbitrariness, exert their power within the party based on their experience, superior will, and tactical skill.

What, then, is the relationship between people and party? What meaning can elections have in modern Western countries? Who does the electing? Whom or what does one elect?

According to the original English system, the people chose a party and not just representatives because the party leadership influenced them in any case. The parties were old and firmly established institutions whose business was to conduct the political affairs of the entire English nation. The individual Englishman realized the practicality of such a system, and from election to election he supported the party whose declared intentions corresponded most closely to his opinions and interests. He also realized the insignificance of the individual representative appointed rather arbitrarily by the party. Indeed, the phrase "fatuous electorate" fit the average representative better than the voting mass itself. It is significant that English workers have quite often voted for an employer who was nominated by one of the old parties rather than for a workman candidate.

In America, where the genuine Englishman no longer upholds the system, the practice now is for the political parties to deliver one set of promises to the people and another to the institution or organization that fills the party coffers. The first set is publicized; the second is kept unpublished.[150]

The vital question is, of course, how the job of politics is paid for in countries that have the parliamentary form of government. The naive democratic enthusiasts refuse to notice that in this day and age, when commercial interests lead all nations, the question of finances is crucial. Guileless believers tend to think in terms of representatives' or party bosses' salaries, but that is a trivial matter. Whereas the monarchs of the baroque period disposed of state income as they saw fit, modern political parties compile, administer, and allocate these funds. It is just a question of expediency as to if, when, or how a big donor decides to mollify the electorate, the representatives, or the party leadership. Such vote purchasing was prevalent where English parliamentarianism was adopted in the eighteenth century; however, in the course of time, this method has become superfluous. Tories, Laborites, Republicans, and Democrats from upper-class groups and having defined social attitudes are now the spokesmen for purely commercial interests; their sponsors differ only occasionally in the most advantageous form and moral rationale for a particular undertaking. Interest groups once divided have gradually merged under the aegis of the democratized parties.

IRRATIONAL VOTERS—INEFFICIENT SYSTEM

Free market–oriented economists have questioned the efficiency of democracy ever since Milton Friedman. They argue that voters are irrational, highly uninformed (especially about economics), and decidedly partial to the few issues about which they happen to possess some knowledge.

The masses are not adequately educated to comprehend and predict the needs and improvement of the community they belong to and, consequently, are unable to cast a vote to that effect. Nevertheless, given voting rights, an uneducated person would indeed cast a vote, which will more likely be wrong as affected by the personal charisma of the candidate or some other superficial reasons. An ordinary voter may also be enticed to cast a vote for the reason of financial help or some other petty promise.

Voter irrationality remains a vulnerable point of democratic government. The problem is not just the lack of information but also that voters poorly interpret and judge the information they do have. The fact is that the investment in learning about a particular issue is very high compared to the cost of not knowing that topic. The lack of information combined with false knowledge becomes an issue as long as otherwise ignorant people vote because of the good feeling it gives them. An additional observation is that as industrial activity in a democracy increases, so does people's demand for welfare. However, because of the median voter theorem, only a few people make the decisions in the country, and many may be unhappy with those decisions.[151] In this way, one can argue, democracies are inefficient.

Machiavelli put forth the idea that democracies will tend to cater to the whims of the people, who then follow fanciful ideas to gratify and amuse themselves, squander their wealth, and ignore looming danger to their rule until it is too late. He famously put forth a cyclical theory of government, according to which monarchies always decay into aristocracies; these then degenerate into democracies, which collapse into anarchy, then tyranny, and then back into monarchy again.[152] An example is a timeline of France before, during, and after the French Revolution until the last Bourbon monarch. The point here is that democracy will, and must, eventually decay; it will destroy itself.

OPPRESSION BY THE MAJORITY: MOB RULE

This author does not agree with statements claiming that there is competition among political parties to prevent oppression by the majority; due to the high cost associated with campaigning, there is, in reality, little competition among political parties (most of them being "conveniently similar") in democracies.

Freedom and democracy are very different concepts. In words (perhaps erroneously) attributed to Scottish writer Alexander Fraser Tytler, "A democracy cannot exist as a permanent form of government. It can only exist until a majority of voters discover that they can vote themselves largess out of the public treasury."[153] Democracy ultimately evolves into kleptocracy.

A majority bullying or ruling over a minority is just as wrong as a dictator, communist, or other doing so. Democracy is two lions and a lamb voting on what to have for lunch.

Yes, there is a difference between democracy and freedom. Freedom is not measured by the ability to vote but by the breadth of those things on which we do *not* vote.

However, it has also been observed that in countries where there are a unified minority and a divided majority, the political parties pamper minorities at the cost of majority for the certainty of votes. For instance, Muslims are considered a minority in India. However, it has often happened that political parties compromise majority Hindu interests (the Hindu community is deeply divided) for the Muslim minority.

US president James Madison devoted the whole of "Federalist No. 10" to a scathing critique of democracy. He offered that republics were a far better solution, saying, "Democracies have ever been spectacles of turbulence and contention; have ever been found incompatible with personal security or the rights of property, and have in general been as short in their lives as they have been violent in their deaths." Madison suggested that republics were superior to democracies because republics safeguarded against the tyranny of the majority, stating in "Federalist No. 10", "The same advantage that a republic has over a democracy, in controlling the effects of faction, is enjoyed by a large over a small republic."[154]

Plato's *Republic* depicts a critical look of democracy through the narration of Socrates: "Democracy, which is a charming form of government, full of variety and disorder, and dispensing a sort of equality to equals and unequaled alike." In his work, Plato lists five forms of government from best to worst. Assuming that *Republic* was intended to be a severe critique of the political thought in Athens, Plato argues that only *Kallipolis*, an aristocracy led by the unwilling philosopher-kings (the wisest men) is a just form of government.

The other types of government place too much focus on secondary virtues and degenerate into each other from best to worst, starting with timocracy, which overvalues honor. Then comes oligarchy, overestimating wealth, which is followed by democracy. In democracy, the oligarchs, or merchants, are unable to rule effectively, and the people take over. They elect someone who plays on their wishes by throwing lavish festivals and spending on entertainment. However, the government grants the people too much freedom, and the state degenerates into the fourth form, tyranny—or mob rule.[155]

Fisher Ames summed it up as follows: the "power of the people, if uncontroverted, is licentious and mobbish."[156]

ANXIETY, GREED, CIVIC INDIFFERENCE, AND THE PERILS OF DEMOCRATIC DICTATORSHIP

The peoples of the Western liberal democracies live daily with the awareness that their station in life is one of variability, potential, and fragility. The result is a society that is, by appearances, industrious but more deeply riven with anxiety. This condition is one of restlessness, or "inquietude—the inability to remain quiet, or still.

In the West, one can find the allegedly freest and most enlightened people placed in the happiest of circumstances that the world affords. However, it seems they are overtaken by anxiety all the time; they are not able to lose it even in their pleasures—they remain permanently serious, forbidding, grave, continuously in despair, and almost sad.

Some people in the West do not think of the ills they endure, while others forever agonize over advantages they do not possess. It is peculiar bewilderment to see with what feverish ardor the people of the West pursue their welfare, and to detect the vague dread on their minds that continually hounds them for fear that they should not have chosen the shortest path that may lead to some accomplishment.

Uncertainty and dissatisfaction are, of course, some of the consequences of democracy. Democracy's relentless drive to equalize our station in life, in fact, makes humans extraordinarily anxious and dissatisfied with their positions in society. Democracies, having rejected the arbitrary inheritance of birthright and rank of aristocratic ages, especially inflate the differences of attainment in the material realm. Citizens of democracies become obsessed with physical signs of success—not only what one should need to have a good and decent life but also how one's achievements compare to others. They become driven chiefly to measure their worth in monetary terms, and economics and business become the most significant activity of a democratic society. They have little patience for theory, demonstrating a preference for practice instead. They demand relevant and practical training in preference to studying in the theoretical areas of humanities, arts, literature, or even theoretical sciences.

Modern liberal democracy increasingly produces workers and consumers, not citizens. Their concerns and obsessions run almost entirely in the private realm, and these same private interests drive the only thoughts they might spare for public life: What is the government doing to pump up economic growth, how much of the earnings will it take away by taxes, is it supporting "upward mobility"?

In an ideal, supposedly real, democracy, independent citizens demand nothing less than active participation in self-rule. They know that freedom can be achieved and maintained only under conditions that permit a flourishing of civic self-government. However, it is precisely the modern liberal democracy, the *democratic illusion*, that inclines people to materialism and privatism, and that defeats real democracy.

Privatism is nothing else but the pursuit of one's interests and welfare to the exclusion of broader social issues or concerns; it is the restless pursuit of material things coupled with a disinterest in the everyday activities of self-government. The tendency toward privatism results in an apathetic and disconnected citizenry whose primary interests are security and comfort amid the unpredictability of their economic lives.

Ever in the past, "tyranny" implied a form of government imposed by force upon a people against their will. In a democracy, one can expect the rise of a kind, gentle, and liberal protective power that seeks to cushion citizens against all the dangers, harms, and risks of the world. Nevertheless, one can argue, this new specter of democratic dictatorship arises from the invitation and desires of the democratic citizenry itself. In fact, they call it democracy, not a dictatorship. However, this democratic dictatorship also comes with a high cost.

After successively having taken each member of the community in its powerful grasp (or "protective embrace"), the protective power then extends its arms over the entire community. It inundates society with a network of small but sophisticated rules and regulations, systematic and pedantic, which the most capable minds and the most energetic characters cannot penetrate or bypass. The will of man is not crushed but lessened, warped, and steered; people are seldom forced to act but are instead continually held back from acting. Such power does not destroy, but it prevents existence; it does not tyrannize, but it weakens, disables, and dazes a people until the nation is reduced to a herd of timid and obedient animals, of which the protective power is the shepherd.

In contrast to the idealistic and theoretical (or communistic) real democracy understood as a discipline of shared self-governance, the people of a democratic dictatorship, or modern liberal democracy, are altogether infantilized by their materialistic obsessions and public indifference. Rather than making them into adults, this form of democracy creates perpetual adolescents, in direct contrast to the utopian real democracy entertaining the idea of self-command and an inclination to obey laws made by oneself.

The answer to this democratic dilemma, then, is not simply "more democracy." Individual arrangements should be preferred in which active self-rule is more likely to occur—primarily local, small-scale settings in which people could develop a strong sense of investment and care in the outcome of decisions. Alas, as our economic interests have overwhelmed our civic commitments, our attention naturally forsakes narrower fields of significance in preference for global markets (beyond our control) and government (no longer in the name of the people).

Today, thought leaders and opinion makers are likely to call for even more democracy, more centralization, and more economic and financial globalization—all of which lead to the further strengthening of democratic dictatorship.

However, what the West needs today is not more democracy but rather the art of self-government closer to home.

LIBERTY (FREEDOM) VS. EQUALITY (DEMOCRACY)

It must be recognized that when we talk about freedom and equality, we are encountered by the relative and not by the absolute terms, by trends and tendencies rather than by pure abstractions.

"Freedom" in this discussion refers to the highest degree of independence possible, feasible, and reasonable under the given circumstances. Freedom is a means of safeguarding man's happiness and protecting his personality, and as such, it is an intermediary toward, and thus forms a part of, the common good. It is evident that freedom must not be readily or callously sacrificed under these conditions to the demands of absolute efficiency or efforts toward a maximum of material welfare. Man does not live by bread alone.

When we speak of equality, we do not refer to equity (which is justice). Two newly born babies are spiritually equal, but their physical and intellectual qualities (the latter, of course, is potency) are, from the moment of conception, unequal. The artificial establishment of equality is as little compatible with liberty as the enforcement of unjust laws of discrimination. (It is of course just to discriminate—within limits—between the blameless and the guilty, the adult and the infant, or the military and the civilian.) Whereas greed, pride, and arrogance are at the base of unjust discrimination, the driving motors of the egalitarian trends are envy, jealousy, and fear. Nature (meaning the absence of human intervention) is anything but egalitarian; if we want to establish a complete flatland, we have to blast the mountains away and fill the valleys; equality thus presupposes the continuous intervention by force, which is an act opposed to freedom.

Liberty and equality are, in essence, contradictory. Moreover, of all political labels, none has been more frequently misused than the terms "liberal" and "democratic."

A *liberal* is a person who is interested in having people enjoy the highest reasonable degree of liberty, ergo freedom—and this regardless of the type of government under which they are living. In this sense, this author is a liberal. It is true that the affinities between liberty and the various political forms are not identical; it is also true that while some political establishments show notable liberal trends, they harbor the danger of far-reaching enslavement nevertheless. The fact remains that the true liberal is not pledged to any particular constitution but would subordinate his choice to the desire to see himself and his fellow citizens enjoying a maximum of liberty.

If the true liberal thinks that a monarchy would grant greater freedom than a republic, he will choose the former; under certain circumstances, he might even prefer the actual restrictions of a military dictatorship to the potential (and inevitable) evolutions of democracy. Thus, any true liberal accepting Plato's evaluation of democracy (a reference to Plato's *Republic*) would reject this form of government because, according to this philosopher, it is fatally doomed to develop into tyranny.

In the United States, a "liberal" has come to mean a person who welcomes change and thus would not be averse to embracing or fostering even a totalitarian ideology. Accordingly, genuine liberals like to call themselves old-fashioned liberals in the United States, to distinguish themselves from leftist sympathizers. On the European continent, liberals have often engaged in the bona fide persecution of those kindred souls who preferred a different scope of views (sectarian liberals).

The philosophical and psychological motives for the liberal position show a great variety. The driving force in Christian liberalism will always be affection and generosity. We also know of liberalism derived from a fundamental philosophical nihilism, which declares that truth is either a mere prejudice, a piece of intellectual arrogance, or a sensory fraud, or that it is humanly unattainable—outside the reach of the faculty of reason. It is evident that such a philosophy of despair, which this author rejects, does not necessarily result in a liberal attitude; it may wind up in its opposite, and the type of its evolution thus depends merely on personal preference or temperament.

The Property is also a means to freedom. Since private capitalism tends to concentrate wealth in fewer and fewer hands, it is, from a genuinely liberal point of view, only a lesser evil in comparison with state capitalism (socialism).

The terms "democracy" and "democratic" are political. Democracy implies power and rule of the people. Mere affection for the lower classes is not "democracy" but "demophilia."

What are the precepts of democracy? It has only two postulates: (1) legal and political equality (franchise) for all and (2) self-government based on the rule of the majority of equals. Depending on the manner of exercise of this self-government—by the whole populace or by representatives—we speak of *direct* or *indirect* democracy.

It is also apparent that the delegates in an indirect democracy have the duty of repeating the views of the electorate; otherwise, we have a republic rather than a democracy.

Respect for minorities, freedom of speech, and the limitations imposed on the rule of majorities have nothing to do with democracy as such. These are liberal tenets; they may or may not be present in a democracy.

Those who want to avoid confusion and insist on clarity in political thinking by carefully trying to distinguish between liberalism and democracy and between democracy and republicanism are probably fighting a losing battle.

The vast majority of Americans and Britons, when talking about democracy, always include the liberal element in their concept of it—and this despite the fact that democracy and liberalism are concerned with two entirely different problems. While *democracy* examines *who* should be placed in ruling authority, *liberalism* deals with the *freedom of the individual*, regardless of who carries on the government.

Democracy *can* be profoundly illiberal; fascism and national and international socialism all repeatedly insisted that they be, in essence, democratic—a claim that must be viewed in a strictly philosophical and historical setting and that, in this light, becomes less hypocritical than observers in the West are wont to admit. The Soviet use of the "democratic" label was by no means just a shrewd political maneuver but a terminology already adopted by Lenin and continued by Stalin through the following decades. Indeed, the "dictatorship of the proletariat" (provided the proletariat form a majority) is more democratic than the US Constitution—in which, in contrast to the "sacred books" of communism, the word "democracy" never figures.

On the other hand, we can imagine an absolute ruler—an autocratic emperor, for instance—to be a thoroughgoing liberal, although it is evident that he cannot be democratic in the *political* sense. Just 51 percent of a nation can establish a totalitarian regime, suppress minorities, and remain democratic, whereas an old-time dictator might reserve to himself only very few prerogatives, all the while scrupulously refraining from interfering in the private sphere of the citizenry.

Democratic Uniformity Leading to Totalitarianism

Among the abundant sociopolitical problems, there are some recurrent psychological factors. One of them we might call man's subjection to the influence of two powerful, mutually antagonistic drives: the *uniformity* or *sameness* instinct and the *diversity* or *distinctness* sentiment. Whereas the sameness instinct belongs, in a certain sense, to the animal nature of man, the distinctness sentiment is purely human. Regrettably, our modern civilization decidedly favors the excessive development of the former. Democracy, mass production, militarism, nationalism, racism, and all tendencies toward simplification emphasize identity and uniformity. It is precisely from this process of leveling and assimilation that one can expect some of the worst menaces to liberty.

Democracy has no enthusiasm for the exceptional. Itself a monstrous product of wily brains and their envy, democracy can use as tools only mediocre people. Nevertheless, the ever-reviving new spirit, coming from below, always gets ahold of the masses so that they, driven by dark instincts, are looking again for the exceptional (leader).

As has already been pointed out, democracy and liberalism are two entirely different principles dealing with different problems. This author is convinced that purely democratic institutions must, sooner or later, destroy liberty, civilization, or both. The most profound cause that made the French Revolution so detrimental to liberty was its idea of equality. Liberty was the maxim of the middle class; equality of the lower classes. Because democracy cannot renounce its egalitarian heritage, the jealousy, envy, and insecurity of the masses tend to stimulate the egalitarian mania, the ever-increasing demands for social security, and the other forms of economic democracy. Equality is a slogan based on envy, and the inevitable result of all leveling tendencies is an antiliberal attitude.

The opposition against the hierarchies of birth—an opposition in itself often healthy—shifts smoothly against the acceptance of all superiority; the leveling then takes on intellectual character, and new steps have thus been made to the direction of totalitarianism. Once the social hierarchies have been destroyed and weakened beyond repair, the political sensibilities are placed squarely on the masses; yet the ordinary person's love for liberty and his readiness to make sacrifices for this ideal have not stood up too well to the test of history. No serious observer today doubts the petit bourgeois character of fascism, Nazism, and Bolshevism.

Conclusion

In conclusion, democracy has far-reaching problems indeed and falls far short of the freedom that it claims to represent. This fact is due to democracy's promotion of disaffection; its reduction of ideas to opinions; its demand for decontextualized decision-making; its basis of majority rule; its inevitability to reproduce itself as a system; its susceptibility to demagoguery, corruption, and special interests; its conflict with irrational voters, mob rule, and moral values; and its bringing about inefficiency, wealth disparity, and political instability.

These are not problems merely associated with the various ways in which democracy is implemented; they are endemic problems of the democratic process itself.

Further accusations against democracy can be summarized as follows:

1. Except for direct democracy, which is practical on a minute scale only, democracy, in reality, is not self-government.

2. The democratic process is emotional, at best irrational, and often antirational and anti-intellectual.

3. Democracy is corrupting in most of its implications and thus morally dangerous.

4. Democracy is wasteful for the "human material."

5. Democracy is historically closely bound up with sectarian liberalism, with the despair concerning the attainability of objective truth.

6. Because of its egalitarianism, democracy is inherently incompatible with liberty.

7. Democracy is the last step in the political evolution toward the modern form of tyranny.

8. Democracy prospers only with the support of strict semitotalitarian or totalitarian societies exercising control in the form of societal pressure.

9. Democracy is collectivistic and anti-individualistic.

Nevertheless, critical remarks on the failings of democracy can have a relative value only. Since governments are necessitated by fallen and sinful human nature, it is questionable whether there can be such a thing as an even *theoretically* perfect form of government—perfect not in its nature or structure, but in its relation to man. In this sense, any government can only be a crutch giving the very best help or service possible to imperfect humans—but no crutch, no government, will make humans perfect. Thus, the question as to whether one form of crutch can be better than another one remains, in a sense, a theoretical notion. We have to ask ourselves whether the shortcomings of democracy are more or fewer than those of other forms of government—for example, aristocracy.

It is evident that the common good cannot be summed up in a simple formula. It abounds with inner conflicts and choices. However, the present tendency of seeing the common good as the sum of material advantages for the community, regardless of the sacrifice of spiritual values, has to be rejected in its entirety.

Moreover, it is highly doubtful whether democracy, with its social controls and pressures, and its functioning with crowds, masses, and parties, can lead us to a rebirth of personal values.

Antoine de Rivarol once said, "The absolute ruler may be a Nero, but he is sometimes Titus or Marcus Aurelius; the people is often Nero, and never Marcus Aurelius."[157]

The democratic principle of "one man—one vote," viewed against the background of voting masses numbering millions, serves only to demonstrate the pathetic helplessness of the inarticulate individual, who functions at the polls as the smallest indivisible arithmetical unit. He acts in total anonymity, secrecy, and legal irresponsibility.

The articulate person, on the other hand, has as great or small a chance to exercise his political influence under *either* form of government. In a democratic society, therefore, the educated, intellectual, and persuasive thinker is depreciated on account of his ineffectuality.

Democracy's justification for existence is not the truth, efficacy, reason, study, or reflection, but volition, pure and simple. The democratic leader coming into power is always unprepared; it is the sudden or quick rise to fame and authority that upsets the mind and disturbs the careerist in a democracy.

Proudhon said it correctly: "Democracy is more expensive than monarchy; it is incompatible with liberty." He also added, "Money, always money, that is the nerve of democracy."[158]

The currently practiced so-called liberal democracy (a blatant misnomer for the reasons mentioned earlier) is only one of the many variations of a democratic system.

Ambassador Daniel Fried of the US State Department, a supporter of the democratic system, stated once in an interview, "I get nervous when people put labels in front of democracy. Sovereign democracy, managed democracy, people's democracy, socialist democracy, Aryan democracy, Islamic democracy - I am not a big fan of adjectives. Managed democracy does not sound like democracy. Sovereign democracy strikes me as meaningless."[159] Well then, let's not try to "improve" this system by attaching adjectives to it, as in the case of "guided democracy" or "liberal democracy" or *any other democracy.*

The globalized world exists on the level of platitude today. People are prevented from thinking; they are supposed to merely regurgitate what they have been taught, such as "imperialism is bad" and "democracy is good." Alas, ironically, most modern progressives embrace imperialism even while they condemn it and kill democracy even as they proclaim it. For instance, they condemn the British Empire as the epitome of imperialism and yet defend the globalism that the British Empire set in place. Similarly, they defend democracy as being "government by the people" and yet promote ever bigger government that is not only further and further away from the people but also increasingly unrepresentative of, and unresponsive to, their will.

Modern liberal democracy is a technologically supported oligarchy wherein the ruling class of elite enjoyers is in collusion with the unproductive majority of the tax users to exploit the productive minority of the taxpayers.

That is why this author, unlike the ruling elites and their political parties, rejects the very notion of democracy as "the ultimate political institution," beyond which any further political advancement is impossible.

8

A Critique of Modern Liberalism

The text below is an excerpt from Rev. Dr. Martin Luther King, Jr.'s "How My Mind Has Changed in the Last Decade," in which he discusses his intellectual evolution, culminating in his embrace of nonviolence. Regarding liberalism, Dr. King praises it for its commitment to the search for truth, its urging an open and probing mind, its refusal to abandon the best light of reason, and its philological–historical criticism of biblical literature. However, he criticizes it for its view on man while ignoring the role of sin concerning reason and the problem of collective evil in the post-Enlightenment era.

> Ten years ago I was just entering my senior year in theological seminary. Like most theological students, I was engaged in the exciting job of studying various theological theories. Having been raised in a rather strict fundamentalist tradition, I was occasionally shocked as my intellectual journey carried me through new and sometimes complex doctrinal lands. But despite the shock, the pilgrimage was always stimulating, and it gave me a new appreciation for objective appraisal and critical analysis. My early theological training did the same for me as the reading of Hume did for Kant: it knocked me out of my dogmatic slumber.
>
> At this stage of my development, I was a thoroughgoing liberal. Liberalism provided me with an intellectual satisfaction that I could

never find in fundamentalism. I became so enamored of the insights of liberalism that I almost fell into the trap of accepting uncritically everything that came under its name. I was absolutely convinced of the natural goodness of man and the natural power of human reason.

The basic change in my thinking came when I began to question some of the theories that had been associated with so-called liberal theology. Of course, there is one phase of liberalism that I hope to cherish always: its devotion to the search for truth, its insistence on an open and analytical mind, its refusal to abandon the best light of reason. Liberalism's contribution to the philological-historical criticism of biblical literature has been of immeasurable value and should be defended with religious and scientific passion.

It was mainly the liberal doctrine of man that I began to question. The more I observed the tragedies of history and man's shameful inclinations to choose the low road, the more I came to see the depth and strength of sin. My reading of the works of Reinhold Niebuhr made me aware of the complexity of human motives and the reality of sin on every level of man's existence. Moreover, I came to recognize the complexity of man's social involvement and the glaring realities of collective evil. I came to feel that liberalism had been all too sentimental concerning human nature and that it leaned toward a false idealism.

I also came to see that liberalism's superficial optimism concerning human nature caused it to overlook the fact that reason is darkened by sin. The more I thought about human nature, the more I saw how our tragic inclination for sin causes us to use our minds to rationalize our actions. Liberalism failed to see that reason by itself is little more than instrument to justify man's defensive ways of thinking. Reason, devoid of purifying power of faith, can never free itself from distortions and rationalizations.[160]

Yes, Dr. Martin Luther King said it all.

THE DEFINITION OF LIBERALISM

The term "liberalism" conveys two distinct positions in political philosophy, the first one a *proindividualist* theory of people and government, the second a *pro-statist*, or what is better termed a prosocialist, conception. Readers of political philosophy ought to be aware of the two schools of thought that reside (or are hidden, rather) under the same banner to avoid philosophical confusions that can be resolved by a clarification of terms. The great switch, or rather great trick, took place in the late nineteenth century—a switch that was the product of shifting the political ground toward socialist or social-democratic policies under the banner of liberal parties and politics.

Etymologically, the former proindividualist theory is the sounder description, since "liberalism" is derived from the word "liberty"—that is, freedom and toleration rather than notions of justice and intervention that were taken on board in the twentieth century.

The second pro-statist socialistic connotation pervades modern thinking so much so that it is hard to separate its notions from the previous original meanings without reclassifying one or the other. The former is often referred to as "classical liberalism," and the latter as "social-democratic liberalism," which is a rather bewildering mouthful; "modern liberalism" is a more straightforward term to master and shall be used here unless the emphasis is laid upon the socialist leanings of such modern liberals.

In the broadest and presently popularly accepted term, the "modern liberal" recognizes the rights of the person and the rights to entitlements, such as health care and education. The two positions are not entirely agreeable philosophically, however, for they produce a large number of inconsistencies and contradictions that can be reconciled only by artificially expanding the definition of freedom to include the freedom to succeed rather than the freedom to try. This intellectual stretching sometimes generates difficult and perhaps insurmountable problems for those who seek to merge the classical and modern doctrines. For those who try, the traditional emphasis on toleration, plurality, and justice accentuate their work; they disagree on their interpretation of tolerance, public and private duties, and the perceived need for opportunities to be created or not.

Some modern liberals, however, do try to remove themselves from classical liberalism and therefore become more like social democrats. They turn into humanitarians of a socialist leaning who assert the primacy of minorities and underprivileged individuals to engage freely in the democratic processes and political dialogues, or whose emphasis on equality demands an active and interventionist state that classical liberals would reject.

A modern liberal, or social-democratic liberal, claims that justice is the essential motif of liberalism and that the state must ensure a just and fair opportunity for all to compete and flourish in a civil society. That may require active government intervention in some areas—areas that classical liberals would reject as being inadmissible in a free society. This position emanates from Aristotle's ethical argument that for a person to pursue the good life, he requires a certain standard of living.[161] Since poverty is not conducive to pursuing the contemplative life, many modern liberals are attracted to redistributive or welfare policies. John Stuart Mill's liberalism can serve as an example of such fairness in the creation of equality of opportunity.

Classical liberals, however, who argue that people are neither born equal nor can be made equal, criticize the modern liberal's emphasis on equality. Talents and motivation are distributed unequally across the population, and attempts to force the same status on different people will reduce the ability (or freedom) of the most talented to act and strive for their advancement. Similarly, the modern liberal's criticism of inherited wealth is scolded as being misplaced; although the policy intends to ensure an equal start for all, not all parents' gifts to their children are monetary by nature. Indeed, some, following Andrew Carnegie's self-help philosophy, may contend that financial inheritances can indeed be counterproductive, fostering habits of dependency.

Both classical and modern liberals may refer to the theory of a social contract to justify either their emphasis on the free realm of the individual or the fostering of those conditions that liberals, in general, deemed necessary for human flourishing.

Classical liberals derive their theory of the social contract initially from Thomas Hobbes's model (in *Leviathan*), in which individuals in a state of nature would come together to form a society.[162] Liberals of both variations have never really believed such a contract ever took place but still envision social criteria they think the contract *should* include. Hobbes leaned toward a more authoritarian version of the contract, in which individuals give up all political rights (except that of self-preservation, which he saw as a natural and inalienable right) to a sovereign political body whose primary duty is to ensure the peace. John Locke leaned toward a more limited government (but one that could justly take the alienable life of an aggressor). Rousseau sought a thoroughly democratic vision of the social contract, and more recently John Rawls has entertained what rights and entitlements a social contract committee would assign its members if they had no knowledge, and hence prejudices, of each other.[163]

Both classical and modern liberals agree that the government has a strict duty concerning impartiality and hence is to treat people equally, and that it should also be neutral in its evaluation of what the "good life" is. Nonliberals, who claim that the assumed neutrality is, in fact, a reflection of a particular vision of human nature or progress, criticize this neutrality. Although critics disagree what that vision may entail, their claim prompts liberals to justify the underlying assumption that promotes them to accept such issues as equal treatment by the law and by the state, liberty to pursue one's life as one sees fit, the right to private property, and so on.

Nonetheless, widespread liberalism accepts and emphasizes that people ought to be tolerant toward their fellow men and women. The contemporary importance of toleration stems from the Renaissance and post-Reformation reactions to the division in the church and the ensuing persecutions against heterodoxy. Freedom of religious beliefs extends to other realms of human activity that do not directly affect neighbors—for example, sexual preference or romantic activities, the consumption of narcotics, and the perusal of pornography.

Moreover, what is philosophically more significant is that the liberal doctrine of toleration permits the acceptance of errors—that in pursuing the good ethical life and hence the useful political life, people may make mistakes and should be allowed to learn and adapt as they see fit. Alternatively, people have a right to live in ignorance or to pursue knowledge as they think best. This doctrine of toleration is held in common with political conservatives, who are somewhat more pessimistic and skeptical of our abilities than most liberals.

Classical and modern liberals do unite in expressing skepticism toward experts knowing what is in the best interest of others. Thus, liberals reject any interference in people's lives as unjustifiable and, from the utilitarian point of view, counterproductive. Life, for the liberal, should be led from the inside (self-oriented) rather than from outside (other-imposed)—but modern liberals add that individuals should have the *resources* to ensure they can live the good life as they see fit. The classical liberal retort is, who will provide those resources, and at what age should people be deemed incapable of learning or striving by themselves?

Despite such differences over policy, liberals of both the classical and social-democratic strain hold a predominantly optimistic view of human nature. That position is derived from Locke's psychological theory as written in "An Essay Concerning Human Understanding," according to which people are born without innate traits, meaning that their environment, upbringing, and experiences must fashion them.[164] For classical liberals, this implies a thorough rejection of inherited elitism and supposedly natural political hierarchies in which power resided with dynasties. For modern liberals, this means the potential of forging appropriate conditions for any individual to gain a proper education and opportunities.

Liberals applaud those institutions that reason sustains as being conducive to human freedoms: classical liberals emphasizing those institutions that protect the "negative freedoms" (rights against aggression and theft) and social-democratic liberals, or modern liberals, the "positive freedoms" (rights to a certain standard of living). If an institution is lacking according to critical and rational analysis—failing to uphold a particular liberal value—then it is to be reorganized for the empowerment of humanity.

At this juncture, liberals also divide between deontological (Rawls) and utilitarian theorists (Mill). Most classical liberals ascribe to a general form of utilitarianism, in which social institutions are to be reorganized along the lines of benefiting the highest number. This utility attracts criticism from conservatives and deontologists: According to what ends? According to whose analysis? Serving which people?

Deontologists are not precluded from supporting liberalism (Immanuel Kant is the most influential thinker in that regard). They hold that the good society, hence political institutions, should generate those rules that are right in themselves, independent of the particular presumed ends we are seeking (for example, happiness).

Modern liberals lean toward an interventionist government and place more emphasis on the ability of the state to produce the right political sphere for humanity; they emphasize reform projects more than classical liberals or conservatives.

Peace, to choose a typical example, could be brought to belligerent peoples or natives if only they admit to the "reasonable proposals" of the liberal creed—that is, they should give up their local prejudices and superstitions and submit to the cosmopolitanism of liberal toleration and peace. Some liberals want to secure peace through the provision of a higher standard of living affected by redistribution policies from rich countries to poor. Others promote the free market as a necessary condition for the growth of the so-called soft morals of commerce. Still others emphasize the need for dialogue and mutual understanding through multicultural educational programs. The modern liberals argue that the world community, through international bodies such as the United Nations, should implement these kinds of programs rather than their being implemented unilaterally, which could arouse complaints against imperialist motives.

However, once the classical or modern liberal framework of action is created, the state and political institutions ought to remain ethically neutral and impartial. The state is to be kept from imposing itself on or subsidizing any belief system, cultural rites, and forms of behavior or consumption (so long as they do not interfere with the lives of others). The similarities of these concepts with the Russian liberal-conservative school are unmistakable, although, as always, the West criticizes the teachings of the Russian school as being naive.

The liberal searches for the best form of government that will permit the individual to pursue life as he or she desires within a neutral framework, and not surprisingly, it is this neutral framework that critics challenge concerning the liberal ideal.

Modern Liberalism and the False Idea of Liberty

Liberalism is also a revolt against any constraints reality might place on humans. It is the disintegrating atmosphere of liberalism that spreads moral disease among nations and ruins the nations it dominates. This destructive liberalism is not to be conceived of as being the prerogative of any one political party; it exercises its baneful influence on all parties, blurring the distinctions between them. It has also created the familiar figure of the professional party functionary.

One of the principles of liberalism is to have no fixed principle and to contend that this is in itself a principle. Modern liberalism is the ideology of Western self-destruction; it is the self-inflicted ruination of the West's prospects and interests.

Anyone carefully examining liberalism would have discovered that people in liberal countries do not enjoy political freedom but, on the contrary, are carefully shepherded by a ruling elite. What this ruling elite means by "liberty" is freedom and scope for *their* intrigues; for all others, it is the freedom to starve. They attain this liberty for the elite by using the parliamentary system that secures the elite enjoyers' absolute power under cover of a constitution and the so-called representation of the people. Such is the specious mask that liberalism wears when it shouts "liberty."

Modern liberalism in the West and around the world is suspect today. This suspicion is directed against a system of nets and trappings set throughout the world, in whose toils Eastern Europe, just to name one particular area, believes itself to be caught.

All the nonsense about Western ideals leads us to the pretense of the Eastern European transition plan that underlies the exploitation of the peaceful political transition. There is no point in contemplating whether the scheme was thought out and agreed on beforehand, because it was undoubtedly existent and effectual. The liberals had left themselves every liberty of action, but when the opportune moment arrived, they speedily reached a practical understanding, as the policy of encirclement and the cordial cooperation of the Western powers abundantly prove. The plan depended on the liberal; it depended on a human, psychological, almost physiological affinity that was quickly translated into political compatibility: a coincidence of impulse and a coincidence of aim.

The liberal dichotomy between the theory of freedom, tolerance, and social contract on the one hand and jealousy, hate, and irresponsibility on the other epitomizes the Janus-faced nature of liberalism.

The liberal is stimulated by the ambition of the aspiring great man who does not want to take second place, the anxiety of the benevolent destroyer, the calamitous powerbroker. The jealousy of power reveals no less than this passion for constitutions that make power dependent on carefully controlled elections, this craze for parliaments to take control of the state, this mania for republics in which the political parties divide the power, the party leaders draw the pay, and the electors enjoy the party patronage.

This rise to power of the modern liberal, the man who delegates responsibility and introduces disintegration just where cohesion is most needed, becomes possible only where the instinct of conservatism has become weakened.

The modern liberal professes to do all he does for the sake of the people but deliberately destroys the sense of community that should bind outstanding individuals to the people from which they spring. The people should naturally regard the brilliant person not as an enemy but as a representative sample of themselves.

Modern liberalism is the ideology of upstart power grabbers who have insinuated themselves between the people and their great men. Liberals feel like isolated individuals, responsible to nobody. They do not share a nation's traditions; they are indifferent to its past and have no ambition for its future. They seek only their own advantage in the present. Their dream is the "great international" having global power in one world in which the differences among peoples, languages, races, and cultures will disappear. To achieve this, they are willing to draw on nationalism, pacifism or militarism, according to the expediency of the moment.

It was this denationalized, irresponsible liberalism that let loose the horrors of World War I, facilitated World War II, and was instrumental in devising every war the West has initiated or instigated since then. It came up with a watchword, "liberty," to entrap the imaginations of people and nations. Moreover, the liberal has flourished in all periods.

The disinterestedness of the conservative cherishes the sacredness of a cause that shall not die with him. While conservatism is rooted in the strength of man, liberalism battens on his weakness. The liberal's conjuring trick consists in turning others' weaknesses to his account, living at other people's expense, and concealing his art with patter about ideas. This chicanery is the accusation against "the liberal," be it called "modern liberal," "social-democratic liberal" or "neoliberal." He has always been a source of the greatest peril.

Liberalism has undermined civilizations, destroyed religions, and ruined nations. Nations, who had already ceased to feel themselves a people, who had lost the state instinct and, yes, the social instinct, gave liberalism its opportunity. The masses allowed a false upper crust to form on the surface of the nation—not the old natural aristocracy whose example had created the state, but a secondary stratum: an upper-middle-class intelligentsia. This is a dangerous, irresponsible, ruthless, intermediate stratum that first thrust itself in between, and then entirely replaced, the upper class. The outcome was the rule of a clique united only by self-interest who liked to style itself the cream of the population to conceal the fact that it consisted of *nouveaux riches* and upstarts. This upper-crust intelligentsia did not care whether its arrogance and new-won privilege were decked out with the conceptions of feudal or radical ideology, though it preferred a delicate suggestion of aristocracy. However, its members found it most useful and fruitful to style themselves as democrats.

Liberalism already caused the ruin of ancient Greece; the rise of the liberal preceded the decay of Hellenic freedom. He was begotten of Greek enlightenment. From the philosophers' theory of the atom, the sophist drew the inference of the individual.

Protagoras, the Sophist, was the founder of individualism and also the apostle of relativity. He proclaimed that "opposite propositions are equally true."[165] Nothing immoral was intended; he meant there was no *general* but only the *particular* truth—according to the standpoint of the perceiver. However, what happens when the same person has two standpoints?

Protagoras also proclaimed that rhetoric could make the weaker cause victorious. Still, nothing immoral was intended; he meant that the better cause was sometimes the weaker one and should then be boosted to victory. However, soon the practice of using rhetoric to make the worse cause victorious became more typical. Not surprisingly, then, the sophists were the first Greek philosophers to accept pay and were indeed the most highly paid. This materialist outlook leads, of course, to a materialist mode of thought; this is very human but true. All this was hailed as progress—but it spelled decay.

So the same course of progressing decay continues: the first generation of the disciples of reason—the apostles of enlightenment, the heralds of progress—are usually great idealists and high-principled people who are sure of the importance of their discoveries and the benefit these confer upon humanity.

However, the strange and unholy connection that exists between materialist philosophy and nihilist interpretation betrays itself no later than during the second generation of these idealists. As at the touch of a conjuror's wand, the scientific theory of the atom reduces society to atoms.

Liberalism had its roots where the individual shook off the conventions of the Middle Ages. The liberal afterward claimed to have freed himself from them—but this freedom of his was merely an illusion.

The conventions of the Middle Ages, of both church and state, were significant achievements; they prevented the disintegration of the ancient world for ten centuries. They were mighty accomplishments, and the people to whom these deeds were due were rooted in these conventions. No one spoke of liberty, because everyone creatively possessed it.

A disintegrating generation took over this great inheritance. Humanism brought the consciousness of human dignity; the Renaissance imposed moderation, form, and a classic attitude on individualism. The people of the Renaissance drew from the literature of classical antiquity the forces they required as models. In the confident assurance that life must have a firm foundation if it is not to fall asunder, the age of the Renaissance made a last desperate effort at linking up with the past.

However, individuals can retain their originality and creative power only as long as their nations are also creative. Alas, the nations of the post-Renaissance era were now developing a society that was divorced from the people. Monumental art was yielding its place to mere decoration; preceding centuries had achieved results in chemistry, physics, mathematics, astronomy, and even sociology, but they made scientific research an end in itself without producing the insight to see that all the discoveries were only partial glimpses into nature. It was like turning an imaginary searchlight onto an imagined truth. This blindness they presumptuously called "enlightenment."

Proud of his reason, the man of enlightenment boasted the right to let go all conventions. As he did so, regardless of the consequences, he also committed life to a reason left to its own devices.

Among the discoveries made by reason, the most fateful was that man is not free. Although it might well have seemed to be the most obviously reasonable and logical thing to protect this unfree man with state conventions, the liberals demanded instead that man, who was biologically unfree, should have complete individual and political freedom. This curious logic showed a deliberate intention to mislead; it bore, in fact, all the characteristically hypocritical signs of liberalism, which is prepared to endorse any contradiction and to look on at any destruction with which the magic word "liberty" can by any means be associated.

Liberalism, therefore, began with a false idea of liberty, which was misunderstood by it from the start. Liberalism also ends with a false idea of liberty, which it employs no longer to defend liberty but to pursue advantages. All human error lies here— and many a crime.

THE AGE OF REASON: THE BIRTH OF PHILOSOPHICAL LIBERALISM

The age of reason was a Western affair—an affair more particularly of England and France.

The English have always talked of freedom, and they have always sought their own freedom—at the expense of everyone else's. The capability to change the viewpoint according to whose aims were in question (one's own or another's) and the firm intention always to pursue what was expedient ultimately led the English to develop a most rational logic of their own. The Renaissance introduced Machiavellianism into English thought; Machiavelli had given passionate expression to a despairing, almost hopeless, love of country—nationalism. The practical Englishman wanted to make sure that the means were available for putting his doctrines into practice.

To the question regarding what freedom was, Hobbes answered, "Freedom is power." Here spoke the practical politician, the positivist, and the loyalist. Hobbes guarded England against the dangers of the age of reason. From this point forward, the English thinker could safely indulge in liberal thought. To the question regarding what power was, the Englishman, who is a blend of the liberal moralist and the political immoralist, answered comfortingly, "Power is right."

Power is so undoubtedly just, proper, and right that it can take precedence of right itself, without right's ceasing to be right. Hence the Englishman was free to assert his right and trample on everyone else's; the logic of this has always been clear to every English mind. Right or wrong, it was ultimately always a question of the welfare of the country, for whose sake its people required political power.[166]

If a link was missing in this chain, it was supplied by the English method of concentrating thought on utility. Utilitarianism became the English national philosophy. Progress, which was the favorite modern conception of the rationalist, could find its apparent justification in utility. Progress became particularly valuable when it marched with the Englishman's advantage and the disadvantage of the foreigner. From the standpoint of utility, every opportunistic thought can be justified, and every lack of principle can be condoned.

Not the least virtue of the English party system lay in the fact that it permitted individuals or groups to shift from one standpoint to another whenever it seemed momentarily useful or necessary, without an overt sacrifice of a principle that was throughout stoutly maintained. Parliamentarianism, which the party system accommodated itself to with a power of adaptation that has never yet failed in England, would seem to have been invented solely to make it constitutionally possible to temper drastic measures with liberal ambiguities.

English liberalism started out by being clean, honest, and law-abiding. An

English freethinker once summed up the very spirit of England in the formula "Freedom, Truth, and Health."[167] (The ambiguous concepts of equality and fraternity would never have occurred to an Englishman.) However, English liberalism, in fact, lived up to these three watchwords only to a limited degree. The practical English and Anglo-American minds were hard and pitiless. England and America have tolerated many encroachments on freedom; they tolerate truth so long as society is not exposed. They are the lands of the pauper and ignore poverty and need so long as these things affect only that stratum of the population that constitutes no danger to the elite.

The English liberals were credulous, well-meaning fellows who liked to cultivate illusions. When Jeremy Bentham worked out his utilitarianism, he genuinely deluded himself into believing that self-interest, if only rightly understood, would contribute to the welfare of all. A certain sloppiness pervades liberal thought: everything is good if it can be dubbed "free," and twice as good if it can be called "useful" as well. Bentham interpreted the psychology of English utilitarianism fairly accurately when he explained duty, conscience, and unselfishness based on a person's self-interest and claimed for his doctrine that it aimed at "regulating egotism." He followed the Epicurean tendency, which has always coexisted with the stoic.[168] This philosophy supplied a self-confidence, to say nothing about arrogance, which became the no-nonsense virtue of the nation. Every English politician took an almost sadistic pleasure in "regulating" English interests throughout the world. This philosophy also supplied a sense of strength—cold, calm and tenacious—taking itself for granted, mindful always of its limitations but, by its concentration on the useful, potent to protect the nation against injury and effeminacy.

The English did not notice how poorly they gave themselves away with such exclusive devotion to utilitarianism. An absolute sense of justice still survived among them, however, which on occasion even looked to the cause and not to the advantage.

During the American War of Independence, for example, Edmund Burke dared to speak in the British Parliament for the Americans. However, Burke was a conservative, a conservative liberal, who became widely regarded as the philosophical founder of modern conservatism.

It must also be pointed out that, as another example, the American and English liberals, who condemned the Peace Treaties of Versailles, St. Germain, and Trianon following World War I, could not be taken seriously, since they could not express themselves in anything more than words. Asquith, the onetime Liberal prime minister of Britain, bemoaned after the war how the peace turned out and that his party had not known in time the line it would take so that they might have worked toward another result.[169] Nevertheless, this liberal eloquence proved nothing without prompting any serious effort to alter the outcome instead of quietly acquiescing to it. It was only content to register emotion and accept advantage. It was just like the US Senate's refusal to ratify the same treaties after signing them in France and then holding on to them without ratification—liberal duplicity based on utilitarian power camouflaged as progressive justice.

French rationalism had deeper roots than *English utilitarianism*. It sprang from the reasoning of the Middle Ages and the casuist philosophy of the Paris scholastics with their doctrine of a dual theological and philosophical truth. As a philosophy of life, it sprang from the Renaissance. Moreover, as long as the French skeptic clung to the cultured and elegant grace of Michel de Montaigne and the harmlessness of François Rabelais, French thought continued to be on the move and make its observations on a superficial plane of wit and wisdom. Humanism brought with it, however, a misunderstanding that proved fateful in the revolution: the dignity of the individual merged with the rights of the citizen. Prussian–German rationalism subsequently had much difficulty in getting back to the line that leads from Luther to Kant and reinstating duty in the consciousness of man.

The Renaissance throbbed with passion; mighty men lived their lives to the full, and their policies were determined by the instincts to which they gave rein. Machiavelli wrote his excellent and ruthless textbook; he was a villain of sheer patriotism, a man full of ambition for Italy, and a thoroughly illiberal man in his fearless honesty.

At this point, weariness overtook humanity. The Renaissance had revealed man as a microcosm; the age of reason showed him as mere matter. Later, it was discovered that man is not free and the notably illogical conclusion deduced that he must, therefore, be liberated and made *politically* free. It was also found that whatever this unfree man does, he does it in his own self-interest. Voltaire expressly declared that self-interest "is the means to self-preservation" and further said, "It is necessary, it is dear to us, it gives us pleasure, and we must take pains to conceal it."[170] So the liberal loyally adhered to this last injunction. Wherever he had good reason to conceal things, he has sought refuge in the following principle: to understand everything is to forget everything.

The Englishman defined the dignity of man as self-reliance; the Frenchman as self-complacency. By a practical application of liberal principles, the Englishman obtained modest but predictable advantages, reaping them surely and silently. The livelier and more passionate Frenchman, however, was not content to do the same; he wanted to boast about them too. France was to be the nation to give the new ideas their historic importance. Montesquieu and Voltaire, therefore, took the conceptions of the English rationalists very seriously, and on their return from London, they trumpeted them aloud for the entire world to hear that France might be the center of people's talk and all eyes might turn to Paris.

The rationalist aristocracy finally fell victim to their age of reason. The nobility and the clergy, the court and the salons, and finally the king himself, were the sacrifice. These circles, which had long since exhausted all the delights that life can give, discovered the "simple man," and they acclaimed him as better than themselves. They took up populist economics, financial speculation, and economic studies; freedom of the corn trade was introduced, and freedom of the press was granted. The Third Estate (i.e., the commons or middle class) was flattered, though it had neither sought this treatment nor done anything to deserve it. Reason evidently never wrought more havoc than in the rationalist circles of France. Everything the rationalists did was done because it was *liberal*—but it all recoiled on them in the end. Alas, in the name of the rights of man and the revolutionary state, they were persecuted, dispossessed, and exterminated by the Third Estate, whom they had preached the outlandish claim to the rights of man.

From the Duke of La Rochefoucauld to the Duke of Saint-Simon, only a negligible number of aristocrats continued to lead along progressive lines of thought, and most of them lapsed into anonymity. The proud aristocracy of France grew effeminate and fatuous in real rococo style; they gave up their knightly virtues to become delicate, ladylike, and artificial. This degeneracy was the aristocracy, which ran away from the Prussians after the shameful defeat at the Battle of Rossbach in 1757.[171]

France had indeed reached the point when she needed a revolution to provide her with new human resources. A new national feeling arose, bestial and cruel. The liberated people ran about the streets seizing everyone who did not acquiesce to get also liberated and simply compelled them to be free, in accordance to the will of the people, who of course could not err. As one of the cruel ironies of history, the first victims of the sovereign people had to be the Girondists, the liberals of the revolution who had dreamed of establishing the Republic of Virtue.

To the seventeen articles proclaiming the rights of man and of the citizen, which had been copied from the US Constitution, there stood in addition to the oddly-interpreted "freedom" a new clause not easily misunderstood—a clause regarding the sanctity of property.[172] This notion is a conception that the Frenchman has never surrendered and that can never become out of date in France. It did not relate so much to the inherited as to the acquired possessions. It referred to the property of the newly rich, who in the sacred names of liberty, equality, and fraternity had divided the wealth of France among them. The security of this newly acquired property was the sole preoccupation of *French liberalism*.

The French have never honestly confessed their attachment to possession, as the Englishmen have admitted theirs to utility. As a nation, they are the incarnation of the pettiest lust for possession, but they need to clothe it with fairer words. For a while, "virtue" sufficed them; but finally they decided on "liberty." In the "Manifesto to all States and Nations, Dec. 29th, 1791," Condorcet wrote, "The French nation will never undertake any war, with a view of making conquests, and will never employ its force against the liberty of any nation, for such is the text of the constitution; such is the sacred vow by which we have connected our happiness with the happiness of all nations, and we will be true to it."[173] Many others have used similar phrases during the world wars, the subsequent French colonial wars in the twentieth century, and ever since.

Napoleon, however, instead of *liberté*, *egalité*, and *fraternité*, gave the French nation "*la gloire*." He gave his Frenchmen Europe and the wealth of other lands, and the intoxicated nation followed him, chanting the popular slogan "The people cannot err." When the intoxicating dream was over, a sobered nation welcomed its Bourbons back again. Then they applauded the House of Orleans, and lastly the Napoleons. For a while, it seemed as if *le roi bourgeois* was the monarchy they needed—the kindly man with his round hat and under the umbrella of *le juste milieu*, who counted lawyers and bankers among his friends. Liberalism, however, had still to be reckoned with; the political battles of the next decade revolved around the electoral law, which was to secure the middle class the right to vote and the right to be elected. So the liberal employed the years of the restoration to stabilize his power. Then he engineered the July Revolution in 1830, the February Revolution in 1848, and the Third Republic in 1870. The aim was always the same: to secure political power for an ever-widening circle. To achieve this goal, the liberal allied himself with clericals and became a nationalist. He never lacked any *raison oratoire* to conceal the real motives of French politics; Gambetta, Boulanger, Clemenceau—they all employed the same liberal rhetoric, resonant with "justice" and "freedom," and concealing all the while the one thought of *advantage*. Raymond Poincaré used the same phrases; the man with the empty face of a grand bourgeois who was one of the most important political players responsible for the outbreak of the First World War fled from its dangers to Bordeaux and afterward played the role of the imperturbable. He used these phrases, knowing that he lied.

Rational Liberalism and the Death of Nations

For the liberals, the end justifies the means, and ideals serve as a means to an end. Thus, liberalism in Western Europe is one thing; liberalism in Eastern Europe another.

When two thinkers of the West meet, they both know what liberalism is: a political trick—the trick with which the upstart society of the Third Estate was able to swindle the tiresome leftover plebs out of the pledges of 1789. The thinkers know what "liberty" means; it is the most alluring of the three slogans with which the defenders of the rights of man lured the deluded masses away from their threatening barricades and shepherded them to the innocuous ballot box.

When the Eastern Europeans and Russians decry themselves as "backward," they shortsightedly overlook a fact that gives them their strength, their advantage, and their future. The illusion that used to pervade Eastern Europe was that first they must copy and introduce all new Western ideas and institutions before they could share on equal terms in civilized history and be accepted in the family of liberalized nations. So at one time or another in their past, they also set foot on the path of liberalism—not to their advantage, not to their credit, but to their doom, as the consequences of their repeated trials and failures, humiliation, and disappointment have shown. Moreover, the Westerners triumph again and again.

Instead of progress, Eastern Europe has always reaped only ruin. Could the Easterners ask, simpletons as they are, for a more terrible proof that the ways of liberalism are not theirs? They have tried to take the path, logically, inevitably, in harmony, as they imagined, with the general trend of Western civilization. It seemed the only path for a civilized person of the twentieth century or even of the twenty-first. Eastern European socialists and liberals alike turned their eyes toward the West, ignoring that socialism and liberalism are mutually exclusive, even becoming allies in united opposition to their newly independent national state. They have been straying among the errors, illusions, and fallacies of liberal democracy, denying the possibility that it might be their nation's death warrant, with their being the signatories.

The opportunity of choosing another path was open to them: the path of national conservatism, inspired by the national spirit based on their identity, values, and all the living and vital institutions of their past.

However, conservatism keeps losing the battles against transitions, transformations, and revolutions, becoming more and more helpless while making more and more concessions to liberalism. Bismarck had already observed that the conservative party in Germany was beginning to lack an inner raison d'être and commended the concept of conservative progress to it. Nevertheless, the continuing and rudderless drift of the conservatives led to a makeshift that strove to unite another two of the incompatibles: liberalism and conservatism. Today we see this development in the Republican Party of the United States or the Christian democratic parties of Europe.

The last century in America was the era of liberalism; however, it was not the loud-voiced national liberalism that made itself so vocal after the founding of the United States of America, but rather freethinking rational liberalism. It was this rational liberalism that undermined all political parties and principles and destroyed the unity of America. Its vices were opportunism and lack of principle; its peculiarity was that its adherents always fell victim to their liberalism because their logic ended in theory and was never, could not have been, adequately translated into practice. Then they gazed in mute amazement at the broken crockery round their feet and fled the scene as betrayers betrayed. Such was American liberalism, and its greatest crime was, and still is, its crass stupidity. Stupidity passed into crime when liberalism ceased to be the toy of idealists, students, and worthy Democrats, as it had been until the First World War, and fell into the hands of economists, publicists, and conservative but helpless Republicans.

The American and European peoples, indeed all the people of the West, are still to inquire, what has become of the ideas of 1789—those of liberty, equality, and fraternity? These were the three principles promulgated by the republicans, or French revolutionists, which were profound absurdities.

Fraternity? President Wilson's "Fourteen Points," the League of Nations, the Treaties of Versailles, Trianon, St. Germain, Sèvres, Neuilly, the Yalta, and Potsdam, and the Dayton Agreements, among many other items, have already devastated the brotherhood of nations beyond repair. Regardless, how can political freedom be granted to humanity when no man *can* be free?

Equality? The doctrine of equality is not merely equality in the eye of the law but rather *absolute* equality. The end of the Cold War would have brought us at least one benefit if it had convinced the peoples of both East and West that the equality of each nation is assured. As it is, Hungarians, for one, can undoubtedly and justifiably feel that, for purely political reasons after their national-conservative party won a two-thirds majority in parliament in 2010, their country has not been treated as equal by the left-liberal European Union. Has the West treated the newly independent Russians as such after the collapse of the Soviet Union? Reflecting on the assertion that "all men are created equal," Fisher Ames quipped, "But differ greatly in the sequel!"[174]

Liberty? There is no need to define the term; the magic of the word suffices. There is no political party in any of the countries boasting enlightenment that does not shrewdly dub itself liberal. In France, the radical, clerical, and socialist are liberal. Laborite, Tory, and Liberal are all liberal in Britain; in the United States, both the main political parties are liberal; in Germany, all mainstream parties in the Bundestag are liberal. In all the parties, the simple-minded are liberal in good faith, the schemers with evil intent. No political party, however, can forgo the advantage of calling itself liberal; while their idea of freedom does not necessarily preclude intolerance, persecution, or subjugation of others, it conveniently coexists with the arbitrary changing of territory and the strangulation of states. The liberal in Eastern Europe should look on with embarrassment and indignation when he sees the old, lofty ideals of nationality and self-determination betrayed, and when he sees the casuistry that is used to throw an appearance of justice over all the injustice that is being wrought at the expense of one's nationality. Government by the people? Goethe believed in no such principle: "Even when you kill the king," he said, "you do not know how to rule in his place … The rulers were destroyed, but who was there to protect the Many *from* the Many?"[175]

Eastern Europeans took as sacred gospel whatever yarns the West chose to spin; they also believed in the great watchwords for which the Cold War was waged. The West gave them the interpretation that happened to suit them. The Eastern European liberals were obliged enough to act as intermediaries, to such good effect that every liberal in Eastern Europe turned his back on his own country's cause. Eastern Europe was safely left to suffer the consequences of Western liberalism; it was thrown to the wolves.

There is a family tree passing from socialism through the '68 generation to Brussels bureaucrats, the red and green parties, the American liberal elite, and the media today. The socialist heritage has a marriage with the radical liberals; this genealogy exists in the West. It is detectable in the doctrine of European human rights and the attempts by the European Commission to impose cultural and constitutional uniformity (meaning socialism embedded in a liberal democracy) on member states.

Western liberalism bears no relation to freedom nowadays. Freedom means for the liberal merely a scope for his egotism, and this he secures using the political devices he has elaborated for the purpose: parliamentarianism and democracy. Liberalism is only self-interest protectively colored.

To the people of the West today, all main established political parties are equally suspect. They are all equally guilty, and they are all tainted with liberal ideas. The conservatives were untrue to their principles; the radicals to their logic. Why is the American political system failing? It is failing because it is infected with modern liberalism. It is modern liberalism that, with cold-blooded calculation and deliberate intent, makes the American workingman a modern slave today.

The modern liberal and socialist are now so discredited that nothing can, or should, save them. The young conservative needs no new proof of the disastrous results of following a mechanical, uninspired liberal ideology for almost one hundred years. The young socialist who has mentally outlived the collapse of Marxism but has retained his labor sympathies has long since been disillusioned by the "progress" that has led only to a phony democracy that is satisfied with the opportunistic enjoyment of apparent power.

If we want to discover the reasons why the conservative and the socialist should so unanimously come to the same conclusion about the principles, points of view, and lines of policy that have led to the present conditions, we shall find that they share a universal contempt and distrust for the liberal ingredient in political thought. This finding is the one common link between the forces of the real right and the real left.

Rational liberalism means the death of nations. However, was it not the liberal nations that won the seventy-seven-year war lasting from the beginning of the First World War in 1914 to the end of the Cold War in 1991?

Today one can answer only that there is some hope that the destruction they prepared for us will recoil on their very own heads. There is a flickering hope that the financial crises, economic stagnation, moral decay, cultural deterioration, and the results of globalization will lead to such exposure in the eyes of all the world that modern liberalism will be unable to survive.

The liberal West has had its past successes. The moment is no longer in its favor; everything is against it. What we can already detect is the beginning of the regrouping of people and nations. All illiberal forces are combining against everything that is modern liberalism. We are living at the time of this transition.

There will be a revolt against the successors of the age of reason. All wars of the last 250 years were the shipwreck of the age of reason. Reason turned thinking man into calculating man; reason corrupted the West thoroughly. It exposed the cunning of the rational calculation that is the political philosophy of America and Britain, which gives moral justification to immoral conduct of life and state, and the tutelage of other nations. It made up the word utilitarianism to cover egotism. It demonstrated the bankruptcy of the rights of man, with which the French Revolution, in the name of democracy, cheated the nations of their nationality. It secured the misuse and abuse of the people by a political caste at the top. The fight against the age of rational liberalism, which we are entering now, is a fight against modern liberalism all along the line.

In the course of this struggle, we shall realize how brief an epoch the age of rational liberalism has been; how circumscribed, superfluous, and feeble its creation; and how ephemeral its legacy. It will also be noted that all great achievements of this world were produced in the teeth of the age of reason and the age of rational liberalism, and the leading individuals producing them were "unliberal," or rather illiberal, people. All momentous historical events have been unliberal events. The only, although not unremarkable, achievement of the liberal was the skill with which he exploited each turn of events and sought to claim the credit for it.

The calculations of the liberal have been successful but false. The moment always comes when the liberal, who likes to consider himself independent of society, realizes his impotence. The moment will come when people and nations alike seek cohesion once more—the cohesion the age of rational liberalism thought it could dispense with, sacrificing understanding to reason. The moment will come only after a hard testing time, which will have tried the betrayer no less than the betrayed. However, come it will.

The successful spread of liberalism is expressly due to the lack of critical thought concerning the tangible across-the-board results of liberal ideas and solutions for society's problems. Indeed, to be critical of or to question liberal prescriptions at all is already considered to be antiliberal. Just like a critic of any religious denomination is labeled a heretic, so is any critic of liberalism labeled "uninformed," "unenlightened" or "illiberal." In other words, one must take the liberal beliefs and accept them even if they are contradictory or counterproductive. Ergo, to accept liberalism, a person must operate almost entirely on an emotional level. Persons steeped in logic or the physical sciences are far less likely to be swept into the liberal camp. It is no coincidence that as people age and undergo the trials of life, they reflect on the cause-and-effect relationship of events and tend to become less liberal and more conservative in their thinking.

Tragically, past events show that young and inexperienced people are the most susceptible to liberal indoctrination. It is a notable fact that the teaching profession, journalism, the general media, and most of the mind-forming and opinion-making fields have a history of attracting persons of liberal or leftist ideology. This ideal circumstance places them precisely where they need to be to spread their philosophy, and the practitioners of liberalism who are in a position to affect public policy too often have real goals or agendas for their beliefs. The standard liberal is but a pawn in the ongoing struggle between socialism and freedom. However, those in power on the left know that the system of representative democracy allows them to pursue their statist-socialist agenda by swaying the majority of the voting public toward their positions and candidates. They also know full well that most people have little time or inclination to study or give considerable thought to far-reaching matters of the day. Instead, scores of voters cast their ballots based purely on emotional terms—the very heart of liberalism's appeal.

One could certainly argue that the average conservative is no less of a pawn of the ruling neoconservative elite. By definition, a conservative arrives at his beliefs through the process of critical thought. As such, he is much less likely to be swayed by wrong-headed proposals should they be offered as "conservative." Most conservatives will consider issues and solutions on their merits and only then decide whether they are worthy of support—however little such decision might weigh.

THE AMERICAN LIBERAL LEFT: TRANSFORMATION FROM CLASSICAL CENTRIST TO MODERN (LEFTIST) LIBERALISM

The French say that one becomes what he hates most, and so Americans ostensibly won the Cold War only to become Marxists, in the primacy of economics and the growing demand for equality.

The contemporary left holds that nonsocialist societies, but only those, are composed mainly of oppressors and oppressed. The alleged cause of this social dispositioning is the economic system of capitalism, which is perceived by the left as the root cause of all social ills and vices, such as racism, sexism, alienation, homophobia, and even imperialism. According to leftist calculations, capitalism is an agent of tyranny and exploitation that presses its boot upon the proverbial necks of a broad range of victim groups, such as blacks, other minorities, women, gays, immigrants, and the poor, just to name a few. For that reason, according to the left, the United States (historically the standard-bearer of all capitalist economies) can only do wrong.

To eliminate America's inherent injustices, the left seeks to invert the power hierarchy so that the groups now said to be oppressed become the privileged races, classes, and gender of the new social order. The left's quest to transform the dominated into dominators, and vice versa, draws its inspiration from *The Communist Manifesto*, which asserts that "the history of all hitherto existing society is the history of class struggle." The struggle identified by the manifesto was that the proletarians and their intellectual vanguard, armed with the radical utopian vision of socialism, were expected to launch a series of civil wars in their respective countries—battles that would topple the ruling classes and the illegitimate societies they had established.[176] According to Marxist theory, these conflicts would rip each targeted society apart and create a new revolutionary world order from its ruins. To accomplish this Utopia, the contemporary left has formed a broad alliance, a united front, comprising radical elements representing a host of demographic groups that are allegedly victimized by American capitalism and its related injustices. Each constituent of this alliance, such as minorities, the LGBT community, women, illegal immigrants, and the poor, contributes its voice to a chorus that aims to discredit the United States specifically and Western culture generally as abusers of the vulnerable. Nor is the left's list of victim groups limited only to human beings; in the worldview of leftist environmentalists and animal rights activists, even certain species of shrubs, trees, insects, and rodents (as elements of the environment) qualify as victims of capitalism's ravages.

The seeds of the contemporary anti-American left sprouted in the new left's rebellion against the classical liberalism of the post–World War II era. True to its tradition of the New Deal, classical centrist liberalism provided active support to the civil rights movement and fought for the eradication of poverty and other social causes to counterbalance inequality. The same centrist post–World War II classical liberalism stood firmly against Communist totalitarianism on the international front. Indeed, they were the "Cold War liberals" rather than the conservative movement who first recognized the Soviet threat and engaged and fought the USSR through a policy of containment.[177]

Then came the New Left in the 1960s—the movement that rejected classical centrist liberalism because of its gradualism in domestic policy and antitotalitarianism in foreign affairs. At its beginning, the New Left also rejected Stalinism, seeing it perilously close to being morally equivalent to "American imperialism." The New Left idealized the charismatic revolutionaries of the Third World as an alternative to the red on the one hand, and the red, white, and blue on the other. As a result, the New Left wound up romanticizing a whole new set of totalitarian heroes—figures such as Mao Zedong, Ho Chi Minh, Fidel Castro, Che Guevara, and Daniel Ortega.

Changed by the Vietnam War from a movement hoping, in theory, to make America a better place into one that regarded America irredeemable, the New Left became an incorrigible revolutionary movement in its approach to domestic policies and foreign affairs. Focusing on Cold War liberals, it made them a threatened species and attacked the Democratic Party, which had hitherto embodied their beliefs and principles. After the ordeal of the 1968 Chicago convention, the New Left progressives not only killed the postwar liberal Democratic Party but also, through the nomination of George McGovern for president, seized and inhabited its corpse. They banished the leading figures of the old centrist classical liberalism, such as Hubert Humphrey and Henry "Scoop" Jackson.

After accomplishing this familicide, the New Left progressives took over and controlled the Democratic Party and appropriated the designation of liberalism, thus promptly accomplishing what the Communist Party USA (CPUSA) had long attempted to carry out when it called the communists "liberals in a hurry." However, now, having their credibility and self-confidence shaken by their backing of the Vietnam War, the genuinely centrist classical liberals were unable to hold the line against attacks from the New Left progressives and lost, in addition to their political party, even the ideological term that had defined their principles. Many of these centrist liberals wound up moving later toward Reaganism and neoconservatism when they saw what those who now called themselves "liberals" actually believed and wanted to accomplish through their control of the Democratic Party.

Calling themselves "liberals" now, today's leftists (descendants of the New Left) claim the moral high ground as self-anointed exemplars of compassion and enlightenment—counterweights to the supposedly reactionary conservatives they depict as heartless monsters. The modern left understands that to win the hearts and minds of Americans and Europeans alike, it must present its totalitarian objective, the uncompromising destruction of the status quo, in the nonthreatening lexicon of traditional Western values. This means, it must cite as its animating purpose the promotion of such lofty ideals as human rights, civil rights, civil liberties, and above all, social justice, or the correction of the free market's inherent inequalities through political interventions of a Marxist nature.

As the perennial socialist presidential candidate, Norman Thomas allegedly once said, "The American people will never knowingly adopt socialism. But under the name of 'liberalism,' they will adopt every fragment of the socialist program, until one day America will be a socialist nation, without knowing how it happened."

Toward this deceitful end, the left co-opted, in the years following the Vietnam War, the name of liberalism. Liberalism has been long honored in the West as the movement that bore freedom and dignity, economic opportunity and legal protection to millions of people around the world who had been denied those advantages since the dawn of history. Cloaking their agenda and objectives in the rhetoric of classical liberalism, the leftists embarked on the revolutionary program of redefining and transforming, subtly and incrementally, what most Americans and people in the West understood liberalism to be. During the following years and decades, the left championed crusades and ideas that step-by-step bore an ever-decreasing resemblance to the liberal causes of a previous era, yet they invariably identified both themselves and their evolving principles as "liberal." Most significantly, the left was exceedingly successful in getting the media and academic elites to publicize the redefinition of that snatched original designation at every stage along the way. Thus, such programs that were, in fact, downright leftist and socialist were passed by legislators in the name of liberalism. Moreover, the reputation for noble intentions of these enacting social reformers served not only to shield those programs from public criticism but also to win de facto public approval of them.

When the term "liberalism" (from the Latin word "*liberalis*," meaning "befitting a free man") first surfaced in the early 1800s, its trademarks were faith in the rule of law, limited government, individual rights, laissez-faire economics, and private property. These beliefs would remain the defining characteristics of liberalism throughout the liberal epoch (generally identified as the period of 1815–1914). However, the modern version of the hijacked and distorted liberalism is a parody of its predecessor.

Modern liberalism is a stalwart champion of group rights and collective identity (e.g., the racial preference policies known as "affirmative action" or the commitment to identity politics rather than individual rights and responsibilities).

Modern liberalism means the circumvention of law rather than the rule of law, as amply demonstrated by the contemptuous disregard of immigration laws and nondiscrimination laws, and by a predilection for judicial activism whereby judges preempt the powers that rightfully belong to legislators.

Modern liberalism represents the growing and spreading of government rather than its cutback and demands ever-increasing taxes to bankroll a bloated welfare state and government that oversees virtually every aspect of human life.

Modern liberalism speaks for the redistribution of wealth through punitive taxes and against the building of a financially healthy and viable state through monitored markets based on private property.

Another hallmark of classical liberalism was its spirit of toleration for different beliefs and ideas and respect for individual freedom of thought. In modern liberalism, social-democratic liberalism—or shall we call it modern leftism—one finds the exact opposite: intolerance of opposing viewpoints and the promotion of group thinking. The left interprets as treason any deviation from its intellectual orthodoxy if exhibited by a member of a so-called victim group that, theoretically, ought to occupy a place in the phalanx of revolutionary agitators. This phenomenon manifests itself with particular clarity by way of black leftists who excoriate black conservatives as "race traitors," "house slaves," "Oreos," and "Uncle Toms."

To question the ideologies of the left, which derive from commitments to an imagined and utopian future, is to provoke a moral response formulated in a counterquestion: Is the questioner for or against the equality of human beings? To decline an unswerving commitment to the progressive viewpoint is thus an automatic unwillingness to embrace the liberated future. It is to will the imperfections of the present order, which, in the current political cant of the left, means to be racist, sexist, classist—a defender of the oppressive status quo. That is why those progressives who call themselves "liberals" are instinctively intolerant toward any conservative opposition.

For leftists, the future is not a complicated and entangled web of social uncertainties and unintended consequences; it is a moral choice. To achieve the socially just future requires only that enough people decide to choose it. Consequently, it is entirely consistent for leftists to consider themselves morally and intellectually enlightened while dismissing their opponents as immoral, ignorant, or much worse.

The old, traditional conservative American values were liberty, trust in God, and unity (as seen in the phrase "E Pluribus Unum," or simply "From Many, One," illustrating the concept of the melting pot). The left has decidedly turned against all three, substituting secularism for God and religion as much as possible, substituting equality of result for liberty, and substituting multiculturalism (the opposite of "From Many, One") for "E Pluribus Unum." Multiculturalism emphasizes not the unity of Americans but the *divisions* that exist between them regarding race, gender, and class.

Contemporary modern liberalism is leftism in disguise. So is the travesty of the "liberal" label being widely attached to individuals such as Michael Moore, George Soros, Noam Chomsky, Al Sharpton, and Jane Fonda, all of whom are opponents of classical liberalism, which defined America and the West for centuries.

The Liberal Metamorphosis of the West: Transformation from Classical Liberalism to Liberal Conservatism

The classical liberal West depends on diversity rather than uniformity, on pluralism rather than monism or dualism, on inclusion rather than exclusion, on liberty rather than authority, on truth rather than power, on conversion rather than annihilation.

The classical liberal West believes in the individual rather than in the organization, in reconciliation rather than in triumph, in heterogeneity rather than in homogeneity, in relativism rather than in absolutes, and in approximations rather than in final answers.

The classical liberal West believes that both man and the universe are complicated concepts and that the apparently conflicting parts of each can be made to conform in a reasonably workable arrangement with a little goodwill, patience, and experimentation. In man, the (classical liberal) West sees the body, emotions, and reason as all equally real and necessary and is prepared to entertain a discussion about their relative interrelationships but is not willing to listen for long to any dogmatic insistence that any one of these has a final answer.

The classical liberal West has no faith in final answers. It believes that all answers are "unfinal" because everything is imperfect although possibly getting better and thus advancing toward perfection, which the West is prepared to admit may be present in some remote and almost unattainable future.

The concepts identified above as Western are to be found in all aspects of classical liberal Western life. The most triumphant of these aspects is science, whose method is a perfect example of the Western tradition. The scientist goes eagerly to work each day because he has the humility to know that he does *not* have any final answers and must work to modify and improve the answers he has. He publishes his opinions and research papers or exposes these in scientific gatherings so that they may be subjected to the criticism of his colleagues and thus gradually play a role in formulating the continuously unfolding consensus that is science. That is what science is—"a consensus unfolding in time by a cooperative effort, in which each works diligently seeking the truth and submits his work to the discussion and critique of his fellows to make a new, slightly improved, temporary consensus."[178]

Because this is the Western tradition, the West is called "liberal." Most historians see liberalism as a political outlook and practice that originated in the nineteenth century. However, nineteenth-century liberalism was merely a temporary organizational or classical liberal manifestation of what had always been the underlying Western outlook.

That organizational manifestation of the Western viewpoint is now mostly dead, killed as much by twentieth-century modern liberals as by conservatives or reactionaries. It was killed because modern liberals took the applications of that manifestation and made them be rigid, ultimate, and inflexible goals.

The classical liberal of, say, 1880 was anticlerical, antimilitarist, and antistate because these were, to his immediate experience, authoritarian forces that sought to prevent the operation of the Western way. The same classical liberal was for freedom of assembly, freedom of speech, and freedom of the press because these were required to form the consensus that is so much a part of the Western process of operation.

However, only twenty years later, by around 1900 or so, these dislikes and likes became ends in themselves. The liberal was prepared, in the name of freedom of assembly, to *force* people to associate with those they could not bear, and he was ready, in the name of freedom of speech, to *force* people to listen. His anticlericalism became an attempt to *prevent* people from becoming religious, and his antimilitarism took the form of opposing funds for legitimate defense. Most amazingly, his earlier opposition to the use of private economic power to restrict individual freedoms took the form of an effort to increase the authority of the state *against* private economic power and wealth. Thus, the classical liberal of 1880 and the New Deal liberal of 1940 had reversed themselves on the role and power of the state, the earlier seeking to curtail it and the latter trying to increase it.

In the process, the upholder of the classical liberal idea that the power of the state should be reduced came to be called a "conservative."

Now, there is a little book that appeared more than a hundred years ago (1912) from the hand of a member of the British Conservative Party. The book is *Conservatism*, by Lord Hugh Cecil. This volume defines conservatism very much as liberalism has been defined—as tentative, flexible, nondogmatic, communal, and moderate. Its fundamental assumption is that humans are imperfect creatures, will probably get further by working together than by blind opposition, and since undoubtedly each is wrong to some extent, any extreme or drastic action is inadvisable. The conservatism of this type was indeed closer to what has just been called "classical liberalism" than the liberals of 1880 themselves were. However, the conservatives of this kind were also perfectly willing to use the church, the army, or the state to carry out their experimental but reasonable projects. Moreover, they were also prepared to use the state to curtail arbitrary private economic power, which the classical liberals of the day were unwilling to do since they embraced a doctrinaire belief in the limitation of state power.[179]

All this is of significance because it directly relates to the fact that the "real" or classical liberals have been battered and destroyed in recent generations. Their contemporary namesakes have either turned into the modern liberal (New Deal socialist) breed or chosen some version of the liberal-conservative (including neoliberal) line. The age-old classical liberal tradition of the West has disappeared; the ongoing and evident decline of the main liberal political parties in the West (the Liberal Democrats in Britain and the Free Democrats in Germany) proves this.

The Emergence of Neoliberalism

Today, neoliberalism is a political philosophy whose advocates support economic liberalizations, free trade and open markets, privatization, deregulation, and the enhancing of the private sector's role in modern society. That is what neoliberalism is about today.

However, neoliberalism was first an economic philosophy that emerged among European liberal scholars attempting to trace a so-called Third Way or Middle Way between the conflicting philosophies of classical liberalism and collectivist central planning in the 1930s. The reason for this development was the desire to avoid repeating the economic failures of the early 1930s that conventional wisdom of the time tended to blame on unfettered (i.e., laissez-faire) capitalism. In the pursuing decades, neoliberal theory tended to be at variance with the more laissez-faire doctrine of classical liberalism and promoted a market economy instead under the guidance and rules of a more active state—a model that came to be known as the social market economy.

In the 1960s, usage of the term "neoliberal" very much declined. Today the term "neoliberal" is used somewhat reproachfully mainly by those who are critical of legislative initiatives that push for free trade, deregulation, enhanced privatization, and an overall reduction in government control of the economy.

The German scholar Alexander Rüstow originally coined the term "neoliberalism" in 1938. To be neoliberal at that time meant that modern economic policy with state intervention was required, turning away from conceptions of laissez-faire toward a market economy under the guidance and the rules of an active state. It was an attempt to formulate a both anticapitalist and anticommunist Third Way. As such, neoliberalism was originally established as something entirely different from the free market radicalism with which it is usually associated today.[180]

The fundamental differences between true neoliberals around Rüstow on the one hand and old-school liberals around von Mises and Hayek on the other were quite unmistakable. While true neoliberals demanded state intervention to correct undesirable market structures, von Mises of the Austrian School always insisted that the only legitimate role for the state be the abolishing of barriers to market entry. Similar differences of opinion also existed in other questions, such as social policy and the scope of interventionism. Over the next few years, the insurmountable differences between Rüstow's neoliberals and the old-school classical liberals became intolerable.

Neoliberal economic ideas were first implemented in West Germany. The neoliberal economists around Ludwig Erhard could draw on the theories developed in the 1930s and 1940s and contributed to West Germany's reconstruction after the Second World War. The alma mater of these original German neoliberals, the *ordoliberal* (or social liberal) Freiburg School, was rather moderate and pragmatic. Although the German neoliberals accepted the classical liberal notion that competition drives economic prosperity, they also argued that a laissez-faire-based economic policy stifles competition as the strong devour the weak; hence monopolies and cartels would pose a threat to freedom of competition. They supported the creation of a well-developed legal system and capable regulatory apparatus. While still opposed to comprehensive Keynesian employment policies or an extensive welfare state, the theory of the original German neoliberals was marked by their willingness to place humane and social values *on par* with economic efficiency. Alfred Müller-Armack coined the phrase "social market economy" to emphasize the egalitarian and humane bent of the idea. Walter Eucken stated, "Social security and social justice are the greatest concerns of our time."[181]

Hayek of the Austrian School did not like the expression "social market economy." In his view, the social market economy, aiming at both a market economy and social justice, was a muddle of conflicting objectives. Ludwig von Mises stated that Erhard and Müller-Armack accomplished a great act of liberalism to restore the German economy and called this "a lesson for the U.S." Nevertheless, von Mises believed that the ordoliberals were hardly better than socialists.[182]

In Germany, neoliberalism, meaning Rüstow's "original German neoliberalism" was synonymous with both ordoliberalism and social market economy in the beginning. However, over time, the original term "neoliberalism" gradually disappeared, since "social market economy" was a much more definite (and for German ears more positive) term and better suited the "Wirtschaftswunder" (economic miracle) mentality of the 1950s and 1960s.

The uncertainty over the real meaning of "liberalism" is commonly reflected in neoliberalism and is the first serious point of confusion.

The second major problem with the definition of neoliberalism is that it went from being a purely theoretical economic philosophy to being a practical and applied political one. From the 1970s on, one saw a surge in the acceptability of neoliberalism, and neoliberal governments swept across the world, promising neoliberal reforms. However, governments hardly ever carry out their promised reforms, either by design or circumstances. This unwillingness or inability to deliver leads to the second serious point of confusion—namely, that contemporary neoliberalism is hardly ever ideologically neoliberal.

The Struggle of Classical Old-School Liberalism in the Twentieth Century

Economists of the Austrian School, including Friedrich Hayek and Ludwig von Mises, revived classical liberalism in interwar Austria. They tried to restate the case for classical liberalism again because they were concerned about the erosion of liberty by both socialist and fascist governments in Europe at the time. In the introduction of his 1970s book *The Constitution of Liberty*, Hayek states, "If old truths are to retain their hold on men's minds, they must be restated in the language and concepts of successive generations."[183]

Hayek's belief in liberty stemmed from an argument about information. He held that no individual or group, including the government, could ever understand everything about an economy or society to be able to design the best system of governance rationally. He argued that this ignorance only gets worse as scientific development progresses and the scope of human knowledge widens, leaving individuals increasingly uninformed in their lifetimes. As a result, Hayek believed, it is impossible for any person or government to design the perfect system under which people can be governed.

The only solution to this, he thought, is to allow all possible methods to be tried in the real world and to let the better systems to beat the worse ones through competition. In a liberal society, he assumed, the few who used liberty to try out new things would come up with successful adaptations of existing systems or new ways of doing things. These discoveries, once shared and adopted by the mainstream, would benefit the entire society, including those who cannot openly partake of liberty.

Hayek argued that, owing to ignorance, a person could not understand which one of the various political, economic, and social rules followed made the successful system prevail. In his mind, this made the superstitions and traditions of the society in which an individual operated critical, since in all probability they had, in some way, aided the success of the individual. This theory would be especially true in a prosperous society, where these superstitions and traditions would presumably be the successful ones that had evolved to exploit new circumstances. Nonetheless, this hypothesis did not excuse any superstition or tradition to be followed if it had already outlived its usefulness: respect of tradition and superstition for their own sake was not acceptable value to him. Therefore, classical liberalism combined respect for the old (drawn from conservatism) with continuous striving for the future (drawn from liberalism).

In emphasizing evolution and competition of ideas, Hayek highlighted the divide between a practical liberalism, which evolved haphazardly in Britain and was championed by such thinkers as David Hume and Adam Smith, and a more theoretical approach of the French, advocated by such philosophers as Descartes and Rousseau. Hayek christened these the pragmatic and rationalist schools—the first evolving institutions with an eye toward liberty and the creation of a brave new world by sweeping all the old ideas away.

Hayek's theories on information and the need of evolving evolutions planted liberalism securely on the pragmatic side, opposite of both rationalist socialists (such as communists, fascists, and social liberals) and rationalist capitalists (such as economic libertarians and laissez-faire capitalists) alike.

Economic and Corrupted Neoliberalism

At the center of liberalism was the rule of law. Hayek believed that liberty was maximized when coercion was minimized. He thought that two things were vitally important when setting up the liberal system of law: the definition and protection of the personal sphere, and the prevention of fraud and deception, the latter of which could be maintained only by the threat of coercion from the state. In delineating a personal sphere, individuals could know under what circumstances they would or would not be coerced, and they could then plan accordingly.

Hayek believed that such a system could maintain a protected sphere by guarding against abuses of the ruling power, be it a monarch, the will of the majority in a democracy, or the government. He considered the essential features of such protections to be equality before the law and generality of the law. Equality meant that all must be equal before and subject to the law, including the legislature and government. The generality of the law meant that the law should focus on nonspecific general rules that could not grant privileges, discriminate, or compel any particular individual to an end. Hayek envisioned that general laws could also transmit knowledge and encourage spontaneous order in human societies, not unlike Adam Smith's "invisible hand" in economics. He also stressed the importance of individuals to be responsible for their actions while encouraging others to respect the law.

Economic neoliberalism stemmed out of the historical rift between classical liberalism and economic liberalism and developed when the economically liberal-minded co-opted the language and ideas of classical neoliberalism to place economic freedom at its heart, making it what is called "right-wing ideology" today. The liberal opposite of economic neoliberalism is modern liberalism, the corresponding left-wing ideology.

Basically, economic neoliberalism can be derived from taking the classical neoliberal definition above and adding to it the protected personal sphere referring solely to property rights and a contract. One of the best-known proponents of economic neoliberalism was Milton Friedman. The most common form of neoliberalism is economic neoliberalism today, and that is what is usually meant by a system described as "neoliberal" in modern times.

In the 1920s, neoliberal economics took the ideas of the great classical liberal economists, such as Adam Smith, and updated them for the contemporary world. The Austrian School systematized Friedrich Hayek's theory of information flow, which is present in classical neoliberalism in economic form. The problem of information flow implied that a decentralized system, in which information traveled freely and was freely determined at each localized point (Hayek called this "catallaxy"), would function much better than a centralized system under a central authority trying to do the same. The previous statement is valid even if the information flow was very efficient and was motivated to act for the public good. According to this view, the free market is the perfect example of such a system in which the market-determined prices serve as the information signals flowing through the economy. Participants in the economy then make prudent decisions by taking into account all the different aspects that determined the market prices without even having to understand or be completely aware of all of the complicated factors.[184]

Curiously enough, in accepting the ideas of the Austrian School regarding information flow, economic neoliberals were forced to accept that free markets were artificial systems and, therefore, would not arise spontaneously; they would have to be enforced, usually by the state and through the rule of law. In this way, economic neoliberalism confirms the role of the state and becomes distinct from libertarian thought. To paraphrase Warren Buffett's famous quote, the market is there to inform you, not serve you.[185]

Nevertheless, in accepting the ideas of self-regulating markets, neoliberals drastically limited the role of the government in managing those forms of market failure that neoliberal economics allowed: property rights and information asymmetry. This constraint restricted the duty of the government to maintaining property rights by providing law and order through the police, maintaining an independent judiciary, maintaining the national defense, and necessary regulation to guard against fraud. This stipulation made neoliberal economics distinct from the Keynesian economics of the preceding decades.

Modern economists critical of neoliberalism's role have often presented the least controversial aspect of neoliberalism in the world economic system. Among these economists, the leading voices of dissent are Joseph Stiglitz and Paul Krugman. Both use arguments about market failure to justify their views on neoliberalism. They argue that when markets are imperfect (which is to say all markets everywhere, to some degree), then they can fail and may not work as neoliberals predict, resulting in some form of crony capitalism. The two primary modes of failure are usually due to imperfect property rights and incomplete information and correspond directly to Friedrich Hayek's assertion that without the protection of the private sphere and the prevention of fraud and deception, classical liberalism will not work.[186] The 1989 Russian neoliberal reform is one of the best and least controversial examples. The economic changes there were justified under neoliberal economic policy but lacked any of the fundamental features of a neoliberal state (e.g., the rule of law, protected personal sphere, free press) that could have justified the reforms.

The failing of property rights signifies that individuals cannot be assured ownership of their possessions and cannot control what happens to these properties or prevent others from taking them away. This lack of protection usually stifles free enterprise and results in preferential treatment for those who can secure the legal status of their properties.

The most brazen scheme of crony capitalism is such a liberal economic system in which only some people (cronies) are permitted property rights by the government in return for the loyal support of the regime, allowing these supporters to expropriate any capital held by opponents. This cronyism is a useful method of control, which is usually seen in its purest form in countries with dictatorships, where the regime can create a liberal system of markets and government without ceding any control of either. Such reforms can also be used to add a sprinkling of liberal legitimacy for the regime and open the country to external capital.

This form can also be useful to explain neoliberal reforms in countries where either the will or ability to enforce property rights is lacking, as was the case in post-Soviet Russia and other Eastern European countries where reformist politicians colluded with politically connected businesspeople. In return for backing democratic and free market reforms, these business figures could expropriate precious resources in a country where ownership was not clear and only sporadically enforced, directly leading to the rise of the oligarchs.

Neoliberal Class Project: Globalization

Even if everyone is theoretically equal under the law, as in a liberal democracy, not all members of society may have equal *access* to the law or information. Real access is not free, as liberals such as Hayek claim, but has associated costs; and therefore, in this context, it is reasonable to assert that the wealthy have greater rights than the poor.

The poor may hardly have any rights at all in some cases if their income falls below the minimum levels necessary to access the law and unbiased sources of information. At the same time, the very wealthy may even have the ability to choose which rights and responsibilities they bear if they can move themselves and their property internationally, resulting in social stratification, also known as class. This alleged tendency to create and strengthen class has led to some claiming that neoliberalism is a class program designed to impose class on society through liberalism.

In practice, less developed nations have less developed rights and institutions, resulting in higher risk for international lenders and businesses, and this means that developing countries usually have less privileged access to international markets than developed ones. Because of this effect, international lenders are also more likely to invest in foreign companies (i.e., multinational corporations) inside a country, rather than in local businesses, giving international firms an unfair competitive advantage. Also, speculative flows of capital may enter the country during a boom and leave during a recession, deepening the economic crises and destabilizing the economy.

Both of these problems imply that developing countries should have both greater protections against international markets and higher barriers to trade than developed ones. However, in response to crises, IMF policy, which is supposed to be guided by neoliberal ideas, is to expand liberalization of the economy and decrease barriers, allowing more significant capital flight and the opportunity for foreign firms to shore up their monopolies. Additionally, the IMF acts to increase moral hazard (meaning increased exposure to risk when insured; for example, a person will take more risks because someone else bears the cost of those risks), since international engagement resulting in an international bailout will usually end up with foreign creditors being treated preferentially. The preferential treatment leads international firms to discount the risks of doing business in less developed countries and force the government to pay for them instead.

The view that international involvement and the imposition of neoliberal policies usually serve to make things worse and act against the very interests of the country being "saved" has led some to argue that the policies applied have nothing to do with liberalism at all but hide some other purpose. The most common assertion given by opponents is that they are a form of neocolonialism, where more developed countries can exploit the less developed ones. However, even opponents do not agree. For example, Joseph Stiglitz assumes that there is no neoimperialist plot but that a mixture of ideology and special interests drives the system. Neoliberal fundamentalists, who do not accept that neoliberalism can fail, collaborate with financial and other multinational corporations that amply benefit from opening up foreign markets. It can also happen that the local elites exploit neoliberal reforms to impose such changes that favor them at the cost of the poor while transferring the blame to the "evil, imperialistic" developed countries, as can be seen from the example of Argentina in 2001.[187]

Opposing Neoliberalism

Opponents of neoliberalism usually argue these following points:

- Globalization can subvert nations' abilities for self-determination.
- Neoliberal economics promotes exploitation and social injustice.
- Neoliberal policies produce inequality.
- Neoliberalism, unlike liberalism, changes the economic and government policies to increase the power of corporations and benefit the upper classes.

Critics of neoliberalism contend not only that neoliberalism's critique of socialism (as "un-freedom") is wrong but also that neoliberalism cannot even deliver the liberty that is supposed to be one of its high points. For example, sociologist Loïc Wacquant argues that neoliberalism has transformed the United States into a "centaur state," or a nation with little governmental oversight for those at the top and strict control of those at the bottom.[188]

Neoliberalism, supporting the omnipotence of the mighty market and personal interests, is nothing but a cul-de-sac. It has not been able to answer the question of how to make a national community productive, efficient, and fruitful. The historical achievements of liberalism concerning individual rights and interests cannot be denied. However, it has nothing more to offer to the national communities of today—becoming ever more one-sided and deformed in the process.

Nevertheless, neoliberalism has maintained its view from the beginning of the 2008 financial and economic crisis that the global market acting upon private interests is the solution to the business and societal problems. Just the opposite, it has become apparent the world over that the market in itself does not create common good. Quite the contrary, it tears societies apart, dividing them into a narrow wealthy elite and the ever poorer masses.

Even more, neoliberalism states that the state should keep itself away from managing the economy and society as a whole; it should not get involved in the lives of individuals. Neoliberalism maintains all of this despite the fact, or perhaps for the intention, that the Western world has lost its Christian faith and values; it has fallen apart morally, becoming not only totally individualized and alienated but also culturally degenerate. In other words, twenty-first-century neoliberalism still sees the solution in the individual good and not in the common good represented by national or community interests. That is why it advocates global rule and interests, which suppress nations and regional communities.

The problem is that human existence is based on individual freedom *and* community life—*both* at the same time. These two must be in balance—contrary to neoliberalism's teachings. Neoliberalism does not protect the national wealth, and it does not create national communities; it creates or increases indebtedness, and it does not live up even to the minimum expectations of national principles.

It must be remembered that the meaning of the word "nonliberal" has been made synonymous with "autocratic" or "antidemocratic" in the Western public life and political science during the past two decades. Since it is hard to change the accepted meaning of an established concept, this author proposes using the term "society-centric" in the twenty-first century instead of using the term "nonliberal" or "illiberal."

LIBERAL DEMOCRACY: THE SUM OF HYPOCRISIES

Both the International Monetary Fund (IMF) and the European Central Bank (ECB) have violated their charters to bail out French, German, and Dutch private banks. The IMF was empowered only to make the balance of payments loans but is lending to the Greek government for prohibited budgetary reasons so that the Greek government can pay the banks. Although the ECB is prohibited from bailing out member country governments, it is still doing that so that the banks can be paid. Moreover, the German parliament approved the bailout, which violates provisions of the European Treaty and Germany's own Basic Law. The case was sent, correctly, to the German Constitutional Court, which, predictably and not at all surprisingly, essentially approved the bailout. All of these acts mean institutionalized hypocrisy.

The unitary executive theory of American constitutional law holds that the President of the United States of America has unitary powers that elevate him above statutory US law, treaties, and international law. According to this theory, the unitary executive can violate with impunity the Foreign Intelligence Surveillance Act (FISA), which prevents spying on US citizens without warrants obtained from the FISA court. The president could violate with impunity the statutory US laws against torture, as well as the Geneva Conventions—in other words, the fictional unitary powers can elevate the president above any laws.[189]

Habeas corpus is a writ prohibiting the government from holding people indefinitely without presenting charges and evidence to a court. It also prohibits the government from denying detained people due process of law and access to an attorney.

However, such constitutional protections as habeas corpus were thrown out the window by the US Department of Justice, and the federal courts obligingly, if not sheepishly, followed suit, as did the US Congress, "the people's representatives"—or rather the representatives of the ruling liberal elite. Congress even enacted the Military Commissions Act of 2006, signed by the president on October 17 of that year. This act allows anyone alleged to be an "unlawful enemy combatant" to be sentenced to death based on secret and hearsay evidence that might or might not be presented in a military court, which is placed out of reach of US federal courts. The crazed politicos in Congress who supported this destruction of Anglo-American law masqueraded as patriots in the war against terrorism. The act designates anyone accused by the United States, without evidence being presented, as being part of the Taliban, al-Qaeda, or "associated forces" to be an "unlawful enemy combatant," which strips the person of the protection of the law. The question is, with US troops fighting overseas for decades without any declaration of war, which foreign person cannot be considered an "unlawful enemy combatant"?

The Taliban consists of indigenous Afghan peoples who, before the US military intervention, were fighting to unify their war-torn country. The Taliban are Islamist, and the US government fears another Islamist government like the one in Iran, which is the direct consequence of previous US interventions in Iran's internal affairs. The US government, for the sake of freedom and democracy, plainly overthrew an elected Iranian leader, albeit a socialist, in 1953 and imposed a despot; US–Iranian relations have never recovered from the subsequent corrupt tyranny that Washington supported for decades.

The US government has always been opposed to any foreign power whose leaders cannot be directly bought, influenced, or otherwise pressured to perform as Washington's puppets. This arrogance is why the United States, with the help of its allies, invaded Afghanistan and overthrew Saddam Hussein in Iraq, Muammar Gaddafi in Libya, and Viktor Yanukovych in Ukraine, just to name a few. Moreover, this historical arrogance is why Washington would prefer to change the governments not only of Syria and Iran but also of Hungary, Russia, and Venezuela, among many others.

With the Western allies having fought another hopeless and reckless war for their usual values in Afghanistan for more than a decade now (longer than World War II but without a victory in sight), the Taliban control more of the country than do the United States and its NATO fronts. Frustrated by their obvious and inevitable failure, the liberating allies increasingly murder women, children, village elders, Afghan police, and aid workers.

There are scores of documented cases that prove Western crimes as powerfully as any evidence used against Nazi war criminals in the aftermath of World War II at the Nuremberg Trials. Perhaps the height of lawlessness was attained when the Obama administration announced that it had a list of US citizens who could be assassinated without due process of law.

Nevertheless, it was not a well-deserving Western political leader but Gaddafi of Libya for whom the International Criminal Court (ICC) had issued arrest warrants before he was murdered. Western powers are using the ICC, which is supposed to serve justice, for self-serving reasons that are unjust.

What was Gaddafi's crime, in any case? Perhaps most importantly, he had unhitched the dollar as reserve currency, thereby removing the greenback as sole means of payment in the oil trade. He attempted to prevent Libya from being overthrown by a Western-supported and -organized armed uprising in Eastern Libya.

Libya was the first armed revolt of the so-called Arab Spring—and reports made it clear there was nothing democratic about the uprising. The West managed to push a no-fly resolution through its instrument, the United Nations. Although the resolution was limited to neutralizing Gaddafi's air force, the Western powers propitiously followed an expansive interpretation of the UN resolution and turned it into authorization to legitimize their direct involvement in the war. Gaddafi resisted, of course, the foreign-incited armed rebellion against the state of Libya, which is the typical response of a sitting government to externally inflamed armed conflict.

In our times, everyone who resists or criticizes the West or its main power players is made a criminal. Anyone who disagrees with the Western policymakers is considered a threat and as such can be killed or arrested as a terrorist suspect or as someone providing aid and comfort to terrorists.

The collapse of law is across the board.

At present, those who oppose hypocrisy and the evil that engulfs the West risk being declared "terrorists." If they are US citizens, they can be assassinated. If they are foreign leaders, their country can be invaded. When captured, they can be executed, like Saddam Hussein and Gaddafi, or sent off to the ICC in The Hague, like the hapless Serbs, who tried to defend their country from being dismantled and their kin being murdered at the instigation and with the help of Western democracies.

The West relies on fear and intimidation to cover up its crimes. America has become a terrified and abused nation—a once proud people cowed, permitting almost any abuses of human dignity. There is not much left of the American character that typified the nation a short hundred years ago. Only people who have lost their soul could tolerate the destructive forces that prevail in their lives. Who is going to march on Washington next?

Western Liberal Machinations around the World

The US Navy's Sixth Fleet moved into position for a cruise missile strike on Syria in 2013. Once again, the United States of America was about to commit an act of military aggression against a state with which it was not at war. Moreover, the United States would have done that without any sanctioning of Syria by the United Nations, without independent verification of the claims leveled against a fellow UN-member state, and without even the slightest threat to US citizens, property, or territory. Brooding in the background, just like in the case of Libya, were two former imperial accomplices, Britain and France, the two nations responsible for igniting ethnic and religious conflicts in the Middle East and elsewhere during the last hundred years.

At the height of the First World War, Britain and France cynically divvied up the former territories of the Ottoman Empire between them. Under the infamous Sykes-Picot Agreement of 1916, France got Syria and Lebanon, and the United Kingdom, in turn, Palestine, Trans-Jordan, and Iraq.[190]

A year later the British Foreign Secretary, Arthur Balfour, promised the Jewish people a homeland in Palestine, elegantly ignoring the fact that the territory had already been populated, overwhelmingly, by Arab Muslims.[191]

A little later, in 1943, the United States appeared on the Middle Eastern horizon. It was under President Franklin Roosevelt that the House of Saud was guaranteed US protection in return for access to a veritable ocean of oil lying untapped beneath the Arabian Desert, about which the New Zealand oil prospector Frank Holmes had assured his American clients.[192]

In 1956, Britain and France used a jacked-up Israeli invasion of Egypt to justify their joint military operation to protect the recently nationalized Suez Canal. The Americans, who had not been invited to participate in this particular Anglo-French adventure, decided to show these two imperial relics what happens to countries foolhardy enough to do a little business on the side without Uncle Sam's permission. Britain, France, and Israel were all forced to withdraw their troops. Sir Anthony Eden, the British PM, resigned in disgrace.

Wars and Western manipulations have been the curse and burden of the Middle East's Arab (and non-Arab) population for many years. T. E. Lawrence, popularly known as Lawrence of Arabia, persuaded the Arab princes and tribal chieftains during the First World War that if they allied themselves with the British fighting the Ottoman Empire, a single Arab kingdom would lie within their grasp. If the British and the French had allowed this promise to be kept, it is conceivable that an Arabian kingdom or an Arabian republic embracing the entire Arabian peninsula and what are now Iraq, Syria, Jordan, Israel, and Lebanon would now be a significant global power.[193] However, of course, even as Lawrence promised the Arabs a rebirth of Islamic greatness, his masters were taking every possible step (see the Sykes-Picot Agreement mentioned before) to ensure that they remained weak and divided under Western, instead of Ottoman, control.

In our time, the United States, Britain, and France are merely attempting to fulfill their internationally recognized "responsibility to protect" the Syrian population from "atrocities" and "war crimes" about to be perpetrated by their rulers—or so said the official Western disinformation campaign.[194] If all this sounds very familiar, it is because of the sequence of events: the refusal to countenance contradictory evidence, and the relentless progression toward the launching of an illegal military attack upon a legitimate state (now suddenly declared illegitimate by the powers attacking it). The events are almost identical to those preceding the US-led invasion of Iraq in March 2003.

How about these same Western powers, who talk so self-righteously about being forced—in the name of humanity, of course—to operate without the blessing of the United Nations Security Council because of Russia's and China's obstruction? Could they be the same ones that unleashed hell in the form of NATO raids and subsequent military occupation, followed by the unilateral changing of borders and carving up of the nations of Yugoslavia? All this had to happen in postwar and post-Communist Europe, at the right strategic moment, when one UN member dared to assert its own "responsibility to protect" its own inhabitants in Croatia, Bosnia, and Kosovo while these were under attack by forces created, organized, financed, and supported by the West?[195]

When masked and armed people occupied government buildings in Ukraine in January 2014, the Western states and their news fabricators told the public that that was a "very good thing." These people, as its political leaders and elite media commentators told the Western World, were pro-democracy protesters demonstrating against the corrupt system and its political leaders, who hesitated to turn against Russia and join the European orbit instead. The US government and its EU allies warned the Ukrainian authorities against the use of force to counter these "pro-democracy demonstrators" even if, according to the pictures shown, some of them were neo-Nazis throwing Molotov cocktails and other things at the police while smashing up statues and setting fire to buildings.

Just a few weeks later, in April 2014, the Western public was told that people occupying government buildings in Ukraine were *not* pro-democracy protesters but rather terrorists or militants.

Why was the occupation of government buildings a very good thing in January but a very bad thing in April? Also, why was the use of force by the authorities against protestors deemed completely unacceptable in January but acceptable in April? Because the pro-democracy hoodlums were pro-Western and anti-Russian nationalists in January, while the other anti-democracy hoodlums were pro-Russian and anti-Western nationalists in April.

"You just don't invade another country on phony pretext in order to assert your interests," US Secretary of State John Kerry said during an interview on NBC's *Meet the Press* on March 2, 2014. "This is an act of aggression that is completely trumped up in terms of its pretext. It's really 19th-century behavior in the 21st century." He was referring to the activities on the Crimean peninsula that were a direct consequence of the coup d'état in Kiev, of course.

Has anyone forgotten the claim that Iraq had WMDs (weapons of mass destruction)? Has anyone forgotten when, in 2002 and early 2003, Western politicians and their media kept telling the world that the freedom-loving Western democracies had to go to war with Iraq because of the threat posed by Saddam's deadly arsenal?

The public is told that radical Islamic terror groups pose the gravest threat to peace, security, and "our way of life" in the democratic West. The public is told that Al-Qaeda, the Islamic State (IS), and other such groups need to be destroyed—that the West needs to have a relentless War on Terror against them. Notwithstanding, the Western political leaders have been siding with such radical groups in their war against a secular Syrian government that respects the rights of religious minorities, including Christians. When the bombs of Al-Qaeda or their affiliates go off in Syria and innocent people are killed, there are no protests or condemnations from Western leaders to be heard. They blame only the secular Syrian government that is fighting radical Islamists and that the Western leaders and their elite media commentators are desperate to have toppled.

In official Western eyes, Russia is a dreadful and backward country because, among others but typically for Russia, it has passed a law against promoting homosexuality to minors. The same Western leaders who boycotted the 2014 Winter Olympics in Sochi because of this law visit the states of the Persian Gulf, where gay people can be imprisoned or even executed, and warmly embrace the rulers there while making no mention of the gay rights issue. Surely the imprisonment or execution of gay people is far worse and more severe than a law that bans the promoting of homosexuality to minors.

Innumerable Western newspaper articles keep announcing that the Hungarian ultra-nationalist party Jobbik is appalling and that its rise is a cause for great concern, even though this party has never been in the government and is not likely to be. However, neo-Nazis and ultranationalists do hold positions in the alleged government of Ukraine that the political leaders in the West enthusiastically support. These far-right elements played a key role in the overthrow of Ukraine's democratically elected government in February 2014—a "revolution" cheered on and financed by the West. Why are ultranationalists and far-right groups unacceptable in Hungary but very acceptable in Ukraine? Because they do the dirty and provocative work that the West wants to be done in Ukraine, and therefore they can be used there.

The Western public is daily reminded that Russia is an aggressive, imperialistic power and that NATO has to oppose the Russian "threat." One can see several countries close to or even bordering Russia that are members of NATO, the United States–led North Atlantic military alliance, whose members have attacked, bombed, and destroyed many lands in the last twenty years. However, there are no states of a Russian-led military alliance that are close to America, just as there are no Russian military bases or Russian missiles stationed in foreign countries bordering or close to the United States.

Having order is one of the essential and necessary components of liberty. No one claims that the Arab dictators or President Yanukovych were ideal. However, prudence dictates that violent revolutions not only are not perfect but also are the definition of tyranny. Violent revolution is the ultimate unraveling of all limits to the evils of human nature in a political community. Wherever violent revolution takes place, sorrow and bloodshed follow. Violent revolution aiming to negate the results of a democratic election is a crime.

In cases of civil strife or civil war, responsible political leaders always attempt to rebuild unity as quickly as possible. Abraham Lincoln famously called for "malice toward none" in his Second Inaugural Address. Yulia Timoshenko, however, fresh from jail, has called for Yanukovych's head and told the "revolutionaries" to stay in Kiev, remain on the streets, and "continue the revolution." The maliciously organized campaign in Kiev was not a replay of the American Revolution. It was not anti-Communist either. It was nothing of a legitimate revolution by the principles of the American Declaration of Independence. What happened in Kiev was the actual destruction of the Ukrainian nation-state: a state that has gone through its second violent revolution of the twenty-first century—a state that has now voided its Constitution three times this century. It is a state impoverished, divided, and manipulated by both East and West, given no room for peaceful civil society to develop.

Thousands of people in Ukraine have been manipulated into risking their lives in the fight to enter the European Union, which is governed by an unelected body of commissars. The first European Council president, Mr. Herman Van Rompuy, has never stood for any election—unlike Mr. Yanukovych, who stood for two of them. Still, thousands of Ukrainians are dead in a maliciously provoked civil war for the adoption of "European standards." What are those sacred European standards supposedly codifying European values? They are the power of Western popular culture, Western materialism, and cleverly sophisticated Western propaganda that are more devastating than the power of Stalin's gulags and indoctrination. For when physical suffering and palpable fear enslave people, their minds remain free, sober, fresh, and hungry for truth. However, when people are made ignorant; when wisdom and education are not honored in a material culture that favors fame, popularity, and money; and when the body is made plump and satisfied, then the mind becomes enslaved, rotten, and mired in lies.

In recent history, at least two European countries initiated actions against separatists on their territories but got two very different reactions in return from the Western elite.

The government of the European "Country A" launched what it called an antiterrorist military operation against separatists in one part of the country. Pictures on Western television showed homes shelled and people fleeing. The United States, United Kingdom, France, and other NATO powers fiercely condemned the actions of the government of Country A, accusing it of committing genocide and ethnic cleansing, thereby causing a humanitarian crisis. Western politicians, together with their establishment journalists, told the world that something must be done. Therefore, NATO launched a humanitarian military intervention to stop the government of Country A. Country A was bombed for seventy-eight days and nights. The country's leader, who was labeled "the New Hitler," was indicted, arrested, and sent on a British Royal Air Force plane to stand trial for war crimes in The Hague, where he died, unconvicted, in his prison cell.

A few short years later, the government of European "Country B" launched what it called an antiterrorist military operation against separatists in one part of the country. However, Western television did *not* show pictures, or at least not many, of people's homes being shelled and people fleeing, although other television stations did. This time, the United States, Britain, and other NATO powers did *not* condemn the government or accuse it of committing genocide or ethnic cleansing. Neither Western politicians nor their establishment journalists told the world that something must be done to stop the government of Country B killing its own people. On the contrary, the very same powers that supported action against Country A now supported the military offensive of the government in Country B. The leader of Country B was *not* indicted for war crimes; nor was he labeled "the New Hitler," despite the support his government received from far-right extreme nationalist groups. On the contrary, he received generous amounts of aid from the West.

Anyone who would dare to defend the policies of the government in Country A is immediately called a "genocide denier" or an "apologist for mass murder."

However, no such opprobrium awaits those defending the military offensive of the government in Country B. No, it is those *opposing* its policies that are smeared.

Of course, Country A *was* Yugoslavia; Country B *is* Ukraine.

The Western elite and their media marionettes routinely deploy lies and insinuations in grooming public opinion for illegal, unprovoked acts. The very different approaches of the Western elite to antiterrorist operations in Kosovo and Ukraine, and indeed elsewhere, show that what matters most is not the numbers killed or the amount of human suffering involved. Instead it is whether or not the government in question helps or hinders Western political, economic, and military hegemonic aspirations. The Western message, in the end, is not about how many innocent people are killed or how reprehensible the actions are but rather whose interests are being served.

OFFICIALLY ENDORSED LIBERAL CONSPIRACY THEORIES VS. THE DISAPPROVED TRUTH

There are formally "approved" conspiracy theories and those that do not receive official approval. Unfortunately, the designating of people as conspiracy theorists has nothing to do with the presence of any objective evidence to support a claim. Rather it is a *political call* based on whom the conspiracy theory concerns and who is developing it. Establishment gatekeepers are not objective judges but are heavily biased and label any idea they do not like as a conspiracy theory. Labeling someone a conspiracy theorist is their standard way of declaring that person to be off-limits (i.e., an unreliable source and a "crank"). It is a way of stifling dissent and debate in what on the surface appear to be free and democratic societies—and deliberately marginalizing people who challenge the dominant establishment narrative.

However, during the last few decades, the most prominent peddlers of conspiracy theories have been the same Western elites and their establishment gatekeepers who are so quick to accuse others of inventing maliciously tendentious intrigues.

In 2013, these establishment conspiracy theorists were at it again, claiming with deep conviction that it was the Syrian government who launched a chemical weapons attack at Ghouta, even though it is still unknown for sure who was responsible.

Other "acceptable" conspiracy theories concern elections. If the "wrong" side (i.e., the side the Western elite does not want to win) happens to win an election, then it is routinely claimed that the election has been fixed, rigged or stolen. Thus the late Hugo Chavez won his regular election victories in Venezuela not because he was genuinely popular but because he fixed the polls. The same was said about Mahmoud Ahmadinejad when he was reelected as Iranian president in 2009. When gatekeepers are asked for objective evidence to back up their claims of electoral fraud, there are only continued accusations without any substantiated proof.

According to Western assessment, the outcome of the election determines whether it has been rigged or not. When (pro-Russian) Viktor Yanukovich won the first runoff election for president of Ukraine in 2004, the "bad" election was declared fraudulent and nullified; (pro-Western) Viktor Yushchenko then "fairly" won the "good" second runoff election following the fortuitous and "good" (Western-supported) Orange Revolution. Nevertheless, the then incumbent Yushchenko failed to secure even a runoff spot during the 2010 Ukrainian presidential election and (pro-Russian) Viktor Yanukovich was elected president of Ukraine in a hotly contested "bad" election (considered to have been manipulated by the West, of course) against the "good" and Western-supported Yulia Tymoshenko. Alas, his "bad" election victory did not save Viktor Yanukovich from getting ousted by the "good" (Western-supported) Maidan Revolution in February 2014.

In Western elite circles, it is acceptable to claim Iraq possessed weapons of mass destruction (WMDs) although it did not. It is acceptable to say Iran has an aggressive nuclear program. It is acceptable to say that the Syrian government launched chemical weapons attacks against its own people. It is acceptable to say that Hugo Chavez engaged in the widespread fixing of elections. When the country being discussed is an official enemy, one does not need much, if any, evidence to make claims against it. The allegation does not even have to be logical.

Common sense suggests that had Bush and Blair genuinely believed Iraq possessed weapons of mass destruction in 2003, they would *not have dared* even to talk about attacking that country. Common sense also suggests that it would have been self-defeating and suicidal for the Assad government of Syria to launch a massive chemical weapons attack close to Damascus on the exact day and hour when United Nations inspectors were in town. The entire world knew that the prowar hawks in the West were looking for any pretext to launch military strikes against Syria. Still, the world as a whole is expected to swallow these elite theories, despite the lack of any real proof and the fact that they make no sense.

However, if the country, regime, or faction (usually a minority) under suspicion is a Western-supported one, anyone making any claims about its actions will promptly be called a "conspiracy theorist" or worse. This charge will be raised even if what they claim is, in fact, quite logical and based on facts.

In many ways, the image of Western presidents, prime ministers, and chancellors is perfect for what Western imperialism needs at present. It is entirely in line with the nonmacho model of Western political leaders: the reluctant warriors—the people who would prefer to spend their time on the golf course or listen to some music on their iPods rather than get involved in yet another brutal conflict somewhere. This image counts for quite a lot in selling US and EU foreign policy and getting support for it in the West.

Here one must give credit where it is due, even if it is through gritted teeth: US imperialism has a genius for reinventing itself. After the Bush years, the empire desperately needed a new kind of front man. The trouble with Bush, Cheney, Rumsfeld, and co. was that they were too obvious, too easy to protest against, and too similar in their apparent love of war and conquest. The hardcore fanatical neoconservatives cheered them on, of course, but the intelligent liberals realized that they had done considerable damage to the cause of Pax Americana and that a new kind of president was needed to extend global US hegemony and take things on to the next stage: one who would talk the language of dialogue and negotiation and stress the need for the US to act multilaterally—someone who would speak of a "new beginning between the United States and Muslims around the world" but would still carry on with the agenda of perpetual policing, or democracy through war.

It was hard to remain unimpressed by Barack Obama speaking about his opposition to the war in Iraq, maintaining that it was the "wrong war." He came across as personable, articulate, and sophisticated—a stark contrast to George W. Bush. The most significant thing about Obama from the viewpoint of the more cosmopolitan left-leaning liberals was that he could regain left-liberal support for Pax Americana and reduce the widespread anti-Americanism in the West, which had reached an all-time high in the Bush years. Obama would be able to rebuild bridges even with Europe; he was, in short, the sort of president that left-liberals craved. Moreover, the fact that he had a real chance of becoming America's first black president increased his appeal even more. Modern liberals and progressives were euphoric when Obama made it to the White House and believed a new era was dawning.

Anyone who predicted amid the euphoria of 2008 that the same Obama, the critic of the Iraq war, would lead Americans to even more military conflicts, would have been dismissed as a hopeless cynic and an anti-American obsessive. However, so it proved. The attacks on Islamic State positions in Syria mean that Obama, the man who won the Nobel Peace Prize in 2009, bombed no fewer than seven different countries in six years. There has been a new cold war too, to go with the hot ones. The president who first promised a "reset" in relations with Russia has taken his country and other Western nations into a second cold war with Moscow following the Western-engineered, highly provocative regime change in a strategically critical European country bordering Russia.

Yes, Obama & co. were what the Western elite needed over the previous few years. They needed a front man who did not *appear* to like war but who nevertheless kept on coming back for more. He was someone who talked the language of peace and conflict resolution and talked about noninterference in other nations' affairs but still worked, like presidents before him, to enforce regime change on governments that the Western elite wanted to be toppled. Those who believed that the Obama era would be radically different from previous US administrations showed a breathtaking naivete regarding the power of the US political elite and the vast influence the political lobbies and interest groups have on both US foreign and domestic policy.

Moreover, the truly depressing thing is that there were, and are, no better alternatives—as the present political system of the Western elite *will not allow* any. Those who think things will improve are likely to be cruelly disappointed. The face, race, or gender of the president may change, but the policies will stay more or less the same.

In any US elections, big business and special-interest groups cannot lose, because all candidates will deliver what is required of them if they win. Anyone who might pose a challenge to the system, from either left or right, will not get the required funding from or the backing of the political elite and will be portrayed as a dangerous extremist, fanatic, or worse by establishment gatekeepers.

Any such figure would not make it through the filter system that weeds out candidates who will not do more or less exactly what the political and business elite and their powerful lobbies want. Donald Trump has tried and unexpectedly triumphed, but the global elite is out to get him even as president of the United States of America when these lines are being written.

So, as the bombs rain down on Syria and Iraq, Libya and Afghanistan, Ukraine and Yemen, it is worth remembering that nothing else can be expected without a profound change of the entire American, and consequently Western, political system. Whether the public persona is President Wimp or President Macho, a Mr. President or a Ms. President, it does not make any real difference at all.

These are the times in which we are living.

9

A Critique of Socialism

The word "socialist" describes a broad range of ideas and proposals that are held together by a central encompassing doctrine: the centralization and state control of society—either because state control is deemed more efficient or more moral. Secondly, socialists agree that capitalism (free market conservatism or classical liberalism) is morally and hence politically flawed. Thirdly, some socialists of the Marxist persuasion argue that socialism is the last historical era that supplants capitalism before communism arrives (a "historicist" conception). This chapter will not focus on the third claim, since history has amply disproved it already.

Central Ownership and the Redistribution of Resources

Socialists claim that the economic system based on free market capitalism should be replaced or reformed. Most of them argue for a radical redistribution of resources, usually to workers—that is, those who, the socialists deem, do not directly own anything. They also advocate for the state or some form of democratic institution to take over the running of the economy. In the aftermath of Bolshevik socialism's collapse (it is a point of conjecture among the historicist Marxist wing as to whether the Soviet system was communist or socialist), many socialists abandoned state ownership and control of economic resources for alternative projects that proposed to be more flexible, democratic, and decentralized.

Economists of the Austrian School (notably Ludwig von Mises and Friedrich Hayek) had long predicted the inexorable collapse of socialism because of its inability in the absence of market-generated price mechanisms to plan resource distribution and consumption efficiently or effectively. Socialist economists, such as Oskar Lange, accepted the critique and challenge but pushed on with state-controlled policies, believing that complex economic modeling could replace the markets' prioritization of values through prices. For example, in Leontief's input-output models, such priorities are given values by either the central authorities or, in more recent turns with the socialist movement, more decentralized institutions, such as worker cooperatives.[196]

Either despite or as the consequence of the empirical challenge of the collapse of the Soviet system and, more importantly, the failure of centrally controlled economies throughout the West and the Third World, socialists have rallied to parade alternative conceptions of the communal ownership and control of resources. Market socialism, for instance, tolerates a predominantly market economy but demands that the state must control certain essential resources. These assets then may lead the general economy in politically desirable directions: for example, developing high technology industries, educational and health services, or the economic and physical infrastructure of the nation. Others argue that the markets should predominate and the state should control only the investment industry. However, the economists' critique that government intervention produces not only an inefficient outcome but also an effect that the planners themselves do not desire is extendable to all instances of intervention and especially to any intervention concerning investment. Here the complexity of the price mechanism deals not just with consumers' and producers' current preferences but also with their more subtle intertemporal choices concerning present and future consumption.

In the face of growing accusations against and unpopularity of central planning, many socialists have preferred instead to concentrate on altering the presiding property relationships, demanding that companies be given over to the workers rather than the assumed exploitive capitalist classes. Resources, most socialists claim, need to be radically redistributed.

Worker-controlled socialism, or rather worker-controlled capitalism, sees the way forward through worker-owned and operated businesses—usually small ones run on a democratic basis. Legislative proposals demanding more discussion and cooperation between management and staff are a manifestation of such beliefs. Nevertheless, the policy of giving control to the workers presumes the following:

- The workers are a definable class and are assumed to enjoy less moral and hence political status than they deserve (which ethically would have to be established).
- The workers are continuously in a condition of being either employed or exploited (perhaps by the same commercial concerns) and do not set up their own businesses or move between employers. An individual can be an employer, employee, worker, and capitalist at the same time, and since people can move between the economic classes, scientific precision is reduced and even abandoned.

The most obvious criticism of socialist plans for the redistribution of income involves the question, according to which moral or political criteria ought resources be distributed? Marx's penetrating clarion call that resources ought to be allocated "from each according to his ability to each according to his need" does not present any practical guidance as to what is supposed to constitute a *need*. Socialists may point, for example, to the disabled as deserving resources they are otherwise unable to attain. Others generate more sophisticated arguments than that (e.g., those are the "deserving" or "needy" who have historically been persecuted). However, this raises not only the question of how far back in history one ought to go but also a multitude of ethical implications of being born either guilty or culpable, and somehow deserving moral and economic reprobation, or needy and somehow deserving unearned resources. The latter certainly presents a paradox for most socialists, who castigated the aristocratic classes for their unearned incomes in nineteenth-century Europe.

Another valid criticism directed against arguments for a redistribution of resources, even if the redistribution criteria could be established, is that in the absence of permanent and rigorous controls, resources will inevitably become unevenly distributed again. Robert Nozick raises a vigorous challenge to socialists in his book *Anarchy, State, and Utopia*, asking what would be incorrect with a voluntary redistribution for, say, supporting a talented basketball player, which would produce an uneven distribution. Socialists may thus either have to recognize the continuously recurring redistribution of incomes and resources within a given band of tolerance or agree to a permanent inequality of revenue and resource ownership once voluntary exchanges are allowed. Faced with such criticisms, socialists can resort to arguments against the morality of capitalism or the free market.[197]

THE SOCIALISTS' MORAL CRITIQUE OF CAPITALISM

The naturally unequal distribution of talent, energy, skills, and resources is not something upon which socialists usually focus their moral critique. Instead they note the historical developments that led to an unequal distribution of wealth benefiting some individuals or nations. Armed conflicts and exploitation by the powerful, they argue, unfurled an immoral distribution, which reformers would prefer to correct to build a society on a more moral basis. Not all would claim that socialism then becomes necessary or that socialism provides the only evaluation of historical injustices, but socialists often refer to the past wrongs that have kept the downtrodden and subjugated poor and oppressed as a justification for current reforms or critique of the status quo. Proposals are wide-ranging on how society should redistribute resources, as are the projects ensuring that present and future generations are permitted at least equal access to a specified standard of living or opportunities. Here moderate socialists overlap with left-wing or modern liberals and pragmatic conservatives, who rely on the primacy of freedom but with a bit of redistribution to ensure that all children get a fair start in life.

Defining "fairness," however, is problematic for all socialists; it brings to the fore the issues outlined above regarding what standards, policies, and justifications are appropriate. If socialists depart from such intricacies, they assert that capitalism is morally flawed at its core—say, from its motivational or ethical underpinnings. The most widespread criticism leveled against capitalism (or classical liberalism) is the unethical or selfish material pursuit of wealth and riches. Socialists often decry the moral paucity of material values or those values that are assumed to characterize the capitalist world: competition, profit-seeking, and excessive individualism.

Socialists prefer collective action to individual action, or at least an individual act that is supportive of the group rather than personal or selfish values. Nonetheless, most socialists shy away from espousing an antimaterialist philosophy; unlike environmentalists, most support the quest for wealth, but only when it is pursued by and for the working class or, in less Marxist terminology, the underrepresented, the underdog, the oppressed, or the general poor. The socialists are often driven by a vision of a new golden age of riches that pure socialism will generate. (How that will be so without the price mechanism is the subject of socialist economics.) Some, however, do desire a lower standard of living for all—for the return to a simpler, collective life of earlier days; these socialists perceive a better life in the medieval socialism of local trade patterns and guilds. Such ascetically leaning socialists have much in common with environmentalists.

Regardless of the moral problem of permanently unequal distributions, socialists have an optimistic vision of what one can be—perhaps not what one now is (exploitive or oppressed) but what one is capable of—once society is reformed along socialist lines. Marxists, for example, assume that inconsistent or hypocritical bourgeois values will disappear; any class-based morality will also vanish (for class distinctions will disappear). However, what will indeed guide ethical behavior is not readily explored. Marx bypassed the topic except to say that men will consider each other as men and not as working class or bourgeois. Most Marxists assume that communism will end the want of religion, private property, and selfishness—all opiates of the unawakened masses that keep them in a state of anxiety and false consciousness. Accordingly, ample amounts of food for all, plentiful resources, unhindered talent, free personal development, and enlightened and willing collectivism will govern. Denying the necessity of all authority that some in the communist camp foresee is something they have in common with anarchists.

STARTING WITH THE FRENCH REVOLUTION

In essence, the French Revolution brought a violent end to monarchy and feudalism and declared the right and sovereignty of the individual free will. The new philosophy and spirit of the rights of all men was expressed in politics.

The political liberalism of the French Revolution inspired liberation, individuality, and the rejection of prescribed rules. Many were stimulated by the ideals of equality, fraternity, and liberty; they revolted against the tyranny of set formulas, practices, and conventions, and asserted the dignity of individual spirit instead. This new form of philosophy became one of the leading guidelines of the new school of Romantic poets, writers, and philosophers. Romantics' search for a new subject, their belief in nature, their emphasis on spontaneity, and their conviction that everyone has a right to express his ideas are the features of individualism that were the primary demand of the French Revolution.

Liberals argued for republicanism, agrarian socialism, and anarchism. Most of those who came to be called "radicals" emphasized the same themes: a sense of personal liberty and autonomy, belief in civic virtue, and hatred of corruption. They also asserted opposition to war because it only profited the landed interest and articulated their repudiation of the monarchy and aristocracy.

The winds of the French Revolution unfurled the fresh, new sails of the modern era. French society itself underwent an epic change as feudal, aristocratic, and religious privileges disappeared under the sustained onslaught of various radical left-wing political groups, the masses on the streets, and peasants in the countryside. The old concepts of tradition and hierarchy regarding monarchs, aristocrats, and the Catholic Church were abruptly overthrown under the mantra of "liberté, égalité, fraternité."[198]

Globally, the revolution accelerated the rise of republics and democracies, the spread of liberalism and secularism, the development of modern ideologies, and the adoption of total war. The fallout from the revolution had immediate and permanent consequences for human history: the Latin American independence wars, the Louisiana Purchase by the United States, and the Revolutions of 1848 are just a few of the numerous events that were ultimately the consequences of the eruption of 1789.

The history and consequences of the French Revolution have received enormous interest and scrutiny not only from the general public but also from scholars and academics. Research and writing on the revolutionary period in France, however, has long mirrored suppositions that were more or less Marxist.

The views of historians, in particular, have been characterized as falling along ideological lines, with disagreement over the implications and significant developments of the Revolution. Alexis de Tocqueville maintained that the Revolution was the manifestation of a flourishing middle class becoming assertive and conscious of its social importance. Other thinkers, like the conservative Edmund Burke, claimed that the revolution was the product of a few conspiratorial intellectuals who brainwashed the masses into subverting the old order—a claim embedded in the absolute belief that the revolutionaries had no legitimate complaints. Different historians, influenced by Marxist thinking, have emphasized the importance of the peasants and the urban workers in presenting the revolution as a gigantic class struggle. In general, scholarship on the French Revolution initially studied the political ideas and developments of the era, but it has gradually shifted toward social history that analyzes the impact of the revolution on individual lives.

The French Revolution is widely regarded as one of the most critical events in human history. The passing of the early modern era, which started around 1500, is traditionally assigned to the outbreak of the revolution in 1789, which is often seen as marking the dawn of the modern era. In France, the revolution permanently broke the power of the aristocracy and exhausted the wealth of the church, although both institutions survived despite the sustained damage.

The revolution produced the most significant and all-encompassing challenge to political absolutism up to that point in history and propagated democratic ideals throughout Europe and ultimately the world.

Both liberal reformers and radical politicians were reshaping national governments, a popular press advanced political awareness, and new values and ideas, such as modern liberalism, nationalism, and socialism, began to emerge.

Having said all that, one must not forget that the French Revolution was also the origin of totalitarian political ideas and of the legitimization of systematic, large-scale violence against social classes considered to be undesirable. Thus, as mentioned before, it had a profound impact on the wave of revolutions in 1848–49 involving about fifty countries around the world. These included the 1849 Baden Revolution with active Marxist participation instigated by *The Communist Manifesto*, published by Marx in 1848, and the Paris Commune of 1871—the first socialist government—following the French defeat in the Franco-Prussian War. The Paris Commune was the prelude to what would happen during the Russian Revolution and civil war, and in Germany, Austria, and Hungary after the First World War; and its ideas inspired Mao Zedong in his struggle at constructing a communist state in China.

The French Revolution's bloodletting foreshadowed the future of the West and reflected the true nature of democracies.

THE DEFINITION OF HORROR: TOTALITARIAN SOCIALISM

The term "socialism" encompasses a wide scope of theoretical and historical socioeconomic systems. Many political movements throughout history have also used the term describing themselves and their goals, thereby generating numerous types of socialism. Moreover, different self-described socialists have employed the name "socialism" to refer to different things, such as an economic system, a certain kind of society, a philosophical outlook, a collection of moral values and ideals, or even a particular kind of human character. Some definitions of socialism are very vague, while others are so specific that they include only a small number of the things that have been described as socialism in the past.

Reading Marx, it seems that socialism could be used as a pretext for just about anything during history: for the confiscation of property, for determining what could and could not be taught in the schools, for pronouncing what did or did not happen—and what should have happened. Since Marx listed more than a half-dozen different kinds of socialism back in 1848, it also seems that socialism is whatever a person says it is—and that all versions of it are objectionable—except, of course, the version of the person who happens to do the writing. Nevertheless, it is clear that there have been numerous political movements calling themselves "socialist" under some definition of the term. While some of their interpretations are mutually exclusive, all of them have generated debates over the real meaning of "socialism." This ideological rendition has always provided an excellent argument to the apologists of socialism, who conveniently ignore or tailor the various interpretations to justify their beliefs and goals.

This author is eager to make the case that totalitarian socialism characterizes the twentieth century more than anything else. Although that is not what most children learn in school or what most people would first think of, it is a reasonable conclusion. Not only was totalitarian socialism directly responsible for provoking the bloodiest war in history, but it has also been the gravest single cause of internal repression and mass murder in modern times.

According to *The Black Book of Communism* (1999), at least 94 million people were slaughtered by communist regimes during the twentieth century.[199] It is an enormous figure, yet that is the lowest estimate. Professor R. J. Rummel, in his landmark study, *Death by Government"* (1997), puts the death toll from communism at over 105 million—and his counts do not even cover the human costs of communism in most of Eastern Europe or countries like Cuba and Mozambique.[200] Nonetheless, his figure is twice the total number of military and civilian casualties killed during World War II.

The full catastrophe of this totalitarian socialist holocaust cannot, of course, be adequately conveyed by these grim statistics. Behind them lies a desolate landscape of economic collapse, mass poverty, physical and mental torture, and broken lives and communities. In fact, nothing illustrates the destructive impact of totalitarian socialism more vividly than the tsunami of refugees it has generated on every continent where it put down roots. Between 1945 and 1990, over 29 million people voted against communism with their feet in Asia, Africa, Europe, and Latin America. Had it not been for the fortified frontiers with their watchtowers and landmines, the world's totalitarian socialist states would have been emptied of their populations long before the fall of the Berlin Wall in 1989.[201]

Totalitarian Logic Disguised as Oxymoron

What generated this torrent of human suffering? What made life so intolerable for most of the inhabitants of these socialist countries?

The great Russian writer and patriot Aleksandr Solzhenitsyn has given us the answer: "Socialism begins by making all men equal in material matters … However, the logical progression toward so-called 'ideal' equality inevitably implies the use of force. Furthermore, it means that the basic element of personality – those elements that display too much variety regarding education, ability, thought and feeling – must themselves be leveled out … Let me remind you that 'forced labor' is part of the program of all prophets of Socialism, including the Communist Manifesto [1848]. There is no need to think of the Gulag Archipelago as an Asiatic distortion of a noble ideal. It is an irrevocable law."[202]

It was therefore always predictable that by requiring the abolition of private property and the family, and monopolistic ownership of agriculture and industry, the socialist pursuit of equality would necessarily produce the evil fruit of totalitarianism. One-party rule, the secret police, the imprisonment and torture of dissidents, concentration camps, mass executions, the political indoctrination of the young, the persecution of religious minorities—all these horrors have been the inevitable result of the centralization and monopolization of power. Power invariably corrupts the ruling elite and the bureaucracies of all full-blown socialist societies. How could it be any other way? How can one talk about freedom when one's livelihood from the cradle to the grave depends entirely on the state, which can with one hand give and with the other take away?

Unfortunately, but not surprisingly, many left-wing intellectuals of today still pursue the phantom of democratic socialism, convinced that democratic institutions will prevent socialism from degenerating into tyranny. The great classical liberal thinkers of the nineteenth century, by contrast, harbored no such illusions. Every single one of them discerned the incompatibility of state socialism with the maintenance of free and democratic institutions. They did so, moreover, long before the advent of the socialist tyrannies of the twentieth century.

John Stuart Mill sounded one of the earliest warnings more than fifty years before the Russian Revolution. In his essay "On Liberty" (1859), Mill declared,

> If the roads, the railways, the banks, the insurance offices, the great joint-stock companies, the universities and the public charities, were all of them branches of the government; if, in addition, the municipal corporations and local boards, with all that now devolves on them, became departments of the central administration; if the employees of all these different enterprises were appointed and paid by the government and looked to the government for every rise in life; not all the freedom of the press and popular constitution of the legislature would make this or any other country free other than in name.[203]

As Mill understood, freedom of speech, freedom of the press, freedom of assembly and freedom of association cannot be maintained if all the means of communication, such as newsprint, radio stations, and more are in the hands of the state. It is equally impossible, in such conditions, for opposition parties to win elections, mainly since a state-controlled economy prevents them in any case from acquiring the capital to finance their campaigns. That is why the oxymoronic phantom of democratic socialism is a contradiction in terms. Socialism must be either diluted or abandoned for the sake of democracy, or democracy (and liberty) will be surrendered in exchange for socialism.

The history of the Russian Revolution and all subsequent socialist revolutions vividly confirmed the inherently despotic nature of socialism, which was also recognized by Mill's Italian liberal contemporary, Joseph Mazzini (1805–72). In the essay "The Economic Question," written in 1858 and addressed to the workers of Italy, Mazzini denounced socialism with a passion. He not only defended private property as an institution essential to human progress and well-being but also pointed out that the establishment of a socialist society would, ironically, create the very worst form of inequality, because universal state ownership would require the creation of an all-powerful ruling bureaucracy. "Working-men, my Brothers," he asked, "are you disposed to accept a hierarchy of lords and masters of the common property? … Is not this return to ancient slavery?"[204]

The prophetic discernment of the nineteenth-century classical liberal critics of socialism is again very apparent in the writings of Frédéric Bastiat (1801–50), the leading French economist and free-trade activist of his generation. A constant critic of statism in general and socialism in particular, Bastiat summarized his objections in *The Law*, a short but lucid pamphlet published in 1850—the same decade, curiously enough, during which Mill and Mazzini raised their warning voices.[205] Bastiat offered many valuable insights in this comprehensive analysis, three of which should be mentioned here.

The first of them called attention to a fundamental contradiction concerning democratic socialism—a contradiction that continues to characterize present-day leftists and modern liberals. On the one hand, wrote Bastiat, socialists are allegedly committed to the cause of democracy, insisting that all responsible individuals should have the vote and an equal share in all political decision-making. On the other hand, they consider the same sovereign people incapable of running their lives without the interference and supervision of the all-powerful state. "When it is time to vote," wrote Bastiat, "apparently the voter is not to be asked for any guarantee of his wisdom. His will and capacity to choose wisely are taken for granted. But when the [socialist] legislator is finally elected—ah! Then indeed does the tone of his speech undergo a radical change. The people are returned to passiveness, inertness, and unconsciousness; the legislator enters into omnipotence. Now it is for him to initiate, to direct, to propel, and to organize."

Socialists were also profoundly misguided as well as arrogant, wrote Bastiat, because they mixed up *society* with *the state* and *altruism* with *collectivism*. As a consequence, he predicted that the socialists' program would not only undermine the spirit of community but also impoverish it, since moral and social progress depends on individual creativity and voluntary cooperation and not on state planning and coercion.

Finally, Bastiat pointed out, by centralizing all resources and decision-making within the state, socialism offered only a recipe for perpetual social conflict and upheaval, since it would awake unrealistic expectations that could never be satisfied and would encourage the people to live at each other's expense through the tax-and-benefits system.

THE SECOND GENERATION OF ANTISOCIALIST CRITICS

The scholarly attack on socialism by Bastiat, Mazzini, and Mill was renewed by the next generation of classical liberal thinkers in reaction to the rapid increase of socialist militancy throughout Europe during the 1880s and 1890s. During this period, its four leading figures in Britain—Herbert Spencer, Charles Bradlaugh, Auberon Herbert, and William E. H. Lecky—condemned socialism with severity and prophetic insight.

"The desire of each man to improve his circumstances, to reap the full reward of superior talent, or energy, or thrift," Lecky wrote in 1896, "is the very mainspring of the production of the world. Take these motives away … cut off all the hopes that stimulate, among ordinary men, ambition, enterprise, invention, and self-sacrifice and the whole level of production will rapidly and inevitably sink."[206]

Bradlaugh's and Lecky's objections to socialism were, of course, not confined to its material destructiveness. They too, like their classical liberal predecessors, recognized its hostility to freedom. Bradlaugh even anticipated that the imposition of socialism would require the ideological reconditioning of the entire population. This phenomenon has proved characteristic of all international and national socialist regimes, notably of Hitler's Germany, Stalin's Soviet Union and its Eastern European satellites, China before and during the Cultural Revolution, and North Korea today.[207]

Herbert Spencer and Auberon Herbert showed the same prudence in their comprehensive analyses of socialism. They not only underlined its incompatibility with liberty but also anticipated the terrible violence and cruelty to which it would give rise. Herbert declared in 1885: "In the presence of unlimited power lodged in the hands of those who govern … the stakes for which men played would be so terribly great that they would shrink from no means to keep power out of the hands of their opponents."[208]

With similar prescience, Spencer wrote, "The fanatical adherents of a social theory are capable of taking any measures, no matter how extreme, for carrying out their views: holding, like the merciless priesthoods of past times, that the end justifies the means. And when a general socialistic organization has been established, the vast, ramified, and consolidated body of those who direct its activities, using without check whatever coercion seems to them needful … [will exercise] a tyranny more gigantic and more terrible than any which the world has seen."[209]

It is undoubtedly a historic tragedy that all these warnings from the nineteenth century fell on deaf ears during the twentieth century. Will those pressing for world government in the twenty-first century heed them?

NIETZSCHE'S ACERBIC CRITIQUE OF SOCIALISM

Friedrich Nietzsche was a prominent critic of egalitarian ideals, as shown by his views on the intellectual forerunners, immediate causes, cognitive assumptions, and errors of socialism. His rejection of socialism is rooted in two essential claims: idealism of socialists—the illusion that the right "social combination" could bring about heaven on earth. Second, he viewed socialism as a particularly objectionable manifestation of the "pessimism of indignation"—a psychological sickness that afflicts individuals who are unwilling to accept responsibility for their wretchedness.

Nietzsche was one of the most scathing critics of many values that are ascendant in the contemporary political theory. Although Nietzsche was critical of many moral and political doctrines, few raised his ire quite as much as socialism. When discussing socialism, his tone became even more caustic than usual.[210]

In *Will to Power*, he contends that "the socialists' conception of the highest society is the lowest in the order of rank," and he describes the doctrine as "the logical conclusion of the *tyranny* of the least and dumbest."[211]

In *The Antichrist*, Nietzsche writes, "Whom do I hate most among the rabble today? The socialist rabble …"[212]

Nietzsche is an influential critic of progressive ideals. Instead of dismissing his political criticisms as the ill-conceived contemplations of a thinker who misread vital aspects of modern society, such as the market and bureaucracy, or trying to explain him as being closer to egalitarianism, contemporary readers would do well to take his critique of social-democratic values very seriously.[213]

Nietzsche's appraisal of the socialist concept of human nature prepares for Freud's misgivings about communism as he saw it evolving in the early years of the Soviet Union.

Nietzsche's critique of socialist idealism also anticipates Michael Oakeshott's skepticism of "rationalism in politics."

I. The Forerunners of Socialism

According to Nietzsche, the socialist ideal represents the "residue of Christianity and Rousseau in the de-Christianized world."[214]

Nitzsche sees socialism as another in a long line of "idealist" systems that are inherently flawed. Idealists renounce *this* world and embrace another. The "mischief of idealism" began with Socrates and Plato, who created a "world of Truth"—a "realm of Being"—and, because of this, brought about a "denaturalization of moral values." Idealism, in Nietzsche's view, "deprived reality of its value, its meaning, its truthfulness," and he therefore believed that "Socrates represents a moment of the most profound perversity in the history of values."[215]

II. The Grandfather of Socialist Thought: Christianity

Nietzsche also identifies Christianity as an idealist philosophy that, like Platonism, rejects *this* world for another. While Socrates and Plato contended that the realm of the Forms, or the "World of Being," is what matters, Christians emphasize the importance of an *eternal* kingdom of heaven for believers. In both cases, it must be noted that bliss is not something that can be achieved through a transformation of *this* world. Rather, both Plato and Jesus can be interpreted as offering people a philosophy of life they can establish within themselves. The essential point for Nietzsche is this: the Christian, in typical idealist fashion, "condemns, disparages, and curses the 'world.'"216

According to Nietzsche, Christ's emphasis on personal transformation was not shared by St. Paul. Whereas "primitive Christianity" is, according to Nietzsche's reading, "possible as the most *private* form of existence," the Christianity of St. Paul is much more public, and thus more like a political doctrine. Once one regards Christianity as a social theory instead of a personal one, it becomes clear how it can be viewed as a forerunner of socialism.

Nietzsche saw the Christian slave revolt in morality as quite similar to future political revolutions. Christianity offers the poor and lowly a gateway to happiness, and for Nietzsche, "to this extent the rise of Christianity is nothing more than the *typical socialist doctrine*." The matters of this world that the gospel passes judgment on, such as "property, gain, fatherland, rank and status, tribunals, police, state, church, education, art, the army," are "all typical of the socialist doctrine."217

The second foundational contribution of Christianity to the socialist doctrine is the idea of "equality of souls before God." Nietzsche is not arguing that socialists accept the tenets of Christianity as a matter of faith. Rather, like so many political actors throughout history, he thinks socialists are adept at using Christian ideas for their purposes: "The socialists appeal to the Christian instincts; that is their most subtle piece of shrewdness."218

In *The Antichrist*, Nietzsche calls the "equality of souls before God" the "pretext for the rancor of all base-minded, the concept that eventually became revolution, modern idea, and the principle of decline of the whole order of society."219 Nietzsche traces the warpath of this idea quite explicitly in *Will to Power*: "Mankind was first taught to stammer the proposition of equality in a religious context, and only later was it made into morality: no wonder that man ended by taking it seriously, taking it practically! – that is to say, politically, democratically, socialistically …"220

Nietzsche concludes that the socialist ideal is "nothing but a clumsy *misunderstanding* of the Christian moral ideal." He identified socialism and other "progressive" theories as "cults of Christian morality under a new name" but thought that they fundamentally misunderstood Christianity. These doctrines represent misunderstandings of the Christian moral ideal because they transfer "the arrival of the 'kingdom of God' into the future, on earth, in human form …" Therefore, the rise of socialism and kindred doctrines can, in part, be explained with the "death of God": without the hope of exultation in the *next* world, socialists and others seek to transform *this* one. The emergence of the socialist ideal is part of our payment "for having been Christians for two thousand years."[221]

To understand the complete development of the doctrine of this-worldly transformation, one must turn from the Christians to the philosopher whom Nietzsche described as the link between Platonic-Christian idealism and the socialist idealism of the nineteenth century—Jean-Jacques Rousseau.

III. The Grandmother of Socialist Thought: Jean-Jacques Rousseau and the Eighteenth Century

The thought of Rousseau and the eighteenth century provides an essential link between the otherworldliness of Christianity and the this-worldliness of socialism. According to Nietzsche, Rousseau was a dreamer. He was the typical personality of a time "dominated by woman, given to enthusiasm, full of *spirit*, shallow but with a spirit in the service of what is desirable, of the heart … intoxicated, cheerful, clear, humane, false before itself, much *canaille au fond*, sociable."[222] This spirit energized an age of ideology when zealous dreamers believed it was in their power to launch the world once more.

What sets Rousseau apart from the Christian tradition is his idealization of human nature and his belief in the transformative power of human institutions; clearly, these two ideas are inextricably intertwined. For Rousseau, man's nature is inherently good, but he was corrupted by various advances in human civilization (especially the institution of private property). Although man's natural innocence has been lost, Rousseau thought that a new form of moral goodness could replace it through the establishment of new political institutions. When we compare this to St. Augustine, we can see what a departure this is from the mainstream of Pauline Christianity.

Augustine held that man is inescapably sinful and concludes that, as such, the city of God cannot be achieved on earth. Rousseau's significant offering to the foundation of socialist thought is in his denial of human sinfulness and his commitment to human betterment through institutional development. With this foundational belief, he set the stage for perfectionist political doctrines that moved the focus from the next world of Christianity by arguing that *this* world can be transformed into heaven on earth.

IV. The Birth of Socialism

In Nietzsche's mind, the rise of socialism as a moral and political ideal can be traced back to the Christian rejection of this world and the moral perfectionism of Rousseau and other eighteenth-century thinkers. Aside from these long-term factors, Nietzsche thought there were more immediate reasons for socialist challenges to the economic and political hierarchy.

First, Nietzsche considered that the "socialist rabble" (political agitators) contributed to unrest by inciting workers to believe that they should be dissatisfied with their station in life.

Second, Nietzsche believed that the ruling class in industrial culture, the capitalists, "lacked noble manners" and as such were not held in enough respect by the working class. In Nietzsche's mind, these two factors played off one another and created the conditions necessary for revolutionary thought and action.

Beyond Good and Evil, Nietzsche argues that "ordinary human beings," especially workers, "exist for service and the general advantage and ... *may* exist only for that."[223] This argument is necessary because, as Nietzsche declares in *The Antichrist*, "high culture is a pyramid: it can stand only on a broad base; its first presupposition is a strong and soundly consolidated mediocrity ... To be a public utility, a wheel, a function, for that one must be destined by nature ..."[224] It is to say that the workers' service is "the only kind of *happiness* of which the great majority are capable."[225]

In short, "for the mediocre, to be mediocre is their happiness; mastery of *one* thing, specialization—a natural instinct."[226] Beyond the happiness attained in performing their particular tasks well, the workers also receive comfort in religion, which

> gives an inestimable contentment with their situation and type. It gives manifold peace of the heart, an ennobling of obedience, a furthering of happiness and sorrow with their peers and something transfiguring and beautifying, something of a justification for the

> whole everyday character, the whole lowliness, the whole half-brutish poverty of their souls. Perhaps nothing in Christianity or Buddhism is as venerable as their art of teaching even the lowliest how to place themselves through piety in an illusory higher order of things and thus to maintain their contentment with the real order, in which their life is hard enough – and *precisely this hardness is necessary.*[227]

Here we have part of Nietzsche's naturalistic safeguarding of the aristocracy. He believes the worker is *naturally* suited for a simple, specialized existence in which he can find happiness in his role and comfort in the assurances of religion.

Many things can interrupt a machinelike high culture, but the focus is on two such things here: the propaganda of the socialist rabble and the lack of noble manners of industrial leaders (or the ruling elite today). In any case, the smooth operation of a hierarchal society depends on the contentment of the various classes. In Nietzsche's view, workers can and "should" (in a naturalistic sense) be content with their lot in life. Alas, this contentment is upset by the socialist rabble: "Whom do I hate most among the rabble today? The socialist rabble, the chandala apostles, who undermine the instinct, the pleasure, the worker's sense of satisfaction with his small existence – who make him envious, who teach him revenge. The source of wrong is never unequal rights but the claim of 'equal' rights …"[228]

Nietzsche views the socialist rabble as the priests of a new slave revolt and the workers as the herd waiting to be led by their noses. The propaganda of the socialist rabble causes the worker to become dissatisfied with his life, and then he begins to ask questions. One of the first questions might be something like this: Why does the boss have a life so much more comfortable than my own? That brings us to the problem of "noble manners."

According to Nietzsche, the propaganda of the socialist rabble is *not*, by itself, sufficient to bring about worker revolt. This is because the recognition that one is "lower" than someone else is *not*, prima facie, a cause for discontent. What matters is not that one is in a subordinate position, but *whom* one is subordinated to: "For the masses at the bottom are willing to submit to the slavery of any kind if only the higher-ups constantly legitimize themselves as higher, as *born* to command – by having noble manners."[229]

In *The Gay Science*, Nietzsche explains the importance of "noble manners":

> Oddly, submission to powerful, frightening, even terrible persons, like tyrants, generals or oligarchs, is not experienced as nearly so painful as is the submission to unknown and uninteresting persons, which is what all the luminaries of industry are. What the workers see in the employer is usually only a cunning, bloodsucking dog of a man who speculates on all misery; and the employer's name, shape, manner, and reputation are a matter of complete indifference to them. The manufacturers and entrepreneurs of business probably have been too deficient so far in all those forms and signs of a *higher race* that alone make a *person* interesting. If the nobility of birth showed in their eyes and gestures, there might not be any socialism of the masses.[230]

Because the "luminaries of industry" lack noble manners, the workers get "the idea that is only accident and luck that have elevated one person above another … and thus socialism is born."[231] Those who fail to exhibit the qualities appropriate to their "caste" undermine the idea of natural hierarchy. Thus, the arguments of the socialist rabble begin to seem more reasonable to the worker.

In *Will to Power*, Nietzsche explains the emergence of Christianity in similar terms: "The degeneration of the rulers and the ruling classes has been the cause of the greatest mischief in history! Without the Roman Caesars and Roman society, the insanity of Christianity would never have come to power."[232]

The base of the broad cultural pyramid is not blind, deaf, and dumb, but it will remain content to be the base only if it knows that the structure it is supporting *deserves* to be supported. The higher-ups must constantly legitimize themselves as higher, or the base will deteriorate.

That makes it clear, according to Nietzsche, that the two immediate causes of the rise of socialism play off one another; the socialist rabble tells the worker that he should demand more from the higher-ups, and the capitalist cannot justify his status and, thus, begins to back down against the working class.

The ruling class bestows upon the worker the right to organize, vote, and serve in the military while simultaneously trying to keep him in a position of economic subordination. Nietzsche sees these concessions as further evidence of the lack of noble manners, or disorientation: "If one wants slaves, then one is a fool if one educates them to be masters."[233] This problem is, of course, the eternal dilemma of the elite: to stand up against the socialist rabble, risking a revolution, or to stand down and compromise, thereby revealing a "lack of noble manners."

One may object that Nietzsche has not made clear whether the socialist rabble causes the worker to challenge the existence of natural hierarchy or whether the lack of noble manners of the luminaries of industry causes the creation of a socialist rabble in the first place. It is a question that has been debated by socialist theorists and others for more than a century and a half. Is there a primary source of class-consciousness? More fundamentally, is there such a thing as class-consciousness? Can a "vanguard elite" accelerate class-consciousness?

It is essential here to mention that Nietzsche diagnosed *both* the indoctrination by the socialist rabble *and* the lack of noble manners of the ruling classes as agents to a fundamental change in worker awareness. With these two sources of the birth of socialism now established, we can now turn to a more detailed account of the psychology of the socialist ideal and consider Nietzsche's criticism of it.

V. Nietzsche's Critique of Socialist Idealism

Nietzsche's critique of socialism can be divided into two major lines of argument. The first line is grounded in Nietzsche's identification of socialism with a Rousseauian perfectionist political theory. For Nietzsche, Rousseau and socialist thought represent forms of idealism that ought to be met with "suspicion and malice" because they promise what they cannot deliver, and even if they could, their ideals are undesirable. The main source of their mistake is the wrong idea about human nature and an unwarranted belief in the life-changing power of human institutions.

Nietzsche's second line of critique is based on his recognition of socialism as a political theory created by resentment and a desire for revenge. In Nietzsche's opinion, socialism is "an attack of sickness" caused by "underprivileged" individuals who blame "society" for their "lack of power and self-confidence." In other words, socialism, like other forms of *ressentiment*, is a manifestation of the "will to power" of the "least and dumbest" members of society.[234]

Nietzsche read Rousseau's political theory as idealist or perfectionist insofar as it was grounded in the idea that man's natural goodness can be restored through the reformation of human institutions. Nietzsche believed that socialists chose to accept this central feature of Rousseau's thought. "How ludicrous I find the socialists, with their nonsensical optimism concerning the 'good man', who is waiting to appear from behind the scenes if only one would abolish the old 'order' and set all the 'natural drives' free."[235]

Nietzsche rejected this form of idealism and contended that the philosophy of Rousseau and the socialists denounced essential elements of life, therefore meaning that their aims were delusionary at best, deceiving at worst.

"Waste, decay, elimination need not be condemned: they are *necessary* consequences of life, of the growth of life. ... It is a disgrace for all socialist systematizers that they suppose there could be circumstances – social combinations – in which vice, disease, prostitution, and distress would no longer grow. – But that means condemning life. – A society is not free to remain young. ... Age is not abolished by means of institutions. Neither is disease. Nor vice."[236]

The socialist belief in perfect social combinations is what Nietzsche sarcastically calls a "gift from the eighteenth century." Indeed, socialism deviates from what Nietzsche identifies as the "progress of the nineteenth century against the eighteenth century." Consideration of this progress reveals the second aspect of Nietzsche's critique of socialist idealism. In *Will to Power*, Nietzsche declares, "We *good Europeans* wage a war against the eighteenth century." Nietzsche was skeptical of not only perfect social combinations but also the revolutionary character of the eighteenth century and the socialist movement. Against these radical dispositions, Nietzsche endorses the central characteristics of the "darker, more realistic, and stronger" nineteenth century: "more and more decisively anti-idealistic, more concrete, more fearless, industrious, moderate, suspicious against sudden changes, *anti-revolutionary*."[237]

According to Nietzsche, Rousseau's "return to nature" was a "dream" and real "progress toward 'naturalness'" demands the repudiation of the romantic idealism of the eighteenth century. In Nietzsche's view, the source of error for Rousseau and the socialists is a flawed theory of human nature.

For Nietzsche, the French Revolution represented the "continuation of Christianity," and Rousseau was its "seducer." The starting point of Rousseau's idealism is the forgetting of man's nature; only by "cleaning the slate" of human nature can perfectionists like Rousseau promise to "begin the world anew."[238] Rousseau and the socialists tell us that the sweeping away the old order and replacing it with something kinder, gentler, and more humane can realize Utopia. With these new institutions in place, Man can recover his lost innocence, and social harmony will follow.

Nietzsche thinks this is pure folly. Against this faith in the infinite malleability and perfectibility of human nature, Nietzsche offers a much more realistic view. In *Will to Power*, he writes: "Not to know oneself: prudence of the idealist. The idealist: a creature that has good reasons to be in the dark about itself and is prudent enough to be in the dark about these reasons too." The act of *forgetting* is a *necessary* step in the idealist projects of Rousseau and the nineteenth-century socialists. Only by forgetting what they know of human nature can they place faith in the transformative possibilities of social combinations. For Nietzsche, the idea of perfecting man through institutional change is impossible and, at the bottom, undesirable.[239]

In sum, Nietzsche's identifying socialism as a form of idealism is based on his dismissal of the improvability of human nature and the transformative power of human institutions. Unlike Rousseau and the socialists, Nietzsche is unwilling to forget man's nature to assimilate him to an ideal. Instead, Nietzsche argues, the only model worth embracing is one that can be reconciled with all that *nature* has to offer—but *not* the idealized, sanitized, and exalted conception of nature proposed by philosophers of the eighteenth century and the socialists of the nineteenth century.

VI. Nietzsche's Critique of Socialism as a Politics of Revenge

A critical aspect of Nietzsche's assessment of socialism is his identification of it as a politics of resentment and revenge. The basis for this facet of Nietzsche's analysis is identical to that which we find at the foundation of his rejection of anti-Semitism. He describes *who* they are he is talking about among others as such: "socialist systematizers," "socialist rabble," and "socialist workers." As noted above, these terms can make his appraisal of the *psychology* of socialism somewhat confusing.

Does the socialist worker grow a sense of resentment on his own volition? If so, is it the consequence of his employer's "lack of noble manners" or the worker's own need to hold someone responsible for his misery?

Alternatively, is there an *external force*—what Nietzsche usually calls "the socialist rabble" convincing the worker that he is oppressed and ought to rebel— that raises worker consciousness? If this second possibility rings true, it gives rise to a new set of questions. Are the socialist systematizers true believers who are genuinely committed to the ideals they are promoting? Alternatively, is socialist doctrine merely a *means* for the elite to maximize their power? If the latter is true, are the workers themselves then just a *means* of this elite? Have the workers been merely duped by a small cadre of intellectuals on whose behalf they are urged to revolt? Nietzsche uses the term "socialist" to include *both* activists *and* workers.

Throughout his writings, Nietzsche identifies socialists as "underprivileged" human beings. They believe themselves to be suffering and seek to find the cause of their pain. However, unlike Christians who blame the entire world, *themselves included*, for their suffering, socialists are unwilling to blame themselves. Instead, socialists "condemn, slander, and besmirch *society*."[240] They are, in Nietzsche's words, the "apostles of revenge and ressentiment" who seek someone else to be responsible and get punished for their failure.

Nietzsche labels this way of looking at the world the "pessimism of indignation." It is manifest when an individual exclaims, "How can *I* help that I am wretched! But somebody must be responsible. Otherwise, it would be unbearable!"[241]

The socialist "discovers" responsibility in those who support and maintain the unjust political and economic system. The socialist then seems to say, "The system has made me wretched. Therefore, if we overturn the system and punish those who supported it, I will not be wretched any longer." Here is the connection, then, between the idealism discussed earlier and the pessimism of indignation. Aside from finding someone to blame, the socialists also produce a model for a new social order that could extricate people from a condition of wretchedness.

Nietzsche's rejection of socialism is fundamentally identical to his condemnation of anti-Semitism. The socialist and anti-Semite are, in Nietzsche's mind, alike because each places a scapegoat at the center of his code of justice. "The underprivileged need an appearance of justice, i.e., a theory through which they can shift responsibility for their existence, for being thus and thus, on to some sort of scapegoat. This scapegoat can be God – in Russia, there is no lack of atheists from *ressentiment* – or the social order, or education and training, or the Jews, or the nobility, or those who have turned out well in any way."[242]

These statements are among the most powerful defenses of Nietzsche against the charge that he was an anti-Semite or proto-Nazi. It is evident that what he loathes in both socialism and anti-Semitism is each outlook's rejection of personal responsibility and fabrication of an excuse that blames others for their own failure. That socialism and anti-Semitism differ in *whom* they blame is, for Nietzsche, irrelevant. What matters is that both have singled out as "evil … precisely the 'good man' of the other morality, precisely the noble, powerful man, the ruler, but dyed in another color, interpreted in another fashion, seen in another way by the venomous eye of *ressentiment*."[243]

Nietzsche identifies the pessimism of indignation as a mental disease that afflicts those who are unwilling and unable to accept their lot in life and seek to blame others for their condition. He asserts that socialists and others suffering from the pessimism of indignation ought to be viewed as "invalids who feel better for crying out, for whom defamation is a relief."[244] In other words, socialist activism and agitation are day-to-day outcries—a form of catharsis for the underprivileged. "In short," Nietzsche explains, "the pessimism of indignation invents responsibility to create a *pleasant feeling* for itself."[245] To the extent that socialists are "crying out" to soothe themselves, Nietzsche says, "there is no reason for taking this clamor seriously."[246] It is when this crying out builds up to the frenzy of revolutionary action that Nietzsche says society ought to get concerned.

Although Nietzsche sees day-to-day socialist agitation as relatively innocuous, he warns that these small symptoms of revenge are but a prologue to what the socialists hope will be the "day of reckoning": revolution. As in his assessment of the French Revolution, Nietzsche sees the socialist hope for revolution as a yearning to join in the ultimate therapy for the pessimism of indignation. A socialist revolution would serve as a "retrograde movement" in Nietzsche's view of progress. That is why Nietzsche believes that the existence of the socialist rabble can be "something useful and therapeutic" for "good Europeans." "It forces the Europeans to retain the spirit, namely cunning and cautious care, not to abjure manly and warlike virtues altogether, and to retain some remnant of spirit, of clarity, sobriety, and coldness of spirit – it protects Europe for the time being from the feminine withering that threatens it … In socialism, we see a thorn that protects against comfortableness."[247]

Nietzsche thought "a few great experiments" in socialism "might prove that in a socialist society life negates itself" and "hence such a practical instruction … would not strike me as undesirable, even if it were gained and paid for with a tremendous expenditure of human lives."[248] In other words, the sacrifice of human lives for the cause of socialism could be progressive for humanity insofar as it helps people recognize ideas that should *not* be pursued.

That provokes a direct but complicated question: Why is the socialist ideal less justifiable than Nietzsche's own model of the "Superman"? In the following brief explanation, I will try to illuminate the reasons behind Nietzsche's rejection of socialism.

Contrary to the interpretation of Nietzsche as an apolitical or antipolitical thinker, he did see a direct relationship between his ideal of the Superman and the sociopolitical systems that were in place at the time. The clearest statement of this link is in *Beyond Good and Evil*:

> We have a different faith: to us the democratic movement [of which socialism is a part] is not only a form of the decay of political organization but a form of the decay, namely the diminution, of man, making him mediocre and lowering his value … The overall *degeneration of man* down to what today appears to the socialist dolts and flatheads as their "man of the future" – as their ideal – this degeneration and diminution of man into the perfect herd animal, this animalization of man into the dwarf animal of equal rights and claims, is *possible,* there is no doubt of it. Anyone who has once thought through this possibility to the end knows one kind of nausea that other men don't know – but perhaps also a new *task!*[249]

Nietzsche saw himself resisting the diminution of man into a "perfect herd animal" and postulating a new meaning of progress. He challenged the sine qua nons and teleological views of humanity and history and believed that man ought to serve as a bridge to conditions under which better and stronger individuals could thrive.

Although it is clear that Nietzsche rejected the idealism and ressentiment of the socialist outlook, it is not clear whether or not he also provided a coherent explanation for the origins of socialist psychology. It seems at times as if Nietzsche believes socialist ideas originate in the minds of workers—his "internal interpretation," as it were. Even if this is an accurate interpretation of Nietzsche's position, the question remains as to *why* these ideas take hold in the minds of workers. In some places, it would seem they emerge because of the ruling class's lack of noble manners; in other places, they seem to surface as a result of the worker's search for an explanation concerning his suffering (the pessimism of indignation).

Alternatively, there is an "external interpretation," according to which the socialist ideas do not originate in the minds of individual workers but are created by an external group that wishes to use the workers as an *instrument* of their will to power. However, even if one accepts this external interpretation, there still exists the possibility of a subdivision within it. It could be asked, perhaps, whether the socialist activists genuinely believe in those concepts they are promoting, but Nietzsche already rejected this option. Idealists are, in his view, shrewd enough to know that they are more likely to gain power if they do everything "for others."[250]

Although Nietzsche did not leave an entirely coherent response to these questions, it can be safely assumed that the external interpretation was the most plausible to him. The strongest argument for the external explanation can be found in *The Antichrist*, where Nietzsche accuses the socialist rabble of subverting the sense of satisfaction a worker can get out of his life. It is the socialist rabble "who makes him envious, who teaches him revenge."[251] Then, it seems, an external source sows the seeds of discontent within the worker.

The substance of socialist psychology becomes relevant at this point; the socialist rabble instructs the worker that he ought to be more demanding. "Why," the once content worker may ask, "should I be subject to constant struggle while my boss enjoys such material comfort?"

The agitating socialist rabble might respond, "Look at your boss, that bloodsucking dog of a man! He sits in his office getting fat while you slave away in the factory! He is capitalizing on your misery. Is that fair? Is that just? He is the cause of your suffering, and it is a due time that we rid ourselves of the system that has allowed him to victimize you all of these years! We can institute a system built on fairness and equality rather than exploitation and inequality. Workers of the world - unite!"[252]

According to Nietzsche, the socialist rabble does not honestly have the interests of the working class at heart. Instead this "cult of altruism" is nothing but a "disguised form of the will to power"; it is, in Nietzsche's words, "a specific form of egoism that regularly appears under certain physiological conditions."²⁵³ The idea of collective aims of the herd is one of the myths of social life, with socialism also being a covert form of it.

> Socialism is merely a means of agitation employed by individualism: it grasps that, to attain anything, one must organize oneself to a collective action, to a 'power.' But what it desires is not a social order as the goal of the individual but a social order as a means for making possible many individuals: this is the instinct of socialists about which they frequently deceive themselves (apart from the fact that to prevail, they frequently *have to* deceive themselves).
>
> The preaching of altruistic morality in the service of individual egoism: one of the most common lies in history.²⁵⁴

It seems that, in Nietzsche's view, socialists recognize that the herd is a means by which one can attain power for himself.

In sum, Nietzsche would not have been taken by surprise by the obtained power of the latter-day vanguard elite fighting for others.

VII. Categorizing Nietzsche's Critique of Socialism: Where Nietzsche's Critique Does Not Fit

At one time in the history of Nietzsche studies, it would have been perhaps reasonable to try to place his critique of socialism within the fascist doctrine. It is apparent today, however, that there is a mismatch; for fascists, socialism was questionable because it "confines the movement of history within the class struggle and ignores the unity of classes established in one economic and moral reality in the State."²⁵⁵ From the fascist perspective, the only aim that matters is the purpose of the state as an organic moral entity. Fascism opposes both socialism and liberalism for emphasizing class and individual respectively.

This fascist critique of socialism cannot be reconciled with Nietzsche's. First, Nietzsche contended that a state has no natural aim, contrary to the fascist assertion that it is a natural entity with an almost supernatural moral purpose. Second, and most importantly, Nietzsche adamantly opposed nationalist beliefs in a "folk soul" since he considered it a basic error to think of collective wills. Instead he instructs us to view the will as resides in individuals and to see the "collective whole" as a means to the exercise of the will to power.

A second area where Nietzsche's arguments should not be placed is alongside liberal critiques of socialism—with two minor exceptions. First, while Nietzsche did oppose acquisitiveness as a philosophy of life, he saw it as *part of* a healthy world. In *Will to Power*, he mentions that the longing to own things is "the oldest and healthiest of all instincts." He even adds that the desire to acquire more than one already possesses is "the doctrine preached by life itself to all that is life."[256] The natural defense of acquisitiveness is *limited* insofar as Nietzsche rejects it as a philosophy of life because it has no aim. It provides the basis for Nietzsche's critique of the nineteenth-century liberal Herbert Spencer, who offered what Nietzsche called a "shopkeeper's philosophy" that was deficient because of the "complete absence of an ideal, except that of the mediocre man."[257]

The second exception is that a case can be made that twentieth-century libertarians have adopted part of Nietzsche's critique of socialism. More specifically, Ayn Rand followed Nietzsche in identifying socialism as a covert form of egoism, and a few libertarians have adopted his interpretation of socialist psychology.

With those two exceptions mentioned, it would be unfair to align Nietzsche's critique of socialism with the liberals for two main reasons. First, unlike most liberals, it does not appear that Nietzsche offered either any moral or utilitarian defense of market economics against the socialist challenge. Second, Nietzsche rejected the liberal conceptions of liberty and equality throughout his writings, and these commitments are central to most liberal critiques of socialism.[258]

VIII. Joining Nietzsche's View of Human Nature with Freud

The fundamental point of agreement between Nietzsche and Freud in their assessments of socialism is the conclusion that the socialist doctrine rests on a flawed understanding of human nature. Socialists, similarly to the philosophers of the eighteenth century, keep forgetting human nature in the interest of absorbing people to their ideal. During the twentieth century, few thinkers were more realistic and pragmatic than Freud. When Freud turned his probing eye to socialism, he saw a delusional philosophy in much the same way as Nietzsche did.

To Freud, the communists of the twentieth century were pursuing a perfectionist political program like that of the nineteenth-century socialists Nietzsche was opposing. In *Civilization and Its Discontents*, Freud writes,

> The communists believe that they have found the path to deliverance from our evils. According to them, man is wholly good and is well disposed to his neighbor; but the institution of private property has corrupted his nature … If private property were abolished, all wealth held in common, and everyone allowed sharing in the enjoyment of it, ill will and hostility would disappear among men … But I can recognize that the psychological premises on which the communist system is based are an untenable illusion. In abolishing private property, we deprive human love of aggression of one of its instruments, certainly a strong one, though certainly not the strongest; but we have in no way altered the differences in power and influence that are misused by aggressiveness, nor have we altered anything in its nature.[259]

Freud, like Nietzsche, retained a deep suspicion of social combinations that promise to bring about Utopia. Both Freud and Nietzsche diagnose in the solidarity of the socialist doctrine *not* the product of love but rather the unifying power of a common enemy—the scapegoat.

The central and fundamental flaw Freud identified in socialist doctrine was the notion that private property is the primary if not the single cause of man's depravity. With this basic concept, socialists were able to claim that man could recover only if the idea of private property itself were abolished and replaced by a kinder, more humane system. To take a conspicuous example, utopian socialist Robert Owen argued that since the "character is universally formed *for*, and not *by* the individual" the "adoption of [socialist] principles of truth … will enable mankind to *prevent*, in the rising generation, almost all of the evils and miseries which we and our forefathers have experienced."[260]

For Freud and Nietzsche alike, the idea that human beings are naturally good or blank slates and that their goodness can be recovered or created through the abolition of private property is sheer nonsense. Man's "depravity" is so deeply rooted and widely entrenched that the abolishment of private property would accomplish little and not change his basic constitution.

The second aspect of Nietzsche's critique that anticipates Freud is the idea that socialism has its roots not in love and fraternity, as the socialists would have the world believe, but in resentment and revenge. According to Freud, "It is always possible to bind together a considerable number of people in love, so long as there are other people left over to receive the manifestations of their aggressiveness." Freud pointed to nascent Soviet Russia as evidence of this phenomenon: "It is intelligible that the attempt to establish a new, communist civilization in Russia should find its psychological support in the persecution of the bourgeois. One only wonders, with concern, what the Soviets will do after they have wiped out their bourgeois."[261]

Nietzsche noted a similar aspect in his assessment of socialism. Socialists, like other underprivileged human beings, reveal their yearning for power by attacking those who are allegedly responsible for their suffering. Nietzsche considers it a basic error to think of socialists, or any other herd morality, as a collectivity with collective or common aims. Rather, he contends, goals exist in "single individuals" and the "herd is a means, no more!"[262] Like Freud, Nietzsche held that what is primitive in socialism is not a love for one's fellow human being but rather a love of power and a desire to find the most efficient way to exercise one's will to power.

In sum, Nietzsche's critique of socialism can be aligned with Freud insofar as both advise us to probe the darkest corners of human nature to find the psychological roots of altruistic projects. When Freud and Nietzsche engaged in this exercise, each emerged contending that socialists are both delusional and predatory. For both thinkers, the fundamental defect of socialist thought is a flawed theory of human nature that forgets man's innate depravity just to be able to offer hope that Utopia can be realized in this world.

IX. Nietzsche and Oakeshott against Rationalism in Politics

Nietzsche's preference for the nineteenth over the eighteenth century was, in part, grounded in his interpretation of the former as "anti-idealistic, more concrete, more fearless, industrious, moderate, suspicious against sudden changes, *anti-revolutionary*." Nietzsche tells us that he is "full of suspicion and malice against what they call 'ideals': this is *my* pessimism, to have recognized how the 'higher feelings' are a source of misfortune and man's loss of value."[263]

This critique of idealistic political theories was echoed in the twentieth century by Michael Oakeshott, who lamented the dominance of rationalism in politics—the view that political justice could be achieved by transforming society in agreement with rational blueprints. One glaring example from today's world: the European Union is holding its member states to some self-proclaimed "European ideals" or "values," which these members, although European, allegedly do not possess.

Like Nietzsche, Oakeshott was suspicious of ideals in politics. For Oakeshott, such suspicion is the essence of the conservative disposition in politics. Oakeshott writes,

> The conservative will be suspicious of proposals for change in excess of what the situation calls for, of rulers who demand extraordinary powers in order to make great changes and whose utterances are tied to generalities like 'the public good' or 'social justice', and of Saviors of Society who buckle on armor and seek dragons to slay; he will think it proper to consider the occasion of the innovation with care; in short, he will be disposed to politics as an activity in which a valuable set of tools is renovated from time to time and kept trim rather than as an opportunity for perpetual re-equipment.[264]

Nietzsche's critique of socialism as the product of systematizers is similar to Oakeshott's analysis of the rationalist approach to politics. For Oakeshott, the fundamental error of rationalists is to think of political society as a chessboard with pieces that can be arranged to achieve the desired perfect outcomes. Like Nietzsche, Oakeshott rejected the idea that social combinations could be laid out by an elite and then forced on the rest of society to bring about heaven on earth. Against the utopianism of socialists and other ideologues, Oakeshott was suspicious of the presumptiveness of utopian politics.

X. Nietzsche's "Vital Socialism" with Human Rights to the Proletariat

Nietzsche stood at the opposite pole of thought from Marx. Marx had offered men, accustomed for tens of centuries to live for and by ideas, the lure of his materialist thought and his materialist conception of history.

Nietzsche foresaw an age of profound reflection that would set in after the "terrible earthquake." However, he warned that it would be an age of "new questions"—eternal questions as he wished them to be heroically thought of, though we should rather call them conservative questions. Among these new questions, he reckoned the proletarian movement; Nietzsche was, of course, the enemy of everything that was ambiguous, characterless, and disorderly mass, and not subordination, order, and organization. He felt himself to be the rehabilitation of rank among men in a time "of universal suffrage; that is to say, where everyone has the right to sit in judgment of everybody and everything." He spoke of "the terrible consequences of equality" and said, "our whole sociology recognizes no instinct but that of the herd: that is to say the total of ciphers where every cipher has an equal right, nay a duty, to be a cipher."[265]

Nietzsche knew that democracy is only the frantic, if perfunctory, occurrence of a dying society. The proletariat, however, was intimately related to the renewal of the human race from below. Nietzsche said of the German people that they had no today—only a yesterday and a tomorrow. He saw that the future, the tomorrow, must somehow also include the proletariat and recognized that socialism—not the mere doctrine of socialism, but a vital socialism that is the expression of an uplifted and inspired humanity—was an elemental issue that could be neither evaded nor overlooked.

There are two faces of socialism: on the negative side, a complete leveling of human values would lead to their total devaluation; on the positive side, it might form the substructure of a new system of new values. Nietzsche saw first the negative side when he explained the nihilist movement (in which he included the socialistic one) as the moral, ascetic legacy of Christianity; Christianity is for him "the will to deny life." On its positive side, however, socialism is the will to accept life; it demands a *real place* in the world for the proletariat—a physical place, for as yet the proletariat knows nothing of models, concepts, or ideals. "That the feeling for social values should for the moment predominate," he notes, "is natural and right: a substructure must be established which will ultimately make a stronger race possible … The lower species must be conceived as the humble basis on which a higher species can take its stand and can live for its own tasks."[266]

The history of every revolution, whether Greek, Roman, English, American, French, Russian, Cuban, or Iranian shows that it ultimately meant a recruiting of new people and new human forces for the strengthening of the nation. The masses are quick to understand that they cannot manage by themselves or provide for themselves and that someone must take charge of them. Individuals rise from the masses and raise the masses with them. These new individuals—and still more their children and their children's children—bring proletarian forces to the nation. They are materialist and shapeless at first, but later, as they become integrated into the nation and absorb its spirit, they grow into shape and become spiritualized.

Rooted in his Prussian–German socialist culture, such was Nietzsche's notion of the proletariat. He thought of its duties, its rights, and its human dignity when he abjured the workingman to remember the following: "Workmen must learn to feel as soldiers do. A regular salary, but no wages." He expresses it elsewhere: "There must be no relation between pay and accomplishment. Each, according to his gifts, must be so placed that he does the best that it is in him to do."

Himself the son of a Lutheran pastor, Nietzsche gave a more dignified interpretation to communism when he anticipated a future "in which the highest good and the greatest happiness is common to the hearts of all." He prophesied and extolled "a time when the word 'common' shall cease to bear a stigma." For equality—with the terrible leveling-down that it implies—Nietzsche thus placed equality of rights on a higher and more moral level. He demanded that the proletarian should be given the right of entry into the kingdom of values that had hitherto been barred to him. He recognized only one measure of human values, and he demanded that the proletarian also should attain it.

Socialism and the Proletariat

Marx wanted to solve the problem of the masses but never asked—still less answered—the first significant question: From where originates the proletariat or industrial working class? Instead of acknowledging that the capitalist mode of production provided, in the beginning, a solution to the population explosion problem, he sought as an agitator to attain power over the masses by political clamor, dogmatic arrogance, biased hypotheses, and the cry of "class war."

As a man of mere intellect, and stricken by an inferiority complex, Marx stood aloof from all national consciousness or ties, so he assured the proletarians that they not only had no property of their own but no country or national home either. He explained to them there was no such thing as a unity of land and nation—that the only shared tie between people was economic interest and that this mutual relationship, discounting the barriers of country and language, united them with the proletariat of all other nations.

Marx considered himself exploited and oppressed: one of the proletariat. Logically, he should then have directed his attack against capitalism, but instead he attacked industrialism and confused capitalist enterprise with generally doing business. From this wrong starting point, Marx set out to help the socially oppressed, the unfortunate, and the misfits. He thrust himself forward without shame, without scruple, preaching the laws of economics that were merely a cash transaction. Marx forced himself into the lives of the people whose traditional, physical, and psychic makeup he did not know; he ignored the imponderables that were the foundation of their lives. By using the distant and cold logic of his reason, he shattered this foundation, robbed their inheritance of its value, rendered it suspect to them, and snatched it from them. As a material compensation, suited to their material ambitions, he turned them into conscious proletarians, and offered them the idea of class as their only home, refuge, and hope from which they might conquer everything that this life provides.

On this false, artificial, and abstract idea of class, he reared the massive structure of his thought, and on the top turret he displayed the garish flag with the wrathful inscription: "Let the ruling classes tremble before the communist revolution! Proletarians, you have the world to win! You have nothing to lose but your chains!"[267]

Marx completely ignored the fact that man had been studying technical problems for his own sake *without even considering* whether the new processes, when introduced into factories, would yield results beneficial to employers or workers or both. Marx, the agitator, deliberately misinterpreted the motives of the enterprising and manufacturing class. He did not want to recognize, among others, that industrial factories had arisen at the very moment of an acute and menacing population crisis, rescuing the proletariat, who otherwise could not have been absorbed and must have had to emigrate or perish.

Marx never even attempted to understand the psychology of the enterprising capitalist. The phenomenon of an enterprise was for him always a materialistic one; he left entirely out the psychological factors: initiative, energy, and imagination. Marx stereotyped an offensive, contemptuous caricature of a slave owner that he could be sure would help his ideas appeal to the multitude. He did not dare to admit that surplus value is the definition of the capacity to create value and as such is inherent in the scientific discoveries, machines invented, factories erected, and capital employed for enterprise and business expansion.

Neither as a theoretician nor as a political agitator did Marx dare to confess that the relation between management value and surplus value, like many other relations in the economic sphere, is not commensurable.

He never dared to point out that after the money has been paid to the manual worker for his work, there is another labor to be rewarded. It is the labor of the mental worker—the inventor, manufacturer, engineer, manager, and capitalist—who contribute to creating the work for the manual laborer and the opportunity for him to turn his work into value.

Socialism is the doctrine of envy and oppression. Achievement is unrewarded and hence implicitly discouraged while mere compliance with the rules is insufficient; one is required to think in conformance with the regulations dictated by socialist dogma. The false theory of socialism creates not only disaffected populations but also distrustful and anxious leaders who regularly take drastic steps against people they suspect may disagree with the system. Socialism has inculcated a belief in entitlements granted without the slightest individual effort and brought about "learned helplessness," resulting in the deliberate destruction of personal responsibility, which crushed the middle class.

The actual agenda of the socialist left is statism, or the control of society by a small elite group. The socialists are a patient lot and are willing to achieve their goals over an extended period through apparently minor and incremental changes in the laws and attitudes of nations and supranational organizations. Through the constant hammering of emotion-driven issues, such as education, the environment, child safety, gun control, nuclear war, human rights, social justice, and gender equality, to name just a few, they gradually affect the laws and policies that govern society. In this insidious process, the masses are being moved closer and closer to the socialist goal, which is a united world of serfs engaged for the benefit of the power elite that will control every aspect of an individual's life.

The beginnings of the modern left can be followed back to the infamous excerpt in Rousseau's "Discourse on the Origin and Foundations of Inequality."[268] In it, Rousseau condemned private property: "The first man, who after enclosing a piece of ground, took it into his head to say, 'this is mine,' and found people simple enough to believe him, was the real founder of civil society."

Added Rousseau: "How many crimes, how many wars, how many murders, how many misfortunes and horrors, would that man have saved the human species, who pulling up the stakes or filling up the ditches should have cried to his fellows: Beware of listening to this impostor; you are lost, if you forget that the fruits of the earth belong equally to us all, and the earth itself to nobody!"

In the 1830s, a faction of French liberals was drawn toward the philosophy of the late Rousseau, proclaiming that capitalism, private property, and the increasing complexity of modern society were means of moral decay, both for the individual and for society as a whole. It became the worldview that has made its way, through history, into the collective mind of the modern left. It is a worldview calling for a change that not only will topple the existing capitalist order but will also replace it with a socialist regime whereby social justice and equality will rule.

Only a totalitarian state can put such ambitions into effect with authority to micromanage every facet of human life—which is precisely the end point toward which the policies and crusades of the modern left are directed.

10

A Critique of Modern Conservatism

This author says, "We are all conservatives." He speaks of all people while referring to conservatism as a natural outlook characteristic of all humans.

Still, it is not easy to be a conservative in the modern world. In fact, it takes a high degree of moral courage, for conservatives are almost always on the defensive, fighting for causes that seem hopeless or lost because they go against the most powerful currents of the modern age.

In praising the courage of real conservatives, one is alluding mostly to cultural rather than economic or political conservatives. The supporters of free market capitalism and limited government who are today called conservatives (in the economic and political sense) are at least tolerated or not vehemently opposed, so they need not think of themselves as defenders of lost causes. However, cultural conservatives are different. They are die-hard adherents of religious, philosophical, and artistic traditions that are out of place in the modern world.

Conservatism is hardly a program, and it is surely neither dogma nor an ideology. It is a way of thinking and acting in the midst of a social order that is too overlaid with history and too steeped in values, too complex and diverse to lend itself to simple reforms. It is a way of thought that not only recognizes different classes, orders, and interests in the social order but also values these differences and is not afraid to cultivate them.

Nevertheless, conservatism must address several problems if it is to avoid further decline and have a chance to realize its potential for changing the West for the better. Following are some points that could be considered relevant:

- Modern Western conservatism and its political philosophy are lacking philosophical depth, continuity, and maturity; their development has been choppy and fragmented, with intellectuals of different orientations showing little interest in actually learning from their predecessors and each other. The conservative movement has not even absorbed the ideas of those of its thinkers who were most original and insightful. In general, Western conservatism needs more philosophical penetration and conceptual precision; it needs a better sense of priorities. Most of all, it has to resist focusing almost exclusively on the practical politics and public policy issues of the day. The future is decided more by society's fundamental moral, aesthetic, and intellectual trends than by politics in the narrow sense.
- The failure or success of Western conservatism ultimately depends on whether it is able to spread "a new spirit of ethical realism."[269] It needs to better understand that true morality is, first of all, a matter of personal character, and that moral virtue shows itself most especially in praiseworthy conduct toward people up close. Western conservatism and its political philosophy have to guard against the danger of morality being mistaken for the merely sentimental benevolence for the world's unfortunate, for which Jean-Jacques Rousseau set the pattern. This self-congratulatory, pseudomoral "virtue" hides dubious motives—usually the will to power—behind humane-looking and deceptively compassionate but cunningly aggressive ploys for the remaking of society and the world. Some of the most passionate do-gooders have done much wrongdoing in the name of helping their fellow human beings.
- Western conservatism has to understand better the extent to which the imagination, ranging from great works of art to mass culture and everyday intuitions about life, shapes our sense of reality and our hopes for the future. The imagination, communicating with the will, whether the effect will be good or bad, does so indeed. Civilization is to succeed or fail because of the attributes of will and imagination that prevail in it. Corrupted imagination warps even rationality, for it is imagination that provides reason with its

sense of reality and balance. Without a fundamental redirecting of the imagination, which prepares the mind to consider even objectionable and discouraging facts, presumed intellectual victories of conservatism will dissipate without transforming society.

- Modern Western conservatism has not done much to effect "a sorely needed restoration of *philosophical reason*."[270] For that situation to change, conservatism has to get beyond a one-sided view of rationality. Being rightly concerned to resist the intrusion of abstract and positivistic rationality into liberal studies, some of its leading thinkers (Kirk, Viereck, and Voegelin) were, unfortunately, suspicious of all systematic and conceptual reasoning, trusting instead in a higher intuition to provide the most valuable insight. They did not consider the existence of such a form of rationality that is very different from rationalistic reductionism. There is deeper rationality that has always been at work in human beings but has been hiding, as it were, behind flawed notions of its character. The recognition of the existence and form of this deeper reason requires the revision of old and ahistorical conceptions of philosophical reason. This recognition does not deny the great significance of "immediate experience" or "moral imagination" but points out that there is a "philosophical reason" that does not distort or kill what it touches but tries faithfully to articulate the actual, living human experience, including experience of the universal.[271]

The problem with even the most profound and sober intuition is that it cannot argue; it is silent in philosophical debates. However, this sound intuition has a partner in historically based rationality that takes account of and tries to sort out the contents of experience, differentiating between what belongs to the world of *action* and what is just imagination or unrealized *desire*. It is this deeper but calm rationality that makes us recognize the crucial importance of history for understanding human life.

A more general philosophical strengthening of Western conservatism is called for, including a value-centered historicism that would reconstitute the theory of knowledge.

A nonphilosophical reader might ask why a discussion of the state of Western conservatism would focus on issues like these and not on the subject of the market economy, foreign policy, education, the welfare state, immigration, the budget deficit, or the size of the government. The answer to the question is that the above points relate not only to each of these more obviously political issues directly but also to how they should be approached. The points help explain the pervasive intellectual confusion of today's Western conservatism, not least its getting mixed up with imperialistic ideology and related causes subversive of traditional Western civilization.

The Western conservative movement has to revise considerably its prevailing notion of what is important and unimportant. It must also recognize that some of its oldest and most deep-seated inclinations have been simply misguided.

American Intellectual Conservatism

Modern Western conservatism and political philosophy have been much affected by a doubtful pragmatism. One visible manifestation of that has been the already mentioned preoccupation with practical politics and a corresponding neglect of philosophy and the arts. These skewed priorities are connected with the assumption that capturing political power is the key to shaping the future.

This is not to deny the importance of politics, of course—just the contrary. Politics forms an essential part of the effort to build and protect civilization. However, in trying to affect the renewal of Western society, winning and exercising political power in the immediate future cannot take the place of the patient and demanding intellectual and artistic efforts that, in time, might change the mind and imagination of people. It is such efforts, together with the practical actions they inspire, that set the direction of society in the long run. Social health depends on morality, but morality urgently needs the oxygen of sound thought and imagination. If a corrupt intellectual and artistic culture is spreading ever-new infections, no amount of political activism can create social health. It is true nevertheless that well-considered political action might have a catalytic and beneficial effect in some particular circumstances, and in a desperate situation, it might at least for a time avert disaster.

The pragmatic preoccupation with practical politics in Western conservatism is closely related to a fondness for economics and business, which is often so pronounced that it amounts to regarding the aims of conservatism and business as the same. However, civilization, including a civilized marketplace, depends, as Wilhelm Röpke has observed, on moral, imaginative, and intellectual preferences that do not arise spontaneously from the economy as such. The priorities set by businesspeople and financiers in their economic activities are *not* ordinarily prescribed by the good, the true, and the beautiful. Too many conservatives with libertarian leanings underestimate the extent to which purely economic considerations need to be subordinated to other motives and the extent to which institutions and individual gatekeepers must help promote moral restraints, good taste, and respect for truth. If many businesspeople in the Western world have demonstrated admirable traits like honesty, good manners, and social responsibility, it is because, like others, they have been the products of an ancient civilization. They have been subject to the elevating influence of priests, thinkers, aristocrats, teachers, and artists. Today, as Western civilization deteriorates, the utilitarian one-sidedness, greed, and insatiableness that politics and business tend to generate are being released from those traditional restraining pressures.

Economics is an excellent discipline that blends into philosophy. However, the "economic" must be part of a larger whole in which business and finance are means to higher ends. There is a form of Western pragmatism that establishes what can work in the real world of action, and as such it rightly refuses to engage in wishful thinking and pointless, merely abstract speculations. Unfortunately, there is also another form of pragmatism that originates in a twisted, truncated view of human beings and their world. This pragmatism expresses a strong anti-intellectual and antiaesthetical prejudice, as in the case of the obsession with politics and economics of so many self-described conservatives.

Despite the West's great universities on the intellectual side and great music and art centers on the aesthetical side, Western life, in general, has a tremendous utilitarian bias. That pragmatic predisposition is exemplified by an inordinate fascination with makers and doers and an inclination to look down on persons engaged in low-paying nonutilitarian pursuits. Since the individual most admired in America may be the self-made person possessing a great fortune, the best and brightest are expected to gravitate in the direction of moneymaking and away from activities whose primary rewards are noneconomic. America and conservatism at their pseudopragmatic and anti-intellectual worst come through in that embarrassing old saying by George Bernard Shaw, "Those who can, do; those who can't, teach."

Then one may think about the correlation between the ivory tower of academia and leftist intellectuals, and the conservatism of makers and doers.

Expressing and fostering a narrow, simplified notion of human beings and their needs, the prejudice against nonutilitarian pursuits has stunted intellectual and aesthetical life and thereby also the moral life. Spreading mass tastes have compounded the harmful effects of this prejudice.

American postwar intellectual conservatism at its best was in considerable part a protest against the contraction and perversion of the human range that is characteristic of pseudopragmatism. This author is critical of utilitarianism and seeks to strengthen a sense of higher values and stress the moral–spiritual and aesthetical bases of civilized society.

Although American intellectual conservatism has had eminent thinkers, its development has been hindered by indifference concerning philosophy, since the movement never even developed a mature philosophical culture. The conservative movement has found it difficult to rank intellectual contributions and differentiate between profundity and superficiality, truth and ideology—a weakness that has festered and worsened with time. So-called neoconservatives asserted that, before they provided fresh firepower, American conservatism was intellectually weak and ineffectual. The neoconservatives' claim of having raised the general intellectual level of American conservatism is plainly calculated to distract attention from thinkers not amenable to "neocon" designs.

However, if the original conservative thought was superior, why would the movement have been attracted to neoconservatism?

The conservative thinkers of the old American school, who worked most diligently to define and enforce a specifically American conservative intellectual identity, were libertarian and individualist in that they promoted a minimum state with maximum freedom for the individual, but they also tried reconciling that view with elements of a traditional understanding of moral virtue. They were also trenchant critics of modern liberalism but lacked something in philosophical subtlety and stringency and offered some less-than-felicitous combinations of ideas. They were less philosophical than ideological in their attempt to define the functions of government and in setting the limit between governmental and other powers. They also underestimated the dependence of freedom and virtue on historically evolved human institutions and associations, including those of government. Some of them were simultaneously defenders of the framers of the US Constitution and admirers of Jean-Jacques Rousseau, not realizing that, despite superficial appearances, the latter advocated a view of human nature, society, and government radically different from that of the former.

Moreover, interestingly enough, many of these thinkers had a history on the extreme left; some had been even ideologically ardent members of the international communist underground. They were now strong anticommunists but had some difficulty shedding reductionist habits of mind. That their separate implicit theories were somewhat distinct, partly even incompatible, was not much recognized by a movement that was more interested in a particular policy than in philosophical consistency and precision. Nevertheless, a comparison of these American conservative thinkers to their counterparts of today strikingly illustrates the intellectual weakening of American conservatism.

The conservative intellectual movement became enamored of free market economics, and it could cite, promote, and publish many sophisticated economists. One of its favorites was Milton Friedman, who would become an icon for the conservative movement as a whole. Though Friedman made compelling arguments for a free market, his notion of capitalism did not dwell on what ordered liberty owes to historical development and noneconomic considerations, or on the need for the market to operate under civilizing pressures.[272]

In sum, the entire conservative intellectual movement was influenced by the ubiquitous pseudopragmatism and had no desire to probe difficult philosophical issues. More concerned about seizing opportunities for antistatist political coalition-building than achieving intellectual coherence, the movement left some of its underlying assumptions regarding human nature and society in provisional, poorly integrated form and got by with a partly contrived intellectual structure. Because of its shaky philosophical foundation and ideology-centered pseudopragmatism, it was also liable to adopting questionable ideas that had politically influential sponsors.

The last few decades have seen a more extreme confusion in American intellectual conservatism than ever before. The movement has increasingly become associated and identified with ideologues whose main ideas had hardly any connection with conservative thinking. In fact, these ideologues bore a closer resemblance to the eighteenth century French Jacobins, the intellectual and political leaders of the French Revolution, than to conservatism. Rejecting beliefs and practices derived from history, the Jacobins wanted to remake society according to allegedly universal, ahistorical principles, which they summed up in the slogan "freedom, equality, and brotherhood." They saw France as called to liberate humanity.[273]

The new Jacobins similarly have a disdain for historically formed societies and want to reconstruct them according to ahistorical and allegedly universal principles. These are summarized as "freedom" or "democracy." America, the new Jacobins assert, is unique in that it was founded on those principles rather than on tradition. According to them, America has the historic mission of spreading "freedom" and "democracy" around the world, bestowing on other nations the kind of model of the "pursuit of happiness" that was bequeathed to them by "the American Founders."[274]

It is absurd, to put it mildly, that a nonideological movement calling itself "conservative" would come under the influence and control of such beliefs and that ideologues attracted to the new Jacobinism would be called "neoconservatives." Even more astonishing is that the promoters of neo-Jacobin ideology would ultimately be allowed to proclaim who was and who was not a true conservative. These neoconservatives could do so by securing for themselves leadership positions in the foundations, media, think tanks, and universities, mainly because of the intellectually eroded and worn-out condition of the conservative movement itself. Had that movement been philosophically and historically better grounded and led, it would have recognized who the new Jacobins were and countered their attempt to divert and transform the entire movement.

Conservatives would have and should have known that modern Western conservatism, or neoconservatism, originated as a reactionary movement along the lines of the old Jacobinism.

The outcome of these comments is not that more philosophical depth and rigor would have produced uniformity and clarity. Any intellectually vibrant movement will exhibit diversity and tension. The point is that philosophical maturity and discipline would have reduced confusion, ideological simplification, and glaring error, and raised the general level of discussion.

The Definition of Conservatism

The philosophically conservative approach plays down the omniscient implications of liberalism with its unifying rationalism and thus accords more respect to those institutions or modes of behavior that have weathered the centuries than liberals do. Philosophically thoughtful conservatives are cautious in tampering with forms of political behavior and institutions, and they are especially skeptical of large-scale reforms. This is not for tradition's sake, but they err on the side of tradition and form a skeptical view of human ability to redesign entire spectra of social values that have developed over and become suited to generations. Damaging values will, conservatives argue, fall into discontinuance without any intervention.

The critical questions facing the conservative are the following: What ought to be saved, protected, and secured? How long must an institution exist before the philosophical conservative approves it? Liberalism turns to reason, still broadly accepted as the unifying element to human societies today, to answer these questions. However, conservatives believe that reason is associated with distinct individuals and, therefore, with their very own political motives, errors, prejudices, and judgment.

Conservatives typically have a pessimistic vision of human nature, drawing on the modern tradition, on Hobbes's belief, according to which, were it not for strong institutions, people would be at each other's throats and would continuously view one another with deep suspicion. Conservatism, to put it a bit simpler, is the philosophy of constructive criticism.

The conservative's emphasis is thus not on the ensuing hypothetical pacifying social contract but on the predominance of fear in human society. Conservatives are highly suspicious of power and man's desire to use it, for they believe it corrupts, over time, even the most freedom-loving possessor of it. Hence, the potential accession to supreme power over others, regardless in what form, is to be rejected as being just as dangerous as Hobbes's vision of the anarchic state of nature.[275]

Conservatives thus applaud those institutions that check the propensity for the stronger or the megalomaniacal to command power; conservatives magnify the suspicion one may hold of one's neighbor. Critics—for example of an anarchist or socialist strain—claim that such fears are a product of the presiding social environment and its associated values, and are the result of neither human nature nor social interaction. Such opponents of conservatism emphasize the need to reform society in order to release people from a life of fear, which conservatives, in turn, consider a utopian pipe dream unbefitting a practical political philosophy.

For conservatives, the value of institutions cannot always be examined according to the rational analysis of the present generation. That imposes a demand on conservatism to explain or justify the rationale for supporting traditional institutions. Evolutionary thinkers from the Scottish Enlightenment (for example Adam Ferguson), whose insights noted the trial and error nature of cultural and hence moral and institutional developments, generated a more accurate and historically ratifiable examination of institutions and morals.[276] On this topic, see the work of Friedrich Hayek especially.

Accordingly, and in contrast to many liberals, conservatives decry the notion of a social contract—or even its possibility in a modern context. They claim that since societies evolve and develop through time, present generations possess duties and responsibilities whose origins and original reasons may now be lost to us but that, for some thinkers, still require our acceptance. As per the liberals, present-day cultural xenophobia may derive from past hostilities against the nation but not be applicable or purposeful in today's more commercial environment; or present-day racism may stem from violent incursions or centuries of fearful mythologies that are no longer pertinent. However, conservatives reply that since institutions and morals evolve, their weaknesses and defects will become apparent and thereby will gradually be reformed (or merely dropped) as public pressure against them changes. What the conservative opposes is the potentially absolutist position of either the liberal or the socialist who considers a form of behavior or an institution to be valid and hence politically binding for all time.

Conservatives do not reject reform per se but are very skeptical of any present ability to fully understand and reshape the vast structures of behavior and institutions that have evolved based on the insight and experience of countless generations. They are thus skeptical of large-scale planning, whether it is constitutional, economic, or cultural. Against socialists, who become impatient with present defects, the conservatives counsel patience—not for its own sake but because the vast panoply of institutions that are rallied against, including human nature, cannot be reformed without the most detrimental effects. Traditional conservatives, following Edmund Burke, typically condemn revolutions as leading to more upheavals than the old regime produced.[277] Consider this against the modern conservatives—the new-Jacobinist neoconservatives, who advocate the spreading of democracy by direct intervention.

Some conservatives argue that a modicum of redistribution is required to ensure a peaceful nonrevolutionary society. Whereas modern liberals justify redistribution on the grounds of providing an initial basis for human development, the conservative's pragmatic fear of the impoverished masses rising to overturn the regime stems from the conservative reaction to the French Revolution. The conservative critique by Edmund Burke was particularly accurate and prescient, yet the revolution also served to remind the political hierarchy of its obligations (noblesse oblige) to the potentially violent masses that the revolt had stirred up. The lesson should not have been lost on either modern liberal or modern conservative thinkers who assert that the state has certain obligations to the poor—including the provision of education and health facilities, among others. In contrast to socialists, with whom some conservatives may agree concerning a socialized system of poor relief, conservatives prefer to emphasize local and delegated redistribution schemes (perhaps even of a wholly voluntary nature) rather than central, state-directed programs.

In affinity with classical liberals, conservatives often emphasize the vital importance of property rights in social relations. Liberals tend to lean toward the practical benefits that accrue from property rights (for example, a better distribution of resources than joint ownership, or a method of providing incentives for further innovation and production). Meanwhile, conservatives stress the role of private property regarding its ability to restrain the power of the state or any individual seeking supreme power. Conservatives consider private property as a sacred, intrinsically valuable cornerstone of a free and prosperous society.

The broad distribution of private property rights complements the conservative principle that individuals and local communities are better assessors of their needs and problems than distant bureaucrats. Since conservatives are inherently skeptical of the state, they prefer alternative social institutions—such as the family, private property, and religion—to direct and assist the maturation of civilized human beings; they also believe that one must have the right and freedom to make mistakes.

Conservatives of the English Whig tradition, such as Locke and Shaftesbury have much in common with classical liberals. Conservatives of the English Tory tradition, however, have more in common with *modern liberals,* agreeing to some extent with the need for state intervention but on pragmatic rather than ideological grounds. Accordingly, those of the Whig tradition associate themselves more with individualism and rationalism than Tory conservatives who emphasize community, "one-nation" politics, and its corresponding duties and responsibilities for the individual. The two initially opposing doctrines merged politically in the late nineteenth century as liberalism shifted its ground to incorporate socialist policies; the two sides of conservatism enjoyed a particularly visible and vocal clash at the end of the twentieth century during the political reign of Margaret Thatcher in the United Kingdom.[278]

There is a seemingly arcane but central philosophical issue whose inadequate treatment by American conservative intellectuals illustrates particularly well how a deficiency in thought can have far-reaching practical consequences. The issue in question concerns the very definition of "conservatism." Oddly enough, the American intellectual movement that claimed the label never developed more than a somewhat vague idea of what was conservative. To answer the question of what conservatism is, a typical representative of the movement would most likely list a set of principles, such as belief in limited government, a free economy, and a strong defense.

However, if doctrines of this type define conservatism, why call it "conservatism"? All belief systems have principles of some kind. The term "conservative" suggests something distinctive—a motive to conserve. Of what, exactly, is conservatism conservative? Of tradition, many would answer. Leo Strauss rejected this view as "historicist," as endorsing whatever history brings up, which he regarded as morally relativistic or nihilistic.[279] In return, traditionalists have bluntly refused the charge, saying that while they believe in respecting tradition, they also believe in universal principles of some sort. If there are principles to guide us, why pay any heed to history? Why be a conservative?

American conservatism has had difficulty understanding and articulating the meaning and significance of the historical and how it relates to universal values. What, then, is distinctively conservative about conservatism?

Many traditionalists, notably Russell Kirk, appealed to Edmund Burke, but on the whole, they did not explain just how Burke's championing of "the general bank and capital of nations and ages" is linked to his acute sense of universal right.[280] Kirk had a strong intuition that the two could not be separated, and he was right. Charges by moral rationalists that Kirk was a historical relativist were unperceptive or were just attempts to damage his reputation. Nevertheless, vagueness on a critical matter exposed Kirk and the traditionalists to criticism.

Value-centered historicism explains how the historical consciousness of Burke is not only in harmony with but also essential for making sound moral, intellectual, and aesthetical choices. Since American intellectual conservatism has not ventured beyond an approximation of philosophy, it has yet to grasp that real universality, as distinguished from abstract rationalistic conceptions or romantic dreams, is in this world indistinguishable from and dependent on historical particularity. The true, good, and beautiful come into being through discriminating incarnation in the concrete—by *synthesizing the universal and particular.*

Recognizing the significance of historical particularity and circumstance—especially the possibility of a union between universality and particularity—focuses attention to the value of individual personality and the demand for creativity in the moral, aesthetical, and intellectual life. Universality can be maintained in changing situations through the creative synthesis of universality and particularity; this idea, so difficult for many to understand, could have enhanced American conservatism time and again. For example, it would have clarified American constitutionalism, making it possible to surpass the artificial opposition between one school of interpretation, called "originalism," and the other one asserting that the US Constitution is a living document. One may retain the concept of an enduring constitutional purpose and yet affirm the need to adapt to new historical circumstances.

The idea of a synthesis of the universal and the particular could also have deepened the understanding of the American constitutional ethos as expressed in the phrase "E Pluribus Unum." Do these words mean that unity must be obtained at the expense of diversity? Must the particular, such as the particular American nation, give up its distinctiveness and independence in favor of some cultural-political homogeneity, or could unity through diversity be achieved by harmonizing the discrete but dynamically interacting parts? Unfortunately, without ever having developed a clear understanding of how universality pertains to historical particularity, American intellectual conservatism has not been able to deal with such questions, despite their importance of illustrating the wisdom of American political tradition.

One of American conservatism's genuinely distinguished social thinkers is Robert Nisbet. His discerning explanation and defense of the quest for community is an enduring achievement.[281] Human beings desperately need the links of intimate associations, starting with the family. Nisbet demonstrated the devastating effects of social atomism, whether in the form of liberal individualism or Rousseauistic socialistic collectivism. Nisbet's acuity is partly due to his appreciation of the role of history and tradition in constituting human groups and societies.

However, his discussion of associations would have benefited from more attention to the simultaneously individual and social nature of man and the needs of individuality as a potential carrier of universality. Without some freedom for the individual to go his own way, a community may become stultifying and suffocate precious personal originality, thereby undermining the community itself. Nevertheless, for all of his deepening and extension of Aristotle, Nisbet does not give human individuality its due. American conservative social thought would have much to gain from scrutinizing further the requirement for balancing the ways of community, on the one hand, with individual freedom and creativity, on the other. These two elements of social life should, as far as possible, be mutually supportive.

In the perspective of value-centered historicism, liberalism and conservatism, properly understood, are aspects of the same desirable approach to life. That Edmund Burke, the great traditionalist, should also be a Whig, a classical liberal of sorts, can be recognized as apt to show that, in life, universality and individuality are mutually dependent on and implicated in each other. A firmer philosophical awareness of this relationship would have enriched American conservative thought on community and identity, tradition and creativity.

American intellectual conservatism has been strongly affected over the years by concerted and persistent Straussian attacks on historicism and real individuality. This crusade has created a presumption that abstract rational principles define higher values than historicism does and must not be seen as, under any circumstances, originated from history or tradition. For the antihistoricists, what is historical is merely accidental and conventional. The stated fondness of many so-called conservatives for ahistorical principles is contradictory, for modern conservatism was born out of the emerging historical consciousness, as in Burke, and was a response to rationalism. Although not explicitly expressed, Burke and others discerned a critical and intimate link between universality and history, which made them respectful, though not uncritical, of tradition.

According to Leo Strauss and the Straussians, the "*highest*" must not be related to tradition or the "ancestral"; to associate them is to abandon philosophy and, with it, universality.[282] The Straussians have not only taught Christians and others who have regarded tradition as one of the pillars of their beliefs to disdain the historical, but they have, in effect, also taught traditionalists self-contempt. Many traditionalists have naively and gullibly adopted the suicidal course urged upon them. What most Straussians call "natural right" bears only a faint resemblance to a traditional concept of natural law. Their advocacy of an antihistorical notion of what is ultimately normative is a prime example of how an error in a supposedly limited and arcane area of philosophy can have not only practical but also disastrous consequences.

Over the past few decades, an abstract neo-Jacobin universalism blended with nationalistic conceit has emerged to form the notion of America as an exceptional, virtuous country called to export its so-called universal principles to the rest of the world. Because of limited philosophical discernment, even persons of some scholarly reputation became supporters of a political cause that has severely damaged America, the West, and the world. Sadly and regrettably, there could hardly be a better proof of the crisis of American intellectual conservatism than the fact that many of its self-designated representatives adopted, or excused, reckless radicalism.

One sign of how American conservatives have exempted themselves from a philosophical effort is their supposition that, mainly when it involves the question of value, what matters is religious commitment. For them, a typical conservative is a sincere and ostentatious believer whose manner announces to the philosophically inclined person that having pious sentiments is much more important than making excellent philosophical points. The proper religious commitment is assumed somehow to guarantee the soundness of thought. There is nothing wrong, of course, with genuine religious devotion, but religion has been so permeated by what Babbitt calls "sham spirituality" in the modern world that it has become a significant contaminant of the mind and imagination.[283] While no one is immune from religious-moral confusion and smugness, there is an urgent need for scrutinizing religious claims.

Also, religious faith is, especially in an intellectual movement, no substitute for intellectual labor. Insufficient philosophical effort and discipline clouds and distorts central questions of human existence and weakens religion itself. Letting pretentious religious sentiment take the place of thought has had just that kind of effect on American intellectual conservatism—a criticism that is directed not against religious faith but rather against a particular and common American form of anti-intellectualism.

There is another weakness of American conservatism: the neglect of the artistic. This weakness is not only analogous to the belittling of philosophy but also has similar origins. Nothing could be more critical to the functioning of a healthy society than exposing perverse, if superficially appealing, imagination and nurturing the creativity of a different quality. The role played by imagination in the shaping of conduct, for good or ill, is central and decisive. Irving Babbitt, who explained the moral-aesthetical dynamic of sound and unsound imagination, has brilliantly, if incompletely, elucidated these issues. Unfortunately, although the phrase "moral imagination" is a part of the vocabulary of American intellectual conservatism, these ideas have been only partially assimilated and applied by a movement with a flawed set of priorities.

American intellectual conservatives do not care much about the arts—at least not above the popular level. Conservatives tend to feel no deep existential need for poetry, novels, paintings, symphonies, films, and such—though some swear by rock music. Any protest to the effect that limited interest in the arts hardly is a major flaw in a conservative person would only confirm the debilitating weakness, which should be remedied. Some will predictably and smugly declare that religion offers all the nourishment for the soul that one needs; they will indicate thereby a deformed and cramped conception of religion as well as life in general. This kind of religiosity often goes together with a utilitarian and pragmatic attitude toward worldly, or material, matters.

It has been suggested earlier that the most basic need of civilization may be moral; "moral-spiritual" might better convey the intended meaning. However, without broad and penetrating imagination, the higher will in man has difficulty finding its way. Some significant reasons have just been outlined as to why American, and Western, intellectual conservatism is in a state of crisis. The reasons discussed involve a deeply flawed pragmatism and an insufficient appreciation for the importance of philosophy and the arts.

Greater philosophical sophistication on crucial issues would have protected American conservatism against intellectual, aesthetical, and moral trends and their political manifestations that owed their momentum not to their intrinsic merit but to the Zeitgeist and the enormous resources wielded by their promoters. Had conservatives been more aware of the close connection between history and universality, they would not have been attracted to Leo Strauss's antihistorical natural-right theorizing either. They would have recognized the siren calls of such neoconservative "universal principles," such as freedom and democracy, which are hard to tell apart, both in ideological content and spirit, from Jacobinism.

Stronger historical consciousness and proportionally better immunity against moral-political utopianism would have made conservatives resistant to imperialistic dreaming and adventurism. Strengths of this kind, combined with more knowledge of the origins of American culture and constitutionalism in the classical Christian and English heritage, would have made them understand that American ordered liberty did not result from implementing abstract principles but from the long gestation of a particular culture. They would have realized that massive and wholesale immigration into the United States was bound to dilute and undermine traditional American culture in general and constitutionalism in particular. Philosophically discerning intellectuals immersed in the spirit of American constitutionalism would have defied a unitary, or imperial, presidency and a national security superstate of the kind promoted by neoconservatives.

It should be obvious, then, that the blatant neglect of seemingly esoteric philosophical issues is no small matter. A weakness of this sort has severely damaged American intellectual conservatism across a broad spectrum of practical concerns.

A better grasp of the significance of imagination and the arts in molding individuals and society would have made conservatives more knowledgeable about diagnosing the problems of America and Western civilization and would have corrected their strategy for dealing with them.

Historians of the future who trace the origins of the curious identity crisis of American and Western intellectual conservatism will undoubtedly record the prominent role of careerism and greed. They will note how effortlessly the powers that be in foundations, think tanks, media, and government were able to buy and manipulate allegedly conservative intellectuals. At the source of this development, one finds, of course, a moral failing.

The persistent weaknesses of human nature would not so easily have broken through the defenses of Western civilization if it had not been for the misguided pragmatism and the related problems of conservatism described here. American conservatism would have avoided intellectual shoddiness, corrupt imagination, and false moral virtue; it could have prevented the damage inflicted upon America and the world by self-described conservatives.

The Perverted Conservatism of America

In the older societies of Europe, conservatism has been made definite and understandable by being manifest in particular classes. Such classes have usually been in a numerical minority and sensed intuitively that only by a carefully preserved balance of power combined with mutual respect could their own survival be safeguarded. These traditional classes were often close to the land and learned the lessons of slow growth and the significance of ceremonies and traditions, which form the inherent wisdom of country people.

This kind of conservatism could mean merely the defenses thrown up by these minorities around their privileges. Alternatively, it could degenerate into an attempt to impose the particular standards and habits of a landowning class on everyone. At its best, the spirit of conservatism transcended the specific circumstances that gave it birth; the things people had learned from their particular way of life became a pervasive force, stimulating an attitude of tentativeness and tolerance.

In the United States, political conservatism has had no such long tradition of established order to grow in. For the most part, American capitalism has been far too dynamic, too restless, and too destructive to foster a conservative approach. It has been too absorbed in its next quest to attain an essential detachment and too bent on novelty—new markets, new products, new employees, and new customers—to appreciate the traditional aspects of society.

The drive to exploit the abundant natural resources has made American capitalism the *opponent* of settled ways. In fact, it is a curious contradiction that conservation (meaning the conserving of natural resources) has never been associated with the so-called conservatism of the business classes in the United States. Both Theodore and Franklin Roosevelt were considered alarmingly radical when they moved to preserve certain irreplaceable parts of the nation's wealth and heritage.

American business developed many of the habits and techniques of centralization and modern liberalism. Commercialism and advertising have pointed the way to the kind of government propaganda that has made Washington more and more the center of gravity of the country. Mass production applied to the automobile has done more than a thousand radical philosophers to encourage a rootless existence in America, to take one other example.

The conservative spirit, therefore, had to be fostered among Americans by a much more subtle process than in older countries; it had to be drawn by perceptive individuals from a wide range of experience of life.

The notable fact about conservatism in the US and the Western world is that it was hideously distorted as a force in the bitter fires of the past eighty years. Whole generations have been brought up to suppose that conservatism is something negative, inherently harmful and unproductive, and represented by the kinds of groups and people who called themselves "conservatives" and fought against the New Deal, Fair Deal, New Frontier, and Great Society.

However, in truth these conservatives were mainly the advocates of a purer and more orthodox brand of liberalism; they objected to the government's programs in the name of *laissez-faire*. They attacked centralization, government by decree, excessive bureaucracy, and the rest not as a Burke or a Disraeli would have attacked them, because they chilled an inner essence of growth and development, but almost precisely in the spirit of the nineteenth-century Manchester economists.[284] The result was that crowds of young people left colleges entirely convinced that conservatism offered no useful insights to any of the problems of the modern world.

The point was almost never made that the rapid and revolutionary developments in Washington, Paris, Berlin, Vienna, and Rome were, in their total impact, a blow against the free, independent, varied, and self-governing life of the Western peoples. Precisely that point should have been the valid basis for a conservative critique.

Bureaucracy may have been expensive, but that was not the real trouble with it. The real problem was that it tended to substitute for the principle of private action and decentralized leadership the methods of direction from above and command from afar. Within the wide-ranging movement of the New Deal, among the many people it drew into its service, there was admittedly some stress on what might be accomplished by the localities. However, in the main, it was the central government that undertook with fierce energy to reform everything, to renovate everything, and to save everything.

The conservatives, however, did *not* attack the centralization as being at odds with the independent, varied, and self-governing life that is the genius of America. Moreover, they did *not* defend and explain what was being done by their underlying philosophy. They merely responded with a violent and irrational outcry.

The New Deal–type experiments were hostile to the genuinely pluralistic nature of the American social order not only because they often crushed initiative but also, in a much more subtle way, because they corrupted action. These programs capitalized for political purposes in the group life of the country. They made people conscious of their particular loyalties and attachments—not so much to develop their natural energies as to give them what they wanted: to cultivate blocs of voters. These programs made Americans aware of the importance of group interests in the national life. Class, professional, and regional ties were deliberately promoted; various industries were encouraged to make their own codes (meaning industrial standards) in return for release from being held liable under the antitrust laws. The expected result was not so much to attain a higher sense of spirit in all parts of the social order but to cultivate an absolute dependence on the central (federal) government.

Each group was emboldened to assert its claims in a most exaggerated form. The farmers, the laborers, the old, and particular industries were all given to understand that if each pressed its claims to the maximum, the whole country would somehow benefit. This idea was a form of the eighteenth-century doctrine of a harmony of interests, but it encouraged the selfishness of groups rather than the intrinsic morality of individuals.

The conservatives should have recognized, interpreted, and explained these alarming tendencies. They should have pointed out that the immediate adverse effect of the transformation may be undetectable at first; ultimately, however, it is the most difficult of all to obliterate or reverse, for one can repeal laws and disestablish agencies, but to reeducate the multitudinous private organizations and individuals that make up the national existence—to make them understand that they exist for some other reason than to raise an outcry for special treatment or entitlements—is a process of years, if it is possible at all. Only the saving instinct for liberty within the people themselves can prevent those harmful culture-changing effects from overwhelming society.

The conservatives, however, did *not* suggest anything like this. They merely iterated that bureaucracy was terrible and centralization upset the balance of the federal budget.

While the conservatives were thus failing to criticize the New Deal-type programs on meaningful grounds, they were also falling into a major heresy regarding the content of their own program. They took the wholly unconservative position of suggesting they would undo and overturn the significant reforms that had become part of American life. They became desperately afraid of seeming "me tooish"—even though the genius of free government (and of true conservatism) precisely is to rally as many people with various interests and outlooks into a common course of action as possible. On the worn-out theme "It is time for a change," they hinted at such profound reversals that democracy instinctively abhors. These conservatives wanted to view *everything* as if nothing had ever been settled and to convince the electorate that they would go about demolishing and upsetting drastically and radically.

Apparently the American conservatives seemed to think that there existed a consistent, understandable, and meaningful body of conservative doctrine, which had to be the exact opposite of what the liberals had already implemented. In their minds, any point of resemblance to existing practice had to be either pure coincidence or treason to the Republican Party. These people never discovered what this program of theirs was, but they were convinced that it existed; pending its discovery and unfolding, they were willing to settle on a point-by-point negation of everything the Democrats had upheld.

True conservatives traditionally mistrust excessive rationalism; they understand that the world moves by values, habits, and faith as much as it moves by having new ideas. When they are in their right minds, conservatives avoid tearing up the roots of something they do not like almost as instinctively as conservatives avoid tearing up the roots of institutions and procedures of which they *do* approve. The undeniable fact that American conservatives forgot, or never learned, this healthy prudence and necessary tolerance can only be explained if one accepts that they had grown so uncontrollably angry. In attacking the left-liberal Democratic plans, the conservatives became inflexible in their thinking, unresponsive to the settled expectations and tacit consent of the general public, and wanted instead to impose a doctrinaire program, without a coherent doctrine of their own.

Because it is a spirit rather than dogma, and because it pervades the whole community in a democracy rather than inhabiting a particular class, American conservatism has been particularly difficult to express in political forms. Although both major political parties have been instinctively conservative in their best period, as soon as one party or one faction within a party starts bragging about its conservatism, it right away departs from the very principles that ought to guide it. It either falls back upon blind reaction or else wants to remake everything by some doctrinaire pattern. The conservative individual in England can be a man like Churchill was: manifold, complex, and overlaid with layers of prejudice, memory, and conviction. In America, an avowed conservative is usually either a young man, proverbial with grandfatherly expressions, or a middle-aged person with a grim expression and a resolve to overturn everything that has developed since the Flood.

The Republican Party has always run the danger of being identified with the "professional conservatives." The long exile from power (from 1932 through 1952) was as bad for the Republicans as the long tenure of power was bad for the Democrats. Outright negativism and obstruction seemed to offer the natural way of winning an election. Within the Republican Party, there was a group that kept rescuing it from its apparent fate but walked out of the Chicago convention with Theodore Roosevelt in 1912 and then walked back in again with Willkie at Philadelphia in 1940. In Chicago in 1952, where General Eisenhower was nominated, it strode triumphantly through the convention hall. It was that wing of the party that was supported by the Eastern Establishment.

This element of Republicanism traced its ancestry to at least three historical sources. James Madison had seen the necessity of balancing groups under a constitution whose rules of procedure were accepted by all. The Whigs had discerned the possibility of harmonizing divergent national interests through massive public works, such as roads and canals. Finally there had been a careful use of federal grants in the Homestead Acts to strengthen the enterprising and independent citizens on the land.

The republicanism descended from these origins had a healthy respect for federal power wielded responsibly for a useful purpose. It upheld the states not to hinder national action but to develop viable communities where citizens could be educated, refined, and engaged, and as "laboratories" where social legislation could first be tried.

The Democratic Party has also had its full share of distorted conservatism. The strategy of simple obstruction—nullification, veto, and threats of secession—was continually advocated in the slaveholding period. Under the New Deal, the reaction within the Democratic Party was toward the other extreme—excessive centralization based on the assumption that a numerical majority was free to act pretty much as it wanted. So persistent have been the reverberations of this period that many people saw Adlai Stevenson as something close to a radical because he bore the Democratic banner. Having failed to discover the true essence of conservatism, they also neglected to recognize that Stevenson was indisputably the most consistent and philosophically mature conservative to have arisen in the twentieth century in either party. Stevenson had a unique sense of the diversity of which American society is composed. He had a feeling for how the separate groups could be brought into the service of the whole.[285]

The failure to grasp the essence of conservatism has made political campaigns in the United States signally barren of any intellectual content. In a debate, it is difficult to admit that one would do the same thing as the opposition, only differently.

The spirit in which things are done does make a difference and can distinguish a sound policy from a flawed one. Social reforms can be undertaken with the result of depleting local vitality and lowering the citizenry to an amorphous mass tied to the cart of the almighty state; alternatively, these social reforms can be set in motion with the effect of strengthening the free citizen's stake in society. The ends are entirely different. The means will also be if people have the wit to distinguish between legislation that encourages voluntary participation on the local level and legislation that bows to special interests and involves unlimited spending and the massive enlargement of the federal bureaucracy.

It is critical how reforms are undertaken. Interest in and concern for the individual, unwillingness to have the central government do what can be done at the state level or to have the public perform what can be done as well by private enterprise—these priorities involve values, and these values should be at the heart of modern conservatism.

Just how far American conservatives can go in their folly is illustrated by the fact that they invented the term "welfare state" as a term of *opprobrium*. Not only is welfare—that is, *the welfare of all the citizens*—a supreme goal of the state, but also it is a concept made familiar by the authors of the constitution and fundamental to conservatism.

Edmund Burke particularly stressed the social progress achieved by a free government in the eighteenth century. "Every state," he said, "has pursued not only every sort of social advantage, but it has cultivated the welfare of every individual. His wants, his wishes, even his tastes have been consulted."[286] As for Britain, it was the state, "without question … which pursues the greatest variety of ends … It aims at raking the entire circle of human desires, and securing for them their fair enjoyment."[287] Burke placed French tyranny in contrast to this, stating that the design "is spirited and daring; it is systematic; it is simple in its principle; it has unity and consistency in perfection."[288] In that country, "to cut off entirely a branch of commerce, to extinguish a manufacture, to destroy the circulation of money, to suspend the course of agriculture, even to burn a city or to lay waste a province of their own, does not cost them a moment's anxiety … The state is all in all."[289]

That contrast should be precisely defined today between the state that "cultivates the welfare of every individual" and the government that, in its quest for doctrinaire unity and efficiency, "cuts off a branch of commerce" or "extinguishes a manufacture." Churchill, for one, as a real conservative, made this his case, and he used it not only against distorted liberalism at home but also against the false lure of communism. However, American so-called conservatives treated welfare as an epithet of abuse and then wondered why radicalism was making giant strides in the country.

It is materialistic to assume that social problems can be remedied by money and the redistribution of wealth alone. It is materialistic to mingle human dignity with one's income and assert that one is oppressed just because another person has a higher salary. Sure enough, when progressives present their views to the people, they often wrap these same fundamentally materialistic premises in their richly moralistic language. Sadly, many voters reward them for it.

Conversely, deep down, conservatives tend to be moralists. Conservatism, at its best, is a series of courageous and subversive moral assertions about what it means to be human.

Conservatism asserts that there is excellent raw material in every single person, regardless of his or her circumstances. This assertion is a radical stance.

Conservatism asserts that providing pathways to work and holding people to high moral standards are acts not of condescension but of brotherly love.

Conservatism asserts that the profound principles of justice require far more of us than just rejiggering the distribution of wealth. Conservatives should fight *for* people, not *against* things.

The notion of security may have been overdone as a political slogan. However, are the conservatives the ones who can afford to denounce security—the security of the individual, the security of the family, the security of the community—as the legitimate and indeed overriding aim of government? Everything conservatives value in the public sphere, such as healthy growth, steady development, and the spirit that avoids violent change and finds utility and promise in established things, depends on an underlying sense of security in the social order. All individuals must know that avoidable catastrophes will not unnecessarily fall upon them, that the worst of fortune will be relieved with the help of the community, and that some safety net will be securely positioned under the regular and predictable dangers of life. It is under such conditions that a person can live, work, and thrive, or an enterprise flourish, and where opportunity is more than just a meaningless word.

All healthy and stable societies had to somehow satisfy this basic need for security. After all, it was for this reason that humans first came together out of the old, wild state of nature and submitted themselves to the inevitable yoke of government. The proper state of affairs is that government should and must concern itself directly, avowedly, and boldly not with the security of the nation only, but with the security (as Burke put it) of every individual.

During the past eighty years, American conservatives have perceived the objective of social security as so distorted as to become one more means of increasing the size of the state apparatus. They clamored against the abuse; unfortunately, they too often cried out against the legitimate concern of government in this field. Many conservatives persuaded themselves that the assurance of a pittance in a person's old age, combined with a guaranty against the shock of unemployment or catastrophic illness, would remove the whole enterprising spirit from life. The scorn poured out by many so-called conservatives upon the objective of social security was not merely inexpedient and misguided politics; it was a shocking revelation of their own limited and narrow-minded vision of human fortune.

The conservatives could have admitted the definite need for a *social security program*, and insisted that it be a means of strengthening *local* ties, the *family*, and the spirit of *independence* in the citizens. Here was a new instrument for the achievement of the fundamental conservative goals. A program conceived and administered in this spirit might not have cost less—it might even have cost more—but a dollar saving is only one of the essential criteria that must be weighed in the making of policy.

If it accepted welfare as its goal, the Republican Party could find in this conservatism a new focus. It could campaign vigorously and creatively, without seeming to adopt the presuppositions of the Democratic regime. Even so, it seems questionable whether conservatism in America should ever become the sole characteristic of one major political party. Since it is a spirit and is widely diffused, it must ultimately involve all politics. Conservatism, at best, remains more profound and pervasive than any political party, and any party exclusively claiming it is likely to deform and exploit it for its own purposes.

Modern conservatives say the government is not the answer but is rather the problem. However, they are badly missing the point; to say that government is not the solution to a nation's problems is to presuppose the wrong incentive for erecting government in the first place. Antistatist conservatives forget that humans left the state of nature in the first place because their souls, which are inherently depraved, need nurturing, and only institutions can provide that.

Alas, democracy will not tolerate institutions of restraint, political or otherwise. Fisher Ames warned us well—if only we could recall his words.[290]

THE DEAD-END STREET OF MODERN CONSERVATISM

There has long been intense criticism of the so-called modern conservative movement; its obsession with politics, including a completely biased foreign policy; and its disproportionate interest in public policy and economics. For a society really to change, its mind and imagination need to be transformed. One can criticize the movement for being less and less attentive to philosophy and the arts. Intellectual and moral confusion made this conservative movement susceptible to manipulation by people with access to money and the media. The decline of conservatism and America was put into relief by absurd claims that conservatism had triumphed; this continues even as it is at its present low point.

To understand the predicament of the present-day conservative movement, it is essential to realize that it originated as a mostly political alliance. It was patched together from diverse intellectual currents, some of which were philosophically remote from each other but could still agree on a limited range of political objectives—mainly the opposition of communism and the defense of limited government. While not even those limited objectives were understood in the same way by all, the lack of intellectual coherence became more glaring than ever with the fall of communism.

It has already been mentioned that most self-described American conservatives would probably define conservatism as a belief in freedom, minimal government, and a strong defense. This interpretation suggests an ideological rather than a philosophical frame of mind and says nothing about what must surely be distinctive to conservatism, which is a heritage that it wants creatively to preserve. Neither does the definition say anything about adapting a universal higher purpose to historical circumstance.

Also, each component of the definition of "conservatism" above can be given vastly different interpretations. Here only the first one, the belief in freedom, will be examined; this is an issue that illustrates well the profound intellectual confusion within the conservative movement. Indeed, it was a simplistic and ahistorical understanding of freedom that made it possible for the neo-Jacobins to invade the movement and cause significant harm to the conducting of US foreign policy.

Many people know the anecdote about Benjamin Franklin being asked, after the Constitutional Convention in Philadelphia, what the convention had accomplished. Franklin answered, "A republic … if you can keep it."[291] Whatever his precise meaning, the Constitution could be maintained only if Americans would shoulder the responsibility for it. For liberty under the law to be possible, they all had to control their emotions and exhibit the "constitutional character."

Edmund Burke's words are also pertinent: "Men are qualified for civil liberty in exact proportion to their disposition to put moral chains upon their own appetites. Society cannot exist unless a controlling power upon will and appetite be placed somewhere, and the less of it there is within, the more there must be without."[292]

That is to say, people wishing to be free have to exercise extraordinary self-control. Human nature being torn between higher and lower potentialities, the latter must be reined in; without this self-restraint, there is no freedom. In case that order does not come from within, it has to be imposed externally; this concept was the moral–spiritual ethos of the American constitutional republic, which was deeply rooted in classical and Christian civilization as transmitted through British culture.

Today most of the defenders of the US Constitution proceed on the naively ignorant assumption that it could be freshly implemented again if only more people could be convinced of its correct meaning. However, the original Constitution and the liberties from which it derives presupposed Americans with certain historically formed character traits that could buttress them. Thus, for ordered liberty to be restored today, an older type of American, the "original type" endowed with the constitutional personality, would first have to reemerge and begin to transform society.

Unfortunately, ordered liberty means something different to many so-called conservatives today than it once did, for example, to John Locke. To Locke, freedom is not the product of lengthy moral conflicts over time; it had existed even before civil society, back in the alleged state of nature in which freedom was simply conferred on human beings as a "free gift." "We are born free as we are born rational," Locke asserts.[293] According to him, nature fully equipped humans to live to good effect, and they left the state of nature only to alleviate a few drawbacks relating to security.

Locke, unlike Burke, was not conscious of what ordered liberty owes to history. He explained the existence of freedom in the state of nature by conveniently alluding to personality traits and ideas in that state that could have evolved only in an advanced society. Seemingly an advocate of rationality and empiricism, Locke was, first of all, a liberal dreamer—an ideologue. He took his bearings not from actual, historical experience but from purely speculative and somewhat naive theorizing.

Locke is one of the originators of the false notion that freedom will flourish everywhere if only, as by getting rid of bad government, external obstructions are removed. Combined with American nationalistic conceit and missionary zeal, this kind of romantic dreaming helped form what could be called new Jacobinism, assigning America the task of bringing in freedom and democracy in all places.

As stated by one American conservative hero: "The American dream lives – not only in the hearts and minds of our own countrymen but in the hearts and minds of millions of the world's people in both free and oppressed societies who look to us for leadership."[294] "America has always recognized our historic responsibility to lead the march of freedom."[295]

The above theory of freedom neither questions the possible existence of any preconditions of freedom nor inquires whether any of the prerequisites for it are already present in a particular society. It simply assumes that freedom will flourish once the bad people and their institutions have been discarded. While utopian idealism used to be a monopoly of the left, it has been the stock in trade of presumed conservatives in recent decades.

Oh yes, Ronald Reagan was the just-quoted conservative hero, and his speeches were full of the idealistic rhetoric of freedom. Like Locke, Reagan had little understanding of the moral, cultural, and social preconditions of freedom. He plainly proclaimed, "Liberty, just as life itself, is not earned but a gift from God."[296] Desperately wanting a political leader, the pseudoconservative movement cheered Reagan's anticommunism and, because of wishful thinking and lack of any intellectual discernment, eagerly gobbled up the sentimental reverie.

Although "Operation Global Freedom" was opportunely restrained by the Cold War in Reagan's case, unfortunately, using 9/11 as the pretense, George W. Bush was able to enlist the United States to remove the remaining obstacles to freedom and democracy in the world, starting in the Middle East. The neoconservative network inside and outside of government, which, in concert with Big Oil, gave Bush its enthusiastic support, had generated the ideological and political momentum for launching this grandiose project and going to war with Iraq.

It is not surprising to a Burkean or a present-day traditional conservative of similar outlook that such ideas should produce disastrous practical consequences; it is clear that the ideology of freedom totally misunderstands the origins of freedom.

Real freedom grows out of historically evolved character traits and institutions and cannot strike roots in the unfavorable soil. It is a prerequisite for maximum economic freedom of such morality and culture that foster a maximum of individual responsibility. In an economy increasingly "managed" by gamblers and crooks and dominated by greed and recklessness, the boundary between honesty and crime disappears and the misuse of economic freedom invites the implementation of regulatory controls.

The conservative movement has not vigorously protested the kind of economism that ignores the moral and cultural preconditions of a sound economy. Neither has it bemoaned the emergence of a crass and callous economic elite. It has not called for the moral and cultural reinvigoration that might shore up economic and other freedom. The new Jacobins and the fanatic worshippers of the theoretically free market do not care about historical circumstances; they care only about adherence to their abstract principles. With friends like them, freedom does not need enemies.

Even after the disasters in foreign and domestic policy in recent years, the so-called conservative movement may not want to give up their ideology and romantic dreaming, but Chapter 11 reorganization will eventually demand it.

Who Still Speaks for Conservatism?

Listening to purportedly conservative American politicians or journalists, one has to ask what these people mean by "conservative." Every time the term is used to describe a GOP position, one has to wonder what makes that position conservative at all.

Why is nation-building abroad a conservative position? It involves the imposition of the latest model of American democracy on populations that are culturally very different from the present decision-making American ruling class.

Why is the outsourcing of American jobs a conservative policy? It involves the merciless letting of American working communities languish.

The obvious answer is that such stands are subjects of interest supported by the Republican Party to hold on to specific constituents that happen to be those of the GOP donor base.

The meaning of "conservative" is blurred even further by the fact that establishment conservative pundits and theorists (they are certainly not thinkers) sound more often than not like the cultural and social left. Popular conservative journalists Jonah Goldberg and John Podhoretz are high on gay marriage, which they argue promotes family values. National Review's Jillian Kay Melchior wishes to see the United States become more fully engaged in Ukraine against Vladimir Putin, lest transgendered Ukrainians come under reactionary Russian sway. Other "conservative" journalists have berated the Russian president for not allowing gay pride parades in Russian cities. National Review Online has paid homage to Leon Trotsky, a cofounder of the Bolshevik dictatorship, for opposing fascism and anti-Semitism. The same fortnightly that once celebrated Joseph McCarthy now denounces him as a dangerous right-wing demagogue, while the same publication now treats its former leftist nemesis, Martin Luther King, as a towering conservative figure and traditionalist theologian. Moreover, when it comes to going after the Confederate Battle Flag and removing Confederate heroes' names from any public site or street in the United States, the Huffington Post has nothing on such stellar "conservatives" as Max Boot and Jeff Jacoby.

Such sea changes are at least partly attributable to the transformation of the American conservative movement falling under the influence and, finally, control of the neoconservatives, who blew in from the left. The designation "conservative" is losing any substantive meaning, except for attachment to Republican operatives and donors, and as a label that particular media personalities choose to give themselves. Although the United States once produced some original conservative thinkers, such as historian Henry Adams and more recently Russell Kirk and Robert Nisbet, the American conservative tradition, going back to the founders, was much closer to eighteenth-century liberalism. The great twentieth-century "conservative" statesman

Robert A. Taft called himself a "liberal," which is what he exactly was in the true historical sense. Taft did not call for Americans to return to a traditional European society of inherited ranks; his primary concern was protecting the system of dual sovereignty and constitutional freedom as set up to endure by James Madison and Alexander Hamilton.

However, the broader application of the term "conservative" concerning social morality must be allowed to designate what just about everyone used to believe but is not supposed to believe any longer. For example, that marriage should be exclusively between members of the opposite sexes, that democracy includes the right to restrict immigration, and that higher education should entail free inquiry rather than continuous sensitivity training. The allowing of such expanded use of the term would require the characterization of almost every American as conservative up until a few decades ago. It is exceedingly odd that what were common American beliefs through 75 percent of US history should now be associated with the far right—and no longer even be shared by mislabeled American "conservatives."

Even more bizarre is the fact that "conservative" advocates of gay marriage and placing illegal immigrants on the path to legalization and eventual citizenship were attacking GOP presidential candidate Donald Trump as a "fake conservative." This charge reeked with foolishness and hypocrisy on the part of GOP boosters who were happy to praise the "conservative" convictions of such lackluster, conflict-averse centrists as George W. Bush, John McCain, and Mitt Romney.

Despite the distaste for his conservative critics, one cannot be fully convinced that Donald Trump is a man of the right. Mr. Trump assumed this role late in life, and he does not play it particularly well yet. It would have been more impressive if in the primaries he had attacked the academic and media efforts to close off discussion on a broad range of "insensitive" subjects instead of, say, the appearance of a female opponent. What may separate a conservative person in the matter of Mr. Trump from the GOP and neoconservative establishment is that, unlike them, a real conservative may like much of what Mr. Trump's message conveys. He has been saying it somewhat clumsily; therefore one just has to see if his actions will clarify, confirm, and reinforce the message the people have hoped to hear.

11

THE GERMAN DREAM COMING TRUE: THE SOCIALIST TRANSFORMATION OF THE WEST

Oswald Spengler once said, "We are all socialists."[297] He meant it as a German, speaking of his compatriots while referring to socialism as a homegrown German ideology characteristic of the German people. Moreover, he was right.

Spengler wanted to liberate German socialism from Marx. For him there was only "German socialism," for there is no other. For him, only the Germans were socialists; no others could be socialists. For him, socialism was Germany's destiny; the spirit of Old Prussia and the socialist attitude were, in fact, the same.

For Spengler, every true German is a worker and German; more precisely, Prussian instinct declares that power belongs to the totality. The individual serves the whole, which is sovereign. Frederick the Great once said that the king is but the first servant of his people. Each citizen has his place assigned in the totality, receives orders, and obeys them. That is authoritarian socialism as we have known it since the eighteenth century. It is nonliberal and antidemocratic, at least when compared with English liberalism and French democracy. It is also evident that the "Old Prussian instinct" is antirevolutionary.

What constitutes, then, the origins of the spirit of German socialism?

Each culture brings together the human beings in its locality and develops them to form a people. In other words, "a people" is not the creator of, but the creature of, its culture. Dorians and Ionians, Hellenes and Etrusco-Romans, the peoples of ancient China, Teutons and Latins, Germans and Englishmen—each people has its peculiar mentality and significance. Each of them stands in a dramatic difference compared to the others. Seen from the outside and compared with foreign cultures, each assumes a unified form: we speak of the Classical man, the Chinese man, and the Western man.

Socialism is not a preference, idea, or inclination of ancient origin but rather a political, social, and economic instinct, and as such, it is a product of one stage of Western civilization.

Spengler stated, "This drive toward universal domination is what I have termed 'modern socialism'. We are now growing more and more conscious of its presence. *It is what we of the Western world have in common.* It is active in every human being from Warsaw to San Francisco, and each of our peoples is fascinated by the spell of its promises and potentialities."[298]

The Germans are the only people who partake of it. Classical, Chinese, or Russian socialism in this sense does not exist.

Still, at the base of this collective consciousness, there is deep-seated hostility and contradiction. Concealed within the soul of every culture—including Western culture, of course—is a single, irreparable fissure. The history of each culture is a never-ending conflict between peoples, classes, individuals, and tendencies within an individual; it is always the same mighty problem. As soon as one historical element makes its appearance, it immediately calls forth an opposing element—a historical duality.

Prussian–German Socialism and Anglo-Saxon Liberalism

With the decline of the Latins, the control of Western Europe's destiny passed into the hands of the Germanic peoples. The birth of the modern English nation occurred in the seventeenth century; that of the Prussian nation, in the eighteenth century. The English and the Prussians have given European civilization universal ideas: capitalism and socialism in a higher sense than the one implied by the words as they are used today; personal independence on the one hand, and suprapersonal community spirit on the other. Today we refer to these concepts as "individualism" and "socialism."

Virtues of the noblest kind are summarized by these words: in the one case "personal responsibility," "self-reliance," "determination," and "initiative"; and in the other, "loyalty," "discipline," "selflessness," and "obligation." To be free and to serve—there is nothing harder than that.

Service—that was the style of Old Prussia. Not "I" but "we"—a feeling of community to which every individual will sacrifice his whole being. For the Old Prussian, the individual does not matter; he must offer himself to the totality. All exist for all, and all partake of that glorious inner freedom, the *libertas oboe dientiae*, which has always distinguished the best models of Prussian upbringing. The Prussian army, the Prussian civil service, and August Bebel's socialist workers' brigades were all products of this breeding principle.

The urge to individuality and independence, however, later drove many of the Englishmen, Germans, and Scandinavians to seek their fortunes on the American prairie, laying the foundation for yet another people with Saxon characteristics. These new people were to arise apart from the maternal soil of the home culture, and thus lacked the "inner basalt" of which Goethe speaks in his poem "America."[299]

Now, there was a difference between the English and German cultural developments. The English soul has developed out of an awareness of insular security as opposed to the German, which has been forced to maintain a frontier without natural borders to protect it from its enemies. In England, splendid isolation replaced the organized state. A stateless nation was possible only under those conditions; isolation was the necessary ingredient in the development of the spirit of modern England (and later of the United States)—a spirit that first gained full confidence in the seventeenth century when the English became the undisputed masters of their island. It is a case of creative topography: England, as a people, shaped and *formed itself*, while Germany, as a people, *was developed* in the eighteenth century by the Hohenzollern, who brought with them the frontier experience of southern Central Europe and who had thus become advocates of the *organized state*.

As real political entities, as state and non-state, Germany and England embody the maximum and minimum functioning of the suprapersonal socialistic principle. The liberal English "state" (a nonstate in the German sense) is completely intangible, undefined, and elusively vague; that nonstate had hardly made any demands on the individual citizen before the twentieth century; nor had it made him a meaningful element in a political system. During the century between Waterloo and the First World War, England went without compulsory education, conscription, and compulsory social security—out of sheer antipathy to these negative privileges. The hostility of the English (and of the Americans) toward centralized organization is neatly expressed in the word "society," which has displaced in their thinking the notion of the state.

Goethe, Schiller, and Herder suggested the word "Gesellschaft," meaning "society" or "community" in English, which then became the preferred expression of the German liberals, too, who used it pretending to eliminate the idea of the state.

England put an end to the principle of the organized state and put in its place the notion of the free private citizen. The citizen demands permission to fight alone in the ruthless struggle for existence. Buckle, Malthus, and Darwin later postulated that the underlying essence of society was the naked struggle for existence. They were right, of course—at least as far as their people were concerned. Indeed, in modern Britain and America, this principle functions in a highly refined and perfected fashion. However, evidence of a more rudimentary adherence to it can be found in the Icelandic and Viking sagas, where such behavior is apparently spontaneous and not borrowed from another culture. The forces with which William the Conqueror took England in 1066 could be called a "society" of knightly adventurers, and English trading companies have subdued and expropriated entire countries—if not continents. Gradually the whole English nation assumed the characteristics of a society. The Old Norse instinct for piracy and canny trading has, in the end, influenced the Englishman's attitude toward all of life, including property, work, foreign cultures, and the weaker individuals and classes among his own people. The same instinct has also yielded political techniques that are handy weapons in the struggle for the Anglo-American and Western elite's mastery of the globe.

A concept complementary to that of society is that of the private citizen. He represents the sum of specific positive ethical qualities that, like all great virtues, are not acquired through training or education but are perfected after passing through generation after generation. The peculiarly English style of politics is necessarily one that involves private citizens or groups of such individuals. That and only that is the very meaning of parliamentary government. Cecil Rhodes was a private citizen who conquered foreign countries. The American billionaires are private citizens who rule foreign countries by employing a junior class of professional politicians.

Among the political attitudes that prevail in Germany today, only socialism has the spiritual roots, value, and integrity inherent in indigenous German culture and mentality. Liberalism is for those who like to chat a great deal about things they can never achieve. That is how the Germans are; they cannot possibly be like the English or Americans but can only be crude caricatures of them—and that they have often been in history.

"Every man for himself" is the English idea. "Every man for every other man" used to be the Old Prussian (German) concept.

"The state for itself; every man for himself" is the message of liberalism. To follow that formula, one must take the liberal course, which is to say one thing while being dead set against its opposite—but, in the end, to let that opposite take over nevertheless.

There cannot be a German type of society quite like the English type. Society made up of separate egos, lacking the single unifying pathos of a common purpose and goal, always strikes the Germans as somewhat ridiculous. The German style of living, in contrast to this, has formed a feeling of unity based on an ethos of work, not of leisure. It united the members of each professional group—military, civil service, and labor—by infusing them with pride of vocation, and dedicated them to activity that benefited all others—the totality, including the state. The feeling of solidarity within each group found symbolic expression in words: respectively "Kameraden" ("mates"), "Kollegen" ("colleagues"), and, with the same sense of pride, "Genossen" ("comrades"). The bond of unity at all levels was a prevailing ethos of dedication, not of success. The distinguishing feature of membership was rank, not wealth. The captain was always superior to the lieutenant, even though the latter may have been a prince or a millionaire. The French used the term "bourgeois" during their revolution to underscore the ideal of equality, but this corresponds neither to the English nor the German sense of distance in social relations. A feel for distance is common to both Germanic peoples; they differ only in the origins of the feeling. When a German worker uses the word "bourgeois," he means a person who, in his opinion, has merely obtained a certain social rank without performing any real work—it is the English ideal seen from the German perspective. England has its snobs; Germany its title-seekers.

The centuries-old feeling of group solidarity in both countries has developed a considerable congruity of physical and psychological attitudes—in the one case a race of successful businesspeople, and in the other a race of workers.

One important symbol of this process, albeit an external one, was the English taste in men's clothing. England had produced civilian dress in the purest sense: the uniform of the private individual. English fashion held unopposed sway in the entire West. England has clothed the world in its "uniform"—the symbol of free trade, private fortune making, and hypocrisy.

The counterpart of this English style was the German outfit: the uniform. It was an emblem of public service, not of separate individual existence. Rather than symbolizing the *success* gained by constant deed, it stood for that *deed* itself. "I am the first servant of my state," said the king of Prussia, Frederick the Great, whose father, the soldier king, had made the wearing of uniforms the established rule among the nobility.

England's fashion in menswear is a matter of social obligation, and it was even stricter than the specifications for uniform-wearing in the Old Prussian state.

To the German way of thinking, the will of the individual is subsumed under the will of the totality. It was not just herd instinct; it was an expression of spiritual strength and freedom—something the outsider could never understand.

The English, the Americans, the French, and indeed the whole world, could never know that the Prussian–German ethic carried with it considerable inner independence. For people with a particular mental framework, a system of social obligations guarantees absolute freedom of the spiritual life, which is not possible under a system of social privileges.

The Englishman pays for his possible freedom with the loss of the other kind of liberty: he is inwardly a slave, whether as Puritan, rationalist, sensualist, or materialist. For three centuries now, he has been the inventor of all philosophies that do away with personal inner independence—for example, Darwinism, which makes man's entire psychic makeup dependent on material forces. The Englishman cares deeply about his right to act as a private citizen, yet for him, there exists no such thing as *real* individual thinking. A unified philosophy governs his life as fashionably as a frock coat and gloves.

Not succumbing to man's inborn lethargy, the German socialist ethic maintains that the chief aim of life is not happiness. "Do your duty," it says, "by doing your work."

The English capitalist ethic says, "Get rich, and then you will not have to work anymore." There is doubtless something provocative about this latter motto. It is tempting; it appeals to very fundamental human instincts, and the working masses of liberal nations have understood it well. The other motto is forbidding; it is for the few who wish to inject it into the community and thus force it upon the masses.

The English maxim is for a stateless country—for egoists with the urge for constant personal combat. It implies maximum independence of mind, the right to gain happiness at the expense of all others, as long as one's strength holds out—in other words, scientific Darwinism.

The German maxim, however, is an expression of the socialist idea in all its profundity: the will to power, the struggle for happiness, but for the happiness of the *totality*, not of the individual. In this sense, the second Prussian king, Frederick William I, the soldier king, and not Marx, was the first conscious socialist. The universal socialist movement had its start with this remarkable personality. Immanuel Kant, with his categorical imperative, then provided the campaign with a recipe.

In the final phase of West European culture, two essential schools of philosophy were founded: the English school of egoism and sensualism, around 1700, and the German school of idealism, around 1800. They express what these nations are as moral, religious, political, and economic entities.

Kant is just as truthful with his contempt for "happiness" and usefulness, his categorical imperative of duty. Hegel places the concrete destiny of individual nations and not the well-being of "human society" at the center of his historical deliberations.

Which is the highest goal, then—freedom *through* wealth or freedom *from* wealth? Ought we prefer Kant's categorical imperative ("Behave as if the precepts governing your behavior were to become law for all") or Bentham's ("Behave in such a way that you will have success")?[300]

The Anglo-Americans are utilitarian, and whenever they try to deny this, the result is the phenomenon that has become famous as cant, pretense, or sham—the maxim of the Western world: hypocrisy. The English are a nation of theologians; the theological mentality tends to avoid naming by its proper name the real goal of all activity: wealth.

Among all the peoples of Western Europe, a rigid social hierarchy distinguishes these two. It is a sign of their drive for dynamic activity; it is an expression of the people's fundamental moral and ethical attitude. Centuries are required for the clarification and realization of this unique feeling for social structure—the ethos of success and the ethos of duty. The English, or rather Anglo-American, people are organized along the lines of wealth and poverty; the Prussian, or rather German, people, along the lines of command and obedience.

The meaning of class distinctions is thus entirely different in the two cultures. In an association of independent private citizens in England or America, the lowest class is the group that *has* nothing; in the German state, the lowest class is the group that has nothing to *say*. In England, or in America, democracy means the possibility that everyone can get *rich*; in Germany, it means to this day that the current ranks are open to everyone with an appropriate political party affiliation. Within the structure of German society, the individual receives his place according to his ability to follow and obey the line of command.

As an example of the first type, one can point to Andrew Carnegie, who first transformed a vast amount of public money into personal wealth, only to distribute it with sovereign gesture among civic activities. His statement "Whoever dies poor dies in dishonor," indicates the admiration for the "will to power" over the totality.

This kind of "private socialism" of the billionaires, or the imperious administration of public monies in extreme cases, ought not to be confused with the socialism of actual civil servants and administrators, who can be quite poor themselves. Examples of this civil form of socialism are the otherwise entirely different personalities of Bismarck and Bebel.

Capitalistic socialism still sees wealth and poverty as the controlling factors in the economic sphere. The worker should try to get rich—this was the policy of the English trade unions right from the beginning. That is why there has never been socialism in the proletarian sense in England or America—it was impossible to distinguish it from the capitalism of the lower class.

For the Germans, the member of a strictly ordered community, be it a political party or the civil service, is a servant of that community who is doing one's duty without surrendering to corrupt notions of private profit. The wages paid to officers and civil servants since the days of Frederick William I have been absurdly small when compared to the sums required to belong even to the middle class in England. The real compensation for the work is rank. This German "workers' state within the state" does not necessarily want to get rich; it wants to rule.

Political economists have often committed the fateful error of thinking solely in materialistic terms. However, the Teutonic knights that settled and colonized the eastern borderlands of Germany in the Middle Ages had also awareness for religion, political and military power, and the authority of the state in economic matters; and later the Prussians, and then subsequently all Germans, inherited that sense. The individual is informed of his obligations by destiny, by God, by the state, or by his talent; these are just different words for the same fact. Rights and privileges of producing and consuming goods are equally distributed. The aim is not ever-growing wealth for the individual or every person, but rather the flourishing of the totality. Thus, Frederick William I and his successors colonized the marshlands in the East, regarding this as their divine mission. The average German laborer, with his sense of reality, has thought and acted along precisely these lines, although the theories of Karl Marx have obscured for him the close connections between his aims and those of the Old Prussians.

The insular English nation has an entirely different understanding of economic affairs. The goal of all is wealth—and God bestows it on the venturesome. The aim is not to work steadily to raise the entire nation's standard of living but rather to produce private fortunes by the use of private capital, to overcome private competition, and to exploit the public. This process is to be performed through the use of advertising, price wars, artificial stimulation of the consumer, and strict control of supply and demand. As Friedrich Engels wrote, "Nothing is more foreign to the English mentality than solidarity."[301]

The economic origin of England and America is synonymous with business (i.e., a subtle form of piracy). The lofty term "free trade" is part and parcel of pirate economics.

The Prussian (i.e., the socialist) term would be "state control of the exchange of goods." That assigns to trade a subordinate rather than a dominant role within the complex of economic activity, while Adam Smith harbored a hatred of the state and the "cunning beasts called statesmen."[302]

Nevertheless, it is paramount that government officials should have the same restraining and forbidding effect on businesspeople as policemen on burglars and naval vessels on the crews of pirate ships.

State regulation of economic affairs, a Prussian–German idea, transformed German capitalism instinctively into a socialist economic pattern—culminating in today's social market economy. The first step in this process was Bismarck's protective tariff legislation of 1879. To political scientist Paul Lensch, a German socialist critic of capitalism, the large syndicates were, in effect, economic states within the state. They represented "capitalism's first practical and systematic large-scale attempt, although it was not consciously planned, to understand the mysteries of its own techniques and to gain control of social forces which up to then had been regarded as natural and unfathomable, requiring passive, blind submission."[303]

Aided by the uncanny German philosophy of idealism, Germany's accomplishments, at least within its economic sphere, received the exalted title of "socialism."

An essential element of any political system is the people who have created this model, which cannot be recreated or imbued with actual reality by anyone else. Each culture and each single people within a culture arranges its affairs and fulfills its destiny according to principles that are innate and virtually unalterable. The ultimate meaning of great political turmoils is something other than a change in the form of government. Following such euphoric moments, a people will always return to its very own political pattern sooner or later. The essential quality of this people-specific political model can almost never be expressed in familiar language.

The instincts and aspirations of a vigorous people are so strong that they can deal with any form of government presented by a historical accident and mold it to their own purposes. When this forming (or reforming) process takes place, no one is conscious of the fact that the political pattern in question has been attained *in name only*. The real political condition of any given country is not to be found in the wording of its constitution; it is instead manifested in the tacit, implicitly stated, and instinctive acts according to which the constitution is put into effect. Without reference to the particular nations under discussion, the words "republic," "parliamentarianism," "democracy," and "autocracy" are utterly meaningless.

It is significant and characteristic of the strength of the national political instinct that the political parties in Germany today—the Conservatives (CDU/CSU), the Socialists (SPD), the Greens, and the Links—are all socialistic in a higher sense. Recognizing neither private nor party interests as the leaders of government, they ascribe to the totality the full authority, the leadership of the individual in the general interest. The fact that one of these parties speaks of the capitalistic state while the other speaks of the working people proves to be only a verbal distinction when we consider that, in Germany, the will of the individual is subject at all times to the will of the totality. They organize entire and well-disciplined battalions of voters, in which the Conservatives (used to) make better officers, the Socialists better troops. They are structured along the lines of command and obedience, and that is the way they conceived of their state, the Hohenzollern state, and the state of the future.

The two great universal principles, the Anglo-Saxon capitalistic utilitarianism and the Prussian–German socialistic idealism, continue to oppose each other in the West: the dictatorship of money *or* organizational talent, the world as booty *or* as a real state, wealth *or* political authority, success *or* vocation.

Authoritative socialism, the old German phenomenon, was by definition monarchist. The Germans envisioned a unified nation in which everyone was assigned a place according to social rank, the talent for voluntary self-discipline based on inner conviction, organizational abilities, work potential, conscientiousness, energy, intelligence, and willingness to serve the common cause. One could plan for "general work conscription," resulting in professional guilds that would administer and at the same time be guided by an administrative council and not by a parliament. In a state where everyone has a job—be it as a worker, civil servant, farmer, or miner—a fitting name for this administrative body might well be "labor council."

Counter to this idea is the currently promoted Anglo-Western vision of a capitalistic, democratic, and globalized world order, which is nothing other than liberal socialism. For the United States and the non-EU Western World, it is a republic, although today the word "republic" refers to government by the successful private individual who can pay for his election and therefore also for his influence. The globalizing liberal socialists dream of the Earth as a hunting ground for those who want to get rich and who demand themselves the right to engage in hand-to-hand combat. Initially, the Anglo-Western liberal socialism wanted to band together against the German type of authoritative socialism, but today we are witnessing the amalgamation of the two.

Western civilization, in all its forms and manifestations, is dominated by industry. The industrial worker originated in this civilization, and he genuinely feels the anomaly of his existence. If others, like the businessman or the engineer, are slaves of the age of technology, then he is also a slave. The middle class comprised those who lived by their work without actually being poor. The upper class was wealthy without working. The lower class worked and was poor.

In old Germany, however, it was rank (i.e., a greater or lesser degree of command and obedience) that separated the classes. Besides the peasantry, there existed a civil servant class; that is to say, there was a unity of function rather than economic distinctions.

The Marxian words "socialism" and "capitalism" are terms for the "good" and "evil" of this irreligious religion. The bourgeois is the devil. The wage earner is the angel of a new mythology, and one need only sample the common paths of *The Communist Manifesto* to recognize behind the literary mask the Christianity of the independents. Social evolution is "the will of God." The "final goal," at an earlier age, was eternal salvation; the "collapse of bourgeois civilization" used to be called the Last Judgment.

Marx succeeded in preaching contempt for work. Work—long, hard, tiring work—is for him a misfortune, and effortless gain a blessing. Behind the typically English disdain for the man who lives by the sweat of his brow, we can feel the instinct of the pirate, whose vocation is piracy and not patching sails. For this reason, the manual laborer is more a slave in England than anywhere else. Moreover, his slavery is moral; he feels that his profession precludes his bearing the title of "gentleman." The concepts of the bourgeoisie and proletariat reflect the typically English preference for business rather than manual work. The former is a blessing, the latter a calamity; the one is noble, the other base. However, with their hatred, the unfortunate ones say, "Business is the evil occupation; manual labor the good."

That is the explanation for the mental attitude that gave rise to Marx's social criticism and that has made him so catastrophic for "true socialism." Had Marx understood the meaning of Prussian–German work, of activity for its own sake, of service in the name of the totality, he would have developed other concepts. Had he been able to comprehend the meaning of "all together" and not for oneself, of duty that ennobles regardless of the kind of work performed, his manifesto would probably never have been written.

Martin Luther praised the simplest physical activity as pleasing to God; Goethe wrote of the "demands of the day."[304]

The Prussian–German socialist state exists beyond this "good" and "evil." It is the whole people, and in the face of its absolute authority, the political parties are simply parties—minorities that serve the general good.

From a strictly technical viewpoint, German socialism is both the principle and outgrowth of public service. In the final analysis, every worker has the status not of a businessman but of a public servant, as also does every employer. There are civil servants of industry, commerce, transportation, and the military. This system was executed in the grandest style in Egyptian culture and again, though quite in another way, in China; work is not a commodity but a duty toward the common interest, and there is no graduation—this is Prussian-style democratization—of ethical values among the various kinds of work. The judge and the scholar perform work just as do the miner and the lathe operator.

The old Prussian–German way of doing things was for the state to determine wages impartially for each kind of work, planning the scales carefully, according to the whole economic situation at any given time, in the interest of all the people and not of any one profession. That was the principle of salary scales for civil servants, made to apply to all occupations. It included the prohibition of the strike, for it regarded this as a single commercial device inimical to state interests. The power to set wage scales was removed from both employer and employee and became the privilege of a general economic council, thus ensuring that each party would operate within the same firm boundaries as they had to in other areas of management and work practice. (One could imagine a system in which every worker—the army officer and administrative official, as well as the laborer—maintained an account with a state savings bank, which received standardized statements from the institutions obligated to pay wages. The individual would then have at his disposal a certain sum to be determined by a standard scale of distribution based on years of service and number of dependents.)

Socialism, as the newly developed version of the Old Prussian ideology, became the doctrine used for the liberation of the working class. It promoted the rise of the fourth class and its incorporation in the political organism of the German fatherland. According to this new German socialist doctrine, the bourgeois was about to leave the old stage, and in its place would come the, heretofore oppressed, class of productive (German) workers, the working class.

The German socialists saw the social question as a matter of necessity and justice for the very existence of a state devised for the German people. The German worker had a claim to a living standard that corresponded to what he produced. Therefore, incorporating him into the state organism was a critical matter not only for him but also for the entire German nation.

THE PATH FROM AUTHORITATIVE PRUSSIAN–GERMAN SOCIALISM TO NATIONAL SOCIALISM

In one form or another, international socialism dominates the political image of the world today. The people of the future will look back with amusement at the "International" of catchwords and Marxism as a set of vapid slogans. This International campaign aims to arouse feelings of solidarity among the peoples of all nations for many decades, but with much less intensity than the various but always noisy socialist conventions and the overconfident public appeals might lead one to believe. Although this solidarity is limited solely to the belief that it exists, it is characteristic of the Western civilization so thoroughly saturated with information that the leaders of the masses, who live in an impenetrable cloud of theory, can nonetheless become the instruments of compelling realities.

Socialism is something different in every country. In the two world wars, it was not only the Allies who fought against Germany but also the liberal pseudosocialism of the Allied nations that opposed the Prussian–German authoritative socialism. By betraying the person of the Kaiser during the First World War, true German socialism betrayed itself, its origins, its meaning, and its position in the socialist world. Therefore, the most dangerous enemy of Prussian–German socialism was not German capitalism, which at one time bore pronounced socialistic features and which socialism itself forced into the pseudosocialist English camp after 1917.

However, only in Germany has socialism, Prussian–German socialism been, as it remains to be, a *weltanschauung*. The Frenchman continues to be an anarchist, and the Anglo-American remains a liberal pseudosocialist.

Socialism has beside and against it capitalism and religion, and thus there are three different forms of the socialist will to power: through the *state*, through *money*, and through the *church*. Their influence extends throughout the political, economic, and religious consciousness of the Western world, and each seeks to subject the others to its will.

The concept of property, a disguise for the businessman's liberalism, is opposed to the Prussian–German view. The German sees property not as private booty but as part of the common good; not as a means or expression of personal power but as assets placed in trust, for the administration of which he, as a property owner, is responsible for the state. The German does not regard national wealth to be the sum of individual private fortunes; instead he considers private fortunes to be functions of the total economic potential of his nation. We must think again and again of the famous words of Frederick the Great: "I am the first servant of my state." As soon as every individual makes this attitude his very own, socialism becomes a fact.

There is no sharper contrast to this idea than Louis XIV with his factual statement "I am the state." Whether on the throne or in the streets, the Western world can conceive of no greater contrast than that between Germanism and Jacobinism, between socialist and anarchist instinct.

Robert Owen (and later Margaret Thatcher) attempted to formulate, as a kind of reform of capital, the desire of the English lower class to adopt for itself the upper-class ideal of property. However, it would be a gross underestimation of the pirate instinct to think that English-American capital will retreat one step on the path toward absolute economic domination of the world.

Unlimited personal freedom and the natural inequality of man based on relative degrees of individual talent are the fundamental articles of the Anglo-Saxon creed. Instead of authoritarian socialism, the English or American billionaire adheres to an impressive form of private socialism, a welfare program on a grand scale, which turns personal power into pleasure and morally vanquishes the recipient of welfare funds. The flashy techniques for distributing the millions are a good cover-up for the methods used to obtain them in the first place. It is the same attitude as that of the old corsairs who, while banqueting in a castle just conquered, threw their table scraps to the prisoners: the voluntary surrender of a property increases the value of what remains. The question of whether or not such voluntary acts should become a legal duty is the chief point of contention among the economic parties of the future in Britain and America. The Western elite is always prepared to transfer considerable commercial assets that are less amenable to speculation (meaning less profitable)—usually old industries; parts of the infrastructure, such as the old mining, steel, and railroad industries; or transportation services—to the care of a pseudostate ("their" state). Of course, they intend to retain the behind-the-scenes prerogative of making this state an executive organ of their own business interests by utilizing the democratic forms of parliamentarianism, (i.e., by paying for election campaigns and newspapers and thus controlling the opinions of voters and readers).

Therein lies the great danger of enslavement of the world by Big Business. Today its tools are the United Nations and its numerous suborganizations—mainly a system of nations, most of whose populations are being exploited by a business oligarchy with the aid of bribed parliaments and purchased laws. Similarly, there was a time when the Roman world was operated by the bribery of senators, proconsuls, popular tribunes, and the robbery of the robbers.

Maintaining full Germanic respect for property, but awarding the power inherent in it to the state—to the totality and not to the individual—was the real (old) German meaning of "socialization." All Prussian–German governments that functioned on instinct untrammeled by theory systematically pursued this concept, from the civil and war chambers of Frederick William I to the social welfare institutions of Bismarck.

German socialization does not involve nationalization by expropriation or theft. It is not concerned with property in the strict meaning of the word, but rather with the techniques of administration. Buying up industries right and left for the sake of some slogan and handing them over to administrative bodies incognizant of the ways of large enterprises instead of leaving them to the responsibility and initiative of their owners is the surest way to pervert true Prussian–German socialism.

The Old Prussian method was to legislate the formal structure of the total productive potential while carefully guarding the right to property and inheritance and to allow so much freedom to personal talent, energy, initiative, and intellect as one might allow a skilled chess player who had mastered all the rules of the game. Old cartels and syndicates mostly functioned this way, and there is no reason this method could not be systematically extended to work habits, work evaluation, profit distribution, and the internal relationship between planners and executive personnel.

German socialization involves the slow, decades-long transformation of the worker into an economic civil servant, of the employer into a responsible administrative official with extensive powers of authority, and of property into a kind of old-style hereditary fief to which a certain number of rights and privileges are attached. In the old Prussian–German socialism, the economy was to remain as free as that of the chess player; only the end effect followed a regulated course.

The Hohenzollern created the Prussian civil servant type—the first of its kind in the world. Because of his innate socialistic abilities, this type practically assures the possibility of new socialization. For three hundred years he has symbolized in his methods what socialism signifies today as a task to be done: the German worker giving up Marxism and beginning to think like a socialist is the Prussian–German type just described. The German state of the future is the state made up of civil servants, and that is one of the conditions toward which German civilization has been steadily moving.

Even a billionaire's socialism could imperceptibly transform a nation into an army of private officials. The big Western corporations have already virtually become separate states exercising a protectorate over the official state. Prussian–German socialism, however, implies the incorporation of these professional-interest "states" into the state as a totality. The point at issue between conservatives and socialists is in truth not the necessity of the authoritarian (German) socialist system, which could be avoided by adopting the American policy (that is the hope of the German liberals), but the question of supreme command.

It may look as though two socialist alternatives exist today, one from above and another from below, both of a dictatorial mold. In reality, either would gradually merge into the same final form. In a political system that intentionally blurs the distinctions between workers and administrators by assuring each qualified individual from menial laborer to foreman and corporation head a secure career, the complete nationalization of economic life is accomplished with the merger of the two socialist alternatives into one by legislation rather than expropriation.

However, the leadership of such a system cannot be republican. Putting aside all illusions, "republic" today refers to the corruptibility of executive power by using private capital.

The individualistic ideal of private property means the subjugation of the state by free economic forces (i.e., democracy, or the corruptibility of the government by private wealth). In modern liberal democracy, the leaders of the masses find themselves in opposition not to the capitalists but to money and the anonymously hidden power it exerts. The question is how many of these leaders can resist such power.

There are three ideals of property locked in conflict today: the communist ideal of equal distribution of the world's goods, the individualistic ideal of using them to create business enterprises, and the socialistic ideal of administering them in the name of the totality. The critical question is this: Shall business rule the state, or shall the state rule business?

As far as this crucial issue is concerned, the German organized state *and* socialism are the *same*. The teachings of Marx, together with class egoism from the German point of view, are guilty of causing both the socialist labor force and the conservative element to misunderstand each other, and thus also to misunderstand (Prussian–German) socialism. However, it is unmistakable that they both have identical goals today. The organized state and true German socialism stand together; solidarity is supposed to mean the fulfillment of the Hohenzollern idea and at the same time the redemption of labor. There is salvation either for conservatives and workers together or neither.

Labor had to get rid of its Marxist illusions; for the workers there is either Prussian–German socialism (meaning the "real" social market economy) or nothing. The conservatives must rid themselves of their egoism.

No matter what one may think of today's liberal democracy, it is the current political reality. For the state, there can only be some form of democratization, and for the conservatives, there can only be conscious socialization. However, each country—each nation, each people—must have its very own form of an indigenous political-economic-social system; this cannot be imposed on from the outside by foreign "helping experts."

The meaning of the old Prussian–German socialism was that life is dominated not by the contrast between rich and poor but by rank as determined by achievement and ability. That was, and still is, the German kind of freedom—freedom from the economic capriciousness of the individual. German socialism means ability, not desire; not the quality of intentions but the quality of accomplishments is decisive.

Now, thoughts and schemes are nothing without power, and the path to power had already been mapped: it resides in the union of the valuable elements of German labor and the best representatives of the Old Prussian state idea, with both groups determined to build a socialist state to democratize Germany in the Prussian manner.

The great Oswald Spengler said, "We are all socialists. Let us hope that it will not have been in vain."[305]

Thus marched Germany on after World War I—straight into National Socialism.

NATIONAL SOCIALISM IS A NATURAL OUTGROWTH OF SOCIALISM

Notwithstanding Spengler's (German) interpretation of (German) socialism, it is an international movement, whereas National Socialism is, as the term implies, a (German) nationalist form of socialism.

National Socialism (Nazism) is a totalitarian system created in Germany immediately following World War I. It is characterized by intense nationalism, mass appeal, brutal use of violence, and the fascist idea of an economic system. Moreover, National Socialism also imposed racial policy underlining the exclusion, domination, and oppression of people regarded inferior by social Darwinism, as advocated by individuals such as Heinrich von Treitschke and Houston Stewart Chamberlain.[306] This philosophy extrapolated Darwin's theory of the survival of the fittest and said that persons, groups, and races are controlled by the same laws of natural selection that Darwin proposed for animals.

The name "Nazi" is a contraction of the full party name, National Socialist German Workers' Party. Nazism, in short, is just one of the several varieties of socialism. As a political party, it controlled Germany under Adolf Hitler during the 1933–45 period, resulting in World War II and a campaign of mostly anti-Jewish and racist politics, culminating in genocide.

Supporters and apologists of modern socialism, in general, including the New Left that incorporated the ex-Communists following the collapse of the Soviet Union, like to pretend that Nazism was not a socialist movement but a right-wing movement.

It has been common to place the socialists and communists on the left and the fascists and Nazis on the far-right of the traditional, or politically correct, left–right spectrum. This deliberately skewed representation of the facts serves to show that socialists and fascists, in fact, stand on opposite ends of the ideological spectrum. The artificial left–right categorization is especially beneficial for the leftists, including socialists and social democrats, since they can, for them very conveniently, separate themselves from the national socialist ideology. Moreover, they can also claim that they themselves, as direct opponents of this criminal ideology, were the victims of National Socialism—an ideology that was utterly alien to them.

However, Ludwig von Mises, for one, knew very differently: National Socialism and Bolshevism both sported the same ideological pedigree of socialism.

"The German (Nazi) and Russian (Communist) systems of socialism have in common the fact that the government has full *control* of the means of production. It decides what shall be produced and how. It allots each individual a share of consumer's goods for his consumption."

The difference between the two systems is, wrote Mises, that the German pattern "maintains private *ownership* of the means of production and keeps the appearance of ordinary prices, wages, and markets." In fact, the government directs production decisions, curbs entrepreneurship and the labor market, and determines wages and interest rates by a central authority. "Market exchange," says Mises, "is only a sham."[307]

There is an accepted mainstream view and widely held belief among historians and academics of the right that National Socialism has its roots in socialism rather than on the right. Nobel Prize–winning economist Friedrich Hayek, in his book *The Road to Serfdom*, has stated that the origins of Nazism lie in socialism, or that they have common roots. He questioned the prevailing sentiment among academics that fascism was a capitalist response to socialism, arguing instead that fascism and socialism had common roots in both central economic planning and state power over the individual. Hayek asserted that socialism undermines human liberty and, if pursued far enough, must result in tyranny.[308]

National Socialism is just one of the many forms of socialism. There is a difference between National Socialism and International Socialism regarding the rhetoric they use, but the result is much the same. National Socialism justifies the subservience of the individual to the state by the propagation of a common racial or cultural identity. International Socialism justifies the subservience of the individual by membership in an international union of proletarians or some other euphemism along those lines.

The result is, of course, the subservience of the individual to the state, which then inevitably acts only to further its pragmatic interests even if they conflict with its stated justification.

Socialism is pragmatic in the pursuit of its interests because there is no one for it to answer. In its purest definition, it does not exclude capital or private ownership, believing instead in a state interested in the (re)distribution of private property (ownership that could not exist with the destruction of that state-recognized entity). National Socialism defines private ownership as being in the interest of its own nationality.

All modern forms of socialism have tended to favor leftist social structures with the line between the definition of socialism and communism becoming carefully blurred, but it all breaks down to how one defines socialism. Different words should, logically and usefully, be assigned different meanings and definitions for them to have a separate use. Therefore, all synonyms are usually colored with some measure of an idea evoking a different perception of the word. Broadly equating two different words as the same has always been a way of including past ideas while excluding present uses for those ideas and those that use them.

In the same way, communists were able to appropriate the philosophical work and political efforts of the socialists to their own ends, obscuring their less emphasized aspects. This appropriation started with Marx himself, and for many people, he entirely made the term as his own. Nearly everyone has forgotten that socialism predated communism and was initially, in fact, a separate political ideology.

However, even as it stands, there are those who want to consider Nazism as a purposeful misnomer meant to deceive, rather than as an appropriately descriptive title, only because they desperately want to decouple the idea of National Socialism as associated with the original construction of what socialism is. Accordingly, two main points must be examined: (1) why Nazi Germany was a socialist state and not a capitalist one and (2) why real socialism, especially the true and pure Prussian–German socialism, understood as an economic system based on government control of the means of production, positively requires a totalitarian dictatorship.

The identification of Nazi Germany as a socialist state was one of the many significant contributions of Ludwig von Mises. When one remembers that the word "Nazi" is a contraction of the "Nationalsozialistische Deutsche Arbeiterpartei," or NSDAP (English translation: National Socialist German Workers' Party), von Mises's identification might not appear all that noteworthy. One should expect, of course, that the economic system of a country ruled by a party with "socialist" in its name is, in fact, socialist; the Nazis were not called "National Socialists" without any reason.

Fascism is regularly described as a creed of the right, although it is decidedly and categorically not. The origins of fascism lie in socialism, and the ideology has far more in common with the left, at least in theoretical political terms. All fascist parties have leftist tendencies, as they predominantly believe in nationalization, collectivism, and the prohibition of free expression, which makes fascism the very antithesis of right-of-center politics. Nevertheless, many present-day leftist adherents of socialism try to show that National Socialism and communism are mostly manifestations of populism—a very derogatory term alluding to the right per modern political correctness. They intend to prove that socialism or social democracy is mainstream ideology and has nothing to do with either extreme-right or extreme-left ideologies.

Not surprisingly, apart from von Mises and his readers, practically no one thinks of Nazi Germany as a socialist state today. Instead it is held in common that it represented a form of capitalism, which is precisely what the communists, Marxists, and socialists want people to believe. The basis for their claim is the fact that most industries in Nazi Germany appeared to be left in private hands.

What von Mises identified, however, was that private ownership of the means of production existed *in name only* under the Nazis, while the real substance of ownership, the actual control of the means of production, resided with the German government. It was the German government and not the nominal private owners that exercised all of the substantive powers of ownership. The German government alone decided, and not the nominal private owners (one would say today "virtual owners"), what was to be produced, in what quantity, by what methods, and to whom it was to be distributed. Moreover, the German government alone decided as well what prices would be charged, what wages would be paid, and what dividends or any other income the nominal private owners were to receive. The status of the allegedly private owners, Mises showed, was reduced to that of government pensioners.

As von Mises pointed out, such fundamental collectivist principles as that "the common good comes before the private good" or "the individual exists as a means to the ends of the State" already hinted at the de facto government ownership and actual control of the means of production. Consequently, if the individual is a means to the ends of the state, so too is his property. Just as the state owns the individual, it also owns his property.

What specifically established de facto socialism in Nazi Germany was the introduction of wage and price controls in 1936. These were imposed in response to the growth of the money supply caused by the expansionary economic policies of the regime from the time of its coming to power in early 1933. The Nazi regime inflated the money supply as the means of financing the vast increase in government spending required by its programs of public works, subsidies, and rearmament. The wage and price controls were imposed in response to the rise in prices that resulted from the inflation.

The inevitable aftermath of the concoction of inflation and wage and price controls is shortages—that is, a situation whereby the quantities of goods people attempt to buy will exceed the quantities available for sale. Shortages, in turn, result in economic chaos—not a situation to which governments typically respond by imposing rationing, but chaos throughout the entire economic system. Shortages introduce randomness in the distribution of supplies between geographical areas, in the allocation of production among the different products, and in the division of labor and capital among the various sections of the economy.

Under the conditions of price controls and shortages, the effect of a decrease in the supply of an item is not to raise its price and increase its profitability, as it usually would be in a free market. Price control rules out the rise in price and thus the growth in profitability, while at the same time the shortages caused by price controls block any increase of supply from reducing price and profitability. Whenever there is a shortage, any increase in supply is merely a reduction in the severity of the shortage. Only when the shortage is eliminated does an increase in supply necessitate a decrease in price and bring about a reduction in profitability.

Consequently, the combination of price controls and shortages allows the random movements of supply without any effect on price and profitability. Under these circumstances, the production of the most trivial and unimportant goods, even chewing gums or popcorn, can be expanded at the expense of the production of the most urgently needed and essential goods, such as medical equipment of life-saving medicines, without any effect on either the price or the profitability of either good. Price controls would preclude the production of the medicines from becoming more profitable as their supply decreased, while a shortage even of chewing gums would prevent their production from becoming less profitable as their supply increased.

As von Mises showed, to cope with such unintended effects of its price controls, the government must either abolish the price controls or add further measures. These actions mean precisely the control over what is produced, in what quantity, by what methods, and to whom it is distributed, as has been explained earlier. The combination of price controls with this further set of controls constitutes the de facto socialization of the economic system, for it means that the government then exercises all of the substantive powers of ownership. In other words, control and ownership are separated.

This separation of control and ownership was the socialism instituted by the

Nazis. Von Mises calls it socialism on the German or Nazi pattern, in contrast to the more overt socialism of the Soviets, which he calls socialism on the Russian or Bolshevik model.[309]

While the origins of Nazism do lie in traditional socialism, this does not mean that, for example, the Social Democratic Party of Germany or any other mainstream socialist party of today has views that are in any way akin to Nazi or other racist dogmas. However, if we refuse to challenge the ideological origins of a movement that culminated in the systematic murder of millions of human beings, we cannot prevent it from happening again.

The best way to prove that the origins of Nazism are not even remotely conservative is to start looking at some defining features of conservatism itself—specifically the European variety of it. These conservative tenets include the belief that a society rooted in monarchy and aristocracy is not necessarily inferior to mass democracy. They also hold that there is a transcendent moral order (what Russell Kirk called the "Permanent Things"), which has been upheld and passed down through the Christian church.[310] Also, property rights are the very foundation of ordered liberty in the conservative view; and of course there is the universal conservative belief that any necessary societal change must occur without any structural damage to established and proven institutions. Moreover, problems in society come not from broken traditions and institutions but rather from broken people and morals.

The National Socialists had no love of monarchy or aristocracy; Hitler did not restore the House of Hohenzollern but made himself dictator, the leader of the movement. The idea that the self-taught son of a minor Austrian civil servant had the opportunity to gain power and rule over Germany can hardly be called traditionally conservative. Moreover, his dislike of the aristocratic military establishment is well known.

The official religion of Nazism was Positive Christianity—a doctrine that cannot be called either positive or Christian. It rejected the Jewish Bible in its entirety, denied Jesus's Jewish origins, wanted to eliminate Catholicism (the stalwart defender of tradition that it is) and create a united Nazi Protestant church.[311]

The conservative argues that socialism is not a cure for the disease of industrial society but a symptom of the same sickness. Nazi property violations were not limited solely to the estate; they also infringed upon life and liberty with spectacular zeal—especially the life and liberty of those they deemed subhuman.

Fascists and Nazis were almost from the start called "right-wing," but this was a slander employed by international socialists meaning to discredit the socialists of a distinctly nationalist bent in the eyes of radical fellow travelers. If they were right-wing at all, they were of the right wing of the left. As Jonah Goldberg explains in his apparently woefully underread work *Liberal Fascism*, this is why street fighting between fascists and communists was so vicious in Germany; these people were fighting for the same hearts and minds—for the same segment of mostly lower-middle-class voters susceptible to revolutionary nonsense.[312] The godfather of fascism himself, Mussolini, was a member of the Socialist International, and the term "national socialist" had been in use in leftist circles well before the Nazi party was created.

Ethnic nationalism, let alone racism, is in no way conservative; the scientific racism of the Nazis, so popular across Europe from the beginning of the twentieth century until the devastating and inevitable result of its assertions, would never have developed if not for the nationalist movements. Nationalism was one of the earliest leftist ideologies closely associated with identity politics. It was forged in the fires of the French Revolution and developed as a means to undermine the old European order of the multiethnic empires of Austria-Hungary, Germany, Russia, and, to an extent, the Ottoman Empire.

The relatively new idea that countries should be based on single-ethnicity groups promoting the nation-states is an ideologically radical position. To a conservative, culture and not race is what matters; the cry of the conservative is "king and country." The cry of the National Socialist is "blood and soil" and "race and nation."

Thus, the intellectually honest must arrive at the inescapable conclusion that Nazism is not conservative. Moreover, if it is not conservative, it cannot be indeed called "right-wing." It is just another grotesque by-product of the French Revolution, another one of Rousseau's overdue bastard children, one more in a long line of deformed, monstrous political creatures to slither its way out of the primordial Jacobin soup.

The fact that all of Europe has a long and at times vicious history with anti-Semitism is well known and frequently referenced when discussing collusion with Nazis in occupied countries. What is noted with far less frequency—but far more critical, however—is the fact that not until the introduction of mass democracy was there any organized or systematic attempt to wipe out the European Jewry. Indeed,

Jews had been periodically persecuted, killed, banished, exiled, evicted, or driven out in several European countries during history, from Portugal to England, from France to Russia, and from Germany to Spain (just to name a few), but never with the explicit intention of wiping them out. In fact, before the French Revolution, there were no deliberate large-scale attempts to eradicate or annihilate *anyone* in Europe (unlike in other parts of the world). This fact is the obvious truth we ignore when we censure and censor people who would accurately link Nazism with leftism. Erik von Kuehnelt-Leddihn, the brilliant political theorist, articulated this truth:

> The roots of the evil are historically-genetically the same all over the Western World. The fatal year is 1789, and the symbol of iniquity is the Jacobin Cap. Its heresy is the denial of personality and personal liberty. Its concrete realizations are Jacobin mass democracy, all forms of national collectivism and statism, Marxism producing socialism and communism, fascism, and National Socialism, leftism in all its modern guises and manifestations to which in America the good term 'liberalism,' perversely enough, is being applied. The issue is between man created in the image of God and the termite in a human guise.[313]

Only a humiliated German people ripped from tradition (except for socialism, their homegrown national ideology) could stand by and watch as millions of human beings were systematically herded up like cattle and sent to be exterminated like termites. This abomination was due to a German people that had lived through political chaos and economic catastrophe after the First World War—a German people starved of all Judeo-Christian morality, drugged with the false promise of a glorious future befitting a superior race, and subjected to the authority of those who shamelessly abused it. They were promised a utopian future, to be attained by sacrificing tradition at the altar of progress, and assured the abolishment of class distinctions as well as the old order, which was politically rooted in feudalism and morally rooted in Christianity. However, as a result, they inevitably ended up with the denial of the sanctity and value of human life.

People across the globe rhetorically ask how humans could participate in something as evil as the Holocaust. Alas, it is the easiest thing in the world to commit a crime when one does not consider it to be such because one lives in a society ruled by moral relativism. The option is indeed between man created in the image of God and the termite in a human guise. So those who would obfuscate the ideological and philosophical origins of Nazism have made their choice known.

"We are Socialists, enemies, mortal enemies of the present capitalist economic system with its exploitation of the economically weak, with its injustice in wages, with its immoral evaluation of individuals according to wealth and money instead of responsibility and achievement, and we are determined, under all circumstances, to abolish this system! And with my inclination to practical action, it seems obvious to me that we have to put a better, more just, more moral system in its place, one which, as it were, has arms and legs and better arms and legs than the present one!" wrote Gregor Strasser, Nazi Party ideologue and organizer, in "Thoughts about the Tasks of the Future" in 1926.[314]

No one would have regarded the above as a controversial statement at the time, and the Nazis could not have been more open with their devotion to socialism. Almost everyone in those days accepted that fascism had emerged from the revolutionary left. Its militants marched under red flags on May Day, and its leaders stood for collectivism, state control of industry, high tariffs, and workers' councils. Around Europe, fascists were convinced that, as Hitler told an enthusiastic Mussolini in 1934, "Capitalism has run its course."[315]

Admittedly, it is a stunning achievement of the modern left to have created such a cultural climate wherein the simple recital of these facts is upsetting. History has been reinterpreted, rejustified, and repackaged, and it is taken as axiomatic today that fascism must have been right-wing, the politically correct rationale seemingly being that "left-wing" means "compassionate" and "right-wing" means "nasty"— and fascists were very nasty indeed. One would expect this level of analysis from Twitter mobs; it should not be expected, or accepted, coming from mainstream commentators. For many apologists of socialism, it is intellectually dishonest to claim that fascism is indeed an offshoot of socialism. According to them, when someone calls a right-winger a "fascist," he is referring not to the economic aspects of fascism but to the belligerent nationalism, xenophobia, and racism found in fascist states.

The economic aspects linking fascism to socialism have already been explained. However, the issues concerning nationalism, xenophobia, and racism are particularly important to elaborate. The left mentions these repeatedly, cynically, and venomously as the most obvious examples of the fundamental differences between socialism and National Socialism, between the left wing and right wing, between progressive and conservative, and between good and evil.

If we believe and accept the tenet that nationalism, xenophobia, and racism are the distinctive characteristics of fascist regimes, how does this fact then automatically confirm that fascism can be linked to "right-wing ideologies? How, then, could the inhumane nature of the unthinkable and unspeakable crimes committed by supposedly non-right-wing regimes be explained or classified? What about the uncounted millions of people deliberately and systematically killed by many a system in human history, from the Greeks and Romans to the Chinese and Mongols, from Stalin to Pol Pot, and from Rwanda to Darfur in more recent times? The modern terms "ethnic cleansing" and "genocide" stand for the timeless act of mass murder, which is as old as humankind. While it cannot be denied that both ethnic cleansing and genocide are linked to nationalism, xenophobia, and racism, does that mean that all regimes and ideologies culpable of these crimes were right-wing ideologies as a matter of course?

Of course not. Who can claim that right-wing regimes committed all genocides in history? Not even the left has submitted as yet that Stalin and the Bolsheviks, Pol Pot and the Khmer Rouge, or the Hutu government of Rwanda were right-wing.

Therefore, it can be stated that very different ideologies and historical circumstances could lead to chauvinistic and racist tendencies involving various cultures in history that could result in genocide.

However, none of the above points directly or indirectly to the political ideology of the right as the potential primary or sole source of nationalism, xenophobia, and racism, just as it does not disprove the link between socialism and National Socialism. Accordingly, it is only the *victims*, the targets of hate, who can be ascertained among the various shades of socialist or not socialist perpetrators of mass murder. The list includes many victims just in the twentieth century, such as the Armenians in Ottoman Turkey, Kulaks in Stalinist Russia, Serbs in the Independent State of Croatia, Jews in Nazi Germany, Kurds in Iraq, and Tutsis in Rwanda, to name only a few.

Whenever anyone points to the undeniably socialist roots of National Socialism and fascism, there are howls of outrage. The apologists of socialism howling the loudest are of course the first to claim some ideological link between fascism and right-wing conservatism. Each socialist idealist believes the other socialist organizations are the wrong form of socialism and deny that those other forms are socialist. Unfortunately, the result is always a bad one for everyone.

SOCIALIST ECONOMY LEADING TO TERROR

Naturally, socialism not only does not end the chaos caused by the destruction of the price system but also perpetuates it. Moreover, if socialism is introduced *without* the prior existence of price controls, its effect is to inaugurate that chaos. This disorder develops because socialism is merely the negation of capitalism and its price system; it is not in itself an active economic system. Therefore, the essential nature of socialism is the same as the economic chaos resulting from the destruction of the price system by wage and price controls. Bolshevik-style socialism's imposition of a system of production quotas, with incentives everywhere to exceed the quotas, was a sure formula for general shortages, as they exist under all price and wage controls. This disorder led, of course, to the final collapse of Soviet-style socialism in the end.

At most, socialism merely changes the *direction* of the chaos. The government's control over production may make possible a higher production rate of some goods of particular importance to itself, but it does so only at the expense of wreaking havoc throughout the rest of the economic system. All this happens because the government has no way of knowing the effects of the securing the production of the goods of particular importance for the rest of the economic system. The requirements of enforcing a system of wage and price controls shed light on the totalitarian essence of socialism—notably, of course, on the German or Nazi variant of it, but also on that of Soviet-style socialism as well.

The financial and business interests of sellers forced to operate under price controls are to evade the controls and raise their prices. Buyers who are otherwise unable to obtain the goods they need are willing, indeed eager, to pay the higher prices as a means of securing the goods they want. Under these circumstances, what is to stop prices from rising and a massive black market developing?

The answer is a combination of severe punishment connected with a high probability of being apprehended and then indeed suffering those punishments.

Since they will be regarded only as an additional business expense, small fines are not likely to provide much of a deterrent. It is necessary for the state to impose substantial penalties comparable to those for a major felony if the government is serious about its price controls.

However, the mere existence of such penalties is not enough. The government has to make it highly dangerous to conduct black-market transactions. It has to make people *fear* that by carrying out such illicit business the police might somehow discover them and they might end up in jail. The government must develop an army of spies and secret informers to create such fear. For example, the government must make a shopkeeper and his customer afraid that if they enter into a black-market transaction, some other customer in the store will report them. Furthermore, the government must also make anyone even considering a black-market transaction fearful that the other accomplice might turn out to be a police agent trying to entrap him. The government must make people afraid of their long-time associates, friends, and relatives, lest even they turn out to be informers.

Finally, the government must place the decision about innocence or guilt regarding black-market transactions in the hands of an administrative tribunal to get the accused convicted. It cannot rely on jury trials, because very few juries would be willing to reach guilty verdicts when, for example, a man would receive a jail term of several years for the crime of selling a few pounds of sugar or flour or a pair of shoes above the ceiling price.

In sum, the requirements for the enforcing of price-control regulations are the adoption of essential features of a totalitarian state. These are the classification of economic crimes, whereby the peaceful pursuit of material self-interest is treated as a criminal offense; the organizing of a repressive police apparatus awash with agents, spies, and informers; and the carrying out of arbitrary arrests and imprisonment.

The enforcement of price controls demands a government not unlike that of Hitler's Germany or Stalin's Russia, in which practically anyone might turn out to be a police spy, and in which secret police exist with the power to arrest and imprison people. If the government is unwilling to go to such lengths, its price controls prove unenforceable and just break down. The black market then assumes significant proportions. Incidentally, this is not to suggest that price controls were the cause of the terror instituted by the Nazis. On the contrary, the reign of Nazi terror began well before the enactment of price controls, which could then be easily enforced in a ready-made environment.

Black market activity entails the committing of further crimes. Under de facto socialism, the production and sale of goods on the black market involve the defiance of the government's regulations concerning production and distribution as well as the disregard of its price controls. For example, the goods sold on the black market are originally intended to be distributed by the government following its plan of distribution instead of being put on the black market. Similarly, the factors of production used to produce those goods are likewise intended to be utilized by the government under its production plan, and not to supply the black market instead.

Under a system of de jure socialism—such as that which existed in the Soviet Union, where the legal code of the country explicitly made the government the owner of the means of production—all black-market activities necessarily entailed the misappropriation and theft of state property. The factory workers or managers who turned out products that they sold on the black market were considered criminals who stole the raw materials, capital, and labor supplied by the state.

Furthermore, in any socialist state, Nazi or communist, the government's economic plan is part of the supreme law of the land. The further disruption of the typically chaotic, so-called planning process by workers and managers purloining materials and supplies to produce for the black market is something that the legal code of a socialist state regards as an act of sabotage of its national economic plan. Consistent with this fact, black-market activity in a socialist country often carries the death penalty.

A fundamental fact that explains the complete reign of terror found under socialism is the dilemma in which a socialist state places itself concerning the masses of its citizens. On the one hand, the state assumes full responsibility for the individual's economic well-being. Soviet or Bolshevik-style socialism openly avowed this responsibility; this was, supposedly, the primary source of its popular appeal. On the other hand, the socialist state makes an unbelievable botch of the job; it makes the individual's life a nightmare.

The citizen of the Soviet Union had to spend much time in endless waiting lines. For him, the problems Americans experienced in the gasoline shortages of the 1970s were routine. Even worse, he was frequently forced to work at a job that was not of his choice and which he, therefore, must have hated (for under shortages, the government came to decide the allocation of labor just as it did the distribution of the material factors of production.) Moreover, he lived in a condition of overcrowding, with hardly ever a chance for privacy. (In the face of housing shortages, boarders—people who live in rented quarters in another's house—were assigned to homes; families were forced to share apartments. A system of internal passports and visas was adopted to limit the severity of housing shortages in the more attractive and desirable areas of the country.) To put it mildly, a person forced to live in such conditions must seethe with resentment and hostility.

Against whom would the citizens of a socialist state (or today's liberal pseudosocialist democracy) more logically direct their resentment and hostility than against that very socialist state (or today's liberal pseudosocialist democracy) itself? The same socialist state that has proclaimed its responsibility for its citizens' lives and promised them a life of bliss is, in fact, responsible for giving them a life of hell. Indeed, the leaders of a socialist state (or today's liberal pseudosocialist democracy) live in a further dilemma in that they daily encourage the people to believe that socialism (or today's liberal pseudosocialist democracy) is a perfect system whose bad results can only be the work of evil people. If that were true, who could those evil people be but the rulers themselves, who have not only made life miserable but corrupted the allegedly perfect system itself?

It follows, then, that the rulers of a socialist state (or today's liberal pseudosocialist democracy) must live in constant fear of the people, knowing that, by the logic of their actions and teachings, the simmering, seething resentment of the people could swell up and turn into an orgy of retribution. The rulers sense this, of course, even if they do not admit it openly, and therefore their primary concern is always to keep the lid on the citizenry.

Consequently, it is correct but very inadequate merely to say such things as that socialism (or today's liberal pseudosocialist democracy) lacks freedom of the press and freedom of speech. Of course it lacks these freedoms. However, socialism (or today's liberal pseudosocialist democracy) goes far beyond the mere lack of freedom of press and speech.

A socialist government (or today's liberal pseudosocialist elite) annihilates these freedoms and turns the press and every public forum into a vehicle of hysterical propaganda on its own behalf. It also relentlessly persecutes everyone daring to deviate at all from its officially approved policy.

The reason for all this is the socialist rulers' terrible fear of the people. To protect themselves, they must order the propaganda ministry and the security apparatus to work around the clock. The job of the propaganda ministry and the official media is to continually divert the people's attention from the responsibility of socialism and its rulers—to deflect attention from those responsible for the people's misery. The job of the security apparatus is to remove and silence anyone who might suggest the responsibility of socialism or its rulers—to spirit away anyone who begins to show signs of independent thinking. Due to the rulers' terror and their desperate need to find scapegoats for the failures of socialism (or today's liberal pseudosocialist democracy), the media of a socialist state is always full of stories about foreign plots, conspiracy, sabotage, and corruption and mismanagement on the part of subordinate officials. It is because of the rulers' terror that it is periodically necessary to unmask great domestic plots and sacrifice top officials and entire factions to keep the lid on the system. It is because of their terror and desperate need to crush every breath of potential opposition that the rulers of socialism (or today's liberal pseudosocialist democracy) must fear the dissemination of, for them, dangerous ideas. Any unauthorized idea is dangerous because it can lead people to begin thinking for themselves and thus to start thinking about the nature of socialism and its rulers.

Socialism cannot be maintained without terror for very long. At the moment when terror is relaxed, resentment, hostility, and opposition against the rulers begin to swell up, setting the stage for a revolution or civil war. In fact, in the absence of terror—or, more correctly, a sufficient degree of intimidation, socialism (or today's liberal pseudosocialist democracy) would be characterized by an endless series of revolutions and civil wars. Without ongoing terror, each new group of rulers would prove as incapable of making socialism function successfully as its predecessors before. The inescapable conclusion is that the terror as experienced before in the socialist countries was not simply the product of evil, such as Stalin, but inevitably sprang from the very nature of socialism. Stalin could rise to the top because his unusual willingness and cunning in the use of terror were the particular characteristics most required in a ruler of socialism to remain in power. He rose to the top by the process of socialist natural selection: the selection of the worst. As a rhetorical question, can, then, any apparent similarity be discerned between socialism and today's liberal pseudosocialist democracy at all?

A possible misunderstanding can be anticipated here concerning the thesis that socialism is totalitarian by its nature. This confusion involves the pseudosocialist countries run by social democrats in Europe, which are not totalitarian dictatorships but only liberal democracies.

The Swedish experiment has been the perfect example of what a European liberal democracy could achieve by being both capitalist and socialist. Sweden has developed a unique approach midway between Anglo-Saxon laissez-faire and actual socialism that once successfully made it a politically, economically, and militarily neutral European power. Promising welfare indicators and social stability once characterized the country, although many in the West had questioned the Swedish model dominated by the state under longtime social-democratic leadership. In any case, both East and West admired Sweden once, and not without reason. Perhaps it was because the Swedes seemingly succeeded at achieving what everyone had longed for: the repair of the failures of the ideologically opposed systems of the world.

However, nothing lasts forever, of course, and the post–Cold War end-of-history spirit won out in Sweden at the end; the Swedes have partially given up their policy of neutrality and entered the European Union in 1995. Accordingly, the structure and volume of immigration have changed; while previously the country had successfully digested—to use today's buzzword, "integrated"—the inflow of people, there is a massive overflow of alienated immigrants today. This overflowing excess, mingled with other factors and actors in its ignorant and helpless rage, and being vulnerable to extremism, can only misbehave—as it has in the streets of Stockholm, Malmö, Norrköping, Borlänge, Uppsala, Örebro, and Nyköping—just to name a few Swedish cities that have been adversely affected. These violent incidents were not unlike those that have occurred in London, Paris, Marseilles, Brussels, Athens, and many other European cities.

What has been happening in Sweden is of particular importance, because if the above symptoms of the disease are present there, then there is no doubt of the epidemic in Europe. Multiculturalism has been defeated, and despite the official propaganda campaigns, there is no need for immigrants. What is required instead is a single-minded local demographic policy. This cannot exist, however, without a robust value system supporting it, such as (horrors!) the restoration of the traditional family as the primary concept.

It is, of course, necessary to recognize the fact that just as these European countries are not outright totalitarian, they are also not entirely socialist. Their governing political parties may espouse socialism as their philosophy and even ultimate goal, but it is not the socialist economic system that they have implemented as the fuel that keeps their countries running. Instead their actual economic system is that of a "hampered market economy," as von Mises once termed it. While more hampered than the American economy in some respects, the European economic system is quite similar to it, in that the natural driving force of production and business activities is not government decree but the private initiative of owners motivated by profit.

The reason that social democrats do not establish outright socialism or introduce the socialist economic system after coming to power is that they are afraid, unwilling, or unable to do what would be required. Namely, the forming of a socialist economy requires a massive act of theft, since the means of production one way or another must be seized from their private owners and turned over to the state. Such seizure is virtually guaranteed to provoke substantial resistance on the part of the owners—resistance that can be overcome only by the use of massive force.

The Bolsheviks were willing to apply such force, as was evidenced in the Soviet Union. Their character was that of armed robbers prepared to murder if that was necessary to carry out their robbery. Contrary to the Communists, the nature of the social democrats is more like that of pickpockets. They may talk of pulling the big job someday, but in fact, they are afraid to do the killing that would be necessary to complete the job, and so they give up at the slightest sign of serious resistance—as the Communists had always accused them of doing.

As for the Nazis, they did not have to kill to seize the property of Germans other than Jews because, as has already been described, they implemented de facto socialism through price controls, stealthily maintaining the outward appearance of private ownership. The private owners were thus not directly (i.e., legally) deprived of their property; therefore, they felt no need to fight for it.

The above is hopefully enough to show that socialism—*pure* socialism—is totalitarian by its very nature. The modern social-democratic version practiced in the West today is only a more liberal, watered-down, and corrupted adaptation of it, camouflaging the essence with the illusion of modernity and progress. The difference lies only in the degree to which those ideological principles are enacted.

German Socialist Domination and the European Union

Germany's domination of Europe is neither unintentional nor accidental. There is no intention or any need to occupy Europe physically, and the current German hegemony has an economic rather than military basis. It is about economic power—and it is interesting to see how the landscape of power in Europe has fundamentally changed.

There is a split between the Eurozone countries and the non-Eurozone countries within the EU. Suddenly the United Kingdom, for example, which used to be only a member of the EU and not a member of the Eurozone, was losing its veto power.

The second split is among the Eurozone countries themselves; it is the critical division of power between the lender countries and the debtor countries.

As a result, Germany, the most influential country economically, has become the most potent EU state; and its austerity policies, in the manner of "divide and rule," are dividing Europe in many ways.

First of all, there is a line of division between northern and southern European countries. The background from a sociological point of view is that they are redistributing the risk from the banks through the states to the middle class, the working class, the poor, the unemployed, and the elderly. This redistribution causes an enormous new inequality, so one cannot keep thinking only in national terms and focusing on the risk redistribution solely under national conditions.

At the same time, there are two leading ideologies concerning austerity policies. The first one is based on what one could call the "Merkiavelli Model"—meaning a combination of Niccolò Machiavelli and Angela Merkel. On a personal level, Merkel takes a long time to make decisions; she always waits until some consensus appears. However, this waiting makes the countries depending on Germany's decision realize that Germany is holding the reins. This deliberate hesitation is quite an unusual strategy implying that Germany has assumed command economically.

The second ideological element is that Germany's austerity policies are based not merely on pragmatism but also on underlying values. The German objection to countries spending more than they can afford is a moral issue, which, from a sociological point of view, directly connects with the Protestant ethic, having Martin Luther and Max Weber in the background. However, this is not considered to be a moral issue in Germany at all but is viewed as economic rationality. They see it not only as a German way of resolving the crisis but also as if they were benevolent teachers instructing southern European countries how to manage their economies.

This "moral–economic pragmatism" creates another ideological split because the strategy, even if it is viable, will take some time to prove itself, and there are many forms of protest already, of which Cyprus, Italy, Spain, and Greece are just some examples. Nevertheless, there is still a very influential neoliberal faction in Europe continuing to believe that austerity policies are the answer to the crisis.

The Eurozone crisis is the proof that we live in a "risk society." This interpretation could easily be misunderstood, because the term "risk" signifies a situation regarding uncertainty. However, risk society is a situation in which we are perhaps not able to deal *with* the uncertainty and consequences that have been produced by society.

A distinction should be made here between "first modernity" and the current situation. First modernity, which lasted from around the eighteenth century until perhaps the 1960s or 1970s, was a period where there was plenty of space for experimentation, and there were many answers for the uncertainties that had been produced: probability models, insurance mechanisms, and so on. However, today we are living with the consequences of this first modernity, for which we do not have any answers, such as climate change, population explosion, globalization, and the financial crises. The last global financial crisis is an example of the dubious victory, or result, of a particular interpretation of modernity: neoliberal modernity following the breakdown of the Communist system. It dictates that the market of the liberal democracy is the solution and that the more we increase the role of the market, the better. Although we see that this model is failing, there are still no clear answers.

Amid living in this risk society, Germany's dream of domination has come true.

There is a saying: "A dream deferred is not necessarily a dream denied." Neither the German kaiser nor the führer could have possibly imagined that the path to direct domination in Europe has nothing to do with war and everything to do with the financial and economic failures of Germany's neighbors. These failures *invite*, and do not resist, German hegemony.

Europe's gathering failure results from a toxic cocktail drunk throughout much of Europe: the potion of liberal democracy mixed with welfare statism, bureaucratization, crony capitalism, and the inefficiencies, excesses, and corruption that inevitably spring from the blend of the former three.

Germans may not need to ride triumphantly throughout Europe on the backs of Panzers (or their modern equivalents). If the West's ruling elites have their way, Germany will use its checkbook and credit to bail out the failing neighbors and save Europe—or attempt to. Germany may still not have the financial or economic muscle to do so, but let us put that aside for a moment. Among the European nations, Germany is the strongest of the lot—hence the reason the Western elite has turned anxious eyes to the Germans.

The *Washington Post* published an article containing the following astonishing comment by Radoslaw Sikorski, the former foreign minister of Poland: "I will probably be the first Polish foreign minister in history to say so, but here it is: I fear German power less than I am beginning to fear German inactivity."[316]

Europe's political and socioeconomic situation is dire indeed. Still, many of the Western elites, who would otherwise be leery of Germany asserting its power, are in step with—if not out in front of—the former Polish minister. Who would have thought that the elite from across the Western world, whose peoples hold a historical distrust of German might, is now practically demanding Chancellor Angela Merkel for deliverance?

Granted, Germany is not seething with brownshirts these days. Totalitarian impulses were finally beaten out of the Germans in World War II, and there is no messianic figure emerging to lead the German people to some ultimate supremacy. Still, there are reasons why sensible Europeans—those not desperate enough to save modern statist and socialist Europe and their positions in it—should pause before making Germany the savior.

Although the German economy is beginning to show vulnerabilities, it is still strong compared to the rest of Europe. Merkel and the German people, heretofore reluctant to bail out their neighbors, may be pressured into trying to do so.

However, little in life is without strings. There is stiff resistance among the German people to any attempt to rescue nations whose peoples are viewed by them as undisciplined and profligate. If Merkel and other German political leaders buckle to pressure from the Western elite, then expect them to exact massive concessions. Merkel or her successors would need to show the German people tangible returns for their playing Atlas; otherwise, they would commit political suicide.

What might those concessions be? A dominant political and economic leadership role in the EU (or whatever could succeed the EU) with preferences for German exports and investments? Greater control by Germany of the political, financial, economic, and social policies in troubled nations?

There is, of course, a real possibility that Europe will fail with or without German intervention. Germany will then still be owed for its efforts, and Germans will have a reasonable expectation of entitlement for their trouble. Even if failed neighbors cannot remunerate Germany, Germans will still expect their leaders to seek repayments in other ways satisfactory to them—or they will find leaders who will do so.

It must also be considered that a Europe of failed nations is very likely to see widespread social unrest and political upheaval. The reality that Europeans' cradle-to-grave welfare states can no longer deliver on their promises will send tsunamis of rage across the continent. Everyone knows from history what a dangerous place Europe is when disordered and roiled.

Germans have an innate and evident sense of order and discipline, as well as a taste for hierarchy. Europe, convulsed, is likely to make Germans immensely uncomfortable. Already having been invited to shoulder more responsibility for Europe's welfare by their neighbors, the Germans will have entrée to assert their will throughout Europe (excepting Russia and its sphere of influence)—that is, if they decide it would be favorable to their interests.

It may just be that a Germany elevated to a first-among-equals status in Europe is the opening of Pandora's box. It most certainly would set Europe on the road toward German hegemony—hegemony that throughout the centuries millions upon millions of Europeans (and other peoples) stoutly resisted, fought, and died to prevent.

A German-dominated liberal pseudosocialist democracy in Europe might seem a welcome development to the left-liberal Western elite, who with each passing day is increasingly desperate for solutions. These elites may persuade themselves that the Germans could lead Europe deftly and benignly down the socialist path. Since World War II, Germans have earnestly reformed their nation, but the preponderance of history will still raise suspicions.

As has already been pointed out earlier, there is an innate anti-Western instinct that exists in Russia. Moreover, a similar feeling, intuition, or pattern is present in just about every Eastern European country. Just as Westernization, imposed by Peter the Great, and Bolshevism, a later outgrowth of a Western ideology imposed by Lenin, had to be first destroyed in Russia to finish the country's liberation from the West, both Western liberalism and German-bred socialism remain suspect and alien ideologies in Central and Eastern Europe today. Their ideological elements have not become parts of the Eastern European culture, mentality, or disposition—and it is doubtful they ever will. The Eastern Europe vs. Western Europe divide will sustain itself based on the invisible ideological curtain.

Better than Germany, or any other country, coming to Europe's rescue would be for the peoples of Europe to throw off their statist and socialist modern liberal yokes and stand up for national governments, national identity, sovereignty, individual liberty, and their initially conceived free markets and trade. They will be surprised to learn how many common cultural ties, social similarities, and mutual interests will be unexpectedly discovered.

The recurrent Freedom House reports, always cited somewhat gleefully in the German press, repeatedly argue, "democracy in Eastern Europe is in peril." Listing a group of Eastern European countries that have "failed to consolidate" their democracies, these reports usually imply that Romania, Bulgaria, Hungary, Slovakia, and the Czech Republic are "failing" in maintaining and enriching their democratic institutions.

It must be, of course, but a pure coincidence that the Czech President has openly called for lifting sanctions against Russia, that the Hungarian prime minister is battling against Western banks and foreign interests plundering his country, and that the Slovaks and Hungarians bordering on Ukraine are hesitant about antagonizing and inflaming the region.

However, what is truly disturbing and deplorable about this spectacle is the presumption on the part of Freedom House and its German partisans that the peoples of Hungary, Romania, Bulgaria, Slovakia, and the Czech Republic need to be *taught* democracy. The presumption is that these nations and cultures are small children born only yesterday, still learning to walk and in peril of falling unless the bastion of liberalism and freedom that is Germany gives them some lessons. This arrogant smugness presumes that the drudgery of communism—on account of which these Eastern European nations suffered occupation, privation, and terror—was a result of their immaturity, not of British treason, French scorn, German bombs, and American abandonment that ended in Soviet tanks.

Noteworthy is the fact that Poland has not usually been on the German list of countries that "failed to consolidate" democracy, according to Freedom House, until recently. Naturally, Poland has been a "success." It has been considered a success because, for several years, until the elections in October 2015, a political party funded mostly by Western interests ruled it. Poland came to be considered a success after its former president, Mr. Lech Kaczyński, by "fortuitous coincidence," crashed in an airplane carrying him and the leaders of his political party. They all died, leaving no one alive and organized to effectively oppose Mr. Donald Tusk's pro-Western, German-supported, and well-funded party in the country.

Upon gaining absolute power over the Polish state, Mr. Tusk conveniently reversed Lech Kaczyński's policies of blocking the attempts of foreign companies to buy majority shares of major Polish firms in strategic sectors of the economy. By trying to eradicate any sense of history and patriotism in his country, Mr. Tusk wanted to create a Poland full of young people wishing to become as progressive, one day, as Germany—because they otherwise should be embarrassed by Poland's traditional Catholic and family culture.

Finally, Germany considers Poland a success because Mr. Tusk headed up a government that first announced that it wished to see Germany lead Europe and Poland lose its sovereignty in a German-led federation. The same Polish government cried out in terror that Russian invasion was threatening Poland and desperately insisted on foreign (Western, of course) occupation to save it. Mr. Tusk, after he had completed his mission of making Poland a German vassal, then decided to move to Brussels, where he was duly rewarded with many times that of the Polish prime minister's salary and the comfortable, if unenviable, position of (unelected) president of the European Union.

Now, if we retake a cursory glance at those unconsolidated democracies, we find that men who happen to oppose foreign occupation of their countries—whether by Russian, German, or any other troops—govern them and have been cultivating good relations with Russia. The prime minister of Slovakia, for instance, has said, "I would sooner resign from politics than let a single foreign army base be opened in my country." The prime minister of Hungary, meanwhile, sensing like the Poles that events in Ukraine may threaten his country, did what any rational statesman would do. He made it clear to the Ukrainian government that Hungary would defend the lives and property of the Hungarian ethnic minority in Ukraine and prudently and pragmatically mended Hungary's ties with Russia while remaining inside the EU and NATO. The Czech Republic and Bulgaria, both of which rely heavily on trade with Russia and peace in the region, have also been working hard toward de-escalating tensions rather than raising them. Thus, while the Western press may blame these nations, their real interests are preserved.

Then Germany, the birthplace of socialism, National Socialism, dictatorships, and aggressive empires in the twentieth century, is suddenly the arbitrator of which

European nations are and are not democratic today? How is it that one measure of democracy is the EU insistence that Serbia, apparently not yet taught democracy by the tonnage of bombs NATO dropped on her in the late 1990s, must now fund a massive gay pride parade to prove how democratic it is? À la Germany and its Western values, of course. How is it that the West is now treating the nations that were not that long ago either forced to succumb to German demands by threats—or simply invaded, occupied, looted, and destroyed by Germany—as culturally backward countries that must learn democracy from Germany?

The answer to these questions has much to do with those left-liberal or socialist elites who exercise political power in the West. However, it also has to do with the fact that unlike Eastern Europe and Russia, the West has never undergone its perestroika, let alone the sort of soul-searching that the entire East has undertaken. Since Eastern European prejudice is still mainly conservative, it is struggling—for lack of a more thorough understanding of itself—under the duress of Western liberal ideologies alien to traditional Eastern European and Russian culture.

Germany's rise to European dominance would come thanks to the doings of the feckless but ruthless, desperately narrow, deceitful, and modern-liberal Western pseudoelite delivering Europe to German socialism on a tray. Should that befall the world, what a strange and ironic twist of fate it would be!

Western Political Correctness: Euphemism with Attitude

The term "politically correct" first appeared in the writings of Anton Makarenko, Lenin's expert on education. Adolf Hitler preferred the term "socially correct."[317] Political taboos are certain subjects that politicians avoid discussing out of fear for their career, political advancement, and success. They fear there is an established consensus against their viewpoint, and since politicians fight for the majority opinion in a democracy, almost any established consensus would satisfy the condition of being a political taboo. Any such agreements are locally subjective; opinions that are an established consensus in one district or nation may not be in another.

Timidity, cynicism, political correctness, and contempt for the electorate paralyzed the political elite into allowing mass and uncontrolled immigration to change the West forever. Only now, at last, is the taboo against speaking out being broken.

As an example, the United States has a de facto policy of open borders and practically uncontrolled immigration along the southern border with Mexico. Americans like to call the allegedly eleven million undocumented people "illegal aliens," a curious misnomer. Theoretically, immigrants who enter the United States without reporting to the Immigration and Naturalization Service (INS) and obtaining the necessary documents are breaking the law. However, a law on paper must be taken seriously by society and meaningfully enforced by the state before that law has a real effect. When only token law enforcement is performed merely for political appearances and many local governments forbid their police to enforce immigration laws, the people will behave as though no law existed at all.

This sham is a de facto policy of open borders because the system, in fact, contradicts the ostensible de jure policy of the US Congress. Moreover, this is also the phony policy adopted by the European Union.

How did this farce come to pass? Why does a political system require having immigration laws but refuse to enforce them? Why is society politically incapable of either openly admitting the policy of open borders or enforcing its immigration laws? What pathology is causing the people to live in fantasy or to tell themselves lies about the de facto policy of open borders? Why can't the political leaders speak honestly about immigration? Like much of the democratic political theater, a combination of political correctness and special interests lies at the bottom of society's inability to have an honest, intelligent discussion about immigration.

Whatever it is the INS and EU are claiming, and whatever they are doing on the southern borders of the United States and Europe, it does not much resemble enforcing the immigration laws. The game the INS is playing can continue as long as powerful political interests in both parties like things as they are.

Democrats like uncontrolled immigration because they think they can manufacture new Democratic voters this way. They have been practicing this ever since Boss Tweed's party hacks presented themselves to Irish immigrants as they disembarked at the port and recruited them as party members.[318]

Influential US Republicans support unlimited immigration because they like cheap labor for the factories and farms and cheap domestic servants for their homes. Republicans have been encouraging massive immigration ever since the Civil War ended and since there was a severe shortage of labor in running the factories and building railroads. This policy was interrupted, however, from 1920 to 1965, when immigration was limited to quotas by national origin that assigned the largest quotas to European nations. After 1965, both political parties reverted to the traditional type of immigration.

The benefits to special interests of unlimited and uncontrolled immigration are easy to understand. Much harder to calculate is whether massive immigration is, on balance, good for America. Americans need to have an extensive, all-embracing, and intelligent national discussion on immigration, and every rational voice must be heard. However, the proposal is blocked in many quarters by the taboos of guilt history and its corresponding political correctness.

One can safely argue that Germans are the most politically correct, taboo-stricken, and psychologically strained people in the world. Traumatic memories about the Nazis have impelled them to fashion a set of politically correct rules against any word, deed, symbol or thought that is reminiscent of anything the Nazis said or did.

German law allows, on demand, the unrestricted abortion of babies who are healthy and normal. However, abortion of a radically deformed baby is forbidden because the Nazis practiced euthanasia and disposed of deformed children. Germans are embarrassed by patriotism and nationalism because Hitler abused patriotism and nationalism.

Just as Germans are frightened of and intimidated by doing anything remotely reminiscent of what the Nazis did, many Americans are frightened of and intimidated by doing anything that will open them to accusations of racism. Just as Germans are uneasy about their Nazi past, many Americans are anxious about their racial segregationist past. Political correctness, impelled by fear of charges of racism or being labeled a bigot, has crippled efforts to think clearly about social issues—for example, education—and improve public schools in the inner cities.

Using the race card as a tool of intimidation is only one peel on the banana of political correctness. Other skins include, among many others, feminism, the gay agenda, abortion, multiculturalism, and hostile opposition to the European cultural past. Knowing that one might slip on any of these banana peels when attempting to explore and communicate forbidden (i.e., not politically correct) ideas will prove to be enough to give up on the subject entirely.

So when the attention of the Western world turns to immigration and open borders, the race card is immediately the showstopper. Is it possible to get around this irrational barrier so that one can have an honest national discussion about the subject? Is it possible to thaw the stubborn ice that prevents real communication from passing through the politically correct censorship?

It will be well-nigh impossible, given the climate of entitlements and special interests already embedded in the socialist liberal democracy. Under such a political system, the elite manipulates the populace by continually appealing to its conscience, guilt, and fear.

The tragic result of the relentless expansion of social justice has been transplanted directly from the Third Reich and the Soviet Union; people have been taught to be afraid of one another.

Women in the United States are afraid of men because "all men are potential rapists." Men are afraid of women because sexual harassment charges hang over their word and action.

If the law permits, the most open-minded employer will stay away from protected minorities because, all too often, lawsuits take the place of honest work.

Parents and teachers are afraid of children; perhaps nothing points to the totalitarian origins of the West's so-called liberals as glaringly as their shameless use (or rather abuse) of children as the front behind which they operate. Commandeering children in the name of appealing to our conscience for political purposes, like carrying placards for or against issues they could not possibly comprehend, has become commonplace today. Every scheme that politicians peddle is being proposed for our kids.

"Voluntarism projects have sprung up telling businesses, for example, how much money they must contribute "voluntarily" to pay those who "volunteer" their time.

To that effect, the following is an old but very typical Eastern European quip:

Truman, Churchill, and Stalin meet for the third time to sort out their differences. Again, it is to no avail. After two frustrating days of talks, Stalin says, "Comrades, we know that cats hate mustard. Whoever can induce a cat to eat some mustard will have his way."

Challenge accepted.

Truman, ever the straight shooter, takes the cat, takes a jar of mustard, and pours it into the mouth of the cat. The cat spits out every last drop.

Churchill, having watched this fiasco, prepares a sumptuous meal of liver, fish, and other cat's delights, with the tiniest drop of mustard in the center of the plate. The cat licks clean the entire plate—except for the drop of mustard in the center.

Stalin shakes his head with mock sympathy. "You have no clue how to do this," he says to the others. "Bring me a pound of mustard and watch!" With that, Stalin takes the mustard and smears it all over the rear end of the cat. The animal frantically chases its tail and licks the area clean to the last drop.

A triumphant Stalin exclaims, "And as you see, he did it of his own free will!"

Focusing on people's national identity is deemed "reactionary"—a harmful throwback to times and places from which we wish to distance ourselves. National identity, we are told, has become an instrument of exclusion—a tool to emphasize differences between peoples—something we need to avoid and eliminate. Consequently, we are actively discouraged to think of ourselves as American, German, or Dutch.

What has caused national identity to be viewed as nefarious?

On the one hand, it was the traumatic memory of nationalism as practiced by the National Socialists. On the other hand, it was the emergence of internationalism, based on the egalitarianism preached by the international socialists. While egalitarianism has become the "ideal" arrangement within a given society, internationalism has become the "preferred" method for the coexistence of different cultures.

The concept of internationalism prescribes that countries and their residents look upon all other countries and their residents as brothers, equals, and partners in various endeavors. Once achieved, such a state of mind is expected to do away with wars, just as communism (or perfect social justice) is supposed to erase economic, intellectual, racial, class, or other tensions within a given society. Consequently, internationalism is useful to socialists and communists as a slogan. It is a euphemism—the substitution of a supranational authority for previously autonomous nation-states.

Internationalism is also useful in separating good people from evil people. Nationalism is "evil," and internationalism is "good." Such examples as the breakup of Yugoslavia and the atrocities in Bosnia were added to the "evil nationalism" side, ignoring the fact that the old Yugoslavia was not a nation to begin with; nor has the new Bosnia become one. The United Nations, with its humanitarian agencies, and the European Union are automatically "good," since they embody the international concept.

Currently fashionable, therefore politically correct, doctrines brand any awareness of one's nationality as "nationalism" because it is supposed to drive a wedge between peoples and, sooner or later, result in war. This rationale ignores the fact that there is a world of difference between nationalism and a healthy sense of national identity.

National identity is an umbrella under which the assets, sentiments, and aspirations of the highest number of compatible people may be combined. Furthermore, war is not a function of national identity. If disputes about possessions, or hostilities between two groups, reach a certain stage, war will break out whether the ground is religious, tribal, or economic. To blame a sense of national identity for war is the ignorance of either history or hypocrisy.

The fact is that national identity is an instrument of internal cohesion and induces people to disregard their differences, including differences of class. Were national identity recognized as an aspiration of citizens, Marx's view of history ("the history of society is the history of class struggle") could not be sustained, because the acknowledgment that national identity unites people within a society causes the Marxist theory of history to collapse.

12

Western Economic Changes

The German economist Friedrich List, doubting the sincerity of calls to free trade from Britain, once wrote: "Any nation which by means of protective duties and restrictions on navigation has raised her manufacturing power and her navigation to such a degree of development that no other nation can sustain free competition with her, can do nothing wiser than to throw away these ladders of her greatness, to preach to other nations the benefits of free trade, and to declare in penitent tones that she has hitherto wandered in the paths of error, and has now for the first time succeeded in discovering the truth."[319]

Capitalism, the Corporate State, and State Capitalism: The First Signs of the Social Market Economy

Are the economic and financial crises that have been afflicting the West since 2008, crises *in* the system or *of* the system? When does a capitalist business enterprise cease to be an economic factor?

It ceases to be an economic factor when its size compels it to be a social factor. The Italian Fascist leader Benito Mussolini claimed, "It is then that a capitalist enterprise, when difficulties arise, throws itself like a dead weight into the state's arms. It is then that state intervention begins and becomes more necessary. It is then that those who once ignored the state now seek it out anxiously." Mussolini stated that the inability of businesses to properly operate when facing economic difficulties proved that state intervention was necessary to stabilize the economy.[320]

Mussolini said in 1933 that, were fascism to follow the current phase of capitalism, its path would "lead inexorably to state capitalism, which is nothing more nor less than state socialism turned on its head. In either event (whether the outcome is state capitalism or state socialism), the result is the bureaucratization of the economic activities of the nation."[321] Italian fascism offered the corporatist economic system as the solution of preserving private enterprise and property while also allowing the state to intervene in the economy when private enterprise failed.

According to Mussolini, "If in all the nations of Europe, the State were to go to sleep for twenty-four hours, such an interval would be sufficient to cause a disaster. There is no economic field in which the State is not called upon to intervene. Were we to surrender – just as a matter of hypothesis – to this capitalism of the eleventh hour, we should arrive at State capitalism, which is nothing but State socialism inverted."[322]

One definition of "state capitalism" is "a close relationship between the government and private businesses, such as when private enterprises produce for a government-guaranteed market." One example of this would be the so-called military-industrial complex, in which pseudoindependent—in reality state-controlled, but technically privately-owned—firms receive lucrative government contracts and are largely protected from the discipline of the competitive market. Some consider this as a compromise of the modern world economy, with normal (or private) free market capitalism at one extreme and a strictly state-controlled economy like that of the former Soviet Union at the other.

State capitalism is pursued by a variety of Western countries when specific strategic resources are vital for national security. These may involve private investment as well. For example, a government may own or even monopolize oil production or transport infrastructure. Examples include Neste Oil of Finland, Statoil of Norway, and OMV of Austria. State capitalism can ensure, among other things, that wealth creation does not threaten the ruling elite's political power, which remains unthreatened by tight connections between the government and industry.

Several European scholars and political economists have been using the term "state capitalism" increasingly to describe one of the three most important varieties of capitalism that prevail in the modern context of the European Union: market capitalism, managed capitalism, and state capitalism. In this context, "state capitalism" refers to a system where close coordination between the state, large corporations, and labor unions ensures economic growth and development in a quasicorporatist model. France and, to a lesser extent, Italy can be cited as the prime examples of modern European state capitalism.

BETWEEN IDEOLOGIES: THE ROAD TOWARD THE SOCIAL MARKET ECONOMY

One could easily imagine a man starving in the streets of a Western city and the reaction of the various economic ideas to it. Capitalism, driven by denial of state interference rooted in liberalism or its radical form, libertarianism, would argue that the man would not starve because there will always be a private benefactor who opens his door to help. The welfare state, rooted in the traditional socialist belief in the communal system, would argue that nobody has to open his door, because the state would prevent such a situation from happening in the first place.

Ideologies are characterized by a self-contained conception of the world that refuses to be questioned and claims to have found the absolute truth. Initially the term "ideology" stood for the "science of ideas"; in the stricter modern sense, however, ideology presents itself to be a comprehensive theory of human experience. Accordingly, based on this supposed experience, it sets out a political program and believes its fulfillment to be the result of a struggle. Ideology seeks not merely to persuade but also to recruit loyal adherents willing to employ violence. It addresses a broad community but may bestow a leadership role upon intellectuals as a privileged vanguard.

The Austrian philosopher Karl Popper (1902–94) stated that ideology is based on a logical error, which is the false belief that history can be converted into science understood as a method of observation, hypothesis, and confirmation. In contrast, Popper described the actual process of science as one of trial and error ("falsification"), not one of confirmation. Popper's fallibilism underlines that we make possible progress in science by deliberately subjecting our theories to critical scrutiny and abandoning those that have been "falsified," or proven false. He blames ideology for attempting to find certainty in history and produce scientific predictions following a false theory of science as a method of self-affirmation.[323] Thus Popper also characterized scientific socialism as a pseudoscience.

The endless row between the proponents of capitalism and socialism shows on both sides the ideological signs of self-certainty and aversion to being scrutinized. Though impervious to their repeated past failures, they were, however, severely damaged by the global financial crisis.

The fundamental crisis of the world financial system has shown what damage the limitless welfare state can do by spending money it does not have—as we have seen in some European countries and the United States. A debt management policy leads to continuously increased budget deficits and, as a natural consequence, to higher taxation, cuts in public services, and future inflation. The examples of Iceland, Greece, Ireland, Portugal, and Cyprus also illustrate why this mentality is endangering individual freedom itself through the drastic economic and financial measures inevitably taken by the state when deficit policies fail.

Many reject, of course, the policy of accumulating debt as a morally unacceptable behavior at the expense of future generations. The promise that the welfare states seem to offer, the living beyond one's means, may be tempting in the short term but is dangerous in the long run. In the end, it is mostly the middle class that will have to pay for the devastations brought about by an ever-increasing fiscal gap.

However, the financial crisis has also shown what harm unregulated markets can do by socializing economic losses while privatizing profits. It became apparent, once again, that pure, unrestricted capitalism leads to a situation in which the financial failure of a few is jeopardizing the wealth of all. "The market has no heart, the market has no brain, it does what it does, which is why the market needs rules and a reliable legal system," wrote Paul A. Samuelson.[324]

Therefore, it is both economically and politically of vital importance to overcome the ideological debate between this construct of a planned economy patronizing the individual on the one hand and the premise of a free market economy with its unconstrained individual on the other. Both ideologies lost further credibility through the global financial crisis, and therefore it is not surprising that new political debate has emerged about how to create a sound and fair economic system.

I. The Social Market Economy as the Third Way

The frequent failures of the welfare and laissez-faire states keep drawing attention to the social market economy as a third-way compromise between the ideologies of socialism and capitalism. The response of the social market economy to the starving man on the streets of a Western city is supposed to read, "Yes, that could happen, so let's see whether somebody will open the door to help. If not, and that could indeed well be the case, the state should be able to help."

Social market economy (German: *Soziale Marktwirtschaft*) is a form of market capitalism combined with a social policy favoring union bargaining and social insurance, and it is sometimes classified as a coordinated market economy.

The notion of social market economy refers to the economic concept that formed the West German economic policy after 1948. The German economist Alfred Müller-Armack introduced the term in 1946. He designed a theoretical concept—an outgrowth of Prussian–German socialism, really—in contrast to both the centrally controlled economy of National Socialism and the familiar concepts of the free market economy.[325] According to Müller-Armack, the social market economy is "to combine the principle of a *free market* with that of *social balancing*," to be a third way between laissez-faire economic liberalism and social-democratic mixed economies. It is a concept in which the core values of liberty and justice represent two sides of a relationship whose tensions and contradictions have to be not only maintained but also tolerated.

The way to the concept of social market economy was prepared by a group of economists of the Freiburg School at the University of Freiburg in the early 1930s. They suffered savage persecution from the Nazis due to their basic common beliefs in ordoliberalism, which is a concept opposed to unbridled capitalism as well as the centrally planned economy. The chief representatives of this group were Walter Eucken, Alexander Rüstow, Franz Böhm, Alfred Müller-Armack, and Wilhelm Röpke, who argued the case for "economic and social humanism" and were strongly inspired by ordoliberalism and the tradition of Catholic social teaching (or, more generally, Christian ethics).[326]

When Wilhelm Röpke set out to write his defense of the humane economy, he had already fallen under the spell of the Austrian school, especially von Mises and Hayek. Hayek's defense of the market against state planning and socialist distribution had taken on new validity, considering the tyranny and economic disorder of the Bolshevik experiment.

Röpke was aware and convinced that markets alone cannot guarantee the goal of economic activity. According to him, the goal must be to provide a community and security where people feel "at home" and at peace with each other. Although the market mechanism is necessary for all the reasons spelled out by the Austrians, it may not be sufficient for the establishment and maintenance of social order. Only in a market economy can prices serve as a guide to the scarcity of goods. Only in a market economy can wages be a guide to the supply of labor. Only in a market economy can individuals plan their budgets and make rational choices for the deployment of their assets, their labor, and their bargaining skills. The argument developed by von Mises in his critique of socialism was demonstrative and convincing; the centrally planned economy destroys the information on which rational economic decisions must depend. This information can be available only in the form of prices and voluntarily negotiated contracts in a free economy, but it is irretrievably dispersed by the attempt to dictate all economic factors from above.

Röpke's interest was in the goal of economic activity, which is the safety and security of the home, where people live in peace with each other. This goal, he believed, is threatened from above by the state—something that he had seen firsthand with his experiences of the Nazis and Bolsheviks—and also threatened from below by the anarchy of unbridled self-interest.

It is quite usual for neoliberals to pay lip service to Hayek's market theory nowadays. Yes, they say, the market is necessary as a transmitter of economic signals. Yes, only market economies can reestablish economic stability following a disruption.

However, markets have no regard for social order, and they neither generate nor maintain the sense of community on which society depends. The markets depend on self-interest, encourage competition, and regard nothing as sacred other than buying and selling. The markets are a useful and necessary tool for the working of a healthy economy but are no more than a means to an end. The markets are only the processors and transmitters of messages, but they neither compose nor interpret them.

Therefore, it is not surprising that capitalist societies of the West are witnessing social breakdown on a hitherto unimaginable scale today as the pursuit of self-interest drives all concern for the community from the thoughts and emotions of consumers. Isn't the consumer society precisely what one must expect of the philosophy that makes consumer sovereignty into the first principle of economic life?

Röpke was determined not to draw the same conclusion that left-liberal thinkers do—namely, that the market needs to be controlled by the state. Powers exercised by the state, he believed, will inevitably end up in the hands of unaccountable bureaucrats controlled by the elite; these powers, functions, or competencies lost to the state can never be taken back by society again, whatever the extent of the wrongdoing. If the market has to be constrained for the common good, as it does, then the constraint must come from below and not from above. It must be a *social* rather than a *political* constraint.[327]

Thus the idea of a social market economy was born—an idea that was to influence German ministers of finance throughout reconstruction following the end of the Second World War. Nevertheless, the West German social market economy, as implemented, was not quite the same as Röpke had intended it to be.

The social market economy was initially promoted and implemented in West Germany by the Christian Democratic Union (CDU) under Chancellor Konrad Adenauer in 1949. It was Ludwig Erhard, a student of the Freiburg School, however, who went on to undertake the practical implementation of the concept of a socially oriented market economy. He became minister for economic affairs in the first government of the German Federal Republic in 1949, until he was elected federal chancellor in 1963. Although Erhard is hailed as the father of the social market economy, the economists of the Freiburg School had laid the theoretical work some years before.

The first phase of its implementation in Germany (1948–66) was distinguished by the accomplishment of economic growth and social security. The so-called German economic miracle of the 1950s led, with American support through the Marshall Plan, to the modernization of industrial production and the rapidly rising standard of living of the population in West Germany.

The second phase (1967–78) was dominated by a policy of demand management, along with the lines of Keynesianism and interventionism. This policy entailed increasing restrictions on the markets.

The third phase (1979–90) started with the policy failure of demand management resulting in increasing unemployment rates and continued with a policy of market stimulation when the government of Helmut Kohl took power.

The reunification of Germany began the fourth phase with a reestablishment of balance between the economic and social dimensions through institutional reforms necessitated by the European integration process.

The Social Market Economy is not explicitly referred to in the German constitution, although some articles contain essential prerequisites for it. For example, Article 14 of the German Basic Law (constitution) guarantees private property, and at the same time, it postulates that this should also serve the general public's well-being.[328]

The Social Market Economy aims to combine a competitive economy, free initiative, and social progress. It is *against* both socialism and laissez-faire economics and integrates private enterprise with regulation and state intervention to establish fair competition and to maintain a balance between a high rate of economic growth, low inflation, low levels of unemployment, good working conditions, social welfare, and public services. The term "social" as opposed to "socialist" was chosen to distinguish the social market economy from a system in which the state directed economic activity and owned the means of production. In the social market model, the means of production are predominately privately owned.

Because a free and legitimate political and economic order should not be used as a force against individuals but to enable them to live together according to their disposition, it is essential to reveal its underlying concept of man. This concept is the benchmark of whether the political–economic order is serving man or vice versa.

The basic values of the social market economy originate from the Christian concept of humanity. The concept of human dignity is the direct result of the essential and immutable being of humans. One individual's dignity cannot be placed above or subordinated to the dignity of another; for Christians, this is the evidence that humans are God's creatures. However, the concept of human dignity can be derived from other traditions or religions as well. Out of the notion of human dignity for everyone arises not only the respect for all people but also the understanding of human individuality. No one is identical to another. From this diversity follows the determination to embrace pluralism in politics and society.

Finally, the Christian concept of man is cognizant of the indissoluble human incompleteness, which nobody can deny for himself or others. If nobody claims perfection, human dignity is secured for everyone. Where one denies human dignity for others, the threat of dictatorship and totalitarianism arises.

II. Christian Social Doctrines

The idea of the social market economy was carried through by critics of traditional economic and social orders, chiefly Adam Smith's laissez-faire liberalism on the one hand and Marx's socialism on the other. The concept of a social ethic was the answer to industrialization and its social question. While Protestant social ethics refers to the Bible, the Catholic Church postulates a universally binding natural law and thus presupposes a social philosophy.

Protestant social ethics was born out of empirical social sciences. The Lutheran theologian Alexander von Oettingen (1827–1905), was the first to use the term "social ethics" in the title of a book in 1868. He distanced himself from an exclusively mechanistic definition of the social process and also took a stance against a one-sided view of ethics as referring only to individual and personal acts.[329]

Protestant social ethics demands that everyone take responsibility for his or her life. To that extent, the individual cannot escape the tension between freedom and responsibility as the two fundamental concepts of Protestantism. Freedom can be substantiated only if individuals have some property and adequate opportunities to be engaged by way of meaningful paid work, since individual freedom is connected to cooperation with others. The reasoning behind this concept is a just society as a fair system of collaboration.

The contemporary Catholic social doctrine starts from a time when Catholicism struggled to find an answer to the social question at the same time that liberalism and socialism emerged as the two predominant economic theories. Liberalism predicted that free global markets would result in the "wealth of nations" (Adam Smith), while socialism maintained the necessity of a "class struggle" that would lead to communism as a "classless society" (Karl Marx).

In the first social encyclical (world circular) of the Catholic Church, "Rerum Novarum" ("of the new things"), published in 1891, Pope Leo XIII dealt with "massification" and anonymity as consequences of industrialization. He emphasized how significant it was to protect and strengthen the individual against these tendencies and criticized the early capitalist class society of the time. He demanded a national social policy for the workers while rejecting the idea of socialism. The encyclical described the possibility of combining liberty, as a fundamental value, and the institution of the market economy with the idea of *"social justice."* These related and combined concepts would then be in such a state of equilibrium that could "carry" the economic system and thus "tolerate" the tension between liberty and social equality.[330]

In 1931, the second papal encyclical, "Quadragesimo Anno" ("in the fortieth year") by Pope Pius XI, explicitly picks up on that plea in the face of totalitarian movements and the arrival of ideologies as new threats to individuals. Pope Pius XI described individuals, family, and social structures as protection against a pervasive state. He said that the "capitalist way of running the economy cannot be condemned as such," but that it is necessary "to organize it properly." "Unhampered competitive freedom" can easily lead to "the survival of the fittest, who all too often tend to be more brutal and to lack in conscience."[331]

Wilhelm Röpke, who had moved from Nazi Germany to Switzerland, thought that he had found a model for social balance in the Swiss style of local democracy. Röpke, although of Protestant background, was also strongly influenced by the social teachings of the Roman Catholic Church and the doctrine of subsidiarity, as expounded in the encyclical "Quadragesimo Anno." Pope Pius XI intended this as a description of the church's organization through the episcopate, according to which decisions must be taken at the subsidiary level (i.e., the lowest possible level still compatible with unified government).

The pope implied, however, that economic and political life might be similarly organized so that power would always be passed up from the bottom and never imposed from above. All that might seem like a call for the empowerment of civil society rather than the state—at least Röpke interpreted it so, and he took it as a foundation for his doctrine of "decentrism."[332]

Now, it should be noted that "Quadragesimo Anno" marked an intrusion of socialist ideas into the teachings of the church. Economic freedom, the encyclical argued, does not lead of its own accord to the "common good" but needs a "true and effective directing principle," and that principle is "*social justice.*" However, behind that dubious phrase, there lurks the whole egalitarian agenda, which, in search of an "equality of condition," looks eventually to the state to impose it. As anticipated, the first draft of the encyclical was created by Oswald von Nell-Breuning S. J., professor of moral theology at the Jesuit School in Frankfurt, a thinker profoundly influenced by Marx's theory of exploitation.[333]

In due course, the term "subsidiarity" was to enjoy a second life through the

European Union, whose official documents declare that all decisions must be taken at the subsidiary level while, regrettably, reserving to the unelected and mostly unaccountable European Commission the right to decide what level that might be.

Unfortunately, social justice, as the term is understood today, is no more a form of justice than fools' gold is a form of gold. It is not a matter of giving each person his or her due, taking account of rights and obligations. The modern-day term "social justice" is interpreted as the reorganization of society with the state in charge—there is no other agent with the requisite power or authority—and with equality as the ultimate goal.

Today's distorted and *"upside-down social market economy,"* a reversal of Röpke's idea that the market constraint must come "from below," is no more a market economy than social justice is a form of justice. As it has developed in socialist Germany and France, the social market has become a statist institution, heavily regulated from above in the interests of ideology-driven political parties and the powerful lobbies of large corporations, trade unions, and the welfare bureaucracy. The "social justice"–oriented social market is suspicious of private property and free enterprise, obsessively concerned with equal partnership, and receptive to every kind of egalitarian dogma. Using the excuse of "protecting" the social market in the name of "social justice," the size of the state has increased to the point of controlling more than half of the French gross domestic product (GDP) and employing more than half of the working population. It has so corrupted the economy of Germany that now some 12 to 13 percent of the official GDP in that once law-abiding country shows up in the black economy.[334]

III. Ethical Goals of the Social Market Economy

The social market economy is dedicated to three main ethical goals allowing people to live under humane conditions:

The first, and most important, goal to attain is an optimal supply of goods, which demands that economic agents have the freedom necessary for their economic creativity.

The second goal to attain is the guarantee of decent conditions at the workplace by way of public legislation. While classical liberalism sees the labor market as exclusively subject to the law of supply and demand, social market economy considers it to be an area where ethics must regulate these laws to secure humane work conditions.

The third ethical goal is solidarity with the economically weak through a system of social security.

In present times, a fourth ethical goal of ecological compatibility and global economic sense could also be added.

On this basis, theoretically, the social market economy is an institutionally order-related program based on the principles of a competition-oriented economy, linking free personal initiative with social progress and made possible by the economic effects of a thriving market. To fulfill this function, the institutional order has to comprise essential structural elements, such as private property, freedom of production, freedom of action, freedom of trade, free choice of occupation, free selection of work, and freedom to consume.

In this context, and as the primary condition of a free market, private property is the *right* of private actors to deal with, manage, and dispose of their goods and services. These private actors must also accept the consequences of their decisions by being liable for them.

However, the social market economy does a lot more than that. It not only provides room for success for everybody in the market, but it also takes responsibility for the losers in the marketplace. Accordingly, it sets up and maintains a social security system to protect all members of society against poverty, hardship, and misfortune and to provide everyone with the possibility to lead a decent life. The idea is to allow all human beings to live in dignity, preferably without continuous outside assistance. To answer the questions of what is, in fact, indispensable to protect human dignity and where state responsibility ends to give room for reasonable individual contributions, the social market economy, at least theoretically, should follow the principle of subsidiarity.

IV. The Concept and Misuse of Subsidiarity

The word "subsidiarity," derived from the Latin word "*subsidium*" ("help")—originates from the encyclical "Quadragesimo Anno," where its classical definition can be found. "Just as it is gravely wrong to take from individuals what they can accomplish by their own initiative and industry and give it to the community, so also it is an injustice and, at the same time, a grave evil and disturbance of right order to assign to a greater and higher association what lesser and subordinate organizations can do. For every social activity ought, of its very nature, to furnish help to the members of the body social and never destroy and absorb them."[335]

The 1991 encyclical "Centesimus Annus" ("hundredth year"), by Pope John Paul II, refers back to "Rerum Novarum" and constitutes a third chapter of the Catholic social doctrine, resulting in the idea of the social market economy. Although it did not use this particular term, it described the issue down to the finest details of ethical principles.[336] While the terms "liberty" and "social justice" define basic moral values, the terms "market mechanism" and "public control" describe the two fundamental organizing features of the social market economy.

The principle of subsidiarity not only demands that the self-sufficiency of the individual be protected from state interference but it also has a dual core: "private before state" and "small before large."

Where a problem arises, the smallest unit should be given the first chance to solve it before large structures can capture it. Priority in assuming responsibility should be given first to the individual and then to the family; the neighborhood is permitted to intervene ahead of the state. The order of priorities moves from local to regional to national to European to global.

The subsidiarity principle is a rule for distribution of the scope of authority. Its ranking is clear: self-help before neighborly help; neighborly help before help from afar and from governmental interference. It is, therefore, crucial how the political and economic order will examine the question of its reach of competence. One cannot insinuate that subsidiarity advocates that the state should not take care of anything. The principle of subsidiarity does not want the state to be so powerful as to interfere everywhere it wants, but it does want it to be powerful enough to act when needed. In addition to its decentralization dynamics, the subsidiarity principle requires the state institution, when it is assigned to solve a problem, to be sufficiently equipped and prepared to complete the necessary tasks.

Theoretically, subsidiarity ("we should keep a sense of proportion") is closely connected with solidarity ("we are all in the same boat"). Subsidiarity promotes freedom and individual responsibility and wants to avoid the dependency and paternalism of the welfare state. It supports the security of the individual rather than the abandoning of the individual to capitalism.

These are great words, a great principle, and a great theory; but how does it work in practice? Who assigns the task to solve a problem—to whom, and at what point in time?

"Quadragesimo Anno" introduced two concepts that became critical in our time: social justice and subsidiarity. Both of them pretend to be about society—its rights, duties, and freedoms—however, both are, in fact, about the state. Moreover, their history shows how easily the original concepts advanced allegedly to defend society from the state can be turned completely around to empower the state against society.

The European Union provides one notable case—a venture *against* which Röpke frequently warned, rightly seeing it as a move toward centralization (euphemistically "federalization") and a blow to the localism that he supported.[337]

The Eurocrats have always stated that national sovereignty would not be sacrificed in the European Union, that the principle of subsidiarity is applied, and that all decisions about a specific nation and its particular interests would be made at the national level by its elected Parliament.

However, then comes the catch: it is the European Commission, *not* the national parliament, that decides that a given issue pertains to the specific interests of a given nation-state. In reality, an unelected commission *delegates from above* national sovereignty, which is in the hands of its permanent staff of bureaucrats rather than in those of the sheepish politicians who have been shunted there from parliaments where they are no longer wanted. The principle of subsidiarity that purports to grant powers to local and national bodies in fact takes them away, ensuring that powers that were once exercised by right are now exercised on sufferance. This bogus subsidiarity today confiscates sovereignty in the same way that social justice confiscates justice and the social market confiscates the market.

What is the alternative? How should one respond to the problems of social fragmentation and the loss of community feeling in the world where the market is left to itself? How would communities renew themselves, and how are fundamental flaws in the human constitution, such as resentment, envy, and sexual predation, to be overcome by something so abstract and neutral as consumer sovereignty and free economic choice?

V. Rules for the Market: Reversed Social Market

With its emphasis on the principle of subsidiarity, the social market economy advocates that every individual has the right and the duty to do what he or she is capable of doing. This argument applies to integration in the job market, the acquisition of knowledge and education, and the ability to accumulate assets and to make financial arrangements for retirement and times of need.

In principle, and as envisioned by Röpke, the social market economy, unlike the welfare state, gives personal initiative priority over state action and stipulates the state to act bottom up instead of top down. Unlike the libertarian laissez-faire state, it does *not* exclude state action as a last choice if the individual initiative is too weak to succeed. The social market economy starts from the premise that the market economy requires a stable legal-institutional framework, which the state can create by making provision for internal and external security, the administration of justice, and a suitable infrastructure.

The government has a responsibility for drawing a charter of general rules for market participants. Markets do not always function smoothly. Open competition is possible only if antitrust laws guarantee a minimum number of competitors and prevent monopolies from dominating the market.

In all free market systems, some economic sectors require special regulations because they deviate more or less sharply from general market principals. Such sectors—basic needs like agriculture and food, water supply, electricity, and health care—are partly exempted from the laws of regular competition in a social market economy. Instruments to be used are state regulations controlling market entry, prices, production and sales volume, investments and capacities, and quality and terms. These rules include the prohibition of cartels and price-fixing, a ban on price recommendations, and monitoring of abuse in cases of exclusivity commitments of customers toward certain suppliers.

The safeguarding of free markets by implementing fair competition is a fundamental purpose of the social market economy. Another is to make sure that human dignity is protected not only for those who can successfully participate in a free market but also for those who fail to survive there.

Röpke's idea was that society is nurtured and maintained at the *local level* through motives that are more than just the pursuit of rational self-interest. There is the motive of charitable giving, the motives of love and friendship, and the motive of piety. All these grow naturally and cause us to provide for each other and to shape our environment into a common home. The true home, which is familiarity based on safety and security, is not an isolated place apart from the rest of the world, in which a solitary individualist enjoys his sovereignty as a consumer. The true home is a place of charity and gift, love, affection, and prayer. Its doors are open to the neighbors, with whom its dwellers join in festivals, ceremonies, weddings, funerals, and worship. The dwellers of the true home are not simply consumers but also members of society, and membership is a mutual relationship that cannot be captured regarding enlightened self-interest; that is the goal—the subject matter of economic theory.

For extreme individualists, life in society is merely a coordination problem, as the game theorists describe it—one area in which my rational self-interest needs to be harmonized with yours. Moreover, the market is the only reliable way that we humans know or could know of coordinating our goal-directed activities, not only with friends and neighbors but also with all the myriad strangers on whom we depend on for the contents of our shopping bags. Membership, if it comes about, is just another form of quasicontractual agreement whereby we freely bind ourselves to mutual rights and duties.

However, two questions arise: How do we spell out, in terms appropriate to modern societies, the implications of Röpke's membership theory? Moreover, is the dispute here to be defined and fought out in economic terms?

In referring to a social market, economists leave an enormous hostage to fortune, for they express the view, endorsed by the socialists, that the social question demands an economic solution. To some extent, Röpke should be criticized on this score. Namely, he believed that a certain form of an economic order could be developed that would result, as a benign by-product, in the kind of social cohesion that he had found in the Swiss villages, which he believed expressed the communal heart of European society. Now, this proposal was to accept, however, one of the most damaging of all of Marx's ideas, according to which social institutions are the by-product: the offshoot or consequence of the economic order, *instead of the very foundation* of it. For if Marx's theory is right, then the cure for social ills must be conceived in economic terms.

That is to say, if the free market of capitalism delivers a fragmented and dysfunctional society, then the answer is to replace the free market, or capitalism even, with another economic system. How could that be done if not by state action, directing the economy toward clearly defined social goals? That much is contained in that troubling expression "a humane economy," which seems to imply that it is the economic organization through which society becomes humane, and not, for example, through love, friendship, and the moral law.

Röpke intended no such implication, of course, but his style everywhere conveys the tension in his thinking between decentrism as a social movement and economic policy.

So again, how, then, could the picture of social membership implied in Röpke's argument be spelled out? Röpke is advocating a community of attachment in which people take an altruistic interest in each other's situations, where distress summons help and success summons congratulation. He is advocating a community in which the pursuit of self-interest is circumscribed continually by a concern for the common good, and in which the bonds of love, desire, and friendship find a socially endorsed pathway to fruition. So understood, social membership cannot be achieved without a settlement, meaning a relationship among neighbors, who are united not by shared ambitions, employment, or wealth but by shared domain and all the obligations that go with that. A small and localized community can guide people through its vigilance toward honest dealing, both to protect the weak from the strong and to channel the profits of the wealthy toward the relief of the poor. This friendly settlement does not happen because the community is organized economically in any other way than the spontaneous way of the market. It happens because people know each other, are subject to common moral pressures, and wish to see virtue rewarded and vice punished. Their self-perpetuating equilibrium occurs, if and when it occurs, because the customs and laws that arise spontaneously among neighbors resolve the conflicts. If they also enjoy a market economy, then this is an additional benefit made possible by having such a background of shared moral order.

The Communist Manifesto contains many half-truths but it also makes an important observation about capitalism. According to the manifesto, capitalism has an inherent tendency to set human communities in motion and to separate people from the place and statuses into which they are born. It also dissolves all traditional arrangements and replaces them with new relationships based on contract rather than inheritance, rendering transitory what had been permanent, and replacing destiny with a choice.

The picture that Marx and Engels drew was true to the experience of nineteenth-century observers, who saw all around them the crumbling of the traditional order and the unsettling of previously settled communities. What was causing the disruption, however, was not, as Marx and the socialists supposed, private property and the market economy—both of which had existed from the beginning of human history as an uninterrupted continuity. The source of the disruption was the very same circumstance that confronts us today—namely globalization: one person's ability to contract with another, regardless of all the physical, moral, and spiritual distance between them.

Industrialization was the first step in this direction, enabling rural workers to move to the towns and exchange their labor for a wage. Imperialism was a further step, allowing industries to outsource many of their inputs and to distribute their goods among distant strangers. Moreover, the modern multinational corporations that outsource everything and sometimes own nothing save a brand, are just the latest move in the same direction—toward a globalized economy in which everything is changed, replaced, or transferred in response to demand and where locality and attachment are discounted.

The obscurity of the global economy goes hand in hand with a ghostly quality—a sense that the agents behind every transaction are not creatures of flesh and blood who live in communities. Instead these agents are "homeless," vagabond, and rogue corporations who take no real responsibility for producing what they sell but merely stick their brand on it, thereby claiming a tariff on producer and consumer alike. It is hard to articulate this complaint, the argument advancing step-by-step to accommodate the latest move toward the global economy. This economy is not dislocated, as the nineteenth-century socialists imagined, but unsettled. Nevertheless, that is precisely why it is so troublesome.

It has become somewhat of a truism that the state is a community of communities. However, the state is not a separate institutional entity tasked with arranging society according to any particular pattern or set of principles. Instead all the communities that by nature constitute society have to work together to establish peace, order, and respect for human dignity. Since conflicts are inevitable in any society, the role of the government in society is limited to maintaining peace among more fundamental institutions and associations.

Unfortunately, while European Christian democracy knew of and valued the church's wisdom regarding human dignity, it sought to pursue it within secular categories and, in particular, the confines of modern sovereignty. The result was the development of modern social democracy. After first arguing for a third way between Soviet-style socialism and a heartless brand of individualistic capitalism, Christian Democrats rather quickly settled into a pursuit of political programs startlingly akin to those of their social-democratic opponents. The only practical issues remaining between them were the respect for the church and its right to participate in public life. Thus, rather than supporting a community of communities based on subsidiarity, they ended up supporting the much simpler fusion of these communities into one body (i.e., a national community under the tutelage of the state.) Alas, that state then might or might not listen to the calls of conscience, perhaps (or perhaps not) as formulated by one or another church.

Everyone knows the proverb, "The road to hell is paved with good intentions." It perfectly fits the road built by the state-as-guardian that led nations and peoples to the supposed paradise of egalitarian left-liberal social democracy, which turned out to be the real hell of lethargic and morally debilitating centralized power with thought police and stifling bureaucracy without cultural cohesion. Sadly, the clock cannot be turned back to undo the damage done in the name of human dignity. However, one ought, at least, to recognize that loss and its source in the abstractions of cosmopolitan ideology that continue to rule international humanitarian thought and institutions.

Economic activity has become disconnected from the building and functioning of communities. Nobody knows the employees or workers who produce the goods that members of a community buy; nobody knows what those workers' working conditions are, or what they believe in, hope for, or desire. Nobody knows, either, the people or their circumstances that provide society with goods and services, except the celebrity CEOs of Apple, Microsoft, McDonald's, or Wal-Mart—individuals who seem miraculously to escape all liability for the products they sell. Local stores, producers, and distributors are successively bought or driven out of business by the anonymous chains. When the hapless members of a local community are trying to defend themselves against an intruding giant, they find that all the cards are stacked against them. Unknown and outside agents, such as the abstract consumer, the dominating state, or special-interest groups, have already announced a preference for a shopping mall, industrial complex, or giant warehouse on the doorstep.

So the faceless and rootless corporation that invests all its capital in a brand thereby escapes liability for the long-term costs of its products. More precisely, the faceless corporation can, in effect, externalize its cost. For example, the cost of producing soya beans in Brazil—the cost of the environmental damage, the devastation of the landscape, aesthetic pollution and so on—is not witnessed by consumers in the United States or the European Union; nor is it controlled by their respective legislations (themselves responsive to lobbying from consumers). The real cost of production to society is a cost that can be, as it were, left in Brazil—and left to the future generations who will have to bear it. This externalization of costs is a practice that under the aegis of globalization is ubiquitous.

The total real cost of packaged food on the supermarket shelf includes the long-term cost of nonbiodegradable packaging. However, neither the supermarket nor its suppliers bear this cost, which is borne by all of our descendants and us over the next hundreds of years. It is the cost of pollution that has been merely externalized. All the personal factors that would compel a supplier or trader under local conditions to behave responsibly are, in this matter, absent. There is no reward for good behavior, and the costs of bad behavior can be mostly passed on; this is a blatant feature of the global market economy—one that is seemingly intrinsic to it.

If one takes the above points seriously, the strength in Röpke's intellectual starting point must be recognized: it is the small local community in which economic activity takes place under the watchful guardianship of the moral sense. However, one must also acknowledge that we cannot return to that community through anything that resembles the social market as adopted by the postwar consensus in the West, for what this social market amounts to in practice is the intrusion into the economy of another big, anonymous entity, the state, which is just as capable of externalizing its costs as any corporation. Even more so, the state can silence its critics as no corporation can.

Thus the social market, as practiced in the Western world today, demands the state to step in and provide for those without work or, among others, for the mothers of children who have no resident father. These are the inevitable results of transferring the responsibility for charity from the community to the state, which is itself an inevitable result of the attempt to make a "humane economy" rather than "humane society"—the exact opposite of what Röpke had envisioned.

Some of the costs of the humane economy must be considered. One is the growth of an underclass of people who do not work but who find every means to avoid work to enjoy the benefits provided by the state. Another one is the growth of illegitimacy, as women find an easy way to provide for themselves and their babies, and men find an easy way to abandon the women they have impregnated. A third one is the growth of antisocial behavior, as fatherless children are released from the dysfunctional households that produce them; and so on and on.

The state has thereby externalized the costs of its social market policies onto society, and the higher the cost, the more the state expands with fictitious plans to reduce them. Never has a better machine for expanding the rentier class of bureaucrats been devised than one that steadily amplifies the problem it was established to solve. Hence, as educational achievement declines in Europe, state expenditure on education increases to the point where there are nearly two bureaucrats for every teacher appointed to deal with the social problems they make a living producing.

These problems are present and very similar also in the United States, of course. However, they have led there to a far-reaching skepticism toward statist solutions and even free market fundamentalism, which insists that the market is the answer to these social ills and not the cause of them. This belief is a straightforward short-term explanation of a complex and long-term problem and is nothing other than a crude way of avoiding the issue.

As things currently stand, this "reversed social market," as practiced, is very far from producing the humane economy that Röpke hoped for. While it may bring a more equal distribution of goods than an entirely free economy, it also produces its own type of social disintegration as the state, by expropriating the charitable motive, also extinguishes it. The world of the underclass knows neither attachment and compassion nor the virtue of charity.

How, then, do we prevent the globalization of everything and the fragmentation of our loyalties and attachments? How do we recover the small community that shapes the moral sense of its members? What, then, is the real solution to the market-induced disorders of modern society?

The answer to these questions is not to be found in any new economic order but rather in the moral foundations of a market economy. Röpke himself saw this predicament and viewed the emergence of mass society and the atheist norm as such a disaster. The disorders of the global market come about for the same reason as the disorders of the welfare state—because people seize every opportunity to externalize their costs.[338]

Moreover, they do this because no vigilant community compels them to behave any other way. One relevant example of this today is the habit of consumer credit, which in earlier times would have been condemned as the most immoral, reckless, and irresponsible form of indebtedness. The conduct of living beyond one's means, which in the still vigilant and small Swiss communities of Röpke's day would have been ample reason for social ostracism, is now regarded as a kind of enviable cleverness. It is a successful way of putting the cost of one's life entirely onto someone else's shoulders and, if necessary, filing for bankruptcy when the going gets tough.

While there is no way forward for humankind that does not involve the restoration of that kind of vigilant community, it can be restored only at the local level by rebuilding the forms of social membership.

Can localization become policy? Would any such suggestion not merely reproduce the problem by giving a new and overmastering project to the state? This dilemma is the problem that the West now faces; the West, victim of its reversed social market, has no means to replace statist policies without involving the state itself.

The state itself must provide incentives to the individuals and localities to start helping themselves, beginning with their own social initiatives (e.g., friendly societies offering nonprofit loans for house purchases, charitable hospitals, networks of doctors, church schools and village schools funded by subscription, and clubs and organizations of enthusiasts devoted to public leisure). The state must forego the externalization of the costs and supply the charitable motive because people give freely what they freely earn and because the foundation of community hope is in the still entrenched local loyalties of the people. Such initiatives will be the engine of the humane economy, which will be humane not because of, but despite, the economy.

VI. Social Security

There are some nonincome periods, such as unemployment, illness, and retirement, for which a social security system should provide a necessary safeguard. The social market economy organizes for this through a compulsory insurance system for everyone because, otherwise, those who are reasonable enough to pay for protection in difficult times would also have to support those who are not.

These compulsory insurance systems against times when there is no income are based on the concepts of solidarity and subsidiarity. They force everybody to show solidarity with oneself by taking bad times into account when one enjoys the good times. Without this imposed precaution, people would live at the expense of others when personal financial crises hit them. Under the principle of the social market, the protection of freedom for all justifies the constraint on individual liberty by the forcing of people to participate in a mandatory insurance system.

In Germany, unemployment insurance, health insurance, retirement pension insurance, long-term care insurance, and accident insurance at work are all compulsory. By contrast with health, long-term care, pension, and unemployment insurance, the statutory occupational accident insurance is contribution-free for those insured. The level of contributions to the mandatory coverages for times when there is no income is connected to and depends on the level of income when it is earned. The insurance premium is divided equally between employers and employees.

While the insurance system is personalized—basically, one gets what one pays—there is also a social security net that is funded by taxes and ensures a minimum standard of living when all other systems fail. Also, beneficiaries are entitled to be reimbursed for their costs of an appropriate home.

With solidarity as one of its principles, the German social market economy is committed to a system of progressive income tax.

In addition to certain tax benefits, such as a tax split for family incomes, there is a different policy to support families, which includes child allowances and parents' money. Time spent on childcare and education is taken into account in the calculation of old-age pensions through insurance contributions paid by the state. The term "family contribution compensation" used for this policy underlines that children do not represent a burden on society and that parents, through their investment of money and labor, are contributors to the preservation and continued development of society. By directly supporting the family policy, the social market economy signifies its commitment to the principle of solidarity.[339]

VII. Compulsory Insurance

Right from the start of its conceptualization, the social market economy was to ensure that the elderly could enjoy their retirement, would be adequately provided for, and would be free from poverty. Retirement pensions should not come across as charity but as a rightful claim derived from contributions made during the acquisition phase.

Pensions are rewards for performance. Therefore, Germany has a so-called contribution-financed pension system for each employee. The employer deposits a fixed percentage of earned income, from which pensioners draw during retirement in proportion to their contributions.

In Germany, for historical reasons, the accumulated contributions are paid directly to the retirees and not placed into interest-bearing investments to be paid out later to the respective contributor. In other words, the pension system works on a pay-as-you-go basis. Retirement plan revenues are based on the contribution average, multiplied by the number of employees. Expenditures are based on the average pension multiplied by the number of pensioners. If the number of retirees rises or the number of employees falls (or both), expenditures will go up, or revenues will go down (or both). Consequently, economic crises and demographic changes have a direct impact on the pension fund, and in the case of a deficit, the taxpayer has to pay the balance. Because of demographic developments (declining population without immigration), these subsidies to the pension fund have become the second-largest expenditure in the German national budget after the interest payments on the national debt. Lowered payouts, extended working age, and incentives for more private provisions for one's old age are the antidotes prescribed by politicians.

The people in Germany have to get health insurance as a protective measure against health risks. Up to a certain income level, they belong to the statutory health insurance system, and about 10 percent of the population also participates in a private health insurance plan. Both plans are financed through contributions that are calculated, based on revenues, to cover current expenditures. The contribution charged is a percentage of income, and free insurance coverage for family members without income is also included. The patient has the right, guaranteed by the system, to select a doctor. In recent years, new medical technologies, new medicines, and the growing number of senior citizens have sharply increased health care costs. Accordingly, the insurance contribution has risen.

Nursing care insurance functions like health insurance, but it is dramatically confronted with increasing costs as a consequence of demographic developments, an aging population, and more people depending on professional care.

Statutory occupational accident insurance, which is fully paid by the employer, covers accidents at work, occupational diseases, and work-related health hazards.

Unemployment insurance guarantees 60 percent (or 67 percent if one has children) of the last wage for twenty-four months, depending on age. After this time, one is entitled to claim basic social security. The primary purpose of this social security system is to reintegrate the unemployed into working life while they are expected to show active participation. Basic social welfare—not the insurance benefits—can be cut if one does not seek a job.

This third-way system of support and demand manifests the continuing ability of the social market economy to fulfill the requirements of freedom and justice while the old ideologies of capitalism and socialism remain stuck in the philosophy that one has to choose between these objectives.

THE SOCIAL MARKET ECONOMY AND ITS FUTURE IN EASTERN EUROPE

After the fall of the Berlin wall in 1989, the formerly Communist-ruled Eastern European countries did not establish a social market economy to follow the successful German model, but one that was "without attributes" as it was described by the former Czech president, Václav Klaus.

As the "victor" of the Cold War, the United States, with its unregulated market economy model, was considered a role model for the new rulers in Central and Eastern Europe, and also in former Yugoslavia. For ideological reasons, Russia could not acknowledge the United States as a role model. However, it moved toward a free market economy with some restrictions that its laws placed on the small social stratum of the so-called oligarchs while the middle layer was left empty-handed.

On the one hand, the excessive welfare state brought about by Germany is a deterrent in Eastern Europe; on the other hand, the social problems of an unregulated economic system are becoming increasingly evident there, especially in light of the financial crisis. Critics of the social market economy see it as an outdated model. Following the collapse of Communism, it was not German ordoliberalism that succeeded in Eastern Europe, but "liberalism without a prefix" and the "market economy without an adjective," as Václav Klaus called it.[340] As

Klaus had so passionately fought against the dictatorship of the Czech communists, any meddling of the state in areas where, in his opinion, things should regulate themselves, was suspect.

It is not a coincidence that the radically free market Klaus completed his economic education at the University of Chicago—from the European point of view a mecca of conservative free market economics. Because of his experience under the Communist dictatorship, which painted a picture of social security and equality through the accumulation of enormous national debt, and his schooling in economics, the social market economy as a way of thinking, which underpins the economies of Germany, Austria, and also France, was highly doubtful. Moreover, the failure of it in Eastern Europe would appear to prove Klaus right.

After the collapse of the Communist regimes, German and French politicians expected the social market economy to conquer Eastern Europe, but this turned out to be a misjudgment. Jacques Attali, the president of the European Bank for Reconstruction and Development (EBRD) at the time, saw exporting the values of Western Europe to Eastern Europe as the task of his bank. Attali was a fierce opponent of radical reforms, such as those being attempted in Russia during that period. When Attali visited Prague in the early 1990s and met with the heads of the government, he found the pro-American attitude in economic matters of the then still Czechoslovakian government as vulgar and, above all, wrong. The French president Jacques Chirac thought the same and also complained about the Eastern European support of the US-led Iraq war.

Socialist Germany and France underestimated the political and economic standing that the United States had in the Central and Eastern European transition states. In the final phase of the Soviet Union, the later Russian economic reformers, such as Yegor Gaidar or Anatoly Chubais, were very interested in the classic American economic model, as they were convinced that the secret to the success of their ideological opponent was to be found there. This belief is critical if one wishes to understand why almost all former socialist nations opted for a pure market economy.

As early as 1990, the then Czech finance minister Václav Klaus predicted that the majority of the Eastern European countries would reject the German-style social market economy, opting instead for a pure free market system. It is noteworthy that even the left-wing intellectuals of most Eastern European countries shared his opinion. Klaus's predecessor as president of the Czech Republic, Václav Havel, wrote in 1992, "… though my heart may be left of center, I have always known that the only economic system that works is a market economy. It is the only one that leads to prosperity because it is the only one that reflects the nature of life itself."[341] Although it is an assessment of the market economy by a left-liberal politician, it is not a commitment to an entirely free market, as Wolfgang Münchau writes in his book *Das Ende der sozialen Marktwirtschaft*. It is merely the eagerness to end the "nannying" that led to the bankruptcy and total collapse of both the economy and society, the effects of which have still not been overcome today.[342]

Alas, very few politicians in the newly democratic Eastern Europe did accept any responsibility for the common good. The already fractured society seemed to be split even further, and the individual was left to his or her own devices. Marxist materialism was just transferred to capitalist materialism.

As Eastern European politicians pronounced themselves to be for the market economy, they had the example of an improved version of a planned economy before them as a deterrent, which is why Václav Klaus labeled the social market economy as "soft socialism."[343] Less dirigisme and a lower public spending ratio—flaws that brought the Eastern European social market economy into disrepute—would certainly increase market dynamics. However, outside the newly rich successful Eastern European economic circles, there is clear doubt that the free market is the solution for everything.

Given the costs of the transformation and the financial crisis, some of the world's leading economists have strengthened their view that the market economy process needs a regulatory framework that meets market requirements in the era of internationalization and globalization.

Nevertheless, it was very problematic to discuss a model seeking to combine economic growth with social equality in the Central and Southeast European countries after the fall of the Iron Curtain. The primary interest of the transition states was a rapid reorientation of the planned-economy model into a free market economic system. Moreover, the epithet "social" was not going to lose the bad reputation it received through its misuse by the Communist system for a long time to come.

Whether the idea of either the real or the reversed social market economy can fulfill the wish for a humane third way between market radicalism and destructive socialism for Eastern Europe is not the least dependent on how Wilhelm Röpke's or Ludwig Erhard's legacy is treated.

Socialist regimes have a peculiar habit of transforming themselves into corrupt crony capitalist ones. The peoples of Eastern Europe must remember that and the common good if they want to prevent societal fractures and safeguard general prosperity.

Russia and the Market Economy

Behind the description "Russian market economy" are the experiences of renowned perestroika reformers, such as Gaidar or Chubais, who adhered to the original liberal American model. Free prices, free external trade, guaranteed property rights, and monetary equilibrium—the rest was taken care of by the market. Distribution of income or policies for medium-sized businesses did not form any part of this model.

The situation of medium-sized companies in Russia is a classic example of the Russian market liberalization, which was shared only by very few mega-rich politically reliable people on the wishes of the government. The problems that enterprising small and medium-sized businesses needed to handle had not changed a great deal before 2002. In 2006, the Russian government not only declared that it wanted to promote medium-sized companies and increase their share of the economy but also offered some help in the form of low-interest loans, microcredit, and venture capital. The attempts, however, have not remedied the most significant problems (i.e., bureaucracy, corruption, and abuse of authority). Russian medium-size enterprises are still a long way from being in a healthy and robust position; growth and innovation are seen only in large companies. Big corporations, such as Gazprom, Rosneft, Sberbank, Norilsk Nickel, Novatek, Rusal, Evraz, and Severstal, dominate the Russian economy. Russian politics that equates diversification with a lack of control is consciously leaning toward large companies or industrial conglomerates, especially in strategic sectors such as aircraft production and some areas of engineering, which contradicts the basis of the social market economy.

The inconsistencies and flaws of market liberalization have not only provoked religious and cultural protests but have also drawn criticism from economists, even when they initially appear to be champions of the free market economy.

The radical "crash model" transition from the planned to the market economy immediately led to high unemployment and created social problems. The Russian liberalization of prices and privatization of state-run businesses did indeed breed some entrepreneurial talent able to flourish in a market economy, although many had had strong doubts about that first. The concentration of market powers that neither Yeltsin nor his successor Putin promoted worsened the social problems. However, there were no political demonstrations in the country, primarily because of the enormous Russian capacity to endure any hardship. In addition to that, civic participation and social partnerships after decades of communism were yet to be accepted, and any such acceptance was not particularly easy in a political landscape often labeled a "controlled democracy."

As previously stated, during the final phase of the Soviet Union, Russia aligned itself first with its powerful economic and chief political rival rather than with its smaller neighbor, Germany, with its social and economic order. The market economy of the United States and the other Anglo-Saxon countries in general was, and perhaps still is, considered a viable and suitable economic and political concept—much more so than the complicated German postwar system. As a consequence, the successor states of the Soviet Union did not assume the intricate West European compromise model called the "social market economy." Instead they opted for the free market model of their ideological opponent that had won the Cold War, been vilified for decades, and was by no means problem-free.

Also, Russian Orthodox Christianity could not approve of an economic system, namely the reversed social market economy, that rewarded laziness and gave the poor the alms of the state to live on, because productive work is an essential part of human life. Nevertheless, while orthodoxy also condemned the unbridled and unregulated capitalistic (laissez-faire) system, it approved of a socially responsible free market system. This position of the Russian Orthodox Church is an explicit criticism of both the excessive social state (or welfare state) of Western Europe and the unbridled free market liberalism that initially entered Eastern Europe.

Many Eastern European economists are also critical of the present-day German reversed social market economy. However, at the beginning of the 1950s, when the concept was still new and balanced and the demands of both employers and employees were satisfied, the criticism was not nearly so loud as it is today.

The changes implemented in Eastern Europe in the 1980s and 1990s diluted the concept of social market economy and considered even social security a severe economic burden. Not only did any social expenditure have to be allocated using insufficient financial resources, but the acceptance of the social market economy would also prolong both structural deficiency and a socialist mentality, which did not want to reject the old system outright. There was also the opposing mentality, which reacted allergically to every supposed leaning toward any new state intervention, seen as popular socialism.

As for the structural deficit, the reformed nations of Eastern Europe were in a fundamentally different situation than Germany in 1945. Russia already had over seventy years of state-controlled economy behind it, without private property, a free market, or any of the characteristics of civil society. In Germany, by the end of the war, there was still a market economy structure present. During the twelve years of Hitler's dictatorship, the economy was controlled by compulsory cartels, but the companies themselves were not nationalized. Only the monetary reform of 1948 had to be implemented to get farmers, workers, manufacturers, and businesspeople back on track.

In contrast, in the Eastern European reform countries, and especially in Russia, there were no companies still intact in the early 1990s. First, the central planning authorities had to be broken up and made independent economic entities through privatization. The victorious allies made sure that the old ruling class was subdued in postwar Germany. On the other hand, in Russia and other Eastern European reform countries, the old monopoly structures still ruled and obstructed all newcomers to the market economy. As an economic area, Russia was not a blank slate to be revitalized by owners with guaranteed property rights in the manner of the University of Chicago under the motto "the market will regulate itself," as a commentator wrote in the Russian financial paper *Kommersant* at the time. Although the all-powerful military-industrial complex was weakened, the monopoly on raw materials maintained its position and influence in politics so that market economy innovation was practically closed off. In such circumstances, a social market economy was almost unthinkable.

The large-scale privatization that began on October 1, 1992, expressly excluded natural resources, power generation plants, and the aerospace and nuclear power industries; these were the assets that were to form the basis of the raw material monopoly of the oligarch system later. State-owned enterprises were transformed into stock companies by presidential decree. Every Russian citizen received a free stock certificate for public (or "national") property to the value of ten thousand rubles. The people were supposed to have the opportunity to buy privatized national property, such as stocks, real estate, or pieces of land. The stock certificates could be sold, exchanged, given away, traded on the stock market, or taken over by investment funds.[344]

The Russian economic reform was based on the floating of most consumer and capital goods beginning January 1, 1992. This decision by the Russian government under Yegor Gaidar was as courageous as it was risky. Since there was no adequate supply of goods at the time, the reformers had to estimate that prices would explode and inflation would escalate. Between July 1, 1992, and November 30, 1994, the ruble–dollar exchange rate on the Moscow currency exchange rose from 125 rubles per dollar to 3,200 rubles per dollar.[345] Gaidar, made a scapegoat for the rising prices, was removed from government as early as December 1992; Viktor Chernomyrdin replaced him.

Nevertheless, the price liberalization was necessary and inevitable. Otherwise there would have been no chance of increasing the supply of consumer goods through imports. Besides, this decision gave the reform process some credibility in the West and made it irreversible for Russia. Other than the price liberalization, the core of the Russian transformation from a planned economy to a market economy was the rapid start of privatization.

The market radicals were victorious in Russia by dividing the raw material market among themselves and taking away society's responsibility—with the relieved blessing of the Kremlin. They quickly made light of the critics of Westernization and the uncritical takeover of the Western free society and economic model. However, representatives of the national Orthodox churches formulate the same criticisms on the transition from Marxist to capitalist materialism. Astonishingly, they refer to the advocate of the social market economy, Alfred Müller-Armack, who perceived Nazi totalitarianism to be a replacement religion at a time of drop in religious belief.[346] Russian and Serbian Orthodox bishops and theologians similarly suspect that neoliberalism and unrestrained capitalism are today's alternative religions.

One could interpret the radical about-face from the absolute dirigisme of the former planned-economy nations to market liberalism with the help of Müller-Armack. He studied the repercussions of cultural concepts on the economy. In his opinion, spiritual legacies proved to have left a deep impression on culture and could also have a significant influence in a very secular society on fundamental values and worldviews. One might ask Müller-Armack whether it is a coincidence that the cultural border running between the Orthodox countries and the Protestant and Catholic countries is almost identical to the EU's eastern border of today. The organically integrated feature of the orthodox view of the world was not unknown to the Western Catholic world either, until the age of industrialization. The goal was an organic interdependence of the economy and society. Although the more secular model gained acceptance throughout Western Europe, Russia, above all, preserved a close affiliation not only between the church and society but also in all areas of society that held a common interest.

This orthodox interpretation carried on even after the 1917 Russian revolution. While Bolshevism used the traditional tendency toward holism to prevent the economy from working freely, the pendulum swung in the exact opposite direction after the collapse of the Bolshevik dictatorship in Russia. The "unexpected" free market economy, as its critics label it, was a holistic and closed model, whereas the social market economy presents a compromise—"soft socialism," to borrow Václav Klaus's exaggerated term again. This compromise is closest to the Catholic social doctrine and was also accepted by orthodoxy. According to Müller-Armack, the trend-setting sense of the social market economy is "to join the principle of market freedom with the principle of social balance."[347]

The remarks by Patriarch Kirill of Moscow and all Russia that the outgrowth of market liberalism in his country could fall under this compromise formula can be taken with a pinch of salt. So can those of his predecessor, Alexij II, who, when asked in 1991 what the church thought of the market economy, said, "The market economy is not so new for us. But when we return to market conditions, we must make sure that souls and fates are not flattened. We will work for more social protection, but that too is still overtaxing us."[348]

Attempted Reconciliation: Economic Dynamics and the Social Market Economy

The social market economy model has raised some serious questions: Is it low in economic dynamics by international standards? In any case, could there be such economic reforms that would substantially raise its dynamics without its character being altered? To what extent would the social market economy have to be dismantled or neutralized to attain a higher level of economic dynamics?

According to the early concept of the desirability of well-functioning capitalism, capitalism should prevail in countries where it can function well. Based on this concept, libertarian-leaning economists argued for a free market economy with a small government. This argument is based on the neoclassical proposal, according to which all that is required for a well-functioning economy is the rule of law and the establishment of private property rights, including the right to own and manage capital. With these minimal institutions in place, the economy will inevitably navigate the optimum path of intertemporal balance.

This argument, however, does not explain much about the essence of capitalism, which is about novelty, exploration, innovative ventures, and discovery—features missing from neoclassical theory.

Political economy has attempted to justify capitalism in two different ways, with Friedrich Hayek contributing to both of them, which understandably has caused some confusion. In his book *The Road to Serfdom* (and later in *The Constitution of Liberty*), Hayek suggested that people ought to have economic freedoms as well as political freedoms.[349] Such freedoms are, for example, the freedom to start a new firm or close one, or the freedom to introduce a new product or production method. Since a socialist system, a statist system, and a corporatist system deny people some of these freedoms, they are wrong, unfair, and unjust. Hayek appears to believe that when allowed these individual freedoms by their government, a people will develop the institutions of the system called capitalism.

However, what if instead people in some countries developed the institutions of a system of cooperatives—such as monasteries or kibbutzim—just because that was well known to them from their ancestral past and not because they had tried capitalism and liked it less. Could that system of cooperatives also be regarded a good economy and good economic order?

In *The Road to Serfdom*, one can find nothing about entrepreneurial activity and innovation—as if the consequences of capitalism were immaterial to its justification. It should be noted that Ludwig Erhard did not advocate the social market economy on the premise that it was the only system that offered people economic freedoms.

Another vulnerable point of this approach is that people might reasonably think that they ought to have the freedom to act in their communities, saying no to a factory they all dislike or subsidizing the relocation to their area of a business they all do like. To persuasively argue that individual freedoms ought to be decisive over community freedoms in every case requires the taking into account the consequences of community freedoms.

One other way of justifying capitalism has been to argue the benefits of its effects—the advantages of its ways, methods, and processes, along with the visible results. For example, numerous American economists maintained in the 1950s that the productivity growth–based rapid economic development justified capitalism, with Hayek opening again that line of argument for capitalism. In writings before *The Road to Serfdom* and after *The Constitution of Liberty*, he presented insights into the mechanisms of capitalism that, taken together, suggested the desirability of capitalism as an economic system and the value of its consequences.[350]

In the 1930s, Hayek had the insight that, in a market economy, every individual in the business sector has experience and observations that no one else has. He then argued that only people possessing this special knowledge are likely to have any idea of how this or that product could be produced and what goods might be remunerative to produce. The implication, which was none too sharply drawn by Hayek, was that these knowledge workers were better able to judge what can or cannot be produced than some state bank or agency, since these would lack the specialized know-how. It is evident that Hayek came to see in the 1960s (if he had not seen it earlier) that out of the specialized knowledge possessed by someone, an original idea may emerge—an idea that, this person could be pretty sure of, no one else has come up with currently or will come up with anytime soon.

So capitalism, a bottom-up system of the private initiative based on unique and individual knowledge, has the potential for creativity. As opposed to this, a top-down system cannot work—a system directed by social institutions too remote to have a wealth of hands-on information possessed by private individuals in business.

Another related theme of Hayek's was that the development and launch of a new and innovative product is a leap into the unknown where no one has been before and, therefore, the law of "unanticipated consequences" applies. There is "imperfect knowledge" about how the economy will receive the novel product; there is a significant amount of uncertainty involved. The uncertainty is even more compounded when many other new products and methods are being launched about the same time. This system, called capitalism is, therefore, a system of a disorder comprising guesses and surprises together with some elements of order.[351] It becomes critical, then, which ideas for the new products and methods are correct and will receive financing for the evaluation and tryout necessary for their widespread adoption. How can this process work?

These fundamental insights have opened the door to a more realistic view of capitalism. The term "dynamics" can be used to mean innovativeness in profitable and commercially viable directions. It can be argued that a well-functioning capitalist system must possess a high degree of dynamics that requires the overcoming of some difficulties. A high level of dynamics requires a lot more than just new commercial ideas. First, it requires entrepreneurs with a range of abilities needed to push the development of a new idea despite unforeseeable hurdles. Second, a high level of dynamics needs financiers, investors, or venture capitalists having a diversity of experience so promising ideas are not abandoned for lack of an investor with the background needed to understand them (to some extent). This way the entrepreneur can have a mentor in each of the development stages. Third, a high level of dynamics requires managers with the vibrancy to be alert to new methods and the education to evaluate them. Finally, a high level of dynamics requires consumers with the "venturesomeness," interest, and financial means to evaluate the new products in the shopping mall and to risk taking some of them home to give them a try.

It is evident, then, that a country's economic institutions and its business culture, and not just the rule of law and private property rights, have a decisive impact on the actors in the innovation process and thus add to or detract from an economy's dynamics. When things go awry, the government has to stand ready to step in, although it will not always know what would be useful to do.

A high level of dynamics expands employment—it generates more jobs than it destroys—through the creation of jobs in development, marketing, and management. It should be pointed out that high level of dynamics has invaluable effects on the workplace experience—benefits consisting of the personal and intellectual development of employees as well as entrepreneurs. In advanced economies, the mechanisms of innovation and discovery form that experience, such as the degree to which employees feel engaged and vital in their jobs, and the rewards, such as job satisfaction and enthusiasm, of participating in the workplace. Without such dynamics, jobs would not offer much in the way of nonpecuniary rewards.

It was thought in continental Europe during the 1920s and 1930s that the bourgeois entrepreneurs were not able or motivated to generate new commercial ideas and that a type of system that was more "coordinated" would be capable of producing faster economic growth. This impression invited the thought of a better system, a tripartite economy, whereby the government, working with leaders of industry and organized labor, would set the main directions of the economy.

Then there was also a thread of equalitarianism—the idea that it is out of place or inappropriate for a person to do anything that would attract attention in the group to which he or she belonged.

There was a de-emphasis on material things. A German person would rather reluctantly concede that he had inherited his wealth than sheepishly admit that he had made his fortune himself.

It was also thought that by setting up institutions for collective bargaining between industries and unions, industrial peace would be served, with the government acting as a mediator if necessary.

Although it is hard to ascertain reliably how well or poorly such systems worked in the interwar period, capitalism in continental Europe continued to be an object of pervasive criticism in the postwar period after 1945.

With the emergence of Ludwig Erhard, West Germany had the opportunity to strike out on a new course. The term "social market economy" arose as a label for the newly emerging system or the main features of it.

Many observers still take the term "social market economy" to mean a capitalist system blended with a welfare state consisting of some basic social insurance and social assistance programs. However, capitalism never implied the omission of any such social insurance programs, and Hayek himself wanted to include some government plans. Then Ludwig Erhard claimed that competition was social because it was in the interest of society—as if to imply that no welfare state baggage was indicated or required.[352]

Nevertheless, in practice, the social market economy has come to refer to an economic system with two new characteristic features: codetermination of the management of corporations by the employees side by side with the owners, and a variety of obligations and penalties imposed on employers and rights conferred on employees. In short, ownership of capital came to be shared between employees and owners. Meanwhile, there continue to be the strands of social thought from the interwar period as mentioned above—the equalitarianism, the antimaterialism, and the idea of social partners.

Concerning capitalism, there is a significant amount of data and empirical evidence based on many decades of observation around the world. It is clear that where well-functioning capitalism is feasible or supportable, for example in Singapore, Japan, South Korea, and the United States, it is *better* for the stimulation, development, and evaluation of new innovative ideas than either socialism or the West European reversed social market economy system.

Incidentally, is capitalism *fair* after all? If so, how exactly might a country move in that direction—what would be the best operational steps? What must be done to create more economic dynamics and better lives?

There is no magic bullet; many initiatives must be taken, and regrettably it will never be known for sure which initiatives were the most important ones.

Some areas can be safely ignored in any program of fundamental reforms. For example, modifying in either direction the duration or the size of the benefit paid to unemployed workers is a step that will not transform the economy into one with high dynamics. In general, it is unfortunate that the political parties are so occupied with moving back and forth some specific standard policy levers, such as tax rates, the budgetary balance, and trade policy. These moves tend to be cyclical, rather than one-way. Moreover, they do not promise to raise dynamics appreciably.

Globalization and Migration

Globalization is the actual and practical erasure of national boundaries with the paving of the way not only to free movement of capital and goods but also to free movement of labor pools in the form of uncontrolled migration from areas of high population growth. The impact of globalization on a national economy, culture, and demography could be devastating.

The prevailing tone that is in favor of globalization, free trade, or free capital movement is not usually or directly associated with migration or demography. Were globalization to be accomplished by free movement of people, demographers would certainly be paying attention. However, since globalization is being primarily driven by free migration of goods and capital, with labor a distant third regarding mobility, few have noticed that the economic consequences of this free flow of goods and capital are equivalent to those that are under a free movement of labor. The same demographic and economic forces drive these economic consequences that would determine labor migration—if only labor were free to migrate.

The economic tendency resulting from competition should be the equalizing of wages and social standards across boundaries. However, instead of cheap labor moving to where the capital is, bidding wages down, capital will mostly move to where the cheap labor is and bid wages up (or would do so if there were not a nearly unlimited supply of cheap labor—a Malthusian situation that still prevails in much of the world). Wages in the capital-exporting rich country are driven down, as if the newly employed laborers in the low-wage country had immigrated to the high-wage country. The determinant of wages in the low-wage country is not labor productivity but an excess or rapidly growing supply of labor at near-subsistence wages. This demographic condition, involving a very numerous and still rapidly growing underclass in the Third World, is one for which demographers have many explanations, beginning with Malthus.[353]

Globalization, fashionably considered by many to be the inevitable wave of the future, is frequently confused with internationalization but is, in fact, something entirely different.

"Internationalization" refers to the increasing importance of international relations, such as international trade, treaties, and alliances. "International," as expected, refers to connections between or among nations, and although relations among the nations become increasingly necessary and important, the nation remains the central unit in the connection.

"Globalization" refers to the economic *integration* of formerly national economies into one global structure, mostly by trade and capital mobility but also by free labor movement by way of uncontrolled migration. Globalization is the practical erasure of national boundaries first for economic, but ultimately for political, purposes. What was once international becomes merely interregional.

The word "integration" derives from the Latin "*integer*," meaning "whole" or a complete "one." The noun "integration" refers to the act of combining the many into one whole. Since there can be only one whole global entity, global economic integration logically implies national economic disintegration. One has to break some eggs to make an omelet, and the breaking of national eggs is necessary to make the global omelet.

It is therefore dishonest to celebrate the benefits of global integration without counting the ensuing costs of national disintegration—and those costs are very significant.

It is also not a random happening that the world's population explosion has only *recently* affected wages in the industrial world. The British did not allow colonial India, for instance, to compete in global markets with its cheap labor; nor did the Chinese seek to do so under the isolation policies of Chairman Mao. Only in the last thirty-five years has the World Bank become converted to the now incontestable orthodoxy of export-led development based on foreign investment as the key part of the structural adjustment. Although "free trade" is the new mantra today, it now means something entirely different from what it represented in the early nineteenth century, when British economist David Ricardo gave it the enduring blessing of his comparative advantage argument.[354]

In the classical nineteenth-century vision of Ricardo and Adam Smith, the national community embraced both domestic labor and local capital. These two factors of production cooperated (albeit with conflict) to make domestically produced goods of the particular country, which then competed in international markets against the goods of other nations produced by their domestic capital–labor factors. That was internationalization, as defined above.

In the twenty-first century, both capital and goods are free to move internationally in the globally integrated world, and capital, or at least money, can be transferred electronically with almost no effort at all. However, free capital mobility undercuts Ricardo's comparative advantage theory of free trade in goods, because that argument explicitly presupposes that capital and other factors remain immobile between nations. Nevertheless, under the new globalization regime and to pursue absolute advantage, capital tends to flow to wherever costs are lowest.

The conventional wisdom is that if free trade in goods is beneficial, then free trade in capital must be even more useful. However, the conclusion of an argument cannot be used to deny one of its premises. Moreover, it no longer makes sense to think of national factors of labor and capital in the globalized economy, since there are competing global capitalists and domestic laborers thrown into the global competition by mobile capital.

So what about the costs mentioned above? What are the consequences of globalization for the national community?

One thing is evident in the West today: the abrogation of the underlying social agreement between labor and capital over how to split up and assign the value they jointly add to raw materials as well as the cost of the raw materials themselves (i.e., nature's often-uncounted value added). That agreement has once been reached nationally—not internationally, and much less globally. That agreement was not reached by economic theory either, but rather through generations of national debate, elections, strikes, lockouts, court decisions, and violent conflicts. That agreement, on which the national community and industrial peace depend, is being repudiated in the interests of global integration; that is a very poor trade indeed, even if one calls it "free trade."

At an even more profound level then, what if globalization began to entail the overt encouragement of free and uncontrolled migration? The radical cosmopolitanism of such a policy would lead to a massive relocation of people between world regions of vastly differing wealth, creating a tragedy of the open access community. The strain on local communities, on both the sending and receiving ends, would be enormous. In the face of unlimited and uncontrolled migration, how could any national community maintain a minimum wage, a welfare program, subsidized medical care, or a public school system? How could a nation punish its lawbreakers and tax evaders if citizens were free to emigrate?

Alternatively, would it not make more sense and be much cheaper to encourage or even force the emigration of a country's poor, sick, or criminal elements instead of running welfare programs, charity hospitals, and prisons? Fidel Castro took this course of action in opening Cuba's jails in 1980; his policy encouraged the migration of prisoners and others that became part of the wave of Marielito immigrants to the United States. Some Eastern European countries have allegedly also tried to unload their Roma and Sinti population on more affluent Western nations.

Furthermore, one might reasonably wonder how a country could reap the benefit of educational investments made in its citizens if those citizens are entirely free to emigrate. Why would nations continue to make such investments in the face of free migration and a continuing brain drain? Why would a country make investments in education if it experienced massive immigration pressures, which would dilute the educational resources of the nation and help subsidize the labor needs of wealthier countries? Why would a country try to limit its birth rate when its youths who migrate abroad and send back remittances can be a sound investment—a fact that might even make that country increase its birth rate? With unfettered migration, a country could never control its population, so why even talk about the controversial issue of birth control?

The global community should be considered as a community of communities—a confederation of nations and states—instead of a foreign and cosmopolitan world government without any historical roots in and direct attachment to real and local communities.

"A world without boundaries" makes for a romantic and naive song lyric, but community and policy cannot exist without boundaries. For mainstream neoliberal economists, only the individual is real (a very liberal position indeed); "community" is just a misleading name for the sum of individuals. From that perspective, national communities impose distorting interferences upon the individualistic free market, and their disintegration is not a cost due to a loss but something to be welcomed. Nevertheless, this aspect of globalization is just another way in which capitalism undermines the very conditions it requires to function; it undermines capitalism itself—and this is the eternal dream of socialism.

Some migration is a good thing—but free migration, where "free" means "uncontrolled; unlimited," as in "free trade" or "free capital mobility," is something entirely different. Immigration is a policy, not a person, and the global cosmopolitans think that it is immoral to make any policy distinction between citizens and noncitizens of a country, and therefore they favor free migration. They also suggest that free migration is the shortest route to their vision of the summum bonum, or the greatest good—equality of wages worldwide. Their point is fair enough; there is some logic in their position, so long as the wages are equalized at a low level. However, those who support free migration as the shortest route to equality of wages worldwide could only with great difficulty try to contend with problems of an open-access community, the destruction of local community, and other issues raised above.

A better moral guide must be the recognition that, as a member of a national community, one's responsibility to noncitizens is to do them no harm, while one's duty to fellow citizens is to do them no harm and always try to do positive good. The many dire consequences of globalization besides those mentioned above amply show that the "do no harm" benchmark is still far from being met. A synopsis of these other consequences must include the overspecialization in a few volatile export commodities (petroleum, timber, minerals, and other extractive goods with little value added locally, for instance). It must also include the crushing debt burdens, exchange rate risks, speculative currency destabilization, foreign corporate control of national markets, unnecessary monopolization of trade-related intellectual property rights (patents on prescription drugs, typically), and, not least, unlimited immigration in the interests of lower wages and cheaper exports.

I. Globalization and Its Effect on the Home Base

What does "globalization" mean again? It is a process in which activities and relations between individuals and institutions expand beyond the local and national all the way to the international or global. Globalization is about economics first, arising from finance, trade, and production, but it very quickly comes to involve social elements, such as tourism and migration, and with the increasing emphasis on communication through the media, it begins to refer to a spreading form of shared political awareness.

"Globalization" is a rather captivating term very much liked by the media and others who live by spinning words. It is something of an enhanced, modernized, and politically correct euphemism for "postnational" and "postindustrial." One vital globalizing force is television, a visual medium; vision, as Hobbes pointed out long ago, is the sense out of our five senses that encourages our propensity to fantasy. What we see is often superficial.[355]

This global visual medium helps create a new situation in which millions of people become increasingly aware of a materially delightful lifestyle available to other people—foreigners, the wealthy—that they cannot possibly share in, because it has taken the West centuries to work it out and develop the capital on which it depends. The resources for everybody sharing it do not exist in current technology. It requires such moral virtues that not all inhabitants of this world possess. These attributes include prudence, self-control, discipline, conscientiousness, regularity of work and, above all, a concept of other people to be treated with respect, dignity, and tolerance as fellow human beings—in contrast with those who take only such people seriously who are kin to them. "Treat a stranger as a thief," states an old Japanese saying, although one would never believe its truthfulness when meeting with present-day Japanese people who possess all those attributes mentioned above.

Regrettably, several nations still lack many of these virtues and have proved, in our time, incapable of running modern societies. The virtues these countries do have—tribal or ethnic solidarity, for example—are self-defeating in market terms, though not, perhaps, in war economies.

Some early form of globalization, or at least economic relations extending beyond the local, occurred for millennia up to 1914. After that, protectionism, mercantilism, and different varieties of war economies dominated the world until after 1945.

The significance of the idea of globalization is that it has become the basis for a political argument, such as "We human beings are now becoming increasingly interdependent and need 'global institutions' to respond to this new situation." Environmentalists are especially prominent in arguing that international authority must supersede national authority. Among many declared foes of any national concept, the European Union makes every attempt to defeat national entities. Hundreds of often coercive international treaties cover such varied issues as the environment, trade, and human rights.

The concept of globalization suggests that the world is moving inexorably toward an achieved unity, a system that embraces everyone; and this unity, though no doubt moral regarding human rights, is based on economic considerations. The assumption according to which the laws of economics are universal and human beings may be understood as pursuers of incentives feeds into the implication that only globalization can assure a peaceful future; it sometimes functions as another branch of the—naturally liberal-democratic—thesis of the end of history. The universal media hype holds that globalization is an unavoidable and unstoppable force, with democracy spreading through the world and the nation-state losing its validity to exist.

Since the United States has become concerned about the flight of high-skill, high-wage information technology jobs to low-wage countries, such as India, China or Mexico, it has become clear that globalization critics were right in arguing that trade agreements like NAFTA (North American Free Trade Agreement) were devastating America's manufacturing base and workforce.

According to the news coverage of the infotech job exodus, "The hemorrhaging of tens of thousands of technology jobs in recent years to cheaper workers abroad is already a fact of life – as inevitable, U.S. executives say, as the 1980s migration of Rust Belt manufacturing jobs to Southeast Asia and Latin America."[356]

Alternatively, there is this statement from Barron's series on the outsourcing wave: "Restructuring and global competition could limit the wage growth of white-collar workers in the same way it did to their blue-collar counterparts when manufacturing began to move outside the U.S. a generation ago."[357]

Indeed, one of Barron's articles was titled "Will US Manufacturing Go to Zero?" It explicitly blamed "the liberalization of world trade and the emergence of nations like China, India, and Mexico as centers of manufacturing and technology for U.S. firms" for "speeding up the decline" of US industry.[358]

That is to say, the new conventional wisdom bears out the worst fears of labor unions, environmental groups, and economic nationalists. These repeatedly warned that by opening the US market indiscriminately to developing countries, which was the hallmark of the globalization decade of the 1990s, a lot more jobs would be lost than created in the United States, driving down the wages of America's remaining workers.

The critics explained that the enormous oversupply of skilled or highly trainable workers in Third World countries would result in stagnant and even declining wages in Asia and Latin America even as workers in these globalizing regions produced ever more sophisticated high-value goods. Thus it would be decades at best before Third World workers could become customers for America's remaining industries and consequently rebalance trade flows. Moreover, by the time these clients appeared, the US economy would have already lost too much productive and innovative capacity to generate a revival, and the unprecedented amounts of deficits and debts could well have sparked a financial crisis.

Some globalization critiques have also exposed the central fallacy of promises that American workers would always beat the competition by reeducating and retraining themselves for the highest tech jobs. The critics observed that white-collar "new economy" jobs had already begun streaming to low-wage countries, and these countries also recognized the importance of educating and training their workers to attract high-value investment.

As American companies talk about sending abroad even Wall Street research and analysis jobs, it is worth recalling just how vigorous the debate was on globalization's impact on US manufacturing—and how confidently globalization cheerleaders derided the critics' contentions.

There was Princeton economist, *New York Times* columnist, and 2008 winner of the Nobel Prize in Economics Paul Krugman, in 1996, dismissed opponents of current globalization policies as "entirely ignorant men" who are "startlingly crude and ill-informed." One year later, Krugman even claimed that the world was witnessing "a convergence of wages (in low-income countries) and in the West through a process of leveling up, not leveling down."[359]

Ivy League economists Robert Lawrence and Matthew Slaughter determined in 1993 that trade had "nothing to do with the slow increase in average compensation" in developed countries like the United States.[360]

Then Lawrence, in 1998, reprimanded critics by stating that "America's growing links with the rest of the world are not responsible for slower average income growth, higher unemployment, or the productivity slowdown … The charge that American workers and companies must compete on an unlevelled international playing field reflects a misunderstanding of what trade and exchange are all about."[361]

It is critical to remember, however, that domestic manufacturing has millions of workers and enormous amounts of capacity left. Moreover, like infotech and other white-collar service jobs today, most manufacturing jobs have fled to Third World countries; this is not because of natural law or some inevitable process but because trade agreements pushed hard by the US government (and, of course, the multinational corporations behind it) have actively encouraged outsourcing.

Liberalizing trade with the Third World was essential to US multinational companies largely because it opened fast-growing, potentially vast foreign markets for their US-made goods. The Third World's poverty was still too big an obstacle to that goal's success. Instead trade agreements ensured that the US market would remain wide open to goods—and now services—that these companies were increasingly producing abroad (whether fairly and lawfully traded or not).

Therefore, reduce or shut off the outsourcers' access to home-country customers and much of this production will feel powerful incentives to come home.

The George W. Bush administration's trade policy objectives were the finalizing of the Chile and Singapore free trade agreements, the extending of NAFTA to the rest of the Western Hemisphere, and the reaching of a new, Third World–tilted global trade agreement. These policies only accelerated the flight of manufacturing jobs, production, and vital technologies abroad.

Globalization today, as in the nineteenth century, is a highly uncertain process, which can, must, and will be stopped in its current form when it becomes intolerable.

II. Globalism's Failed Promise and Its War on the Nation-State

The disaster in Ukraine has done more than just reveal weaknesses in regional security arrangements. It has exposed fundamental flaws in the basic assumptions underlying that secular faith known as globalization.

Since the 1960s, many liberal opinion-makers, politicians, and their paid stooges have stated and restated, explained, and interpreted the first axiom of globalism, declaring the nation-states obsolete. All of that has been unquestioningly accepted as an article of faith by the smart set. The Western liberal elite has come to believe that nations will wither away in a brave new economically integrated world. Progressive-minded people are to believe that national flags are simply vestiges of a bygone era rather than touchstones of national identity. Individuals' self-identities will be tied not so much to their countries of birth as to their smartphones, whose parts have crossed more borders than five generations of migrants. "iPhone or Android" will mean more to "*Homo modernicus*" than "American or Australian."

Humanity has been promised deracination would lead inevitably to world peace: "Nations that trade with each other do not go to war with each other."[362] Free trade apologists keep repeating this fallacy, facts notwithstanding. It is conveniently made forgotten, for example, that Germany and France were major trading partners before World War I; instead, the "improved" aphorism was coined: "*Democratic nations* that trade with each other do not make war on each other." No rational head of state would upset the harmonious workings of the global economy; nationalist passions would be tempered by "market realities."[363]

It is clear now that the Russians and Ukrainians did not get this message at all; although they have been significant trading partners, the economic realities did not stamp out nationalism. It is a modern Western conceit to view all human aspirations strictly through a materialistic lens. Aleksandr Solzhenitsyn decried Western society's tendency to focus on the accumulation of material goods to the exclusion of all other human characteristics.[364]

Of course, this stubborn insistence on seeing the world in purely economic terms blinded the West to anticipating that President Vladimir Putin could do just what he did regarding Ukraine. President Putin was not supposed to risk upsetting the market, but he did. He was expected to fear sanctions and economic backlash, but he did not.

Therefore, to the "enlightened, reasonable, and sensible" Western intellectuals, the only possible "rational" explanation was that President Putin was disconnected from reality, as German Chancellor Angela Merkel reportedly said.[365]

Blind faith in economism supplies false solutions to puzzling problems proposed by many across the political spectrum. According to them, economic sanctions will promote good behavior in Eastern Europe, and at the same time, economic engagement will promote human rights and religious tolerance in East Asia. In Ukraine, we can even conveniently have it both ways—sanctions *and* engagement: exporting loads of cheap American natural gas will reward our friends and punish our enemies in the future.

Despite developments in Ukraine, Western globalists continue to pursue their postnationalist agenda based on transnational projects envisioned by liberal thinkers fifty years ago. This program rests on the mistaken assumption that nationalism is a thing of the past and that people around the world think, believe, and conduct business in the same manner as the Western elite.

Fortunately, they do not.

The West has come to believe that raising everyone to the Western standard of living will spread Western values. The naively simplistic assumption is that having the same kind of material goods will make everyone the same; that the software will follow the hardware, making it work. President Clinton once used this formulation concerning China: democracy would flourish in China in tandem with a middle class.

However, nationalism and national differences are still alive and well.

Free Trade's Hidden Shackles

Free trade and global integration mean that individual nations are no longer free not to trade. Freedom of *not* to trade is undoubtedly necessary if trading is to remain voluntary—a precondition of its mutual benefit.

To avoid war, nations must both consume less and become more self-sufficient, said the age-old adage. However, free traders say we should become *less* self-reliant and *more globally integrated* as part of the main quest to consume ever more. We must lift up the laboring masses, which now include the formerly high-wage workers, up from their subsistence wages. We are also told that only massive growth can do this.

Can the environment sustain so much growth? It cannot. Moreover, how will the growth dividend—whatever growth dividend there is—ever get to the poor (i.e., how can wages increase given the nearly unlimited global supply of labor)? How could it ever be even expected to have high wages in any country that becomes globally integrated with the globe, which has a vast oversupply of labor? In the desperate struggle to attract capital and jobs, there will always be a standards-lowering contest to keep wages low and minimize any social, safety, and environmental requirements that raise costs.

Some are seduced by the idea of simultaneously "solving" the South's excess population problem and the North's labor shortage problem by migration. However, the North's labor shortage is entirely a function of below-equilibrium wages. The shortage could be instantly removed by an increase in earnings that equated domestic supply and demand—by merely allowing the market to work.

However, the cheap-labor lobbies of the West, mainly multinational corporations, think that we must import workers to keep wages from rising (reducing their profits) and export competitiveness. Of course, this also prevents the vast majority of Western citizens from sharing in the increased prosperity through higher wages. It does not matter; they will still benefit, because the importing of workers is the key to saving Social Security and pension plans—which, we are told, will collapse without growth in the cohort of working-age people provided by immigration. Oh, and when the large group of worker immigrants retires? Well, we will repeat the process, right?

The only solution to the Western countries' problem with Social Security imbalance is the raising of the retirement age and the lowering of benefits—and remembering that paid-in contributions would also rise with the offering of higher wages.

The only real solution to the South's problem is for those countries to lower their birth rates and put their working-age population to use by producing necessities for the home market locally.

Politicians, economists, and demographers are understandably disinclined to prescribe birth control to any country. Who is to say a sovereign country is wrong to choose a large and growing population, low wages, and high inequality over fewer people, higher wages, and less inequality? All nations have to make their own choices, and it is they who will have to live with the consequences, too.

However, while that may be a defensible position under internationalization, it is not justifiable under globalization. After all, the essence of an integrated world is that the consequences of actions, such as cost–benefit decisions concerning the costs of overpopulation and benefits of population control, are externalized globally to all nations.

The costs and benefits of overpopulation in a globalized world are now shared more by class than by nation; labor bears the cost of reduced wage income, and capital enjoys the advantage of reduced wage costs. Both Malthusian and Marxian considerations seem to promote inequality, since both regard wages to tend toward subsistence under capitalism. Marx would probably see globalization as one more capitalist strategy to lower wages, while Malthus might agree, arguing that it is a fact of overpopulation that allows the capitalists' strategy to work in the first place. Therefore, one could only lament the recent tendency of the environmental movement to court political correctness by soft-pedaling issues of population, migration, and globalization.[366]

One of the pits into which the globalizing Western elite falls is undoubtedly the lust for commerce. The Western elite preaches about the global economy, believes in the self-proclaimed myth of an overarching global culture, and piously states that this is all inevitable. However, behind the facade of political correctness, the elite wants nothing else but flat uniformity in the name of governing and commercial convenience.

Unfortunately, Marx was right when he wrote in *The Communist Manifesto* that "the bourgeoisie has set up one solitary unscrupulous freedom – freedom of trade."[367] What communism could not do, the commercialism of capitalism is doing. When commerce dominates, the culture dies.

We all watch the same silly programs on television and are subjected to the same propaganda from governments and industries. The global attack on culture in the name of business is an enormous social cost that must be compared with the imaginary gains of raising Western living standards by creating more low-paying jobs, reducing or eliminating tariffs, and bringing in more cheap goods.

How is the Western standard of living increased if Western culture (what is left of it) deteriorates despite more jobs, goods, and services?

What other painful social and economic adjustments will have to be made to gain these "benefits"?

Is further instability and insecurity what the West needs or wants?

To the degree that some international trade is desirable, are there no alternative ways of securing these benefits without intensifying our dependence on a global economy?

Wilhelm Röpke reminds us of the close relationship that necessarily exists between economic and political order. Intensive international trade tends to induce the formation of a corresponding politics; that is why we all should worry about centralizing trends, such as European political unification and the World Trade Organization (WTO). Röpke's humane economy requires us to keep the beast of economics and trade in its proper place, while at the same time it means the rejection of the mythology of destabilizing, unlimited growth.

THE SUPRANATIONAL CORPORATIONS AND THEIR IGNORANCE OF SOCIETY

The business, media, and financial elite practically beatified Jack Welch, the CEO of General Electric Company (GE) during the last two decades of his rule. The lavish praise continued not only after the release of one of the most heavily promoted books in history but even after his retirement. GE under Welch indeed was a leader; it set the tone for the hard-edged, stock price–obsessed, supranational, ruthless, and cutthroat orientation that is now accepted as the norm or, at least, a shared aspiration for corporations.

However, there was also another side of the Welch era—the immense costs of GE's relentless focus on short-term earnings and share price. GE's business model is a global system of management by anxiety, with the company considering stress as the engine of efficiency; GE believes stressing its workers beyond all limits improves their productivity. It believes that stressing its global production system by always looking to cut costs through layoffs, subcontracting, outsourcing, or moving production to lower-wage and nonunion environments enhances company performance. It believes in stressing its suppliers, going so far as to order both US and foreign businesses to migrate to low-cost countries to service the already relocated production facilities of GE. It believes in stressing—or blackmailing, rather—local neighborhoods by always using the threat of plant closings to secure tax breaks from communities that can ill afford to subsidize GE but can even less afford to lose the GE jobs. It believes in stressing the regulatory system, pushing to the edge—and too frequently beyond—of legal bans on environmental damage, tax evasion, defense contractor fraud, and anticompetitive practices, and it uses its political muscle by employing lobbyists and special-interest groups to stretch the legal limits of what is permissible.

The results concerning human lives have been disastrous. Welch has left behind communities across the United States suffering from mass layoffs and disinvestment. While it is difficult to get a fix on the number of GE layoffs over the last three decades due to the constant convulsing of its businesses, well over one hundred thousand well-paid workers have been dismissed in the United States alone. The company has practically abandoned its once strong and world-renowned research-and-development infrastructure while it has compiled a shameful record of repeated violations of workplace safety rules, defense contractor safeguards, and other public interest regulations, with workers' lives put at risk and taxpayers bilked as a result.

In typical GE style, the company usually responds with full-blown campaigns relying on many management tactics carefully fabricated by one of its lobbying dream teams, enormous tax (avoidance) departments, or law firms. What all of GE's record reveals is the strident opposition to any societal rules that impose costs on GE, and the company's willingness and ability to leverage its economic power into political influence—and to use that political influence to enhance its economic power.

The global financial crisis shook the $170-billion-a-year conglomerate in 2008, almost destroying its financial services unit, and sent its share price from twenty-nine dollars in the days before Lehman Brothers crashed to below six dollars. (It has since recovered somewhat, together with other blue-chip stocks, but it is still only a fraction of what it once was in the year 2000.)

Conventional thinking would suggest that General Electric's diversification across product lines and geography should have done a much better job protecting it from the maelstrom of 2008. However, as the crash of 2008 proves, the problem with major financial crises is that the correlations among assets tend to increase in the moment of truth. In other words, the various businesses of a conglomerate with different exposures to the ebbs and flows of the economic cycle suddenly all react negatively to it, thereby defeating the diversification theory itself.

Looking at GE, one sees a massive, diversified, and profitable conglomerate with a lot of good but very unrelated businesses. Aircraft engines, freight locomotives, and commercial financing carry only limited opportunities for cost reduction and economies of scale. GE's businesses also include medical devices, power generation, consumer lighting, energy management systems, and mission-critical equipment used in oil and gas drilling (subsea, offshore and onshore), as well as liquefied natural gas (LNG), distributed gas, pipeline, storage, refinery, and petrochemical applications.

Within the power generation business segment alone, the company sells gas turbines, generators, integrated gasification combined cycle technology used to convert coal and other hydrocarbons into synthetic gas, steam turbines, nuclear reactors, nuclear fuel and support services, and motors and control systems for oil and gas extraction and mining. In just that one business segment alone, there is an astonishing range of products, any one of which would serve as a significant and viable business in and of itself—but GE has them all rolled up under its corporate umbrella.

Analyzing and evaluating GE's business and where it is going is an absolute nightmare. One could, and should, expound on any one of those products ad nauseam, but GE's current composition requires such a massive amount of analysis to assess and understand the company and the risks involved with it that nobody has any chance to see through the maze. This criticism can be levied on many large conglomerates today.

Since the financial collapse, investors are far more risk-averse—and naturally so. Looking at GE with all of its seemingly unrelated businesses and subsidiaries, it is easy to see why investors and analysts have said "why bother" to the daunting task of evaluating the company's exhibiting only moderate revenue growth over the past decade.

The implications of this for GE are that its decades-long efforts to become a diversified company have been for nothing, because the primary argument for that diversification, namely safety during crises, has been proven invalidated by severe liquidity events in the financial markets. The conglomerate structure has become contradictory to the idea of diversification, where diversified assets are supposed to be independent of one another. However, in a conglomerate like GE, the combination of businesses serves to support each division; in effect, all of the businesses become correlated although they would not be if separate.

Another aspect of a supranational company's governing strategy is the emphasis on using government contracts and bailouts to bolster its business.

For example, by way of a loophole in the regulations underpinning the Federal Deposit Insurance Corporation (FDIC), GE was able to rescue its borderline insolvent GE Capital division by using the Temporary Liquidity Guarantee Program to issue nearly $74 billion in debt.[368] Without that guarantee, it is unlikely GE Capital would have been able to continue to function, since—like so many other financial institutions that stood on the precipice in 2008—it was dependent on borrowing short and lending long. Once the short-term markets tightened up, firms whose operations depended on such cheap financing faced severe liquidity issues. What this means is that GE Capital encumbers General Electric with such financial risk that bankruptcy becomes a real danger not only to that subsidiary itself but also to the entire firm during turbulent times. This risk correlation has to be factored in to any analysis of supranational corporations, including General Electric.

The *Wall Street Journal* published an op-ed entitled "The Great Misallocators" in 2011. The essence of the piece was that politically allocated capital is inherently less efficient than privately allocated money and will lead, as a result, to slower economic growth than the alternative. The *Wall Street Journal* epitomized the relationship between General Electric and the United States government with the following quote from Jeffrey Immelt, GE's CEO: "The interaction between government and business will change forever. In a reset economy, the government will be a regulator; and also an industry policy champion, a financier, and a key partner."[369]

Quite understandably, the government needs to make purchases from private companies, and for many of those purchases, GE is an ideal supplier. However, GE has been going to the US government, including the Obama administration, hat in hand and pushing the administration's policies, such as cap-and-trade and the expansion of wind generation, to curry favor among federal appropriators. Cap-and-trade is an environmental policy tool that is supposed to deliver results with a mandatory upper limit on emissions while providing the responsible sources flexibility in how they comply.

Given the historical inefficiency of state-owned enterprises as observed across multiple countries, such cozy relationships between corrupt, incompetent, and politically motivated governments and power-hungry supranational companies motivated solely by the profit motive should make anyone feel very uncomfortable.

Whenever the government serves as partner, financier, and regulator in one (see the housing market), there is an inherent conflict of interest. How such a relationship could rebound on GE is impossible to foresee and, therefore, impossible to price. The government does not give federal contracts solely based on merit (much to the chagrin of most of the electorate).

For a supranational firm like GE wanting to ingratiate itself to such a murky, if undoubtedly profitable, state-controlled market serves as a legitimized escape from appealing to the private-customer-driven market it should be working to win over instead. Alternatively, it is a tacit admission that it cannot win over that market any longer. Therefore, it can be expected that General Electric, like many other supranational firms with oversize greed and undersized social responsibility, has every intention of significantly expanding the company's dealing with not only the US but also any and all governments.

Concerning GE, analysts have often criticized its management's ability to state the operating results of the company's myriad businesses unequivocally. It is complicated to evaluate each business segment on its own merits and then compare it with appropriate peers in the industry and determine whether managers of a particular business segment are allocating resources in the most optimal way for shareholder growth. Being a jack-of-all-trades is not necessarily a bad thing, and when an organization like GE has its hands in multiple businesses, it also has the potential to reduce the cyclic nature of its net earnings.

On the other hand, when the organization has several hitherto successful businesses, it can be hard for management to focus on building out one particular business. By extension, this may prevent the company from becoming (or remaining) the best in any one business—and investors tend to flock to companies that are best in class, not secondary or tertiary players.

The False Fetish of Economic Growth

The usual defenders of the free market, the modern Western political and financial elites, are not primarily concerned with private property or liberty. They are firstly concerned with economic growth, which mainly means constant economic, technical, and social change.

When airplanes became popular, air travel would have been challenging and costly if traditional rights in the air had been respected (flying through airspace was a trespass). Instead these rights were dismissed to accommodate air travel in the 1920s, since a free market with traditional air and property rights would have impeded growth. The growth of this sort ultimately uses property rights as its disposable tools. The full pursuit of this ideology gives rise to some social and economic problems, which were the subject matter of some of Wilhelm Röpke's work.

Two kinds of goods or markets must be set apart. The first market includes material goods that can be mass-produced, such as cars, clothing, consumer electronics, and Big Macs; the second market includes all those goods that not only cannot be mass-produced but, in fact, must remain in limited supply no matter how much they are in demand. These goods of the second market involve social and economic positions of prestige and high income, such as the desire to be a corporation's president.

Furthermore, the commitment to unlimited growth in the first kind of goods, which may be mass-produced and so made available to everyone, also whets the appetite for things that cannot be mass-produced and made available to everyone. All can have Big Macs, but not all can be presidents of corporations. Alternatively, we might like to have a cottage on the shores of a secluded lake. However, as more people buy cottages, the lake is no longer secluded, the price rises dramatically until perhaps only the wealthy can afford it, and the result is inextricable frustration.

In a like manner, one generation may work to provide the basics of a good home and other material necessities, and when these needs are met through economic growth, the family demands the nonproducible or nonexpandable goods for their children, such as important positions commanding higher incomes. "I do not want my children to labor as I did, but to be plant managers or executives." That sounds very admirable, but what if all factory workers want their children to become plant managers too? Since employers must have some way to decide among potential managers, education becomes the standard before commensurable experience: one must have a high school degree first. This standard education works for a while, but word leaks out and more people get high school degrees. Therefore, the standard is raised again so that plant managers must have college education now. This cycle keeps repeating, and in the next go-round the requirement is raised again to the now typical master of business administration (MBA).

Just as in the case of the secluded lake problem, demand is greater than the limited supply, which cannot possibly be increased to the satisfaction of all. In this particular case, more and more has to be invested in education to get the good jobs, which is the final goal here. However, the lengthening of the educational process—the buying of more education—is (indirectly) a cost and not an immediate benefit; it is an intermediate product that we have to buy to get what we want.

The problem of excessive growth can also be illustrated in another way by looking at an imaginary person, Mike Moreless. Twenty years ago, Mike got up at seven o'clock in the morning to get to work and arrived at his office at eight o'clock. Today Mike must get up at six o'clock to arrive at the same time.

Why is Mike less efficient in getting to work today? He must spend more time getting ready for work, and especially more time driving to work, to get to the office on time. The lengthened commuting time results in higher costs for more gasoline and auto maintenance (e.g., tires, oil changes, brakes, and eventually the entire vehicle). Mike also has to buy another radio for the kitchen so he can listen to the traffic news to avoid congested roads if possible, and he buys a GPS to find these routes. He must spend more time preparing and planning for his trip and its delays. Mike's insurance rates go up too, because he lives in a congested area now and because he drives more miles than twenty years ago. His taxes similarly go up to cover the increased costs of police, fire department, and ambulance services needed to clear the highways after accidents and to minimize traffic delays. Mike buys a battery-operated razor to shave in his car during the inevitable delays, along with a smartphone to conduct business en route, not even mentioning the increased stress, air pollution, and corresponding health costs.

Nevertheless, the same radio news that reports on the latest traffic jams also gives the most recent economic reports (or rather government propaganda), reassuring Mike that his life is getting *better* because of his consumption. His spending for all these things he has bought has gone up, and so, with the help of his fellow citizens, he has helped increase the gross national product (GNP). Mike knows he consumes (spends) more, but he somehow feels he is getting *less*. These extra, and ever increasing, amounts of consumption are not his primary goals. They are merely in-between items—things necessary to get what he wants. That makes them a cost to him, not a benefit. Unfortunately, because of the nature of the GNP and its manner of calculation, we cannot see this difference in the reported numbers; no economic report separates out the growing need for in-between goods from those of primary satisfaction. So it looks like life is better than before, and the elites of the world rejoice. However, Mike's life becomes ever more hectic, frustrating, and increasingly one of "getting ready to get ready" as the chain of in-between goods gets longer.

One only hears that many Americans must now work four or five months out of a year just to pay taxes. How much time out of every working day must Mike sacrifice just to be able to get to work? At the very best, he must work harder and give up more just to stay in the same place and keep the same social and economic position.

Economists and their employers are fond of comparing economic growth with a rising tide that causes everybody's ship to be raised. The tidal wave of material growth means that everyone today consumes more than he did before—certainly more than his grandfather did. However, after we have satisfied our basic needs, this becomes less and less relevant. People today do not care that they earn and consume more than their ancestors. If they want that secluded lakeshore cottage, for example, they must make not only more money than their ancestors did before but also what their presently living neighbors earn today. This means that in a prosperous economy (all ships having plenty of clearance above the seafloor or the ship's height above the seabed) the demand necessarily expands to include all the aspiring to become relatively still wealthier. That is, one's ship must rise *higher* than the others to get the desired nonproducible goods and services.

Apparently, no matter how high it is, the tide in itself will not change one's position relative to the position of one's neighbor. This fact makes all the extravagant promises of growth economists (seemingly most of them) deceptive; these are nothing but a mirage, because once you get to the good life, it vanishes or moves still farther away. Our expectations increase, but their fulfillment diminishes.

The resulting inevitable frustration is manifested in several ways, but perhaps the most significant is the tendency to acquire those advantages we could not obtain in the market by changing the government policies in our favor instead. In this way, the glorification of economic growth induces still more government growth.

If we want to reduce the ever-increasing size of government and be less frustrated economically, we must abandon our commitment to limitless economic growth by reorienting national policy to the issue of distribution—not as socialists conceive the problem but in the manner of Röpke's "Third Way."

The following two main points must still be discussed: unlimited economic growth ultimately undermines the moral foundations it presupposes; this occurs because of a confusion of logic.

I. Undermining the Foundations

In the Middle Ages, Christian philosophers were concerned with questions of justice in economic exchange. The problem of rationing out the economic pie or who acquires what in the economy was answered concerning the economic justice rooted heavily in religious doctrine, social structure, the concept of social status, and the afterlife. However, with the rise of the modern industrial economy, the appeal was made to a doctrine of "natural harmony." This theory claimed that there is natural coordination in the workings of the free market system so that if society follows the economic laws, things generally will turn out all right and all people will benefit economically.[370]

Recently that doctrine was modernized to be dynamic; that is, there is a natural harmony through time. If a person is poor today, that is one thing, but with hard work in a free economy, he or she will be less poor tomorrow and eventually perhaps even rich; there is certainly nothing locking someone into poverty, such as a rigid and static social system.

However, when one also applies this same reasoning to morality—that is, to make moral questions unpolitical by designating them as a purely subjective preference, the unintended social consequences are always unhealthy. Any policy that seeks to smooth over the issue of economic distribution to dodge the question of who gets what also necessarily avoids the issue of morality by assuming economic growth is a substitute for justice. If injustices exist, they will be corrected over time through economic growth in a mostly propitious market system.

Nevertheless, this naively optimistic blindness to the social and historical conditions of market realities increasingly neglects the moral aspects of life. It has been assumed that pure self-interest acting in a moral vacuum is both sufficient to produce economically good results and also socially benign. Some point with pride to the past successes of capitalism but fail to understand that the West has been living off the moral capital of earlier centuries over the past two hundred years. The legacy of the precapitalist and preindustrial past is the social morality that has served as a foundation for economic individualism. This legacy has diminished not only with time and the corrosive contact of capitalist values but also with the increased anonymity and mobility of the industrial society.

The philosophical force behind this corrosion is pragmatism. Pragmatism is the philosophy that claims the test of truth or belief lies exclusively in its practical consequences; beyond this, our beliefs and conceptions have no meaning. This has led to such a narrow interpretation of "consequences" that only what can be manipulated and controlled is what counts. With that has come the natural reliance on quantification as the touchstone of truth. The bottom line of pragmatism is the material success of the individual; if it works, in this crass sense, it is true.

Just to avoid the red tape, "false interpretation," and subjective judgments of the results, the evaluation of the effectiveness of military units during the Vietnam War was finally reduced to the simple but gruesome reliance on mere body counts instead of the broader and qualitative military objectives. Let us take as the second example the case of public education teachers who are evaluated by the number of students passing quantifiable tests easily. A third, more ordinary, example is familiar to sales clerks in retail stores who are awarded extra pay based strictly on their volume of sales.

What does all this mean morally? It tends to eliminate reliance on internalized moral standards and turns our dependence on those things that give immediate, tangible, or material rewards. Those internal moral checks become another name for "character," which is what a person does when no one is looking.

Pragmatism, which places strict emphasis on consequences, encourages us to do only what people see us do and get paid for, and it leads to easily foreseeable abuses: leaders of military units ignored other military aspects and focused only on the body counts—and sometimes fudged these. Teachers also ignored other aspects of teaching—for instance, personal attention to an interested student—and merely taught to the test because that is all they were evaluated on. Because they are rewarded for sales only and not on other aspects, the most aggressive sales clerk who gets the highest commission is often the one who most neglects the other aspects. These aspects, such as cleaning the merchandise and the store or displaying products tastefully, must be taken care of by others, if at all. Anything that broadly involves taking extra time or qualitative aspects is understandably neglected. In all three cases, the more critical objectives—such as the war, education, and excellent service—suffer.

All three cases show a bias for proxy and statistical methods: body counts, multiple-choice tests, and numbers of sales. In such a pragmatic world, doing right because it is right does not count; the character does not pay.

Moreover, this pragmatism is revealed not only in economic theory or in the way economists think professionally but also how people behave in the actual market. The very essence of the market process itself is that individuals always try to get the best deal they can have. The efficient allocation of resources by the market requires that individuals then use their available resources for whatever objective they happen to have. It is not surprising, then, if the people of a society entirely devoted to this principle of individual self-interest cannot enjoy sociability and friendliness as individuals. They can have those qualities only collectively as communities that believe in more than a me-first lifestyle, or greed.

It is hard to see that people have much room in their lives for more than immediate material benefits, given this individual self-interest. Greed will not recognize any inner necessity of work but will only acknowledge money, wages, or profits—the economist's useful proxy for what is economically sound or healthy—and this is then rendered the absolute and perfect essential element of economic activity.

A similar story is true concerning the increased dependence on GNP statistics. This addiction to statistics erodes the reliance on internal moral checks—on doing what is right because it is right and not because it brings immediate consequences, material or otherwise (save, perhaps, inner satisfaction). It detracts from the broader human aspects of the economy, focusing attention and efforts on the quantifiable instead. Such statistical measures as the GNP, kept since about World War II, have themselves contributed to the rising demands and expectations. The renewed interest in economic growth that took place following World War II was itself a product of the statistics. A run of numbers, showing a decided tendency to upward movement demonstrated a pattern of growth with a regularity that might not otherwise have been discerned.

Owing to improved statistical techniques and the employment of high-speed computers, workers in all occupations have now become hypersensitive to movements in their real wages and positions in the pay structure. They are inspired by the growth gospel and encouraged by government pronouncements helped by the spread of news media and the surge of materialistic expectations.

The same emphasis on the quantifiable explains why pure capitalism as an economic system, not a social one, is biased in favor of material goods and services as opposed to those aspects of life that are impossible to quantify, such as neighborliness, solidarity, community, altruism, friendliness, or sociability. In this way, if statistics and numbers are the official manifestations of economic pragmatism, then the GNP is the body count of the economy, and unlimited growth is its Vietnam.

II. Confused Thinking

The liberal-libertarian arguments for ever more individual freedom and consumption (growth) are flawed on logical grounds. What is good or rational for the individual is not necessarily good or rational for society. What is correct in the short term is not necessarily right in the long term. If more freedom and growth benefit individuals who pragmatically pursue private ends but at the same time undermine those social structures and values that such action presupposes, such as the family, the community, and those internal moral checks, the argument is not even economically sound.

Increased specialization, another name for economic growth, reduces market coordination and gives us the business cycle instability—the boom and bust of the capitalist system. As Röpke argues repeatedly, growth in the division of labor renders coordination among the various firms more difficult. Also, as workers specialize in narrower and narrower fields and new jobs are generated in the marketplace, it is harder for the price mechanism to coordinate investments and expand credit properly; the harmonizing or coordination finally comes to correct economic overexpansion only in a recession. Moreover, these effects are worsened by the individualistic (greed) ethic as the scope of coordination is proportionately reduced by growth with technical specialization; that is, more new jobs exist with narrower fields. The harmony is reduced still further by the encouragement to focus on self: each investor or consumer is concerned only about what is in it for him or her. There is no thought concerning the common good, and even if there were, it burdens individual effort to comprehend how all these different parts connect. During the business cycle, some employers lay off employees, which leads to the laying off of other workers, which eventually leads to still more employers firing workers elsewhere, and so on, until the result is a depression that no one wanted but all helped bring about.

This same complexity obscures the relationship between effort and reward. One's additional hard work will not prevent that person from being unemployed by automation, and if the person retrains, that will only delay another round of unemployment. Why should this individual work harder then? All this also heightens the fear of economic loss (unemployment). The effect is to increase reliance on the individualistic ethos of "what's in it for me now," and one will want higher wages regardless of one's productivity. One deserves the rewards of any increase in output no matter where one comes from. This demand can be seen as a way of protecting oneself from the fallout of growth. The combined effects of the interlocking economy encourage the individual to act in his or her self-interest. However, these effects will probably have an adverse impact on the person's job and income in the future, and when this is coupled with the individualistic ethos, the result is the belief that all must share—indeed, have a right to—whatever growth there is (to redistribute). It is easy to recognize from this how special interests will dominate politics, which is treated as a personal market, and budget agreements are painfully difficult to achieve.

There are many other typical examples. If people in the front rows of a football stadium stand up, they may see better at first, but everyone else behind them also has to get up just to preserve the same view.

If the city bus service raises its fares and loses some customers and so raises its fares again and then loses still more passengers and so on until it goes out of business, each customer who dropped out helped contribute to the collapse of the service even though it was not his or her plan to do so.

In the arms race during the Cold War, each side increased its quantity and quality of weapons and escalated matters to dangerous levels that neither side wanted but both helped create.

In the beginning days of oil well drilling, every company in that business wanted to pump out oil as fast as they could before the competition would get more oil out, thus wasting tremendous amounts of the resource, which nobody wanted but everybody helped bring about.

If a few early capitalists compete with one another and generate families like the Morgans, Rockefellers, and Carnegies, with large landed estates, portrait collections, and yachts, society and the economy can bear all that. However, if people are told that all of them can live like this through economic growth over time, the result is unmitigated frustration, the same as if all soldiers were told that with patience and hard work they could all become generals someday; this just cannot be done. Until this is realized, we will continue to face economic and political frustrations.

The automobile, starting out first as a rich man's toy, has eventually become available to all. However, by the time all people could have a car, the environment had changed entirely. The same mass production that makes the car available to all today makes it also a necessity, in that all other alternative modes of transportation have been either eliminated or neglected. The car has become an embedded part of life, and one must have one to get along and live in society. An entire pattern of life has emerged that is increasingly dependent on the automobile. Also, various restrictions, rules, and regulations on the freedom of its use, which were unnecessary when only the wealthy could afford a car, have become indispensable because many have one. The experience with the car for the poor man today is not the same as was for the rich man at the beginning of the twentieth century. Plato's saying "necessity is the mother of invention" has been reversed: the invention of the automobile is the necessity of today.

The figure of a marching column can more broadly illustrate the same problem. The vanguard of the column is always the first to enjoy the fruits of economic growth; the rest of the column following it eventually arrives at where the vanguard has been before. In economic terms, it means that most people can have tomorrow what the wealthy can have today. Now the problem is this: by the very act of marching and by the time the end of the column reaches the point where the vanguard had been before, the economic and social "turf" has become so deteriorated that what the rest of the column gets is *not the same* as what the vanguard got first. A middle-class professional who now could afford to go on an exclusive tour to visit a once exotic site would find the place ruined by mass tourism today.

Finally, the most readily felt cost of our growth obsession is the common problem of the time crunch. Although both production and consumption levels have gone up, the amount of time people have for the stress-free enjoyment of these products remains constant. The result is the feeling of being harassed.

III. Conclusion

The commitment to endless increases in consumption and growth is ultimately counterproductive, since the social and moral costs are higher than the economic benefits. In fact, the experience of people living in modern Western societies is one of *constraint* rather than freedom—of dearth more than abundance. One of the paradoxes of history is the sense of abundance perceived by older and simpler societies as opposed to the sense of scarcity felt by the ostensibly wealthy societies of today. This contradiction is the reason for modern man's feeling of slow economic strangulation—his sense of never having enough to meet the needs that his pattern of life imposes on him. Standards of consumption that he cannot meet and does not need to meet come virtually in the guise of duties. As the scarcity of the complicated life has replaced the abundance of simple living, it seems that in some still unexplained way we have formalized prosperity until it has become, for most people, only a figment of the imagination.

We understand how a society based on modern capitalism can be prosperous materially but still feel poor. We can explain how the free market system can struggle along a path of growing decay and why the practicing of individual freedom, choice, and rationality will still not produce a healthy and happy society. Man is a spiritual being, and his freedoms presuppose and are always circumscribed by moral duties. When he neglects these, he may still have a kind of liberty, but it will not give him the satisfaction he wants.

Economic growth does not stop the cultural decline.

13

The Crumbling of the American Middle Class and the Proletarianization of Society

The character of society is determined mostly by the picture it has of itself and what it aspires to be. From this point of view, American society was mainly middle-class one hundred years ago. Its values and aspirations were middle-class values, and power or influence within it was in the hands of middle-class people.

To be sure, even the most vigorous defenders of bourgeois America did not pretend that all Americans were middle-class. However, they did see the United States as organized in middle-class terms, and they looked forward to a not remote future in which everyone would be middle-class except for a small, shiftless minority of no importance. To these defenders, and probably also to the idle minority, American society was regarded as a ladder of opportunity up which anyone could work his way, on rungs of increased affluence, to the supreme positions of wealth and power near the top. The same standard, based on money, obtained all wealth, power, prestige, and respect. This criterion, in turn, was based on pervasive emotional insecurity that sought relief in the ownership and control of material possessions. The basis for this may be seen most clearly in the origins of this bourgeois middle class.

THE HISTORICAL APPEARANCE OF THE MIDDLE CLASS

A thousand years ago, Europe had a two-class society in which great masses of peasants supported a few upper-class nobles and high clergy. While the peasants provided the food and all other material needs of society, the nobles defended this world, and the clergy opened the way to the next one. All three estates had security in their social relationships in that they occupied positions of social status that satisfied their psychological needs for companionship, economic security, a foreseeable future, and purpose of their efforts. Members of both classes had no apprehension about the loss of these things by any likely outcome of events, and all thus had emotional security.

The intrusion of a small, active, distinctly different, and new class between them changed the uncomplicated two-class society in the course of the medieval period, chiefly in the twelfth and thirteenth centuries. Because this new class was in between, it is called "the middle class" today, just as it is also called "bourgeois" (after "*bourg*," meaning "town"), from the fact that it resided in towns, a new kind of social aggregate. The two older, established classes were almost entirely rural and closely associated with the land economically, socially, and spiritually. The permanence of the land and the intimate connection of it with the most basic of human needs, especially food, amplified the emotional security associated with the old classes.

Now the new middle class, the bourgeoisie, who had grown up between the two older classes, had *none* of these things. They were mainly commercial people—merchants concerned with the exchange of goods, mostly luxury goods, in a society where all of their prospective customers could already have every necessity of life, which could be provided only by their privileged status.

The new middle class had *no status* in a society that was based on status; they had *no security* or permanence in a society that placed the highest value on these qualities. Since the old law was mostly about past customs and their activities were not conventional ones, the new middle class had *no law* in a society that highly valued legalities. The flow of supplies, notably food, to the new town dwellers was so precarious that some of their earliest and most decisive actions were to ensure the continuous flow of goods from the surrounding country to the town. All the things the bourgeois did were new things; all were precarious and insecure; their whole lives were lived without the status, permanence, and security that the society of the day most highly valued. The risks and rewards of commercial enterprise, well reflected in the fluctuating fortunes of figures such as Antonio in *The Merchant of Venice*, were extreme, and a single deal could ruin a merchant or make him rich.[371] This insecurity was intensified by the fact that the prevalent religion of the day disapproved of what he was doing—seeking profits or taking an interest—and could see no way of providing religious services to town dwellers because of the intimate association of religion with the existing arrangement of rural landholding.

For these and still other reasons, "psychic insecurity" became the most original description of the new middle-class ideology. The only remedy for this vulnerability of the middle class seemed to be the steady accumulation of ever more material possessions that could demonstrate the world of one's importance, power, and success. For the middle class, the general goal to seek future salvation in the hereafter was secularized to an effort of finding the security of the future still in this world by the acquisition of wealth, its accompanying power, and social prestige. However, the social prestige of wealth was most available among the fellow bourgeoisie rather than among nobles or peasants. Thus the opinions of one's fellow bourgeoisie, by wealth and by conformity to bourgeois values, became the motivating drives of the middle classes, creating what has been called the "acquisitive society."[372]

In that middle-class acquisitive society, prudence, discretion, conformity, moderation (except in acquisition), decorum, and frugality became the marks of a stable and sensible person. Credit became more important than intrinsic personal qualities, and credit was based on the appearances of things—especially the appearances of the external material accessories of life. The facts of a person's qualities, such as kindness, affection, thoughtfulness, generosity, personal insight, and such, were increasingly irrelevant or even adverse to the middle-class evaluation of that person.

Instead the middle-class evaluation rested instead on nonpersonal attributes and external accessories. Where personal qualities were admired, they were those that not only directly contributed to acquisition but also were often opposed to the established values of the Christian outlook, such as love, charity, generosity, gentleness, or unselfishness. These middle-class qualities included decisiveness, selfishness, impersonality, ruthless energy, and insatiable ambition.

As the middle class and its commercialization of all human relationships spread through Western society in the following centuries, it to a great extent modified and to some extent even reversed the values of earlier Western society. In some cases, the old values remained but were redirected, such as future preference and self-discipline. Future preference ceased to be transcendental in its aim and became secularized. Self-discipline ceased to seek spirituality by restraining sensuality and instead pursued material acquisition. In general, although the new middle-class ideology had a substantial religious basis, it was the religion of the medieval heresies and Puritanism rather than the religion of Roman Christianity.

This complex outlook that we call middle-class or bourgeois is, of course, still the primary basis of our world today. The reason that Western society is the wealthiest and most powerful society that has ever existed is that it has been impelled forward along these lines, beyond the reasonable degree necessary to satisfy basic human needs, by the irrational drive for achievement regarding material ambitions. To be sure, Western society always had other kinds of people, too, and the majority of the people probably had other outlooks and values, but it was the middle-class urgency that pushed modern developments in the direction they took. There were always dreamers, truth seekers, and tinkerers in Western society. They, as poets, scientists, and engineers, thought up innovations, which the middle class adopted and exploited if they seemed likely to be profit producing. Middle-class self-discipline and future preference provided the savings and investment, without which any innovation, no matter how appealing in theory, would be set aside and neglected. Moreover, the innovations that could attract middle-class approval (and exploitation) were the ones that made our world today so different from the world of our grandparents and ancestors.

Middle-Class Ideology: Outlook and Values

This middle-class outlook was imposed most firmly and characteristically on the United States. At its basis lies psychic insecurity founded on a lack of secure social status. The cure for such insecurity became insatiable material acquisition, from which flowed a large number of attributes. Only five will be mentioned here: future preference, self-discipline, social conformity, infinitely expandable material demand, and a general emphasis on externalized, impersonal values.

Those who have this outlook are middle-class; those who lack it are something else. Thus, middle-class status is a matter of perspective and not a matter of occupation or rank. There can be middle-class clergy, teachers, and scientists; indeed, most of these three groups are middle-class in the United States, although their theoretical devotion to truth rather than profit or others rather than self might seem to imply that they should not be middle-class. Honestly, they should not be; for the urges to seek truth or to help others are not compatible with middle-class values. However, in Western culture, these have been so influential and pervasive that many people, whose occupations seemingly should make them other than middle-class, nonetheless have adopted significant parts of the bourgeois ideology and seek material success in religion or teaching or science.

The middle-class outlook born in the Netherlands, northern Italy, and other places in the medieval period could pass on by being instilled in children as the proper and desired attitude for them to emulate and refine. It could be passed along from generation to generation and from century to century, as long as the parents continued to believe it themselves and disciplined their children to accept it. Those children, a minority for sure, who did not accept this outlook were not only disowned by, and fell out of, the middle class but also were, until recently, pitied and rejected even by their own families. Therefore, only those who accepted the outlook could march on in the steadily swelling ranks of the thriving middle class—until the twentieth century.

THE MIDDLE CLASS UNDER ATTACK: TRIALS, TRIBULATIONS, AND DECLINE

For more than a century, from well before World War I, the bourgeois ideology has been under relentless attack, often by its most ardent members who often thoughtlessly and at times even unconsciously have undermined and destroyed many of the essential social customs that preserved it through earlier generations. Some changes occurred in child-rearing practices, and some arose from the very success of the middle-class way of life, with the material affluence that tended to weaken the older emphasis on self-discipline, savings, future preference, and the rest of it.

One of the significant changes, fundamental to the survival of the middle-class ideology, was a change in Western society's basic conception of human nature. This idea had two parts to it.

The traditional Christian attitude toward human personality was that human nature is inherently good and formed and modified by social pressures and training (this is also the basis of socialist ideology). The goodness of human nature originated in the belief that every human being was a kind of weaker copy of God's nature, lacking many of God's qualities (in degree rather than in kind) but still perfectible and perfectible mainly by its own efforts with God's guidance. In this Christian outlook, the chief task was to train men and women so that they would use their fundamental freedom to do the right thing by following God's guidance.

From the beginning, there was another view opposed to this outlook of the world and the nature of man that received its most explicit formulation by the Persian Zoroaster in the seventh century BC and came into the Western tradition as a minor, heretical, theme. From this dissident Western minority point of view came seventeenth-century Puritanism.

According to the Puritan viewpoint, from Zoroaster to William Golding (in *Lord of the Flies*), the world and the flesh are real evils and man, in at least this physical part of his nature, is inherently evil.[373] Therefore, he must be disciplined to prevent him from destroying himself and the world. In this view, the devil is a force or being of real malevolence, and man, by himself, is incapable of any good and, accordingly, he can be saved in eternity by God's grace alone and can get through this temporal world only by being subjected to a regime of total despotism. The direction and nature of this despotism are not regarded as relevant, since the essential thing is that man's innate destructiveness be controlled.

Nothing could be more sharply contrasted than the above two points of view: the orthodox (human nature is inherently good), and the puritanical (man is inherently evil).

The Puritan point of view, which had been struggling to take over Western civilization for its first thousand years or more, almost did so in the seventeenth century. It was represented to varying degrees in the works and agitations of Martin Luther, Jean Calvin, Thomas Hobbes, Cornelius Jansen, Antoine Arnauld, Blaise Pascal, and others. In general, this point of view believed that the truth was to be found by rational deduction from a few fundamental revealed truths, in the way that Euclid's geometry and Descartes's analytical geometry were based on logical deduction from a few self-evident axioms.

The result was a mostly deterministic human situation, in sharp contrast with the conventional point of view, still represented in the Anglican and Roman churches, which saw man as generally free in a universe whose rules were to be found most readily by tradition and consensus. The Puritan viewpoint tended to support political despotism and to seek a one-class uniform society, while the older orthodox view put much greater emphasis on traditional pluralism and saw society as a unity of diversities. The newer Puritan idea led directly to mercantilism, which regarded political-economic life as a struggle to the death in a world where there was not sufficient wealth or space for different groups. To them, money was limited to a fixed amount in the world as a whole, and one person's gain was someone else's loss. That meant that the major struggles of this world were irreconcilable and must be fought to a finish—corresponding to the Puritan belief that nature was evil and a state of nature was a jungle of violent conflicts.

Some of these ideas were changed, some rearranged and modified, and some others retained in the following periods of the Enlightenment, the Romantic Movement, and scientific materialism.[374] All three of these periods returned to the older orthodox idea that man and nature were essentially good. To this restored belief in the garden of Eden, they joined a mostly optimistic faith in man's ability to deal with his problems and to guide his own destiny.

Not man but society and its conventions came to be regarded as evil, and the late Enlightenment and the early Romantics rejected the guidance of traditions. Nevertheless, the excesses of the French Revolution drove many of the later Romantics back to having confidence in history, culture, and established practices because of their growing feeling of the inadequacy of human reason. One large change in all three periods was the community of interests, which rejected mercantilism's insistence on limited wealth and the fundamental incompatibility of interests for the more optimistic belief that all parties could somehow adjust their interests within a community in which all would benefit mutually. The application of Darwinism to human society changed this idea again toward the end of the nineteenth century and provided the ideological justification for the National Socialist wars of extermination. Only after the middle of the twentieth century did a gradual reappearance of the old Christian ideas of love and charity modify this view, replacing it with the older idea that diverse human interests are reconcilable.

All this shifting of ideas, many of them unstated or even unconscious assumptions, and the gradual growth of affluence helped to destroy middle-class motivations and values. American society had been mostly, but not entirely, middle-class. Above the middle class that dominated the United States during the first half of the twentieth century were a small group of aristocrats. Under the middle class was the petit bourgeoisie, who had middle-class aspirations but were in most cases even more insecure and often bitter because they did not obtain middle-class rewards. Below these two middle classes were two lower classes: the workers and the "Lumpenproletariat," or socially disorganized outcast elements, who had little in common with each other.[375]

Outside this hierarchical structure of five groups in three classes (aristocratic, middle, and lower) were two other groupings that were not part of the hierarchical structure. On the left were the intellectuals, and on the right were the religious. These held in common the idea that the truth, to them, was more important than interests; but they differed greatly from each other in the fact that the religious believed they *knew* what the truth was while the intellectuals were still *seeking* it.

This whole structure was much more like a planetary arrangement of socioeconomic groupings than the middle-class vision of society as a ladder of opportunity. The ladder, in fact, included only the middle classes with the workers below. The planetary view, becoming increasingly widespread, saw the middle classes in the center with the other five surrounding these. Social movement was possible in a circular as well as in vertical directions (as the older ladder view of society believed) so that the sons of workers could rise into the middle classes or move right into the religious, left into the intelligentsia, or fall even into the declassed dregs. So too, in theory, the children (or more likely the grandchildren) of the upper middle class could move upward into the aristocracy, which could also be approached from the intellectuals or the religious.

Strangely enough, the nonmiddle classes shared more with each other than they had in common with the middle classes. The main reason for this was that all other groups had value systems different from those of the middle classes and, above all, placed no emphasis on publicly flaunting their material affluence as proof of their social standing.

All placed more emphasis on personal qualities and less on such things as clothing, residence, academic background, or kind of transportation used—all of which were important in determining middle-class reactions to people. In a sense, all were more sincere, personally more secure (except for the Lumpenproletariat), and less pretending than the middle class, and accordingly, they were much more inclined to judge any new acquaintance on his merits. Moreover, the middle classes, to provide their children with middle-class advantages, had few children, while the other groups placed little restriction on family size (except for some intellectuals). Thus, aristocrats, religious, workers, the declassed, and many intellectuals had large families, while only the uppermost and most securely established middle-class families, as part of the transition to the aristocracy, had larger families.

Ideas of morality also tended to set the middle classes off from most of the others. The latter tended to regard morality in terms of honesty and integrity of character, while the middle classes based it on actions—especially sexual actions. Even the religious considered sin to be based to some extent on purpose, attitude, and mental context of the act rather than on the act itself and did not restrict morality as narrowly to sexual behavior as did the middle classes.

However, the middle-class influence has been so pervasive in the modern world that many of the other groups fell under its influence to the extent that the word "morality," by the early twentieth century, came to mean "sex." Sex was mostly regarded with greater indulgence by aristocrats, workers, intellectuals, or the declassed than by the middle classes or the more Puritanical religious.

In America, as elsewhere, aristocracy represents money and position grown old and is organized in terms of families rather than of individuals. Traditionally, the aristocracy was made up of those families that had had money, rank, prestige, and social status for such a long time that they became naturally accustomed to them without ever having to even think about them. The members of the aristocracy never had to impress any other person with the fact that they had these privileges; they simply accepted these attributes of family membership as a right and an obligation. Since it never occurred to them that their advantages could ever be jeopardized or lost, they had underlying psychological security, which made them self-assured, natural, but distant. Their manners were gracious but impersonal, with their chief characteristic being the conviction that their family position came with obligations. This noblesse oblige made them participate in school sports and serve their universities, their local communities, their churches, their states, and their countries. They often scandalized their middle-class acquaintances by their unconventionality, eccentricity, and social informality, such as greeting workers, recent immigrants, or even outcasts by their given names.

The type of car a person drove was, until very recently, one of the best measures of middle-class status, since a car to the middle classes was a status symbol, while it was a means of getting somewhere to the other classes. Oversize Cadillacs, Lexuses, Mercedes, or BMWs are still middle-class cars, but in recent years, with the weakening of the middle-class ideology, almost anyone might be found driving a Volkswagen or a Toyota. Another real evidence of class may be recognized in the treatment given to service personnel: the middle classes consider them as inferiors, while aristocrats look upon them as equals or even superiors.

The real working class in the United States is much smaller than one might assume, since most American workers seek to rise socially, help their children to advance socially, and are considerably concerned with status symbols. Such people, even laborers, are not of the working class but instead belong to the petit bourgeoisie. The real working-class people (mainly unionized workers) are somewhat more relaxed; have present rather than future preference; generally worry little about their status in the eyes of the world; enjoy their ordinary lives, including food, sex, and leisure; and have little desire to change their jobs or positions. They have a taste for broad humor and are natural, direct, and friendly without significant underlying insecurities of personality. The Great Depression in the 1930s, by destroying their jobs and economic security, much reduced this group, which was always proportionately smaller in America, the land of aspiration for everyone, than in Europe.

The petit bourgeoisie is the second most numerous group in the United States, including millions of people who consider themselves middle-class and are under the typical middle-class anxieties and pressures—but often earn less than unionized laborers. As a result, they are often very insecure, envious, and filled with hatred, and they are typically the chief recruits for any extremist or hate campaigns against any group that refuses to conform to middle-class values. Made up of clerks, shopkeepers, and vast numbers of office workers in business, government, finance, and education, these people tend to regard their white-collar status as the chief value in life and live in an atmosphere of envy, pettiness, insecurity, and frustration.

In general, these class and psychological considerations have influenced the political alignments in the United States even more than income and economic or occupational factors.

Traditionally, the Republican Party has been the party of the middle classes, and the Democratic Party has been the party of the rest.

In general, aristocrats have tended to move toward the Democrats, while semiaristocrats often remain Republican (with their middle-class parents or grandparents), except where historical circumstance (chiefly in New England, the Midwest, and the South, where Civil War memories remained alive) operated. All that meant that the Republican Party, whose nineteenth-century superiority had been based on the division of farmers into South and West over the slave issue, became an established majority party in the twentieth century, then once again becoming a minority party because of the disintegration of its middle-class support following 1945.

Even during the period of middle-class dominance, the Republicans were already losing control of the federal government. This political decline came about because of the narrowly plutocratic control of the party that split it in 1912 and alienated most of the rest of the country in 1932. Twenty years later, in 1952, although the country looked solidly middle-class following World War II, in fact, even by that date middle-class morale had almost been destroyed, the middle classes themselves were in disintegration, and the majority of Americans were becoming less middle-class in outlook. The events of 1968 proved to be detrimental to the political control of the middle classes, the influence of conservatism, and widespread respect for the Republican Party; these changes were one of the most significant transformations of the twentieth century.

The future of the United States, indeed of Western Civilization and of the world, depends on what kind of outlook replaces the dissolved or dissolving middle-class ideology in the next generations.[376]

The weakening of the middle-class ideology was a chief cause of the panic of the middle classes, and especially of the petit bourgeoisie, during the Eisenhower era. Eisenhower had been preferred by the Eastern Establishment of old Wall Street—Ivy League and semiaristocratic Anglophiles whose real strength rested in their control of eastern financial endowments, operating from foundations, academic halls, and other tax-exempt refuges.

This Eastern Establishment was more concerned with policies than with party victories and remained above political parties. It had been the dominant element in both political parties since 1900 and practiced the political techniques of William C. Whitney and J. P. Morgan.[377] Its members were Anglophile, cosmopolitan, Ivy League, internationalist, astonishingly liberal, patrons of the arts, and relatively humanitarian. All these characteristics made them anathema to the lower-middle-class and petit bourgeois groups, chiefly in the small towns of the Midwest. Despite supplying the votes in Republican electoral victories, these groups found it still difficult to control the nominations because the big money necessary for nominating in a Republican National Convention was allied to Wall Street and the Eastern Establishment.

The ability of the latter to nominate Eisenhower over Taft in 1952 was a bitter pill to the radical bourgeoisie and was not sugarcoated sufficiently by the naming of Richard Nixon, a man much closer to their hearts, for the vice-presidential post. The split between these two wings of the Republican Party and Eisenhower's preference for the upper bourgeois rather than for the petit bourgeois wing paralyzed both of his administrations and was the significant element in Kennedy's narrow victory over Nixon in 1960 and Johnson's much more decisive victory over Goldwater in 1964.

John F. Kennedy, despite his Irish Catholicism, was also an Eastern Establishment figure. This fact did not arise from his semiaristocratic attitudes or his Harvard connections. These helped, but John Kennedy's introduction to the Eastern Establishment resulted from his support of Britain, in opposition to his father, while at the American Embassy in London during the critical days of 1938–40. His acceptance into the English Establishment opened its American branch as well.

The period since 1950 has seen a revolutionary change in American politics. This shift is not so closely related to the changes in American economic life as it is to the transformation in social life. Nevertheless, without the changes in economic life, the social influences could not have operated the way they did.

What has been happening is a disintegration of the middle class and a corresponding increase in significance by the petit bourgeoisie at the same time that the economic influence of the older Wall Street financial groups has been challenged by new wealth springing up outside the eastern cities, notably in the Southwest and Far West. These new sources of money have been based mainly on government action and government spending but have, nonetheless, adopted a petit bourgeois outlook rather than the semiaristocratic outlook that pervades the Eastern Establishment. This new wealth, based on oil, natural gas, other natural resources, the aerospace industry, military installations in the South and West, and the computer and electronics industry with all its attendant activities, has centered in the South and on the West Coast. Its existence, for the first time, made it possible for the petit bourgeois outlook to make itself directly felt in the political nomination process instead of the unrewarding effort to influence politics by voting for a Republican candidate nominated under Eastern Establishment control.

In these terms, the political struggle in the United States has shifted in two ways, or even three. This conflict, in the minds of the ill informed, had always been viewed as a struggle between Republicans and Democrats at the ballot box in November. Wall Street, however, saw long ago that the real battle was in the nominating conventions the previous summer. This realization was forced upon the petit bourgeois supporters of Republican candidates by their antipathy for Willkie, Dewey, Eisenhower, and other Wall Street interventionists and their inability to nominate their congressional favorites, such as Senators Knowland, Bricker, and Taft, at national party conventions. Just as these disgruntled voters reached this conclusion with Taft's failure in 1952, the new wealth appeared in the political picture sharing the petit bourgeoisie's suspicions of the East, big cities, Ivy League universities, foreigners, intellectuals, workers, and aristocrats.

The main political issue by the 1964 election was the financial struggle behind the scenes between the old wealth and the new wealth. The old wealth was sophisticated, cultured, liberal, and international in foundations, while the new wealth was virile, unaware, and chauvinistic, rising from the flowing profits of government-reliant corporations in the Southwest and West.

Here was the entire future face of America at issue. The older wealth stood for values and goals close to the Western traditions of diversity (the globalism of today), while the newer money stood for the narrow and fear-racked aims of petit bourgeois insecurity and egocentricity (the nationalistic conservatism of today).

The formal issues between them, such as that between internationalism and unilateral isolationism (which both its supporters and foes preferred to rename "nationalism"), were less fundamental than they seemed. The real issue was the control of the federal government's tremendous power to influence the future of America by the spending of public funds. The petit bourgeois and new-wealth groups wanted to continue that spending on the military-industrial complex, such as defense, aerospace, and electronics, and on agriculture and industry. The old-money and nonbourgeois groups wanted to direct expenditures toward social issues, such as diversity, amelioration for the aged, education, health care, and the protection of natural resources for future use.

The newer wealth, even though it had very legitimate concerns, was arrogant, ignorant, inarticulate, and misinformed. In their growing anxiety to control political nominations, the principals of the new wealth ignored the even greater need to win elections. They did not realize that the disintegration of the middle classes, mainly from the abandonment of the bourgeois ideology, was creating an American electorate that would never elect any candidate the newer wealth would care to nominate. Time had run out on the newer wealth, and it has been running out on the Republican Party ever since. As part of this lack of vision, the newer wealth and its petit bourgeois supporters ignored the well-established principle that a national candidate must have a national appeal, which can be obtained best by a candidate close to the center.

Moreover, the center, the "target," has been moving, in a seemingly unstoppable way, to the left. The more the once newer wealth, the petit bourgeois, tried rather desperately to stop this leftward shift, the more ground they lost. Later, the onetime Eastern Establishment reinvented itself to become the modern liberals, putting the final nail in the Republican coffin.

In American politics, there are several parties included under the blanket words "Democratic" and "Republican." In oversimplified terms, the Republicans were the party of the middle classes and the Democrats were the party of the fringes. Both parties were subdivided, each with a much stronger congressional and a rather weak national party wing. The Republican Congressional Party (representing localism) was much farther to the right than the National Republican Party and as such was closer to the petit bourgeois than to the upper-middle-class ideology. The Democratic Congressional Party wing was much more clearly on the fringes and thus often further left than the Democratic National Party itself. The party machinery in each case was in congressional party control during the intervals between the quadrennial presidential elections. However, to win these elections, each main political party had to call into existence its shadowy, middle-of-the-road national party wing in presidential election years.

All this meant that the Republicans had to appear to move to the left, closer to the center, while the Democrats also had to move from the fringes toward the center, usually by moving to the right. As a result, both national parties and their presidential candidates, with the Eastern Establishment busily promoting the process from behind the scenes, kept converging together and nearly met in the political center with almost identical candidates and platforms. Nevertheless, the real and orchestrated process was concealed, to a feasible extent, by the resurrection of zealous, emotional, and chauvinistic war cries and political slogans. No sooner was the presidential election over than the two national party wings vanished and party controls fell back into the hands of the congressional parties, leaving the newly elected president in a delicate position between the two congressional parties, neither of which was to be anywhere close to the short-lived national coalition that had elected him.

The main problem of the dominating and controlling Eastern Establishment, which with time changed itself to the modern liberal and cosmopolitan ruling elite, has been how to make the two main congressional political parties more national and international. The innocent argument that the two parties should represent, perhaps, contending principles and policies of the right and the left is to the ruling elite a foolish idea acceptable only to doctrinaire and academic thinkers. Instead this elite believes that the two parties should be almost identical so the elite can safely control the democratic process without it resulting in any profound or extensive shifts in policy. The ruling elite believes that policies that are vital and necessary for America are no longer subjects of significant disagreement but are disputable only in details of the procedure, priority, or method.

Accordingly, we must remain strong, continue to function as a great world power in cooperation with other powers, keep the economy moving without any significant slump, and help other countries do the same. Also, we must provide the basic social necessities to all of our citizens and create jobs for them. We must open up opportunities for social shifts to those willing to work for them and defend the fundamental Western outlook of diversity, pluralism, cooperation, and the rest of it, as already described. These are the things that any national American political party hoping to win a presidential election must accept.

To be sure, either party in office over time becomes corrupt, tired, unimaginative, and impotent. If that came to pass, it should then be possible to replace it by the other party, which will pursue—with new vigor, of course—approximately the same basic policies. That is the system trick of the American liberal democratic ruling elite controlling the world today.

On the other end of the American spectrum, the petit bourgeois mentality has been driven to near despair by the disintegration of the middle classes and the steady rise in prominence of everything they considered anathema. These are the minorities, immigrants, liberal intellectuals, aristocrats (and near aristocrats), people educated in liberal schools, people from the major cities or the East Coast and West Coast, cosmopolitans and internationalists, and, generally, modern liberals who accept diversity as a virtue.

The Tea Party movement and the Trump revolution are the direct consequences of the clash between the (up to now advancing) modern liberals and the (thus far withdrawing) petit bourgeoisie.

Along with the aforementioned political manipulations by the ruling elite, the disintegration of the middle classes had a variety of causes: some intrinsic, many of them accidental, a few obvious, most of them deliberate, and several of them going deep into the very depths of social existence.

THE DESTRUCTION OF THE MIDDLE-CLASS IDEOLOGY

All of these causes acted to destroy the middle classes by working to destroy the middle-class ideology. This outlook was killed by middle-class adults abandoning it and by the failure, unwillingness, or inability of middle-class parents to pass it on to their children any longer. Moreover, the failure was restricted mainly to the middle class itself and not to the petit bourgeoisie (lower middle class), which, if anything, was clinging to its particular version of the ideology more tenaciously and was passing it on to its offspring in an even more intensified form.

In short, the disintegration of the middle class arose from a failure to transfer its outlook to its children. This failure was thus a deliberate breakdown of education, since the modern American school system had been consciously organized as a mechanism for indoctrination of the young in secularism, socialism, and internationalism, not in traditional middle-class ideology.

It would appear that the traditional American educational system, unlike those of continental Europe, was more concerned with the indoctrination of middle-class ideology than with cultivating patriotism or nationalism; it has been more concerned with instilling attitudes and behavior than with mental training. The so-called American way of life identified more with the American economic and social system than with the American political system. Children of racial, religious, national, and class minorities all passed through the same procedure and received the middle-class formative process with incomplete success in many cases. All this refers to the public schools, but the Roman Catholic school system, especially on its upper levels, was doing the same things. A large number of Catholic men's colleges in the country, especially those operated by the Jesuits, had as their primary aim the desire to transform the sons of working-class and often immigrant people into middle-class citizens in professional occupations (mainly law, medicine, business, and teaching).

On the whole, this system has become less and less successful in turning out middle-class people, especially from its upper educational levels. This failure can be attributed to a failure of the system itself, and it occurred chiefly within the middle-class family, a not unexpected situation, since outlook is still determined rather by a reaction to family conditions than by submission to a formal educational process.

Only a few of the internal factors that have influenced these changes are mentioned here. Much of the disintegration of the middle-class ideology can be traced to a weakening of its most important aspects, such as future preference, intense self-discipline, and, to a lesser degree, a decreasing emphasis on infinitely expandable material demand and the importance of middle-class status symbols.

The most significant external factor in the destruction of the middle-class ideology has been the relentless attack upon it in the media, literature, drama, and arts through most of the twentieth century. In fact, it is hard to find works that defended the middle-class outlook or even assumed it to be true as was frequently the case in the nineteenth century. It is not that such works did not exist at all even in recent years; on the contrary, they have been avidly welcomed by the petit bourgeoisie and by some middle-class housewives. Lending libraries and women's magazines of the 1910s, 1920s, and 1930s were full of them, but by the 1950s they were mostly restricted to television soap operas. Even those writers who explicitly accepted the middle-class ideology tended to portray middle-class life as a horror of false values, hypocrisy, meaningless effort, and insecurity.

In the earlier period, even down to 1940, literature's attack on the middle-class ideology was direct and brutal. Works like Upton Sinclair's *The Jungle* and Frank Norris's *The Pit* dealt with the total corruption of personal integrity in the meatpacking and wheat markets.[378] These first assaults were aimed at the commercialization of life under the bourgeois influence and were reformist in outlook by assuming that the evils of the system could somehow be taken out, perhaps by state intervention. The following attacks saw the problem, however, in moral terms so fundamental that no remedial action was possible, and only complete rejection of middle-class values could remove the corruption of human life as perceived by Sinclair Lewis.

After 1940, writers tended less and less to attack the bourgeois way of life; that job had already been done. Instead they described situations, characters, and actions that were simply nonbourgeois: violence; social irresponsibility; sexual laxity and perversion; miscegenation; human weakness concerning alcohol, narcotics, and sex; and domestic and business relationships conducted along entirely nonbourgeois lines. Ernest Hemingway, William Faulkner, and a host of lesser writers, many of them embracing the cult of violence, showed the trend. A few, like Hemingway, found a new moral outlook for replacing the middle-class ideology they had abandoned. Hemingway left upper-middle-class Oak Park, Illinois, indignantly and immersed himself in the Spanish tragic sense of life, with its constant demand for men to demonstrate their masculinity by casual illicit sexual relations with women and heroic bravery in facing death. To Hemingway, this could be manifested in the bullring, African big-game hunting, and war, or in a more symbolic way, in prizefighting or crime. The significant point here is that Hemingway always recognized in his embracing the outlook of the Pakistani-Peruvian axis (as a token of the rejection of his middle-class background), a pretense, and when his virility, in the crudest sense, was gone, he blew out his brains.[379]

The literary assault on the bourgeois outlook was directed at all aspects of what has earlier been mentioned: at future preference, at self-discipline, at the emphasis on material acquisition, and at status symbols.

The attack on future preference appeared as a demonstration that the future is never reached. The argument was that the individual who continually postpones living from the present to a speculative future eventually finds that time has gone by; death is nearing without one having lived yet, but one is unable to do so any longer. If the central figure in such work has successfully achieved his materialist ambitions, the suggestion is that these goals, which looked so attractive from a distance, are but impediments to the real values of life when fully lived. This motif, which goes back at least to Charles Dickens's *A Christmas Carol*, continued to be presented to the twentieth century and often took the form, in more recent times, of a rejection of a man's whole life achievement by his sons, his wife, or himself.[380]

The latest form of this attack on future preference has appeared in the existentialist novel and the theater of the absurd. Existentialism believes that both reality and life consist only of the particular, concrete personal experience of a given place and moment and ignores the context of each event and thus isolates it. However, an event without context has no cause, meaning, or consequence; it is absurd, as anything is that has no relationship to any context. Moreover, such an event, with neither past nor future, can have no connection with tradition or with future preference. This point of view came to saturate twentieth-century literature so that the initial rejection of future preference was expanded into the total rejection of time, which is now merely conceived as a mechanism for enslaving man and depriving him of the opportunity to experience life. The bourgeois time clock thus became a tomb or prison that alienated man from life.

A similar attack on *self-discipline* had a philosophical basis in an oversimplified Freudianism that regarded all suppression of human impulse as leading to frustration and psychic distortions, which made subsequent life unattainable. Thus novel after novel and play after play portrayed the wicked suppression of healthy and natural impulse versus the salubrious consequences of self-indulgence, especially in sex. Adultery and other manifestations of undisciplined sexuality were described in increasingly clinical detail. They were associated with excessive drinking or other evasions of personal responsibility, as in Hemingway's *A Farewell to Arms* and in John Steinbeck's love affair with personal irresponsibility in Cannery Row and Tortilla Flat.[381] The total rejection of middle-class values, including time, self-discipline, and material achievement for the admiration of personal violence, was portrayed in a multitude of literary works from James M. Cain and Raymond Chandler, as well as the more recent shenanigan of James Bond. The result has been a complete reversal of middle-class values by presenting as impressive or admirable the mere negation of these values by aimless, shiftless, and irresponsible people.

A similar reversal of values has flooded the market with novels filled with pointless clinical descriptions presented in an obscene language and fictional form of swamps of perversions including homosexuality, incest, sadism, masochism, cannibalism, necrophilia, and coprophagia. These performances represent not so much a loss of values as a loss of any conception of the nature of man.

The Greeks and the following Western Civilization regarded man as a creature halfway between God and animal, a little lower than the angels and capable of an infinite variety of experience. However, instead of seeing man the way the tradition of the Greeks regarded him, these twentieth-century writers have completed the revolt against the middle-classes by sinking from the late nineteenth-century view of man as merely a higher animal to their brutally modern view of him as lower than any animal could naturally descend. From this the Puritan view of man has emerged (but without the Puritan view of God) as a creature of total immorality in a deterministic universe without any hope of redemption.

This point of view, which justified despotism in a Puritan context between 1550 and 1650, now may be used, with petit bourgeois support, to justify a new tyranny to preserve by force instead of conviction the petit bourgeois values in a system of compulsory conformity. George Orwell's *1984* has given humanity the picture of this scheme as Hitler's Germany showed its practical operation.[382] However, today, given the present upsurge of nonbourgeois social groups and social pressures, this possibility becomes decreasingly likely.

The destruction of the middle classes through the collapsing middle-class ideology was brought about to a much higher degree by *internal* than by *external* forces. Moreover, the most destructive influences have been operating within the middle-class family.

One of these has been the growing affluence of American society, which has removed the pressure of want from the childbearing process. The child who grows up in wealth is more difficult to instill with the frustrations and drives that were so fundamental to the middle-class ideology. For generations, even in relatively affluent families, this indoctrination continued because of enduring emphasis on thrift and restraints on consumption. However, by 1937 the Great Depression showed that the underlying economic problems were not savings and investment but distribution and consumption. There appeared a growing *r*eadiness to consume, and as a result, an entirely new phenomenon appeared in middle-class families: the practice of living up to, or even beyond, their incomes—an unthinkable scandal in any nineteenth-century middle-class family. One incentive to consume was the increased emphasis on status and the accompanying display of wealth instead of on the elements of frugality and prudence. Thus, affluence and success undermined both future preference and the training for self-denial and self-discipline.

Somewhat related to this was the aftereffect of the 1929–33 Great Depression. Having been born in the period 1905–15, the generation that was entering manhood at that time felt that the strenuous attempts to fulfill their middle-class ambitions had involved them in intensive hardships and suffering. These adversities included the difficulty of finding a job or enough to eat, working while going to college, and doing without leisure, cultural expansion or travel. By the 1950s, the generation of the Great Depression was determined that their children must never have it as hard again as they had had it in their youth. They did not recognize that the very efforts making things easy for their children were removing precisely those obstacles or qualities from their children's training process that had helped to make them, the parents, achieving and successful middle-class people. They did not see that their very efforts to do this were weakening the moral fiber of their children.

Still another element of this development was a change in the educational philosophy of America and a somewhat similar change in the country's ideas, on the whole, about child training. Earlier generations had continued to adhere to the vestiges of the Puritan ideology, according to which children must be trained under strict discipline, including corporal punishment. This seventeenth-century idea in American family thinking by 1920 was being replaced by the view of the nineteenth century that child maturation is an innate, natural process not subject to modification by outside training. In educational theory, this false idea went back to *Emile*, a 1762 treatise on education by Jean-Jacques Rousseau.[383] Rousseau's work idealized the state of nature as equivalent to the garden of Eden and believed that education must consist of leaving a youth completely free so that his innate goodness could emerge and reveal itself. This idea was developed, intensified, and given a pseudoscientific foundation by advances in biology and genetics in the late nineteenth century. By 1910 or so, child-rearing and educational theories had accepted the concept that man was a biological organism, like any animal, that his personality was a consequence of genetic traits, and that each child had within him a rigid assortment of inherited talents and a natural rate of maturation in the development of these abilities. These ideas were consolidated into a series of slogans, such as "Every child is different" and "He will do it when he is ready."

From all this came a sweeping abrogation of discipline, both at home and in school, and the onset of permissive education, with all the things that logically follow from it. Children were emboldened to have opinions and to speak out on issues of which they were completely ignorant, the acquisition of information and intellectual training were shoved into the background, and restrictions on time, place, and movement in schools and homes were reduced to a minimum. Every emphasis was put on spontaneity, and fixed schedules of time periods or subject matter to be covered were belittled. All this significantly weakened the disciplinary influence of the educational process, leaving the new generation much less disciplined, less organized, and less aware of time than their parents.

Naturally, this disintegrating process was less evident among the children of the petit bourgeois than in the middle class itself. These influences alone would have contributed much to the weakening of the middle-class ideology among the rising generation, but other, much more profound forces were also operating, most importantly within the middle-class family structure.

As in so many other things, also concerning marriage has Western Civilization been subjected to somewhat antithetical theories; these can be called the romantic and the Western ideas of love and marriage.

The romantic theory was that each man or woman had a unique personality consisting of inborn traits, accumulated by inheritance from a particular combination of ancestors. That is, of course, the same theory that was used to justify permissive education. In romantic love, however, the theory went on to assume that for each man or woman there existed in the world a person of the opposite sex whose personality traits would just fit those of his or her destined mate. The only difficulty was to find that partner, which discovery, it was believed, would be done when an instantaneous flash of recognition would reveal at first sight to both that they had met their one possible partner in life.

The above concept was closely related to the Manichaean and Puritan theories concerning God's truth coming to men in a similar flash of illumination—an idea that goes back to Plato's theory of knowledge as reminiscence.[384] This romantic theory of love in its most extreme form assumed that each of the two intended lovers was only part of a person, the two parts instantly fitting together on meeting into a single personality. Associated with this were some other ideas, including the idea that marriages were made in heaven and should be eternal, and that such a romantic marriage was completely satisfying to the partners.

The middle class embraced these ideas about romantic love and marriage, but not to any significant degree did the other classes. Like so much of the middle-class ideology, the theory of romantic love and marriage also originated among the medieval heresies, such as Manichaeism.[385] It stemmed, therefore, from the same tradition as the bourgeois outlook in the Middle Ages and its reinforcement by the closely associated Puritan movement of modern times. The romantic theory of love was spread through the middle class by incidental factors, such as that the bourgeoisie was the only social class that read much. Romantic love was a literary convention in its propagation and made no real impression on the other social classes in European society, such as the peasants, the nobility, and the urban working craftsmen.

Strangely enough, romantic love, accepted as a theory and ideal by the bourgeoisie, had little influence on middle-class marriages in practice, since these were usually based on middle-class values of economic security and material status rather than on love. More accurately, middle-class marriages were based on these material considerations while everyone concerned *pretended* that they were based on romantic love. Any subsequent recognition of this clash between fact and theory, which is hypocrisy and is one of the fundamental characteristics of modern Western liberal democracy, often gave a severe jolt and had sometimes been a subject of literary examination, as in the first volume of John Galsworthy's *The Forsyte Saga*.[386]

Opposed to both the romantic theory of love and marriage and the bourgeois practice of sensible marriage was the Western theory of love and marriage. This theory assumes that personalities are dynamic and flexible beings formed mainly by experiences in the past. Love and marriage between such personalities are, like everything in the Western outlook, diverse, imperfect, adjustable, creative, cooperative, and changeable. The Western idea assumes that a couple comes together for many reasons (sex, loneliness, shared interests, similar background, economic and social cooperation, mutual admiration of character traits, and other grounds). It further assumes that their whole relationship will be a slow process of getting to know each other and of mutual adjustment—a process that may never end. The need for constant change shows the Western recognition that nothing, even love, is final or perfect. This understanding is also demonstrated by recognizing that love and marriage are never total and all-absorbing and that each partner remains an independent personality with the right to an independent life. This concept is found during the whole of Western tradition and stems from the Christian belief that each person is a separate soul having its own and separate fate.

Thus there appeared in Western society at least three kinds of marriage, which can be called romantic (middle-class *theory*), bourgeois (middle-class *practice*), and Western. The last one is, without being much discussed (except in current books on love and marriage), presumably the most numerous of the three; regarding the first two, if they prove successful at all it is because of their gradually developing into this third kind. Romantic marriage, based on the shock of recognition, has, in fact, come to be based very largely on sexual attraction, since this is the chief form that love at first sight can take. Such marriages often fail because even sex requires practice and mutual adjustment and is too momentary a human relationship to sustain a permanent union unless many other shared interests can be found around it. However, even when this happens and the marriage becomes a success in the sense that it persists, it is never total. The romantic delusion that marriage should be all-absorbing of the time, attention, and energies of its partners, which was expected by many women brought up on the romantic idea, merely means that the marriage becomes an enslaving relationship to the husbands and a source of disappointment and frustration to the wives.

Middle-class marriage, in fact, was not romantic, for marriage, like everything else, was subject to the middle-class system of values. Within that value system, middle-class persons chose a marriage partner who would assist in achieving middle-class goals of status and achievement. A woman, with her parents' approval, wanted a husband who could show promise to be a good provider and a steady, reliable, social achiever. She wanted a husband who would be able to give her a material status at least as high as that provided by her parents. A man wanted a wife who showed promise of being an aid, comfort, and guidance in his upward struggle, a wife able to act as hostess to his aspirant activities and to provide the domestic decorum and social graces expected of a successful businessman or professional.

Such a marriage was based, from both sides, on status factors rather than on personal factors. A man could have been a Harvard or Yale graduate, educated and trained for a profession, had a position with a good firm, driven an expensive car, ordered dinner in a fancy restaurant, and already applied for membership in a golf or country club. These were merely the accessories of his status but not the reasons for loving him as a person. Nevertheless, middle-class people married for reasons such as these and at the same time hypocritically tried to convince themselves and all others that they were marrying for romantic love—based on the fact that they were also sexually attracted.

For a time, perhaps, the new marriage could keep up these pretenses, especially as the elements of sex and novelty in the relationship helped conceal both the contrast between theory and fact and that the marriage was an external and superficial relationship. Alas, the fact remained, and slowly unconscious frustrations and dissatisfactions, which did not necessarily reach the conscious level for a while, began to surface. At least unconsciously, the realization had set in that the marriage was *not* based on love. A loving relationship must be a recognition and appreciation of personal qualities instead of status accessories. Without personal feeling based on such personal qualities, the relationship was not a personal relationship and was not based on love, even when the middle-class partners, with their usual lack of introspection, still insisted on it. The consequences of such unconscious recognition of the real lack of love in the bourgeois marital relationship are not only significant but also decisive.

This hypocrisy of love occurred in a hypocritical society that never stopped repeating the absolute necessity of love for human happiness and fulfillment in the theater, cinema, magazine, and literature.

Women became "emancipated" as a consequence of World War I, but even more significant was the appearance in the outside world of a significant increase in the number of jobs that could be done best, or only, by women. As part of this process, considerable changes took place in bourgeois morality, such as greater freedom between the sexes, the acceptance of divorce as morally possible in bourgeois life (a custom that came in from the stage and cinema), and the ending of chaperonage.

A dramatic event of great social significance also occurred in this whole process: the reversal in longevity expectations of men and women. In a mainly rural context, a twenty-year-old man could expect to live longer than a twenty-year-old wife a little more than a century ago. In fact, such a man might well bury two or three wives, usually from the mortality associated with childbirth or other female problems. Today, a twenty-year-old man has little expectation of living as long as a twenty-year-old woman. Moreover, a twenty-year-old woman a century ago married a man considerably older than herself, at least in the middle classes, only because future preference required that a man be economically established before he began to raise a family.

Today, as a result of a series of causes, husbands die before their wives in most cases. The causes are, just to mention a few, the extension of female life expectancy, the increased practice of birth control, coeducation (which brings the sexes into contact at the same age), and the weakening of future preference and middle-class ideology leading to marriages by couples of about the same age. The recognition of this, plus the increased independence of women and their adapting to tax and other legal practices, have given rise to joint financial accounts, to the property put in the wife's name, and to significantly increased insurance benefits for wives. The wealth of the country gradually became female-owned, even if still mostly male-controlled, but this had subtle results; it made women more independent and more outspoken. Bourgeois men gradually came to live under a regime of persistent nagging to become better providers. For many men, work became a refuge and relief from domestic revelations of the inadequacy of their performance as economic achievers. This growth of overwork, constant tension, and the frustration of emotional life and leisure began to make more and more men increasingly willing to accept death as the only method of achieving rest. Bourgeois men began to kill themselves by unconscious psychic suicide from overwork, neurotic overindulgence in alcohol, smoking, work, and violent leisure, and the middle class slowly increased its proportion of materially endowed widows.

The marked change in this whole process was a switch over the twentieth century from the male-dominated family to a female-dominated family. Closely related to this reversal of the social roles of the sexes was the decreasing sexual differentiation in child-rearing practices.

Because the middle-class marriage is based on social rather than personal attraction, the wife's emotional relationship with her husband is insecure, and the more the husband buries himself in his work, hobbies, or outside interests, the more troubled and unsatisfactory the relationship becomes for his wife.

The point of all this is that typical adolescent rebellion has become, in America and generally in the West today, a radical and wholesale rejection of parental values, including middle-class values, because of the protracted emotional warfare that now goes on in the middle-class home with teenage children. These tensions threaten to destroy the family and are already in the process of destroying much of the middle-class ideology that was once so distinctive of the American way of life.

From this has emerged an almost total breakdown of communication between teenagers and their parents' generation. An entirely new teenage culture serving as a protective barrier has grown up, and its chief characteristic is the rejection of parental values and the middle-class culture. This new teenage culture has its own taste in leisure, music, and dance, its emphasis on sex play and group solidarity. It almost entirely rejects any future preference and struggles to free itself from the tyranny of time.

This infantilization of Western society is gradually spreading with every passing year to higher age levels in the culture and is having profound and damaging effects on the transfer of middle-class values to the rising generation.

In general, the negative attitude appears in a profound rejection of abstractions, slogans, clichés, and conventions; these are treated with tolerant irony tinged with contempt. The targets of these attitudes are the general values of the petit bourgeoisie and middle-class parents. What are these values? Position in society, concern about what people think, self-respect, keeping up with the Joneses, the American way of life, virtue, making money, destroying our country's enemies, respect for established organizations, and such.

While rejecting material acquisitiveness and even sensuality, the younger generation's outlook concentrates on experiences without context. Their experiences are necessarily limited and personal and never fitted into a broader picture or linked with the past or the future. As a result, they find it almost impossible to imagine anything different from what it is or even to see what it is from any long-range perspective. Therefore, their outlooks, despite their extensive exposure to various situations through the mass media or by personal travel, are very narrow. They lack the desire to obtain some experience vicariously from reading, and the shared experiences they do get from communicating (usually with their fellows) are rarely much different from their own experiences. Consequently, their lives, while erratic, are strangely dull and homogeneous.

Efforts by middle-class parents to prevent their children from developing along these non-middle-class lines are futile. An attempt to use parental discipline to enforce conformity to middle-class values or behavior means that the child will refer to the many cases where children are not being punished. He is encouraged in his resistance to parental discipline by its large-scale failure all around him. Moreover, if his parents insist on conformity, he has a powerful weapon to use against them: academic failure. From this whole context of adolescent resistance to parental pressures to conform to middle-class behavior flows a significant portion of middle-class juvenile delinquency. It involves all kinds of activities: earliest efforts to smoke or drink, speeding, car stealing, vandalism of property, major crimes, and perversions.

These remarks, it must be emphasized, apply only to the middle class and are not intended to apply to the other classes of American society. The aristocrats, for example, have considerable success in passing along their ideology to their children, partly because it is presented as a class or family attitude and not as a parental opinion. Also, partly because their friends and close associates are also aristocrats or semiaristocrats, rejection of their point of view tends to leave an aristocratic adolescent much more personally isolated than the rejection of his parents' view would leave a middle-class youth. (The latter finds group togetherness only if he does reject his parents.) Further, there is much more segregation of the sexes among aristocrats than in the middle class, chiefly because the aristocrats use a separate school system, including disciplined boarding schools. The use of the latter, the key to the long persistence of the aristocratic tradition in England, makes it possible for outsiders to discipline adolescents without disrupting the family. Among the middle class, the effort to discipline adolescents is mostly in the hands of parents, but the effort to do so tends to disrupt the family by setting husband against wife and children against parents. As a result, discipline is usually held back to retain at least the semblance of family solidarity as viewed from the outside world, which is what counts with middle-class people.

Unfortunately for the aristocrat who wishes to expose his son to the same training process that molded his own outlook, he finds this a difficult thing to do. The organizations that helped form him outside the family such as the Episcopal Church (or its local equivalent), the boarding school, the Ivy League university, and the once-sheltered summer resort have all changed and are being invaded by a large number of nonaristocratic intruders who alter the atmosphere of the whole place. How did this come about?

In the end, the American Establishment, which is so aristocratic and Anglophile in its foundation, came to accept the liberal ideology. The Episcopal Church, the exclusive boarding schools, and Ivy League universities like Harvard, Princeton, and Yale all decided that they must open their doors to the abler of the nonaristocratic classes. Accordingly, they established scholarships, recruited for these in lower schools they had never thought of before, and made efforts to have their admission requirements and examinations fit the past experiences of nonaristocratic applicants.

As a consequence of this, the sons and daughters of aristocrats found themselves being squeezed out of the formative institutions that had previously trained their fathers, and at the same time, they discovered that these establishments were themselves changing their character and becoming dominated by petit bourgeois rather than aristocratic values. At the alumni reunions many years ago, the president of Harvard was asked in an open forum what the questioner should do with his son, recently rejected for admission to Harvard despite the fact that the son descended from the Mayflower voyagers by eleven consecutive generations of Harvard men. To this tragic question, President Pusey replied, "I don't know what we can do about your son. We can't send him back because the Mayflower isn't running anymore."[387] Despite this sarcastic retort, which may have been called forth by the inebriated condition of the questioner, the fact remains that the aristocratic outlook has a great deal to contribute to any organization fortunate enough to share it. Among other things, it has kept Harvard (where aristocratic control continued almost to the present day) at the top of the American educational hierarchy decade after decade.

Petit Bourgeois Rising

The effort, by aristocrats and Democrats alike, to make the social ladder in America a ladder of opportunity rather than a ladder of privilege has opened the way to a surge of petit bourgeois recruits over the faltering bodies of the disintegrating middle class.

The petit bourgeois is rising in American society along the channels established in the great American hierarchies of business, the armed forces, academic life, the professions, finance, and politics. They are doing this not because they have imagination, broad vision, judgment, moderation, versatility, or group loyalties but because they have neurotic drives of personal ambition and competitiveness, great insecurities and resentments, narrow specialization, and fanatical application to the task before each of them. Their fathers and grandfathers, earning $100 a week as bank clerks or insurance agents while unionized bricklayers were getting $120 a week when they cared to work, embraced the middle-class ideology with tenacity.

In this thinking, they saw the principal means (along with their white-collared clothing) of distinguishing themselves from the unionized labor they feared or hated. Their wives, whom they had married because they held the same outlook, looked forward eagerly to seeing their sons gain the kind of material success the father had failed to reach. The family accepted a common viewpoint of believing that specialization and hard work, either in business or profession, would win this material success.

The steps up that ladder of success were unmistakably marked: to be the outstanding boy student and graduate in school, to gain entrance to and graduation from the best university possible (naturally an Ivy League one), and then to spend the final years of specialized application in a professional school.

Many of these eager workers headed for medicine, because to them medicine, despite the ten years of necessary preparation, meant a tremendously high average annual income. As a consequence, the medical profession in the United States ceased to be a profession of fatherly confessors and unprofessing humanitarians and became one of the largest groups of hardheaded petit bourgeois hustlers in the country, and their professional association became the most ruthlessly materialistic lobbying organization of any professional group. Similar persons with lesser opportunities were shunted off the most advantageous rungs of the ladder into second-best schools and third-rate universities. All flocked into the professions, even to teaching (which profession, on the face of it, might have expected that its practitioners would have some allegiance to the truth and to helping the young to realize their less materialistic potentialities), where they quickly abandoned the classroom for more remunerative tasks of educational administration. Moreover, the great mass of these eager beavers went into engineering, science, or business, preferably with the largest corporations, such as General Motors, AT&T, General Electric, and Microsoft, where they looked with fishy-eyed anticipation at the rich, if remote, plums of vice presidencies.

The success of these petit bourgeois recruits in America's organizational structure rested on their ability to adapt their lives to the screening processes that the middle classes had once set up covering access to the middle-class organizational structures. The petit bourgeoisie, as the last fanatical defenders of the middle-class ideology, had in excess degree those qualities of self-discipline and future preference that the middle classes had established as the unstated assumptions behind their screens of aptitude testing, intelligence evaluation, motivational research, and potential success measurements. Above all, the American public school system, permeated with the tacit premise of middle-class values, was ideally suited to demonstrate petit bourgeois success quotients. These successive barriers in the middle-class screening process, which were almost insurmountable for the working class and outcast, also became difficult to overcome for the new generation of middle-class children who rejected their parents' value system but were ideally adapted to the petit bourgeois anxiety neuroses.

Soon, however, big business, government civil service, and the Ivy League universities were becoming disillusioned with these petit bourgeois recruits. The difficulty was that the new volunteers were rigid, unimaginative, narrow, and above all illiberal at a time when liberalism was coming to be regarded as the proper approach to large organizational problems.

The West needs a culture that will produce people eager to do things, but it also needs a culture that will facilitate and encourage the decision-making process; that is the old division of means and goals.

To be able to decide about goals require values, meaning, context, and perspective. They can be set, even tentatively and approximately, only by people who have some inkling of the whole picture. The middle-class culture of our past ignored the whole picture and destroyed our ability to see it by its emphasis on specialization. Just as mass production came to be based on specialization, so human preparation for making decisions about goals also became based on expertise. The free elective system in higher education was associated with the choice of a major field of specialization; all the talk about liberal arts, outside electives, general education, and required distribution was mostly futile. It was futile because no general view of the whole picture could be had just by attaching some specialist views of narrow fields for the simple reason that each specialist field looks entirely different, presenting various problems and requiring different techniques, when it is placed in the general picture. This mere fact still has not been realized in those circles that talk most about "broadening outlooks."[388]

Means are almost as difficult as ends. In fact, the character traits of personal responsibility, self-discipline, some sense of time value, future preference, and, above all, the ability to differentiate between "essential" and merely "nice to have" are all required.

On the whole, neither America nor the West, in general, can be saved by a wholesale recreation of nonachieving social realities in consequence of our rejection of the middle-class ideology that has brought us this far. Here we must discriminate; let us not throw the baby out with the bathwater. The West has an achieving society today because it has an achieving outlook, and precisely this achieving outlook has been the middle-class ideology over the last few centuries.

A New Performing and Achieving Ideology Is Needed

Are there any other achieving outlooks? Could an achieving society be constructed based either on the aristocratic outlook or scientific outlook (pursuit of truth) or perhaps on a religious basis? Yes, there are probably a large number of other achieving outlooks.

There is no need to go back to the middle-class ideology, which killed itself by successfully achieving what it set out to do. However, the West must have an achieving society and an achieving ideology, and these will inevitably contain parts of the middle-class ideology. Nevertheless, these parts will unquestionably be fitted together to serve entirely different purposes. For example, future preference and self-discipline were initially necessary so people would restrict consumption and save instead for investing in capital equipment required for production. Although flows of income through the economy provide these investments on an institutional basis today, society still needs the qualities of future preference and self-discipline for young people to undergo the years of hard work and training in preparation to work in a complex technological society.

We must bring *meaning* back into the human experience. That can be done, just as with the establishing of an achieving outlook, by going backward in the Western tradition to the period *before* there was any bourgeois outlook. Western society had both meaning and purpose long before it had any middle class. In fact, the middle-class ideology obtained its meaning and purpose *from* the society where it grew up; it did not give meaning and purpose *to* society. Moreover, capitalism, along with the middle-class ideology, became meaningless and purposeless when it so absorbed man's time and energy that he lost touch with the meaning and purpose of society, in which capitalism was a brief and partial aspect.

However, as a consequence of the influence and success of both capitalism and the middle classes, the tradition was broken; the link between the meaning and purpose of society as it had existed before the middle-class revolution is no longer connected with the search for meaning and purpose by the new post-middle-class generation. This disconnect can be seen even concerning the Christian clergy, who insist that they still cling to the Christian tradition of Western society. They are doing no such thing but instead usually offering us meaningless and hypocritical verbiage or unrealistic and pretentious abstractions that have little to do with the experience of living in a Christian way here and now.

The real worth of any society rests in its ability to develop mature and responsible individuals who are prepared to act independently, make decisions, and accept the consequences of their decisions and actions without protest or self-justification. This ideal was the Christian doctrine established long ago, and as a consequence, Western society, although not without deficiencies, has done better than any other. If it has done less well recently, this can be remedied only by some reform that will increase its supply of mature and responsible adults. Once that process is established, the adults thus produced can be relied upon to adopt, from the Western heritage of the past, a modified ideology that will fit the needs of the present as well as the traditions of the past. If Western culture can do that, it need fear no enemies from within or from without. Moreover, it has no alternative.

THE NEW PROLETARIANIZATION OF THE WEST

The modern liberal who lives on the product of human labor and the proceeds from trade or dividends is causing a full retreat of Western civilization before the modern proletarian.

Who is this modern proletarian? Following the industrial revolution, the people who sold their labor for survival in the newly emerging modern societies were usually labeled as "working class" or the "proletariat." Today the term "proletariat" can be defined as the people who earn their living through wage labor, do not own any assets or capital, do not possess any authority in the workplace, are unskilled, or are legal or illegal immigrants; to put it in an all-encompassing phrase, they are working people without property.

Over the years, scholars have even argued that the working class differs from the rest of society it belongs to with its politics, culture, family structures, and the conditions in which its members live.

Today, the bourgeoisie, the middle class, has become moribund, and the professionals have been reduced to paid wage laborers. The masses, falsely, continue to regard the problem as an economic one. Materialism is also a proletarian attribute, not only a principal value of the disappearing middle class.

The proletarian has always developed into the socialist of the day, but he also toyed with communist modes of thought. On the other hand, the proletarian has no feeling for the nation or community; he thinks first, last, and only *of* himself. He does not even suspect this, and it is the fact that he does not that stamps him as a proletarian. The actual world around him is a hateful bourgeois world that he hopes to alter.

Perhaps in the entire West, no one condemns democracy more severely than the proletarian; he condemns a democracy that selected him to bear the burden of the impossible fulfillment. This disapproval is the natural reaction to the promise of socialism; the masses have been reduced to following the upstarts and exploiters of socialism and modern liberalism. The intellectuals of every revolution, every progressive change, and every political transition use the strength of the masses to put themselves in power. They call their power democracy.

The trust of the masses is lacking. However, any leadership can be based only on mutual trust between the leader and the led. New America and New Europe, the very pillars of the left-liberal-socialist West, are the shipwreck of leadership; the secret of leadership, *trust*, appears to have been lost.

The modern Western proletariat of today painfully lacks leadership other than that of the established political party organizations. This proletariat is led to support a dangerous brew of modern liberalism (represented by various democratic, Christian-democratic, or liberal parties) and socialism (represented by a medley of socialist, social-democratic, green, or other parties).

The proletariat sees the present only and dreams of a more just future; it does not consider itself part of a community but a body misused by society. So the proletarian demands a share not of the values of which he knows nothing, but of the goods he sees in possession of more privileged persons.

The more gifted man who takes a share in the spiritual and intellectual values of a broader community absorbs from these the strength to rise above class distinction, to extricate himself from the masses—to become nonproletarian.

The proletarian has no political tradition; his school has been the political party. Today, in the age of globalization, the awful reality makes known to him that he is living in a world of his own doing. Moreover, in his present world, things, far from getting better, are getting worse every moment because there were gullible people who believed that all would be well by now. The proletarian will find salvation only when he can rise to a supraeconomic and supramaterialistic thought and concerns himself not with building up a proletarian world but with finding a niche for the proletariat in the actual world.

The proletariat has a right, of course, to a recognized and stable position in a society dependent on industrial enterprise and proletarian labor. However, it is not entitled to the superior position of power that the socialist and communist parties wanted for it during the radical periods of the past 150 years. The more moderate and prudent position is of vastly greater value; it is more genuine, justified, and enduring.

The Right must finally recognize the pressure, needs, just claims, and weight of the masses. The conservative is the guardian of values and feels it his fundamental mission to prevent their falling victim to the leveling forces of democracy or the proletariat. However, the people who traditionally stood for these values all proved their political incompetence during the century of the Democrat and the proletarian; the position of the conservative has been completely undermined, and the things for which he stands have outwardly lost their value. The champions of these depreciated values are indeed themselves threatened with "proletarianization," which is a form of downward social mobility. Respected ranks, honorable and reserved professions, and the entire Western middle class are sinking into the proletariat, despite how desperately the individual may seek to avert such a fate from himself.

It is the issue of people who seem destined to become, though they are not yet, proletarian; it looks as if whole nations are doomed to become proletarian. Therefore, the problem of the masses becomes urgent also on the right.

14

Deteriorating Social Values

The idea of the new Soviet man was intended to reflect the new political–economic reality of revolutionary change in the Soviet era of social engineering, instead of carrying the baggage of peasant and religious superstition that had dominated czarist Russia.[389] The Soviet writer Alexander Zinoviev created the expression "Homo Sovieticus" as a sarcastic and critical allusion to ordinary people of the time being subjected to Frankenstein-like experimentation, which in the end turned on its master.[390] In our age, the experiment has been resurrected in the West, this time with the help of cutting-edge technology to control and manipulate in the service of ideology and mass propaganda. It also has the purpose of creating a new and improved version of the previous Soviet failure: *Homo westernicus*. It is the modern, better fed, entertained, overworked, distracted, and dressed up version of its poor Soviet cousin, but both will end up on the scrap heap of history, fed on a steady diet of ideological "hopium" for a better tomorrow, which will never come.

Education

Leftist activists dominate American colleges, and radicalism of the American political spectrum has established a central place in the curriculum of American universities. The California Association of Scholars lamented the widespread politicization of teaching, pointing out the extraordinary imbalance of liberal to conservative scholars at California universities (29:1 in the Berkeley English Department, for example), a situation that certainly applies not only to North America but also to the entire Western world. Many professors, particularly in the humanities and social sciences, devote themselves less to teaching their particular disciplines than to decrying the presumed crimes of the United States; sympathizing with Islamic terrorists, leftist radicals, and other violent dissidents; or calling for the overthrow of the capitalist world order.

With political commitment often necessitating the abandonment of scholarly integrity, the radicalization of the humanities and the drop in academic standards are closely related. Many teachers of English no longer care much about prosody or literary history or correct grammar because such subjects seem trivial beside the grand social struggles that claim their allegiance. It may well seem more urgent to combat racism than to fight the comma splice, to analyze patriarchal privilege rather than Jane Austen's irony; and when (politically) correct thinking is more important than rigorous thinking, details can be overlooked on the altar of student enlightenment. Combining this with an administrative emphasis on filling seats and a state commitment to student access, and one has the perfect academic turmoil—one that sweeps away scholastics and whirls in crude social engineering.

That many professors seem sincere in their commitment to history's underdogs cannot excuse the damage caused by their policies and by their skewed teaching practices. Their ideological convictions are often imported into the classroom, where a balanced overview of the course material is sacrificed to the politics of race, class, and gender. Students quickly learn that success requires them to adopt approved and preferred positions. Lesbian identities, aboriginal culture, and sharia law are protected from critical appraisal by charges of homophobia, genocidal racism, or cultural imperialism. Instructors often choose the texts on their syllabus not to represent the traditional scholarly consensus on the important and best literature of the period but rather to pose a range of victim groups presented in a noble struggle against the forces of social prejudice. Literature is taught not because it is necessary and worthwhile in itself but because it teaches students to denounce inequality, empathize with victims, and feel either appropriately empowered in a complaint or guilty by association. Some students become so absorbed in leftist ideology that they believe it to be the only possible view of the world; therefore, they would never even seriously consider any alternatives. Their conviction of correctness has revealed itself in a multitude of repressive behaviors on university campuses.

Is there anything to be done? Unfortunately, the ranks of the professoriate are filled with political ideologists who consider their primary responsibility to be that of advancing the goals of leftist orthodoxy. Someday, perhaps, if the decline is not irreversible, and if more courageous professors stand up against the corruption of the academic enterprise, English departments might once again become places where teachers and students can pursue a love of literature.

Economic and Social Life without Objective Truth

If we turn to a brief discussion of the patterns of economic and social life, we see a most extraordinary contrast. While the economic life of Western society has been increasingly successful in satisfying our material needs, the social aspect has become increasingly frustrating.

Not that long ago, the chief aims of most Western people were greater material goods and rising standards of living. These were achieved at enormous social costs by the attrition or even destruction of much of social life, including the sense of community fellowship, leisure, and social amenities. Today we are acutely aware of these costs in the original industrial cities and urban slums, but looking around us, we are often not conscious of the high, often intangible, costs of middle-class living in suburbia or in the dormitory environs that surround European cities. These costs also include the destruction of social companionship and solidarity, and the narrowing influence of exposure to persons from a restricted age group or a narrow segment of the social class. All know the horrors of commuting, the incessant need for constant driving about to satisfy the usual requirements of the family for groceries, medical care, entertainment, religion or social experience. In general, the whole way of life of the suburban rat race, including the large-scale need for providing artificial activities for children, is typical of modern Western civilization.

Rebellion against this rat race began a long time ago, not from the lower middle class or petit bourgeois, who still aspire to it, but from the established middle class, who have, as they say, "had it." On the whole, the efforts to find a way out while still retaining a high standard of material living have not been successful, and the real rebellion is coming, as we have already seen it, from their children. These have expanded the customary adolescent revolt against parental dominance and authority into a large-scale rejection of parental values.

One form this rebellion has taken has been to modify the meaning of the expression "high standard of living" to include a whole series of desires and values that are not material ones and thus were excluded from the nineteenth-century bourgeois understanding of the expression "standard of living." Among these are two disconcerting elements in the rudimentary tribal understanding of the standard of living: small-group interpersonal relationships and sex play. These changes have come to represent a challenge to the whole middle-class ideology.

The social costs of the contemporary economic system are staggering. On the whole, they have been widely discussed and are recognized. As commercial enterprises have become larger and more tightly integrated into one another, freedom, individualism, and initiatives traditionally associated with the modern economy (in contrast to the medieval rural economy) have been sacrificed. The self-reliant and independent individual has gradually changed into the conformist "organization man."[391] The routine has displaced risk, and subordination to abstractions has replaced the struggle with various concrete problems. The steadily narrowing range of possibilities for self-expression has given rise to deep frustrations with their concomitant growth of irrational compensating customs, some of which are the obsession with speed; vicarious combativeness, especially in sports; the use of alcohol, tobacco, narcotics, and sex as stimulants, diversions, and sedatives; and the rapid appearance and disappearance of fads in dress, social customs, and leisure activities.

Because of advancing technology, the demands of the modern industrial and business world for a more highly trained workforce have been most crucial. Such training requires a degree of ambition, self-discipline, and future preference that many persons lack or refuse to provide, with the result that a growing class of social outcasts (the Lumpenproletariat) has reappeared. The groups rejected by the bourgeois industrial society provide one of the most intractable future problems because they gather in urban slums, have political influence, and are socially dangerous.

In the United States, where they congregate in large cities and are often African Americans or Latinos and Latinas, they are regarded as a racial or economic problem but are, in reality, an educational and social issue for which economic or racial solutions would help little. They are most numerous in the more advanced industrial areas and now form more than 20 percent of the American population. They are a self-perpetuating group, have many children, and are increasing in numbers faster than the rest of the population. Their self-perpetuating characteristic as a group is based not on biological differences but on sociological factors. Disorganized, undisciplined, present-preference-minded parents living under chaotic economic and social conditions are most unlikely to train their children in the organized, disciplined, future-preference-minded manner and instill those orderly habits that the modern economic system requires from its workers. As a consequence, the children, like their parents, grow up as unemployables.

This problem is not a condition that can be cured by providing more jobs, because the jobs require characteristics these victims of anomie do not possess and are unlikely to acquire.

All this leads to the most significant of current changes—the changes in attitudes and outlooks. At this point, the middle-class ideology and its challenges that are the central issue in the West shall not be discussed again. Instead, an equally broad subject, the changes in the *outlook* of Western society as a whole, especially in Europe, will be examined.

The intellectual and religious aspects, including the pattern of outlook, of a society change at least as rapidly as the material dimensions of it but are typically less noticed. Among these, the most significant and least noticed are the categories into which any society divides its experiences and the values this society places on these categories. In every society, there are particular groups, perhaps the intellectual elite, who think out new thoughts or have new ideas—new at least in comparison with what went on before. In time some of these ideas spread and become familiar, until it may seem that everybody is thinking them. Of course, everybody is not, because there are three other groups in every society: a large group that does not think at all, a sizable group that is not aware of anything new and retains the same outlook for years and even generations, and a small group that is always opposed to the consensus only because the opposition has become an end in itself.

The problem is how to preserve the historical life of the West—namely the characteristically American, British, French, or German lives that shall make the American, British, French or German peoples embrace all who belong to those nations. Revolutions and transitions may change a person inwardly, but this inwardly changed person must continue the great and historical life of the West, whether to find in it his or her rise or fall.

The battle for civilization is being lost in the West because Western nations have plunged into the tide of neopaganism and are abandoning the foundations for a just and peaceful society. It is insufficient to save the environment, for example, if the underlying social order is collapsing and, in the end, such a cause will merely be a stepping-stone to tyranny.

The nonphilosophy of relativism is now the mainstream default setting in Western society. Relativism has become mainstream because there is no rational debate about it in the absence of objective truth. Without the truth to be debated, one person's opinion on a matter must be as valid as the next (see the many useless and senseless television roundtable discussions).

If there is no objective truth, the only way to make a decision is by utilitarianism or sentimentality. If there is no truth, there is indifference, there is emotional anger, and there is the force of power.

"Objective truth" means not only verbal propositions believed to be factual but also a cohesive and integrated system of thought that makes sense in every aspect of reality. This cohesive system of thought includes even that what is erratic, unstable, and incomprehensible by bearing in mind particular uncertainties. The objective truth is not only a cohesive system of analysis and integration but also a model for life, a code of behavior, and a blueprint for community coexistence. For this truth to be *real*, it must work and keep on working; it must be practical, durable, alive, active, and real.

This cohesive, integrated system of thought that we regard to be true is what the poison of relativism has destroyed, and the result of relativism can only be a dictatorship.

The strong must prevail; Nietzsche was right in a way he did not foresee. Nihilism will produce the "Übermensch," the superman, because there is no other alternative to the nihilism of relativism than the triumph of the superman.[392] If all is relative, who wins the argument? The strongest.

The most stupefying but sobering aspect of this truth is that the indifferent, unconcerned or neutral will *demand* the tyranny of the superman. Most dictatorships are welcomed for what they offer, and in the lack of objective truth and morality, what the strongman says and does is right and proper. Out of the quicksand of relativism comes salvation; finally a light shines in the darkness. Even if the dictator is unable to bring meaning out of senselessness, at least he can bring order out of the chaos. Even if he cannot bring beauty out of the beastliness, at least he can promise security in the midst of terror. Even if he cannot bring morality out of the morass, at least he can impose law on the lawless.

The strongman will only stand there, and he will be worshipped, adored, and glorified, for he will rescue his people from their relativism. He will vow to deliver them from their self-created hell while still allowing them all their decadent pleasures. He will be someone, at last, to believe in and serve, and they will fall at his feet, longing to be his devotees, his debauchees, his supplicating victims, and his willing slaves.

Question: "Do you think immigration should be sensibly moderated, welcoming the deserving but screening possible terrorists?"

Response: "So cruel! So heartless! How can you reject these poor homeless refugees! And you call yourself a Christian!"

Question: "Do you think that the unborn child deserves the right to live and that to cut him up and sell his body parts might be a crime?"

Response: "No one wants to criminalize these poor women who need to move forward in life! How could you deny them the right to choose? Are you in favor of enslaving women once again? How can you be so judgmental?"

This reasoning is sentimentalism, which is one of the serpent heads of the hydra demon called relativism. It is tenderness without truth, mercy without justice, and compassion without morality or meaning.

This way of thinking is no longer the triumph of sensitivity but the tyranny of tenderness, and the final result will be a real tyranny. Pope Benedict XVI's famous phrase *"the dictatorship of relativism"* will eventually lead to political dictatorship because human beings cannot live in the anarchy of boundless and undiscerning compassion for very long.

Ultimately, the pendulum will swing back. People will demand justice, and if we thought compassion without truth was terrible, justice without truth will be no more than the rule of brute force.

Is truth one's own conception of things? It is not, of course. The thought is an attempt to discover whether one's understanding is correct or not. Is truth merely subjective, something that we come up with in a manner that suits our tastes and preferences, or is it objective, something that exists outside ourselves whether we know it or not or like it or not?

For the relativist, just like goodness and beauty, the truth is also in the eye of the beholder. A thing is true, good, or beautiful insofar as one finds it so. All truth, goodness, and beauty are dependent upon the individual. It is self-referential and therefore self-centered; the truth is self-centered; goodness is self-centered; beauty is self-centered. Goodness, truth, and beauty are ultimately about the individual: me, the self, or I.

For the realist, truth exists whether one beholds it or not, and so do goodness and beauty. It does not depend on the individual; I depend on it, whether I know it or not. Realism, as the phrase is used here, is the philosophers' term for those who believe that the cosmos contains independent objects that are perceivable to the senses and include transcendental realities such as love, goodness, beauty, and truth. Realism is, therefore, the antithesis of relativism—the very antidote to the poison that relativism spreads.

Egoistic insolence is the making into God of oneself. It is the placing of oneself in the center of the cosmos and deciding that something be true only if it is one's own conception of things. It is the decision that something is beautiful only if one finds it so. It is the decision that "I" am the only one to judge whether something is good or bad. Egoistic insolence is the totalitarianism of the self.

THE DECLINE OF MORALITY IN WESTERN SOCIETY

I. Judeo-Christian Values vs. Western Values

Judeo-Christian values are *not* the equivalent of Western values; they are, in fact, a subset of Eastern *and* Western values. As self-evident as it should be, both Judaism and Christianity are religions born in the ancient Middle East and rooted in *biblical text* and *faith*. Western values were born primarily in ancient Greece and Rome and rooted in *reason*.

When Jews migrated to Europe during the Diaspora and Christianity finally prevailed on that continent, a merging of the Eastern religious values of biblical faith and morality with Western reason started to happen. This cross-pollination benefited both, as reason was brought under the umbrella of biblical morality and faith was made compatible with reason; thus, Judeo-Christian values were born.

The merger of East and West can also be seen in the writings of Saint Augustine, Maimonides, Saint Thomas Aquinas, and John Locke, and, ultimately, in the American Declaration of Independence. The writings of C. S. Lewis, in particular, paint a beautiful picture of this hybrid between biblical faith, wisdom, morality, and Western reason.[393]

After Emperor Constantine had established Christianity as the official religion of the Roman Empire, a paradoxical situation arose: Christianity became entangled with the authoritarian power of the empire, and the Medieval European Christian Church began to lose sight of its biblical morality. Theocratic authoritarianism ("reason" prevailed!) ensued in the West, and because of this, Medieval Western values cannot be construed as being Judeo-Christian values. This time was an age of brutality, and there was no assurance of the sanctity of life; there was no liberty, and creativity was reserved for the privileged few. During the Reformation, biblical morality was reasserted in the European Church, and there was then a rebirth of Judeo-Christian values among both Catholics and Protestants; the concept of liberty, however, was still rudimentary.

The modern Western notion of the death of God and the perfectibility of man evolved in Europe after the Renaissance and Reformation. This new ideology was based on reason alone—or, more correctly, it was based on Western reason and atheistic faith. This theophobic ideology began to truncate the hitherto Eastern religious and moral nature of Renaissance civilization and resulted in the Western totalitarian evils of Communism and Nazism in the end—modern European amoral legacies of the Roman Empire.

Although Judeo-Christian values were forged in Europe, they have not always found a welcome home there. European Judeo-Christian values were supplanted in turn by Western theocratic authoritarianism during medieval times, by Western Communism and Western Nazism during modern times, and are replaced by Western socialism today. The current and prevailing postmodern European socialism is merely a milder form of Western theophobic ideology and as yet has not turned entirely totalitarian.

As Judeo-Christian values have evolved, they have been reflected in the writings of philosophers, with Middle Eastern religious morality mixing with Western reason in varying combinations particular to each writer; but from the outset, Judeo-Christian values have stood upon the unchanging bedrock of the biblical God. The American Judeo-Christian values have taken on incremental improvements as they have challenged each new generation of lesser values, with a quantum leap occurring as the Founding Fathers of America recognized the God-given individual rights to life, liberty, and creativity.

Although Judeo-Christian values still hold fast to reason, Western values have time and again rejected biblical morality. The European Western values of today lean toward recognizing both the measurable value of the individual and the reversible human rights, which are *not* from the biblical God but are derived from and documented by an elite group of men.

Western values without biblical morality are often in conflict with Judeo-Christian values and promote self-idolatry, but in the end, they demote the individual as state idolatry ensues. Undoubtedly, many Europeans still adhere to some Judeo-Christian values, but they are dwindling in numbers, and theirs is no longer the prevailing culture of Europe.

It fell to the American Founding Fathers to reestablish Judeo-Christian values. However, this time, as outlined in the Declaration of Independence, the God-given and irreversible right to life, liberty, and creativity was asserted as well as the previously identified Eastern values of biblical faith and morality, and the Western value of reason.

The church, but *not* the biblical God, was separated from the government, and there is therefore in America a 1789 constitutional separation of church and state with a preexisting 1776 declarational unity of God and state. The genius of the American Founding Fathers was to reprocess and reintegrate the best of East and West. American Judeo-Christian values assert the infinite value of the individual made in the image of God and promote the unity of free individuals rather than the coerced group conformity of Europe-based Western socialism, communism, and Nazism.

Slavery, begun on American soil by the British before America was a nation, was a violation of American Judeo-Christian values and required the shedding of much blood and the wasting of much treasure to erase it from America during the nineteenth century. American Judeo-Christian values were the source of moral opposition to American slavery. Judeo-Christian values were the moral basis for Europe to rid itself of the theocratic authoritarianism of medieval times, and the

Judeo-Christian values of America also provided the moral foundation for the defeat of Nazism and communism.

The question now is whether Europe will establish Judeo-Christian values similar to the American model with God-given human rights based on biblical morality or whether it will again degenerate into a tyranny of one sort or another.

That question also applies to much of the rest of the Western world.

II. Relative Morality or Absolute Moral Standards?

Past generations through the first half of the twentieth century seemed to live by a general agreement on what was right or wrong, acceptable or unacceptable, moral or immoral. Ostensibly there have always existed those on the edge of society who rejected the necessary standards and morality of the majority. However, in the past, such individuals would have remained in the background, unwilling to be recognized or be blatantly rejected by the accepted norms.

The reality of current Western society appears to be the polar opposite of that scenario. The necessary (biblical) morality that used to be the standard has been replaced by ambiguous norms that are equivalent to a lack of morality, and those who in the past remained in the shadows of society's edges now appear to be in the mainstream. Anyone who would dare to question this new reality is marked "politically incorrect" at best or ignorant and prejudiced at worst.

The primary reason for this shift is the belief that morality is not absolute but evolving as society grows and changes.

That conviction was revealed in 1948 when Alfred Kinsey, the widely acknowledged "father of the sexual revolution," published his unprecedented report on human sexuality, *Sexual Behavior in the Human Male*, followed by his companion book on females in 1953.[394] Kinsey's theme of "free love" was reinforced by a well-timed media blitz, and the American public was receptive. Kinsey greatly helped with the abandoning of absolutes in the social or judicial interpretation of America's Judeo-Christian moral system. As Kinsey biographer James H. Jones writes in *Alfred Kinsey: A Public/Private Life*, "Kinsey loathed Victorian morality. He wanted to undermine traditional morality, to soften the rules of restraint, and to help people develop positive attitudes toward their sexual needs and desire. Kinsey was a crypto-reformer who spent his every waking hour attempting to change the sexual mores and sex offender laws of the United States … For Kinsey, no sexual behavior was bizarre, deviant, or antisocial. The ends justified the means. Adultery could be considered no more immoral than having dessert after dinner. Thus, Kinsey opened Pandora's box to the coarsening, degradation, and abuse of sexuality that have become the hallmarks of the modern world."[395]

Believing that morality naturally changes as society advances may seem the reasonable point of view—if one makes only a limited analysis of the issue. For example, most would agree that the treatment of minorities, particularly African Americans, in the United States during its early decades was undoubtedly immoral—and now we have progressed to a new level of moral consciousness in regards to civil rights. Consequently, one would argue that just because the majority accepts a particular policy (e.g., segregation), it does not make it morally acceptable (see the criticism of democracy). In this particular case, the history of the United States concerning race relations was never the moral high ground. The same cannot be said in regard to other moral issues. Despite the denials of many, American common law was constructed on biblical principles to protect and order society's most essential building blocks: marriage and family.

Avoiding sexual depravity, dressing modestly instead of provocatively, having a sense of civility, avoiding obscenity, treating women with respect, being honest, upholding the family, respecting the parents—all these qualities, as well as others like them, exemplify the moral high ground.

This author believes that morality is an absolute—there is no gray area. Even if a majority of the population considers an action, belief, or concept to be acceptable or even desirable, that fact does not change the reality of absolute moral truth. In ancient times, people accepted as fact that the earth was flat, but that did not change the absolute truth that the earth is a sphere. Modern doctors and scientists have been forced to correct erroneous beliefs that they "knew" to be true over the centuries. By rejecting the truth about gravity, one will soon discover that this belief is not essential for it to function.

The same standard holds true with morals. Will we someday reach the "enlightened" state when we realize that it is a good thing to murder people we do not like or who have offended us? Alternatively, at some "informed" day in the future, will we finally accept the benefits of stealing something of value if we want it? Is the "civilized" time going to come at last when we can share our wives with our neighbors without feeling guilty? Can we ever conceive a "liberal" day when having sex with a child is going to be acceptable? If one believes that none of these things should ever be tolerated, should this person be considered ignorant? Why not?

Because there are absolute moral lines that must be drawn to distinguish humans from the lower animals. We can and must make intelligent choices. People should not act on every physical impulse with impunity as if merely instinct controlled us.

Nevertheless, while the vast majority of people still believe murder, stealing, and pedophilia to be abhorrent and intolerable, they have seemingly accepted other acts previously considered immoral. However, once society starts going down the slippery slope of lowering standards in one sphere of morality, is there a line drawn, or can the downward spiral even be halted?

How wise is it to allow those who were formally considered outsiders because of their immoral actions or those who have now acquiesced to their viewpoint to gain control of the entertainment industry, the arts, the media, the fashion trade, advertising, and other outlets that promote their agenda?

It is unclear whether the majority of people genuinely believes this new view of morals to be something that is real or is only afraid to be labeled as insensitive, uninformed, intolerant, or ignorant. In any case, history is full of examples in which the majority of a population allowed itself to be wrongly influenced by an immoral minority owing, in large part, to the fear of otherwise appearing different, intolerant, cruel, outdated, primitive, or plain stupid. None of those examples had a happy ending.

It must be acknowledged that people, by their very nature, desire freedom. This desire extends to moral freedom, which is the idea that individuals should be able to decide for themselves what it means to experience a good and virtuous life. Since this author wholeheartedly believes that morality is not an ever-changing set of guidelines but instead a set of unshakable standards that transcends all generations, he also opposes efforts by the state or a government or the elite to impose morality (their morality) on any population. In fact, those who are genuinely motivated by moral veracity do not need a set of laws to be in place to follow their conscience—and that is the Russian interpretation of the law.

Personal morality cannot be legislated; nor can it be feigned. Even though standards of morality in the Western world have changed, those who still attempt to live by a congruous and steady moral code should not allow the actions of any individual or group to influence their course of life, even if the particular group of people becomes the majority.

The concept of morality is somewhat straightforward at its absolute core, since it stands for a set of conducts and duties ensuing from what are right and wrong. Morality is the basis of character, wrapped around ethics, and is a challenging subject these days. Most people would agree that society needs some standards of morality; the problem is for them to agree on what those standards should be. Even religion is divided and confused on the subject, as is much of secular society. Meanwhile, as debate and discourse continue, moral standards are indeed changing.

What we are experiencing now is an assault that aims at, and mostly accomplishes, sweeping changes across the entire Western cultural landscape. Large chunks of the moral life and significant features of the culture have either already disappeared or are in the process of extinction. These have already been or are being replaced by such new modes of conduct, new ways of thought, and new standards of morality that should be unwelcome to most of us.

As moral standards in Western society have come under attack, there has been a predictable reaction. Those who believe that morality has no permanent basis for validity rejoice as barriers and social taboos are broken down. Those who believe that society without clear moral underpinnings will disintegrate are alarmed by the discernable trends in this direction. One group sees progress, while the other sees a degenerating society.

III. Right or Wrong?

Mark Twain once suggested, "Always do right. This will gratify some people and astonish the rest."[396] The thought of astonishing people is certainly appealing, yet we need at least a general idea of how to define "right" before we can do it. How do we determine what is correct? That can be difficult, despite the fact that there is a vast field of study devoted to the topic, which is described using terms like "ethics" and "moral philosophy." Nevertheless, even philosophers could hardly improve on the age-old dogma "Treat others as you want to be treated." Albert Schweitzer rephrased it this way: "A man is truly ethical only when he obeys the compulsion to help all life that he can assist, and shrinks from injuring anything that lives."[397]

Regardless of the fact that religion and morality are sometimes treated as interchangeable ideas, moral standards are necessary whether one believes in a higher power or not. Specific standards of behavior are needed to make society work and to establish the basis by which human beings can safely and comfortably relate to each other. If ethical lines shift erratically, no one can anticipate our responses or predict our stance on any issue. However, we all have a strong desire to know where we stand with respect to others or whether they care about us. In most cases, we know that based on their attitudes toward us, their treatment of us, and their responses to our actions. The best relationships we have are with those who will respond as we expect. Accordingly, we strive to be reliable as well, since we know this works both ways; we have to treat others with the same regard and respect as we expect them to extend us.

One could rightly ask why old values failed to inspire a younger generation. A simple answer would be the discernible results of such values. As we witness divorce rates, corporate greed, self-serving political leaders, violence, hypocrisy, and depravity all around us, the next generation is bound to question the values that have produced these results.

Young people have been taught to question and reject morality based on values with any absolute substance; that what is taught in school, church, or home will eventually find its way into the political and moral fiber of our society; and that what is depicted as acceptable on television and in movies eventually becomes the politically correct stance everyone is expected to embrace.

Because of human beings' high propensity to always treat the effects instead of addressing the cause, the solution to wavering moral values will continue to prove elusive.

Until Western society comes to a full realization of what is moral and what is immoral (right and wrong), no practical solution will ever be possible.

Western Values Imposed on Eastern Europe

Today the progressive and liberal opinion leadership of the Western world espouses socialism, globalism, interventionism, egalitarianism, gender equality, environmentalism, social justice, human rights, and a host of other tired mantras of the Left. According to them, Eastern Europe is a place that is provincial, backward, and mired in religious dogmatism. Their vision is a useful one for those wishing to pretend that Eastern European culture and tradition are not an essential part of the European heritage but rather something that the progressive West must go about fixing.

The progressive West wants to convey that Poland, Hungary, Ukraine, and Russia were not participants in European culture and history for a thousand years. "Europe" and "European," according to the Western line of thinking, do not mean "arising from European history" but instead refer to the acceptance of homosexual marriage, secularism, and a globalizing and homogenous technocracy ruling from Brussels.

In this sense, more than 300 million Eastern Europeans who always thought of themselves just as countless others across the continent, as European, have awoken to the world where they hear every day that they need to be "more like the Europeans." That, in fact, means more like what the progressive ideologues want them to be. It is subtle propaganda intended to convince millions of Europeans that they are, in fact, not European at all—unless they support a very narrow political ideology that, like communism before it, was thrust upon parts of Europe by a small but powerful elite. However, the tenacity of this elite is not to be underestimated.

The intellectuals on the Left were wrong about communism for most of the twentieth century. What makes them think they are not wrong about where progressive left-liberal ideology might lead the West today?

Communism, socialism, and modern liberal ideology seek to use government to transform culture to remake humankind and result in its ultimate liberation from all physical and material constraints. We see the effects of this movement in practice in the West. The most compelling diagnosis came from none other than the esteemed Aleksandr Solzhenitsyn in his address to Harvard University in 1978. Every word in that address is apt and prophetic, but none more so for Eastern Europe than these:

> But should someone ask me whether I would indicate the West such as it is today as a model to my country, frankly I would have to answer negatively. No, I could not recommend your society in its present state as an ideal for the transformation of ours. Through intense

suffering, our country has now achieved a spiritual development of such intensity that the Western system in its present state of spiritual exhaustion does not look attractive. Even those characteristics of your life, which I have just mentioned are extremely saddening. A fact, which cannot be disputed, is the weakening of human beings in the West while they are becoming firmer and stronger in the East – 60 years for our people and 30 years for the people of Eastern Europe. During that time, we have been through a spiritual training far in advance of Western experience. Life's complexity and mortal weight have produced stronger, deeper, and more interesting characters than those generally [produced] by standardized Western well-being.[398]

However, the Western progressive intellectuals do not share Solzhenitsyn's view in this or, one would imagine, much else. Instead they embrace what Solzhenitsyn precisely warns against—the West as it is now. Aleksandr Solzhenitsyn certainly experienced the physical and material depravity of the Soviet gulag. If Western luxury did not fool a man like him into the mistaken belief that such a society where, as Dostoyevsky's Ivan from *The Brothers Karamazov* put it, "everything is permitted" was a superior society, then what weight do the musings of the Western elite have on this subject?[399]

The church understands that man is body and spirit, and as Solzhenitsyn taught, both are to be guarded against the radical ideologues who would substitute the perfect love of utopian liberation for the imperfect love of families, citizens, and friends. For Solzhenitsyn, it was enough to look at the soul of the American republic to see that while the bodies of Americans were in relatively good condition, the character of their nation was not.

Ironically, as Solzhenitsyn noted, no amount of physical pain under Soviet Communism could produce such spiritual suffering as American liberalism. Indeed, the people of Eastern Europe and Russia, following their Communist sojourns, were hardened and more firmly grounded in reality—the reality of mortality, the importance of seeking real meaning in life. Harvard University might have "Veritas" as its motto, Solzhenitsyn suggested, but the carefree Americans who passed through it had no understanding of what "truth" meant, because their lives had been soft.

Why should we care? What does it matter if individuals choose to do something? It matters because, if we think about the fate of civilization in this context for a moment, we realize that it matters a great deal.

We might agree, for instance, that an individual has the right to smoke if he wants to. But would we want a society in which every young person smokes when we know of the ills of tobacco use?

We might also agree that women should not be forced into relationships they did not choose and in which they feel oppressed. However, do we feel comfortable with a society where people exchange marriage vows, have children, and then give up on them on a whim as a matter of normalcy?

Do we like a society in which even the suggestion of morality is treated as an insult to someone's lifestyle and the philosophical dialogue about how we ought to live is repressed through political correctness? Can we have free government and free institutions if people are unreflective slaves to their passions? It is not without reason that the scope of constitutional freedom Westerners enjoyed was broader when their culture was more Christian and rational. This scope has now considerably diminished, and their culture continues to become more secular and nihilistic.

There is no denying that the frontal assault against traditional values and modes of (moral) behavior in the West has been increasing of late. Nevertheless, the conservative nations of Eastern Europe, including Russia, want none of that. There is no need to mention the crude escapades, absurd and outrageous rigmaroles, and eventual arrest of the punk provocateur group Pussy Riot, for example, to appreciate that Russia is not going negotiate when it comes to maintaining some level of decency and morals in society.

Russia's law regarding the dissemination of gay propaganda is a perfect example. The law does *not* infringe upon anyone's freedom to engage in whatever sort of sexual activity the individual prefers, while at the same time ensuring the freedom of children not to be forced or publicly encouraged to consider such matters. This law sounds nothing more than the soundest common sense. However, predictably, this easy-to-understand law did not stop dozens of Western media commentators unleashing a torrent of lies regarding the subject. The West, which is becoming increasingly wicked regarding its hyperliberal prerogatives, wants to unleash any and all subjects of carnal interest into the public square.

One attempt to impose a warped vision of humanity, the celebration of transgender individuals, arrived courtesy of the 2014 Eurovision first-place winner, drag queen Conchita Wurst. While some may say that for this persona to enter the global consciousness is just a harmless artist cashing in on his/her uniqueness, others would disagree. Considering that millions of people, many of them impressionable children and adolescents, watch this annual and increasingly bizarre program, should we be so quick to dismiss what kind of psychological impact a bearded transgender woman might leave on this group? Are these the heroes that our children should be emulating?

Shortly after that Eurovision show, Russian President Vladimir Putin gave his view on the winner: "For us, it is important to reaffirm traditional values. People have the right to live their lives the way they want. But they should not be aggressive, or put it up on a show." Many Russians sided with their leader on the matter, as thousands signed a petition demanding Eurovision be removed from the TV lineup and accusing European liberals of exposing children to a "hotbed of sodomy." Indeed, over the long term, such outrageous displays of culture must eventually take their toll on society.

Because Vladimir Putin and some other—albeit not enough—Eastern European leaders are fighting against the steady encroachment of increasingly aggressive, provocative, capricious, and irresponsible acts saturating the world by way of the West, the Russian leader is met with scorn of both sellout Western politicians and their media outlets the world over. However, he has also won over the hearts and minds of millions of individuals, Westerners included, who understand that Putin is fighting for traditional conservative values in a world gone mad. For that, he deserves to be not merely applauded but followed.

The Problems of Immigration: Multiculturalism Creates Multiple Problems

In the midst of the ongoing global experiment, unprecedented in its scope, the melting pot concept of integration is unable to digest the growing migration flow. The reason is that the move toward multiculturalism, as implemented by the left-liberal elite, rejects the notion of integration through assimilation.

Multiculturalism elevates the idea of the right of minorities to be different to the absolute. At the same time, it insufficiently balances this right with civil, behavioral, and cultural obligations regarding the indigenous population and society as a whole. What multiculturalism is leading to in Western countries is the formation of closed national and religious communities that not only refuse to assimilate but do not even adapt. It is astonishing and preposterous that whole neighborhoods and entire cities where generations of immigrants are living on welfare do not even speak the language of the host country.

There can be just one outcome for such a social model: xenophobia on the part of the indigenous population, which understandably seeks to protect its interests, jobs, and social benefits from the foreign competitors.

Immigrants can bring a host of skills and expertise and fill the gaps in the labor market, making the Western economies stronger and Western countries more prosperous. Regrettably, during the past quarter century at least, a reasonable, fair, and controlled position on the subject of immigration has been wholly forsaken. Instead successive Western governments have decided to pursue a policy of massive and uncontrolled immigration from the whole world, whereby the citizens of the West do not even get a say as to who enters their countries. Immigration is not bad for the West, but pursuing a de facto open-door immigration policy that all member countries of the European Union or the United States must follow is.

Within the last fifteen years, immigration has soared to unsustainable levels. In Britain, for example, more immigrants have entered the country between 2004 and 2014 than during the previous nine hundred years.[400] How can that possibly be sustainable? Schools, hospitals, housing, and public transport are all seeing higher pressure than ever before.

Over recent decades, Europe's liberal elite, socialists and leftists, trade unions, and employers have opened their borders to undocumented immigrants for all the wrong reasons: ideology, political correctness, social engineering, and greed. As a result, European immigration policy has been less than successful in assimilating waves of these newcomers. The French riots of 2005 were an indicator of uncontrolled immigration and failure to assimilate.

Along with France, other European Union (EU) nations have experienced religious strife arising from conflicts between Muslim strictures and European secularism. With an estimated twenty million Muslims currently residing in Western Europe, six million of them in France, many remain unassimilated on the lower economic and social rungs of society.[401] Islamic law (sharia) is already firmly established in the EU, and the number of sharia courts is on the rise in each country. Sharia courts prescribe a pattern of personal conduct rather than following a set of rules to govern civil society. Thus some Muslims claim that international human rights, as products of Western culture, are repugnant to Islam. Also, sharia interpretations differ from country to country and even from imam to imam. By allowing different laws for different ethnic groups, sharia has the potential to balkanize a nation.

The recent history of US immigration is a mirror image of Europe's except that the United States has fewer Muslim immigrants than the EU countries. United Nations (UN) officials complain that public opinion polls in Europe and America show a growing intolerance toward undocumented immigrants and their impact on national sovereignty, social and welfare programs, and the environment. These officials contend that this immigration heresy is neither politically nor globally correct. In line with the UN, immigration advocates in the Obama administration also argued that the United States must welcome and provide for undocumented newcomers.

Meanwhile, more and more European nations realize that open borders and waves of unassimilated immigrants undermine national sovereignty and integrity—but they still refuse to do anything about it. In typically hypocritical Western fashion, the EU signed a pact in 2008 that includes a pledge to deport undocumented migrants from European countries and to strengthen border controls; nevertheless, illegal immigrants continue to stream into Europe from the Middle East, Africa, and Asia—encouraged and welcomed by the EU.

In 2009 already, France dismantled camps that had been set up by illegal aliens in the Calais area, from which undocumented immigrants were attempting to cross to Britain. Italy used to intercept illegal immigrants at sea and send them back from whence they came. In response, twenty-four undocumented migrants from Eritrea and Somalia sued Italy in the European Court of Human Rights, claiming that interception is a violation of a person's human right to enter another country legally or otherwise. Lawyers for the twenty-four East Africans argued that the interception of their clients violated Article 3 of the European Convention on Human Rights, which prohibits torture and inhuman or degrading treatment or punishment.

Supporting their case were immigrant advocates who held that interception of persons attempting to enter another country illegally is cruel and inhuman treatment. They also held that illegal migrants have an unfettered right of entry and that the national sovereignty of a detaining country needs to be stretched to include international waters.

Italy and other European countries answered that foreign nationals allowed into Europe pending a human rights lawsuit tend to disappear into Europe's ghost population of illegal aliens and thus fail to show up for their court hearings. In the end, the court ruled in favor of the twenty-four claimants in 2012, mostly clearing the way for the free and uncontrolled entry to Europe of more than a million people in 2015.[402]

The Obama administration, aided by congressional Democrats and lobbyists, sought amnesty for those undocumented aliens who are presently and illegally in the United States, even if their numbers were as high as sixteen million men, women, and children. The official estimate of eleven million people cannot be accepted, since that figure has not changed for many years. Just as in the Obamacare debates, the president and congressional Democrats chose to ignore the voices of the majority of US citizens who said no to socialized medicine and no to European-style immigration.

Many Americans are questioning government accommodations made to Muslims, such as installing footbaths in public educational buildings and prayer rooms at airports. They also question the failure to raise the American flag at Islamic schools operating in the country or the downplaying of the number of hostile acts whereby Americans are threatened or murdered by Islamic terrorists.

The demographic changes brought about by unfettered illegal immigration together with a redistribution of wealth could evolve into the borderless nation proposed by Saul Alinsky, founder of the community organization that inspired young Barack Obama.[403] President Obama openly sought to accommodate undocumented immigrants who demand "no borders, no states."

Illegal and uncontrolled immigration poses a real and present danger to all sovereign nations. Although everyone has an opinion on migration, only very few can justify it; identity and fear fuel the passion underpinning ideas on immigration.

All high-income, primarily Western, societies have developed robust conventions or taboos based on intimidation by indoctrinating political correctness against intergroup violence. This intimidation is one of the defining and distinctive characteristics of high-income societies, and it is a relatively recent achievement, according to left-leaning liberals.

Let us consider some points that would be required for any reasoned analysis of migration:

Some 40 percent of the population of developing countries says they would emigrate if they could.[404] However, if migration happened on any level approaching this scale, the host societies would suffer substantial reductions in living standards. Hence, in attractive countries, immigration controls are essential.

Diasporas accelerate migration. Those immigrants and their descendants are meant by "diasporas" who have retained strong links with their home countries or societies rather than integrating into the host societies. These links not only lower the costs of migration but also fuel it instead; as a result, while diasporas are growing, migration is accelerating. Diasporas continue to increase until immigration is matched by the rate at which immigrants and their offspring are absorbed into the general population. A crucial deduction from this interconnection is that the policies for migration and diasporas must be compatible.

Most immigrants prefer to retain their culture and hence cluster together. This clustering reduces the rate of absorption at which the diaspora is integrated into the general population. The lower the rate of absorption, the lower the rate of immigration that is compatible with stable diasporas and migration. By design, absorption is slower with multicultural policies than with assimilative policies.

Migration from underdeveloped countries to developed ones is driven by the vast gap in income between them; this gap is the moral horror story of our times. The difference in earnings is ultimately due to differences in political–economic systems and social structures, combined with historical and cultural circumstances. Migrants from underdeveloped countries are escaping the consequences of their systems but usually bring their culture with them;

While migrants are the principal beneficiaries of migration in economic terms, many suffer a wrenching cultural and psychological shock. As far as it can be determined from the net effect on satisfaction, the economic gains and psychological costs broadly offset each other, although the evidence on this is currently sketchy.

Since migration is costly, the migrants who can afford it are not among the poorest people in their native lands. The effect on those left behind depends on whether emigration speeds up a political and social change in the home country or slows it down; a modest rate of emigration as experienced by China or India helps, particularly if many migrants return home later. However, the exodus of the young and skilled—as suffered by Haiti, for example—causes a hemorrhage that traps the society in poverty.

In high-income countries, the effect of immigration on the average incomes of the indigenous population is trivial. Immigration does not damage economies, but nor is it necessary for them. The distributional effects can be more substantial, but they depend on the composition of immigration.

In Australia, which permits only the immigration of the skilled, the working classes probably gain from having more qualified people in the workforce. In Europe, which attracts many low-skilled migrants, the indigenous poor probably lose out through competition for social housing, welfare, training, and work. The most apparent effect on the job market is that new migrants compete with existing migrants, who would consequently be substantial beneficiaries of tighter controls.

The social consequences of immigration far outweigh the economic ones, so they should be the primary criteria for policy. These results come from diversity. Diversity increases variety, and this widening of choices and horizons is theoretically a social gain.

However, this diversity also potentially jeopardizes cooperation and generosity. Cooperation rests on coordination stratagems that support both the provision of public goods and myriad socially enforced conventions. Generosity rests on a general sense of mutual regard that supports welfare systems. Both public goods and welfare systems benefit the indigenous poor, which means they are the group most at risk of loss. As diversity increases, the additional or marginal benefits of variety decrease, whereas the risks concerning cooperation and generosity increase. There is an ideal level of diversity, and hence an ideal size of diasporas in each host society.

The control of immigration is a human and sovereign right of every nation. The group instinct to defend territory is common throughout history; it could be even more fundamental than the individual right to property. All societies assert the right to control immigration: one does not have the automatic right to move to Kuwait, the Chinese do not have the automatic right to move to South Africa, and Indians do not have the automatic right to move to the UK and claim the use of its social services and economic wealth.

It is sometimes reasonable to grant the right to migrate on a reciprocal basis; for example, thousands of Germans want to live in Britain, while thousands of Britons want to live in Germany. Nevertheless, if flows become too unbalanced, rights derived from mutual advantage can be withdrawn: Australia, for instance, withdrew them from Britain. The expansion of the EU has created these unstable situations, and the original reciprocal right may, therefore, need modification.

Migration is not an inevitable consequence of internationalization between similarly developed countries. The vast expansion of trade and capital flows among developed countries (see the Western industrial countries of the European Union) has coincided with a decline in migration between them. However, mass migration is an inevitable consequence of globalization.

Left-leaning liberal intellectuals want to combine rapid immigration, the multiculturalism that entitles migrants to remain within a distinct cultural community, and egalitarian society. This amalgamation is a naive, idealistic, and therefore dangerous vision that does not ensure its feasibility.

The open-door policy, multiculturalism, and generous provision of public services are an impossible trinity. It is so because the main social risk posed by rapid migration combined with multiculturalism is not that the society polarizes but that it atomizes. It is not that England, Germany, or Sweden would immediately descend into violence but that their tacit norms of cooperation and generosity would gradually be undermined.

The weight of the evidence overwhelmingly suggests that if a society fragments between an indigenous population and a variety of diaspora communities, cooperation will weaken. More surprisingly, diversity even appears to reduce cooperation *within* the native population; as indigenous networks are disrupted, people withdraw into more isolated lives.

The evidence for these adverse effects of diversity is partly analytical, partly statistical, and partly the results of experimental games. In a book such as this, there is only enough space to present one practical example of a well-known social convention that could be threatened by immigration:

Britain has an unarmed police force. The rarity of this practice rests on a convention among criminals, according to which when faced with unarmed police, the criminals should also be unarmed. Naturally, criminals would gain an advantage by arming themselves, so for the convention to remain in equilibrium depends on an unlikely pattern of collective behavior among offenders—a bizarre code of decency among crooks.

This highly attractive convention is under threat. One reason is that criminals in some diasporas have brought with them entirely different protocols. Jamaica has a murder rate that is forty times that of Britain, and so its criminals have an ingrained gun culture.[405] Somalia has had interclan warfare for a generation, so its criminals are socialized into extreme violence. A sufficiently frequent presence of Jamaican and Somali criminals in Britain would be liable to change the behavior of indigenous offenders; why follow a personally disadvantageous convention if many others are breaking it? At some threshold of criminal violence, the unarmed police force would become quixotic, and British society would lose something it cherishes. Given the difficulty that practically all other societies have had in establishing such a convention, it is likely that this precedence could not be reestablished once it is lost.

Nevertheless, Jamaicans and Somalis are not genetically prone to crime and violence; race and culture are distinct. Anyone of any race can comprehend and absorb any culture; ethnic Jamaicans and Somalis can become culturally indistinguishable from the native English, and many have done so, just as ethnic English criminals might adopt the norms of Jamaica and Somalia.

Diaspora is, of course, not a race; it is a social network associated with a particular culture, and it becomes identified with race only if there is no cultural assimilation or absorption.

Multiculturalism, as its name also implies, is also about culture and not a race; it intends to slow or prevent the assimilation of diasporas into the mainstream indigenous culture. In so doing, multiculturalism reduces the rate of migration compatible with both a stable diaspora and steady migration.

With an open-door policy, migration keeps accelerating beyond this level so that diasporas keep expanding, thereby increasing diversity. In turn, beyond a point diversity starts to undermine the cooperation and generosity on which egalitarian policies rest. This gradual erosion of trust is why the trinity of policies judged desirable by liberals is unattainable.

The analyses and experience suggest that moderate migration is modestly beneficial, whereas rapid migration carries potentially high risks. The West lacks the research to determine where Western society is along this dangerous path.

One can only guess whether to date Britain, Germany, or France have had net benefits. We do, however, know that uncontrolled migration is accelerating. Consequently, at some point, the costs of additional diversity would outweigh the benefits.

We do *not* know the rate at which diasporas are being absorbed.

We do *not* know what rate of migration would be compatible with stable diasporas to establish an ideal level of diversity and the ideal size of diasporas in the host societies.

We do *not* know at which point particular social conventions would start to crack when confronted with the increasing diversity.

Finally, but perhaps most importantly, we do *not* know what the costs of such cracks would be.

In these circumstances, modern liberals who dismiss concerns about future migration as distinct from the complaints about its past effects are being cavalier, as usual, at other people's expense. It is the indigenous poor, existing immigrants, and people left behind in the countries of origin who are potentially at risk, not only the middle classes.

If future migration is to be controlled and the permitted rate related to the size of the diaspora stabilized, immigration policies and the supporting data will need thorough examination and revision. Both the rate of illegal migration and the size of the diaspora are unknown in the West today.

The core objective of migration policy should probably be to stabilize the size of the diaspora, culturally defined. There are evident legal, political, and ethical limits that will need to be respected—not least arising from the EU—but a commitment to the reasonably defined and measured stabilizing of diversity must be a meaningful and implementable objective.

Although we do not know whether the current estimated size of the diaspora is correct, both the caution appropriate to scientific ignorance and the evidence of widespread concern among the indigenous population suggest that stabilization would be a sensible medium-term objective until we know better.

All forms of temporary migration, such as international students studying in a host country, are benign and should be excluded from targets. Students who return home after graduation are highly beneficial to those left behind; in addition to the acquired skills they take back, students' exposure to the political and social values of their host societies rubs off on them; once they return, they spread these practical benefits. It is true that student visas are open to abuse; students refusing to go home are not just a problem for the host society but are also debilitating for their home countries.

There is sufficient scope for a deal between the state and universities: more students in return for adequate controls. Universities have very effective control points at their disposal (e.g., the award of a degree and prepayments), which they already use without compunction to ensure that students pay their bills. The same system could be used (by the state) to make sure that students leave the host country upon finishing their studies.

The composition of migration matters more than its rate; the more skilled and employable the migrants, the more beneficial they are. Whereas a points system can assess skills, only employers can determine employability, and so a reasonable requirement is that migrants should already have a job offer.

Existing migrants want to bring in their dependents, and this occupies migration slots that could otherwise have been filled by skilled workers. Furthermore, this family reunification process is likely not only to slow the rate at which diasporas absorb into mainstream society but also increases the burden on the welfare system of the host country.

A particularly sensitive issue is the migrant's right to bring in a prospective spouse. Although indigenous citizens have the right to bring in foreign spouses, it is viable as a right only because few native citizens wish to use it. To extrapolate from this mostly unexercised right of the indigenous to infer a right that would be utilized very frequently by immigrants is wholly unreasonable. A similarly contestable extrapolation to the rights of immigrants concerns social housing and related benefits. Many migrants from developing countries will have needs that exceed those of the low-income indigenous population—but should they preempt limited provision?

Granting the right to immigrate can be part of a package of rights and obligations designed to protect the rights of the indigenous. This package is particularly important where entitlement to welfare systems is needs-based, as in Britain, rather than dependent on past contributions, as in continental Europe. Migrants to high-income countries from developing countries have won the lottery; in return, the poor indigenous population must also be protected of its rights.

Parents incline to pass on their culture to their children; this desire is true both of immigrants and of the indigenous population. It has become an unshakable belief in liberal and official circles that cultural diversity must be respected and promoted. However, although the cultures that immigrants from poor societies bring with them may have some attractive features, they are naturally implicated in the social failures from which these migrants are escaping. For example, poor societies typically have far lower levels of trust and higher levels of violence and intolerance. There is, therefore, a real and objective reason why we should want the children of immigrants to absorb the Western culture.

Left to their inclinations, migrants cluster. This fact reduces the rate of absorption of even essential attributes, such as language. High concentrations of diaspora clusters in schools are so likely to slow absorption that it may be sensible to cap the proportion permitted. Some countries have had more active policies of dispersal: location is made part of the package of rights and obligations.

The consequences of uncontrolled future immigration are potentially severe, dangerous, and possibly catastrophic. Designing controls that are effective, just, and advantageous to citizens will be complicated and contentious. The task cannot be avoided.

Some political parties, particularly those of the Left, encourage mass immigration to rub the Right's nose in diversity, calculating that it will boost the number of their voters. The rate of migration has been so high that irreversible changes have been made to vast swathes of several Western countries. Ethnic division is a reality, and the problem is getting worse. Although much of the blame lies with leftist, socialist, green, and liberal politicians, the so-called conservatives are little better.

The British must build a new home every seven minutes for new migrants. England is, with Holland, the most crowded country in Europe, with 380 and 500 people per square kilometer, respectively, compared with 232 in Germany and 121 in France.[406]

Conservative and socialist, Republican and Democrat, green and liberal politicians alike have been lying to the people as to the scale and effect of immigration for many decades. Their stock riposte to those speaking out has been to accuse them of being racist, but the debate has never been about the preservation of the West's cultural identity.

The age of mass uncontrolled immigration in the West must come to an end. Since 1990 immigration has added almost sixty million new people to the populations of North America and Europe; this figure does not include illegal immigrants, the exact number of which is unknown but is probably, or officially admitted to be, at least eleven million only in the US—and probably much, much higher.

Europe as a whole is very densely populated. One of the most densely populated countries in the world is England; it is more densely populated than China, India, and Japan. It just cannot sustain an immigration level that adds another one million people to the population every four to five years, putting an intolerable burden on the infrastructure and public services there.

A minimum of a five-year freeze on immigration for permanent settlement should be introduced immediately, at least until the time the United States and EU regain command of their borders, institute effective immigration controls, and deal with the problem of illegal immigration. Overstaying a visa should be considered a criminal offense and treated accordingly.

Future immigration for permanent settlement should be on a strictly limited and controlled basis when it can be shown to benefit the people as a whole and their economy. Immigrants would not be able to apply for public housing or benefits until they had paid tax for at least five years.

The responsible authorities, using a points-based work permit system, should enable people to enter and work in Western countries for limited periods of time to fulfill specific gaps in the job market that the existing workforce cannot fill.

Measures must be taken to identify illegal immigrants and remove them to their countries of origin. Exceptions may be made in limited circumstances, but there would be no general amnesty for illegal migrants.

Affected Western countries could, would, and should withdraw from the European Convention on Human Rights and the European Council on Refugees. This withdrawal would enable them to deport foreign criminal and terrorist suspects where desirable. However, the states involved would still allow genuine asylum applications in agreement with their international obligations.

None of these policies can be implemented, however, while the political leadership of the Western nations remains under the left-liberal-socialist influence.

Principles of Media Criticism

The Western world, circa 2017, resembles a rudderless ship drifting aimlessly, without any political leaders of conviction and moral authority to steer its course.

The social-engineering project that Western democracies are currently pursuing distorts human reality and pretends that human existence can be tailor-made to the specifications of our caprice. Part of this has come about by creating not only self-doubting and self-loathing individuals but even entire nations that fail to understand the fragile nature of human liberty. This moral vacuum must be filled somehow.

Contemporary politics, political scientists, and philosophers pay next to no attention to the role that Marxist and neo-Marxist disinformation plays in Western countries. This disinformation cleverly exploits the reality that insecurity and anxiety ultimately rule human existence.

Disinformation is effective because it places carefully selected and damaging lies and slander in the ears of unsuspecting people and institutions that spread them at will. Disinformation is effective because it creates a web of deception that weakens a person's capacity for inference and perception. Through disinformation, truth no longer corresponds to what one sees but to what the official censor makes one believe. Disinformation has a consciousness-altering power, which is why disinformation tactics are fine-tuned by taking the pulse of Western man's moral–spiritual convictions. In the deceptive communication of disinformation, Bolshevism and its many subsequent variants discovered a tool that is effective in undermining Western man's morals and morale but that few would ever come to suspect.

Humanity has always known despotism but not totalitarianism. The dialectical malice of disinformation dawned on communist despots in the twentieth century. The assault on Western civilization is encountered on many fronts and has proven very effective since the 1960s. We witness this numbing moral–spiritual infirmity in our self-indulgent, life-negating art and literature, the proliferation of what is essentially a death-of-God Christianity, and modish, self-mutilating nihilism. Western man is being strangled by nihilistic passions and the compulsion to abuse freedom in democratic societies.

The enemies of Western civilization have gotten delighted by their own tricks and become emboldened by the recognition that the ideological hegemony of cultural Marxism, combined with patience and persistence, pays consistently high dividends in the culture war. Theirs is a win-win game of opportunism, and they are cynical debasers of democracy from within. Their democracy is gracious enough to accommodate them—a condition which, as modern history shows, makes democracy a willing participant of its own demise. This curious fact is one reason why people who have lived in communist countries are amazed at the insipid, self-destructive complacency of Western man.

Socrates believed the fallacious nature of "seeming wise while not being wise" will sooner or later reveal itself. His opponents, the Sophists, retorted by saying that words were always subject to interpretation, so someone controlling interpretation will eventually control reality. In our times, Sophists would probably find their golden age, since words and images are twisted in unimaginable ways.

The Western media, which ascribes itself the right to be the translator of things, regularly misinterprets what the leaders of other countries, such as Russia, China, Iran, and Hungary, have to say. These "interpreters" follow the principle that if reality does not correspond to Western stereotypes, formed of course by the ruling elite and their media, then so much the worse for reality. Accordingly, the media translation of reality looks more and more like manipulation.

Moreover, media criticism is undeveloped today, primarily because the mainstream media allows virtually no open discussion of the subject. Some criticism does get out to the public, of course, but the same forces that have turned the media into a source of manipulation corrupt most of it.

The selections below attempt to correct this conspiracy of silence by offering an introduction to the field that will allow seeing the broader trends that define mainstream media today. These selections focus on the following characteristics of contemporary culture and society:

All centers of power rely on the media today using sensory manipulations and stimulations, along with story lines, rhetoric, and acting to sell the public their ideas, candidates, and packaged products.

The mainstream media, from the news to advertising, relies on spectacle, simplification, manipulation, and exaggeration to snatch and grip audiences.

The media has become part of the power and economic system on which it is supposed to report, instead of standing at a distance from events and trying to provide an accurate account. All too often it is just another inside player manipulating information for its own ends. This means not only that media companies have a conflict of interest but also that even those journalists who would perhaps prefer to be honest end up subordinating themselves to those in power and shaping their coverage accordingly. It also means that media criticism that is not afraid to report on what is taking place is, or should be, now essential to the maintenance of democracy.

Much of the media is beset by idealization and demonization both to create exciting stories and win battles. The media manipulators depict themselves and their cronies as heroes and saints, and their opponents or victims as villains, fools, and disturbed characters.

The missing information pervades the media today. What is missing is precisely the information that should bring about improvements and reforms, which would dismiss those who work the system for their own benefit.

All mainstream media today is a form of action; stories, rhetoric, visual images, and manipulated impressions are all efforts to influence people's perceptions and reactions, evoke their fears and desires, and play to values. The deliberate omission of information by the media is a form of action as well.

The above items have to form the core of any theory of media criticism and any theory that seeks to describe contemporary society.

There is an unmistakable difference between the ways the media covers liberals versus conservatives. Regarding leftist economic and social policies, the media functions more as supporters than reporters. Media bias is so rampant nowadays that journalism is collapsing before our eyes. How could the institution that claims to be impartial and objective in its reporting turn out to be so blatantly biased?

There was a time when journalism embraced its role as a political advocate. For most of the nineteenth century, printed media was explicitly partisan in its perspectives and openly sought to convey particular political viewpoints and theories to an increasingly educated public.

Then, journalism, along with Western society as a whole at the beginning of the 20th century, went through two fundamental changes, indicating a cultural turn toward modern liberal values.

First, journalists began to reconsider their trade as an appendage of scientific rationalism, seeking to analyze events objectively and impartially, regardless of the predisposition of the reporter. Under objectivity, journalists supposedly adopt the pose of scientist and vow to eliminate their own beliefs and values as guides in ascertaining what was said and done. Purportedly avoiding all subjective judgments and analysis, the journalist strives to become a rigorously impartial expert collector of information. That is why the journalist is never part of the story he or she is covering, since such an inclusion would violate the perception of objectivity. This perceived absence is a primary way in which journalists establish themselves as mediators of information composed of data and facts.

While the first change involved the journalist's conception of *knowledge*, the second change involved the journalist's orientation toward *values*. Scientific rationalism erects new boundaries of knowledge that effectively censor religions, traditions, customs, and cultures from the realm of what can be known. Indeed, scientific facts are considered objective precisely because they transcend the biases and prejudices innate to cultural values and norms.

What emerges from this precommitment to scientific rationalism is what has been called a fact/value dichotomy: facts are objective while values are subjective; facts apply to all while values apply to only some. Thus, as the journalist transforms into an impartial observer of economic, political, and social events, he or she begins to view moral and religious sensibilities regarding personal lifestyle values that are relative to individuals or cultures. Today virtually every media outlet features prominently a Lifestyles section, where we can learn about everything from the sex habits of entertainers to our horoscopes.

There is an inescapable global consequence to these twin commitments of modern liberalism. Inexorably, the modern liberal reimagines the world through bifocal lenses as comprising those who embrace modern liberal values on the one hand (no doubt "distant vision" for the liberal) and those who reject them on the other ("near vision"). Those who embrace modern liberal commitments are by definition rational and progressive, while those who reject them are by definition irrational and repressive.

Moreover, when journalists transcribe this bifocal vision to the political arena, it is applied to two political factions. The first one, which, through its support of abortion, LGBT rights, and strict separation of church and state, demonstrates its commitment to modern liberal values, while the other, through its insistence on traditional morality and social structures, shows its resistance. Thus, one party is viewed consistently as rational and liberal while the other party is seen as irrational and repressive. When challenged on such a perspective, journalists can always fall back on objective and impartial "facts."

The "unsophisticated" Communists of the formerly subjugated Eastern Europe used the media to make their lies believable but failed miserably. The "sophisticated"

Western elite uses the media to sell their hype to the public, and many, but not all, people in the West not only believe this propaganda but even enjoy it.

The Soviet and Eastern European populations used to turn to the BBC, Voice of America, or Radio Liberty for news and information during the Cold War. Today, in another twist of history, more and more people in the East and West turn to Russia Today or China's CCTV to gain insight into non-Western-influenced viewpoints.

The Western ruling elite and their official news fabricators know and feel that they are slowly but surely losing the disinformation battle for the control of the minds of the general public, but they do not care, since they have a monopoly on deceiving the people.

WHAT HAPPENED TO THE WEST? THE FALSE FAITH IN PROGRESS

All about us, we can see now that the West is passing away. In a single century, all the great houses of continental Europe fell, and all the old European empires that ruled the world have vanished.

Not one European nation, save Muslim Albania and Bosnia, has a birth rate that will enable it to survive through four or five generations. As a share of the world population, peoples of European ancestry have been shrinking for three generations. The character of every Western nation is irrevocably altered as each undergoes an unresisted invasion from the Third World.

Having lost the will to rule, the Western man seems to be losing the will to live as a unique civilization as he feverishly indulges in *La Dolce Vita* with a yawning indifference as to who might inherit the earth he once ruled.

What happened to the Western World?

When the twentieth century opened, the West was everywhere supreme. However, sometime during that century, the Western man suffered a catastrophic loss of faith in himself, in his civilization, and in the faith that gave it birth.

There can be no dispute about the physical and psychological wounds that may yet prove mortal. This catastrophe was the seventy-seven years of war from 1914 to 1991: the two world wars, which could be called the "Western Civil War," and the subsequent Cold War. Not only did the two world wars carry off scores of millions of the best and bravest of the West, but they also gave birth to the fanatic ideologies of Leninism, Stalinism, Nazism, and fascism. All of these were outgrowths of socialism, whose massacres of the people they misruled accounted for more victims than all of the battlefield deaths during those seventy-seven years.

Who is responsible for the decline of the West? Who blundered into the seventy-seven years of war, the costliest and bloodiest period of war in the history of humanity, which may have brought on the end of Western civilization?

Without a doubt, the Western elite did so by reneging on their responsibility to the people, by becoming tired of their riches, and by becoming corrupt, immoral, and wicked—in short, by giving up on all of the Judeo-Christian values. By adopting the left-liberal-socialist mindset instead, by abandoning the middle class, and by making deals with the devil to save their position (which they will inevitably lose in the end), the Western elite gave us the present calamity. If not exposed and checked, they will produce more wars and disasters in the name of making the world safe for democracy and protecting human rights.

Over fifty years ago, Wilhelm Röpke was warning the postwar Western world of the dangers of mass culture, mass society, and mass man, where the soul of man is neglected in pursuit of material gain—"where," he said, "the dignity of man is sacrificed on the altar of efficiency and where the media is employed for the dissemination of economic and political propaganda aimed at directing and controlling the masses."[407] Regrettably, neither the elite nor the masses have heard or heeded his warning.

Carefree and secure, but with no requirement for intellectual activity or exertion, the peoples of the West have become slightly insane. Their minds have become shallow and unstable, and their lives have degenerated into a quest for leisure and amusement, looking for solace in the bustling yet malcontented world.

The soil of Western Civilization, which in the Dark Ages was left uncultivated, is now exhausted. Bewildered by opulent materialism, men and women travel everywhere but live nowhere, know everything but understand nothing. Amid this constant turmoil and anarchy, there is no opportunity to find solitude for the mind or quiet for the soul. The world of socialistic liberal democracy has killed the human personality.

In such a paradise of the traveling salesman, where life is rationalized and added with every material comfort, there is not much satisfaction for the genius of man.

The essence of civilization lies in man's defiance of an impersonal universe. It makes no difference that a mechanized world may be his creation if he allows his handiwork to enslave him. It is not for the first time in history that the idols that humanity has shaped for its own ends have become its master.

A sense of disorientation has become the Western reality, and the people do not understand what is happening to them. They are bewildered and perplexed—sensations that have always beset men and women in times of crisis. Their bewilderment leads first to exasperation and a world overflowing with extreme yet transitory phenomena with which they intoxicate and stupefy themselves. Then desperation follows with the recognition that there is no hope of respite or escape. Although people continue to live, they find no idea or action satisfactory; they move like machines and conduct the necessary business of life but find in it little of joy and nothing of value. They have come to feel an intractable loathing for the world at last.

In the very distant past, people who were lost, embittered, and estranged retired to the desert or the mountains or found some other secluded place where they could hide. They wanted to simplify, clarify, and solve the problems of life this way by reducing contact with the world to a minimum. This retreat came amid, and indeed because of, the expansion of knowledge, and yet none of it enough; the splendor of riches, appetites, and pleasures, and yet none of them fulfilling or complete; the persistent stir of activity, and yet none of it endowed with meaning or purpose. Under those circumstances, life became empty, incompetent, and unpredictable, dominated by fictions and falsehoods.

Our age is an intermission between a past period in which much of the old world and way of life died and a still-coming period in which the promising new world and way of life will ripen into what they will become—if they have not already gone rotten. Doubt and insecurity abound.

Three characteristics mark periods of cultural disintegration. First, culture becomes too intricate and abstruse, overwhelming human intellectual and moral capacities. Second, ideas lose their vigor and standards of conduct lose their force. Third, the culture ceases to be authentic, honest, natural, and instinctive and becomes instead inconsequential and disconnected from the flow of life. Under such conditions, no one can be who he or she is except by retreating into the self and remaining alone to determine what thought, opinion, idea, belief, or action is one's own. However, before expressing any of these, one must pause and enter into the self.

Since the only alternative to a hectic, unruly, deranged, and falsified life is to remain centered in the self, people prefer hypocrisy instead. Although the hypocrite pretends to think or believe something that he is not, he at least understands what his real ideas and beliefs are, even as he conceals them in an attempt to deceive.

So the modern Western man has become a fake hypocrite in his hypocritical society. If people live on borrowed ideas, embracing and repeating them only because they have heard someone else do so, then, unlike the real hypocrite, they will not be deceiving others. They will deceive only themselves.

Farewell, then, to repose and serenity. Farewell to modesty and humility. Farewell to truth and honesty. Farewell to all that is real.

Beneath what we presume to be the progressive and revolutionary character of our time lurks an extraordinary intellectual stagnation. It can be anticipated that ideas move with a deadening sluggishness and lassitude during this cultural devolution, with people continually mistaking appearances for reality.

This author has lived in a period that saw the most rapid changes take place in the minds of people. However, it will inevitably happen that the principal human opinions will be more stable than they have been in the preceding centuries of Western history. Western societies will end by being too invariably fixed in the same institutions, the same prejudices, and the same mores. As a consequence, humanity comes to a stop and becomes limited; the mind eternally turns back on itself without producing new ideas; man becomes exhausted in small, solitary, and sterile movements; and, even while always moving, humanity no longer advances.[408]

Many in the West refuse to abandon their faith in progress and continue arrogantly to believe that it is assured to them. In time, progress will return and all will again be well, and all manner of things will be well—or so they think. The unmentionable contradiction of progress is that, although it promises to liberate—to make life better by making it easier—the so-called progress has always and everywhere diminished the need for human effort and creativity. It finds ever-new ways to eliminate the *necessity* of using the muscles and the brain. Progress thus makes us weaker, more stupid, and more dependent.

For that reason alone, George Orwell contended, "Nowadays, every intelligent person is a reactionary," or ought to be.[409]

For Americans, history must always have a happy ending; there can be no calamities or tragedies. However, the American commitment to progress and happiness has by now come to rest on little more than wishful thinking. American optimism (not unlike the unbounded confidence of many other high cultures in the past) denies the limits of power. It would be more prudent to trust the goodness of life without either ignoring the restrictions it imposes on us or denying its ultimately tragic character. The idea of progress seduces us with promises of unlimited desire and ambition, neither of which can ever be satisfied.

In their persistent unwillingness to accept or even acknowledge human limitations, Americans have become more the victims than the beneficiaries of progress. Perhaps their embrace of it in the face of the economic and spiritual crises has been the antidote to despair, a mistakenly optimistic fatalism, or fake hypocrisy to counter an equally mistaken pessimistic resignation. In any case, the dogma of progress has exhausted its usefulness and no longer has the capacity either to explain or to inspire.

The stubborn progressive orthodoxy, now so firmly embedded in popular culture, political and business life alike, has thus rendered impossible an imaginative reinterpretation of the past, a sober assessment of the present, and a realistic vision of prospects. The worst of all is that the expectation of progress without end (permanent double-digit growth) obscures the many blessings that Americans have long enjoyed and distorts the old truth that life is a gift and not an affront to the power of the human will. Such ingratitude and arrogance are at once the renunciation of virtue and the essence of sin.

During the Anglo-Saxon days, God was supposed to have made the laws, and the king and his council only declared what they were. After the reign of King John, who signed the Magna Carta, all kings succeeding him on the throne admitted that their sovereignty over their subjects was limited. Philosophers, such as Browne, Hobbes, Milton, and Locke, stated in broad, abstract terms the theories of limited sovereignty. The scholars of the American Revolution stated these principles more clearly and made them the foundation of the American State.[410]

According to these principles, the right to self-government is sacrosanct, the government was made to serve man, and man was not made to serve the government. When the government fails to serve man, it should be changed—peaceably if possible, forcibly if need be.

Conservatism is based on the cardinal principle of self-government, which is the direct consequence of understanding human history. Any government from a great distance is an ignorant government because it has no understanding of the local situation; it is a despotic government because the opinion and wishes of the people are not considered or even known. The Western elite has maliciously transformed society by not bringing freedom and happiness to the people but rather to the great bankers and industrialists. In reality, the globalizing industrialists and multinational but homeless corporations gained control of the national governments and made them over according to their own desire.

One of the leading causes of the social and cultural dislocation in the modern-day West concerns married women as mothers. Most of the modern emancipated women lost their connection with the traditional role of wife and mother not by some accident but by choice. Modern women are free; they work and provide for their families—many because they have to, others because they choose to. Modern society dictates that course.

It could be argued, though, that the modern woman does not *want* to live in a genderless society, regardless of a gradual push in that direction. These women do not want their husbands' jobs; they do not want to take men's places. Today when women are told that liberty means fewer children and a career, it is almost forgotten in the West that women have long been the standard bearer for the tradition, stability, and unity of society. Women rear their children on the history and culture of their people, provide a link to the past, and nurture future generations to develop respect for place and tradition; women are the key to cultural independence.

Another reason for the social and cultural dislocation of the modern-day West is the destruction of the old order. Man, living in the modern industrial state, lost his connection with the past, his economic freedom, and his belief in the old doctrines. Man, in essence, had by inertia been dislocated from his traditional mores. He has no dock, no compass, no map, and no reference point; *he is lost*.

Before modern Western society robbed man of the good and the beautiful, man, as representative of society as a whole, mostly retained the ancient doctrines of his ancestors. These were grounded in religion, in the belief of free will, and in the doctrine of eternal reward and punishment. The modern man has instead substituted all religious values; he now solely worships man and his creation.

This shift allows for the modern man to be reduced to a wage-slave, a tool at the hands of the plutocracy, because he has no more conception of independence and no attachment to the land. Modern society has made him weak, and the loss of tradition has made him intellectually unable to deal with or resist the drastic changes that usurped his independence.

All these shifts, changes, and events indicate a move toward the reestablishment of slavery, because to be compelled to work not by one's own initiative but at the initiative of another is the definition of slavery. Whether enslavement shall come first in the form of slavery to the state or employer before it arrives at the final, natural, and stable form of slavery to individuals, it is still slavery. The free, liberated, and democratized modern man accepts such slavery in the unshakable belief that it is inevitable, being in the nature of things.

This author used to be compelled to be a good team player by his employers and do what they expected of him, which was to use *his* intellect and own initiative based on *his* education and experience—but only as *tools*. He was never to come up with new ideas or establish new parameters of his own; he was only to bring *their* ideas, orders, and parameters to fruition, with the help of *his* tools. The result of this modern form of slavery is the decline of our civilization.

The remedy may be found only in a change of philosophy; only by instructing man in the forgotten order of things, including the possession of the land, would man be able to restore his independence. Nevertheless, this task has become exceedingly trying to achieve. Ownership, property, freedom, respect for the old order, the understanding that change and tradition must be reconciled, community, and the imperfectability of the soul must all be part of the crusade to save man from himself. However, cultural independence will breed political and economic independence.

The above is the practical application of the conservative mind—a political, economic, and cultural prescription for the restoration of the Western order. It is the culmination of centuries of wisdom, a philosophical critique, but more of a call to action—partly political, partly economic, and wholly cultural.

Independence can be achieved. It used to be the Western way.

15

The Decay of Culture, Arts, Sports, and Environment

A society going through rapid technological changes, political upheavals, devastating wars, and social restructuring is bound to experience enormous strain within that is reflected in its culture.

Only after the Roman Empire began to lose its internal cohesion, patriotism, and fighting spirit over the centuries did it start to give way to its adversaries and finally collapse.

Indeed, it is the same course Western civilization is taking today.

Internal Cohesion

Today's Western society not only has a "do your own thing" attitude but also glorifies the defying of rules and the flouting of authority. Balkanization through multiculturalism has become dogma.

It is almost forgotten that national consciousness once articulated the idea of "we"—the conviction of togetherness. The willingness to accept responsibility as a community, the feeling of belonging in a time of need, has mostly faded away. We do not even know who we are any longer. There is hardly any talk about a nation, as if history besmirched even the term. What is a nation after all? Is it an anachronism, a bellicose right-wing concept, a reminiscence of the past?

The words "nation" and "national" have become negative terms or even taboos in the West ever since the Second World War. The most extreme example is Germany, of course, where National Socialism, with all its aftereffects, caused not only hitherto irreparable psychological damage but also a profound identity crisis.

When the concept of Europe is detached from the idea of the nation and "Europe" replaces "the nation" in the public political arena, it is a telling sign of serious weakness. The nation-states have not disappeared; Europe is and will remain the product of such nation-states even if the socialists disavow it. The individual countries have many different, varied, and justified interests that should not disappear behind a European haze.

Can Western society and culture remain the anchor uniting its various nations, or are we on the road to Balkanization and the breakup of the West into ethnic enclaves?

Western countries are no longer distinct nations descended from the same ancestors, speaking the same language, professing the same religion. They are from every continent and country; they are multiracial, multilingual, multicultural societies in the world, where many countries are being torn apart by race, religion, and roots. Nearly four in ten Americans trace their ancestry to Asia, Africa, and Latin America.

The people of any Western nation no longer speak the same language, worship the same God, honor the same heroes, or share the same holidays. Christmas and Easter have been privatized. The politics of a Western country have become poisonous; their political parties are at each other's throats; Christianity is in decline. Traditional churches are sundering over moral issues like abortion and same-sex marriage. Islam is surging.

The societies of Western countries seem to be disintegrating. Over 40 percent of all births now are illegitimate in the United States; the figure is 52 percent among Hispanics and 73 percent among African Americans. The drug use rate, dropout rate, crime rate, and incarceration rate are all many times higher among children born to single mothers than among children born to married parents.[411]

More and more, all of the twenty-first-century nations of North America and Europe seem to meet rather well Metternich's depiction of Italy in 1847—"a geographic expression."[412]

Patriotism

Not only is patriotism disdained in the West; the very basis of pride in one's country and culture is systematically undermined in practically all of the educational institutions. These teach history that conceals the achievements of Western civilization and portrays every human sin as if it were a Western peculiarity.

The classic example is slavery, which existed all over the world for thousands of years and yet is incessantly depicted as a characteristic of Europeans enslaving Africans.

The Arab slave trade originated before Islam and lasted more than a millennium. Arab traders brought Africans across the Indian Ocean from present-day Kenya, Mozambique, Tanzania and the Far East, Eritrea, Ethiopia, and elsewhere in East Africa to present-day Iraq, Iran, Kuwait, Somalia, Turkey, and other parts of the Middle East and South Asia (mainly Pakistan and India). Unlike the trans-Atlantic slave trade to the New World, Arabs supplied African slaves to the Muslim world, which stretched over three continents from the Atlantic to the Far East at its peak. According to historians, it is estimated that from ten to eighteen million Africans were enslaved and transported across the Red Sea, the Indian Ocean, and the Sahara desert by Arab slave traders between the years 650 and 1900.[413]

To a smaller degree, Arabs also enslaved Europeans. Robert Davis, professor of history at Ohio State University, has calculated that at least 1 million and possibly as many as 1.25 million European Christians were abducted between 1530 and 1780. They were captured by the Muslims of the Barbary Coast, vassals of the Ottoman Empire, mainly from the seaside villages of Italy, Spain, and Portugal, and also from more distant places, such as France, England, the Netherlands, Ireland, and even Iceland. They were then enslaved and forced to work in North Africa. The impact of these attacks was devastating. France, England, and Spain each lost thousands of ships, and the inhabitants almost completely abandoned long stretches of the Spanish and Italian coasts.[414]

Also, both the Ottoman wars in Europe and the Tatar raids brought large numbers of European Christian slaves into the Muslim world. Crimean Tatars were known for frequent, at some periods almost annual, devastating raids into what is Ukraine and Russia today. The Crimean Khanate continued a massive slave trade, which was the basis of its economy, with the Ottoman Empire and the Middle

East through the late eighteenth century. One of the most important trading ports and slave markets was Kefe (modern-day Feodosiya). Slaves and freedmen formed approximately 75 percent of the Crimean population.

Researchers estimate that altogether more than two million people, predominantly Ukrainians but also Russians, Belarusians, and Poles, were captured and enslaved in what was called "the harvest of the steppe" during the time of the Crimean Khanate. In 1769, a last major Tatar raid that took place during the Russo-Turkish War saw the capture of twenty thousand slaves.[415]

It is instructive to compare the Mediterranean and Crimean slave trade with the one across the Atlantic. Over the course of four centuries, about ten to twelve million black Africans were taken to the Americas.[416] According to Paul E. Lovejoy, "It is now estimated that 11,863,000 slaves were shipped across the Atlantic."[417]

However, from 1500 to 1650, when trans-Atlantic slaving was still in its infancy, probably more white Christian slaves were taken to Barbary than black African slaves to the Americas.[418]

Now, how many schools and colleges are going to teach that today? How many of them would go against political correctness to undermine white guilt? How many people have any idea today that it was Western civilization that eventually turned *against* slavery and began stamping it out while non-Western societies still saw nothing wrong with it?

The fact is easily overlooked that no patriotism can be born, cultivated, nurtured, and developed without a positive approach toward the concept of the nation. The individual nations always find themselves in a difficult transitional phase between established history and a hoped-for great future. For this reason they must be mindful of their values and sense of direction, prepared and ready to defend their cultural and religious heritage and political convictions.

Xenophobia is dangerous, but patriotism is a good and healthy concept.

Fighting Spirit

Western culture and Western civilization have been trashed in their institutions, taught to tolerate even the intolerance of other cultures brought into their midst, and conditioned to regard any instinct to fight for their survival as being reckless, irresponsible, dangerous, unscrupulous, and thoughtless. Accordingly, Western nations that show any sign of standing up for self-preservation are rare exceptions today. Any nation in the West that would dare do that would immediately be demonized not only by its enemies but also by the other Western nations. Russia and Serbia are good examples: they have been stigmatized for not having European values and excluded from the "community of nations"—the well-known euphemism for the West. How many Western nations are there that have not yet succumbed to the destructive and suicidal trends of our times?

If and when we all succumb, the epitaph of Western civilization will say that we did have the power to annihilate our enemies but got so confused in the process that we ended up destroying ourselves.

Repudiation of the Past: The New Culture of Imposed Arts

The term "West" denotes a comprehensive form of human life that was once flourishing and expanding but is now declining into sterility and self-doubt. It is not just that the people and their elite in the West have developed a critical response to their traditions. Self-criticism is a virtue, and all the historic turning points and renewals of the Western spirit have come about through questioning things—at the Renaissance, at the Reformation, and at the Enlightenment. Nevertheless, through all such critical changes, our ancestors always kept a continuity of involvement, participation, commitment, and inspiration, which can be recognized in the institutions that survived into modern times, and of course in the extraordinary artistic traditions that are the glory of Western civilization.

However, by the end of the nineteenth century, self-criticism gave way to outright repudiation. Instead of subjecting the Western inheritance to a critical evaluation, a great many of those appointed as cultural stewards—artists, producers, critics, cultural advisers, and composers—chose to turn their backs on it. Instead of seeking what was good in this inheritance and trying to understand and endorse the ties that bind us to it, they chose to embrace the prevailing idea, which seemed to be "This is all dead and gone." This renunciation of the tradition has been accompanied by vigorous denunciations of the social order and traditional morals of those who formerly enjoyed or created it, whose sexist, racist, or hierarchical attitudes distance them incurably from us living now.

Two examples of this culture of repudiation illustrate the enormous damage that has been inflicted on Western society. The first is architecture, and the second is classical music, both of which have been betrayed by the experts into whose hands they were placed.

Architecture and music are worth comparing for one critical reason. While music is a fine art, and one that entirely draws on its resources for its own spiritual ends, architecture is a skill that is measured partly in terms of its utility and cannot, therefore, demand genius or originality from its ordinary practitioner. This distinction is of increasing importance in an unfortunate age when critics and impresarios count originality, creativity, and challenge as the primary aesthetic values, dismissing the yearning for beauty as a chronic and nostalgic form of sentimentality.

Building a city is an enterprise undertaken by many hands over many years. Its principal goal is to create an enduring community united by the sense of settlement. It is rarely possible to call on a single architect to create the final result. The great and prosperous cities of Western civilization, such as Paris, Florence, Venice, Amsterdam, Barcelona, Edinburgh, and the old German cities, have surely not been conceived as works of art and certainly not built with originality in mind. They have evolved practical solutions to the dilemma of settlement. They achieve order and unity by striving to conform to a project that was started by others. They use patterns, materials, and details that naturally fit together; they exhibit the feel for proportion and scale that people understand without knowing how to explain it. They are organized according to a kind of natural order that is similar to a language that anybody can learn and use to make his own remarks but that is usually spoken in straight and unoriginal prose. Anybody can learn this natural order and the adaptation of it to new uses and materials.

Quite suddenly, however, in the aftermath of the modernist movement, architects turned their backs on this natural order and the tradition that it represented—a tradition as old as Western civilization. They were in a state of complete repudiation: the past was the past and was no longer available. One was to begin again with something entirely new. The building was to start a priori from wholly new assumptions, and any attempt to fit into the old idea of the street was a kind of betrayal—a lapse into nostalgia, and fakeness.

However, whatever we think of the old ways of building, it is to these that people gravitate—not only as tourists but as residents too. People flee the new structures, which are imposed on them by planners and managers seeking to claim credit for their advanced and sophisticated taste but who would not want to live in the result. Why, then, was it not possible to go on pursuing the old way—not to repeat what had been done but to adapt and develop it according to our changing uses? What caused the radical break? What caused the complete repudiation? Why is the adaptation, on which all communities, species, and individuals depend, no longer available?

These same questions haunt the world of classical music, too. As has been suggested, the two cases are distinct, in that most surviving architecture is the product of ordinary and uninspired people, whereas most surviving music is the result of artistic inspiration. However, this difference makes the comparison all the more illuminating.

The classical tradition in music has evolved through continuous dialogue and exchange between creative composers and a self-sustaining community of performers and the listeners and concertgoers of the public. Unlike architecture, which is imposed on all regardless of being liked or not, music can only be imposed on those who are willing to listen to it or perform it, and therefore it survives only through its appeal. When a style becomes tired, when a musical vocabulary declines into repetition and cliché, it loses its audience or retains their interest only in an uninvolved way, like background music in a restaurant. The tradition then depends on renewal—on the artist who, like Beethoven, discovers a new application, a new way, and a new territory into which the old devices can be extended. This evolution is beautifully dramatized in "Die Meistersinger von Nürnberg," in which Wagner epitomizes the dialogue between the musician and the audience. The new melodic language of Walther von Stolzing *adapts* to the musical tradition of Nuremberg, which in turn *adapts* to Walther's melody. The drama shows the audience evolving in response to the music and the music shaping itself in response to an existing tradition to become part of it by also changing it.

The intention should be to renew a tradition and not to turn one's back on it. Alas, the culture of repudiation has taken over classical music too. It is not anymore a question of adjusting and adapting music to the audience and the audience to the music. It is a matter of starting again, from a new conception of the art of sound.

Moreover, if the audience does not like the result, that is only further proof of its reality as a challenge and a transgression. Besides, in the state-controlled culture of the liberal West, an audience is no longer necessary or required. The state can entirely fund the politically correct arts, and the state, as today's socialist institution, could be controlled by the modernists—those believers in progress and the future for whom the past finally refuted itself. That was the cultural bequest of postwar Germany, and it proved infectious everywhere in the West. Every attempt by composers to establish some continuity with the existing repertoire and to appeal to a community of listeners whose ears had been shaped by the tonal language has been regarded with suspicion by the avant-garde and, as a rule, dismissed as pastiche or cliché.

Most people live in cities now—or, rather, they congregate around cities while increasingly avoiding the center of them, escaping for the protection of the suburbs. If one asks what draws them, nevertheless, into the heart of the city, two things seem important: first, traditional architecture, which creates the vision of a community of free beings; and second, the symphony hall or music center, which invites the listener into another, inward, vision of the same free community. Moreover, just as a city renews itself through adapting to new needs while maintaining continuity with its past, so does the classical tradition in music renew itself by incorporating new feelings and forms of social life into the living tradition of polyphonic sound. Repudiation never achieves this kind of renewal. Only by adapting what has worked before can the present embrace and give form to what is new.

Therefore, the Western model for the future should not be the sterile projects but rather the quiet efforts to adapt the old to the new and to find the means that touch the hearts of the audience—because they express the spirit of the artists.[419]

Cultural Degeneration: A Critique of Contemporary Art

What is happening to Western culture and Western values? The more senior reader probably still remembers when people in rural areas used to be able to leave their house doors unlocked at night. The windows could be opened wide, knowing that your belongings were safe. You could even leave the ignition key in your car without any fear of it being stolen. Some would say those were the good old days, and most of us would solemnly agree—especially us baby boomers.

Our culture has changed so drastically that we are even afraid to go outside in the inner cities of some metropolitan areas after dark for fear of losing our lives. It is easy to blame law enforcement by claiming they are not doing their jobs, but would that be entirely fair? The sad truth is that this might be just the beginning of our woes. In the past, we had opportunities to speak up, and we remained silent.

What's next? Are we going to be branded with numbers on our foreheads or have detection devices implanted under our skin? When do we say, "Enough is enough?" We are going to have to make a stand soon. If a culture can be renewed at all, it would have to begin with outstanding leadership.

The modern proletarian appears everywhere in dramas, films, and on television, the latter being a media outlet it has long dominated. The new proletarian holds sway in many art forms, such as opera, popular singing, composition, ballet and modern dance, fine arts, sculpture, and writing in all its manifestations.

Art is universal. However, it is not a universal language understood by all people everywhere in the world. Art is universal in the sense that it is not restricted to any particular country or civilization and is as much a part of a human being as eyes, ears, hunger, or thirst. There has never been a race or tribe that did not have either art or religion, because humans wish to reach beyond their own meager limitations and express the higher inner cravings of their souls for the good and the beautiful.

The arts, whether painting, sculpture, music, dance, or literature, are united in a common purpose—the integration and communication of experiences—but each technique employs its own means. Painting has continually striven to increase its representational power—not to imitate nature but to make plausible reconstructions of life; to make forms that are real and convincing, that strike us with the force of life experiences.

We long for substance, content and context, real subject matter, something bearing on life as it is experienced.

However, the purpose of this chapter is not to enter into a broad philosophy of art. Firstly it will focus on a particular phase of art—namely, painting and sculpture—as well as a given period, which is classified as contemporary.

Secondly, even the meaning of the controversial term "art" will have to be left to the disputes of the philosophers, although subsequent writing will reveal the accepted understanding of that term.

Finally, this shall not be a discussion of personalities and their worth or failure but a survey of the field of modern or contemporary art and its effect on or relation to our present society.

Although differences of opinion have always existed, for generations people more or less agreed on general views of art regarding its meaning, purpose, and function. Never in the history of Western civilization has there been such confusion and controversy upon the significant part of the public as there exists today regarding so-called contemporary art. Moreover, so great have become the confusion and controversy that a significant portion of the public has become outright inimical to it. Admittedly, it may also be true that there has often been a rift between the most vibrant form of art of a given period and the general public.

For example, the great masters of the Middle Ages may not have been immediately comprehensible to the people of that time—and for that matter, they are not entirely understandable even today to those whose education or sensitivity is deficient. Nevertheless, the rift today appears to be more profound. The question is, can our civilization continue without the harmonizing influence of living art that is understood, accepted, and enjoyed by the majority of the public?

In such a complicated and controversial subject, this author would like to be objective above all—but it is most difficult given the situation. It is something that affects us personally and today, not tomorrow or yesterday.

The problem began a little more than a hundred years ago. Previous to that, art had passed through a series of intriguing stages, which must be understood in a broad sense to appreciate the current trends. The first animal drawings of cave dwellers developed into the marvelous wall paintings and ornamentations of such cradles of civilization as Egypt, Babylon, Assyria, and Persia. As we slowly approach the Christian era, the instinct to record the beauty of form, color, and movement becomes even more fully developed.

Four centuries before Christ, the Greeks brought sculpting to a point of perfection and physical beauty that has never been surpassed, while their architecture still influences us in this day and age. The Dark Ages left the East still supreme with its oriental love of color and decoration, as exemplified in Byzantine art, until the spirit of faith swept all of Europe and a new civilization with its culture came to overshadow it.

All the arts, with the exceptions of music and literature, reached their highest form of perfection in the Middle Ages. Moved by a living faith, the arts sought to reflect the beauty of God's handiwork (which is the first essential condition of art) to please us, to enchant us, and to transport us into the ideal world. Secondly, the arts sought to do all things well (which is the other requisite of art) and as perfectly as possible.

I. Spirit of the Renaissance

In this vitally alive concept of art began the spirit of the Renaissance, with its humanist philosophy, to sow the seeds of destruction. Then came the Reformation; the impact was too massive, and under it, a high culture began to crumble. It was the death warrant of art when the reformers rejected all that made life brighter, happier, or pleasurable for people and protested against all that was motivated by the spirit of the church, since this greatest of art was decidedly Catholic.

Once art lost its close association with religion, a significant change slowly overcame the culture of the West. This change came slowly because the gigantic stature of the old masters was too immense to be lost overnight. However, divorced from this vital, living force, the arts began to look inward instead of outward—and man is a most limited subject at best.

For three hundred years following the Reformation, history records a general downward trend of Western civilization. So apparent has this become that some historians claim the Reformers made not one single contribution to culture. Nevertheless, there were a few throwbacks to the glory of the Middle Ages and the spirit of the Renaissance even during that time. Such men as El Greco, Tintoretto, Rembrandt, Velasquez, Rubens, Titian, and Goya deserve our recognition and attention—but they were great because they were *heirs of another age.*

With the coming of the Reformation, art ceased to be an active force in society. The love for beauty instinctively continued in secular life for a time, though with a diminishing force that was finally to be extinguished in the nineteenth century. The impulse was *dead*.

Art became merely representational; it had no vitality or inner spark of life; any reasonably good photograph was more charming than a painting, which became emotionless, dull, and stale. To make matters worse, it took up a romantic air in the nineteenth century; the exponents of this Romanticism indulged in sentiment, nostalgia, heroic fervor, and languid musings, ending in the degradation known as Victorianism.

II.   From Impressionism to Expressionism

Now the stage was set. Art could sink no further—or so it was thought. A change had to take place lest it disappear from the face of the earth. Then came the revolt, and as in the case of any revolution, it was not without connection to the past at first. This initial step of a radically new movement in art was called impressionism. It meant just that—the representation of nature as it impressed the artist at a glance. Two factors helped considerably in developing this.

For one thing, up until this period (the middle of the nineteenth century), the artist had mainly worked indoors, whether painting interior or exterior scenes. Then, when the idea of moving their easels outdoors became popular, they discovered many exciting qualities of color in light, which was not true of the color that could be found in their pigments.

Secondly, the introduction of photography forced the artists to attempt to do what no camera could do—and that was to reproduce color as contained in light.

A whole new school of painting, as well as a whole new palette of colors, developed from this movement. The results were interesting, if only as an experiment in light and pigment. In place of mixing pigments to produce varieties of color, the impressionists placed one pigment dot or band next to another to reproduce the color effects of light. Shadows remained no longer an absence of light but became another kind, quality, and value of light instead. Black color did not exist; in its place, they used the darkest tones of blue, violet, or green. Nor was there any brown; here they put the components of that color—green, red, and yellow—side by side. The juxtaposition of yellow and violet formed the color of gray. This juxtaposition of pure color, which at a certain distance fused in the eye of the observer and produced the effect of the tint desired, captured every tone or chromatic quality. This method is known as optical mixture because the mixing is done in the observer's eye. The impressionistic method may also be called luminism, since the aim of the process is mainly to represent the color of light with all its sparkle and vibration.

This impressionist school brought about a decided innovation: the dazzling color dabs delivered a radical obliteration of distinctly clear contour. It specialized in fleeting surface impressions, tempting to the eye by way of a rainbow-color display. Nevertheless, though it spread rapidly throughout the world, impressionism never amounted to much outside of France; its limitations were several. It was not entirely new, since Titian and Velasquez had already experimented with it centuries before. The great old masters had used it only sparingly, not more than a means to an end—and not as an end in itself, as in the case of the impressionists.

Impressionism started the schools of the technicians instead of the painters. Moreover, one must fear that the hazy approach of such artists was entirely suitable to shroud a complete assortment of a painter's deficiencies. Indeed, anybody could paint an impressionistic picture who dared to splash wrong colors, preferably combinations of blues, yellows, and violets. By 1910, impressionism had hazed itself into obscurity; although some traces of it may still be found, it does not exist as a school of painting today.

III. Expressionist Reaction Sets In

The most powerful reaction began from the heart of impressionism itself. A new generation of artists began to argue that, after all, painting was not a science but art. As such, its primary function was not the precise representation of nature but rather the expression of emotion.

Accordingly, a fresh start was made in a new direction with the emphasis on expressing an *idea* rather than depicting *appearances*. It was also thought that by scaling down the facts known through senses to a minimum, the idea might be able to stand out more clearly.

So, in due course, the visible world began to be reduced to its essential geometric forms of the cube, cone, and sphere. Trappings were discarded, and only the necessary forms were used to give painting a rugged simplicity, to put it gently. So was modern art, as we know it, conceived, and the four proponents of this new school were Seurat, Cezanne, Van Gogh, and Gauguin.

Since expressionism attempts an extreme vehemence of expression and feeling; the visible matter becomes secondary. Unlike other art forms, it is not limited in the range of technique, color, or theme and does not disdain to draw from all sources available. It aims to attain a highly personal and dramatic expression, and to do this the expressionist does not vacillate to employ dissonance of colors and distortions of forms.

Similarly to impressionism, expressionism is not a school without precedent either. Not only can many ancient works of art be classified as expressionistic, but all art, in fact, worthy of the name is the expression of the inner feelings and convictions of the artist. The entire history of Western art, from Giotto and Cimabue to the breathless intensity of Michelangelo and Da Vinci to the extreme asceticism of El Greco, breathes a deep expressionism, but with limitations. In the modern innovation, there are no limitations any longer as the artist removes himself from the pale of any confinement to express his inner emotions.

This vibrantly alive and colorfully flamboyant form enthralled the world, and by its very limitless and unrestricted manner of expression, it led to many schools of art. One should remember both the four proponents of expressionism mentioned above and the different impulses of their work, and the subsequent developments will be easy to understand and will even appear logical.

IV. Modernism: Schisms in Art

Since the days of Cezanne, there has appeared a succession of movements, which has shocked, under the collective name of "modernism," the complacency of the orthodox for the past hundred years.

In 1909, the geometric concoctions of Picasso made their appearance and were to be treated with contempt by the name "cubism." Simultaneously, two Americans in Paris professed to combine the properties of architecture and music into what they called "synchronism." They were followed by futurism, orphism, purism, surrealism, vorticism, and a dozen other equally sonorous and Latin-sounding movements, or rather sects. The distinctions between the sects were immaterial at least and trivial at most, which made the rivalry among them absurdly acrimonious. As a climax to all this school-founding, sect-creating, and schism, a group of cynical renegades contrived a campaign of clever parody to burlesque modernism to death under the title of "dadaism."

These cults with their pompous denominations were, for the most part, technical schisms. Today many of them are rightly dead and, thankfully, all but forgotten; there is nothing to be gained by discussing them individually. Since the picture is unjustifiably complicated, only the most critical schools will be discussed—those that still have a bearing on art today. These, for all practical purposes, may be grouped under the two general headings of "cubism," or "abstract art," and "expressionism."

There is absolutely nothing mysterious about a cube or a cone or a triangle or a square; nor is there anything mysterious in cubism if taken for what it is—an experiment in structure. However, cubism as a distinct school of painting owes its origin to Cezanne, whose forms were composed of colored planes. Picasso, in his first phase, enlarged the planes and changed the contrasting colors into simple areas of light and dark. This process, carried further, abstracted an object into its nearest geometrical equivalent; that is, a human head, though still recognizable as a head, was reduced to an assemblage of geometrical fractions. In his second phase, Picasso split the head into sections and then arbitrarily shuffled the parts together again to bring into a single focus different aspects observed from several points of view. The head is now only an eye, a nose, and an ear scattered among the splintered wreckage. In its last phase, cubism went flat. The three visible planes of the cube, by process of extension, were projected beyond the limits of vision, ceasing to function as indications of solidity and becoming automatically three flat tones; the head, needless to say, disappeared. Representation was thereby annihilated. Art was pure, absolute, and abstract at last.

By dictionary standards, to abstract is to draw out or distill the essence of something. A landscape or cow can end up in squares and triangles if distilled far enough, and only the artist alone can name the natural parent of his child. Since to the layman abstract painting can be readily confused with a nonobjective, there is no point in trying to find any distinction between the two. The most interesting and valuable thing about abstract art was the practical influence it had on modern design rather than any intrinsic worth of the painting itself.

Even in abstract or nonobjective art, we find traces of expressionism at times, with Kandinsky being an example of this. According to him, he tries to transfer emotion to his outlines and uses color to express mood rather than for decoration. His compositions are amorphous (that is, without definite shape) in order to convey a musical ebb and flow. In fact, the nonobjective painter considers his combinations of colors and forms similar to a mix of tones in music.

The last of the shockers was futurism, a cult manufactured in Italy and launched in Paris. It had propaganda to offer and was bent on driving it home in the most sensational manner: break with the past, abolish tradition, step out into a world of freedom, invest life with new symbols, feel and express—thus to create art.

According to the futurists, everything was art so long as genuine feeling inspired it.

The influence and existence of futurism were short; it is worthy of note only because it represents the turmoil and revolutionary spirit of the age. It was also the only school that developed outside of France at the time, and the only thing it did for Italy, where it originated, was to produce Mussolini—he adopted futurism's radical philosophy to suit his ends.

Futurism, like many of the minor schisms in the modern era, became absorbed by expressionism, the movement, which in turn gave rise to the greatest freedom and divergence in the art. Where cubism meant analysis of underlying forms and resulted in the abstract, expressionism tapped the emotions. They were not pretty feelings but passionately sincere. The brushwork is correspondingly slashing, and much detail is suppressed or slurred over to point up a dominant trait or attitude.

Expressionism states unequivocally that the artist must have a natural interest in his subject. If this interest or feeling is genuine and not forced, the condition of true art is granted; true feeling makes true art.

As a consequence, expressionism runs into many vague symbols and forms of expression known only to the artists. The final stages of expressionism were the fantastic or dream world. At first the artists were visited by dreams—ominous presentiments or affectionate inconsistencies, as with Chagall. Later, in their sense of futility over the destructive force of war, another group set out to laugh certain traditions to death (dadaism). Lastly came the surrealists, who have deliberately and artificially attempted to raise the submerged half of the mind (our subconscious) and weave dream and waking into a new irrationality. From its thesis, expressionism has run into cracked symbolism and pathological trances, and abetted by Freudian research, it ends up in the dream world of surrealism.

All have seen it in the galleries; each picture is a gruesome manifestation of some private and incommunicable agony, and all have seen the spectators—little knots of serious folk seeking in each picture the unique key, the password without which there is no possibility of entrance into the artist's soul.

That the artist is sincere and original is no recommendation; the world has been flooded with shapeless forms and confused jumble offered in the name of pure expression for too long a time now. Much of the stuff is childishly immature and has no more right to be considered as art than the bawling of a child—also pure expression.

The above, in brief, is the story of modern art. It holds that the emotional power of art is its abstract organization.

The modernist movement appears to be on the wane; it went over in a remarkably short time. The time has come for advancement, but sadly enough, modern art does not even have the seeds of that within itself; it has been concentrating on the method to the exclusion of content, reflecting the realities of life in the West.

V. The Placing of Modern Art

The twentieth century has seen an almost complete transformation of society in its mechanism, its motives, the tools with which it works, its mental processes, and even its ethical standards. Everything that conditions life in its material aspect today and all those things that have made possible an incredible technological civilization are the products of a period within the memory of people.

Only the Fall of Rome, the Renaissance, and the French Revolution have marked essential transformations in society comparable to what has happened in our own time. Indeed, one could expect that this enormous change would present itself also in an adequate art. Unfortunately, this is not at all the case.

The old forms continued to be used in the clumsiest way, being arbitrarily imposed on an alien and unsympathetic base. Take, for example, the early American skyscrapers, which assumed the general form of a medieval church tower of incredible dimensions and were overlaid with Gothic ornamentation produced by mechanical means.

Modernism tried, theoretically and logically, to correct this—to create art that fitted a technological, materialistic, and despiritualized society. In a way, it succeeded. Jazz, futurism and cubism in painting and sculpture, modernism in architecture, free verse—all these things relate themselves to contemporary life, and nowhere more intimately than in their severance from all precedent, their denial of any fundamental law, and their devotion to ugliness.

The strangeness of the modernist movement—its obsessions and eccentricities—could point to a charlatan mutiny organized in Paris for notoriety and profit. This impression is perhaps erroneous but far too flattering to the artists.

In a society with no common purpose, no unifying religion, and no general idealism, and in a world that encourages pretense, hypocrisy, sham, and factitious achievement, it is to be expected that art, too, should be polluted by snobbery, inanity, and commercial cunning. Only in this respect does modern art resemble modern life; it includes in its ranks the upstart, the cheap exhibitionist, the politician, and the virtuoso, together with the deluded visionary who sees a new world where there is only chaos. Moreover, most artists have paid a hefty penalty for their devotion to a dying cause.

If by the question "Is modern art indeed art?" one means "Is it great art?" then of certainty, it is not, because admittedly it possesses neither the communication nor the receptivity of *great* art. That is, it does not make itself understandable; nor is it accepted or followed by any significant number of people.

If this is asked about the general acceptance of the term "art" as involving beauty and perfection, then the answer must again be in the negative. As far as the former is concerned, the modernists have spurned the beautiful for the cult of the ugly. As for perfection, here they are divided. The cubist or abstractionist seeks perfection in basic geometric forms in his arrangement and technique. The expressionist, on the other hand, is interested solely in manifesting his innermost thoughts, feelings, or aberrations, and nothing else matters. The latter is to be taken in its most literal sense, because the expressionist is entirely indifferent to form, medium, and technique.

Admitting the very limited good that modern art has accomplished, it is high time that we weighed this art objectively, critically, and openly. Its protagonists have tried to defend it with a whole new vocabulary of gibberish that has done more harm than good by discouraging the intelligentsia and frightening the sincere.

The modern art movement is obviously suspect. Not only from the point, as mentioned earlier, of hiding under a whole array of confusing jargon but also from this one simple fact: the defenders of the movement have never yet *adversely* praised any work of the so-called masters. In its current stage, Picasso and Matisse are held to be the painters without peer, mighty geniuses of this cataclysmic art. Moreover, nobody has ever heard an apologist of modernism explain why specific works by these artists are mediocre or trivial. Is it perchance possible that Picasso or Matisse do not slip? Rembrandt did, and El Greco—even Michelangelo. In point of fact, the greatest of men used to err once in a while, and the greatest among us still do so.

There are any numbers of valid charges that can be hurled at the modernists based on their own admissions. There have been too few masters in the movement, leaving much of the work a product of mediocrity and charlatanism. Like real revolutionaries, they have revolted against existing forms of art, but once they destroyed the past, they found they had nothing to put in its place. They claim to have made a complete break with everything in the past yet ape the ancient forms of art or the distortions of uncivilized tribes. Continuing their contradictory bent, they claim to represent the present age while yet abhorring the technological progress of the twentieth century, isolating themselves from all society in the profligate haunts of decadent Paris. They bizarrely hold that the uglier a thing is in nature, the more beautiful it becomes in art; thus, they come to uphold and depict the grotesque for its own sake.

Finally, to dispel all dissension within or without its ranks, they put themselves above all law and here, in their own little world, it is only they who can legislate. But must the legislator explain his timeless designs to the vulgar?

If one were to criticize the childishly simple and ineffectual line work of Matisse's paintings, the apologist is wont to remark, "Yes, but he can really draw, you know, when he wants to." That leaves the observer to believe that Matisse is merely capricious; that he is mystifying the public for some ulterior purpose when he might be doing beautiful work. Whereas the line work of Matisse does not matter since he is mistaken for a painter instead of the printmaker that he is, his work might be interesting if applied to silks, cretonnes, or ceramics, but it should never be considered as something to be framed and hung on a wall.

Everything is done to bewilder the observer; everything is, in fact, except for the attempt to lead him to judge a painting on its own terms. Here confusing verbalism achieves its ultimate goal; by dragging on a false philosophy, the connoisseur evades the real issue of art and yields to parlor mysticism. What is by its very nature an affair of visual perception becomes, in our so-called advanced age, a philosophical, ethnological, liturgical, and what-have-you problem. That this is done for clarification of art issues can be seriously doubted, since after such treatment matters can emerge only warped beyond all recognition.

There is no doubt that most of the professional art critics, journalistic and otherwise, have proved unequal to their task when commenting on contemporary art. It is not that the critics lack information; they are, for the most part, well versed in the current art gossip. They know the facts and official findings of the art historians, and their mental larders are well stocked with professional-sounding patter and standardized phraseology. However, in the course of time, all this has been conveniently tailored to cover any emergency or shortcomings.

To sum it up, they are governed by the mode of the marketplace rather than by aesthetic and technical principles, by shifting standards rather than by explicit, immutable criteria.

That the modernist has discredited, if not wholly destroyed, the stale and sterile formulae of Victorian art is undoubtedly correct. His success amounts almost to a revolution, but in one crucial respect it differs from all other antecedent revolutions and finds its fellow only in the Russian social and political revolution of 1917. An old system was overthrown in the past because particular individuals or groups already had formulated another, and to establish their new order, the old had to be destroyed.

In the case of modern art and Bolshevism, the old system was assailed because it seemed to some that it was terrible and therefore had to go. This laudable act accomplished, the workers of the revolution found themselves in the embarrassing position of having nothing valid to offer in its place. One after another, new devices were brought forward (with the statement "Nobody has ever tried this before") only to be in turn discarded; and now, after more than a hundred years of chaotic effort to discover or create new art, we—or, rather, they—are further from success than ever.

VI. Cult of the Ugly

Perhaps in one sense modernism does express the spirit of the age through its ugliness and chaotic qualities. However, even if we did not agree with the contention that man and his machines cannot be reduced to a common abstraction, there is a meaningful contact with life that modern art has sadly neglected, and that is its inability to discriminate between the new things, which are perhaps most transient and need expression, and the old things, which are eternal although quite alien to these new days. Among these one can certainly think of religion in its traditional forms.

As for the modernist cult of the ugly, one cannot say enough. The search for and the creation of beauty through art has always been the possession of humanity from the beginning of time. The quality and the nature of its manifestation have varied with the culture of a given race or period. However, at no point in Western history has there been a conscious turning to, searching for, or creation of ugliness in place of beauty, other than the last 150 years.

Moreover, if we take the pursuit of beauty to be an essential requisite of art, then we may add that there have been but two periods when art suffered a temporary but almost complete eclipse in all of history. These were the Dark Ages of Western Europe, between the years AD 500 to AD 1000, and the time dating from about 1850 (with the exceptions of music and poetry that flourished during the second half of the nineteenth century).

There is a great deal of significance in this search for the ugly. The perception of beauty synchronizes with the appearance of culture. However, the decadent Western civilization, having reached the allotted height of development, now prepares to yield its place to another as yet only in the earliest stage of emergence into the light. Indeed, from all indications of the past more than 150 years, we are entering a new Dark Age, since except for our technological progress we find nothing but deterioration on every side, in education, culture, and the very heart of society itself—the family.

Whatever the explanation, the results are unmistakable. For the first time in the memory of man, the modern artist pursues and accomplishes ugliness and declares that there is no such thing as beauty in any sense that permits definition. In the Dark Ages in Western Europe, the culture was at very low ebb, admittedly; but even then the arts, while crude and illiterate, showed a real desire for beauty and a pathetic desire to accomplish this.

However, the "dark ages" of this past century are entirely different: There is no suffering from an inferiority complex but rather a self-assurance that is all the worse for having no foundation. All the old art of Christianity has been scorned, and there is no searching for the best artists and artisans. With rare exceptions, the most incompetent tyros have been accepted rather than those a shade less futile in their ideas and accomplishments.

This last reflection leads to the last charge made against the modernists—namely, the arrogant manner in which they have withdrawn themselves from all possible criticism, as well as from all possible contact with their public, by denying the existence of all law and criteria and admitting only of complete freedom of expression. They have aimed to place the artist in a world of his own where only he may legislate, interpret, judge, and dispense the aesthetic joys of life. From this premise, we can readily see the reason behind the resultant chaos, since it is only through observance of law that we can produce order.[420]

i. New Standard of Values: Mirroring the Rejection of Moral Standards

We are confronted today with a new estimate of aesthetic values on the nature and function of art. In the place of the word "beauty," we now have "significant form." This highly superior and supercilious intelligentsia of the domain of aesthetics rejects the idea of the existence of any standard of values apart from the personal equation.

Since any existence of the absolute is in doubt, any essential differences between a frieze on the Parthenon or Temple of Hephaestus in Athens and a comic strip in a popular daily are also denied. The words "art" and "artist" have a new but mutable connotation, while "truth," the "ideal," and "good" are similarly discarded as no longer representing anything in the realm of reality. All in all, the old terminology, even when it is retained for lack of a sufficiently ingenious and mystifying substitute, is given a new content and so becomes not an agent for the clarification and expression of ideas but, as has been brought out before, a method of *concealing* them. There are those who maintain that ideas, by themselves, do not exist—hence the practical usefulness of the new method.

Nevertheless, the reality is that significant form is permanently joined to qualified matter in such fashion as to be embedded in the matter and so is peculiarly unsusceptible to abstraction. This truth is what makes abstractions in the art so artificial—that precisely what is most connected with matter is *removed* from it in the process of overintellectualization.

Abstraction as such is a blind alley, and when a work of Picasso in the cubist style is the source of aesthetic experience, it is because of his grasp of color and certainly not because of the overintellectualized form depicted therein.

Let us enter this inviolable world of the artist now and consider his claim that we cannot compare the old with the new and that to judge quality by a system of comparison is an utterly false concept. This author begs to differ with such a false assumption, since it denies the necessity of sense perception for the intellect to form judgments. How else would we judge the quality of music, violins, prima donnas, and any standards in art without making comparisons? How would one know that a Stradivarius, for example, is a better instrument than one can buy in a bargain basement unless one compares their properties? Alternatively, suppose that all the music one had ever heard in life had been some of the modern popular tunes. How could one know that such tunes are utter abominations as compared with tunes composed by Schubert? Of course, one may enjoy any noise without attempting to evaluate its artistic merit, but once a person seeks for a standard of value, he or she will first have to establish a scale of values.

What would such a paradigm be? In the case of Gothic architecture, for example, that could be the cathedrals of Chartres, Rheims, Rouen, or other great Gothic masterpieces. Now, assuming that an Asian person who has never seen a Gothic edifice goes to New York. We could safely point out to him the Rockefeller Church on Riverside Drive as a splendid example of Gothic architecture, and the unsuspecting soul would have no idea that we were only being facetious.

There are some who hold that we cannot compare the classic with the new art and in so doing arrive at a common denominator of quality. The truth is that there is no difference in the issues involved. Whether in the old or new art, the aesthetic laws, which rule the art of all times, are immutable.

Today, because of the dual standard, there is much confusion in the matter of evaluation. In our contemporary system of criticism, we have ample evidence that the quality of art is determined by means as dependable as reading leaves in a teacup or by crystal gazing.

The protagonists of contemporary art often complain that the adversaries of modernism most commonly take refuge in generalizations and attack without having looked first to see whether the object has fulfilled its aims. In short, they feel that the theories and assumptions of the unenlightened seem to obscure their perception.

However, could it be, perhaps, that the perceptive faculties of the so-called enlightened have been dimmed and damned by the mortal dread of appearing uncouthly rustic and lacking in sophistication? Is it not, perchance, the ludicrous disease of *Homo westernicus*, born out of insecurity concerning taste, that is responsible for the virulence of the bandwagon chasers?

Spurious ideas of sophistication and glamour seem to be the chief obstacles standing in the way of developing an independent taste in the Western mind.

ii. Symbols in Art

In 1948, a roundtable group composed of art critics and connoisseurs from England, France, and America felt that it was the use, or misuse, of symbols that removed the work of the contemporary artist from the public.

Symbols are a real part of the art, of course. They consist of an object or image that is intended to represent a whole field of reality; their creation is perhaps the highest artistic act. Great symbols grow to be accepted and recognized by everyone; moreover, they grow out of, other than the artist, the being that is the man—out of his religion, his society, his race, and his times. One of the leading characteristics of contemporary art, derived from its high emphasis on individualism, is that the symbols have become increasingly private, and this sometimes raises insuperable barriers for the observer. Thus the modernists have deliberately destroyed communication with the public.

The extent of privacy of the communication is the measure by which the public will accept or reject the work of art. Here the roundtable agreed that the artist must begin striving, within the limits of his vision and resources, to collaborate in the direction of intelligibility; only then could modern art become acceptable to the public and achieve the social validity that its critics demand.

So where do we go from here? Anyone aware of the trends of contemporary art cannot help but feel the inadequacy of the movement. For one hundred fifty years, there has not been a single development of any one of the revolutionary changes introduced by the pioneers. Art has been stripped to its essential elements of line, form, color, and texture, and the artist has further stripped it of its relationship to the fundamental values of life, even denying that such values exist.

These destructive tendencies cannot be denied, but on the other hand, we cannot allow the artist to deny the existence of all values to cover up his lack of intelligence and skill in forming the elements of art into an intelligible picture.

For well over five generations now, artists have been playing with the elements that go into a great work of art but to date have failed to produce one. For decades before 1948, critics were already asking the same question: "Where do we go from here?" The sad part of it is that the answer still has not been found.

iii.   The Ugliness, Themes, and Death of Modernism

Critics of modern and postmodern Art have turned to the "isn't that disgusting" strategy for a long time, pointing out that specific works of art are ugly, trivial, or in bad taste, or that a five-year-old could have made them. Those points have often been true, but they have also been tiresome and unconvincing—and the world of art has been entirely unmoved.

Of course the major works of the twentieth-century art world are ugly; of course many are offensive; of course a five-year-old could, in many cases, have made the same product. Those points are not arguable—and they are beside the central question entirely.

Why did the art world of the twentieth-century adopt the ugly and the offensive? *Why* did it pour its creative energies and cleverness into the trivial and the self-proclaimed meaningless? *Why* did cynicism and ugliness come to be the game one had to play to make it in the world of art?

Standard histories of art tell us that modern art, with its themes and strategies exhausted, died around 1970 and that we now have almost a half-century of postmodernism behind us. The big break with the past occurred, of course, toward the end of the nineteenth century. Until the late nineteenth century, art was a vehicle for sensuousness, meaning, and passion, and its goals were beauty and originality. The artists were skilled masters of their craft and able to create original representations with social significance and universal appeal. By combining skill and vision, artists were exalted beings capable of creating objects that in turn had an awesome power to exalt the senses, the intellects, and the passions of those who experienced them.

Again, up until the second half of the nineteenth century, the goals of art had been beauty and originality. The break came when the first modernists systematically set themselves to isolating and eliminating all the elements of art or completely opposing what seemed sensible or reasonable.

There were several causes of the break: The increasing naturalism of the nineteenth century led those who had not shaken off their religious heritage to feel desperately alone and without guidance in a vast and empty universe. The rise of philosophical theories of skepticism and irrationalism led many to mistrust their psychological and cognitive abilities of perception and reason. The advancement of scientific theories of evolution and entropy contributed to the pessimistic opinion of human nature and the destiny of the world. The spread of liberalism and free market capitalism caused their opponents on the political left, many of whom were members of the artistic avant-garde, to see political developments as a series of profound disappointments. The technological revolutions stimulated by the combination of science and capitalism led many to project a future in which humanity would be dehumanized or destroyed by the very machines that were supposed to improve its lot.

The nineteenth-century intellectual world's sense of disquiet had become full-blown anxiety by the beginning of the twentieth century. The artists (including composers, writers, and poets) responded, exploring in their works the implications of the world in which reason, dignity, optimism, and beauty seemed to have disappeared.

The new theme was that art must be a quest for truth, however brutal, and not a quest for beauty. So the question became, what is the truth of art?

The first significant claim of modernism is a content request—a demand for recognition of the fact that the world is not beautiful. The world is fractured, decaying, horrifying, depressing, empty, and ultimately unintelligible.

That claim by itself is not uniquely modernist, though a number of the artists who signed on to that claim were uniquely modernist. Some past artists had believed the world to be ugly and horrible, but they had used the traditional realistic forms of perspective and color to say this.

The novelty of the early modernists was the assertion that form must match the content. According to them, art should *not* use the traditional realistic forms of perspective and color, because those forms presuppose an orderly, integrated, and knowable reality.

Edvard Munch got there first with *The Scream* in 1893: if the *truth* is that reality is a horrifying, disintegrating swirl, then *both* form and content should express the feeling.

Pablo Picasso got there second with *Les Demoiselles d'Avignon* in 1907: if the *truth* is that reality is fractured and empty, then *both* form and content must express that.

Salvador Dali's surrealist paintings go a step further: if the *truth* is that reality is unintelligible, then art can teach this lesson by using realistic forms *against* the idea that we can distinguish objective reality from irrational, subjective dreams.

The second and parallel development within the boundaries of modernism is reductionism. If we are uneasy about the idea that art or any discipline can tell us the truth about external, objective reality, then we will retreat from any content and concentrate solely on art's uniqueness. Moreover, if we are concerned with what is unique in art, then each artistic medium is different.

For example, what distinguishes painting from literature? Literature tells stories, so painting should not presume to be literature; instead it should concentrate on its very own uniqueness. The truth concerning painting is that it is nothing more than a two-dimensional surface with paint on it. Therefore, instead of telling stories, the reductionist movement in painting asserts that the painters must find the truth in painting by deliberately eliminating whatever can be removed from the picture and seeing what survives; only then will we know the essence of painting.

Since we are eliminating in the iconic pieces of the twentieth-century form of art, it is often not what is, or remains, on the canvas that counts but what is not there. The significant is what has been eliminated and is now absent; art comes to be about absence.

So we eliminate from art a cognitive connection to an external reality. What else can be removed? If traditional skill in painting is a matter of representing a three-dimensional world on a two-dimensional surface, then, to be faithful to painting, we must eliminate the pretense of a third dimension. It is the paint on canvas and *only* the paint on canvas. We are now as two-dimensional as possible, and that is the end of this reductionist strategy—the third dimension is gone.

What about composition and color differentiation? Can we eliminate those? Furthermore, if traditionally the art object is a particular and unique artifact, then we can eliminate the art object's special status by making such artworks that are reproductions of agonizingly ordinary objects. Andy Warhol's paintings of soup cans and duplications of cardboard tomato juice boxes show the outcome.

Similarly, in a variation on that theme, we can take objects that are in fact special and unique—such as Marilyn Monroe—and reduce them to two-dimensional mass-produced commodities.

Additionally, if art traditionally is sensuous and perceptually embodied, we can eliminate the sensuous and perceptual altogether, as in conceptual art. Here the perceptual appeal is minimal, and art becomes a purely academic enterprise—and we have eliminated painting entirely.

Adding all of the above reductionist "strategies" together, the course of modern painting has been to eliminate the third dimension, composition, color, perceptual content, and the sense of the art object as something special.

In modernism, art becomes a philosophical enterprise rather than an artistic one. The driving purpose of modernism is not to *do* art but to *find out* what art is. We have eliminated X; is it still art? Now we have removed Y; is it still art? The point of the exercise was not aesthetic experience; instead the works are symbols representing a stage in a philosophical experiment. In most cases, the discussions about the works are much more intriguing than the works themselves. We keep the works in museums and look at them not for their own sake but for the same reason scientists keep lab notes: to record their thinking at various stages. The purpose of modern art objects is like that of road signs along the highway; they are not articles of contemplation as a result of their own merit but markers to inform us how far we have traveled down a given road.

The work itself is not art; it is merely an instrument utilized for an intellectual exercise in understanding why it is not art.

Modernism, by the 1960s, found it had reached a dead end. To the extent modern art had any content at all, its pessimism led it to the judgment that nothing was worth disclosing. Insofar as it played the reductive elimination game, it found that nothing uniquely artistic survived elimination.

Art became *nothing*.

Andy Warhol found his usual smirking way to announce the end when asked what he thought art was anymore: "Art? – Oh, that's a man's name."[421]

iv. Themes of Postmodernism

Where could art go after the death of modernism? Postmodernism did not go far. It needed some content and some new forms, but it did not want to return to either classicism or romanticism or traditional realism.

Finally the art world reached out again, as it already had at the end of the nineteenth century, and drew upon the broader intellectual and cultural context of the late 1960s and 1970s. It absorbed the trendiness of existentialism's absurd universe, the failure of positivism's reductionism, and the collapse of socialism's New Left and was strongly influenced by their abstract themes of antirealism, deconstruction, and their heightened adversarial stance to Western culture. From those themes, postmodernism introduced four variations on modernism.

First, postmodernism reintroduced content—but only self-referential and ironic content. As with philosophical postmodernism, artistic postmodernism rejected any form of realism and became antirealist. Art cannot be about reality or nature, because, according to postmodernism, reality and nature are merely social constructs. The social world and its social constructs are all we have—one of those constructs being the world of art. So we may have content in our art as long as we talk self-referentially about the social world of art.

Secondly, postmodernism sets itself to an even more ruthless deconstruction of traditional categories, such categories that the modernists had not eliminated. Although modernism had been reductionist, some artistic targets remained.

As an example, stylistic integrity had always been an element of great art, and artistic purity was one motivating force within modernism. Therefore, one postmodern strategy has been to mix styles eclectically to undercut the idea of stylistic integrity. An early postmodern example in architecture, for instance, is Friedensreich Hundertwasser's *House* (1986) in Vienna—a deliberate slapping together of a glass skyscraper, concrete, stucco, and occasional bricks, along with oddly placed balconies and arbitrarily sized windows, and completed with a Russian onion dome or two.

Putting the above two strategies together, postmodern art will become both self-referential and destructive—a continuity from modernism. Picasso took one of Matisse's portraits of his daughter and used it as a dartboard, encouraging his friends to do the same.

Postmodernism allows one to make content statements as long as they are about social reality and not about an alleged natural or objective reality and—here is the variation—as long as they are *narrower* race/class/sex statements rather than pretentious, universalist claims about something called the human condition.[422]

Postmodernism denies universal human nature, substituting it with the claim that we are all created as competing groups by our racial, economic, ethnic, and sexual circumstances. The postmodern claim suggests that there are no artists, only adjectivized artists: black artists, female artists, homosexual artists, poor Hispanic artists, and so on.

The third variation is the issue of money. There is the long-standing rule in modern art that one should never say anything kind about capitalism. German artist Hans Haacke's *Freedom is now simply going to be sponsored – out of petty cash* (1991) is one great example. While people were celebrating the end of Bolshevism behind the Iron Curtain, Haacke erected a huge Mercedes-Benz logo atop a former East German guard tower. Men with guns previously occupied that tower, but Haacke suggests that the only change is the replacing of the Soviet rule with the equally heartless reign of the corporations.

The fourth and final postmodern variation on modernism is a more ruthless nihilism. The earlier version, while always focusing on the negative, still dealt with important themes of power, wealth, and justice. As mercilessly negative as modern art has been, what has not been done? How can any remaining positivity in art be eliminated more thoroughly? Apparently by employing the following:

Entrails and blood: An art exhibition in the year 2000 invited patrons to place a goldfish in a blender and then turn the device on—art as life reduced to indiscriminate liquid entrails. One artist collected his own blood over the course of several months and molded into a frozen cast of his head. That is reductionism with a vengeance.

Unusual sex: Alternate sexualities and fetishes have been pretty much worked over during the twentieth century. However, until recently art has not explored sex involving children. Now we can move on to extreme bestiality, child sexuality, and sex with animals; nothing is left out in the name of artistic freedom.

A preoccupation with urine and feces: *Kunst ist Scheisse* ("Art is Shit") became, fittingly, the motto of the dada movement.[423] One representative of this art form canned, labeled, exhibited, and sold ninety tins of his own excrement—one of which was purchased by a British museum for about $40,000.[424]

So again, one cannot consider all that as a significant development over the course of a century.

VII. The Future of Art: Not Without Moral Renewal

The heyday of postmodernism in art was the time during the 1980s and '90s. While modernism had become stale by the 1970s, postmodernism also reached a similarly well-deserved dead end—a "what next?" stage. Postmodern art was derision that played out within a narrow range of assumptions, and we are weary of the same old vulgar tricks with only minor variations. The gross-outs have become mechanical and repetitive, and they no longer gross us out.

So what next?

One must remember that modernism in art came out of a very particular intellectual culture of the late nineteenth century and has remained loyally stuck in those themes. However, those are not the only topics open to artists, and much has happened since the end of the nineteenth century.

We would *not* know from modern art that average life expectancy has doubled since Edvard Munch screamed or diseases that routinely killed hundreds of thousands of babies each year have been eliminated. We would *not* know from modern art anything about the rising standards of living, the landing on the moon, or emerging markets.

Although we are brutally aware of the horrors of National Socialism, we are much less cognizant of the sins of international socialism—and art should have a role in keeping us informed of both. Nevertheless, we would *never* know from the world of art the equally important fact that those battles were *won* and brutality was *defeated*.

Moreover, if we knew only the contemporary art world, we would *never* get a glimmer of the excitement in evolutionary psychology, big bang cosmology, genetic engineering, the beauty of fractal mathematics, or the remarkable fact that humans are the kind of beings that can come upon all those extraordinary things.

The world is ready for bold new artistic movements and artists, and the art world should be at the edge. Alas, the art world is marginalized today. It is inbred and left behind, and for any self-respecting artist, there should be nothing more demeaning than being left behind.

This author's argument is with the uniform negativity and destructiveness of the art world. When did art in the twentieth century say *anything* that was encouraging about human relations, about humanity's potential for dignity and courage, about the sheer positive passion of being in the world?

Here we face the most bizarre contradiction of all between an imposed modernist ideology and the actual feelings of people. While the general public is fully aware that modern art has reached a dead end, the art establishment of museums and schools of fine arts still uphold modernism. Most people see that the rejection of beauty and the contempt for visible reality by modern artists is absurd, and most are offended by art that has been reduced to gimmickry or shock value or the nihilism of general chaos.

Beneath the calm surface, nearly everyone thinks about modern art like the little boy in *The Emperor's New Clothes*: "There is nothing there!" Unfortunately the inner voices of people are still stifled by fears of sounding philistine.

As with other modern ideologies, however, modernism in the art will eventually give way to the natural demands of the body and the soul—in this case, to the request for depictions of visible realities and beautiful forms.

Modern architecture, too, that has rejected higher beauty for the cold and lifeless utility of abstract functionalism will eventually be transformed into something better; the seeds of response are already evident within the architectural establishment. To Mies van der Rohe's lapidary dictum of modernist dogma that "Less is more," Philadelphia architect Robert Venturi famously responded, "Less is a bore."[425]

The point here is not to return to the 1800s or to turn art into the making of lovely postcards. Rather it is about being human and looking at the world afresh. In each generation, there are only a few who can do that at the highest level, but that has always been the challenge of art and its highest calling.

The world of postmodern art is a run-down hall of mirrors tiredly reflecting some innovations introduced a century ago. It is time to move on.

This author pleads with all earnestness for the recovery of beauty as an essential part of life in its quality as an expression of the best and highest things, as a stimulus to greater endeavor, and as a sound method of testing values. He looks for the recovery of art as a singular source of joy, as the truest public expression, and as the symbolic manifestation of those things that are too high for another voicing. By this he means art as an everyday thing, not an added amenity of life, or art as the peculiar possession of the few. If we continue to make beauty a cult isolated from life, if we accept it only after the pagan and Renaissance fashion as sensory perception and a stimulus either to intellectual or voluptuous enjoyment, then we are lost indeed, as shown by the sad events of the past few hundred years.

Art is an expression of flourishing life; it is not a product of propaganda, publicity, or pedagogy. Unless beauty can become an active principle in life, visible and operative in our institutions and methods, it will remain far afield; unless art can become the healthy and instinctive mode of expression of all people, it will continue to be decadent, as it is now.

Is it an impasse in which we find ourselves—a situation that either denies us the good life unless we first acquire beauty or denies us beauty unless we first obtain the good life? We have the will now, and in good measure, but there is an error in the direction in which this will is applied. We still rely on machines and mass action for the redemption of society; we still adhere to our art-museum propaganda and our art-school pedagogy for the recovery of beauty and the recreation of art, because we have not been able as yet to emancipate ourselves from the old intellectualistic methods that wrought our undoing.

Now is the time for them to seek redemption. We must win back the impaired consciousness—the consciousness that life itself is greater than any of its parts, that it is more than the sum of its individuals, and that it has, in a word, unity, and personality. When we see this, we shall know that life cannot be divided into separate categories, each part functioning in individualism and methods of high specialization, but that vitality can be attained only by coordination.

The possession of beauty and the role of art are intimately and thoroughly integral parts of life itself. As such, neither is attainable or usable, not even desirable, unless they are so related.

Therefore, beauty must be linked again with life, and art must be given back its true service—starting with the reestablishment of our moral standards. One of the troubles with the Western culture is the breakdown of rules so that modern man cannot make value judgments. Once one uses the words "genuine" and "authentic" in art, morality and truth cannot be separated from the work of art.

If we had this spirit of faith back in its old nature and power, we should not need to trouble ourselves about the problems of art. It would burst forth into a glorious flowering as before, when people were not mired in the haze of their confused souls but expressed the beauty that was above and beyond them. Perhaps through the conscious attempt at recovery of art and its right application, we may be making more comfortable the way toward regaining this greater thing that, once achieved, would solve more than just aesthetic problems.

Again, modernism is an old concept dating back to the nineteenth century. The idea passed through artists like Matisse, Gauguin, and then Picasso and a whole school of thinkers. However, its culminating point—and also death—came only some fifty-odd years ago in the 1960s, which itself culminated in the youth revolutions of 1968. "Modern" meant anti-Victorian, the rejection of any old value, of anything old-fashioned, regardless of whether it was worthwhile or not.

Typical of this culmination of modernism were the Second Vatican Council, liberalism, recreational drug use, alcoholism, pornography, feminism, abortion, divorce, and the collapse of marriage and stable family life. Then, a decade after the culmination of modernism and the rejection of any tradition, good or bad, came the inevitable climax of postmodernism—that is, cynicism, skepticism, disbelief, and nihilistic deconstruction. Although postmodernism is also an old concept, its climactic point could come only after the 1960s, in the cynical destructiveness of the period between the 1970s and 1990s. Typical of postmodernism are the lack of belief in anything constructive or positive, spiritual emptiness, depression, nothingness, an "anything goes" attitude, the mocking of sincere belief, irony, throwaway products, shallowness, cheapness, fads and fashions, and superficiality. Most of its bitter and disbelieving advocates are now aging or else are already dead.

If postmodernism comes after modernism, what comes after postmodernism? Metamodernism? It is a question that intellectuals have debated for decades and about which they still have not come to any conclusion. The lack of any answer is due to the spiritually empty nature of postmodernism. After a vacuum, anything is possible. A consensus on what makes an epoch cannot be achieved while that epoch is still in its early stages. On the one hand, it is possible to continue to wallow in the negativism of postmodernism and make a cult or delusional consciousness out of it. Notwithstanding, it is—theoretically, at least—equally possible to reject something as primitive and harmful as postmodernism with something positive and constructive.

Something positive and constructive? These are words that have little meaning in today's Western society, which alone has generated both modernism and postmodernism. Interestingly, it may be that the Western world will have to stop being ethnocentric and look outside its self-absorbed culture to find the qualities to regenerate itself. The fact is that "something positive and constructive" can only be built on a spiritual rebirth, which is the very baby that was thrown out together with the bathwater in the Western modernist '60s, postmodernist '70s and after.

Contemporary artists apparently believe that beauty is an old and silly concept.

Representational art is dead, having been killed by the camera, by technologists, and by scientists. Contemporary artists also feel that they are painting *ideas* now. What do we other mortals know about beauty? Nothing?

Einstein describes the three elements of scientific beauty: "A theory is the more impressive, the greater the simplicity of its premises is, the more different kinds of things it relates, and the more extended is its area of applicability."[426] According to Einstein, the first element of beauty is simplicity. He expresses how a theory harmonizes dissimilar things with "the different kinds of things it relates." So the second element of beauty can be identified as harmony. The extended applicability is a theory's splendor, or radiance—how clear, direct, and pure it is, and how much light it sheds upon other things, clarifying and explaining something unknown.[427]

Composer and conductor Leonard Bernstein's comments on Beethoven's *Eroica* symphony are as follows: "The element of unexpected is so often associated with Beethoven. But surprise is not enough; what makes it so great is that no matter how shocking and unexpected the surprise is, it always somehow gives the impression—as soon as it has happened—that it is the only thing that could have happened at that moment. *Inevitability* is the keynote. It is as though Beethoven had an inside track to truth and rightness so that he could say the most amazing and sudden things with complete authority and cogency."[428]

The four marks of beauty, then, are simplicity, harmony, radiance, and fitting surprise.

Modern Music: Akin to Modern Art

A full century after Arnold Schönberg and his students Alban Berg and Anton Webern unleashed their dissonant chords on the world, modern classical music remains an unattractive proposition for most concertgoers. In 2009 at the New York Philharmonic, several dozen people walked out of a performance of Berg's *Three Pieces for Orchestra*; about the same number exited Carnegie Hall before the Vienna Philharmonic struck up Schönberg's "masterpiece of dodecaphony," *Variations for Orchestra*.[429]

For decades, critics, historians, and even neuroscientists have been pondering the question of why so-called modern music seems to perplex the average listener.

After all, adventurous artists in other fields have met with a very different reception. Once, these cultural untouchables were dismissed as charlatans—merchants of the emperor's new clothes, to employ a phrase that remains commonplace among unappreciative concertgoers.

Explanations for the abiding resistance to musical modernism have proliferated, their multiplicity suggesting that none quite holds the key. One theory maintains that a preference for certain tonality is wired into the human brain. Babies hear tonal music almost from the moment of birth and so are conditioned to accept it as natural. Moreover, visual arts research demonstrates that children prefer representational images to abstract ones; the same can happen with music.

Earlier classical music, specifically that of the Romantic period, is more complex than modern music because of the intricacy of sound and *purpose*. One can define "earlier classical" as pre-twentieth-century classical music beginning around the late seventeenth century.

Modern music, which includes rock, hip-hop, rap, and modern classical music, is post-nineteenth-century music.

Modern music tends to have fewer types of chords, has less and simpler harmony, and fewer chord progressions, and it is lacking in purpose. Modern—thus post-nineteenth-century—classical music does occasionally use more complicated chords in an acoustic sense; however, these chords are a construction of the composers' tendencies to exclude purpose in their arrangements of sounds. Consequently, pieces lose their attractiveness and may seem to listeners to be arranged randomly.

If one wants to make the point about various levels of complexity, music can be compared to writing. In its essence, music is composed of sounds arranged in a certain way, similarly to words arranged in an essay. If the sounds are not skillfully arranged in a recognizable pattern, the music has no meaning; likewise, if words are unarranged, the writing also has no sense or meaning. Music pattern is not exclusive to the melody but pertains to all the notes as well; the patterns in music are expressed by the blending of sounds, called harmony, and scales, also known as keys. Harmony has a particular structure, in the same way a sentence does. Like any language, music is composed of sentences; if these musical sentences do not show the way or connect to each other by a change in harmony (chord progression), the composition loses its meaning, or sense of purpose.

The Baroque period, especially Bach, expanded harmony and chord progressions (changes in harmony) to nearly its maximum degree. Music should also have at least one set of sections—an introduction, a climax, and a conclusion—giving a musical piece a fuller and deeper meaning, such as the case with the structure consisting of the sentence, paragraph, chapter, and story. These sections in music are a trademark of the Romantic period and can be easily recognized by their dramatic changes in harmony and volume or dynamics. They are the rudiments of program music, telling a story that makes Romantic music so emotional.

In conclusion, purpose (purposeful complexity) is formed from harmony, chord progressions, and scales. The deeper purpose also includes sections, all of which are arranged in a way that makes them seem connected in a meaningful and distinct manner. The elements collectively will be considered a musical piece's acoustic complexity, and the connections holding all these elements together are created by the music theory required to achieve purposeful complexity.

The Romantic period, which extended through the eighteenth and nineteenth centuries, was the peak in the evolution of music and the last period of earlier (pre-twentieth-century) classical music. It was a time when new, talented composers reached outside of the boundaries set by the Classical and the Baroque periods. They had a high reverence for Bach and his conventions, which greatly influenced the structure of their pieces. Bach's rules for harmony and chord progressions (harmonic changes), along with traditional styles (fugue, sonata, concerto), formats (musical notation), and melodic formation, were all present. Moreover, thanks to the new instruments introduced in the symphony orchestras and the expanded keyboard (both developments instituted by Beethoven), many more possibilities opened up to be explored. Accordingly, the new composers added sections characteristic of program music that gave pieces deeper purpose, which made their music more emotional. For example, Richard L. Crocker wrote the following about Wagner, an "epitome of the Romantic period": "For the greatest effect, Wagner gave each harmony the richest spacing, position, and orchestration he could, sustained the chord as long as he dared, and then moved to a second chord whose relationship to the first would be as exciting as possible. His purpose was to produce feeling – not vague, indefinable feeling, but a prickle on the back of the neck."[430]

Audiences who could afford the luxury of attending a performance would marvel at the famous master musicians and composers of the time.

The modern classical music that followed the Romantic period slowly started to degenerate in purposeful complexity, deviating from traditional harmony, chord progressions, styles, and purpose. This slow decadence can be seen in the many strange and dissonant sounds and harmonies of impressionist composers. The impressionists, whose trademark composers were arguably Debussy and Ravel, concentrated their efforts on making radically new sounds while being content to attach these sounds to relatively traditional shapes (shapes being similar to chords). They also found it difficult, if not impossible, to create new shapes with purely traditional sounds. The "radical new sounds" are mainly composed of dissonance, which gives the impressionist period its nickname, "the Dissonant Period." The objective of this period is less concerned with emotional expression and more with qualities of sound and style, meaning that the deeper sense of purpose included with program music is lost. Another aspect of impressionist music is that the harmony changes less frequently than in classical works before its appearance. Thus, complexity regarding both sound and purpose decreased over time.

Theodor W. Adorno summed up the transformation in music around the 1920s as "a condition of chaotic fermentation, that is, the end of which could be foreseen and which would restore order from disorder."[431]

The most conspicuous composer to mention is the notorious Arnold Schönberg, who is considered an expressionist. The founder of atonality (the condition of having no particular scale) and the twelve-tone technique, his music would use a lot of dissonances without *any* reference to traditional functions. Again, purpose in such music is almost entirely lost, while strange sounds and a peculiar style not only individualize the music but also make the piece acoustically very complex. In such a way, patterns are difficult to recognize, and the music is made truly chaotic, lacking any sense of meaning and purpose. What else is the music, then, than a "randomization" of notes?

Some other composers of neoclassicism, however, still stayed with the strictly classical Western past and tried to create new pieces that replicated the previous styles (Prokofiev, Ravel, Stravinsky).

Since the end of the Romantic period, music theory has been increasingly neglected, the media being the major, if not entire, cause. As much as the media has influenced our clothing, lifestyle, politics, and other things, it has also affected music. This control resulted in a switch of the culture from being driven by highly educated individuals to a mass-consumer society, giving birth to new types of popular music that are generalized to the public and kept alive solely by the media. Others try to create new sounds—be original—by avoiding music theory altogether, and some have idealized notions that the future will expand music theory into something new and better, making early classical music obsolete.

Popular music is one of the main components of modern music. Popular music has always been around, whether it has taken the form of singing folk songs in pubs in the 1600s or blasting metal in a car. Surprisingly, popular music has increased in acoustic complexity—thanks to new electronics able to play such music anywhere—and is now, by some people and critics, considered to be art. Nevertheless, modern popular music does not have the exact purpose that folk songs had long ago. Nowadays it combines accompaniment and prerecorded performances that would obviously not have been available before and is entirely under the control of the music industry and its institutions of mass production.

Pre-twentieth-century popular music consisted mainly of various types of folk songs. Attempts to make these folk songs more artistic have been made by such composers as Brahms but were afterward considered as endeavors in classical music.

The generalization of the audience in today's popular music by the mass-consumer society is the main reason it lacks the same elements that earlier and modern classical music contain. A person needs to be well educated in its components if he or she is to understand classical music's various complexities. However, most people do not listen to music to analyze it. Moreover, not all of the early classical music is as complicated as it seems and is popular in modern society—such as, for example, Beethoven's seventh symphony. It has a simple recurring melody that each time repeats in slightly different variations. Its purpose and intense emotions of anger, joy, sadness, and love are easily discerned, giving it purposeful complexity.

Notwithstanding how old classical music may be perceived, its popularity has increased over time. Classical music is growing, not shrinking, in demand today, and we should expect that demand to grow even more in the coming years. Its complexity influences many people to practice instruments, sometimes for most of their lives, to gain the satisfaction of playing a musical piece and having the ability to interpret and change the music as desired.

In contrast to classical music, modern popular music is heavily edited and seems to have a short period of popularity, lasting about one to two years. For a long time, classical music has been considered rich and elegant and has played a significant role in modern culture. When dining at a city's most renowned restaurant, would someone expect a rap group or a string quartet playing Mozart? Also, practically all movies include some form of classical music.

When composers switched to the alien languages that repelled everyday people with natural instincts, feelings, and drives, the core of the audience headed for the door. Nevertheless, we officially joined the modernist cult, in which everybody is required to endure the harsh notes of the modern classical pieces and compliment the emperor's new clothes to fit in and to keep up with the fashion.

Today's composers suffer from, in the words of Léon Krier, "the fear of backwardness."[432] It could be added to that, that musicians, too, not unlike teenagers, feel awkward—trapped in a "fear of backwardness." They want so much to be cool; they want everyone to like them. Eventually they will have to grow up and realize that trying to be all things to all people is a fool's game. The cool kids usually peak in high school; it is the nerdy or socially unimpressive kid who goes on to do something remarkable. We are that nerdy kid who has to endure the stupid teacher and stupid classmates at school, and we have to withstand the agony imposed on us by modern classical or popular music.

Every day there are third of a million children born in this world who have never heard Beethoven's fifth symphony. A good number of them will want to listen to it again and again because the very nature of the classical music makes it a thing that is not disposed of after enjoying it; it is eternal. Time even enhances its value—its quality; it gets better and better upon repeated listening. One keeps coming back to reconsider a piece over the years as it opens up to the listener adopting it. The classical music experience is about living with a work, getting to know it intimately. New compositions can also become part of the canon, provided they demonstrate that perennial quality of the eternal things.

During this undeclared war of sorts with living composers, orchestras let a few of them appear on their repertoires, but the audiences still do not trust them—and neither do the musicians themselves. Too many of them feel already betrayed by the contemporary composers with their ugly and inhuman sound art—rather like the obnoxious cityscapes of concrete, glass, and metal that have chased human settlement into the suburbs.

The audiences, voting with their feet when they smell a modernist lurking, are probably the musicians' best friends in this respect, as the patrons have been the protective barrier preventing the musicians from jumping headfirst into the shallow end of the avant-garde.

However, some happy and notable exceptions still exist in the popularity of new music composed for video games and film. Both of these genres employ perfectly understandable and coherent musical ideas to drive real human emotions, without any progressive agenda to be original or groundbreaking. The top compositional talent is going into these applications of orchestral music because there is a living to be made there. There is also a great lesson to be drawn from the way audiences embrace new music that plays on real and natural human responses.

In the past, classical music, with its intelligently arranged harmony and melody to show an obvious yet beautiful progression, was created to please the upper-class audience. In the sense of purposeful and acoustic complexity, nothing can compare with the classical music of the Romantic composers.

Commercialism, the generalization of the audience, and continuing attempts to revolutionize sound have caused the decline in complexity of modern music. Popular music is written to entertain a more general audience, thus requiring less knowledge and attention in the field—although exceptions can be found. Modern classical music tries to create new sound, thus also straying away from any limitations.

I. Perverting Opera

The disappearance of the bourgeoisie has led to a crisis in the arts. How can the defeated remnants of the philistine class be tracked down just to be disturbed with the proof of their irrelevance? Theaters, galleries, restaurants, and public resorts all offer impeccable postmodern fare addressed to nonjudgmental people. Television has been dumbed down below the horizon of bourgeois awareness, and even the churches are rejecting family values and marital virtues. The world of art lacks a target without the bourgeoisie, forever condemned to repeat empty gestures of revolution to an audience that long ago lost the capacity for outrage.

Luckily, not all is lost, however. There is one last redoubt where the bourgeoisie can be corralled into a corner and spat upon, and that is the opera. Believers in family values and traditional marriage are romantics at heart who love to sit through those fantastic stories of intrigue, betrayal, and reconciliation where love between man and woman is exalted to such incredible height that can never be reached in real life—where the whole fable is presented through magnificent music and magical scenes that take the audience, for an enchanted three hours, into the world of dreams.

Siegfried's love for Brunhild shot through with unconscious treachery, or Butterfly's innocent passion built on self-deception—these are exciting ideas that could never be realized through words but that are burned into our hearts by music. Is it surprising that the surviving remnants of the bourgeoisie, surrounded as they are by a culture of flippancy and sacrilege, should be so drawn to opera? After a performance of *Onegin*, *Pelléas*, *La Traviata*, or *Aida*, they stagger home amazed at those passions displayed on the stage by creatures no more godlike than themselves. They will come to sit through their favorite fairy tales from miles away and drive home singing in the early hours. They will pay 200 dollars or euros for a mediocre seat to hear their favorite soprano or tenor and will learn by heart the arias that they are never satisfied to hear unless in the flesh. One can take any performance of an operatic classic anywhere in the world and find, sitting in close confinement, motionless, and devout for the space of three hours, the assembled remnant of the bourgeoisie, innocent, expectant, and available for a shock.

The temptation is irresistible. Hardly a producer today, confronted with a masterpiece that might otherwise delight and console such an audience, can control the desire to desecrate. The more exalted the music, the more demeaning the production.

This author has come across many horrifying stagings: Siegfried in schoolboy shorts cooking a sword on a mobile canteen; Mélisande holed up in welfare accommodation, with Pelléas sadistically tying her to the wall by her hair; Don Giovanni standing happily at ease at the end of the eponymous opera while unexplained demons enter the stage, sing a meaningless chorus, and exit again; Rusalka sitting in a wheelchair from which she stares at a football in a swimming pool while addressing the moon; Tristan and Isolde on a ship divided by a brick wall, singing vaguely of love while each remains hidden from the other; Mozart's *Entführung aus dem Serail* ("The Abduction from the Seraglio") set in a Berlin brothel; and Verdi's *Masked Ball* with the assembled cast squatting on toilets so as to void their bowels; not to speak of the usual Hitlerization of any opera, from *Fidelio* to *Tosca*, that can be squeezed into a Nazi uniform. Wagner is always mercilessly mutilated, of course, lest those misguided bourgeois fall for his seductive, and often artificially implied, political message. As for *Madama Butterfly*, what an opportunity to get back at the Americans for that bomb dropped on Nagasaki!

The outrageous thing is not that this distortion occurs but that the taxpayer pays for it. The more ridiculous the staging of an opera, the more recognition and acknowledgment are needed to attract the attention of an audience lost in wonder as to the meaning of it all. Both the opera productions and the producers are expensive. People like Peter Sellars, who have made a living out of the effort to shock, startle, appall, and offend, have become international celebrities. There is a feeding frenzy among such avant-garde directors and producers as to who can provoke the greatest emotional reactions—positive or negative; it hardly matters—from the critics and other reviewers of the media. As far as claiming subsidies from city councils, arts bureaucracies, institutional sponsors, or the state, what counts is not what the critics say but how loudly they say it. An opera house must be contentious, given to path-breaking and challenging productions presented in a politically correct manner to apply for the standing required for a state subsidy. The bureaucrats need to be persuaded that something very crucial to the future of the community, city, or nation will be jeopardized without a grant to the opera company, whose importance is proved by the protests that are stirred up by it.

A typically encountered argument goes like this: operas are very expensive to put on, and to charge the full price to the patrons would be tantamount to pricing the art form out of the market. Therefore, subsidies are necessary, but these are obtainable only if those who provide them can be persuaded that they are not funding outdated bourgeois audiences who have already had their share of life and are soon to disappear in any case. Accordingly, contentious, indoctrinating, propagandistic, and politically correct productions are required as the only alternative to no productions at all.

While there are some valid points in the above argument, the bizarre truth is that precisely the same old-fashioned and slowly disappearing bourgeois audience is needed to inspire the modern producer, since otherwise he has no one to offend. However, the offense is necessary; otherwise, the bureaucrats (who are the producer's handlers) will think that they are subsidizing, heaven forbid, the bourgeoisie.

Not only the opera productions but also their directors are expensive. They are expensive because, like Richard Jones, Peter Sellars, David McVicar, Dmitri

Tcherniakov, or Pierre Audi, they have a psychological need to draw attention to themselves at the expense of the work itself. This chronic ego aggrandizement means outlandish props, lighting effects, and strange gestures imposed on the singers as opposed to the natural movements inspired by the music.

What modern producers seem to ignore is that audiences are gifted with the faculty of imagination; this faculty is not extinguished or impaired by being bourgeois. The very fact that opera, sung rather than spoken, stimulates the imagination by presenting a drama with music, seemingly escapes the attention of the new school of producers—perhaps because so many of them spend their training years in the spoken theater as apprentices. They do not fully understand that music, by existing and moving in the space of its own, automatically transports the audience to an imaginary world. The singers, put in costumes that distance them from the audience, will move in a world of their own—even without stage sets and props. The music itself will direct them how to move, where to turn, and with which expressions on their faces. With an additional accessory or two, all the meaning that the composer intended is there on stage, and only the quality of the performance will affect whether the audience can grasp it.

This disregard of the original work is the point where the greatest *disservice* has been done to opera by modern production. In the past, the production was designed to *present* an opera; now it aims to *interpret* it, to attach a perhaps new meaning to it, regardless of whether it conforms to the work or not. The work itself is seen merely as a vehicle for the ideas of the producer rather than a drama whose meaning lies in itself—as was intended by its composer and librettist. Instead of allowing the work and the music to speak, the producer, who is now a paid interpreter of some politically correct ideology, stands in front of it and moralizes at the assembled bourgeoisie by saying that this or that feature of the text or the music must be pinned to some allegorical or symbolic meaning. In any event, the whole thing has to be made into a relevant commentary on the psychic traumas of the day—otherwise, how can we take it seriously? In short, the magic of the opera, its capacity to create an enchanted world of its own, must be neutralized by an interpretation that brings it down to earth. That pins it into some sordid corner, as Peter Sellars did with *Pelléas et Melisande*, so that the imaginary world intended by the composer is blotted out by a screen of the producer's usually half-baked and in any case self-aggrandizing ideas.

II. Classical Music Means Beauty

Those who reject the idea of beauty, those who deny its value, and those who relegate it to meaninglessness are at a loss to explain what it is that music offers us. What is classical music about, then, if not beauty?

It is risky to defend beauty today. The most apparent efforts denying beauty in classical music are the attempts to make the music itself ugly or ridiculous. With that tactic alone, orchestras have managed to drive away a great many decent people during the last century.

Music, the modernists told us, has to be ugly because modern life is ugly. Webern and his modernist comrades may have been quite confident we would all one day be whistling their horrendous atonal tunes, but they would be hard-pressed to find anyone who could recall them today.

The postmodernists tell us music must be ridiculous because life is ridiculous. They brought us stuntmen like John Cage, with bizarre acoustic noises perpetrated by grotesque gadgets designated as instruments. To drive the point quite literally home, modernists house orchestras in beastly buildings of rust and algae-streaked concrete, and postmodernists impose on us concert halls that look like crash-landed spaceships. Nevertheless, it is true, perhaps much about the way we live is ugly and ridiculous, but it is mostly the crackpot theories of the modernists and postmodernists that make it so.

Perhaps it was difficult not to sympathize with the modernists' sentiment following the sickening devastation of the First and Second World Wars. The horrors of industrialized warfare must have suggested that the modern condition was one of abject and novel ugliness. What the argument depends on, however, is the assumption that, in an ugly world, Beauty is no longer relevant.

Nevertheless, that is a losing argument. The human ear has unequivocally rejected the ugly and ridiculous musical compositions in the concert halls. When they, regrettably, do appear in a concert program today, they are shrewdly and quite ingeniously sandwiched in the middle of the program because organizers know that audiences will arrive late or leave early to avoid them. However, it is no good scorning at the audience for its philistine appreciation of beauty; they will elect not to show up at all. In fact, and not surprisingly, that is what happened as naturally conservative audiences abandoned their symphony orchestras.

One cannot help noticing the fact that while art galleries devoted to ugly modernist art are full, concert halls featuring the musical equivalent are empty. When a person views an abstract or expressionist canvas, time is in his or her control. One may spend as much or as little time at the gallery as one pleases, but when a person listens to atonal music, he or she is stuck in the seat for as long as the wicked composer wishes to keep him or her there. That hapless person is in the position of the trendy but naive wide-eyed left-wing intellectual who made the fatal mistake of actually moving to Moscow in the 1930s rather than admiring it from a safe distance.

Music, perhaps for precisely this reason, has resisted the ideological uglification that the brave new world order has imposed more successfully on its cousins: art, poetry, and literature. Standing like a fortress above the onslaught and built on a canon to which we still respond and always return, classical music is still an unconquered repository of beauty. However disheartened the snobbishly self-avowed connoisseurs of modern music may profess to be at the prospect, orchestras will always perform Beethoven's fifth symphony because audiences will ever want to hear it. In fact, the uglier their world and its modern music become, the more likely the concertgoers will understand and appreciate classical music. That is because beauty does not deny the ugliness, the pain, the torments, the sorrows, or even the ordinariness and baseness of existence; it transforms them. This miracle is often performed in the canon of classical music, and people attend concerts precisely to witness that miracle and take part in it. When we reject beauty, when we insist on wallowing in vulgarity and ugliness, what we ultimately reject is this possibility of transcendence.

So what is next for those who insist that music is not about beauty? If music cannot, through beauty, transform our relationship with or transcend the ugliness of reality, then it must change physical reality itself to eliminate ugliness; it must change what we can believe in. Music must change society: it is about making our world a better place.

Modern Sport: Professionalism, Entertainment, and Business

Among the activities through which people seek release from everyday life, games offer, in many ways, the purest form of escape. Like sex, drugs, and drink, they remove awareness of daily reality, not by blurring that consciousness but by enhancing it to a new level and intensity of concentration. Moreover, games have no side effects; they produce no hangovers or emotional complications. Games satisfy the need for free fantasy and the search for gratuitous difficulty simultaneously; they combine childlike exuberance with deliberately created challenges.

By establishing conditions of equality among the players, games attempt to substitute ideal conditions for the common confusion of everyday life. They recreate the freedom, the remembered perfection, of childhood, and mark it off from ordinary life with artificial boundaries within which the only constraints are the rules to which the players freely submit. Games enlist not only skill and intelligence but also a total concentration of purpose on behalf of utterly useless activities that do not contribute to the struggle of humanity either against nature or for the wealth or comfort of the community or its physical survival.

In communist and fascist countries, sports were organized and promoted by the state—for essentially self-advertisement.

In capitalist countries, the uselessness of games makes them offensive to social reformers, improvers of public morals, and functionalist critics of society, who see in the futility of upper-class sports anachronistic survivals of militarism and tests of prowess. However, it is precisely the futility of play that explains its appeal—its artificiality, the arbitrary obstacles it sets up for no other purpose than to challenge the players to surmount them, and the absence of any useful or uplifting object. Games quickly lose part of their charm when pressed into the service of education, character development, or social improvement.

Modern industries having reduced most jobs to routine, the games in our society take on added meaning. People seek in play the difficulties and demands, both intellectual and physical, that they no longer find in work.

The history of culture appears from one perspective to consist of the gradual eradication of the elements of play from all cultural forms—from religion, from the law, from warfare, and above all from productive labor. The rationalization of these activities leaves little room for the spirit of the arbitrary invention or the disposition to leave things to chance. Risk, daring, and uncertainty, all critical components of play, have little place in industry or in activities infiltrated by modern methods, which are intended precisely to predict and control the future and to eliminate risk. Accordingly, games have assumed an importance unprecedented even in ancient

Greece, where so much of social life revolved around contests. Sports, which also satisfy the starved need for physical exertion—for a renewal of the sense of the physical basis of life—have become an obsession, compulsion, and mania not just of the masses but also of those who set themselves up as cultural elites.

The rise of spectator sports to their current importance coincides historically with the rise of mass production, which intensifies the needs that competition satisfies while, at the same time, also creating the technical means to promote and market athletic contests to a vast audience. Alas, according to a common criticism of modern sport, these same developments have also destroyed the value of athletics.

The commercialized play has turned into work, subordinated the athlete's pleasure to the spectator's, and reduced the viewer himself to a state of passivity—the very antithesis of the health and vigor sport ideally promotes. The mania for winning has encouraged an exaggerated emphasis on the competitive side of the game, to the exclusion of the more humble but more satisfying experiences of sportsmanship, cooperation, and competence. The cult of victory has made savages of the players and rabid fanatics of their followers. The violence and partisanship of modern sports led some critics to insist that athletics impart false values to the young and irrationally inculcate false pride in the spectator.

A shift toward overseriousness had ruined modern games and sports. At the same time, the playing had lost its element of ritual, had become profane, and as a consequence ceased to have any organic connection with the structure of society. The masses now crave trivial recreation and crude sensationalism and throw themselves into these pursuits with passion above and beyond their intrinsic merit. The crowds play with the blend of adolescence and barbarity today, investing games with patriotic and martial fervor while treating serious pursuits as if they were games.

Far-reaching contamination of play and serious activity has taken place, with the two spheres getting mixed. While in the activities of an outwardly serious nature hides an element of the game, the recognized play is no longer able to maintain its true "play-character" as a result of being taken too seriously and being technically overorganized. The essential qualities of detachment, artlessness, and gladness are thus lost.

When the television networks discovered surfing, they demanded that events be held according to a prearranged schedule, without any regard to weather conditions.

A surfer complained, "Television is destroying our sport. The TV producers are turning a sport and an art form into a circus."⁴³³ Substituting artificial surfaces for grass in tennis has slowed the pace of the match, placed a premium on reliability and patience, and reduced the elements of tactical brilliance and overpowering speed. However, this lends itself to television producers perfectly by making tennis an all-weather game and even permitting it to be played indoors.

Spectators keep becoming more sensation-hungry and bloodthirsty. The rise of violence in ice hockey, soccer, and basketball, far beyond the point where it plays any functional part in the game, coincided with the expansion of professional sports into cities without any traditional attachment to that particular sport—cities where weather conditions had previously precluded any such tradition of local play to develop. At this point, sport ceases to be enjoyable and becomes a business.

The degradation of sport consists not in its being taken too seriously but in its subjection to some ulterior motive, such as profit making, flag-waving nationalism, character building, or even the pursuit of health. Sport may facilitate all these things, but ideally, it produces them only as by-products having no organic connection with the game. Moreover, when the game itself comes to be regarded as merely incidental to the benefits it supposedly confers on participants, spectators or promoters, it loses its unique capacity to transport both participant and spectator beyond everyday experience.

Unfortunately, the recent history of sports is the history of their steady submission to the demands of everyday reality or the entertainment business. The recognition that sports have become a form of entertainment alone justifies the salaries paid to star professional athletes and their prominence in the media. However, even as the television audience demands the presentation of games as a form of spectacle, the widespread envy of star athletes among followers of sport indicates the persistence of a need to believe that sports represent something more than just entertainment. It is the belief that though they are neither life nor death in themselves, games retain some lingering capacity to dramatize and clarify those experiences. On the other hand, the envious resentment of star athletes is directed against the inflated salaries negotiated by their agents and against the athletes to become hucksters, promoters, and celebrities.

The rise of a new kind of journalism helped to professionalize formerly amateur athletics, assimilate sport to promotion, and make professional athletics into a major industry. Until about hundred years ago, professional sports attracted little public attention. Then, following World War II, entrepreneurs extended the techniques of mass promotion, and television and mass journalism elevated sports to new heights of popularity while reducing them to entertainment at the same time.

The invasion of sports by the entertainment ethic breaks down the boundaries between the ritual world of play and the sordid reality from which it is designed to provide an escape. Newspapers and magazines report sports-related business news on the sports page instead of confining it to the business section, where it belongs. The fact that the faithful sports fan can only find the spread of entertainment ethic today sheds more light on the degeneration of sports than all the strictures of left-wing critics, who wish to abolish competition, emphasize the value of sports as health-giving exercise, and promote a more cooperative conception of athletics—in other words, to make sports an instrument of personal and social therapy.

Today work tends to be permeated with behavior formerly confined to after-work hours; one example is the manipulation of personal relations in the interest of political or economic advantage. At the same time, (professional) play is measured by standards of achievement previously applicable only to work.

The development of (professional) sports follows a similar pattern. Sports are not separate and apart from life today but are a business aided by the evolution of the spectacle as the predominant form of cultural expression and the assimilation of sport into show business.

I. Amateurism in Sports

Amateurism is essential; in its primary meaning, it is inherent in all organized sports. We can abolish specific rules of amateurism, but other rules will spring up in their place. Society can recognize and promote professionalism in sport, but this cannot eliminate or reduce the problem of amateurism for the 99 percent of athletes at the lower levels of performance.

Amateurism is valid for all cultures and times. Some fundamental truths or concepts define amateurism in sports for all cultures and institutions, just as certain truths are eternally valid in such other areas of human affairs as economics, ecology, biomechanics, and social ethics. The fundamental fact is inexorable and unchanging, though its application may be over a wide range of possibilities.

Sports morality is an essential aspect of social morality; as hard as the International Olympic Committee has tried to separate amateur sports from politics and international conflict, the problems of sports are inseparable from the morality and values of the whole society. Each nation or institution interprets amateur sports in terms of its belief and practice of social benefits in general.

In nineteenth-century England, the aristocracy dominated all phases of life, including sports. Naturally, amateur sports were interpreted from their viewpoints, with a high valuation of honor in keeping agreements and rejecting foul play of all kinds. They valued the importance of leisure time as well as sports for sport's sake—for the fun of it. If material rewards resulted from winning, as they often did, this merely enhanced the pleasure; to work harder at sports to ensure greater material rewards would be dishonorable.

Amateurism cannot be policed. The rules of amateurism are mostly unenforceable unless we accept Big Brother and digital society. Conformance can be achieved only within a community whose beliefs, values, and practices are at a consistently high level.

Someone once said that the worth of any society, institution, or individual could be judged by the degree of its free adherence to rules of social conduct that are unenforceable. Indeed, this applies to amateur sports.

The fundamental truths and essentials that underlie the amateur idea in sports include the following:

The demands of sports as related to time, energy, and commitment, are secondary to other aspirations: studies, vocation, social service, or any challenging pursuit in life. This tenet forces the acceptance of a limitation on the daily time, energy, and commitment that can be devoted to sports, even though this produces a restriction on performance.

This first tenet is the crux of amateur sports. It is this principle that separates it from professional sports, which accepts no such limitations. The word "amateurism" is derived from the Latin, meaning "lover." However, the love of sports—even for sport's sake—is not proscribed from professional ranks. Human motives are complex and intermingled, never all this and none of that. In fact, a person committed without reservation to a sport can love it in a way and to a degree that is not possible for the part-time participant.

Again, amateurs proclaim fair play on the field of competition without being alone in this. Professionals must also adhere to the rules of the game, even though fairness may not be a primary concern.

Amateurism agrees with and conforms to the prohibition of all material rewards and incentives for success in sports that induce competitors to break the rules and regulations of the first tenet. Among such incentives are such highly valued methods of recognition as money payments, job promotions, life pensions, and others.

To break the first tenet of amateurism is likely to give a direct and unfair advantage; the greater is the time-energy ratio for preparation, the better the performance. Nevertheless, a material reward in itself does not enable a person to run faster or make a higher percentage of baskets in foul shooting. The first tenet is the primary end; the second tenet is but the means of ensuring that end.

The third essential of amateur sports is a sense of honor: personal integrity or pride in practicing the agreements of amateurism—especially the off-the-field agreements, though recognizing that these are mostly unenforceable by those administering sports.

Concerning sports morality in modern Western society, it has already been stated that the problems of sports are inseparable from those of society as a whole. Although any society can place any degree of value on the tenets of amateurism, it is evident that modern Western society puts little value on the points of view stated in the above three principles, not merely in sports, but in all walks of life. Private profit is a significant and even primary goal in all professions. Honor in maintaining social codes is neither a respected nor extensively practiced concept. There is hardly any recognition of the fact that a limitation on human performance in all walks of life is not only inevitable but also desirable if a necessary balance of life is to be achieved. It is inevitable then, in today's Western culture, that there should be a general disinterest and nonconformance with even a low-level interpretation of the amateur code.

ENVIRONMENT: CLIMATE CHANGE CAUSED BY POPULATION GROWTH

The West is solving the wrong problems. Although climate change is real, the political and business elites believe that it is just an engineering problem for which there will be an engineering solution.

Earth has an enormous dilemma causing the climate change: exploding population growth. But the truth cannot be admitted! Everybody on earth is in denial about the issue of global population growth, which totals about 80 million new people a year.[434]

Thousands of scientists worldwide are trying to come up with brilliant technical solutions to reduce the impact of global warming, but population growth is the primary cause, or root cause, of global warming—and it is an issue no politician will touch. Nobody is working on the real solution; no one has the courage. Why?

It is a tragic measure of how far the world has changed—and how no subject can get one more swiftly into political trouble than motherhood.

As for motherhood, the fertility of the human race, we are getting to the point where one cannot even mention it; the world is thereby refusing to say anything sensible about the most significant single challenge facing the globe. The biggest problem is *not* global warming; that is a secondary challenge. The primary challenge facing humanity is the reproduction of its species.

The population of the earth is growing with every word that skitters beneath the eyeball, depending on how fast one reads. More than two hundred eleven thousand people are being added to the world's population every day; and a population the size of Germany, the most populous European country, every year.

If someone had been traveling around the world for decades, that person could see and feel this change. One can smell it in the traffic jams all over the world and see it flying over Africa at night when mile after mile of fires burn in the dark as the scrub is cleared away to make way for human beings. One can see it in the satellite pictures of nocturnal Europe, with the whole place lit up like a fairground. One can see it in the crazy dentition of the Shanghai skyline, where new skyscrapers are going up around the clock. One can see it flying over Mexico City, a vast checkerboard of smog-bound, low-rise dwellings stretching from one horizon to the other. When one looks at what we are doing to our planet, one has a horrifying vision of habitations multiplying and replicating like bacilli in a Petri dish.

The world's population is now 7.4 billion—roughly *triple* what it was when this author was born. The UN has revised its forecasts upward, predicting that there will be 9.55 billion people by the year 2050—but no one discusses this impending calamity, and no world political leader has the guts to treat the issue with the seriousness it deserves.[435]

How can we talk about dealing with global warming and reducing consumption and pollution when we are continuing to add so relentlessly to the number of consumers? The answer is politics, political cowardice, and the loss of the middle-class ideology—including future preference.

During the 1960s and 1970s, when people were becoming interested in demography and the United Nations was holding essential conferences on the subject, it was quite respectable to talk about saving the planet by reducing population growth. However, over the years, the perspective shifted, the argument changed, certain words became taboo, and specific theories became banned. We have reached the stage where even the mere discussion of overall human fertility—global motherhood—has become more or less suppressed.

The world seems to have given up on population control, and all sorts of explanations are offered for the surrender. Some say Indira Gandhi gave it all a bad name by her deliberately misconstrued and misdirected plan to sterilize Indian men. Some attribute the complacency to the Green Revolution, which seemed to prove Malthus wrong. It became the accepted wisdom that the world's population could rise to umpteen billions as humanity learned how to make several ears of corn grow where one had grown before.

Then, more recently, a pincer movement from the Right and Left has more or less enveloped and stifled the whole concept of global population control. While religious fundamentalists of the Right disapprove of anything that sounds like birth control, the US government even withholds the small American contribution to the UN Fund for Population Activities, ignoring the effect on the women's health in developing countries.

As for the Left, they dislike any suggestion concerning population control because that, for them, seems to smell and taste of colonialism and imperialism, telling the Third World what to do. So humanity gripes about the destruction of the environment, and yet there is not a word in any communiqué from any summit of the EU, G7 or G8, G20, or UN about the global population growth that is causing that destruction.

The debate will inevitably become unavoidable. One should only look at food prices, driven ever higher by population growth in India and China, or the insatiable Chinese desire for meat, which has pushed the cost of feed so high that Russia has been obliged to institute price controls.

This issue is not an argument about immigration per se, since it does not matter where people come from, and with their skills and their industry, immigrants can add to the economy. This issue is a straightforward question of population growth and the eventual size of the human race. The world can reduce population growth and poverty by promoting literacy, female emancipation, and access to birth control. Isn't it time politicians stopped being so timid and started talking about the real number-one issue?

There is, of course, an even more sensitive taboo topic related to this, and particular interest groups may perceive it as borderline racism. Namely, the question arises: Which parts of the world's population are responsible for most of the population growth? However, in the interest of objectivity, it must be said that the population in developed countries is aging and declining, while most of the population growth occurs in Third World countries, which are unable to sustain even the existing population adequately, let alone impose some form of one-child policy, as China did. The political correctness in avoiding the discussion of this problem in, say, India or Africa, will eventually lead to a future humanitarian catastrophe. With most of the population living in those places in horrible hygienic conditions as it is, every family still tends to have five children at least, owing to cultural factors and the prevailing mindset. This fact may cause huge problems twenty to thirty years down the line.

16

THE CULTURAL ABDICATION AND INTELLECTUAL ARROGANCE OF THE WESTERN ELITE

On one side, there is the 1 percent Western elite, while on the other one finds the rest of the planet. Who is this elite?

According to the Oxford Living Dictionaries, "elite" means "A group or class of people seen as having the most power and influence in society, especially on account of their wealth or privilege."

In political and sociological theory, the elite is a small group of people who control a disproportionate amount of wealth or political power. The inner core of the power elite involves individuals who can move from one seat of institutional power to another, therefore having a broad range of knowledge and interests in many influential organizations and being professional go-betweens in economic, political, and military affairs.

This elite is the controller of governments, commerce, industry, finance, energy, media, science, and technology. Most of the elite are unelected men and women deciding what paths our futures hold. Although there are many members of these groups, it is only a select few that hold immense power and wealth.

Felix Frankfurter, a US Supreme Court justice, said in 1952, "The real rulers in Washington are invisible and exercise power from behind the scenes."[436]

The ideals of the postwar elite and their hopes for social democracy, for international institutions, and for European unity are looking more and more threadbare. Their policies and the reasonable fear that our children will be less well off than we are have dealt a blow not only to those ideals but also to the educated, arrogant, left-liberal class that did most to promote them. The peoples of the West have been led astray by their rulers—the scheming, hypocritical, vainglorious, pretentious, and value-relinquishing elite masquerading as guardians of human rights and socially conscious democrats.

The Western elite of today is *against* the people; they are *destroying* the Western identities—ethnic, national, and religious. It is they who are sabotaging the welfare states by rewarding the lazy, spending uncontrollably, bankrupting the nation-states, and robbing countries of their sovereignty, all while blaming the Right for the problems thereby created.

The Western elite is responsible for the destruction of customs and traditional communities, for the moving of entire industries from continent to continent, for the creation and dominance of globalized financial centers that have become more influential than governments. The Western elite is also responsible for those people and nations who feel left behind and marginalized, and for the resulting politics of resentment and hatred that has never resulted in anything good.

While preaching the modern liberal shibboleths about internationalism, the richness of immigrants' cultures and the horrors of racism, the Western elite has created a borderless economy without any tempering of the growing inequalities or shielding of the vulnerable from global market forces. If they want to stave off the storm of destructive hatred, they had better come up with some ideas of their own on how to temper the market forces from which they have profited so well.

Libya's autocratic ruler, Muammar Gaddafi, was brutally tortured and killed in 2011, after France, Britain, the United States, and NATO had actively given military support to rebel troops that were known to include groups with ties to terrorist organizations such as al-Qaeda.

However, Gaddafi was *not* killed in retaliation for his attacks on American servicemen in Berlin in 1986. He was *not* killed for the downing of PanAm Flight 103 over Lockerbie, Scotland, in 1989. Neither was he murdered for his central role in the USSR's terror networks going back to the 1960s and 1970s.

No, Gaddafi was killed *after* coming over to the Western side of George Bush's notorious War on Terror in the final phase of a civil war in Libya in which his regime fought al-Qaeda affiliates. Gaddafi was killed *because the West had joined the other side*—the Western elite, that is.

The day before he quit as Egypt's president after the popular uprisings in February 2011, Hosni Mubarak had some harsh words for his former US allies and their misguided crusade for Middle Eastern democracy. "They may be talking about democracy, but they don't know what they're talking about, and the result will be extremism and radical Islam," said Mubarak.[437]

Mubarak kept stability in Egypt during his three decades in power; maintained peace with his neighbors, including Israel; and promoted decent economic progress in his country without being cruel. Despite this, the Western elite quickly turned their backs on him when protests began. As a result, the Muslim Brotherhood gained in strength and won the allegedly first democratic elections in Egypt, and since then the attacks on Coptic Christians have escalated. The Western elite, probably disappointed with the outcome, turned around again and started supporting the Egyptian Army in overthrowing the freely elected regime. The so-called Arab Spring, enthusiastically backed by the Western elite as the long-awaited democratization of Islam, has ruined many Muslim countries but, other than creating chaos and war with ever-increasing terrorism in North Africa and the Middle East, achieved nothing.

Many ordinary citizens, when witnessing their sham leaders supporting the enemies, wonder whether the Western political elite has completely lost their grip on reality. What are they trying to achieve with such senseless and destructive policies? Why do they want to export liberal democracy to Islamic countries even if this would bring radical organizations with hostile agendas to power, at the same time as the democratic system is being de facto abolished in Europe by the European Union?

The cultural, economic, and immigration policies currently promoted by the ruling elite throughout virtually the entire Western world are detrimental to the long-term interests of all the peoples who created this civilization. One fundamental question is whether this trend is entirely accidental and exclusively reflects the purely impersonal forces of technological globalization or whether there is also a purpose and a plan behind some of these changes.

The world is shifting in countless ways that should make all citizens of the

West feel very uncomfortable. Non-Western powers are rising fast, a Western sense of moral superiority is becoming harder to maintain, demographic changes both inside and outside of the West bode future catastrophe, and Western economic and political leadership is fast turning obsolete.

This author strongly suspects that there is a method behind the trend of breaking down Western nation-states. The all-pervasive indoctrination with non-Western diversity as well as the systematic demonization and ridicule of all traditional practices, cultural symbols, and national identities of the Western world amply demonstrate this fact. The arguments continually presented for continued globalization, mass immigration, and multiculturalism are remarkably similar in all Western countries—too similar to be entirely coincidental.

Why? What do those promoting such policies hope to achieve? No possible explanations should be ruled out that may supplement rather than contradict the previous claim of the systematic ruination of the West.

One could argue that there are profound underlying ideals embedded in Western culture and mentality at work here—for example, the concept of universal egalitarianism already found in Greco-Roman antiquity, and especially in Christianity. This tenet was secularized after the Enlightenment in the form of human rights. Present-day globalists, regardless of whether they present themselves in a socialist or a capitalist guise, can exploit these ideals. Lastly, there is no doubt that many people vote for open-border globalists of their free will. Their decision can partly be attributed to media convincing and decades of indoctrination, and partly to a new electorate comprising immigrants who tend to vote for globalist parties, which give them access to more welfare payments than other parties.

Nevertheless, the fact remains that tens of millions of Westerners more or less freely vote for parties that not only rob them of their heritage but also dispossess them in the long run. The West is full of decadent and indifferent consumers (one should not call them citizens) who live only for the moment, are cut off from their historical roots, and have little regard for the future of their nations. They care little for what will happen fifty to one hundred years from now, as long as they can still enjoy a steady supply of material comforts, welfare payments, some new electronic toys, plus football and sex on TV.

One of the factors behind the budget deficits in many Western countries is the *short-term focus* inherent to the democratic system. Accordingly, people prefer short-term gain now at the price of long-term pain later and vote themselves into possession of other people's money. Tradition-conscious people coming from nondemocratic cultures, such as the Chinese for example, seem to be able to think and plan for future generations centuries ahead.

Ironically, the handful of arguably right components that democracy may contain have also been undermined by the hollowing out of this system from above through international organizations, which in many cases promote bad programs and policies against the wishes of the majority.

This author claims the following:

The political, financial, and business elites *purposely* flood the West with millions of immigrants to socially engineer a truly multicultural society without consulting the citizenry. The huge increases in migration over the past twenty years were due in part to a politically motivated attempt to radically change the West and to rub the Right's nose in diversity.

The mass immigration has been the result of a deliberate plan, but the elite refuses to discuss it for fear of alienating the core working-class voters of the left-liberal political parties.

The Western elite has been lying to the people about the extent of immigration—causing a massive rupture of trust. The elite has launched a full-front attack on their peoples, amounting to the ethnic cleansing of distinct national groups.

In 1998, former Democratic US president Bill Clinton publicly stated that Americans should be mindful of their nation's rapidly changing demographics.[438] He also told an Arab-American audience that the United States will no longer have a majority of people of mainly European descent by 2050 and claimed, "This is a very positive thing."[439]

One would never hear representatives of the Chinese, Russian, or Japanese leaderships boasting about the fact that they welcome the change in demographics of their respective countries by replacing ethnic groups in their ancestral homelands. Only leaders of the supposedly democratic West do that.

For another extreme example of the bizarre ideological views of the Western political elite, one should remember a less-promulgated detail of President George W. Bush's immigration reform plan trumpeted during his 2004 reelection campaign. This clause would have allowed any foreigner anywhere in the world to immigrate legally to the United States if he or she accepted a minimum-wage job that no Americans were willing to fill—an utterly insane proposal that would have transformed America's minimum wage into its maximum wage. Naturally, his opponent, Senator John Kerry, saw absolutely nothing wrong with this idea, though he did criticize various other aspects of Bush's immigration plan as being "somewhat mean-spirited."[440]

The buying and selling of citizenships, often to people thinking of it purely as a *right* and never as a *duty*, have become common throughout the West. The political elite sees nothing wrong in individuals collecting passports as they might collect club memberships.

The Western elite suffers from the urge to denigrate the custom and culture of their peoples while, in their own eyes, defending enlightened universalism against local chauvinism. The continuing moral decline of the West itself is a sign of the weakening of national consciousness among the Western elite, who no longer feel attached to their peoples but see them as obstacles to be overcome or silenced through public antiracism campaigns and doctrinal guilt imposed from above.

All this does not mean that there is no grassroots support at all for multiculturalism. But support for mass immigration is lukewarm at best among the population as a whole, whereas the ruling elite in politics, media, and academia promotes it enthusiastically. If anything, this pan-Western disconnect and the deficit of trust between rulers and the ruled are growing ever larger. If unchecked, the widening political chasm seriously threatens to undermine stability in the Western world.

Britain, Germany, France, the Netherlands, Italy, Sweden, Ireland, Spain, and other Western countries, with their native peoples and majorities, are no longer nations with a distinct heritage; they are only random spaces on the map waiting to be filled with a collage of different cultures.

North American authorities and mass media are little better than European ones, and sometimes worse. In 1965, the United States was the first Western country to open its borders to mass immigration from anywhere in the entire world as a matter of ideological principle. US authorities have been promoting similar policies elsewhere in the Western world ever since.

Perhaps the best authoritarian key to the crushing of the traditional Western desire for self-determination is to paralyze it by flooding these lands with non-Western ethnic groups who themselves often come from repressive and authoritarian cultures.

The phrase "political correctness" first came into use under communism and meant that all ideas had to conform to and support the agenda of the Marxist movement. History and philosophy were the first to be forced into line, but as is evident from the career of Trofim Lysenko, science was made to conform, too.[441] Those who dissented from the official doctrine were judged to be psychologically imbalanced or evil.

At a certain stage, Western self-criticism gave way to repudiation. Instead of subjecting the Western inheritance to critical evaluation and trying to understand and endorse the ties that bind us to it, a great many of the Western political and cultural elite choose to turn their backs on it. This outright repudiation of tradition has been accompanied by vigorous denunciations of the social order and mores of those who formerly enjoyed or created it, whose sexist, racist, or hierarchical attitudes distance them incurably from us living now.

Today the ruling Western ideology is absolute egalitarianism that amounts to saying that all cultures have an equal right to exist except the Western one, which is evil.

Whether the Western elite truly believes all that is less important than the benefit they gain from its promulgation. The primary advantage is that it paralyzes the natural preferences for national preservation by characterizing opposition to elite doctrines as immoral, indecent, and inhumane. It allows the unelected and invisible elite to aggrandize their power by obliterating national sovereignty and nullifying democratic accountability. Many are, without exaggeration, real leftist totalitarians that have no regard for the well-being of those they control, since the only way they can consolidate their dystopian plans is through brute state power. While there is no doubt that many well-meaning individuals join their efforts, they are the kind of useful idiots who excused and covered up communist atrocities during most of the twentieth century.

Members of the Western elite overwhelmingly subscribe to a neoliberal world outlook in general and the tenets of multiculturalism and globalization in particular. They tend to agree with the principle that recognition, positive accommodation, and even celebration of demands and unique political and moral claims of various ethnic, religious, or sexual minorities are *obligatory* through "group-differentiated rights."[442] The result is obsessive favoritism of allegedly disadvantaged groups, such as immigrants from Third World societies in general—Muslims in particular, who are often hostile to the European-descended majority of Western countries.

The political, academic, and media elites culturally and institutionally internalize these assumptions. However, behind the veneer of all-embracing diversity, one finds a carefully calibrated scale of approval or denial of "the other"—depending on the ideological, political, and cultural preferences of the elites themselves. These elites insist that there are many self-validating, closed systems of perception, feeling, thinking, and evaluation, each associated with a racially, ethnically, religiously, or sexually defined group. This explanation forcefully rejects the legacy of Western civilization and specifically its reliance on the standards and principles of reason, evidence, objectivity, justice, and freedom that apply to human beings.

The inevitable result is a postmodern moral and intellectual relativism, in conjunction with its accompanying hypocrisy. It enables the elite to elect which group will be blessed with the approval for the status of sanctified martyrdom and which will be denied the benefit of the doubt, let alone sympathy. The denial is automatic, of course, in the case of all members of the extended European family (in the Old Continent, Russia, and North America), who are not ashamed of who they are.

This multicultural madness has dangerous secondary manifestations that are presently packaged and instituted as "-isms" by the elite. These include "tolerancism," millenarian one-worldism, inclusivism, humanitarianism, and antidiscriminationism, which not only demand engagement abroad but also advocate open-door immigration at home. The Western elite picks and chooses the definition based on their vision. The impulse is neurotic and the justification entirely esoteric; it also reflects a collective loss of nerve and faith of a sick society. This societal mental breakdown has produced an obsessively self-hating elite—an occurrence unprecedented in history.

The entire monstrosity is built on the arrogant conviction that human reason, reinforced by science and technology and wrapped in modern liberalism, contains the solution to the dilemmas, challenges, and mysteries of human existence. It holds that specific enlightened abstractions, such as democracy, human rights, and free markets, can and should be spread across the world, since only they are capable of transforming it in a way that will, for example, turn Muslims into secularized global consumers.

The above forms of insanity have a left, or Wilsonian, variant (one-world, postnational, compassionate, multilateralist, therapeutic, Euro-integrationist) and a right, or neoconservative, alternative (democracy-exporting, interventionist, monopolar, boastfully self-aggrandizing). While often differing in their practical manifestations, the overall paradigm is the same—and utterly idealistic. The roots are in the legacy of the Enlightenment; both alternatives maintain that man is inherently virtuous and capable of improvement, and both are sects of the same Western heresy that has grown out of the Renaissance seed. Its fruits are shaping the decline of the West, which is becoming terminal.

The shared attributes of Western Europe and North America are no longer discernible in what they cherish but in what they *reject*: societies founded on national and cultural commonalities, stable elite and constitutions, and independent national economies.

They look upon all enduring values, institutions, cultures, and traditions with open hatred. They reject the concepts of limited government at home and nonintervention abroad. They assert their commitment to the free market, but in fact, they promote a type of state capitalism carefully controlled by a network of global financial and regulatory institutions. They insist that countries do not belong to those people who have inhabited them for millennia but who happen to find themselves within their boundaries at any given moment in time.

The resulting random mélange of mutually disconnected and incongruous multitudes is not a boon but a blow. The assertion that one should not feel a special bond to any particular country, nation, race, or culture but should instead transfer preferences to the whole world equally is not new. However, that open assertion being made by the elite is.

By 1992, the then deputy US secretary of state, Strobe Talbott, was ready and willing to declare that the United States of America may not exist "in its current form" in the twenty-first century because the very concept of nationhood, in the United States and throughout the world, will have been rendered obsolete. "All countries are social arrangements, accommodations to changing circumstances … they are all artificial and temporary."[443] To the members of his class, nations are merely transient entities.

We are faced, then, with a global problem that is a synthesis of all others and goes way beyond culture wars. It is the coming end of culture itself.

Now, for many millennia, people lived in communities in which links were direct and emotional. Those communities eventually merged into society, in which relations were measured and formalized; nevertheless, the human being remained the subject of his own activity generated by his emotions and needs as a living, feeling, thinking creature.

However, by the mid-twentieth century, when science and technology ushered in the information era and society became a vastly more complex sociotechnological system, man was reduced from the subject of activity to a mere element of it—the human factor.

True, all impulses for action still pass through the individual, but the system initiates, dictates, and controls these impulses. Having been integrated into the network of connections as a distinct reality, man has to act in agreement with the system's procedures.

The real world becomes symbolic rather than actual; the natural is dismissed, with nature merely providing the component segments for the artificial. Most relationships between people cease to be regulated by feelings, customs, faith, love, hate, considerations of good and evil, sin and punishment, and beauty and ugliness.

What the elite would call "ideology," and what would be known as spirituality until not too many decades ago, is substituted for false content by information. And that is why the survival of culture is uncertain.

Multiculturalism generates the dreary sameness of predictable, barren, and lifeless monism. If it continues its destructive course, by the end of the twenty-first century there will be no Europeans as members of ethnic groups sharing the same language, culture, history, and ancestors, and inhabiting lands associated with their names. The shrinking native populations will be either indoctrinated into believing or else simply forced into accepting that the demographic shift for unassimilable, unwilling, and ominous outsiders is a boon that enriches their culturally wanting, morally and socially unsustainable societies.

According to Jean Raspail, "no other race subscribes to these moral principles, because they are weapons of self-annihilation."[444]

Society's metamorphosis into a mass of techies signifies its death. With the impending revolution in genetic engineering, culture, as a means of passing on values that contribute to society's cohesion, will no longer be needed. The only required "values" will be money, success (power), and health. The soul, emotional experiences, and personal beliefs are but burdens that distract from production and the precise execution of directives. Culture itself, as a whole, is merely a relic or a heritage—part of the tradition. The transformation of society into a sociotechnological system regulated by "the market" signifies the end of man's cultural history and may mean the end of humanity as such.

The apparent disharmony between real conservatism and the ruthless ideology of democratic capitalism is lost on the average citizen of Western liberal democracy. So-called democracy in America and Western Europe alike is a corrupt democratic process run by an elite that conspires to make secondary issues relevant and essential matters irrelevant or illegitimate. One party or politician may be in, another out, but the elite's regime remains permanently in power.

It must be mentioned that the common ground between the Western elite and Islam is that they both pursue globalization; both have as their objective the destruction of the old nation-state system based on nationhood defined by ethnolinguistic, cultural, and territorial commonalities. The Western elite betrayers, for all the outward differences, share with ISIS, the mullahs, the sheiks, and the imams the desire for a monistic single world. They both long for Talbott's single global authority, postnational and seamlessly standardized.

A century ago, Talbott and his class shared social commonalities that could be observed in Monte Carlo, Karlsbad, Biarritz, or Paris, depending on the season. Englishmen, Russians, Prussians, Frenchmen, and Austrians shared the same outlook and sense of propriety; they all spoke French, but they nevertheless remained rooted in their national traditions—the permanent vessels in which *weltanschauung* could be translated into *kultur*.

Today's West, by contrast, does not create social and civilizational commonalities except by wholesale denial of old mores, disdain for inherited values, and an overt rejection of traditional culture. It is in the refusal of the modern Western elite to confront the threat to Western civilization that Europe and North America most tellingly certify they share the same cultural chromosomes. The same traits of decrepitude are present everywhere; topping the list is the elite's hostility to all forms of solidarity, with the majority population sharing historical memories, common ancestors, beliefs, and culture.

The consequences are predictable: the loss of a sense of place and history among Europeans and North Americans; the rapid demographic decline, particularly in Europe (unparalleled in history); the rampant Third World—in Europe overwhelmingly Muslim—immigration. The further consequences are also the collapse of private and public manners, morals and traditional commonalities, the imposition of multiculturalism, and the criminalization of any opposition to it.

The result is the Westerners' loss of sense of property over their lands. The elite casts aside any concept of an explicitly Western geographic zone, cultural space, or intellectual property that should be protected. The West faces an elite consensus that de facto uncontrolled immigration, as the solid bedrock of multiculturalism, is an immutable fact that must not be scrutinized.

The depraved mass culture and multiculturalist indoctrination in schools and by the mainstream media have already largely nullified the sense of historical and cultural continuity among young Europeans and North Americans. The revolutionary character of the multiculturalist project is revealed in the endless mantra of "Race, gender, and sexuality," the formula now elevated to the status of the postmodern philosopher's stone. It is the force that moves the historical process forward, toward the grand "Gleichschaltung" (or standardization, synchronization, and bringing into line) of nations, races, and cultures.

Race, gender, and sexuality have replaced the proletariat as both the oppressed underclass (hence the cult of the nonwhite, nonmale, nonheterosexual victimhood) and the agent of revolutionary change—as preordained by history. Classical Marxist political economy identified the primary source of revolution in the unavoidable conflict between the proletariat, which has nothing to sell but its labor and nothing to lose but its chains, and the capitalist owners of the means of production.

Nowadays, however, latter-day Marxist revolutionaries go beyond dialectical materialism by introducing the metaphysical concept of victimhood with an array of associated special-rights claims that have worked such wonders for the enemies of the Western world. The majority native populations of "old" Europe and America, according to this psychotic but all-pervasive paradigm, are guilty of oppression by their very existence and therefore must not protest the migratory deluge—let alone try to oppose it, since that would amount to racism.

The fruits are with us already. Edward Gibbon could have had today's London, Marseilles or Los Angeles in mind when he wrote of Rome in decline, its masses morphing "into a vile and wretched populace."[445] On present form, the native Western majorities will melt away within a century; on par with "fat-free" and "drug-free," "child-free" is the precise yuppie lifestyle term. However, whereas the threat of extinction of an exotic tribal group in Borneo or Amazonia, let alone a species of spotted owl or sperm whale, would cause alarm and prompt activism among the modern liberal elite, it is deemed inherently racist to mention that Europeans and their trans-Atlantic cousins are, literally, endangered species. The facilitators of our destruction must be neutralized if we are to survive.

To explain how the Western elite's conception of the world is shaped, the phrase "engineering mentality" has already been used. This engineering mentality has been one of the main factors in the West's brilliant success. It means that one approaches problems with a can-do attitude. One rules out extraneous, distracting cultural and historical factors to figure out a practical way to fix things. Damn the torpedoes; full speed ahead! Construct buildings, roads, and bridges; invent new products; revolutionize production methods. Do not be intimidated by the traditional; do not be afraid of change. Just because it has never been tried before or has been tried but failed previously does not mean it cannot be done today. Forget about ideology or preconceived notions; get the job done as quickly, cheaply, and efficiently as possible.

Such energetic and fearless pragmatism conquered continents, industrialized agrarian nations, and won wars. A century ago it allowed America to turn disparate ethnic and religious groups into a single nation. In recent decades, with remarkably little violence or disruption, it broke down long-prevalent racial, gender, and other barriers.

Now, how does this engineering approach deal with the outside world? Not so well. By ignoring historical, cultural, ideological, religious, and other factors, one is not going to understand, appreciate, or comprehend foreign countries. One can try to understand them (from a skewed perspective) or get them to change ("Just do it!"), but these interpretations do not work, and the efforts to change will fail. The idea, for example, that American know-how will go into a country like Iraq, Haiti, Libya, Afghanistan, Kosovo, or Ukraine and succeed in nation building is greatly exaggerated.

How have Western (American, British, etc.) leaders in the past found ways to overcome this engineering bias? By acknowledging differences and comprehending that other countries and peoples have their very own orientations, worldviews, and cultures. Far from being something objectionable, the idea of American or British exceptionalism was a useful concept once. Realizing that the United States has been more successful than other countries was an essential element in dealing with reality because one then had to ask and evaluate *why* America had done so well, which would also imply not only the question of why others had not followed but also the question of why they *could not* follow this pattern.

For example, the weight of tradition in other societies was too overwhelming to permit easy change. Class distinctions were more rigid than in the West. Ideas and institutions that might have worked in the past were now blocking development. The move had to come from *inside*; backwardness was not the result of external oppression but internal stagnation. All of these points are the opposite of the radical ideas currently prevailing in the West.

The Western elite seemingly fails to understand that others can take some of the elements that have worked in the West, perhaps adapt them for themselves, and possibly combine them with the best homegrown ingredients. Incredible ignorance and arrogance are shown in denying there are fundamental differences and in failing to understand that there are valid reasons—rooted in different conditions, history, and many other factors—for those differences. It is no wonder that, when this ignorance and arrogance are combined with the West's engineering mentality, it produces blindness and hence disastrous policy.

Ironically, the "highly sophisticated," politically correct multiculturalist view has much in common with the worst provincialism of the past. Everyone in the world is just like us; to think otherwise is considered to be a crime and in practice often means that those who think otherwise are not just like us and only care about their material well-being.

In the past, Western thinking was far more sophisticated. Let us take the modernization theory as an example.[446] In the 1950s and 1960s, Western social scientists asked how Third World countries could go from being poor and underdeveloped to becoming prosperous and stable. That was an entirely antiracist viewpoint; anyone could succeed if they were only willing to implement the proper combination of internal reforms and changes.

There needed to be urbanization, better education, more democracy and civil rights, a more significant share of private enterprise, and equal treatment of women. Along with these were a series of economic steps, starting with import substitution and leading to industrialization. While modernization theory was not entirely accurate, it did offer a good description of what happened first in Japan and then in places like South Korea, Singapore, India, and China.

Today the leading theory is that underdevelopment is merely the result of Western exploitation. Such a view, aside from its political implications, will do nothing to help countries improve themselves, while it makes the West a cheerleader for stagnation and reactionary forces. Endless aid is handed over either to keep regimes in power with subsidies or to go into the elite's Swiss bank accounts. Such an international entitlement approach is the welfare state on a global scale, with all the failings of that system.

So while the Western engineering approach—"Just do what works best"—may be part of the problem for the United States in dealing with Third World countries, the far more significant issue is the contemporary refusal to discuss what is wrong with other societies. That also implies the understanding of what is right about the West and the nature of the West's problems.

Similarly to so many issues, neither academia nor the mass media nor the policy elite is even considering the need for an honest discussion of differences among countries or the road to development for the Third World. Without doing so, the world becomes incomprehensible and Western foreign policy fails.

It is true that the United States of America, this author's land, is a very wealthy and powerful country; fate and its system have created it and made it so. Nevertheless, its system also creates appalling mass poverty. Supporting the state and the elite who profit from it places a crushing burden on the American people. Surely that is not what this author wants for the America he loves.

All of history shows that corruption arises when the elite uses the government to loot the people. In the past, the people were robbed by force and superstition. In the new system, they are to be robbed by fraud—by laws, taxes, insurance, stocks, and government bonds. There is a class established that is wealthy because of its influence on the government and whose unearned wealth comes from the labor of the people. All the evils of old Europe are reproduced, and they are destroying the chance that America has for something better concerning human happiness. Moreover, all the setting up of constitutional contraptions that were supposed to thwart majority rule are ridiculous and will ultimately fail.

The Persistence of Nationalism

In this supposedly postmodern era, people live allegedly freed from the old, unhealthy, and petty anxieties emanating from that provincial concept of national interest and, even worse, nationalism. A new, happy, and progressive era of peaceful globalism was supposed to have dawned.

Alas, then came Turkey's fusion of Islam and nationalism under Recep Tayyip Erdoğan, Sri Lankan leader Mahinda Rajapaksa's use of militant Buddhist nationalism to defeat the Tamil insurgency and construct an authoritarian state, and China's increasingly assertive territorial demands in the South China Sea. Also, there was the election and reelection of Hungary's national-conservative Viktor Orbán, Moscow's seizure of Crimea in the name of ethnic Russians, India's election of Hindu nationalist Narendra Modi, the Scottish and Catalan independence movements, and a lot more.

Far from being dead, nationalism is back with a vengeance.

Historical fashion varies over time. Early peoples organized themselves by gathering with those who looked alike and talked and acted similarly. Multiethnic empires also emerged as the strong dominated, even subjugated, the weak. Then, a century ago, three great European multiethnic empires—Austro-Hungarian, Ottoman, and Russian—collapsed. That process unexpectedly led to horrors beyond imagination as their rapacious and more powerful neighbors absorbed the resulting "Saisonstaaten" ("states for a season"), as some Germans called the new countries.[447]

A similar collapse happened in 1989 when the Soviet Empire dissolved. Western commentators were quick to proclaim the triumph of liberal democracy; Francis Fukuyama famously suggested that humanity had just reached the "end of history," with "liberal democracy" representing the "end point of mankind's ideological evolution."[448] Of course, the move from totalitarian communism to democratic capitalism did not progress so smoothly. Although the Western elite does not share and deliberately misinterprets Russian leader Vladimir Putin's view that the fall of Soviet Union was a geopolitical catastrophe, the process was excruciating, painful, and messy for the peoples involved.[449]

The Communist collapse and its aftermath immediately raised a fundamental question: What is the best way for polities to be organized or arranged under the newly changed circumstances? The overwhelming response of the progressive intellectual elites—or at least the answer that politicians, bureaucrats, businesspeople, journalists, academics, intellectuals, and other elites pushed hardest—was that in a postnational globalized world, internationalist and multinational systems were the answer.

Indeed, the United Nations was offered as the solution to humanity's problems.

Never mind that the UN's predecessor, the League of Nations, had failed to deliver on its promise to bring international peace and harmony in the wake of World War I. Never mind either the inherent limitations of an organization made up of self-seeking and often authoritarian governments. Never mind the fact the UN has been under the careful guidance, or control, of the five victors of World War II.

The European leaders responded to the breakup of the Soviet-led Eastern Bloc by expanding the then-existing international organization of their own, the European Community. A political idea that had been discussed ever since the end of World War II, the first economic-turned-political European Union (EU) became a reality in 1993. It attempted to suppress traditional national differences and established an unelected executive for the entire union. It gave the European Parliament control of the budget but left the new entity without a military—the typical signature of a sovereign state. Soon enough, the EU installed a unified currency, the euro, on the assumption that it would force additional monetary and fiscal cooperation, as well as further political consolidation.

Despite these victories for internationalists, concern for national sovereignty did not disappear. In fact, opposition to transnational organizations grew. Although American administrations routinely attempted to use the UN to their advantage—winning UN Security Council approval for military operations and economic sanctions, for instance—Washington resolutely resisted unfavorable UN decisions. American administrations also refused to fund UN operations with which they disagreed. Even when successive administrations pressed for acceptance of UN initiatives, such as the Law of the Sea Treaty, the US Congress balked out of concern for national sovereignty.

Meanwhile, the peoples of Europe grew less accepting of the EU and its grand ambitions. In 2005, French and Dutch voters rejected the proposed Treaty Establishing a Constitution for Europe, or TCE, also known as the Constitutional Treaty. In response, the Eurocratic elite reissued the constitution as the Treaty of Lisbon, also known as the Reform Treaty, removing the word "constitution" from the charter.

Only Ireland put the now infamous document to a vote, and the Irish people voted no, to the outrage of Eurocrats across the continent. They debated whether to sideline Dublin as a second-class EU member or make the Irish vote again until they got it right. The EU leadership chose the second course, and Ireland then ratified the treaty.

Although the Eurocrats triumphed with that strong-arm "democratic" measure, they have not been able to eliminate opposing views. On the contrary, the financial and economic crises that erupted in 2008 have only strengthened popular dissent and nationalist sentiment. When several countries turned to the EU for bailouts, Europhiles pressed for even more centralized fiscal and political power, giving Brussels control over national budgets and continental borrowing through Eurobonds. Nations requiring bailouts were forced to accept humiliating and painful economic reforms, essentially transferring control of economic policy to a European troika. (The term "troika," which comes from Russian and means "group of three," was increasingly used during the eurozone crisis to describe the European Commission, International Monetary Fund, and European Central Bank. These three organizations formed a group of international lenders that laid down stringent austerity measures when they provided bailouts, or promises of bailouts, for indebted peripheral European states—such as Ireland, Portugal, and Greece—during and after the financial crisis.)

In Greece, one of the countries bailed out, the anti-EU left achieved substantial electoral gains, becoming first the main political opposition and then taking over the government while the Golden Dawn party gave a hard right-wing edge to antigovernment protests. In France, Marine Le Pen moved the nationalist-populist National Front to the center of the country's politics. Similar currents reached even the stolidly bourgeois Germans, with the government resisting proposals to turn the country's debt rating over to its profligate neighbors, the constitutional court limiting power transfers to Brussels, and the Alternative for Germany party rising to challenge the EU. Eurosceptics have been winning increasing representation not only in national bodies but also in the European Parliament.

Outright secessionist sentiments have also threatened the European structure. Belgium has become so bitterly divided that it went without an elected government for 589 days in 2010 and 2011; moreover, the largest party in Flanders favors splitting the country entirely. In Spain, the province of Catalonia announced a referendum on self-determination, while Scotland scheduled, and held, a referendum on Scottish independence from the United Kingdom in 2014. These and other secessionist movements promote new, smaller, and more unified sovereign states by expanding nationalistic feelings.

Nationalism took an even more aggressive form when Russia completed the breakaway of Crimea from Ukraine. The collapse and breakup of the Soviet Union left substantial numbers of ethnic Russians scattered throughout the newly independent countries. At the time of disintegration, Moscow was too weak not only to defend its geopolitical interests but also to assert itself on behalf of those ethnic Russians who suddenly found themselves outside of the new Russian borders. However, Vladimir Putin, after successfully restoring state authority and military capability, seems very much interested again in power politics, geopolitics, and ethnic solidarity. Nationalism can offer him a means to advance Russia both internationally and intranationally while strengthening himself politically.

These various and controversial moves toward greater national unity may be natural reactions to the almost frenzied demand by the Western elite for a greater diversity of subject peoples combined with increased authority for central governments. Ethnic or cultural unity does make it easier to form a cohesive policy; by itself, however, nationality offers no independent grounds for sovereignty. The presence in a given territory of a majority with a particular immutable characteristic provides no principled justification for joining other areas with similar national majorities. Shared ethnicity cannot supplant consent.

Consent is of particular importance where territories contain substantial national, ethnic, and other minorities. In practice, national and ethnic homogeneity becomes less likely as boundaries are drawn farther apart. As such, nationality almost always fails as a basis for sovereignty. Attempting to create ethnicity-based nations after World War I merely shifted the plane of the conflict downward. For instance, at the Paris Peace Conference, Woodrow Wilson was surprised to learn that three million Germans lived in Bohemia, which he supported transferring to the new nation of Czechoslovakia. These Germans had as much justification in seeking inclusion in Germany as the Czechs had had in separating from Austria-Hungary.[450]

It would be much better to rely on prudence organizing societies. The more diverse the population, the better the case for a looser federal arrangement with weaker central power. Such methods seem the best means of resolving some of today's more intractable territorial disputes. There is no apparent reason to link Dutch-speaking Flanders and French-speaking Wallonia together, as Belgium currently does—especially when both would remain within the European Union. However, just because separation would be legitimate does not necessarily mean that it would also be the most practical or prudent course. Nevertheless, maintaining a single nation with a looser federation lessens tensions between Flanders and Wallonia by reducing transfers from and controls over the other.

Although the dramatic return of nationalist sentiments may horrify the elite seeking to empower supranational organizations, the fact is that such emotion is a common popular impulse that cannot be ignored without peril. Perhaps the greatest danger is to force having transnational governance that failed so many times before and sparked bitter opposition, nationalist fervor, partisan conflict, and even war.

International institutions did *not* arise to create universal people, and nations did *not* join them to wipe themselves out. International institutions were conceived as a forum for international politics to play itself out peacefully rather than violently. Whenever an international body, organization, or institution takes it upon itself to reeducate its members or attempt to superimpose a universal culture upon sovereign nations—and that is what the EU is doing now—it will only lead to tumult and war sooner or later.

THE WESTERN ELITE AGAINST THE NATION-STATE

Political parties are like people: they must conform to the categorical imperative. They must not practice or justify murder and must not incite hatred toward any minority or subcommunity; if they do those things, the state has the right and duty to disband them.

It should be pointed out that socialist parties have not always obeyed the ground rule against incitement. For many years, the leftist parties existed on a diet of class hatred similar to the hate that had been a cornerstone of communist ideology between the two world wars. The most striking feature of the leftist movements of the 1960s—movements to which many of today's political elite or their forefathers belonged—was the hatred they expressed toward the bourgeoisie, meaning anyone who owned property. Since incitement is omnipresent in politics, people must continually examine their conscience to confirm that they are not also guilty of this crime, of which it is so easy to accuse their opponents. Only then can we begin the urgent task facing the West today, which is that of achieving a new negotiated settlement that will embrace all citizens, indigenous and new, of states that have been irreversibly changed by immigration.

That is why the charges of racism and xenophobia that have been leveled at national-conservative parties are so serious. These charges are designed to suggest that any such party offends not only against the ground rules of democratic politics but also against the primary goal of the West, which is to incorporate large immigrant populations into a form of citizenship that transcends race, religion, culture, and creed. If we do not establish this type of citizenship, then we can look forward to a future of conflict and disaffection, in which intercommunal strife is the norm.

The current Western political culture denies the existence of serious social problems, condemns those who seek to discuss it, and tries its best to silence them. For a long time now, the Western elite has been in denial about the enormous problems posed by the mass immigration of people who do not enter the Western way of life. This elite has turned angrily on those who warned against the disruption that might follow and who affirmed the right of indigenous communities to refuse admission to people who cannot or will not assimilate. The charges of racism and xenophobia are weapons that the elite has used against those wishing to discuss the problem—to ensure that it is never troubled by the truth it denies.

People of the current generation have been brought up in fear of this charge, just as the people of Salem were brought up in fear of being denounced as witches. People saw what happened to Enoch Powell as a result of a public speech that warned of the dangers in 1968.[451] That was virtually the last time that a British politician dared to warn against the effect of large-scale immigration.[452] Since then an uneasy silence and frightened discomfiture have prevailed at the political level while discussion at every other level has been hampered by the periodic show-trials of those judged to be guilty of racism—because they have argued, for example, that immigrant communities must integrate and that separatism is intrinsically dangerous.

By denying a problem, its discussion is prevented until a dialogue is too late. The European political elite lived in denial over German rearmament throughout the 1930s. By the time reality began to set in, it was too late to prevent Hitler's seizure of Czechoslovakia. Reflecting on such examples, it is surely reasonable to conclude that we have a duty now to brave the charges of racism and xenophobia, and to discuss every aspect of immigration. We owe this not just to the indigenous people of Europe but also to the immigrants themselves, who have a just as keen interest in peaceful coexistence as the rest of us.

Every society depends on a membership experience: a sense of who we are, why we belong together, and what we share. This experience is prepolitical: it precedes all political institutions and provides our reason for accepting them. It unites left and right, blue-collar and white-collar, man and woman, parent and child. To threaten this first-person plural is to open the way to atomization, as people cease to recognize any general duty to their neighbors and set out to pillage the accumulated resources while they can. Without membership, we risk a new tragedy of the commons as our inherited social assets are seized for present use.

"Membership" can be defined in different ways at different times and places. For many societies, religion is a very significant part of it, and the infidel is cast out or marginalized, as in traditional Islamic society. Although religion has also been an essential part of European identity, it was, under the influence of the Enlightenment, gradually pushed into the background by nationality, and subsequently by the rise of the nation-state.

It is thanks to the nation-state that we enjoy the freedoms and secular jurisdictions that are so attractive to immigrants—and especially to those immigrants who define their prepolitical membership in religious, rather than national, terms. National loyalty is a form of neighborliness; it is the commitment not only to a shared home but also to the people who have built it. National loyalty makes no specific demands of a religious or ideological nature and is content with the simple conformity to the rule of law and a common sense of belonging to the homeland and following its customs and habits of peaceful coexistence. Communities founded on national rather than religious conceptions of membership are inherently open to newcomers, in the way that religious communities are not. An immigrant to a religious community must be prepared to convert; an immigrant to a national community need only obey the law.

The European nation-states have encapsulated the prepolitical idea of national loyalty in the legal benchmark of citizenship. The citizen's relation to the state is understood in terms of reciprocal rights and duties. To claim the citizen's status is not only to bring the power of the state to one's aid against malefactors but also to promise one's help when the country is in danger. It is to enjoy state-protected rights that make one, legally speaking, equal to all other citizens in any conflict and as bound by the duty of obedience as they are.

Hence we, as citizens of nation-states, are bound by reciprocal obligations to all those who can claim our nationality, regardless of family and regardless of faith. Freedom of worship, freedom of conscience, freedom of speech and opinion offer no threat, we believe, to our mutual loyalty. Our law applies to a particular territory, and our legislators are chosen by those whose home it is. The law, therefore, confirms our shared destiny and attracts our humble obedience. Law-abidingness becomes a way of life, part of the scheme of things, and part of the way in which the land is settled. Our people can quickly unite in the face of a threat, since they are joining in defense of the thing that is necessary to all of them—their territory. The symbols of national loyalty are neither militant nor ideological but consist of peaceful images of the homeland—of the place where we belong. National loyalties, therefore, aid reconciliation between classes, interests, and faiths, and form the background to a political process based on consensus rather than on force. In particular, national loyalties enable people to respect the sovereignty and the rights of the individual.

For those and similar reasons, national loyalty is not merely an issue concerning a democratic government but is profoundly assumed by it. People bound by a national "we" have no difficulty in accepting a government whose opinions and decisions they disagree with; they have no difficulty in accepting the legitimacy of opposition or the free expression of outrageous-seeming views. In short, they can live (even) with democracy, and express their political aspirations through the ballot box. None of those good things are to be found in states that are founded on the "we" of tribal identity or the "we" of faith. In modern conditions, all such states are in a permanent conflict and civil war, with neither a bona fide rule of law nor durable democracy.

It must be pointed out that the account of national loyalty that has just been offered does not even fit the case of the country that gives a home to the European Union: Belgium.

Modern Belgium is a state in which two nations are being held together, mostly against the will of one of them. Belgian citizenship is not rooted in a shared national loyalty and has become a purely legal privilege that can be bought or sold with the passport. This buying and selling of citizenship to people who think of it merely as a right and never as a duty is common throughout Europe. The political elite sees nothing wrong with people collecting passports as they might collect membership cards. However, it seems that the trafficking in Belgian passports is especially prevalent, perhaps because there is no prepolitical loyalty, which the passport represents.

For the same reason, no effort is made to ensure that immigrants to Belgium acquire loyalty to the secular state or respect for the customs that have shaped it. Belgian *citizenship* is what immigrants are seeking, and indeed the political class has treated Belgian citizenship as a commodity to be bought and sold like any other.

Finally, the Belgian political elite has fixed its sight on Europe as the collective enterprise that will extinguish all those old national loyalties and put a cosmopolitan indifference in their place. The European Union has meant a lot to the Belgian elite. It places them at the heart of the continent, transforms Brussels from a provincial town in Flanders to the capital of Europe, and provides a project that will distract attention from the growing disintegration of the country and from the problems they are determined to deny in any case. No wonder they are angry when a popular party calls for the separation of Flanders and its reconstitution as a self-governing nation-state. Even if there is no ground for the charge of racism and xenophobia, one can be sure that the plan is to make it stick.

Just imagine what would happen to the EU were Flanders to become a nation-state. What a step backward this would be—a step toward loyalty, accountability, democracy, and all the other superannuated things that the EU seeks to extinguish.

The charge of racism is regularly leveled against innocent members of the indigenous majority, and almost never against guilty members of immigrant minorities. This bias is not a European phenomenon only. On the contrary, there is a kind of collective feeling of guilt feeling that imbues all discussions of racial difference in the West today. According to politically correct official policy regarding multiculturalism and the treatment of minorities, all whites are racist, whether knowingly or not.

That is, of course, a racist remark of the lowest kind—one that attributes to people of a particular skin color an enormous moral fault—a fault they can do nothing to overcome, since they possess it unknowingly. It is indicative of a general approach to racial and cultural relations in the modern world. Racism is defined as a disease of the indigenous Western majority from which incoming minorities are genetically immune, even when they bring with them the visceral anti-Semitism that prevails in much of the Arab world or the Malaysian hatred of the ethnic Chinese.

Why is the Western political elite so eager to charge its own people of racism while disregarding the bigotry of immigrants? The answer can be found in another double standard planted in the charge so frequently associated with that of racism—the accusation of xenophobia.

Xenophobia is very different from racism. Etymologically, the term "xenophobia" means "fear of, and therefore aversion toward, the foreigner"; it suggests a differentiation between the one who belongs and the one who does not. In inviting us to jettison our xenophobia, politicians are asking to extend a welcome to people other than ourselves—a welcome predicated on the acknowledgment of their otherness. It is rather easy for an educated member of the liberal elite to discard his xenophobia: typically, his contacts with foreigners help him to strengthen his power, extend his knowledge, and polish his human skills. However, it is not so easy for an uneducated worker to share this attitude when the incoming foreigner takes away his job, brings strange customs and an army of dependents into the neighborhood, and finally surrounds him with the excluding sights and sounds of a ghetto.

Again, there is a double standard that affects the description. Members of the modern liberal elite may be immune to xenophobia, but there is an equally grave fault that they exhibit in abundance, that being their repudiation of, and aversion to, "home" as the meaning of "homeland," "motherland" or "native land." Each country exhibits this vice in its own domestic version. For example, nobody who was brought up in the postwar United States can fail to be aware of the educated derision that has been directed at American national loyalty, or patriotism, precisely by those who, because of their social status and wealth, would not be prepared to die for their country in any event.

The *loyalty* that people need in their lives, and which they affirm in their unaware and spontaneous social actions, is now habitually ridiculed, jeered at, or even demonized by the mainstream media and the education system. National history is taught as a shameful and degrading made-up story; Western art, literature, and religion have been just about excised from the curriculum, and folkways, local traditions, and national ceremonies are routinely ridiculed.

The repudiation of the national idea is the consequence of a peculiar mindset that was instilled throughout the Western world after the Second World War and is particularly prevalent among the intellectual and political elite. There are no adequate words for this attitude, though its symptoms are instantly recognized: namely, the disposition, in any conflict, to side with "them" against "us," and the strong desire to disparage the customs, culture, and institutions that can be identified with "us." There is a definite aversion to home—by way of emphasizing its close relation to its mirror image: xenophobia. This attitude is not only a stage through which the adolescent mind passes typically but also the stage in which intellectuals tend to become arrested. As George Orwell pointed out, intellectuals on the left are especially prone to it, and this has often made them willing agents of foreign powers.[453] The Cambridge spies—educated people who penetrated the British Foreign Service during the war and betrayed many Eastern Europeans to Stalin—offer a telling illustration of what this attitude has meant for the West.[454]

When Sartre and Foucault draw their picture of the bourgeois mentality, the mentality of the "Other in his Otherness," they are describing the ordinary decent Frenchman and expressing their contempt for his national culture.[455] A chronic form of fear of the home has permeated the American universities in the guise of political correctness and loudly surfaced in the aftermath of September 11, to pour scorn on the culture that allegedly provoked the attacks and to side, by implication, with the terrorists.

The domination of the national parliaments, particularly the German Bundestag, and the EU machinery by "home-haters" is much responsible for the acceptance of subsidized immigration and the attacks on customs and institutions associated with traditional and native forms of life.

The home-hater repudiates national loyalties and defines his goals and ideals against the nation, promotes transnational institutions over national governments, accepts and endorses laws that are imposed from on high by the EU or the UN. The home-hater defines his political vision in terms of cosmopolitan values that have been cleansed of all reference to a real historical community.

The home-hater is, in his own eyes, a defender of enlightened universalism against local chauvinism. Moreover, it is the rise of the home-haters that has led to the growing crisis of legitimacy in the nation-states of Europe, for we are seeing not only a massive expansion of the legislative burden on the peoples of Europe but also a relentless assault on the only loyalties that would enable them to bear it voluntarily.

Where national ideas, beliefs, or sentiments constitute a danger to the centralization of power, the European machine is determined to extinguish them. Such is the case, for example, when it comes to Flemish nationalism, which threatens the very heart of the European Moloch.

Therefore, the charge of racism and xenophobia should be assessed in the light of these double standards. It is a charge almost invariably leveled at members of the native communities of Europe and at the political parties that attempt to represent those people, promising them some relief from a problem that no other party wants to address. Those who level the charge are almost invariably in the grip of the home-haters. These people do not have any sense of belonging and look down on the old forms of the European Community—in particular on the old national identities that shaped the European continent—with barely concealed distaste. By focusing on their cosmopolitan visions of politics, they deliberately ignore of the fact that the West, including the European Union, is settled with an ever-increasing number of people who have no national loyalty to connect them with either the land or the members of the native community. Looking at it this way, therefore, it should become clear that the charge of racism and xenophobia originates from the guilty conscience of a liberal elite living in denial.

What is wrong with this kind of existential dishonesty? The ordinary people of Europe and America, becoming deeply anxious about their future, keep looking for someone who can represent their anxieties and take measures to reduce them. When people are in a state of anxiety, they pose a threat both to themselves and to those whom they fear. It is vital, therefore, that the Western countries come to a solution and achieve effective integration of their immigrant communities. However, if the liberal ruling elite will not even discuss the matter and continue to blame the racism and xenophobia of the native population for the growing anxiety, then the likely long-term effect will be an inevitable explosion. Moreover, if the liberal elite keep supporting home-hating, which is a corresponding contributory cause of the problem and one from which none will benefit, least of all the immigrant communities, then the further degeneration and alienation of society will indeed be assured.

The Death of Nations, the Death of Freedom

The freedoms that the peoples of the West have taken for granted are being taken away from them in many ways. One of the most grievous of these is the method by which the rise of globalism has brought the continuous erosion of national sovereignty.

Nations serve the same function as the law; in the absence of law, the strongest will devour the weak. Similarly, if globalization does away with all nations or erodes their sovereign right to self-determination, there will be no international community of world citizens, as the globalists believe (or say they believe), but a globalist tyranny. In this tyranny, the most powerful corporations, financial institutions, and political, business, and financial elites and their supranational organizations will have free rein.

What sort of political freedom will be left to the ordinary citizen on the street when all government powers are centralized in global bodies? What voice will the individual have? Who will hear it?

The global corporations and financial institutions want a level playing field without the irritating obstacles that nation-states present to them with their annoying laws. It is in their interests that national sovereignty should be eroded, and this is why the globalists support tyrannical political empires, such as the European Union, that undermine the sovereignty of their member states. It is much easier for the globalists to deal with relatively few multinational empires than to deal with a multitude of individual and sovereign nations. The nations have to be sacrificed on the altar of Mammon so that Mammon can have its will. Small nations must be crushed, and so must the people living in them who cherish their local freedom and culture.

In George Orwell's *1984*, the world is divided into three vast empires: Oceania, Eurasia, and Eastasia. Each is a tyranny in which nations do not exist any longer, and the individual has been reduced to a powerless, alienated, and forlorn figure bereft of all freedom. This predicament is the fate that awaits us all if we allow the globalists to destroy our national liberty in the name of globalization.

The surprise victory of "leave" in the Brexit referendum on Britain's membership in the European Union has been praised as a win for national sovereignty. It also has been lambasted as a sign of racism and xenophobia among the English and Welsh—though not among the overwhelmingly socialist Scots, who voted for "remain." Stock markets and currency exchanges have been uneasy as left-wing celebrities, the punditocracy, and various globalist elites exploded with rage into antidemocratic hate speeches.

Nevertheless, one thing is clear: the British referendum was merely the opening shot in an impending war for control over the destinies and lives of peoples within the West.

The concern is not just with Britain's leaving the European Union. It is with the entire notion of devolution—of people's demanding a return to self-government in the face of ever-larger and more distant supranational bureaucratic organizations taking control over more and more of their lives. The principle involved in devolution is that people in their local communities should control their own destinies and forge larger alliances from real, culturally based shared interests. This principle is both universalist and localist; it requires greater self-government for meaningful geographically and culturally based communities everywhere.

Globalists generally deride this principle as intrinsically racist because it entails peoples' control over their own borders. Still, these globalists have long recognized the natural drive for self-government; in Europe, they have mastered the art of providing relatively meaningless forms of autonomy over cultural issues as a way of buying off the local elite. Scots even claimed a significant measure of self-government within the United Kingdom, in part on the understanding that the European Union would foot much of the bill for their socialist policies. However, crumbs and backdoor arrangements are no longer enough for millions of Europeans, particularly in the midst of the Muslim invasion visited upon them by their rulers. Today, the demand is for local control over lawmaking and enforcing, budgeting, and social and moral issues. The struggle for self-government, so long suppressed, is finally beginning.

One cannot expect neutral, unbiased, and fair reporting on this struggle for the simple reason that the mainstream media is a built-in, critical component of the coalition fighting on one (globalist) side. Thus, the narrative coming from the media, academia, and the political establishment of the West remains the same: a few cleverly evil people are using racism and economic fear to herd the mindless masses into the supporting of policies that all sensible people should oppose. However, conservatives, in particular, need to understand that the populist movement taking shape in Europe and the United States, while not intrinsically conservative, is the only action available to counter the ever-greater centralization under a solidifying regime of globalist economics and political correctness. While avoiding foolish and objectionable appeals to racism and religious hatred, we must support, wherever possible, the demand for self-government at the heart of the popular revolt against the globalist elite.

There is not necessarily a grand conspiracy at work in centralizing power. What the West has been experiencing is a global joining of the cosmopolitan elite into an increasingly single-minded group made up of individuals who see themselves as righteous rulers pushing the rest of the population toward a better, more egalitarian, secure, and (of course) environmentally friendly future. Most of these people see themselves as special because they either directly work for or are closely associated with those who work for the same international system of money, business, and political management. They also consider themselves as people of the world and therefore identify less with their own cultures than with a liberal ethos entitling them to organize other people's lives and minds to make them better, more tolerant individuals. Moreover, whether on Wall Street, in Berlin, in London, or in Silicon Valley, they see ordinary people everywhere as mostly interchangeable labor inputs whose political voices and cultural aspirations must be finessed or suppressed to nurture ever-growing global structures of economic and environmental security and managed free trade.

The United States—for most of its history the home of local self-government—has become almost as much of a casualty of cosmopolitan centralization (federalization) as Europe during the last few decades. Conservatives, in particular, have resisted this development for a while, defending the family, church, and local associations against the claim that equality and progress require uniformity and conformity enforced from Washington. That tentative defense broke under the pressure of the second Bush presidency—that president being perhaps the most profligate and expansionist in half a century—and was left helpless in the face of the Obama administration, which turned out to be the most radical in modern US history. Corrupted by power, privilege, lackadaisicalness, and connection with the Republican Party establishment, the official conservative movement quietly quit during the 2016 primary season. Nevertheless, there remains real hope that the central conservative principle of local self-government now may receive renewed attention.

A significant transformation is needed in the United States, Europe, and throughout the Western World—namely that devolution will be fought in the name of self-government and conservatives will have to join forces with many who do not share all of their principles. Many of the Brexit supporters were socialist Labour Party supporters who are attached to an intrusive welfare and administrative state. Similarly, many populists want their government to organize their lives for them, rather than to build their own lives in conjunction with their local communities.

Devolution is a vital step toward open debate with those hooked on state-provided security. Only when local communities, regions, and sovereign nations have some real control over their own affairs can they have any serious conversation about how the good life is led, and how much of it can or should be directed through political means. Without devolution, the people can have no hope of renewing their particular cultures and communities. Indeed, until the native people can—or, correctly speaking, are rather allowed to—control their borders, they cannot ensure the survival of significant communities at all, as they will be swamped not only with people having different customs than their own but also with "helpers" from the government. These government helpers will reconfigure the native traditions in the name of tolerance, but in reality they will be following faceless bureaucratic structures.

The globalist elite will, of course, charge that the aspiration to maintain into the future the character of one's community and culture is intrinsically racist, rather than an essential element of self-government. In combatting this lie, conservatives must work hard to keep any real racial or ethnic hatred from rearing its ugly head. The actual difference between globalists and the rest of the population is that globalists see people as little individual units—as specks to be organized by themselves according to a grand plan for equality and security. Only by breaking through this fundamental misunderstanding and misrepresentation of human nature to the recognition and acceptance of our shared identities and the various associations in which those identities are formed, developed, and exercised can there be any chance of a renewal of ordered liberty and public sanity.

War on the Middle Class

The Western political elite has been waging class warfare on the middle class. From the corporate ownership of the political system to the near extinction of labor unions and the outsourcing of millions of jobs, any insightful look at the divergence of interests between those that run the countries of the West and the rest of us who live in it can paint only a grim picture indeed.

The middle class is, to a great extent, left without a political party; these are the people who are married with kids in school; college graduates, with bills and commitments everywhere; people trying to make sure that they have a job at a livable wage and that all their bills are paid.

The political and business elite, in favor of grand and ultimately failed intellectual experiments, has ignored the basic economic self-interest of the middle class. Illegal immigration devalues labor, as does any trade agreement that fosters the offshoring of jobs. Illegal immigration, the other side of the same coin as international trade agreements, is the result of the fact that businesses and employers want to do business in a formerly middle-class society but do not want to pay middle-class wages. Instead they search for cheap labor somewhere and then move jobs there. Alternatively, as in the case of illegal immigration, they encourage the cheap labor to come to them. The result of all these policies is growing misery in the form of higher taxes (or increased debt for our children) and stagnant wages. This predicament is for those who play by the rules and try to do the right thing every day the middle class, of course.

Especially America has become a society owned by corporations and special interests that dominate its political system. There is no countervailing influence. Labor unions are nearing extinction; the media takes the easy way out (equal time to both sides) and does not investigate; universities are dependent on the federal government, corporations, and the wealthy; and churches tend to expand their political energy on issues like gay marriage.

The middle class is being beaten down by illegal immigration, inability to pay for health care, declining availability of pensions, outsourcing, corporate bankruptcies, an increasing share of taxes, rising income inequality, and ever-increasing deficits.

Corporate income taxes made up about 30 percent of federal revenues in the United States fifty years ago; now they make up less than 10 percent—but Washington DC has between fifteen thousand and ninety thousand lobbyists.[456] Corporate taxes, in spite of the high corporate tax rates, are at the lowest level in about one hundred years; profits account for the largest share of national income in forty years, and the percentage going to workers is at its lowest level in fifty years.[457]

What are the main reasons (other than the self-inflicted wounds discussed in earlier chapters) for the decline of the middle class during the last two decades?

Governments have become pawns to the elite, large corporations, and powerful special-interest groups. The political parties have succumbed to corporate contributions and squadrons of well-financed lobbyists. Labor unions—once the foremost defenders of working men and women—have lost power, and some union officials seem preoccupied with pleasing large corporations rather than defending their members. National sovereignty is steadily being eroded by free trade agreements and a global marketplace. National interests are being replaced by international dictates and fast-track trade agreements signed by governments and are cheered on by multinational corporations.

What say do middle-class citizens have in their respective countries about globalization, the job market and unemployment, immigration and population control, national sovereignty and national debt, social and internal security, and education and health care?

Nothing.

The War on Terror

What is the West fighting for in the so-called War on Terror? Terrorism has always been merely a tactic, and arguably the most effective tactic, of various real or perceived national liberation movements of the past centuries.

Terrorism was used, to name a few examples, by the Irgun to drive the British out of Palestine, by the Mau Mau to run them out of Kenya, and by the EOKA to fight them in Cyprus. Terrorism was the tactic of the Front de Libération Nationale (FLN) to drive the French out of Algeria and by the Vietcong to defeat them in Vietnam. It was the tactic of the African National Congress (ANC) to fight against apartheid in South Africa; it was the tactic of the FRELIMO in Mozambique against Portuguese rule; it was the tactic of the Committee for the Liberation of South Tyrol (BAS) to gain autonomy for the German-speaking province in Italy.

What did the FLN, Vietcong, Mau Mau, EOKA, Irgun, Mandela's ANC, and the FRELIMO have in common? All sought the expulsion of foreign rule and the independence of their respective nations. All used terrorism for the same purposes as the Uighurs do in China, the Chechens in the Caucasus, and the Kurds in the Middle East.

In his declaration of war on America, Osama bin Laden specified as his casus belli the presence of US troops and their "temple prostitutes" on the "sacred soil" of Saudi Arabia. He wanted the United States out of his country.

What are the alleged terrorists, jihadists, and radical Islamists fighting? What are the goals of ISIS and al-Qaeda, Boko Haram and Ansar al-Sharia, the Taliban and al-Shabaab?[458] All want the foreign troops, the alien Western culture and its infidel faith, out of their lands, and all seek the overthrow of regimes that collaborate with the West. All wish to establish their own systems that comport with the commands of the Prophet. That is what they are recruiting for, killing for, and dying for. We hate their terror tactics and deplore their aims, but they *know* precisely for what they are fighting.

What is the West fighting for? What is the Western vision that will inspire Muslim masses to rise, battle alongside the West, and die fighting Islamists? What future does the West envision for the Middle East or Africa? Is the West willing to pay the price to achieve it?

The usual, often-heard, and politically correct reply is "The West is fighting, as always, for democracy, freedom, human rights, and the right of people to rule themselves." However, if democracy and self-determination are the goals of the West, why did it not recognize the election of Hamas in the Palestinian territories or of Hezbollah in Lebanon? Why did it condone the overthrow of the elected regime of Mohamed Morsi in Egypt or the elected government in Ukraine? Why does it demand democracy in Syria but not in Saudi Arabia?

There is no wonder that billions of people around the world, such as Muslims, Eastern Europeans, and Asians reject the false values of the West. They do not believe that all religions are equal, and they do not believe in freedom of speech if the press can blaspheme their Prophet, their leaders, and their culture. The Muslim world rejects not only the Western presence on its territory but also Western culture and beliefs. Moreover, it is precisely this Western presence that spawns more terrorists than the drones can kill.

The millions of Muslims in Western countries have become an indigestible minority that imperils the survival of those states. The liberal West has embraced a malignant diversity that will inevitably lead to a future like the recent past in Palestine, Cyprus, Lebanon, Sri Lanka, Sudan, and Yugoslavia.

The Western elite has no more religion; they have an ideology: secular and liberal democracy. However, the Muslim world, for one, rejects secularism and will use democracy to free itself from the West and establish regimes that please Allah.

What can the mindless Western elite offer as the apotheosis of democracy?

Nothing but hypocrisy.

LIBERAL DEMOCRACY: THE TERROR IDEOLOGY OF THE WEST

According to biblical scripture, God revealed the holy Ten Commandments to Moses: "I am the Lord, your God, who brought you out of Egypt, out of the land of slavery. You shall have *no other gods* before me. You shall *not bow down to them or worship them; for I, the Lord, your God, am a jealous God*, punishing the children for the sin of the parents to the third and fourth generation of those who hate me, but showing love to a thousand generations of those who love me and keep my commandments" (Exodus 20:2–4 NIV, emphasis added).

This author holds that Jewish-Christian monotheism, which is also a significant source of the Islamic faith, is the origin of most forms of "do-gooder terrorism." Christianity had a universal appeal already early on, and proselytization spread quickly over the borders of Israel.

The longest-lived Western civilization ever was Rome. The Romans could rule over many lands on three continents for fifteen hundred years not only because of their military and technical superiority and civilizing power but also because of their cultural and religious tolerance. Their enormous staying power manifested itself in religious and racial tolerance and not in political leniency. The Greeks and Israelites, Galls and Egyptians, Armenians and Celts could all keep their respective religions, enjoying equal treatment before the law as citizens of Rome.[459]

Christianity, the new religion based on "equality" (for Christians), changed all that. Christianity introduced *intolerance* in that it promised hell to all who did not subscribe to it. All heretics and non-believers were *excluded, banned and isolated*, if not burned or otherwise eliminated during the period between the end of the Roman Empire and the Age of Enlightenment.

Yes, the Christians also have suffered terrible persecution in the Roman Empire for about three hundred years. However, they could still proselytize and disseminate the tenets of Christianity in many regions mostly undisturbed over an extended period. By Roman tradition and for political reasons, the emperor was invested with the characteristics of a God, and sacrifices had to be offered to this God on a regular basis. Christians, just like the believers of *all* other religions, again for political reasons, were supposed to take part in the exercise if they wanted to be considered loyal citizens of Rome. Their refusal to participate not only cast doubt on their loyalty and commitment to the state but was also seen as a provocation and became the reason for their persecution. On the other hand, this Christian refusal to offer sacrifice was consistent with their Christian beliefs, if one took monotheism seriously.

With Emperor Constantine's conversion to the Christian faith, Christianity practically became the state religion of Rome; the initial promises of religious tolerance had only a very short lifespan, and that tolerance was done away with for the next thirteen hundred years.

State and church marched arm in arm by the end of the fourth century already—under the leadership of the clergy. This change had, of course, a direct effect on the freedom of expression and freedom of opinion. Any dissenters from the Christian faith were *severely persecuted* from the early Middle Ages on and, if possible, exterminated.

Now, what does the "do-gooder terrorism" have to do with all this?

While the Greco-Roman culture of the Antique World brought with it the freedom of thought, a diverse view of the world, and a multiplicity of lifestyles, its destruction was due more to Christianization than to the invasion of the barbarians. Then again, perhaps the victory of Christianity was also the consequence of the tiresome worldly diversity and the search for the truth.

In any case, the ancient heritage of spiritual freedom sank into a relatively deep slumber for another nine hundred years until it was again discovered with the Renaissance during the fourteenth century. Moreover, this return of the secular world to the center of interests concerning the arts and science started the gradual retreat and decline of Christian ideas.

Nevertheless, the do-gooder-terrorism survived all this. The idea that there is an absolute truth for man, for his destiny, for the meaning of history or whatever else, changed little—and only in its external form. In the interest of this absolute truth, and for its protection from the damaging heresies, the struggle must continue. These secular forms of the do-gooder mentality, from the social welfare committees of the French Revolution through Stalin's gulags to the Red Khmers' tyranny, could compete on equal footing with all terror species once developed in the name of the Christian faith, like the Holy Inquisition and witch hunt.

According to the logic of monotheistic beliefs, with their claim to be the sole representatives and exclusive possessors of truth (the absolute truth), they had to control also the thoughts of all the faithful. Their successors, the left-liberal socialist do-gooders, the modern elite, think along the same lines today. The church of the old world, just like the elite of the modern democracies, see themselves authorized and entitled to convince the dissenters to give up their heretical ways. The church of the old world, just like the elite of the modern democracies, sees itself authorized and entitled to proceed with the elimination of these dissenters by using various forms of punishment (not always necessarily violent in recent days, but just as effective).

Equality and freedom (or liberty) are the two great codes of Western thinking. In the American Declaration of Independence, they are masterfully reconciled with each other: equality of men before God and before the law is the starting point, the source of a free life, which nevertheless can lead to entirely different directions and entirely different outcomes.[460]

The relationship between equality and freedom in the French Revolution is something altogether different again. As Louis Antoine de Saint-Just pointed out in 1791, "If all men are free, they are all equal; if they are equal, they are just."[461] However, this is the core of a quixotic program—a reversal of and in contrast to the thoughts on equality of the American Declaration of Independence, which created the scope for human development.

The free development of people always leads to inequalities. Moreover, where one wants to have equality, freedom must disappear. In the French Revolution, equality was supposed to be established by virtue, and for virtue to prevail, terror was needed. That was the logic of the French Revolution, which thereby radically differed from the American Revolution—although both were the children of the Enlightenment.

The idea of the revolutionary radicals was the state of virtue. It was not oriented to one God and the afterlife according to Christianity; its goal was the attaining of the perfect order (good and virtuous life, the absolute truth) in this world. To achieve that, all real and potential enemies of that order (of *their* order) had to be eliminated.

How is all this reflected in today's Western democratic societies?

The Western ruling elite claims the absolute truth concerning people, society, and the meaning of history; all with a different perspective are driven to moral and social isolation. That makes these systems both totalitarian and hypocritical, since they are the antithesis of what they claim they are—namely, democratic.

From the equating of freedom with equality and equality with justice grew out the real terror of the do-gooders, first philosophically and sociopolitically, but then also in reality, wherever and whenever this kind of thinking could achieve political power.

This equality code, negating all differences found in man and morally condemning all differences originating from external circumstances, has become not only a dominant Western secular religion today but also the heart of the currently prevalent terror of the do-gooders.

European Union political leaders disregard national interest through the promotion of unification and mass immigration; the upper class disenfranchises America's more secular working-class voters; college students find solidarity in identity politics as universities abandon liberal education for technocratic agendas and diversity mantras. Each time, populist representatives arise where elites fear to go, the latter forfeiting their claims to real representation and national leadership, often by scorning (or condescendingly giving in to) the vox populi and their concerns.

The defection of the elite is their abdication of any identification with lower classes. Westerners have gradually removed the embodied forms of what we have and do in common, which enables us to see and speak politically.

Seeing politically means, like the Machiavelli dictum, reading ancient things to understand the experience of modern things. One uses political science, from Thucydides to Tocqueville, to comprehend contemporary life; speaking politically applies that knowledge in shared reflection and public deliberation. However, political correctness *opposes* speaking politically; it derives from the disorder of an absent ordinary life that otherwise permits seeing things politically.

The EU ignores disunity among its member nations and between their native populations and unassimilated Muslim immigrants, but *political correctness* also mutes political speech when representation and its preconditions are abolished. As the implicit rule of what and how one says something, political correctness is a top-down method, absenting common identity, imposing the appearance of order, and ignoring real disorder. Political experience enables political epistemology; its absence blinds us from seeing things politically.

The welfare state, for example, illustrates the removal of preconditions of representation. Since the welfare state allows democratic states to extend their inclusion of working classes, these are no longer represented at all. Being represented in government presupposes that a unified group exists prior to its representation; however, the state providing welfare eliminates the working class as a class that works, which can then be represented. Therefore, it is no wonder that this ignored and unrepresented working class, together with the remnants of the lower middle class and petit bourgeoisie, is most likely to see Donald Trump as their representative. With stagnant wages, job losses, and lack of representation, Trumpism means the entire American working class has legitimate reasons to be angry with the ruling elite.

It is important to understand here how Tocqueville distinguishes *aristocracy* from *democracy*: aristocracy possessed stable, though unequal, bonds among its members; modern democracy erodes these bonds by having comparatively equal individuals. The result is two alternatives: equal subjection to bureaucracy and equal rights exercised in civil society.

The nature of democracy tends to erode social capital, but the art of democracy means rebuilding it through voluntary associations. Tocqueville found that Americans understood the art of upholding the substance of civil society in this way.

Americans have cultural inequality today. Once, they bragged about having a civic culture uniting them across classes by means of shared daily experiences and assumptions about marriage, industriousness, honesty, loyalty, and religion. Regrettably, by today that common civic culture has unraveled into a class society; the liberal-democratic upper / upper-middle class, possessing advanced education often through graduating from elite schools, shares tastes and preferences isolating it from Middle America. The populist lower class has withdrawn from America's core cultural institutions. Personal politics at universities is an upper-class phenomenon; support for Mr. Trump a lower-class phenomenon. Both exhibit a segregated culture: politically correct identity politics defines the former, and politically incorrect identity politics the latter. The upper class practices but does not preach our core institutions, while the lower class has left them altogether.

Liberal democracy has been living off the borrowed capital of moral and religious traditions antedating the rise of liberalism. That capital was borrowed from aristocratic institutions—but either not practiced or not preached. Political correctness and populist reactions suggest the loaned money is defaulting.

Any response to this inequality in a democratic system requires examining the totalitarian temptation. The demands of college protesters and strongman politics indicate a ruling system, which embodies a breakdown of what the people hold in common. The soft despotism of current liberal-democratic American politics is the evidence that modern egalitarian man has spent the political capital inherited from aristocracy and is thus in danger of losing the institutions, mores, and practices that sustain his way of life.

The Western way of devising the new means by which to put things in common reflects the Western belief in conversion: the soul's ability to change while fundamentally remaining the same. This idea was reflected in the invention of the nation-state, a political metamorphosis unseen since the Roman transformation from city to empire. The homogenous city was intimate but exclusive; the homogenizing empire was orderly and universal. Today the *nation* embodies the city in its civil society, and the *state* represents the empire in its sovereign authority, assuring that under its umbrella all individuals are equal. Here the representative regime of the nation-state mediates the forms of the city, with the state allowing for equality (and potentially liberty) by presupposing nationhood.

Europe forgot this political science because it forgot how to see and to speak politically. Though Europe invented the nation-state, the EU alienates Europe from its achievement, for the Western elite is in the thrall of a postpolitical, postreligious, and postfamilial fantasy in which one can live untethered without institutions designed for beings who were born to know, love, die, and be from somewhere in particular. Europe's fantasy entails the politically correct elite refusing to see the obvious disorder, while America's fantasy consists of the disorder of cultural inequality and dual-class pathologies. Both are chimeras that require our putting political things in common again.

Man, Men, and Misanthropy

Philanthropy, as far as one can see, is rapidly becoming the mark of the wicked man.

Man is not merely clever, selfish, and a mere slave of his genes but is one who transcends instinct in his desire for spiritual meaning, with a life that is a journey with the goal of drawing ever closer to the goodness, truth, and beauty of divine perfection. So claim the do-gooders, at least.

It is the crucial connection between man and men, which condemns philanthropy as the mark of a wicked man. This statement is provocative because it is counterintuitive; if philanthropy means the love of man, the love of humanity, which it does, how can it be wicked? It becomes wicked when the love of man destroys the lives of men.

For instance, as the direct consequence of the French Revolution, the Reign of Terror was conducted in the name of "Liberté, Egalité et Fraternité." The revolution's barbaric savagery slaughtered people on the guillotine in the name of freedom, equality, and brotherhood. The same philanthropic spirit was the crux of the Marxist demands for justice and the consequent Communist bloodbaths of the twentieth century. As merely thousands were earlier offered on the altar of the noble savage, millions of people have already been destroyed for the Marxist man since the Bolshevik Revolution.

It would, however, be a grievous error to believe that philanthropy is deadly only when espoused by those who call themselves socialists, communists, or Marxists. Those who call themselves capitalists have also spilled the blood of men in the name of the love of man. Much of G. K. Chesterton's spleen was vented against the philanthropy of John D. Rockefeller and his ilk.[462]

Once one has ascertained the damage done by such philanthropists as Jean-Jacques Rousseau, Karl Marx, Armand Hammer, or George Soros, among many others, with their love for the false notions of man, the wisdom of Chesterton's provocative assertion that "philanthropy is rapidly becoming the mark of a wicked man" can be appreciated. Chesterton also declared, "the quite simple objection to philanthropy is that it is religious persecution."[463] The essence of Chesterton's religious persecution is this: the person who happens to have the power and means, either by wealth or by official position, will govern his fellow citizens not according to *their* religion or philosophy but according to *his* own.

In short, and to agree unequivocally with Chesterton, modern philanthropy is the imposition by a wealthy and powerful elite of their false religion of man on the vast majority of men. Thus the love of man becomes the enemy of men, and the philanthropy of the elite becomes their misanthropy.

17

Western Renewal Philosophy: Conservatism and Subsidiarity

The West is now faced with a new ideology whose overarching ethic consists in what Pope Benedict XVI called the "dictatorship of relativism."[464] The first behavioral expectation of this dictatorship is nonjudgmentalism—that is, refusing to pass judgment on the lifestyle choices of others.

As Alexis de Tocqueville warned in the preface to *The Old Regime and the Revolution*, a shortcoming of democratic societies is that "the ruling passions become a desire for wealth at all cost, a taste for business, a love of gain, and a liking for comfort and material pleasures." These failings are the results of a tendency for citizens of democracies "to wrap themselves up in a narrow individuality in which public virtue is stifled."[465] What we suffer from now cannot be remedied by appeals to increased individual liberty as it could in the face of mass political movements—or "political religions," as Eric Voegelin called them—like communism and fascism, because the ailment is not one of too little individualism but too much.[466]

Nor can appeals to American values or European values be useful, because the trajectory of *modern Western culture* is essentially a reductio ad absurdum on a certain understanding of "American values." The interpretation of the "expressive individualism" meaning of the American founding documents that is articulated most poignantly in the jurisprudence of Justice Anthony Kennedy has remade American principles in a mold that is unrecognizable to many. Especially the notorious passage from the famous 1994 case *Planned Parenthood v. Casey* can be considered controversial: "At the heart of liberty is the right to define one's own concept of existence, of meaning, of the universe, and of the mystery of human life."[467]

Accordingly, if one's destiny is not determined by social class or race or religion or even the body (the focus of the sexual revolution), why, then, should culture define it? If the dream of freedom is prized above all else, the most American thing would be to deny the authority of Western culture; anti-Americanism thus becomes a kind of hyper-Americanism—something that many American conservatives fail to recognize. A repudiation of America goes against still greater freedom; if we take America down a notch or two, we disenchant the inherited social norms that control us, giving ourselves mental space to live according to whatever values we prefer. If we think this way, being antipatriotic is the highest and most noble way to be patriotic.

American secularism rebelliously rejects its given world after judging it unworthy of its abstraction of "freedom."

The idols of postmodern materialism are health, wealth, and pleasure. When these become the highest things on offer, they then provide the ideals for the elite; the one who is slimmest, richest, and drinks the best wine in the most luxurious private jet wins. And those who, for whatever reason, cannot compete in the pursuit of these "highest things" are simply left behind. Even more perversely, the reduction of human flourishing to being given choices allows these elites to guiltlessly dismiss those who are left behind in this brave new world as deserving their lot because, after all, they made their choice.

Cosmopolitan corporatism has given rise to a global elite harboring little sympathy for traditional societies of whatever form. Utilizing leftist critiques to understand how power structures operate to subvert traditional societies is a task that conservative scholars should take up as corporate power increasingly shows itself to be hostile to conservative understandings of the human person and human flourishing, both at home and abroad.

This author's vision is about providing space and legitimacy for conservatives to speak up as conservatives; this becomes increasingly important as the fruit of radical movements begins to manifest itself in the West. Finding a renewed conservative form of solidarity may be the only way to counterbalance the growing dichotomy between, on one hand, secular, corporatist, technocratic, nonjudgmental globalism and, on the other, left–right extremism.

The dichotomy that has developed is causing a considerable amount of dissatisfaction with the status quo on both the left and the right. This dissatisfaction indicates that there is an opportunity for the articulation of a renewed vision of a just and humane society that promotes human flourishing for everyone.

Decadence is a moral and spiritual disease, resulting from too long a period of wealth and power, that produces cynicism, pessimism, and frivolity. The citizens of such socicty will cease to make an effort to save themselves because they are not convinced that anything in life is worth saving.

We live in very mean-spirited times and, despite all the hypocritical cant about "love," "tolerance," "human rights," and "self-determination," there is little real difference between the superciliousness of progressivist snobbery and the most pernicious forms of discrimination.

If, for example, one were to visit a village in a remote corner of Africa, witness children playing with crudely crafted toys, and presume from his observations that these kids must be inferior to their Western counterparts because Western children have iPods and smartphones, that person would rightly be accused of patronizing condescension. However, precisely this is what "progressivists" do when observing cultures separated by *time* instead of *space*. The past is deemed by them to be inferior and can be treated with scorn or, perhaps even worse, with patronizing condescension.

If the ancient Greek philosopher Plato were to walk into a room of impeccably progressive moderns today, he would no doubt become the cause of a good deal of humor on account of his quaint ethnic clothing. His appearance, however, would be nothing compared to the laughter that would ensue upon his inept attempts to make sense of the automobile parked outside. Not only would he not know how to drive it, but he would probably not even know what it was. Perhaps, if he surmised it was indeed some carriage, he might look in vain for a horse attached to it. "Now, aren't we superior to those early primitive cultures?" the progressive moderns would no doubt think.

If, however, Plato deigned to linger with us for a few days, despite our decidedly uncivilized behavior, he would soon master the relatively simple skill (it is scarcely an art) of learning to drive. He might even buy some suitably modern clothes to avoid standing out in the crowd. In short, Plato would have mastered the niceties of our technological culture within a few days and would no longer be the object of ridicule. Notwithstanding, he would soon become a nuisance at parties with his insistence on defining the terms under discussion and his frequent interruption of polite conversations. Plato would probably quickly come to the inescapable conclusion that this strange race of progressives were, in fact, barbarians who adorned themselves with the contraptions of technology but had no concept whatever of the meaning of life or the nature of reality.

These analogies illustrate that progressivism is as arrogant and ignorant as the worst sort of redneck discrimination. It looks down its supercilious nose at the *Untermenschen* (subhuman beings) who inhabit the developing world of the past, self-confidently convinced of its inherent superiority and wanting to ensure that these Untermenschen or their friends be excluded from the polite and politically correct society in which the progressives reside.[468]

Tradition may also be explained as the extension of the right to vote. Tradition means giving votes to the most obscure of all classes—namely, to our ancestors. Tradition is the enfranchisement of the dead; it refuses to submit to the small and arrogant ruling elite, who merely happens to be on a present-day walking tour.

All democrats object to people being disqualified by accident of birth; tradition disagrees with people being disqualified by accident of death. Democracy instructs us not to disregard a good man's viewpoint even if he is our groom; tradition appeals to us not to neglect a good man's opinion even if he is our father.

This author cannot separate the two ideas of the right to vote and tradition. Tradition is the extension of the right to vote through time, the proxy of the dead, and the enfranchisement of the still unborn. Respect for tradition is merely a popular demand for majority rule. Progressivists, however, look upon the dead as savages and sanction the systematic extermination of the unborn. The contempt for tradition inherent to and endemic in progressivist circles is fundamentally undemocratic insofar that it excludes the vast majority of humanity.

The past is not dead and buried; it is more real and alive than either the present or the future. The expression "people living in the past" is commonly applied to old or old-fashioned people. However, we all live in the past, because there is nowhere else to live.

To live in the present is like proposing to sit on a pin. It is too minute, it is too slight to support, it is too dangerous, it is too uncomfortable a posture, and it is of necessity followed immediately by entirely different encounters, analogous to those of jumping up with a yell.

To live in the future is a paradox—a contradiction in terms. The future is dead in the perfectly definite sense that it is not alive. It has no nature, no form, and no feature—not even a vague aspect of any kind except for what we choose to cast on it from the past.

No, the past is not in the least dead in the sense in which the future is dead. The past can move and excite us, the past can be loved and hated, and the past consists of lives that can be regarded as complete and finished. On the other hand, nobody knows anything about any living thing in the future except what he makes up out of what he regrets in the past or desires in the present.

There is an existence in the universe beyond time and space in which the past, present, and future all exist together and are not only known but also eternally present. There is no past or future for nature; there is only the eternal ever-present now.

Accordingly, not only is real and true conservatism not dead, but it even has eternity on its side. We live to bequeath.

The conservative is the person who refuses to believe that the aim of our existence is fulfilled in one short span. The conservative sees that one life is not enough to create the things that a person's mind and will can develop. The conservative sees that we, as people, are born each in a given age, but we only continue what other people have begun, and others again take over where we left off. The conservative sees that individuals perish while the whole continues, series of generations are employed in the traditional service of a single thought, and nations are busy in building up their history. The conservative ponders on what is ephemeral, obsolete, and unworthy; what is enduring; and what is worthy to endure. The conservative recognizes both the power linking past and future and the permanent element in the transitory present. The conservative's far-seeing eyes range through space beyond the limits of the short and temporary horizon.

The liberal's thinking follows other lines; for the liberal, life is an end in itself. The liberal is the person who demands liberty in order to enjoy life to the utmost and to procure the maximum of happiness for the individual. Provided one generation enjoys life and another follows and enjoys, man's well-being is assured. At any rate, personal well-being is always the liberal's first consideration.

The liberal is, however, careful of using the word "enjoyment" and prefers instead to talk of progress. Humans are continually perfecting means to lighten the burden of life, and the path of liberty leads, through progress, to gradual perfection. Thus the liberal tries by generalities not only to divert attention from the egotism that liberalism invented but also to have some philosophy of its own.

The real conservative sees through this nonsense and understands that everything the liberal undertakes is contingent upon the life of the existing community. Liberalism seeks to enjoy the fruits garnered by an earlier conservatism.

The revolutionary holds yet another opinion. The revolutionary is the person who does not want to create. The revolutionary's immediate aim is to abolish. The revolutionary renounces the past, swears devotion to the future, and talks of millennia that will dawn someday, but these are the immaterial figments of an ever-receding future.

The revolutionary shares, or rather presupposes, the liberal's idea of progress, leaping from the real to the utopian. The revolutionary shares the biological illusion, which dominated all thought during the nineteenth and on into the twentieth century, that life is based on evolution and, as a consequence of that, the evolutionary prospects of all human actions are infinite.

The conservative recognizes only Genesis. The conservative does not deny the phenomena of evolution but contends that nothing can evolve that was not already in existence. Evolution is a secondary phenomenon; Genesis is the first event.

One can examine the past, the history of all ages and peoples, yet never discover progress. We see values created whenever people of strong will or strong popular movements are in play. When we investigate how they came about, we find that neither nature nor the universe nor history know any progress other than continuity and tradition.

Values themselves are a matter of grace and emerge suddenly, spontaneously, and mysteriously when their time comes. Not surprisingly, the rationalist's creative power always fails when deliberately set out to make values—whether with reactionary or progressive intent. Since people invented the idea of progress and the liberal century was upon us, there has been nothing but retrogression.

The liberal, of course, even in the face of irrefutable evidence to the contrary, contends there has been democratic progress and will deny that we owe the decline and retrogression in the West to the principles of liberalism.

The real conservative, at once both conserver and rebel, seeks to discover where a new beginning may be made and what is worth conserving. The conservative despises the juggling, mystery mongering, and chicanery that are the liberal's stock-in-trade.

The real conservative's enemy is the modern liberal. The conservative knows that people can achieve just about anything when they unite to defend their existence, to fight for their future, and to maintain their freedom. The conservative also knows that when peoples or nations or epochs give their egotism free rein and live for their lusts, existence becomes no more than waste.

The Eastern European Velvet Revolution, or political transition, at the end of the Cold War was the work of liberals, not of revolutionaries. It was the work of opportunists; it was a pacifist revolution to end a socialist struggle, the burden of which had become intolerable and its continuation aimless. The Velvet Revolution had no ideal of its own but snapped at an ideology whose expounders were trusting in promises that came from the West, the home of liberalism. This Velvet Revolution hoped, by naively surrendering to the will of the West, to obtain conditions that would make life possible again; the liberal tendencies, which exist in all democratic parties, were given play.

Liberalism also corrupted European socialism. Its basic idea of social justice gave birth in the nineteenth century to a party of enlightenment that played lip service to progress, liberty, equality, and fraternity but was satisfied to become nothing more than a party of adaptive transformation. The social-democratic party became the party of evolution, which characterized the nineteenth century and transferred the idea from the sphere of natural science into that of universal history.

Is it to be wondered at that social democracy was, and still is, blind to the fact that industrious and expanding (Asian) nations rise while dwindling (Western) nations, consumers rather than producers, must slump? That recognition would seem a rather vital consideration for a movement whose primary concern was, and remains, professedly, social justice.

Instead social democracy adapted itself to the liberal age; it soon exchanged its revolutionary stride for the parliamentary jog-trot.

The state must exist for the sake of the nation. A nation is a people conscious of its nationality. We must face the fact that the European Union of today—the socialist decision-makers—along with their Green allies and progressive modern liberal supporters do their best to eliminate the individual nations' national consciousness.

What does that all mean? Let us examine one example: after the collapse of Yugoslavia, the Western allies created a country called Bosnia and Herzegovina. The liberal was crying out that the Bosnian people must be made politically minded. The liberal was immediately thinking of democratization and parliamentarianization but did not see that the people (they had not been "a people" yet) must first be nationalized (or developed into a nation) before they were democratized. To democratize the people without having them first nationalized (meaning the creation of national consciousness) leads only to democracy for the sake of democracy. For a people with no developed national consciousness, this is just a substitute that lacks both internal cohesion and external protecting power. Instead of waiting until the (Western-incited) Yugoslav civil war ended, with all of its human rights violations, ethnic cleansing, war crimes, and at least one hundred thirty thousand dead, all of which should have been surely expected, the West was so unwise as to involve itself in an internal political crisis. That gave the Western democratic parties the right to substitute the policy they were the sponsors of—for the only policy worthy of a state is the one willingly adopted by the people. This hypocrisy led—or, rather, misled—Bosnia to democracy. Such was the catastrophic fate incurred by a (nonexisting) people that lacked all the qualities of nationhood and had allowed itself to be talked over by liberals into abandoning conservative principles.

The conservative is not a conservative for the sake of the state but for the good of the nation. The power of the state is welcome only in the interests of the nation's freedom. The hour that sees this freedom established will not be the time of the liberal, of parliament, or of a party—but of the Western renewal.

The Western renewer will be able to rise to the height of that hour only if he recognizes that the chasm that sunders right from left is the chasm between two mutually hostile philosophies—a gap we have so far failed to bridge.

The Western renewer will rise to the height of that hour when he recognizes that those who upheld the conservative ideal of state in the nineteenth, twentieth, and twenty-first centuries were false to the spirit of true conservative thought;

The Western renewer will rise to the height of that hour only if he proves himself not only manfully ready to act but also spiritually capable of acting.

The Left has the *reason*; the Right has the *understanding*. It is characteristic of the confusion of our modern political thought that we confuse the two concepts.

The trouble began with rationalism, with the inference "Je pense, donc je suis"

(I think, therefore I am).[469] The age of reason adapted this and said, "I reason, therefore my reasoning is correct."[470] The *result* of thought was identified with *truth*. This fallacy underlays the destructive influence that reason exercised on understanding; reason trespassed outside its intellectual domain. The true reason should guide emotion, not destroy it, but this false reason ruined the feeling and thereby forfeited all guidance, all inspiration, and all intuition. The reason should be one with perception, but this false reason ceased to perceive; it merely reckoned. Understanding is spiritual instinct; reason became mere intellectual calculation.

The consequences showed themselves first in the political sphere. Reason was seemingly capable of drawing any deduction that self-interest wished to draw. Reason concluded that the greatest wisdom is to be found when each contributes his own wisdom. However, only understanding is capable of drawing the simple inference from the empirical fact that when all act as they like, the net result is bound to be an infinity of unreason. What everyone thinks is for the best proves to be the worst for everyone.

Understanding and reason are mutually exclusive, whereas understanding does not exclude emotion. Rousseau perceived this and took his stand against rationalism by the "reason of feeling."[471] Nevertheless, he was not able to unsettle the position of rationalism; the merger of reason and sentiment only made reason the more rabid. When the French Revolution raised it to the rank of a goddess, reason formed all the political ideals of Europe and developed into that "*idle reason*" Kant exposed as our most dangerous self-deceiver.[472] Its baneful influence brought us eventually to such a pass that we lost our hold on moral values and imagined that reason was the guarantor of justice.

In the West, people soon discovered that it might be extremely advantageous to talk of the rights of man—of liberty, equality, and fraternity—but highly dangerous to put these rights into practice. Reason then acquired a second application, according to whether a man's own interests were at stake or another person's. A mood was skillfully created in the world at large that uncritically accepted as progress everything that happened in countries of the West or was imported from them. France no longer spoke of the sovereignty of the monarch but of the sovereignty of the state—and gave the state over to party corruption. England talked about public welfare and left her people socially backward. In later days, extending into the present, the Western powers hypocritically spoke of peace, peaceful coexistence, disarmament, and peace treaties while they prepared themselves for war.

The true conservative has always had understanding enough to see the devastation that reason would wreak among people. All that the conservative stands for—security for the nation, preservation of the family, devotion to the state, the discipline that regulates life, the authority that protects it, and constitutional self-government in professional and corporative organizations—are the functional derivatives of this knowledge of people.

CONSERVATISM AS PART OF THE WESTERN RENEWAL

Conservatism, not any political party but a conscious principle, was the one thing the West needed to overcome the Cold War. Now, after the Cold War allegedly has been won, it is only the conservative who understands and can interpret the events—who feels no surprise that the Velvet Revolution misled Eastern Europe or that the Cold Peace brought nothing but deception.

However, it was not European but American and British conservatism that possessed sufficient knowledge to lead their peoples to victory. European conservatism failed in its allotted task.

To discredit the right in the West after the Velvet Revolution or political turnaround following the collapse of Communism, the New Left asserted that every political crisis, economic slowdown, and financial collapse owed to the breakdown of the conservative or, for them equally evil, capitalist system. This allegation is untrue. The system that broke down was not the conservative but the *constitutional* system.

The failings of conservatism lie not in its principles, which are sound and unalterable. The guilt rests with the inept representatives of modern conservatism, whose spurious tenets lost all spiritual content because of the moral bankruptcy that overtook the West.

The Western conservative had long forgotten that he had first to create what he was to conserve—that only by being incessantly rewon can a thing be conserved. The cause of true conservatism was lost when European conservatives neglected to complete the work that Freiherr vom Stein had begun more than two hundred years prior.[473] They felt themselves initially more at home with Metternich at the Congress of Vienna and in the status quo–strategy atmosphere of the Holy Alliance, and they then started letting themselves be dragged further and further to the left first by the liberals, then by the nationalists, and finally by the socialists. Conservative intellectual circles did *not* throw up one single person in later days to lead the cause; they never touched on the question of spiritual and intellectual deterioration but took refuge only in lifeless, stale, and worn-out phrases. Again, no conservative seemed to remember that a conservative's primary function is to create values that are worth conserving.

The political parties of the right could do nothing to avert the conservative collapse because they not only failed to live up to the heritage that had been handed down to them but also lost touch where they had formerly been leaders.

The parties of the New Left seized the opportunity and claimed the right to that apparent leadership; the same process can be observed in all parliamentary states.

Meanwhile, democracy was vocal: before the Cold War, still somewhat shamefaced; during the Cold War, more and more shameless. Democracy was supplied and armed with all the weapons of intellectualism and reason, which subsequently was to prove that it had been unreason. Nevertheless, the conservative thinker, who had lost the habit of independent intellectual thought, was powerless against this modern sophistry.

The conservative parties were more and more squeezed out; their adherents were bewildered. These all conspired in the name of reason to give a turn to Western civilization: liberal political leaders, denying the conservative foundations of their creed; politicians, scenting a chance of making a career; journalists, no longer disguising their socialist leanings; a press that seems predestined to misinform. The parties of the right still had the understanding on their side. They had no illusions. They faced realities. They foresaw the actual consequences that must follow. Although understanding remained a conservative monopoly, it was not possible to make it prevail against reason, to which the Left unremittingly appealed.

Every person of the West should realize what is at stake today. All individuals, whether they owe allegiance to the Right or the Left, must feel again that they all are members of one body—the nation to which they belong.

Conservatism must continually be rewon. Conservative thought perceives the eternal principle, which, now in the foreground, now in the background, but never absent, ever reasserts itself because it is inherent in nature and humans. This eternal principle must be continually recaptured amid the transitory.

The Western renewer must recover the idea that conservatism must be creative and inclusive—a mighty legacy of thought that the conservatives failed to conserve.

All states have been founded on conservative thought; a nonconservative state is a contradiction in terms. A state must conserve.

The conservative tradition still lives in the blood of the modern conservatives, but no longer in their spirit. They consider this tradition their political privilege; they lost touch with the people. The deterioration of the West reveals the calamity that overtakes a civilization, which puts its faith in reason and not in understanding.

We have all learned much since the Velvet Revolution—the collapse of socialism in the East. Socialists observed how the postulates of a socialist system broke down in the face of such an age, which adapted to advanced capitalist development. The incalculable happened, for which the socialist was not prepared. It was not possible to realize socialism by succeeding to the economic power of a single class. Socialism, social democracy, acquired a meaning only when it embraced the whole people and their economic necessities.

The Western renewer, for his part, must overcome the mechanical socialism, which is purely theoretical, with an organic social system that could be put into practice. He must conceive a new social order that will start with the group, with the community, and with the corporative unity of the entire nation. Such a social system should be familiar to the conservative from the idea of guilds and callings and professions, which he inherited from the specifically European past.

Western renewers must be united in their distrust of political parties and in their suspicion of the liberal and egotist taint in party life that attaches more importance to the program than to the cause.

Western renewers must be united in their distrust of the parliamentary party system that necessarily sets the party before the nation even though it acts within the framework of the nation. The thought should further unite them in the conviction that human welfare cannot safely be left to human caprice but can be attained only by compulsion and leadership.

The thinking of the Western renewer must concern itself with the problems of every sphere—those that are peculiarly conservative and those of the opposition that must be solved if stable and secure life is ever to be possible again. To this end, the conservative should be driven to reexamine his very own postulates and search his very own conscience; creative and inclusive conservatism is not a reaction. The reactionary clings to existing conditions or wishes them back if they have changed. The reactionary can conceive the world only as it was on the day of his birth. His thought is, in its way, as circumscribed as that of the revolutionary, who can picture the world only as it was the day he overturned it.

In contrast to these, the Western renewer must get busy and create something new. He has no ambition to see the world as a museum; he must prefer it as a workshop, where he can create new things that will serve as new foundations. His thought differs from the revolutionary's in that it does not trust words that were hastily begotten in the chaos of upheaval; things have a value for him only when they possess certain stability. Stable values spring from tradition. We may be the victims of catastrophes that overtake us, of revolutions that we cannot prevent, but tradition always reemerges.

Revolutions have eternity against them; conservatism has eternity for it. Nature is conservative; the cosmos itself, spinning on the axis of law, is no revolutionary phenomenon but one of conservative statics. The mightiest events of destruction are insignificant compared with the power of procreation, which immediately takes effect again and year after year and century after century brings similar forms of life to birth.

The conservative recognizes that human life maintains itself in communities, in nations. He therefore seeks to maintain the life of that nation to which he belongs. The reactionary puts his faith in *forms*; the conservative, in the *cause*. What is the only possible reason? Which purpose must be ours? On one point the conservative is clear: his only objective, now and forever, is the cause of his country, his nation, his community.

Socialists never ask what would become of their countries; they think of humanity (Europe, the West, the world), and the masses think of themselves. If the thought of humanity were victorious, so reason the socialist leaders, the individual Eastern European countries, to give an example, would be cared for among the rest of Europe. However, these socialist leaders do not think of their respective countries at all. These amazing world-upheavers only wait anxiously to see what the world—and for them the world (or humanity) this time means the European Union—would permit them to do or to leave undone, although they would have the opportunity to experiment with many a daring plan.

The Western renewal needs leaders who feel themselves one with the nation and identify the nation's fate with their own—leaders who, whether they spring from the old leader class or themselves create a new one, will devote all their powers of decision, will, and ambition to securing the future of the nation.

It is possible that the West shall need a long and changing succession of such leaders to nationalize the people and then to make the West politically minded.

The West needs such leaders under whom the history of yesterday can work through the effects of the past and pass on into the history of tomorrow; without these leaders, the West will drift leaderless into this tomorrow.

The West needs leaders who will know how to hold the scale even between the possibilities that remain to the people and the new opportunities that are only opening before them.

The West needs leaders who are not concerned that a political party should always be right, but who in the uncertain future into which the West is sailing will steer a straight course and through all vicissitudes and storms will keep their bearings and pass on the chart to their successors.

Leadership is not a matter of ballot boxes but a choice based on confidence. The disillusionment the political parties have wrought has created receptivity for the leader-ideal.

For the sake of ending the insecurity of the West, it is easy to imagine a republic reverting to conservative traditions—worthier, more deeply rooted, and of greater antiquity than those abandoned one hundred years ago—and reviving a form far more genuinely Western than parliamentary government and party systems.

Fulfillment cannot come until the new Western renewer is sure of his nation—until the pressure of life has wrought a mental preparation for the people. Not until then shall we be ready to alter that fate for which every person bears in his own way a measure of responsibility. To be a Western renewer means to help the people of the West to discover the form of their future today.

The question "What is conservative?" leads on to another: "When will conservatism become possible again?"

The confusion of "conservative" with "reactionist" arose when our political life lost its conservative basis and was invaded by reactionary phrase-mongering on the one side and revolutionary ideology on the other, the latter ultimately gaining the upper hand. The confusion will end only when today's modern pseudoconservatism itself becomes conservative once more.

There must be a united Western renewal countermovement active all through the West, leading the fight against both left-liberal socialism and neoliberal conservatism—an effort to call a halt. It must be at the same time, however, a reckoning between the conservative and the reactionary.

The reactionary lives with his eyes in the past; the conservative, from his point of vantage, looks before *and* after, from what was in the past to that which is still to come.

The revolutionary, on the other hand looks forward only. The revolutionary is the heir of the liberal, who invented progress and who today is selfishly intent on enjoying the loot that he secured. The liberal is the reactionary of yesterday's revolution seeking to enjoy his today. The revolutionary movement is against him, shaking the foundations of today.

However, the Western renewal countermovement would secure for today its due position in eternity and aim not at restoration but a new linking up with the past.

The socialist will deny the Western renewal countermovement and oppose it, of course. The socialist has always intended to make the world entirely different from what it was before but dares not confess that he deceived the world and himself. He will himself, however, succumb to the influence of the Western renewal countermovement, though he will not care to admit it. He promised once—to quote *The Communist Manifesto*—"the overthrow of all hitherto existing social order"; here spoke revolutionary thought.

However, the socialists' program hurls at imperialistic capitalism the age-old criticism that it is unable to bring about either the political or the economic stability of the world and powerless to create a stable and enduring world order. There speaks conservative feeling, does it not?

The communist believes that the proletariat was once very near the Marxist goal during Soviet-style Bolshevism but is reluctant to admit that the forces that defeated it were eternal conservative forces. Every revolution is wrecked on the same rock, and socialists and communists are compelled to find out that there are in the world forces of tradition, survival, and unalterable law.

If the proletariat were utterly alone in the world, living an existence regulated on the strictest Marxist principles, the great conservative law of gradation would immediately begin to assert itself, and the primeval instinct to form groups, families, and nations would prevail; order would ensue, and history would inevitably repeat itself.

At this point, the socialist will protest that he never spoke of any equality other than that which would follow from the elimination of economic contrasts and that social order founded on this equalization is entirely feasible. Communists would contend that their equality means the communization of the means and the products of production. Democrats would accept the equality of people that would also affect governmental and economic institutions.

Equality has been the compelling principle of socialism, just as love was the compelling principle of Christianity. However, the principle of equality is a false ideal. From the triad of the French Revolutionary catchwords, the socialist yanked out "equality," left "liberty" and "fraternity" for sentimental liberal idealists, and adopted the fiction that equality and justice are one. This bogus identicalness of equality and justice became the center of the socialist ideology.

At an earlier stage of development, Henri de Saint-Simon's demand was "To each man, a vocation according to his capacity, and to each capacity a recompense according to its worth!"[474] Marx picked up on the appeal and advocated a future when "the slavery arising from the subordination of the individual to the division of labor" should be abolished; the materialist interpretation of which was "*From each* according to his ability, *to each* according to his needs!"[475]

Lenin also took up Saint-Simon's challenge, and, recognizing that *equal* rights for *unequal* individuals results in injustice, he drew the conclusion that the Bolshevist's equality of work and reward established only "formal justice" and that the task of creating an "actual justice" lay still ahead.[476] Lenin could not admit, of course, that his conclusion brought him back exactly to the point where people had always stood when they tried to order their existence in a state. That leads to the very point where a new state with a new system seeking to evolve a just system is bound to result not in ultimate equality but only in new *inequality*.

Leninism, meanwhile, had the opportunity of doing experiments with reality. The Bolshevists experienced what the transition period between a capitalist and communist society is like and what is called "the dictatorship of the proletariat."[477] The Soviet state moved not in the direction of communism, of which Lenin spoke, nor in the direction of realizing Utopia, but in the course of political realities.

The revolutionary lives in the illusion that the coveted collapse gives him the opportunity for providing existence to an entirely new set of values according to laws evolved in his head, which he can compel the present to accept. The revolutionary separates the past, a time of history but no happiness, from the future, a time of happiness but no history. However, the *continuity* of human history bids defiance to this illusion. If, for one moment, we suppose that the revolutionary were to succeed in overthrowing and annihilating all traces of the previous social order, the conservative law of movement would reassert itself on that same day.

The effect is never a revolutionary reorganization—which is a contradiction in terms—but always a conservative restructuring. The revolutionary believes that man is by nature good, and that only history and economics have made him bad; the conservative knows that man is weak and must be compelled to develop his strength. The revolutionary trustfully believes in progress and imagines that as lessening economic exploitations cease to foster evil, the good in man will assert itself. The revolutionary anticipates that the majority movement will produce genuine mass progress in all domains of public and private life.

The conservative is much more skeptical and does not believe in any such progress for the sake of progress as reason demands. The conservative believes much more in calamity, in man's powerlessness to avert it, in the march of fate, and in the disillusionment awaiting the overly credulous. He believes only in the power of election granted to the individual.

While the revolutionary seeks to enlist believers in his Utopia, the true conservative fears that democracy will prove to be the *tertius gaudens* (rejoicing third). It is the international, globalizing, formal, and corrupt left-liberal democracy, composed of an "immense minority" of the wealthy (rulers and nations) who, completely lacking scruples, have hitherto understood only too well how the "immense majority" can be controlled.

If it proves impossible to harness the forces of the democratic struggles that tear the West to pieces, the suffering, the discord, and the pettiness of this democratic strife may well last for centuries.

Only a Western renewal countermovement can offer salvation if it is not the movement of a party but the involuntary effort at self-preservation of a desperately threatened civilization—a supreme effort of self-defense in the face of danger.

The revolutionary and the conservative have always had a common foe—not in the reactionary; he is merely an obstruction. The revolutionary has succeeded in getting the better of the reactionary; the conservative has to overcome the reactionary in himself. Their common foe is the liberal. The revolutionary instinctively feels it;

the conservative consciously knows it. The revolutionary gives the liberal another name and calls him "capitalist." He takes the economic point of view and calls him the exploiter of the masses, who is withholding the rights of life from the proletariat.

The conservative recognizes in the liberal an age-old enemy; mentally a freebooter, politically a rationalist and a utilitarian who can sneak in disguise into any form of government and has even been able to destroy conservatism itself. The liberal grasps at power in the name of liberty; he may be known alike by the lying plausibility of his words and unscrupulousness of his deeds. We could see this in the political outrages of the Eastern Establishment of America, the *grande bourgeoisie* of France, and the socialist-liberal European elite, who have brought about many wars for their own ends in recent times.

The conservative, who takes his stand not only on economic but also on political and moral data, cannot ignore the economic question because it is far from being proven that the capitalist epoch is nearing its close—as the revolutionary hastily maintains. He, the real conservative, knows only that the world always tends to become, by the law of nature, conservative. He also knows that the world, which until the appearance of the liberal was still conservative, cannot become conservative again until the liberal is finally defeated. In embarking on his fight against the liberal, the conservative is aware that it is only the continuation of the great struggle between two principles that began when the age of enlightenment came to bring darkness rather than light to the world. This fight has been going on for hundreds of years; the conservative is prepared to believe that it may last for many more years until it is fought to the finish.

The Western renewal thinking cuts across all political party lines; it repudiates the political thought that brought the West to ruin and appeals to every Western person. The Western renewer trusts that there still exist in America and Europe many people whose reason has not been darkened by enlightenment but who have preserved clearness of understanding—people with genuine, straightforward insight; strong passions; and the will to act accordingly. He trusts that such people still live in the West, and he also presumes that the degenerate Western world will allow itself to be set in order once again.

It is possible to turn the tide, but only a large number of intelligent people can gradually form the attitudes of the culture and thus of the nature of its political and economic system. No single individual can do it alone; everyone must get involved. A slave is one who waits for someone to come and free him.

Conservatism is the complete opposite of Marxist socialism, which is the materialist conception of the history of human civilization explained with the conflict among various social groups and by the change and development in the means of production.

Conservatism believes in actions influenced by no economic motive, direct or indirect.

Conservatism denies that class war can be the preponderant force in the transformation of society.

Conservatism combats the whole complex system of democratic ideology and repudiates it, whether in its theoretical premises or its practical application.

Conservatism denies that the majority, by the mere fact that it is a majority, can direct human society. It denies that numbers alone can govern using a periodic consultation, and it affirms the immutable, beneficial, and fruitful inequality of humanity that can never be permanently brought to a common level through the mere application of a mechanical process, such as universal suffrage.

Conservatism denies in a democracy the absurd conventional untruth of political equality dressed in the garb of collective irresponsibility and the myth of happiness and indefinite progress.

From the given facts that the nineteenth century was the century of socialism, liberalism, and democracy, the twentieth century of socialism, fascism, Bolshevism, and democracy, it does not necessarily follow that the twenty-first century must also be a century of socialism, liberalism, and democracy. Political doctrines pass, but humanity remains, and it may somewhat be expected that soon will come an era of conservatism. For if the nineteenth century was an era of individualism and the twentieth was the time of collectivism, it may be expected that this will be the century of conservatism.

Conservatism must have a striking dislike for both Marxism and liberalism. Conservatism must reinforce authority in the war declared against certain principles of democracy, in its accentuated national character, and in its preoccupation with social order. Conservatism cannot think of avoiding certain limits of the moral law, which it may consider indispensable to maintain in favor of its reforming action.

Conservatism demands not only discipline and the coordination of all forces but also a deeply felt sense of duty and devotion. This fact explains the necessarily severe measures that must be taken against those who would oppose this spontaneous and inevitable movement in the twenty-first century. They would fight it by recalling the outworn ideologies of the twentieth century, which, however, must be repudiated; for never before has the world stood more in need of authority, direction, and order.

The continuous gaining ground of extreme liberalism, the individual selfishness of the societies living in the intoxicating salvation of consumption, and the profit hunger of the multinational corporations have together led to the present situation in the West. Also, the lack of coherent strategic vision, the distortion of the Founding Fathers' American and European ideas, and the extinction of real political leaders have only multiplied the problems.

These questions keep raising their heads as the symptoms of an underlying disease—perhaps in different forms depending on time and place, but still infected by the same virus. Moreover, those institutions and persons from whom the solutions would be expected by the quietly tolerant, dazed, enfeebled, and helpless population not only do *not* alleviate the problems and ills but also, in their hunger for power, feigned and pretentious pseudoelitism, and real mediocrity, even further aggravate them.

The political–social irony of the West today is the fact that the people have been led to expect entitlements, expect good government, and expect to be socially protected and taken care of by the state—and these are all socialist-oriented, liberal-conceived expectations. The peoples of the West have abandoned an ethical basis for society, believing that all problems are solvable by a good government. The government says, "Give me a popular mandate, and I will solve all problems of society."

Now, what is a good government? Where do the concepts of private initiative, individual responsibility, and self-reliance, all traditional Western values, fit into this picture?

The globalizing, internationalist progressives deny the importance of these values, claiming that Western culture is neither homogeneous nor unchanging and, as the case is with all other cultures, that it has evolved and gradually changed over time. However, these values are moral values, and the question is whether moral values can or should be modified over time.

This author's eagerness to seek the truth as an ordinary and customary act is a personal reaction to the age of communist dictatorships. That is why he is greatly alarmed and disappointed by the political correctness rampant in the West.

Political correctness, the communication of hypocrisy, is emasculating cancer and neuters opposition by stigmatizing it as hateful and bigoted. In essence, it makes the weak strong and the strong weak.

THE WESTERN RENEWER: THE NEW CONSERVATIVE

Polarity, opposition, and contradiction also belong to the essence of life. These enrich and energize the broader context of which they are a part when integrated, harmonized, and synthesized; their warring forces harnessed by the sovereign personality, institution, or society.

However, the organic union of opposites is not a central intellectual concern today. Today's age of ideology demands conformity, and the conservative intellectual is impotent to do more than grieve over the passing of an era in which variety and the dialectic of opposites produced a vibrant and dynamic society.

The liberal intellectual desires movement but refuses to pay the price for it; he wants individuality and creativity but refuses to tolerate the divergences of viewpoint and the frequent eccentricity that are the price of nonconformity. The liberal wishes creativity but is uncomfortable with the messiness of failed experiments and failed lives that creativity produces. For the organic reconciliation of opposites, which is the measure of a healthy society, the liberal has substituted the myth of pluralism—the dream of a multitude of mutually exclusive and hostile social units and individuals that coexist but fail either to stimulate to action or to enrich the collective group.

Conservative thought has not avoided the static and weary spirit of the age, and it is neither broader nor more inclusive, neither more dynamic nor more creative, than the doctrinaire liberalism that is its counterpart.

The blunt truth is that most modern conservatives have no clear concept of the society they wish to create, have no organic relationship with either the present or the past, hold no grand design, entertain no enduring principles, and are responsible for no whole and healthy vision either of individual or society. Their discourse consists of the platitudes of political criticism, but it is neither a substitute for principle nor a guide for action.

Conservatism tends to disintegrate because the centrifugal forces are much greater in it than in modern liberalism. Liberalism is a body of coherent doctrine, deductively derived from a set of central propositions. Conservatism is a synthesis of contradictory principles: the principle of *authority* and the principle of *freedom*. These principles are held in precarious balance by individuals and societies; the resolution of their forces is never final; their synthesis is never complete. The drive they impart to society is in a measure the product of their instability. If conservatives are finally to achieve the universal agreement necessary to the establishment of principle and ideology, they must reconcile themselves to the dialectic of freedom and authority and capitalize on the values of their divided heritage.

They can achieve this by following the essential option and becoming Western renewers.

The Western renewers must reconcile in their lives and their thinking both authority and freedom, anticipate the problems of the modern world, and work toward viable and optimistic solutions.

The Western renewers must stand in the center of power while mistrusting power itself, and never forget its corrupting influence.

Whether active or inactive in practical politics, Western renewers should be contemplative by nature, preferring the study of power to its exercise.

Western renewers should suspect the worst of human nature but optimistically hope for the best.

Western renewers should have an aristocratic outlook and be receptive to an aristocratic order, which they must attempt to understand, and they must assimilate themselves into the new social processes that are transforming Western society.

Western renewers must be ethical thinkers of the highest order who shall tolerate no concession of principle to practical politics.

Western renewers must combine in their thoughts and lives such devotion to both principle and freedom as ought to distinguish the contemporary conservative.

Not only extraordinary personalities but also history itself, by slow conjunction, unites the opposites that people so often find in contradiction. Prudence disposes, and wise men conform themselves to the world whose ordering was only partially theirs. It is only through historical understanding, through action, and finally through prudence that the reconciliation of opposites becomes possible. Western renewers must understand both the necessity of prudence and trust and the need for immediate political action. Although Western renewers will tend to be pessimists about human nature, they are at the same time also optimists—mostly because of their belief in prudence and trust.

Both Acton and Tocqueville recognized already that if it is hard to put up with the necessity of understanding and action in a world ordered by providence, it is even harder to accept the concept of providence itself.

The attack upon prudence, providence, and purpose has been the distinguishing characteristic of modern society; the abandonment of trust and value, its unique mark. The general conception of creative prudence, foresight, and care, which establishes a purpose and imposes meaning upon the events of history, had already been denied by the eighteenth century. The revolt against the eighteenth century had been well underway before the eighteenth century was halfway through. It was only incidentally a revolt against reason, but reason, too, was forced to abdicate its sway, once purpose had been banished. The era of nihilism and the utterly absurd begins with the doubt as to the nature and purpose of God in history. The nineteenth-century attempts at the restoration of order, value, and purpose all revolved around the central problem of finding and giving back meaning to history. Even Marxism is an attempt to bring back purpose, to restore ends, and to reestablish values. That it restores these to history without restoring prudence and trust is the most valid reason for its failure; it is impossible to justify the course of dialectical materialism as it reveals itself in its subhuman and antihuman processes.

Humanity must move into the realm of order, value, purpose, and trust if it is to escape absurdity.

Remembering the Old Liberals

Some claim that "liberalism" has meant two very different things. In the modern use, a liberal thinker is a proponent of redistribution of wealth. However, in the eighteenth through the twentieth centuries, a liberal would have been identified with one who was "willing to respect or accept behavior or opinions different from one's own; open to new ideas" and "favorable to or respectful of individual rights and freedoms" (Oxford Living Dictionaries).

Old liberalism was indeed about liberalizing—freeing something up and becoming more permissive. Nevertheless, this is not the case in the way the word is used today.

If the old liberals of the nineteenth century were one thing, they were not revolutionaries. What did Burke's old liberals, the not entirely conservative conservatives, represent? They were surely neither reactionaries nor radicals.

Burke and his "Old Whigs," the original classical liberals, defended the institutional monarchy and aristocracy while encouraging reforms that would give the ordinary people greater access to mercantile and farming opportunities. The Old Whigs supported the emancipation of Catholics, and many (including Burke) were suspected of being Catholics themselves.

Could it possibly be that the liberals of old believed in land reform or parliamentary reform for the sake of improvement—not necessarily to spite or change the establishment? Could they have even supported the monarchy and aristocracy on principle and yet still accepted that changes were necessary? If so, modern progressive liberals will have to face an uncomfortable truth: their forebears were far from slaves to compulsive progress but instead stood behind fixed principles rooted in a particular vision of society.

This author believes in political equality but does not think that either God or nature created an egalitarian world. A king or queen can also be a necessary part of civilized society; merely putting the matter out of one's mind cannot fill the void that could be filled with millionaires, athletes, film stars, and all the poisons of the soul instead.

The progressives are far less preoccupied with questions of permanence. Unlike the old liberals, they believe that political justice is derived from natural rights, which the progressives call "fundamental human rights." Among these are the rights for same-sex couples to be married, for women to have access to abortions, and for refugees to seek asylum. They believe these rights are guaranteed solely by them having been born.

Burke and his Old Whigs, however, were leery of the notion of natural rights. Instead, Burke claimed that rights were won and gained by "an entailed inheritance derived to us from our forefathers, and to be transmitted to our posterity; an estate specially belonging to the people of this kingdom without any reference whatever to any more general or prior right."[478] For the old liberals, there was no such thing as advantage by right. The only assurances were the laws of nature; from there it is man's responsibility to build a just and happy society and to pass that culture on to their children.

"Change" is the progressive's battle cry; "Reform" is the liberal's.

Chesterton's warning was "The whole modern world has divided itself into Conservatives and Progressives. The business of Progressives is to go on making mistakes. The business of the Conservatives is to prevent the mistakes from being corrected."[479] We have to wonder what, exactly, is that error the traditionalists saw in their contemporary conservatives.

The one great and all-pervasive conviction that unites these critics of both modern conservatism and modern liberalism is distributism.

G. K. Chesterton and Hilaire Belloc, of course, formulated distributism.[480] One cannot be both a distributist and a supporter of neoliberal economics—the sort touted by Reagan, Thatcher, and most of the center-right parties in the Western world. One might be a distributist with a more or less laissez-faire approach, but a firm distributist opinion would surely snub Reaganomics or the trickle-down scheme. Distributism has always been more than a mere mathematical method of scrutinizing human interaction and is undoubtedly the most counterintuitive philosophy in modern times. It is adherent to both the organic structure of society and a revolt against man's inherently selfish nature. It is a desire to improve the lot of every person without making him or her obsessed with that lot. At its heart, distributism is at once a traditionalist and reform-oriented philosophy; it is a relic of the old liberal spirit.

Now, it is true that the old liberals, like the neoliberals, believed that governing forces (be they aristocrats or kings or republics) ought to have greater autonomy in the market. However, the critical question is whether they believed in a free market economy for its own sake or if they believed individual freedom was the ideal. Would the old liberals have been comfortable with heavily centralized wealth in the hands of corporations, a large banking sector, the exportation of labor and agriculture, and the decline of independent artisanship?

This author would incline to say no. The avowed distributists have always opposed the rise of modern capitalism, which they considered to be a form of social Darwinism. The distributists, like the old liberals, thought that neither governments nor corporations have any right to deprive workers of the ownership of their labor or to exert a strong influence over the affairs of the common man. This belief is the strain of liberalism that believed that man ought to be rooted and free, autonomous, and deferential to the natural order of things. It is the sort of democracy that mistrusts any one fallen man to lord over any other fallen man and yet respects the traditional institutions that know how to govern justly.

Preferring a corporate master to a government master is the conservation of the wrong thing. It belongs to a deadly strain of conservatism that, rather than respecting all things sacred—kings and ordinary men, communities, and individuals—picks one and holds fast. The old liberals understood this need for perpetual reform—constant rebellion against the corrupt, wicked, and unjust world. The old liberals knew as Christians and students of natural law that although the world is unfair, men ought to strive to be fair themselves. They knew that kings and presidents were often the most just rulers of all, but to expect perfection of them was in itself a significant error; idolizing does great harm to one's self, but it also hurts the idol, who might think himself far more formidable than he indeed is.

This careful balance between adapting and questioning is the most precarious of all. Indeed, it is always easier to say, "This is as good as it gets" or "Everything needs to go." However, as Chesterton said of Christianity, it has not been tried and found wanting; it has been found difficult and not tried.[481] The same may well be true of good old liberalism.

DISTRIBUTISM: THE SUBSIDIARIST ALTERNATIVE TO SOCIALISM AND PLUTOCRACY

This author claims that practically all nations of the West are polarized and coming apart. No reasonable person can deny that the West needs to mitigate the effects of extreme individualism, especially the erosion of national unity.

There is a battle raging between two conflicting yet inadequate visions of Western society. Simplifying a bit, one is a conservative West that yearns for the security of moral values and social unity. The other is the progressive West, which longs for the heady idealism of extreme individualism, income equality, and governmental safety nets. One side longs for the stable 1950s and the other for the restless 1960s. All elements of unity and broad political consensus have eroded or broken down over the last several decades. The institutions of family, community, and faith that typically stand between the individual and the state are being undermined and worn away. These middle layers are where people see each other face-to-face and offer a middle ground between radical individualism and extreme centralization.

The competing two visions are blinded by their prejudices and eroded by the culture; neither of them has the power to recapture the mainstream. Neither one can afford to follow the present narrative, which does not address the current reality. Something different must be done.

The remedy can be summed up in one word: subsidiarity. The definition of this social concept is "Putting power, authority, and significance as close to the level of interpersonal community as reasonably possible." That is to say it means letting each social unit take care of itself while relying on larger institutions, especially government, only when necessary. The conciliating institutions of family, community, and faith need to be revived, reinforced, and empowered.

Agreed, this is easier said than done; it is more problematic how such a remedy might be implemented. The present judicial and regulatory infrastructures may not be so willing to relinquish their stranglehold on Western life, cease their hostility, and reverse the inebriating freedom of extreme individualism. Laborious virtue has found it always trying to contest easy vice.

"Distributism" is the name given to a socioeconomic and political creed initially associated with G. K. Chesterton and Hilaire Belloc. Belloc was merely the propagator and the popularizer of the church's social doctrine of subsidiarity as expounded by Pope Leo XIII in "Rerum Novarum" (1891).[482] That doctrine would be restated, reconfirmed, and reinforced by Pope Pius XI in "Quadragesimo Anno" (1931) and by Pope John Paul II in "Centesimus Annus" (1991).[483]

As such, it is essential first and foremost to see distributism as a derivative of the principle of subsidiarity.

Subsidiarity is discussed in the catechism of the Catholic Church under the condition of the inherent danger present in too much power being accumulated by the state: "Excessive intervention by the state can threaten personal freedom and initiative. The teaching of the Church has elaborated the principle of subsidiarity, according to which a community of a higher order should not interfere in the internal life of a community of a lower order, depriving the latter of its functions, but rather should support it in case of need and help to coordinate its activity with the activities of the rest of society, always with a view to the common good."[484]

Simply stated, the principle of subsidiarity rests on the assumption that larger communities (e.g., the state or centralized bureaucracies) should not violate the rights of small communities (e.g., families or neighborhoods). To give an example in practical terms, parents' rights to educate their children without any politically correct school curricula imposed by the state would be upheld by the principle of subsidiarity. Parental influence in schools is subsidiarist; state control is antisubsidiarist.

"Subsidiarity," although an awkward word, serves as an adequate definition of the principle for which it is the label. "Distributism," on the other hand, is both an awkward word and an awkward name. What exactly does it advocate distributing? Are not communists and socialists distributists in the sense that they seek a more equitable distribution of wealth? Belloc vehemently argues that distributism is radically at variance with the underlying ideas of communism and socialism. Therefore, it is for reasons of clarity that modern readers might find it useful to translate "distributist" as "subsidiarist" when reading Belloc's critique of politics and economics.

Put succinctly, distributism was the name that Belloc and Chesterton gave to the version of subsidiarity they were advocating in their writings.

Unlike the socialists, distributists were not advocating the redistribution of wealth per se, though they believed that this could be one of the results of distributism. Instead, and the difference is crucial, they were advocating the redistribution of the means of production to as many people as possible.

Belloc and the distributists drew the vital connection between the freedom of labor and its relationship to the other factors of production (i.e., land, capital, and entrepreneurial spirit). The more labor is separated from the other factors of production, the more it is subjugated to the will of powers beyond its control. In an ideal world, every man would control his destiny by having control over the means to his livelihood (i.e., he would own the land on which he worked and the tools with which he worked). According to Belloc, this is the most critical economic freedom. If a man possesses this freedom, he will not so quickly succumb to encroachments on his other liberties.

Belloc was also a realist and knew that man does not live in an "ideal world," which, in the absolute sense, is unattainable. Indeed, if Belloc erred at all, it was on the side of pessimism. As a Christian, he believed that man is called to strive for perfection by imitating Christ, even if he cannot be as perfect as Christ is perfect. Moreover, what applies to man in his relationship with God also refers to man in his relationship with his neighbor (i.e., we are called to strive toward a more virtuous and satisfying society, even if it can never be perfect). Accordingly, every policy and every action leading to man's union with (i.e., ownership of) the land and capital assets on which he depends for his sustenance is a move in the right direction. Every policy or action that subordinates him to those who control (i.e., own) the land and capital assets on which he depends for his livelihood, thereby also controlling his labor, is a move in the wrong direction.

In practice, the following would all be distributist solutions to current problems:

> policies that create a favorable climate for the establishment and subsequent thriving of small businesses

> policies that discourage mergers, takeovers, and monopolies

> policies that promote the breaking up of monopolies or larger companies into smaller businesses

> policies that encourage producers' cooperatives

> policies that privatize nationalized industries

> policies that decentralize power from central government to local government, from big government to small government, and bring real political power closer to the family level

All the above are practical examples of applied distributism.

As the preceding practical examples suggest, distributism/subsidiarity is *not* an esoteric idea without any practical applicability in everyday life; on the contrary, it is at the heart of political and economic activity. Since power becomes centralized in the hands of fewer and fewer people in politics and economics, subsidiarity is the antidote to this centralization (i.e., it is the principle at the heart of the forces of decentralization, the law that demands the rights and protection of smaller political and economic units against the encroachments of a central government and big business).

Many other practical examples can be presented, of course, starting with the Constitution of the European Union, which is fundamentally centralist by its very nature—so much so that all reference to "subsidiarity" in EU documents amounts to the scandalous employment of Orwellian doublethink. Euroskepticism, the view that the European Union is an offensive monolith that needs to be either reorganized or broken up, is fundamentally subsidiarist. Similarly, the rights and demands of rural cultures to be able to enjoy their traditional ways of life are subsidiarist, whereas urban-driven legislation officially forbidding traditional rural pursuits is an infringement of subsidiarity. Gun ownership in the United States or the right to hunt foxes in the United Kingdom would fit into this category. It is not a question of gun control or animal rights but of the right of rural cultures to choose their own way of life without the imposition of unwanted urban value judgments.

The continued erosion of states' rights in the United States and the corresponding increase of power by the federal government is an encroachment on subsidiarity.

In short, and in sum, distributism as a variation of the principle of subsidiarity offers the only real alternative to the preferred obsession of the modern Western world.

We should indeed begin taking a look at Wilhelm Röpke's work in drawing out the market economy's dependence on a humane and ethical social order. Röpke is counted among a group of thinkers known as the ordoliberals, who recognized that state intervention was needed to ensure that a healthily competitive environment was guaranteed against monopoly.

Distributism is in line with Röpke's humanism and the ordoliberals' recognition of the need for relatively small-scale participation in the economy for markets to function properly; distributism might even be called a radically localist ordoliberalism. Distributism is not only feasible but also necessary; it conforms with and is an expression of subsidiarity. Distributism puts the family at the heart of economic and sociopolitical life and calls for the protection and preservation of small government and small business against the power encroachment of big government and big business. In today's age of secular fundamentalist monoliths, such as the European Union, supranational institutions, and global corporations, the creed of distributism, which Chesterton called "the outline of sanity," is needed more than ever.

18

Proposal for the Future: The Essential Option

It is much easier to diagnose a problem and then conclude with a vague, dishonest solution for resolving it. It is not known what kind of mysterious backroom deals prompt modern Western conservatives to do that, but they effectively keep declaring themselves traitors to their cause. They offer only vague and anodyne suggestions to go back to church and vote conservative so that "we" can turn the tables on the declining Western Civilization. They must know that "we" are not going to save the West by those methods.

Exploring Alternative Methods

First, it is perfectly acceptable for people to think nationally—and they must do so. Western civilization cannot preserve itself if we are too afraid to say that we belong to nations that need preserving and that we are proud of it. We have to stop being scared of being called nationalists. That does not mean being a dreaded Nazi; it only means, as the Latin root "*natio*" implies, that we belong to particular, respective cultural–political communities that have become conscious of their coherence, unity, and specific interests.

Secondly, we need to acknowledge that the West is not going to survive merely through the ballot box. If the West, with all its national elements, wants to survive as a civilization, the people, the citizens, are going to have to step up and fight for it. The modern Western elite has lost the consent of the governed, and their rule needs to be ended. They will not go voluntarily; they never do. We must begin to embrace the concept of alternative methods, and we must prepare to exercise that human right.

In addition to proposing the long view, people must be urged to stop thinking in terms of historical progress in a logical and linear direction and to think instead in cycles of civilization. The assumption is that civilization has its ups and downs but beneath the fluctuation is an order of nature—a set of laws, patterns, and forms that give human nature and the natural universe an enduring structure. Narrow trends play themselves out over finite periods while the full range of human possibilities remains permanently viable.

The natural patterns will survive as long as the created being endures. The implication is that human nature may be temporarily distorted (sometimes for centuries) by the rise and fall of historical civilizations, but specific natural patterns will persist and reassert themselves. What looks inevitable today—democracy, industrial and technological society, and even modern science—can be seen more realistically as a transitory phase in the rise and fall of civilizations.

The currently existing order of things is therefore not merely the culmination of history in the inevitable destiny but a diluted and opaque version of a shifting but livable ephemeron until past patterns, including old patterns of greatness, can reemerge. How and when and in which form this will occur is impossible to predict. Therefore, let us not confuse the last few centuries with a "necessary" or "best" order due to progress, and let us remain open to the permanent possibilities of the human soul.

Duality vs. Absolutes

Be it philosophy, theology, the natural sciences or politics, the ever-present existence of some duality, bipolarity, or a yin and yang in the universal structure is easy to recognize and obvious to see. Chinese philosophy stated thousands of years ago that opposite or contrary forces not only exist and are interconnected and interdependent, but also that they also give rise to each other as they interrelate to one another. Various natural dualities, such as light and dark, high and low, hot and cold, fire and water, life and death, and male and female, to name a few, are considered as physical manifestations of the yin-yang concept within Taoism. Numerous branches of classical Chinese science and philosophy originate from this duality concept, which is a primary guideline of traditional Chinese medicine as well.[485]

This duality must be thought of as complementary (instead of opposing) forces interacting to form such a synergic system in which the whole is greater than the sum of its parts. All things possess both yin *and* yang aspects (for instance, shadow cannot exist without light; everything has its advantages and disadvantages, or pros and cons), and either of the two fundamental facets may be revealed more strongly in a particular object, depending on the criterion of the observation.

In Taoist metaphysics, distinctions between good and bad, and other dichotomous moral judgments, are perceptual, not real; so yin and yang are an indivisible whole. In the ethics of Confucianism, on the other hand, most notably in the philosophy of Dong Zhongshu (c. second century BC), a moral dimension is attached to the yin-yang idea.[486]

Even though this duality also manifests itself in ethical aspects, it is certainly *not* to be interpreted as the justification for moral relativism. On the contrary, it is duality that mandates moral guidance to be followed in all human endeavors if we want to stay on the road that nature and the universe have destined for us. It is true; there are no right or wrong, black or white, or yes or no decisions on most critical problems in nature—and there is no definite solution to everything at all times either.

As such, it is human nature always to look for security, and we also feel instinctively safe and satisfied in finding solutions to our problems. However, since nature, life, and the entire universe are full of singularities or discontinuities for which no explanations can be delineated, there are many challenges and dilemmas we encounter in our lives for which, although desired, no exact solutions can be offered or found. It is a hard-to-swallow fact for modern man that he must accept the inevitable; there are problems and challenges for which he cannot and will not find solutions.

The above problem is magnified when one looks for the perfect sociopolitical–economic system, which does not exist. All extreme—meaning utopian—idealist trials conducted in the name of liberty, freedom, and equality have ended up in some form of uncompromising regimes, leading to inevitable disasters. The search for perfect solutions has always resulted in complete failures.

The issue is no longer between absolute and relative values. The absolute must set limits; meaning limits based on duality. The relative values can then be accepted strictly within those absolute limits that have been established by duality.

The Essential Option

Having learned the lessons of perfect solutions, one would be wise to draw the consequences from the failures and successes of the past.

Based on the positive aspects of the Anglo-American classical liberal system emphasizing the responsibility of the individual and unleashing the creativity of private enterprise, the healthy political system of the future must include some, but not all, of the characteristic features of contextual existentialism. This philosophy emphasizes the uniqueness and isolation of individual experience in a hostile or indifferent universe, considers human existence as unexplainable, and stresses freedom of choice and responsibility for the consequences of one's acts.

Concurrently, the complementary Franco-German system promoting the responsibility of the state has to be also recognized; the idea of the social market economy connected to an efficient government cannot be left out of any future socioeconomic system;

The teachings of the Russian liberal conservative school have to be considered to counteract the destructive forces released by modern liberalism. Accordingly, the principle of state supremacy in areas where it has competence but abstaining in those areas in which it does not must be taken into account.

This author argues *against* both totalitarianism and formal democracy and *for* an alternative way of building a new political system in the West.

The combination of Anglo-American individualism, Franco-German collectivism, and Russian liberal conservatism will be called "the inclusive Western alternative option," or, in short, "the essential option."

I. Elements of the Anglo-American System

Few Western ideas have been the subject of more unrelenting corrosion than the notion of man in modern times. Moreover, this notion has been shared by two strange political bedfellows, namely many Catholics and almost all communists: that of the self as inherently sinful, whether against God or state—a repository of living shame, guilt, greed, and antisocial attitudes. According to this degenerate view, the human is a helplessly weak being whose self-interest is usually malevolent and whose dignity is inevitably disgraced.

This corrupted notion of the individual has fundamentally rendered the massive problems of the West, particularly in the United States, no longer merely political but philosophical. The corrupted philosophy, in turn, has been the result of two vastly different understandings of democracy of which the West, especially the United States, has lost sight. The first one is aristocratic democracy, which is what the American Founding Fathers initially intended; and the second one is egalitarian democracy, which is what has been created instead, much at our peril.[487]

On this point, one is referred to Federalist 9, 10, 47, 49, and 57 of the Founding Fathers, and to Thomas Jefferson's self-admitted search for the "natural aristoi," whom he wanted to cultivate for public service.[488] Jefferson argued that education in a republic must be "democratic and aristocratic."[489] One should also remember Madison's and Hamilton's almost obsessive fear of "mobocracy" and their revulsion toward the idea of direct democracy.[490] "When I mention the public, I mean to include only the rational part of it. The ignorant vulgar are as unfit to judge of the modes, as they are unable to manage the reins of government," wrote John Randolph in 1774.[491]

The following must be clear: the term "egalitarian" does not mean "equality" here; it means "the lowest common standard," which has the highest possible cultural and political influence, either elite-directed or mass-driven. Also, the term "aristocratic" is used here not in the sense of baronies, barbicans, or bloodlines; it is meant in its original, philosophical sense, best summarized as self-reverence, self-sufficiency, and self-perpetuation.

It is this last quality of the long view—the concept of time or future preference—inherent in the aristocratic outlook that is its most important aspect. It is what integrates the sustainability of the individual's freedom with what enables him to sustain himself in society in the first place: his means of production—or capitalism.

That is to say, a proper society, in which the self-reverence and self-perpetuation required of the citizen is of supreme significance, will at the same time be a properly capitalistic society in which the citizen's long-term self-perpetuation is made possible. The future of any society is a contest between these short- and long-term views, and the outcome will determine whether the United States, and ultimately the West, will manage to find the way out of a state of decline in the coming decades or not.

If Western society is to survive, it must incorporate that which it has long regarded as its diametrical opposite: the aristocratic (the long view). If Western society is to perish, it will continue promoting that which has been falsely regarded as its best element: the egalitarian (the here and now—the mass appetite).

One remarkable intellectual social trend that highlights all these factors at once is the corruption of the very concept of the individual. There is a mass preference for the appetites and impulses of the present; modern societal contempt for the future and future planning may be seen in the "sophisticated" intellectual trend of attempting to convert capitalism into something else that it is not and should not become. Subtly distinct changes of terminology have been gaining currency since the onset of the economic crises, and one hears calls for communitarian capitalism, the social market, social entrepreneurship, and the end of something called "Gucci capitalism." On the face of it, all of this seems harmless, even reasonable; for many, including business leaders, these new categories represent an intelligently progressive step in the right direction, ostensibly respecting the productive ends of capitalism while mixing some social oversight into those ends. As a side benefit, say supporters, the word is purged of its recently tainted connotations.

However, therein lies the danger. Such nuanced language means that the traditional center and spirit of capitalist enterprise, the individual—his gain, his search for profit, his self-interest, his distinction or even glory—represents something distasteful at best and inherently criminal and corrupt at worst. According to such thinking, the only legitimate and, by extension, morally superior economic behavior is the social–communal group mindset. This mentality uses guilt; the crimes of oligarchic, financial, and political gangsterism; and a troubled economy to undermine the theory and working of capitalism and reverse the very premise of it. It puts the group ends of distribution as the ethical objective above and beyond the protection of the fundamental means of production: the individual and his mind. The egalitarian becomes the goal, while the aristocratic—the primary driver of standards, long-term planning, and generational perpetuation—becomes the object of resentment.

Ignoble elements of a nation can exert a marked influence on its course because they are without reverence toward the present or the future. They see their lives and the present spoiled beyond remedy and are ready to waste and wreck both; hence their willingness regarding chaos and anarchy. That is the egalitarian on the path of destruction. The egalitarian creates for the short term because the present is an ordeal to get through, the past invariably is a source of evil, and the future is beyond his control or care. The short term is convenient and instantaneous—the whetting of an appetite.

Soon the short term becomes not only the economic but also the political, cultural, and social mentality of choice. Everything becomes short term: the short term in financial practices, the short term in political expediency, the short term in art—all recycled, disposable and forgotten. It is the short term in educational standards, the short term in the durability of a product or a service, the short term in human relationships, in concentration and commitments—all of it leading to today's crop of human capital.

Then popular opinion and its elite mass representatives bemoan the individual as a rapacious, quick-scheming wretch. Well, they should know; they created him.

At present in the West, there is a population of the human capital, created through political decisions, that is not fit for democracy—certainly not economically. Lo and behold, capitalism is blamed for the decline and fall, while that same capitalism is being taken hostage by politically correct terminology that it may still be coaxed into showing up and saving the day.

Dramatic as it sounds, there is a consequential end to all of this. If society does not demand far higher specific character standards of itself, it will eventually and by default become proletarian. That is, if more is not asked of the individual, then nothing at all will be requested of the mass. One person, one will, will be invested with the responsibility for the many, making of him the dictator he will inevitably have to become—Jefferson's "elected despot."[492]

How many times has this happened in the West since the French Revolution, and with what result? Assuredly, it *will* happen, indeed *must* happen, again—provided things do not fundamentally change.

The aristocratic element of society is its long-term quality. It has reverence for the past and plans for the future. It is the basic instinct that Western society would need once more, while capitalism, the practical support of society, should be free of guilty-conscience modifiers or apologetic labels tacked onto it. Once upon a time in Europe, this view meant vast fortunes made with the goal of sustaining generations of the family name. In the United States, it became the outlook of Madison, Adams, and Jefferson, who referred time and again to the need for a gallant citizenry to uphold their immense and awe-inspiring undertaking. It is the outlook of the kind of individual whom no great force—emperor, soldier or government—can replace.

Only the element of individual responsibility taken from the Anglo-American system and put within an aristocratic framework, instead of egalitarian order, can provide society with any long-term future planning quality.

II. Elements of the Franco-German System

The West needs an ideological system that applies the concepts of management by objective on a national scale (i.e., within the political life of the people). The achievement of those objectives is entrusted to appointed leaders who must exercise their skills and talents in the most helpful, efficient, and honorable way possible.

The underlying principle is that the welfare of the whole outranks the well-being of the individual. It means that, in a situation where conflicts of interests arise, the lesser is sacrificed to the greater in pursuit of quality. (This is the German system.)

The political system appoints a leader in a particular position, and he is, on account of his appointment, granted the power and freedom to make decisions. The results of those decisions determine whether the incumbent will remain in that position, because he, and only he, is responsible for the consequences of his choices. If these go wrong, as measured against set principles and goals, he has to accept accountability for his errors and vacate the position of power.

Freedom is offset by responsibility, fulfillment of duty is rewarded by more power, and failure is met with accountability. (This is the Roman system.)

Democracy itself can never be called to account for anything, since the right of decision is not vested in any cabinet but in the parliamentary majority. The cabinet always functions as the mere executor of the will of the majority, and its political ability can be judged by how well it can adjust to the will of the majority or can persuade the majority to agree to its proposals. However, this means that the ruling body must descend from the level of real governing power to that of a mendicant who has to beg the approval of a majority that may have gotten together only for the time being. Thereby the chain of command and, with it, all responsibility are abolished in practice.

The principle of combining full responsibility with full authority will gradually cause a selected group of leaders to emerge, which is not even thinkable in our present epoch of irresponsible parliamentary democracy. As soon as the concept of power is discussed, democracy-minded people are quick to quote Lord Acton's adage: "Power tends to corrupt, and absolute power corrupts absolutely."

While this wisdom might be true, one must also not forget that (1) no society or organization can function unless power, with a commensurate amount of responsibility, is entrusted to distinct and officially recognized individuals, and (2) responsibility must always rest with individuals, meaning specific people, and it cannot be delegated; only authority can be. In a democratic government, in which committees and commissions arrive at decisions based on majority votes, responsibility and authority are so mixed-up and dispersed, confused and comminuted, that in the end they practically disappear.

The current Western liberal democracy neither assigns responsibility to its leaders nor holds them accountable for their actions.

Has anyone been identified or held accountable as the political leader responsible for the Vietnam War? Was it President Kennedy or President Johnson? Did that leader have the authority to bring the United States into such a military conflict without Congress declaring war? Did the US Congress surrender its constitutional right and duty by not declaring war but letting half a million troops be sent to Asia and authorizing the funds required? How did this supposedly superior democratic political system work while violating its own alleged principles for more than fifteen years? Could such things have happened had the Franco-German system of government been in place at the time?

Before the American military operations in the First Iraq War started in January 1991, there was a US congressman who introduced Congress and the American public to a fifteen-year-old Kuwaiti girl. Her testimony as a key witness before Congress in October 1990 was widely publicized and was cited numerous times by

US senators and the president of the United States in their rationale to back Kuwait in the Gulf War. In her emotional testimony, the girl stated among other things that after the Iraqi invasion of Kuwait, she had witnessed Iraqi soldiers take babies out of incubators in a Kuwaiti hospital, take the incubators, and leave the infants to die.

Then, in 1992, it was revealed that the girl was the daughter of the sitting Kuwaiti ambassador in Washington. She had been used and coached to be an eyewitness testifying under oath about her "suffering," thereby justifying direct US intervention on human rights grounds.[493]

Was this congressman ever tried for perjury, for the deliberate misleading of the American people, for abusing his office, or for having been involved in atrocity propaganda and starting a war? Never.

In how many overseas wars has the United States been militarily involved since the Second World War? One can count somewhere between eighteen and twenty major interventions, meaning large-scale or long-term troop deployments associated with direct combat in Korea, Vietnam, Iraq, Afghanistan, Panama, Bosnia, and the like. (See appendix A). Short-term policing actions and deployments in Somalia, Haiti, and others are considered minor skirmishes only. How many of these wars have been duly declared by the US Congress as the Constitution demands? Not one.

How many individuals have been prosecuted for the unauthorized use of force, for the tens of thousands of American lives lost, for the trillions of dollars of American money and wealth wasted? Not one.

Considering the above simple but obvious and pertinent examples to elucidate the case, this author proposes that taking the elements of the Franco-German system enforcing the direct, clear, and unambiguous responsibility and accountability of the state will result in a fairer, more just, more efficient, and incorruptible government. Any such government and socioeconomic system shall be based on a real bottom-up social market economy.

III. Elements of the Russian System

The primary sources of the West's problems are corrupted and degenerate moral and legal consciousness. Given this, democracy is *not* a suitable form of government.

There must be a single responsible will at the head of the state. United and strong state power is needed; at the same time, there must be clear limits to these powers. The political leader must be elected and have popular support; the state organs must be both responsible and accountable; the principle of legality must be upheld, and all people must be equal before the law. Freedom of speech, conscience, and assembly must be guaranteed. Private property must be sacrosanct. The state should be supreme in those areas in which it has competence but must stay out of those areas in which it has none, such as private life and religion. That is the meaning of a long-standing, peculiarly Russian, tradition of liberal conservatism.

To Westerners, Russian liberal conservatism is somewhat incomprehensible, as its core beliefs seem paradoxical, even contradictory, which indeed they are. However, it is a position with deep roots in Russian philosophy stretching back to the mid-nineteenth century and thinkers such as Boris Chicherin, followed by Vladimir Solovyov and Pyotr Struve.

The roots of Russian conservatism can be found in the resistance to the momentum of individualistic Western liberalism. There was never a Russian Edmund Burke to make a sophisticated plea for the powers of tradition and community over rationality as a guide to how to live, but there was always the Russian Orthodox Church to bluntly dismiss pure reason as anathema.

The Russian philosopher Ivan Alexandrovich Ilyin's liberal–conservative doctrine divides sovereign authority between the state and private spheres based on the supremacy of the law and sets legal limits. Only by embracing the relevant elements of the doctrine can the West successfully combat the destructive forces released by modern liberalism.

The West's resurrection depends on the revival of the true spirit, love of one's country and people, respect for the law, a sense of duty and honor, devotion to the state, general well-being, and prosperity instead of personal or party interests. It will suffice to mention here but three themes that stand out: statehood, legal consciousness, and nationalism.

Statehood: To view the state as a balance of competing material interests is profoundly mistaken; the state should work for the general good. To this end, it must be strong and just; a weak state would result in anarchy. This author favors autocracy, but one filled with a creative spirit—an autocratic–aristocratic confederacy or sovereignty. One single will must stand at the head of the state. The state should be absolute in those areas in which it has competence but should not have jurisdiction over everything; it has to be bound by law and accountable to the people.

Legal consciousness: One of the modern West's greatest failings is its peoples' misguided sense of what is right and wrong and whether they should obey the law. One of the most important tasks of the autocratic state must be to develop and nurture the people's legal consciousness. The single correct path to any reform is the ever-continuing education in legal awareness. Theoretically, the state can be reduced to self-government of the people. However, the single and objective aim of the state is so high and requires from the citizenry such mature legal consciousness that historically the people turn out to be incapable of self-government. It must be one of the future tasks of political philosophy to uncover the root of this divergence; state power must find the way to correct it.

Nationalism: This author is a nationalist; love of country is a central part of his philosophy. Every nation should develop in its own way. Thus the West has no right to tell others how to run their country; in other parts of the world, the conditions are not the same as they are in the West. The West is *not* entitled to impose any political forms whatsoever on others.

At the same time, this author rejects imperialism. Precisely because each nation should develop in its own way, all those powers and empires comprising several different and distinct entities (e.g., the European Union, Russia, and China) should not seek to absorb and destroy them but let them develop their own cultures (see Canada or Switzerland).

REBUILDING THE WEST BASED ON THE ESSENTIAL OPTION

Was not Japan able to find a way and reconcile to its situation, renouncing its sense of international mission and the pursuit of tempting political ventures—and did not that country flourish as a result?

The time is long overdue for an uncompromising choice between a Western Empire—of which we, Americans and Europeans, are the primary victims—and the spiritual and physical salvation of our peoples.

Pursuing and holding on to a vast empire means to contribute to the extinction of the Western peoples and Western civilization. What need is there of this odd and heterogeneous amalgam? Do we want Europeans (French, Germans, British, Danes, Hungarians, Portuguese, Greeks, Finns, among others), Americans, Canadians, and Australians to lose their unique characteristics? What hope can there be for preserving and developing their culture amid the chaotic jumble of today? There is less and less hope, surely, as things are becoming ever more mashed and pounded together.

The spiritual life of a nation is more important than the size of its territory or even its economic prosperity; the health and happiness of the people are of incomparably greater value than any external goal based on prestige. A nation must develop its fate *for itself*, and this is a question that cannot be decided without a national plebiscite.

Western recovery today is not merely a matter of identifying the most convenient system of government and then hastily cobbling together a marvelous constitution. Unless one craves revolution, a state must possess the qualities of continuity and stability while providing security and peace to its citizens. In this sense, a strong presidency will always prove useful for many years to come.

What is clear is that the process must always start at the local level with grassroots issues. While preserving a stable central authority, the people must patiently, persistently, and permanently expand the rights of local communities. While the information-gathering and communication process must flow from the local level in bottom-up fashion, the decision-making process must proceed from the top down.

I. Political Philosophy of the Western Renewal: The Sandys Doctrine

This author writes and advocates for the political philosophy of a Western renewal. His purpose herein is to reflect on the firm belief that ideas, facts, and keen perception will be victorious against lofty rhetoric and mind-conditioning based on primitive propaganda.

The essential option advocates that human action develops alternative methods of living in different places and from different historical circumstances. This explanation directly leads to a political philosophy that rejects rationalist designs (e.g., to overthrow all political institutions so as to begin afresh according to some utopian blueprint) and emphasizes the continuity of wisdom instead—as contained in institutions and the language of politics—over the generations and in specific localities.

Dostoevsky pronounced the idea of universal and equal suffrage "the most absurd invention of the nineteenth century."[494] At any rate, it is not Newton's law, and it is permissible to have doubts about its alleged merits.

Does not "universal and equal" clash with the tremendous inequality among individuals regarding their talents, their contributions to society, their ages, their life experiences, their degrees of rootedness in the country and the locality? It represents the triumph of bare quantity over substance and quality. What is more, such elections assume that the nation lacks all structure—that it is not a living entity but a mere mechanical conglomeration of disparate individuals. Nor does secret voting represent something to be admired in and of itself; it facilitates insincerity or is an unfortunate necessity born of fear.

Well-established and dominating minorities rule all democracies. Democracy is a means whereby a well-organized ruling minority holds sway over an unorganized majority. A flexible and smoothly functioning democracy is adept at deflecting popular protest and depriving it of any great outlet. Boris Chicherin pointed out in the nineteenth century that of all the varieties of the aristocracy, one that rises to the surface in a democratic system is the aristocracy of money. One cannot deny that money can bring real power in a democratic setting and that an inevitable concentration of power occurs in the hands of those with vast fortunes.

European democracy was initially permeated with a sense of Christian self-discipline and responsibility, but these spiritual principles have been gradually losing their influence. The dictatorship of various group interests and their self-satisfied vulgarity keep the pressure on spiritual independence from every direction.

Why would we continue to embark on democracy at a time when it has already proved its declining state?

The bipolar conflict between classical liberalism and the preeminence of freedom in the economic realm continues today. The tension between social conservatism on one side and economic liberalism on the other continues into our present era. Owing to this dualism, we will fail to see the full dimensions of ordered liberty. Such division also undercuts inherent conservative political power, dividing it into two warring camps of social vs. economic conservatism. A cohesive model of the real social market economy offers a viable alternative.

A suitable legal–social framework of the economy must be guaranteed, since private property and free price movement themselves do not constitute a social order.

Free markets require a moral framework outside themselves to work optimally, because the market is only defensible as part of a broader system encompassing ethics, law, the state, politics, and power.

The Western renewal's political philosophy must be that the authority of the local communities is expanded at the expense of the central, or federal, state bureaucracy, as the goal is to reduce direct central involvement in urban affairs. For example, federal land owned by the central government must be returned to the cities; city council members must be compelled to resume municipal authority, even against their will; and the financial burden of the cities and local communities must be made dependent on investment rather than set up as a compulsory tax.

The author's following doctrine is the basis for the essential option's, and consequently Western renewal's, political philosophy. The doctrine is as follows:

The first objective is to stop the spread, rule, and domination of modern left-liberal, socialist, and communist ideologies on the territories of Western countries or elsewhere that pose a threat comparable to that represented formerly by the Soviet Union. This objective is a dominant consideration underlying the political philosophy of Western renewal and requires that we endeavor to prevent modern liberalism associated with neoliberalism, neoconservatism, socialism, or communism from controlling a region whose resources would, under consolidated authority, be sufficient to generate global power.

That needs to be defended and saved which the West has accomplished concerning knowledge, the advancements in health, education, and technology for the past twenty-five hundred plus years. That traditional Western world is worth defending from its main enemy, which is Western liberalism. However, what is being defined as Western liberalism is not the liberalism of the nineteenth century. Marxism, with all its horrible symptoms—usually referred to as "communism" and "socialism"—has hijacked Western liberalism. Eradicating communism and socialism would return the world to a somewhat safer state.

II. Hierarchical System of Government

To illustrate the way the Western renewal must challenge the present order, this author would once again like to speculate about one false idol of the modern age—democracy. Contrary to conventional wisdom, it is doubtful that this phenomenon is as inevitable or desirable as the dogma of historical progress wants the people to believe it.

Is democracy the best form of government or the one toward which all nations must converge? The Western renewal must wrestle with this question, because the most rooted prejudice of the present age is the firm belief that democracy based on human rights (liberal democracy) must be not only the best but indeed the *only* legitimate form of government. Thomas Jefferson said the idea was "self-evident" to all enlightened minds and with that shut down any further discussion of the issue. He made it seem unpatriotic to question this view—although patriots like Alexander Hamilton did entertain the possibility that elective monarchy was better than democracy.[495]

A monarchy is both a political system and a form of government in which one person, the monarch, exercises the role of sovereignty and embodies the country's national identity.

In contrast, democracy is a political system in which sovereign power is invested in the majority of the people. In today's world, as prone as we are to the prejudices of our own time and culture, most Westerners would feel that democracy is obviously the fairer form of government—completely disregarding the fact that the principle does not work very well in practice. As Plato tells us, democracy tends to descend into anarchy—a system of political chaos with the majority, and particularly the weakest members of the majority, suffering the most.

What about monarchy then? Mindful of Lord Acton's famous maxim that power tends to corrupt and absolute power tends to corrupt absolutely, who would advocate a system whereby absolute power is placed in the hands of a single person? If monarchy condemns us to a system in which tyranny is allegedly much more widespread than justice, democracy condemns us to a system in which politicians tend to become both increasingly powerful and corrupt. The governments of democracies tend to become ever more powerful and more distant from the people, becoming more and more corrupt. The apparent difference between monarchy and democracy is that good kings are more common and more forward-thinking than sound democratic governments.

It seems, then, that monarchy leads to corruption, which leads to tyranny; and that democracy leads to anarchy, which also leads to tyranny in the end. We are thus condemned to choose between two tyrannies: between the rule of the king and the rule of the mob.

This author has already elaborated on and demonstrated the numerous and inherent weaknesses of democracy inevitably and invariably leading to corruption, anarchy, and tyranny. What could be considered, therefore, is a political structure that might be called controlled aristocracy: a political system utilizing and combining the advantages of monarchy, a hierarchical system with a top-down decision-making process, and bottom-up subsidiarity.

A true monarchy is a political system that is subject to the one king from whom all authority flows. However, instead of the absolutist monarchy that advocates the so-called (and heretical) divine right of kings, an idea that tyrannical kings have employed to justify their tyranny, what is needed is a hierarchical and aristocratic system that is not only subject to the moral law but has no right to break it. What is therefore needed is a controlled aristocracy that is subject to the principle of subsidiarity and that consequently has no right to supersede the power that is invested in legitimately elected local, regional, or state government.

This author advocates a hierarchical and aristocratic political system that has limited power and is both a servant of the people and answerable to the moral law.

One should always remember that most of the great political thinkers of the classical and Christian tradition were at odds with our current way of thinking. Despite the differences among Plato, Aristotle, Saint Augustine, Saint Thomas Aquinas, Martin Luther, John Calvin, and the early American Puritans, all agreed that democracy is not the best form of government and that monarchy, aristocracy, or some mixed constitution is the best regime in most cases. It would be a significant step in liberating our minds if we could recover their reasoning and take it seriously once again.

Their argument, briefly, is that democracy is not the best system, because it levels the distinctions between high and low in society and the souls of citizens, and this leveling tendency undermines the quest for virtue or human excellence, aspiration, and achievement. Instead of judging life by the peaks of humanity (the philosophers, saints, and heroes), democracy worships the preferences, judgments, and opinions of the average man, producing a popular culture or mass society that weakens the highest impulses of the soul. In extreme forms of mass democracy, the people, as well as the educated elite, become ashamed of the moral superiority implied in real virtue and tear it down by treating it with indifference or contempt. That leads to democratic tyranny—something we have witnessed in violent fashions under various forms of socialism and softer models in the debased mass culture of America and the social democracies of Europe.

Since democracy leads to the leveling of distinctions between a high and low degree of merit, the classical and early Christian thinkers preferred hierarchical regimes to democracy. Heeding Plato's dictum that the "regime in the city shapes the regime in the soul," they preferred monarchy or aristocracy to perfect the minds and characters of citizens. Alternatively, they defended mixed systems that combined wisdom and virtue of the rulers (or top-down order) with the demand of the people for concurrence (or bottom-up order).

One of the various models proposed is Saint Thomas Aquinas's idea of a mixed or constitutional monarchy—a regime that combines elements of kingship, aristocracy, and democracy in a balanced order.[496]

In fact, this was the form of the English constitution for centuries—a balance of king, lords, and commons. It was also the organization of the Spartan regime, which combined kingship (actually two kings) with an aristocratic body of venerable elders and the elected representatives of the people. The mixed constitution was also the political order endorsed by the great conservative Edmund Burke, Plato in his *Laws*, and Cicero in his *Republic*.[497] It is the system underlying most corporate hierarchies in business, the military, and tribal life where one boss or chief governs by consensus in partnership with the qualified elite and the broad body of people.

Is it possible to believe that those favoring mixed and hierarchical regimes are right and that advocates of pure republicanism or democracy are wrong about the best form of government?

It is not only possible but also paramount to hold this view, even if it seems politically incorrect in the present age. This author is convinced that the time will come when it will be successfully implemented.

Wherever work is considered as universal duty and the meaning of life itself, individuals will differ not in wealth but in accomplishment. Their local professional associations will be arranged according to the relative importance of each occupation to the society as a whole. There will be a representative hierarchy, capped by the state council, with mandates at all levels to be revocable at any time. There will be neither organized political parties nor career party leaders nor periodic elections. Just as an aircraft needs a trained pilot to fly it, a proper state needs the state council led by the head of state (or governor).

III. National-Conservative Ideology

The Western renewal appeals for national conservatism, the aiming to the preservation of the nations' political sovereignty and their right to self-determination. The Western renewal also promotes the principle of individual responsibility and is skeptical of the uncontrolled expansion of governmental services or military involvement abroad. It stands for strictly controlled government spending on social welfare and education.

Western nations are just that: various nations—and the great mission of the West must be to unite and bind them into civilization. The civilizational identity must be based on the preservation of Western cultural identity, which must be carried not only by ethnic Germans, English, Italians, or Spaniards but also by all carriers of this identity regardless of nationality. This cultural code must prevail; it needs to be nourished, strengthened, and protected. This *weltanschauung*, or the whole world-view of the Western renewal, must include and be based on the following principles:

Man, a fallen, incomplete creature, must recognize his limits, for he is fallible.

Each person is unique, one of a kind, and irreplaceable. This uniqueness also means diversity, differentness, and distinctness. We are all different from each other as a result of our sex, age, talent, wisdom, and experience. We all have similarly diverse characteristics but also in various proportion and degree; adverbial equality does not mean real sameness.

Humans are social beings whose reasoning and enjoyment of the diversity of nature differentiate them from animals.

To overcome the Western moral crisis, people need to return to the endless moral values of love, freedom, conscience, family, homeland, and nation. Only these values can assure safety, security, and the corresponding feelings of belonging, fulfillment, and happiness.

The one thing learned from both the 2016 US presidential election and the EU (Brexit) referendum in the United Kingdom is the fact that modern politics have nothing to do with lofty principles, such as truth, integrity, or freedom, and everything to do with fearmongering of the most pernicious kind.

The trouble, of course, was that the voters had seen only the headlines—the endless and gloomy TV analyses explaining that if they failed to vote to keep their chains in place as obedient slaves of the US elite and EU tyranny, the world would fall on their heads.

That, at least, was the original game plan. How shocking it was for all concerned when the British and American voters ignored the threats and the doomsday predictions, which had been dropped like journalistic bombs on a regular basis throughout the whole referendum and election campaigns. How shocking it is that, in this meretricious age, people can vote for their political freedom in spite of the threats of penury if they do so.

This author was as shocked as the globalist elite by this unexpected and defiant resistance on the part of the British and American populace. He had fully expected shameful capitulation in the face of the bullying. He had fully expected both the British and the American people to weep their way to full compliance with the will of their tyrannical masters, going to the polls with their tails between their legs.

He has never been so pleased to be proved wrong.

The world woke up to a changed Europe on the morning of June 24, 2016. The United Kingdom voted to leave the European Union with the so-called Brexit referendum, and the EU lost one of its most valuable and influential member nations.

On the morning of November 9, 2016, the world awoke to a changed United States of America. With the presidential election, the American people voted to leave the old system, and as such, the American elite lost their hitherto unchallenged monopolistic status.

Because globalization challenges the traditions, customs, religions, and even the languages of local cultures, its methods tend to be resisted with the unintended adverse results of both political action and countercultural situation. Against threats to localized identity markers, people assert their religiosity, kinship, and national symbols as mechanisms of resistance against globalizing dynamics.

Few nations exemplify this connection between a resurgent nationalism and a revived conservatism as the Russian Federation. There has been a self-conscious distancing from globalism by Russia, drawing inspiration instead from the ideals of a neo-Byzantium, which involves a considerable admixture of Orthodoxy, ethnic mysticism, and Slavophile tendencies that have deep resonance in Russian history. Moreover, with this national revival comes a reembracing of traditional moral values.

Indeed, the current rise of national conservatism throughout Europe and the West will continue. This resurgence is not a temporary political fad, since globalization necessitates its own futility. As was found with the attempt to bring liberal democracy to the Middle East, few are willing to die for emancipatory politics, feminism or LGBTQ (lesbian, gay, bisexual, transgender, and queer) rights, but the willingness to die for LNCLR (land, nation, custom, language, and religion) is seemingly universal. Though a formidable challenger, globalization appears to have no chance of overcoming such innate fidelities.

Both the Brexit referendum and the US election not only signify the rise of national conservatism in the West but also suggest the inexorable revival of traditional values and norms. Although there are many current cultural peculiarities and paradoxes indicative of stubborn secularism and left-liberal socialism throughout the West, we can expect social and cultural trends to resolve such inconsistencies in favor of traditional beliefs and practices in the end.

IV. Building on the Principle of Subsidiarity

This author's reasons for favoring nations and nationhood are based on the principle of subsidiarity, which holds that political and social problems can be resolved best and most justly when dealt with at the most immediate level suitable for their solution. In practical terms, this means that many political and social problems currently being addressed by supranational organizations on international levels could and should be dealt with by newly empowered or reempowered national, local, and regional governments. Subsidiarity is, therefore, consonant with localism and the decentralization of political power.

"It has become fashionable in recent times to talk of the leveling of nations, and of various peoples disappearing into the melting pot of contemporary civilization. I disagree with this, but that is another matter; all that should be said here is that the disappearance of whole nations would impoverish us no less than if all the people were to become identical, with the same character and the same face. Nations are the wealth of humanity, its generalized personality. The least among them has its own special colors, and harbors within itself a special aspect of God's design."

Aleksandr Solzhenitsyn's above-quoted words, delivered in his Nobel Prize acceptance speech in 1972, tell us that we are to be good multiculturalists in the international sense, which is the complete opposite of the kind of multiculturalism that the globalists are seeking to force on us. For that reason, we are accustomed to the false multiculturalism of the globalists and not to the correct multiculturalism of the subsidiarists, such as Solzhenitsyn. His words explain that true multiculturalism is good—in the form of a plurality of thriving national cultures. The problem is that the model of multiculturalism sold to us by the globalists is not multiculturalism at all.

The globalist variety of multiculturalism does not want a multiplicity of diverse *national* cultures at all. It wants a melting pot, in which all cultures blend into one global culture in which everyone wears the same global brands of clothing, shops at the same global chain stores, watches the same global movies and TV programs, plays the same global games, and listens to the same global music. What the globalists want, in fact, is not any real form of multiculturalism but a global monoculture of standardized people reduced to being mere consumers of the bread and circuses that the global plutocracy provides for them. This mad and manic monoculture is what the globalists call "multiculturalism."

By contrast, the subsidiarist view of multiculturalism, as envisaged by Solzhenitsyn and those of similar ilk, calls for the thriving of independent national, regional, and local cultures. It calls for a Europe of the nations and not the European Union. It seeks a patchwork-quilt cultural landscape in which local customs and cuisines flourish and are not mown down by the globalist insistence on standardization by a low standard in which the global brand is invariably bland.

The globalists seek temporary multiculturalism only as a means to a global monoculture. Theirs is false and sinister multiculturalism designed to destroy the authentic multiplicity of cultures, which have grown naturally from the soil and soul of their peoples. The globalist form of multiculturalism is cultural imperialism in which a global plutocracy imposes its will on the people and poisons the roots of all cultures it comes into contact with. Such willful destruction of the cultural environment can be called many things, but it is Orwellian newspeak and doublethink to have the temerity to call it "multiculturalism."

Similarly, one should not lose sight of the fact that the way political referenda are manipulated by Big Brother (big business and big government) ensures that the results reflect the big-is-best agenda. It is evident in the numerous referenda controlled and finessed by the European Union, the big political parties, and international business interests.

Whenever opinion polls show that the majority of those polled is opposed to issues supported by the Western elite, the respective ruling parties, government agencies, opinion-makers, and propaganda arms of international organizations start persuading voters—financed, of course, by taxpayers' money—that they are wrong to oppose the elite.

Big government is always joined by big business in the campaign to influence Western public opinion. Big business continues to support big government in Brussels and Washington, DC. This unholy alliance is enhanced still further by the power of the media, with every single major newspaper coming out in support of the Western elite. The public is bombarded with a one-sided view of the issues during the referendum, with much more money usually spent on proelite propaganda compared with that of the antielite campaign. Eclipsed and outmaneuvered by the sheer financial power of the alliance of big business, big government and big media, the arguments of the antielite campaign, usually supporting the country's economy and its political freedom, are both unheard and unheeded. Allayed into passively accepting the claims of those who are making the most noise, the befuddled electorate duly ratifies the program of the elite. This ludicrous process already has a disastrous history behind it.

Nevertheless, the same pattern emerges every time: after an opinion poll shows that those intending to vote against the wishes of the elite are in the majority, the hydra-headed power of big business, big government, and big media are immediately unleashed again. Big business threatens with big moves if the projected majority wins; big government flexes its political muscle to warn of the dire consequences, and the media presents an overwhelmingly biased perspective of the arguments. Faced with this juggernaut of manipulation, the "reasonable" voters change their minds at the last moment and vote for the "reasonable proposals" of their rulers.

Were there any proposed referendum or initiative announced by the representatives of the people against some unilateral decision on the part of the ruling elite, this would immediately be declared as antidemocratic. Stating that a constitution or some basic law makes it illegal for one part of the electorate to unilaterally make decisions that affect the whole, a court or other governmental organization will dismiss the notion that the proposed referendum is legal. "We can't allow the will of the few to deprive everyone else of their rights."

Such reasoning is not only dangerous but also profoundly antisubsidiarist. Multinational bodies, such as the European Union, could, for instance, use it to declare that all referenda held by individual member states to decide on continued membership of the EU or independence from it are antidemocratic. According to this reasoning, such polls allow the will of the few (for example, the British or the French) to deprive everyone else (the people of the European Union) of their rights. This reasoning is the antithesis of subsidiarity, which holds that political and social problems are best managed at the most immediate level.

A just solution to the problems caused by the globalization, centralization, and uniformization of our age is the empowerment of local and regional governments and the devolution of power away from a Machiavellian and macro-level-oriented central state.

V. Real Social Market Economy Based on Incentives

Economics is a utilitarian and materialistic study today. It is concerned with maximizing profit, with describing the actions of man as an economic being, and with explaining the allegedly inevitable results of supposed economic laws.

The Western renewer must practice a political economy that is concerned with human well-being. The Western renewer does not assume that man is to be understood wholly or chiefly as an economic being. He does not believe that abstract laws entirely determine the economic conditions people face; instead they are the result of human decisions—some of them the product of corrupt politics.

Contrary to Marxists and the kinds of capitalists they decried, the Western renewer does not believe that material conditions control the thoughts of man; instead, he believes that the human mind creates material conditions. The Western renewer does not think that maximum wealth is the proper goal of productive work. There are such things to be considered as widespread and comfortable prosperity and stewardship instead of maximum exploitation of bountiful nature. People must eat, but they do not live by bread alone. Economics, being the product of human acts and decisions, is part of the moral realm and not merely technical knowledge.

Most of all, the Western renewal's political economy insists that the health of society is *not* represented by great wealth but by widespread ownership of real and tangible physical property. Without the broad ownership of all such property, which makes the vast mass of people free and independent citizens, there could be no healthy society and indeed no free society.

Still, the West has installed and is devoted today to an advanced (or rather distorted and manipulated) form of capitalism, by which is meant not free enterprise but private profit subsidized by the government.

The Western renewal's conception of the good society must become the central pillar of opposition to big business. In the modern pseudocapitalistic Western world, nobody can think of anything except government bailout. The Western renewer must not allow such an atrocity; nor must he approve of such trade bills like TPP (Trans-Pacific Partnership), TTIP (Transatlantic Trade and Investment Partnership), or CETA (Comprehensive Economic and Trade Agreement). The secret contents and false promises of these trade bills are being promoted with all the tricks in the inventory of big business against the will of the people and will accelerate the destruction of small business enterprises and the dispossession of workers in the West.

Who owns America today? Both liberals and socialists take for granted the enormous concentration of power over the economy by a few gigantic corporations and argue over details; in fact, there is little difference between them. Both are for preserving a system in which the masses of the people are wage earners at the mercy of owners.

The above is the wrong kind of society. The United States began as, and for a time continued to be, a society of independent citizens having widespread property ownership. "Private property and free enterprise are good things, and we are all for them," says the Western renewer. He rejects socialism, but he also questions the current domination of America and the West by corporate capitalism. A rich country is not synonymous with happy people. Also, a rich government is not the same thing as a prosperous people.

If we ask today who owns America, here is what we get: the wealthiest 3 percent of families own 54 percent of the national wealth. The wealthiest 10 percent of households own 75 percent of the national wealth.[498] Most of the rest own nothing except mortgages perhaps; the people are at the mercy of large institutions. We are not the independent citizens that would be necessary for a free, healthy, and happy society. In fact, the inequalities of wealth are worse today than they were in 1936 and have been steadily increasing since the 1970s.

The large corporations in effect own the country and the politicians; they are the owners of the West today.

What is a corporation? It is a legal person except, unlike a person, it is immortal and cannot feel pain or guilt. Also, like a real person, it is said to have rights that may not be interfered with.

An individual owns stock in a corporation. What does that ownership mean? He holds a right to dividends if there are any and may sell his stock with a gain or loss. He is hardly liable for the corporation's debts personally, which is a significant advantage to all those participating in the company. Contrary to a farm or a family business, the corporate stockholder has no functional responsibility at all for what the corporation does, and most importantly, he has no moral responsibility for turning out a good product either to society or the workers.

The corporation is in the power only of a few men. This fact is true whether these are business executives of the capitalist order, the expert economic planners of socialism, or the party officials of communism. In each case, the happiness or satisfaction of the people is dependent upon unknown forces over which they have almost no control. Unlike a society with widespread ownership of productive property, this is not a healthy or free society.

The liberals yell about threats to free enterprise and the evil effects of interference with the law of supply and demand. The trouble is, big business has never practiced free enterprise; it is too powerful to tolerate competition. Big business *controls* rather than *participates* in the free market.

During the Great Depression, prices of farm products declined by over 30 percent—but the prices of steel and automobiles did not fall at all. If the law of supply and demand is correct, prices should have dropped with falling demand; consequently, something had to interfere with the free market.[499] What happened was that the large corporations reacted to declining demand by reducing wages, firing workers, and cutting production rather than lowering prices, which would have been the economically sound and socially useful thing to do. They preserved their profits because government tariffs excluded foreign competition and their size assured their ability to suppress any potential domestic competition. The New Deal–offered real solution was to flood the economy with cheap money to increase demand, which might help unemployment but would also keep profits up. So much for free enterprise.

Furthermore, the giant corporations exist not solely because concentration is an inevitable result of the law of economics. Entrepreneurs and managers do not control industry; *bankers* control it. Wealth is made up of entries on banks' books and securities that are incredibly manipulable for private profit.

John D. Rockefeller controlled Standard Oil, which commanded a large part of the US market. It was not the socialists who hated the fabulously wealthy Rockefeller; they were glad to see the concentration of industry he had brought about, which he claimed was a socially beneficial thing. It was a perfect move toward their socialist goals; unlike widely dispersed property, it would be easy for the government to take over. No, it was not the socialists but the *entrepreneurs* who hated Rockefeller—the men who used their knowledge and risked their money to get the oil out of the ground. They found that the Rockefeller capital had bought refineries, rigged railroad rates, bribed state legislatures, and obtained and held in check new patents that would have lowered production costs for small producers. The real makers of wealth were not able to sell their product except on Rockefeller's terms, which usually meant turning over control.[500]

The power of the banks, similarly to other nebulous establishments, is almost never questioned in public discussion. Now that is real power—when you can prevent yourself from even being mentioned, as some other inconspicuous organizations and special-interest groups can. Moreover, when somebody does bring up the subject at all, he is immediately branded a loony conspiracy theorist.

Incidentally, is a large company necessarily more efficient than many small enterprises spread through the countryside? No, there are giant corporations not because they are competent but because that is what the bankers want. It makes their control easier and firmer, and it will fortuitously also cloud transparency. It is no wonder that the same establishments support globalization, centralization, and supranational organizations.

The Western renewer does not want to do away with private property; he wants to see policies that will spread it around—that will curb the power of large corporations and multiply the number of people who have enough property to make an independent living. The Western renewer not only wants to see a genuinely free market but also wants to see the West become free.

This author realizes that the above program is too charitable and sounds too idealistic, too lacking of money to buy politicians and media, and too unattractive and unprofitable to the vast herd of petty intellectuals who dominate the Western discourse. It could not succeed before, and the West has gone on its current way.

The conflicting ideas of the good society that compose the economic concept of the Western renewal need to be understood. On the one hand, humans are flawed, imperfect creatures; and as a consequence, they need to be governed by their betters. Conversely, a government must be strong and active to protect the country and promote its welfare.

So then, from where do these angels, these superior creatures who have the right to govern others, come?

A new wage-enhancement system should be introduced that directs national state (federal) money toward *supplementing* the income of only those people who work in qualifying low-income jobs, meaning a real increase in their—and *only* their—minimum-wage limit.

The idea of wage subsidies accepts the Left's proposition that the problem is purely a monetary (economic) one; giving poor people more money merely to make them feel more comfortable in their poverty is the solution. That is the opposite of a safety net, which, if properly designed, offers peace of mind to the most vulnerable in the event of a total disaster.

Mass society and the proletarianization of the middle class are central to the twenty-first-century crisis. The Western political elite, with its globalization and distorted capitalism, has created the dispossession of the middle class but cannot dispose of the proletarians and the social catastrophe that comes with them. The controlling elite has made interest-group politics possible, and liberal democracy had long allowed vested interests to flourish unchecked.

As has often occurred in history, the apparent antidote should be widespread ownership of productive assets—deproletarianization by gaining possession of profit-producing properties. Wherever possible, the realm of self-provision outside the market should be expanded, and competition enforced.

However, the state and the economy cannot be entirely separated.

Special-interest-group liberalism is damaging diversity; it does not limit the power of the state but tries to use it for its own purposes and make it subservient to those purposes.

There should be strict legal limits on the unchecked concentration of capital; preferably, only expansion through organic growth should be encouraged. "Organic growth" refers to business expansion by increased output, new product development, or customer-base expansion, as opposed to mergers and acquisitions.

For centuries, manufacturers, artisans, builders, and owners were proud of the quality and durability of their products, but today in the West we see a numbing sequence of new and flashy but cheap and dubious models while the sound notion of repair is disappearing. Items that are just barely damaged must be discarded and replaced by new ones—an act inimical to the human sense of self-limitation.

To this one must add the psychological plague of inflation: as labor productivity increases, prices do not fall; they rise. It is not progress but an all-consuming economic fire.

For economies with the size and wealth of those of the United States, China, the European Union, India, Russia, or Brazil, it is possible to manage with the domestic market alone for a considerable time. Those large economies can develop and nourish the local, native industries and markets (just as happened in the past) without exposing them to the harmful effects of international financial markets and international trade. It is not advocating protectionism or autarchy but recognizing, acknowledging, and reversing the destructive forces inherent in globalization and antisubsidiarity.

To restore the economy requires that offshoring be reversed and the jobs be brought back, say, to the United States; changing the way corporations are taxed would undoubtedly help to do this. The tax rate on corporate profit should be determined by the geographic location where businesses add value to the products they market in the United States. If the goods and services are produced offshore, the tax rate should be high. If the goods and services are produced domestically, the tax rate should be low. The tax rates must be set to offset the lower costs of producing abroad. The lobbying power of transnational corporations, supranational institutions, and Wall Street must be broken.

Following the Civil War, and over the final decades of the nineteenth century, real GDP and employment doubled in the United States. Thanks to the marked improvement in productivity, annual average real earnings rose by over 60 percent, and wholesale prices fell by 75 percent during the same period.[501]

What is the difference between that age and ours? One of the main differences concerning the economy is that an income tax rate of 35 percent on individuals and corporations did not exist in the United States then.

Admittedly, today's world is a lot different from that of the nineteenth century. The populations of the Western countries demand at least a limited welfare state, limited working hours, assured security, and affordable education, to mention a few benefits, all of which cost much money. The state would not be able to fulfill these expectations without any individual and corporate taxation.

A corporate (and individual) tax avoidance strategy is to move overseas to a corporate tax haven like Bermuda or Switzerland. As an example, by reincorporating offshore, companies avoid paying federal income taxes on profits earned outside the United States.

The Western renewer, realizing the above, must demand a new tax policy based entirely on incentives. These incentives must take into account whether the particular expenditure draws money *from* the state (that expenditure will have to be more highly taxed) or will reduce the demand for current or future financial assistance by the state.

There is no point in getting into a discussion about what constitutes consumer goods or luxury items, or whether these should be taxed progressively or not. Anyone can start an argument about whether an expensive luxury yacht or a private jet aircraft should be considered a necessary consumer good or not, or whether the design and manufacturing of this high-tech equipment would require capital investment, create highly paid jobs, and help the economy. These are legitimate questions, of course, but as examples, they are extreme cases deliberately chosen and not the typical or ubiquitous problems occurring across the national economy on a daily basis.

The more typical cases requiring due consideration would be individual savings plans for medical expenses, individual retirement savings plans, and savings plans for education. Even the issue of setting up new savings plans for people investing in various public infrastructure projects must be considered, as should companies investing in design, development, infrastructure, or the education of their employees. These are some of the fields that require state or public funds one way or another;

if they could be financed with more private instead of public funds, the burden on the state would *decrease*, and public participation and support would significantly *increase*.

In other words, private financing of the welfare state should be and must be encouraged. It is the only way the eventual bankruptcy of the state can be avoided and the national debt can be reduced.

Let us take a look at the economies of the United States and Germany. How could Germany, even though it is based on a topsy-turvy reversed social market economy, support a socialist welfare state with all its funds-draining programs and still have a booming economy for the last sixty years—at least compared to the United States?

The answer is, the way this author sees it, the smart, intelligent, consistently flexible, and far-reaching German tax policy—a tax structure that, in spite of the high tax rate by US standards, is considered fair by most Germans. The German tax system not only encourages burden-sharing but is also synchronized with the country's economic, financial, monetary, and social policy. It is like a finely tuned machine—a system that is hard to reproduce (see not only the United States but practically all the other European states).

What the German system seems to say is that we can turn globalization to our advantage only if we save and strengthen our *national* economy; it is a zero-sum game. So much for globalization's "advantages."

VI. Foreign Policy Based on National Interest, Sovereignty, and Self-Determination

The Western renewal encourages the involvement of the nation-state in intergovernmental and supranational organizations but strictly on the principle of national sovereignty and self-determination. The Western renewal prefers strict neutrality of the nation-state and the preservation of a national army as the institution responsible for national defense. The military shall remain a militia force and should never become involved in interventions abroad.

After the First World War, Poland, freshly emerging from the collapsed Russian Empire, and Czechoslovakia, resulting from the collapse of the Austro-Hungarian

Empire, both made the catastrophic decisions to trust British and French war guarantees, which lost them their freedom. They did not understand that the only means of gaining and preserving independence were not pieces of paper but military victory. Mustafa Kemal Atatürk did not make the same mistake—and was able to save Turkish sovereignty. After World War I, Poland became a nation-state because of its superior army; then Poland lost its nation-state status because of its inferior army in World War II.

One cannot help noticing the continuation among segments of the Eastern European liberal elite of a tendency to think in British or American (which is to say foreign) terms because of their attachment to London and Washington, rather than thinking in, let's say, Polish or Romanian terms. One can also note the skepticism of the vast majority of Czechs, Croats or Bulgarians toward the enthusiasts of American or Russian benevolence and the lack of a strictly home-oriented national political elite. Eastern Europe always repeated a simple error during the twentieth century: rather than following the Latin maxim of "do ut des" ("I give that you might give"), expressing reciprocity of exchange, the politics of the various Eastern European nations *relied*, for the preservation of their respective statehood, on other countries.

During the Cold War, American and British rhetoric regarding Iron Curtains and anticommunism were just that—rhetoric. In fact, the United States and its Western allies silently conceded the total elimination of all remnants of anticommunism in Eastern Europe during the 1950s, and the Soviet Union acknowledged the neutralization of communist forces in the West. Where any internal conflict raised the prospect of tactical gains, as in the case of Greece, Hungary, Cuba, or Vietnam, the superpowers engaged in the sort of proxy or limited wars that would characterize the Cold War.[502] The explanation for this strategy was the nuclear age, which necessitated the consolidation of imperial spoils of war by the world's two superpowers and ideological antagonists. Both anticommunist rhetoric in the West and anticapitalist rhetoric in the East served domestic ends of the consolidation of political power; one can compare the Stalinist show trials in Eastern Europe to McCarthyism in the United States. The United States occupied Western Europe, and the Soviet Union occupied Eastern Europe; Europe became a pawn of the ideological successors of the Enlightenment, both of which were exponents of revolutionary universalist doctrines running roughshod over the old, traditional European modes and orders of the Continent.

Cold War America's democratic pretensions can be considered to be an extension of the nineteenth-century policy of Manifest Destiny, albeit carried from the New Continent onto the Old, with deleterious effect.[503] This view is only incomprehensible to those who maintain that Nazi Germany was a totalitarian enemy of liberal democracy. However, Adolf Hitler was the child, the direct descendant, the final result, and the answer to the alien liberal democratic modes and orders forced on Germany at Versailles. A man like Hitler, who was the embodiment of socialist populism, would never have come to hold political power in the (imperial) Germany of the House of Hohenzollern. At worst, Germany might have come under the sway of a man like Ludendorff, but never Hitler—and not without the leveling tendencies presented by Anglo-American democracy and thrust upon the German nation with age-old traditions of military honor and aristocratic hierarchy.[504]

American liberal democratic values in Europe were an equally foreign body, just as European socialism and liberalism were in Russia—or in the United States.

European identity is rooted in Christianity and its secular alter ego, socialism, and is antithetical to liberal democratic traditions. The only sort of universalism that is manifested in the various cultures of Europe's nations is Christian Universalism. The content of national patriotism could be judged as more or less ethical by its approximation of Christian ethos. At the core of this ethos is the notion that human institutions are inherently fallen; that government cannot be absolute; that man, be he the ruler or ruled, is always under the obligation to God; and that no social institution will ever prevail if it wants to change rather than temper human nature.

The West is in a blind alley today, and it will not succeed in getting out soon. For what has always distinguished the liberals, as it does the left-liberal internationalists today, is their breezy optimism that experiments, adventures, and wars will end well and make everything better.

Russia has withdrawn its military from all the lands occupied during World War II and permitted the peaceful secession of components of the Soviet Union. Russia has recovered, thereby, its national identity and made possible the application of statecraft to the issues of the nation rather than to the problems of managing an international imperial order. It has abolished the Soviet Union and ultimately acquiesced to NATO membership for the Eastern European satellite states and the Baltic States.

Nevertheless, real Russian liberality would be possible only under the condition of a free, friendly, and secure Eastern Europe guaranteeing Russian safety from Western designs on its security and national identity.

Regrettably, the condition of a free, independent, and secure Eastern Europe has not come to pass. Eastern Europe is not free, and therefore it is not safe. Eastern Europe is not free because it slowly, consistently traded away the sovereignty it had won from Moscow to the European Union and NATO in exchange for Keynesian economic stimulus, lucrative posts for its political elite in Brussels, and security guarantees from the United States. These guarantees, even if they were ever to be honored, would be fulfilled under the full control and in the sole interest of the West and could not prevent the destruction of Eastern Europe in any large-scale war.

Eastern Europe's economy, which grew at 5 to 10 percent per annum following the Velvet Revolutions but before joining the European Union, has now slowed to a growth rate of 1 to 3 percent per annum. Millions of Eastern Europeans, tired of waiting for their political elite to create conditions for growth, have fled to the West.

Rather than doing the strenuous work of building a strong and free Eastern Europe, its political elite was immediately seduced to a quick and easy path to apparent prosperity and security within the European Union. However, with each passing year of EU membership, the economic growth of the Eastern European countries has slowed as they have been compelled to take up liberal socialism.

Meanwhile, the effectiveness of the Eastern European political class at retaining power through artful public relations has also grown. Western liberal democratic methods of political discourse and liberal democratic standards of education have slowly transformed the political dialogue in Eastern Europe from an amateur but elevated discussion into a mirror image of the ignorant, childish partisanship of the Western "tabloid democracies."

The onetime Russian interior minister Pyotr Nikolaevich Durnovo wrote a historic memorandum to Czar Nicholas II in February 1914, warning of the dire consequences that would result if Russia continued to ally itself with France against Germany and went on to war with the latter.[505] Durnovo saw it correctly: the central fact in European politics was the struggle between Germany and England for European dominance and geopolitical security, the epitome of the interwoven family ties based on sentiment. This conflict was bound eventually to produce war, which would not be confined to those two nations.

As Durnovo correctly pointed out, the vital interests of Russia and Germany did *not* conflict. A foreign policy based on national interest (raison d'etat) rather than sentiment would have aligned Russia with Germany and so could have prevented the war that eventually destroyed both countries.[506]

Just as the price of the Russian and Soviet Empires was the subjugation of Russian national interest rightly understood, with the periodic utilization of Russian nationalism for imperial ends, so too the price of the American Empire is the systematic impoverishment of the American people. The American imperial government is so busy trying to manage its provinces that it fails to serve its own citizens. Just as the Russian and Soviet Empires introduced foreign elements into the Russian body politic, which paradoxically led to politically paralyzing interethnic strife in the Soviet sphere, so have American imperialism, and its European marionettes now introduced tens of millions of foreign elements into the American and European body politic. There are nations within a nation that cannot and will not be assimilated but forever change the political character of the West and demographically erase the possibility of restoration, say, of American constitutional republicanism—the defining characteristic of the American nation.

Instead of antagonizing Russia to punish Vladimir Putin for standing up for Russian traditions, values, and interests, and for supporting law and order in Syria, perhaps the politicians of America and Europe should undertake the real work made necessary at home by the crises of our times. These officeholders should apply themselves, for example, to the restoration of limited constitutional republicanism in the United States and the establishment of a free, independent, and healthy Eastern Europe. They should do all that instead of failing to see that law and order is preferable to the multiplication of Islamic fundamentalist strongholds, instead of setting the Middle East aflame and triggering mass Islamic migration into Western Europe, and instead of provoking a constitutional nightmare in Ukraine by creating chaos and supporting extremists.

The citizens of the West will have to make up their minds very soon which of these views to trust and then live with the consequences.

Thus, in the waning days of Western unilateralism, American "unipolarism," German arrogance, and European federalism, the diplomacy of the West sinks into a mode of semiautism, able to perceive and express its own interests, perceptions, and desires, while oblivious to the concerns of others.

The Western renewal therefore refuses to subjugate national interest to ideological sentiment. Realism is often denounced as immoral, as if the crude pursuit of national interest inevitably produces terrible results. However, a foreign policy based on rational calculations of national importance is likely to alleviate hasty adventures and produce more ethically desirable outcomes than one based on ideological moralizing.

VII. Leadership Principles Based on Proven Merit, Not on Electioneering

The West needs political leaders who, even if they hold a weak hand at a critical moment in history, through guts and determination, knowledge and perseverance, can still manage to win. The West needs leaders with the courage to practice long-term thinking, future planning, and the making of courageous, bold, anticipatory decisions at the right time, when problems have become perceptible but before they reach crisis proportions.

Great leaders, political and business leaders alike are born, and political science, just like management science, is more of an art than science. Calling a discipline a science gives it more perceived legitimacy and creates the false feeling that by studying its structure one can learn to be a manager or a business or political leader. Just as with music, one can study it and practice long hours playing an instrument, but all that does not automatically make one a great musician or a great performer. That requires more—a lot more—and this extra ability cannot be acquired solely by studying the technique. Whether this extra ability is present or not should be judged by the musician's accomplishments—and this should be the same evaluation with political leaders too.

Even purely theoretical work, which cannot be measured by a definite rule and is preliminary to all subsequent technical discoveries, is exclusively the product of the individual brain. The broad masses do not invent; nor does the majority organize or think—but always and in every case does the individual, the person. Thus, the leadership principle is not based on the idea of the *majority*, but on that of *character*.

The leadership principle may be imposed in a top-down way on an organized political community. However, this principle can become a living reality only by passing through the stages that are necessary for its evolution. These steps lead from the smallest cell of the state organism upward and require a body of people who have passed through a selection process lasting over several years and been tempered by the hard realities of life.

A healthy political system does not need any deceitful electioneering in the way democracy does. Issues can be settled by (at least advisory) referenda; leaders should rise gradually higher in the organizations by virtue of character, competency, and efficiency as demonstrated by their track records.

Democracy totters from one election to the next with flexible agendas. The intervals between the replacements of one person by another have gradually become shorter, finally ending up in a wild relay chase. With each change, the quality of the statesman in question deteriorates until finally only the petty type of political huckster remains. In such people, the merits of statesmanship are measured and valued according to the adroitness with which they either cobble together one coalition after another or reach compromises successively. In other words, their talent lies in their craftiness in manipulating the pettiest political transactions.

There is a better chance of seeing a camel pass through the eye of a needle than of seeing a leader discovered through a democratic election; this is a political system that, far from co-opting the best of its citizens, alienates them profoundly while promoting the most immoral and corrupt ones into the positions of power.

The leaders of the state must be developed naturally—without any democratic hypocrisy. Democracy may well mean perfect equality of opportunity, whereby every person shall have equal chance to make himself or herself fit for the tasks he or she suited. Nevertheless, democracy does *not* assure that *only* those who have proved their talent, vigor, and character, and have emerged from all tests with the insignia of skill, shall be eligible to lead.

In a healthy political system, public officials shall be chosen not by votes or by secret cliques pulling the unseen wires of democratic pretense, but by their ability as demonstrated and proven in an equal race. Nor shall any person hold office without specific training or hold high office until filling a lower office first.

Is this aristocracy? One must not be afraid of the word if the reality it betokens is good. We want to be led by the best. Regrettably, we have come to think of aristocracies as hereditary; it should not be that kind; one should instead call it a "judicious aristocracy"—an aristocracy based on merit.

Rather than blindly electing the lesser of two evils presented to them as candidates by the ruling elite, the people themselves will be here the candidates. There is no caste here, no inheritance of position of privilege, no stoppage of talent born penniless. Career will be open to talent wherever it is born.

VIII. Supporting Forgiveness, Distinction, Achievement, and Aspiration

Since most people, in general, need managing, political philosophy needs to reflect on what it is of human nature that creates this need to be chaperoned. There are certain aspects of the human condition people are reluctant to think about. They are all averse to think about things that they know not to be agreeable to themselves and others. Moreover, there are also general features of the human condition we find difficult to think about.

The first such aspect is envy and resentment. People feel resentment toward the goods, the status, and the talents of others, and this is normal. Nietzsche thought that ressentiment was the default position of human communities. He argued it is resentment that makes the world go round and is why the world is so awful. One of the things we resent in others is that they are doing better than we are; that resentment is going to be always there—especially when we are in close competition for something we want, such as a job, lover, social position or status, and we see the other person getting it. We cannot control what we feel.[507]

There is another side of humans that needs managing, however, and it is the desire for orthodoxy—the desire to conform. John Stuart Mill believed that orthodoxy, rather than freedom of opinion, is the default position for human societies.[508] He felt that conformity prevails and we take refuge in it; we recognize that if we repeat what everybody else says, even if we do not find it to be true, we are safe, secure and not going to be attacked. To stand out, however, and say the thing that is disapproved of, even if it is quite obvious, requires courageous character.

A third feature of the human condition, which has been much emphasized by the French philosopher, critic, and anthropologist René Girard, is that humans have an inbuilt need for scapegoating, for persecuting the heretic, for finding the fall guy.[509] If society is in an awkward position or people are faced with some real or perceived threat, it helps, in order to protect oneself, to find a person to blame.

It does not matter that he is not actually to blame; people all unite against him and feel good about it. They believe the trouble has been found, and they are getting rid of it. If one looks back over history, it becomes apparent that scapegoating, the disguise of self-protection, is indeed one of the critical features of human society.

All three of the above elements point to the fact that forgiveness is hard to convey to both human communities and individuals. It is hard to forgive people for being better than oneself, to forgive people for standing out with an opinion of their own (especially if they are right), and to forgive people for being heretics. Penitence is very rare; people do not often confess to their faults; nor do they undergo any repentance in order to atone for them or make amends.

Nevertheless, forgiveness is essential and fundamental to healthy social order. People can get along with each other in a sound, robust, and thriving society only if they are willing to forgive others' faults and to confess to their own shortcomings.

In light of the above statements, it becomes apparent why it is somewhat difficult, sometimes inconvenient or embarrassing if not outright dangerous, to be or to aim to be a member of the elite. In modern Western liberal democratic society, it has become a relatively common thing even to apologize for it. By apologizing, one spontaneously feels guilty and takes the blame for everything that is considered to be wrong in order to have a kind of preemptive, peaceful relation. Although apology has become a sort of quiet exit from the ghastliness of human society, it does not, of course, solve all problems—just the contrary.

Curiously, members of the hypocritical modern elite, who are only too eager to relinquish their responsibility to society, usually choose philanthropy instead of apologizing for their wrongdoings.

The consequence of this preemptive, detached, disingenuous, and withdrawing behavior of the Western elite is a kind of pretentious clamor for equality—and this is apparently the case, especially in a democratic society. In every sphere today, there is a desire to equalize. People do not like hierarchies and privileges, and there is a natural disposition to say that they are not deserved.

When anybody claims some hierarchical status, the question is raised immediately, "Who does he think he is? By what right does he claim superiority over me?" Hierarchical organizations, therefore, such as the Catholic Church, monarchies, the military—anything with a chain-of-command structure—are frequently attacked as anachronisms. People say, "Perhaps that was all right in the Middle Ages, but we cannot have things like that today; they are inherently incompatible with the kind of society that has evolved since."

People are loath to accept the idea that there is an authority handed down from above, embodied in the individual and the office of the pope, king, president, or CEO and filtering down through all the bishoprics, political bodies, government organizations, and corporate governance to the ordinary person. In opposition to that idea, we have the evangelical churches saying that the Holy Spirit visits us all equally, and elections and corporate rules pretending to bring everything up from below. Alas, what a beautifully democratic idea, and how hypocritical again, based on the upside-down reversed social market economy's deceptively mandating top-down rule.

Then again, wealth, privilege, culture, and intellect are all targets of resentment in our society because it is hard to take pleasure in assets that you do not share. To take pleasure in somebody else's good fortune is a rare thing and involves a work of forgiveness: you have to forgive that person for being better than you, for getting the girl that you wanted, and on and on. Forgiveness is very rare but essential.

Because of the legacy of resentment, because forgiveness is rare, and whenever people feel judged by someone else's success, there is a desire to bring down the mighty and make any distinction either nonexistent or worthless. There is a motive for the alienated to gang up to dispossess the beneficiaries in human society. One sees this happening in the political arena too; the majority will vote to divest the successful because they believe that wealth does not belong to those people who have got it. Instead, the thinking goes, wealth is a social asset, and it should be distributed more equitably. Moreover, they think, we can distribute it more equitably through the state. We can tax the rich and spread the wealth among the rest of us.

Many political philosophers justify this, claiming that wealth is a social asset and is not even owned until it is distributed. Not only that, but it has to be distributed according to a plan that takes account of the social needs of all people and has, therefore, to be implemented by the state. So, because of this feeling that assets are indeed in some way socially owned, the majority of people vote not only to redistribute the economic resources of society but also somehow to abolish the "threat" posed by universal education.

The above statement needs to be further explained. The majority of people cannot easily distinguish genuine culture, which is the province of a minority, from fake culture or popular culture, which we can all easily acquire. The advocates of classical music, for example, know that the classical tradition of music contains within it precious achievements, valuable knowledge, and a cherished world of feeling that requires a certain effort to enter. There are a great many things like this in life; one knows and appreciates the value of something only when one has become acquainted with it. However, to get acquainted with it, one has got to be persuaded of its value. Indeed, it is a kind of paradox, and the following are some of its aftereffects.

One of them is the desire and attempt to seize and redistribute the assets of the successful. The problem is that the process penalizes success, and soon after the redistribution begins, the assets will no longer be there. We saw this incongruity in the former Communist countries: the confiscation of the profits of any enterprise led to the diminishing and final disappearance of those profits, so there was nothing to redistribute in the end, and society became poorer and poorer. However, the majority clamors for more and more, which, as a result, forces governments to borrow from the future. The people want to have what they are used to—not just the opportunities but also the entitlements that their government has promised them—even though there are fewer and fewer economic resources (assets) from which to renew those benefits. We have seen this in our societies all across the Western world—the borrowings from the future. There is a growing indebtedness coupled with a looming fiscal crisis, and most people would say that the day of reckoning will have to come, but nobody knows what it will look like.

Another consequence of the paradox is the destruction of high culture—the kind of culture that universities should be committed to purveying. There is not only hostility toward distinction in all its forms but also a correspondingly expanding culture of mediocrity: "It's okay to be what I am, and I don't care if you think you're better than me. I'm just happy as I am." The elite could, and can, get through it. We all know that instead of leading and taking responsibility for something, people will leave you alone if you keep your head down—precisely what the modern elites are doing. That is already at least a temporary solution to the problem.

However, people are not consciously committed to mediocrity, since they recognize in their hearts, especially if they have any children, that they want opportunities to succeed in every aspect of life for themselves and their children. Therefore, people need a culture whereby success is distinguished from failure; they may not know in what sphere their children are going to be competing, but they do know the difference between success and failure and certainly do not want their children to fail. Every parent has a desire for high standards in education, and all people who are making the sacrifice to achieve an educated worldview accept that there must be such standards.

Parents are, therefore, competitive; competition lies in the nature of the reproductive process. Parents are in charge of their children's lives; they are going to protect them and want them to succeed—and that is an inherently competitive attitude because the world is harsh. Real egalitarians—the modern and "sophisticated" do-gooders, the people who believe that equality is everything—tend to be childless or, like the elite and their politicians, they secretly secure advantages for their children while imposing mediocrity on everyone else.

Looking back at what happened to Europe and the West during the terrible twentieth century, it becomes evident that everything beautiful, excellent, satisfying, and pleasing was sacrificed, wasted, and destroyed. Nevertheless, the West had to go on, and it devised constitutions, which are obstacles to majorities so they cannot tyrannize over the minorities that want to improve themselves. The West needed a kind of virtual political discourse—indeed, original hypocrisy—that would conceal this fact from the majority.

Here is where things become difficult: The West had to keep pretending, relying on more and more lies. The elite said, "Of course, this society is all about *equality*." Americans have always said so, even though the US Constitution was carefully designed to prevent that from being the sole truth.

The West increasingly practices the ancient art of concealment: whenever confronted by another, learn how to say that you believe just as he believes, that you live your life exactly as he does. However, inside, suffering plaintively but not revealing itself, is that soul who knows the truth. This concealment—this act of pretending, this political correctness—is the problem that afflicts us all; the advice that should be given must not be given openly. You have to conceal your distinction in many circumstances of modern life; you do not necessarily allow that you are less ignorant than your neighbor. Do not confess to your own culture or make any effort to criticize the other's lack of it, but joyfully condemn yourself as an idiot like the other ones are. In the end, you have to confess humbly to the right of the other, as part of the majority, to shape the future of the society that includes you. You do not let on that you have the secret desire to pass on another kind of culture.

So what kind of culture is that?

We want to pass on a culture that is based on knowledge and the distinction between real knowledge and mere opinion. This knowledge must pronounce judgments, set standards, and distinguish the true from the false, the good from the bad, the virtuous from the vicious. This knowledge is there because people who made sacrifices so that it should exist have bequeathed it to us. We must honor those sacrifices and do our part in passing on the institutions and traditions in our turn. However, we do not have to accept everything about them. On the contrary, we have to make our living contributions to them, and they have to be amended in many ways.

Above all, we have to preserve the collective memory of what we are as a people. That does not reduce to what the majority of individuals presently happen to want. The demographic nature of the West changes rapidly from generation to generation, and yet there is a sense that we belong together and share the things we have inherited. We want to change aspects of it, but without it, we would not be peacefully together in the same place; this involves an active work of memory in which we confront the terrible things that have happened and rescue the good things that we want to perpetuate. This collective consciousness must, in turn, be open to the concept of achievement, aspirations, and ideals that people can still have under the changed circumstance.

IX. Overcoming Evil with Grace, Integrity, Morality, and Virtue

We must use strength, if required, but never violence in our struggle, because violence is the sign of weakness. One who cannot win the heart or the mind with moral power, courage, determination, and logical reasoning seeks success through violence. However, each act of violence is vivid proof of pure incompetence, moral turpitude, and sheer desperation. The greatest enduring battle known to man, known to history, is the battle of ideas. The most pitiful and insignificant actions are the violent ones. An idea that requires weapons to defend it will die on its own account. An idea that can only live by violent means is sheer abuse. An idea that is capable of life conquers on its own; such an idea will find millions of spontaneous followers. Therefore, never get engaged in armed revolution, insurrection, or any form of mass coordinated popular violence.

This truth is a rather simple one: although Lloyd George, Clemenceau, Wilson, Orlando, Churchill, Hitler, Roosevelt, Stalin, and all their new progenies attempted to reconfigure the world every which way, they failed to get any closer to truly full justice at the end. After humanity found itself stuck at the brink of nuclear war between two hegemonic superpowers, no one remembers today that the vast armies and great battles were and are meaningless. Only the battle of *ideas* has any meaning; the simple truths, like all truths, change the world for the better. History's fanatics, megalomaniacs, and psychopaths can win some battles, even wars, by violent means for a short period, but only ideas will triumph in the long run. The Soviet Union collapsed, the Berlin Wall fell, and human liberty was restored where all the guns of the world and cold wars failed to plant it.

The calling to freedom is intricately rooted in the nature of each person and within a mature national consciousness; therefore, it is connected with both law and duty. It is related to law insofar as every limit of freedom necessarily leads to the suffering of every person and every nation. Limiting man's inalienable right to liberty leads to rebellion—even to war. The calling to freedom is therefore connected with the duty in understanding that liberty and not a license is the challenge standing before each person, and it requires reflection, prudence, and the ability to choose and make decisions.

If we look at the "wise men" who whispered war, revolution, regime change, democracy, free markets, nation-building, or the end of tyranny over the past hundred years, we find that none of them whispered the overcoming of evil by grace, integrity, morality, virtue, humble suffering, and prudence. Moreover, if we read the "wise literature" about the end of the Cold War, we learn about economic factors, politics, arms races, and statesmanship, but we do not learn of the preeminence of hope, faith, patience, endurance, and perseverance.

The West has had many wise men giving wise speeches and making wise plans since the end of the Cold War, and yet we have come to ruin. We do not understand this destruction; we grope to find answers as to how we might get ourselves out of this wise mess, but we fail to understand the superiority of morality and virtue over human wisdom. How many of the military planners and builders of the new world order have spent time considering the forces of moral obligation, respect, loyalty, patriotism, or conscience that might have given rise to the stupendous end of the Soviet Union and tyranny, rather than the "miraculous events" caused by these planners? Maybe, just maybe, this is why the Middle East burns, why Ukraine burns, and why the whole world will burn until we relearn that liberty and peace begin with morals and nothing else.

X. Overcoming Angry Politics by Rebuilding Trust

There is something different about today's angrily bitter politics. The major issues that have shaped the political debate for years have remained mainly the same. The finances are still in bad shape, the deficit is still growing as fast as ever, education is in a shambles, and terrorism remains a top concern.

The mood of the West, however, has undergone a significant change. People are not just annoyed today but angry—very angry. They are venting their rage neither *about* something nor *at* any particular individual, but rather at classes, institutions, or groupings of people. Targets include incumbents, corrupt politicians, bureaucrats, lobbyists, members of the mainstream media, politically correct academics, clergy, or just the everyday establishment, the elite—whatever that might mean. According to this uncertain and unfocused shotgun approach, the people need to throw the bastards out and start over again to bring about real change.

The causes of this widespread discontent are likewise uncertain and unfocused; there are genuine, rational reasons for this dissatisfaction, but it usually manifests itself more through feelings than facts. There is a general (and often legitimate) sense of betrayal, dishonesty or falseness on the part of the ruling elite and governing institutions that have failed to be responsive to an assortment of conflicting concerns. People sense that things are stagnant, lifeless, dead, and not moving forward; many people feel left behind.

The result is a very real divorce between the present policies shaping the Western nations and what the people of these nations genuinely need and want. Like every divorce, this separation is also very messy.

As in a broken marriage, the missing element is trust. Public confidence in the leading institutions, the media, academia, corporations, and religious groups has plummeted over the past four decades. Anti-institutional candidates and political parties are not only the rages in the Western World today, but they also win by railing against anyone even remotely connected with the system.

The erosion of the public trust has been building for decades, but only now are the political implications becoming evident. The giant edifice of Western society, seemingly robust and resilient, is only as strong as the trust that binds people together for virtuous life in common. These ties can be found in families, communities, and other intermediary associations that hold a nation, a society, together in trust. However, it can be obvious to all that the strength of these social ties has dramatically weakened over the years and the vital lines of communication in society have even been severed from top to bottom. The respect, affection, and courtesy flowing from these social connections no longer exist, and intermediary groups, such as parishes and local communities, are disappearing, together with the feeling of security they once contributed. People no longer identify with the surviving institutions that are usually remote, impersonal, enormous, and bureaucratic. Hence comes the sensation of alienation, decline, and desperation that is so much connected with angry politics.

For the sake of a misplaced diversity without unity, some progressive people go about defining their identity, loyalty, sexuality, and other distinguishing marks without much concern for society or the common good. Moreover, anyone opposing this "diversity disordered from above," is angrily labeled "bigoted," "intolerant," or worse.

The result is a frenzied disintegration of society in which people stiffen in their positions and the world becomes a meeting place for individual wills, each with its own set of attitudes, preferences, and the understanding of that world solely as an arena for the fulfillment of their personal preferences. The outcome, of course, is a political climate of mistrust that leads to polarization, which is a shattering of the West into thousands of little poles that make angry politics happen, and this is only logical, since broken trust tends to beget ever more angry distrust. Therefore, the existence of a healthy society becomes a contradiction if anger leads to the conviction that each should become his or her own authority and law.

If we are to return to order, there will be a need for those who rise above self-interest and truly grieve for the nations. Such representative figures have always appeared in times of crisis to unite, never shatter, their nations. They will need to restore trust by remaking the social bonds and rebuilding society and its structures. They will need to rally the Western nations around those permanent virtues that encourage moderation and build strong social bonds, such as courage, duty, courtesy, justice, and charity.

XI. Education: Returning to the Humanities and Recognizing the Individual

The Western renewer knows the vital role education must play in the saving of the West. The primary goal of education, the purpose of the entire educational system, should be to give every person the required volume of knowledge of the humanities, which forms the basis of people's self-identity.

Education in the West today suffers from an unprecedented amount of aimlessness and confusion. This recognition is not to suggest that education in the West, as compared with other parts of the world, fails to command attention and support. In the laws, it is endorsed without qualification, and the provision for it has been on a lavish scale.[510]

However, we behold a circumstance whereby, as the educational plants and equipment become ever larger and more meticulously appointed, what goes on in them becomes more diluted, less serious, and less effective in the training of mind and character, and what comes out of them becomes less equipped for the rigorous tasks of carrying forward an advanced civilization.

Today, for an alarming percentage of Western citizens, the word "education" is a kind of conjuror's word that is expected to work miracles by the very utterance of it. If politics becomes shortsighted and corrupt, then the cure must be education. If the juvenile delinquency is growing out of hand, then education is to provide the antidote. If the cultural standard of popular entertainment declines, then education is to arrest and reverse the downward trend. A whole society expects to be saved by a word to which it cannot even give any content.

Most people see education merely as the means by which a person can be transported from one economic plane to another or, in some cases, from one cultural level to a more highly esteemed one. There is some truth in these assumptions, for it is correct that people with a good education can receive, over the period of their working life, higher earnings than those without, and it is true that almost any schooling brings with it a certain amount of cultivation. However, these people are judging education by what it does for one in the general economic and social ordering only.

In both of the above aspects, education is appreciated as an instrument of succeeding in life—a reasonable and legitimate goal, of course, but hardly one that sums up the whole virtue and purpose of an undertaking that, in a modern society, may require as much as one-quarter of the lifespan. Both "education" as a conjuror's word and "education" viewed as a means of ensuring one's competitive advantage relative to one's fellows distract from what needs to be done for the individual.

Education is a process through which the individual is developed into something better than he or she would have remained otherwise. How does the process go about taking human beings and making them better?

For one thing, it involves the premise that some human beings can be better than others, a supposition that is resisted in some quarters. Nothing can be plainer when we consider that education is discriminative. It takes what is less good physically, mentally, and morally and transforms that by various methods and techniques into something that more nearly approaches our ideal of the good.

The vast majority of people would hopefully agree that the purpose of education is to make the human being more and a better human. Every generation is born ignorant and unformed; it is the task of those whom society employs as educators to bring the new arrivals up to some degree of humanity.

All human beings have a distinguishing attribute in the mysterious entity of the mind, which is disciplined through the language of sign and symbol. Unfortunately, modern Western education has worked to undermine the very discipline that made human beings more aware, resourceful, and responsible through the centuries. Contemporary educators have been attacking those studies that, because they make the greatest use of symbols, are the most intellectual: mathematics and language study, with history and philosophy also catching a significant share of their disapproval. There are excellent reasons for naming certain subjects "disciplines" and for insisting that the term be preserved, for "discipline" denotes something that has the power to shape and control by objective standards. It connotes the authority to repress and discourage those impulses that interfere with the proper development of the individual. A disciplined body is developed and trained to do what its owner needs it to do; a disciplined mind is prepared and trained to provide its owner with real causal reasoning about the world. A person with a disciplined will is trained to want the right thing and to reject the wrong out of his or her own free volition. Discipline involves the idea of the negative, and this is another proof that man does not unfold naturally, like a flower. He unfolds when a sound educational philosophy is developing him according to known lines of truth and error, right and wrong, and correct and false.

Mathematics lies at the very basis of our thinking about various scientific disciplines, numbers, magnitudes, and position. The number is the very language of science. So pervasive it is in the work of the intellect that Plato would not have allowed anyone to study philosophy without having studied mathematics first. Mathematics works entirely through symbols and makes real demands upon the mind.

Language has been called "the supreme organ of the mind's self-ordering growth."[511] It is the means by which we not only communicate our thoughts to others but also interpret them to ourselves. Language has the public aspect of intelligibility and thereby imposes a discipline upon the mind; it forces us to be demanding with our own thoughts so they will be comprehensible to others. At the same time, language affords us practically infinite possibilities of expressing our particular inclinations through its variety of combinations and nuances. Humans even think in language; thought would be impossible without language. Those who attack the study of language (whether in the form of grammar, logic, and rhetoric or the mold of a foreign language) because it is aristocratic are attacking the core medium of the mind.

History presents the story not only of man's achievements but also of his failures. Since history explains the past and the future, it is mercilessly exploited by all. It contains many vivid lessons of what can happen to man if he lets go his grip on reality and becomes self-indulgent; it is the record of the race, which can be laid alongside the dreams of visionaries, with many practical lessons.

Still, the modern tendency is to drop the traditional history course and to substitute something called "social science" or "social studies," which could be dubbed "social stew." What this often ends up to be is a large amount of wild speculation based on a small amount of actual history. The speculation is, to a certain extent, subtly slanted, of course, to show that society should move toward socialism or at least some other do-gooder type of collectivism. This kind of study is often frivolous; the student is invited to give his thoughts on the dating patterns of teenagers instead of explaining the rise and fall of nations. More can be discovered about the nature of man as an individual and member of society from any book explaining history than from all social studies put together by dreamy, idealistic, and politically motivated progressive educators.

Philosophy alone can provide a structure for organizing our experiences and a ground for the hierarchical ordering of our values. Nevertheless, under progressive education there is but one kind of philosophy—that of experimental inquiry in adapting to an environment. This simple query is unable to give any insight or indication as to whether one type of life is higher than another if both merely show an adjustment to the externals around them.

Thus, with incredible audacity, the progressive educators have turned their backs upon those subjects that have provided the foundations of culture and intellectual distinction throughout civilized history. If this has been stressed at some length, it is to deny the claim that modern progressive education fosters individualism. In the true sense, individualism is a matter of the mind and the spirit. Individualism means the development of the person, not the well-adjusted automaton. However, what the progressives really desire to produce is the smooth individual adapted to some favorite scheme of collectivized living, not the adroit person of strong convictions, refined sensibility, and a deep personal feeling of direction in life.

The first loyalty of education must be to the truth, and the educator must be free to assert unpopular, unappreciated or politically incorrect points of view. Education has a major responsibility not only to the objective truth but also to the person. One can expand on this even further and state that education must consider two concepts as sacrosanct: the truth and the personality that is brought into contact with it.

Education cannot be civilizing and humane unless it respects the person as individual, and no educational institution is doing its work or performs its duty if it treats the individual just like everybody else. Education must take into account the distinct competence produced by nature and personal character, and these differing aptitudes are extremely varied. Humans widely differ in their capacities to see, to taste, to bear pain, to assimilate food, and to tolerate toxic substances, as well as in many other physical respects. Then there are the varied ways in which individuals psychologically differ through their nervous systems. Moreover, on the top of this are the various ways in which individuals differ physically in their ways of intuiting reality, their awareness of ideas, and their desires for diverse, supersensible satisfaction. Therefore, if one carefully considers all of the above factors, it becomes clear that every individual is a unique creation—something fearfully and wonderfully made—and that the educator who does not allow for personal development within the discipline he or she imposes is a repressor and a violator.

Present-day education and the pressures of modern life treat the person as if he or she were a one- or, at best, two-dimensional being. They tend to simplify and indeed even brutalize their treatment of the individual by insisting that certain ways be good for everybody.

However, the kind of self-mastery that is the most valuable of all possessions is not something imposed from without; it is a gestation within us, growth in several dimensions, integration, which brings into a whole one's *private* thoughts and feelings and one's *individual* acts and utterances. A private or secretive world alone is indeed dangerous, but a person whose frame of reference is entirely public is disposed to be dull, unoriginal, and unexciting. Any individual who does not develop within himself or herself some specific psychic depths cannot meet the crises of life with any real staying power. His or her fate is to be moved along by circumstances that in themselves cannot bring one to an intelligent decision.

One should have an authentic inner life in which one reflects deeply on matters until one makes them a kind of personal possession. The individual then learns to think about things in a way that can enable one to transcend time and place. This is what "developing a personality" means.

It may seem paradoxical to insist upon both discipline and the development of private and inner resources at first, but the cooperative working of the two is the essence of education.

The reason for not only permitting but also encouraging individualism is that each person is individually related to the source of moral impulse and should be allowed to express his or her unique capacity for that relation.

Still, there is a real sense that one does not become such an individual until he or she becomes aware of the possession of freedom. The people in this world who impress us as nonentities are those who have no means of evaluating themselves except through what other people think of them. These nonentities are those people whose speech and actions are only reflections of what they see and hear from other people about themselves. These nonentities are controlled and directed people; they are hollow people who have to be filled with stuffing and manipulated from the outside, and who increasingly glut our civilization.

In contrast to the hollow people, the "real person" is the individual who senses in himself or herself an internal principle of control to which his or her thoughts and actions are related. Ever aware of this, this person makes his or her choices, thereby asserting his or her character in the midst of circumstances. Then the feeling of freedom comes with a tremendous upsurging sense of triumph: to be free is to be victorious; it is to count, whereas the nonentity, by his or her very nature, does not count.

XII. Controlled Immigration Based on National Interest, Merit, and Employment Opportunities

The massive immigration streams representing millions of people worldwide in search of a better life is a significant problem in the modern world. The surging numbers of migrants who are fleeing from hunger, poverty, social unrest, ethnic or military conflicts, and political or religious persecution are forcing even the most developed and tolerant nations to address the national question.

The entire Western world, including North America and Europe, is being forcibly changed because politicians have pushed non-Western immigration upon the people—and the people are fed up. Only the political and business elite and their elected representatives are in favor of any policy that makes Britain into a non-British country, France into a non-French country, and Germany into a non-German country or adds a vast number of culturally alien newcomers for the sake of change. The neurotic instincts of the Western elite and their politicians to debase nations and force unwanted and undesirable change upon many a country for the sake of business interests is not normal. To call out this destructive behavior, reverse these policies, and restore the sanity and health of the Western nations is a praiseworthy exercise, and cheap slander should not dismiss its necessity and wisdom.

The Western renewer demands laws that authorize the deportation of criminal foreigners and prevent immigration into the social welfare system in order to reduce the high proportion of foreign nationals among public insurance benefits recipients and social welfare programs. Immigration problems can be solved only by controlling limited employment opportunities to nonresidents—against the business lobby, against big business, and against multinational corporations and their vested political and business interests.

It would be worth examining the immigration policy of the wealthiest oil-producing countries. There are some (such as Saudi Arabia) where individual tourists are not even allowed to enter, and if someone wants to work there, he must submit to a lengthy and exhausting admission process. Low-wage and unskilled workers are permitted only from Muslim states—from a similar cultural background; people with other religion are accepted to work there only if they possess such unique skills that are indispensable for the country. All such people must leave their passports with their local sponsor, who is responsible for the actions of the invited person. With the expiration of his working permit, the person involved must exit the country immediately; obtaining local citizenship is practically impossible.

However, these "friends of the West," such as Saudi Arabia, the United Arab Emirates, Qatar, Bahrain, Kuwait, and the other oil-rich countries of the Middle East, do not receive nearly as much Western attention or criticism about their refugee policy than the "intolerant, prejudiced, and illiberal" Eastern European nations, which are allegedly betraying European values. Of course, the oil-rich countries are the friends of the West; the poor European cousins are not.

The idea of multiculturalism is ancient; all high cultures were multicultural in their final end phase because the immigration and subsequent mixing caused their downward leveling and eventual collapse.

Therefore, the Western renewer demands the introduction of another immigration system: a strictly controlled naturalization process based on merit and national interest; economic refugees or guest workers cannot become citizens and must return to their home countries after reaching retirement age.

XIII. Judiciary: Upholding the National Law

The Western renewer fights against the increasing influence of the judiciary in politics. This control, in particular through international law, increasingly puts the sovereignty of nation-states in question and undermines the functioning of the state by rendering unconstitutional the outcome of legitimate and free elections. *National* public law, based on *national* elections, is legitimized by democratic standards and should be agreed to by the *national* high courts. International law, which is not democratically legitimate, must therefore always be subordinate to the national law.

The Western renewer is critical of the judiciary as undemocratic if the courts keep making decisions against the will of the people and in the interest of the political elite.

XIV. Environment: Protecting from Uncontrolled Population Growth

In the context of reducing CO_2 emissions, the Western renewer supports only globally and legally binding agreements to address global climate change while demanding, as a prerequisite to any environmental agreement, controlled and enforced population growth.

Ever since the black death back in the fourteenth century, the human population has not stopped growing. The most significant boost happened in the past fifty years, and that is because of advancements in agricultural productivity and medical developments. As of January 2017, the world's populace was estimated at more than 7.4 billion, according to the United States Census Bureau. The recent increases in human population are triggering some serious concerns; for example, according to the UN, the population is rising at a frenzied pace in sub-Saharan Africa. By 1960, the world population had reached three billion people; by 2040, experts of the United Nations predict that at least nine billion people will inhabit the planet.[512] Overpopulation is a fact, not a myth. If we accept the theory that climate change is human-made, we have to concede that it is only so because there are too many human-made people.

XV. Social Policy: Supporting the Return to Meritocracy

In social welfare policy, the Western renewer rejects the further expansion of the welfare state and is skeptical of governmental support of an "identicalization" of both genders. In its education policy, it opposes tendencies to shift the responsibility for the upbringing of children from families to public institutions. In general, the Western renewer supports the strengthening of all crime-prevention measures against social crimes and, particularly in social welfare and education policy, a return to meritocracy.

XVI. Self-Limitation: Emphasizing Moral Justice Instead of Social Justice

"Human rights" has become the most fashionable and most eagerly repeated slogan in the West. However, we all have rather different things in mind; for example, the educated class in capital cities visualizes human rights in such terms as freedom of speech, freedom of the press, or freedom of public assembly. However, many would angrily demand to curtail rights as ordinary people see them, such as the right to live and work in the same place where there is something to buy—which would bring millions into the capital cities.

Human rights are an excellent thing, but how can we make sure that our rights do not broaden at the expense of others? A society with unlimited rights is incapable of standing up to the adversities in life.

If society does not wish to be ruled by coercive authority, then each of us must rein in himself or herself. No constitution, laws, or elections will by themselves assure equilibrium in society, because it is human to persist in the "pursuit of happiness"—meaning one's interests. Most people in a position to enhance their rights and seize more of it will do precisely that—hence the demise of all ruling classes throughout history.

A stable society is achieved not only by balancing opposing forces but also by conscious self-limitation and by the principle that we are always duty-bound to defer to the sense of moral justice.

Human freedom includes voluntary self-limitation for the sake of others. Our duty must always exceed the freedom we have been granted. Therefore, the Western renewer is guided by the conviction that freedom is linked to our various responsibilities and our self-restraint. For neither the individual nor the state can have freedom without discipline and honesty.

Humility is required for forgiveness; it shows gratitude and opens the door to truth.

When people display humility, weaknesses become strengths, and the humble, because they place less importance on the self, exhibit higher self-control in many situations.

XVII. High Culture Supported by the Meritorious Elite of the Hierarchical System

There is a definite connection between a hierarchical political system and the need to maintain a high or noble culture over popular or mass culture. Without high culture, the human soul is degraded to the point where human existence does not rise above comfortable self-preservation. However, for anyone concerned with human excellence, character, spirit, magnificence, refinement, taste, or elegance, it is vital to establish a system that promotes high culture over popular culture—that promotes Mozart over Madonna, as it were, or Michelangelo over Hollywood, or opera over rap music, or the classical liberal arts over professional training. Since all high culture is aristocratic culture (taking "aristocratic" in its broad sense to mean rule by the best souls rather than a mere hereditary privilege), it follows that hierarchical regimes would be better at promoting high culture than purely democratic or republican systems.

Although one can ponder upon the freedom, prosperity, and dynamism of modern liberal democracies, no one can excuse the cultural wasteland they have produced through the leveling of high culture by the masses. Nor can one absolve the even more devastating deconstruction of high culture by the educated elite of the democratic age.

What is unnatural about the present arrangement is precisely the contempt shown by the Western elite for true and meritorious elitism. The natural inequalities of mind and spirit cannot be eliminated from human nature, and the elite, in healthier ages, channeled them into great and spiritual cultures that spoke to all classes of society.

Under present conditions, the mission of the Western renewal must be the defense of high culture over popular culture and the advocating of traditional hierarchies wherever possible while waiting for modernity to spend its last energies on nihilistic self-destruction.

Fortuitously, time is on our side. Modernity is not a permanent stage but a brief period in historical civilization, temporarily supported by the distortions of modernist ideologies and modern technology.

There are other tools, such as the performing arts, television, cinema, the internet, and popular culture in general that shape public opinion and set behavioral examples and standards for the promotion of Western cultural norms.

This author is not directly advocating here some encroachment on the freedom of artistic creativity or censorship, but rather that the nation-states must have the right to direct their efforts and resources toward the resolution of recognized social and public problems. That includes the formation of a worldview that binds a particular nation.

19

Reflecting on the Forms of Government—Ars Politica

While this author does not consider himself a pessimist, he approvingly remembers Clare Boothe Luce's words: "In this world, there are two kinds of people – optimists and pessimists. The pessimists are better informed."

The patient reader who has followed the author to the bitter end has probably often asked himself or herself already what sort of blueprint for the establishment of a lasting, just, and genuinely free order the writer of these reproving lines would propose.

Whoever peruses this book cannot fail to notice that these studies have by and large a negative, critical character; the reader may have expected the rejection of totalitarian tyranny, but probably not the no less unequivocal condemnation of the "only alternative," the universally accepted palliative of democracy.

One must also be acutely aware of the fact that there are countries, circumstances, historical times, and psychological settings that narrow the scope of practical choices. A harmony between constitutional forms and national characters is necessary. Political theory, political practice, and human realities are, to some degree, distinct elements, but the necessity of having them brought into some organic relationship cannot be disregarded.

Good Government, Good Society

A government differs from an administration (in the sense of bureaucracy) in that a government must solve *new* problems while an administration deals only with familiar and conventional ones. It is for this reason that ministers must be highly qualified, and if a government slips into a bureaucratic mode of thinking, it will lose its ability to lead the nation.

What a reasonable citizen has to wish for is a stable, just, efficient, and consequently minimal government.

What the citizen of a Western democratic country usually gets today is unstable, quasijust, inefficient, and oversize government, while stable, unjust, relatively efficient maximal government is the norm in totalitarian dictatorships. Therefore, we have to look for a third way, which, it so happens, resembles in many respects the old way.

We are being forced to rely more and more on government by *experts* today, and the discrepancy between the things that are theoretically known and those that ought to be known by the politicized masses and their leaders is increasing by leaps and bounds.

To ask a farmer in central Wisconsin whether a concession should be given to a cheese factory is one thing, but to ask a man on the street in Milwaukee what sort of diplomacy should be used toward Afghanistan is quite another. This discrepancy is equally apparent concerning the modern politicized leaders, executives, and managers. At the Congress of Vienna in 1815, it was sufficient for a diplomat, besides the mastering of the French language, to have a good grasp of history, geography, and human psychology. The reliance merely on these topics, even theoretically, would be entirely insufficient today. The delving into such additional subjects as international law, economics, military affairs, geopolitics, and a whole score of other disciplines, not to mention decades of studying and hands-on experience, seems to be indispensable in our time. Nevertheless, the fact is that most of the modern-day politicized foreign ministers, diplomats, or statespersons have not 10 percent of the knowledge, the insight, the manners, and the experience of a Metternich, a Castlereagh, a Talleyrand or a vom Stein. Aptitude, knowledge, talent, intelligence, and acumen cannot be disregarded but must be respected, put to use, and appreciated.

The political objective of our time, of all times, remains a political paradox: to have a good government with assured personal liberty and to have a maximum of security with the maximum of freedom. Democracy offers no solution to resolve such a problem, since the masses, choosing between freedom and the illusion of economic security, will usually head straight for the elusive dream. Nevertheless, freedom also remains only an unattainable goal when one reflects upon the tricky process of enslavement in the West. Popular representations today, resting on the comfortable fiction that the parliaments are us, "the people," control every aspect of the citizens' private lives to a far greater extent than the monarchs of the past would ever have dared to command the lives and doings of their "subjects."

So the historical problem of our day is, and will always remain, the establishment of minimal government from above that will assure and maintain personal liberty. This issue cannot be shirked or permanently delayed by preserving the illusory fluidity of democratic institutions, which have ultimate control of the central government. Since only authentic, meaning meritorious, elites have a genuine (i.e., psychological and intellectual) interest in liberty, it is axiomatic that they must have a position in political life that is more substantial than their numerical share. Needless to say, such elites are not identified with classes or castes here, but instead they embody the best-qualified people capable of creative action. Both creating and creativity stand in constant need of liberty.

Democracy, despite the ubiquity of the term, has failed the expectations of the world. It failed as a guarantor of freedom, the role in which it has posed for so long; it has betrayed its own idealism with greater levity than any modern despotism. Liberal democracy is morally dead today.

Therefore, the West needs another form of government that can give it both freedom and strength—the kind of government that fulfills the ethical as well as the practical demands of the times. The West would do well if it returned to its great traditions and eternal wellsprings, because the lies, illusions, and myths of the last hundred years are going to save neither its soul nor its precarious physical existence.

Government alone is incapable of building any enduring civilization. The social structure always precedes the political structure, with the former being a more fundamental entity. Those who cave in to fleshly appetites will never rise from being mere beasts. Those who do this choose anarchy instead of order and peace.[513] Spengler correctly pointed out that the "idea of the state" is differently understood in different cultures and that there is no definitive "best" form of government that needs to be borrowed from one great culture for use in another.

For a given people, and for a given nation with its particular geography, history, tradition, psychological makeup, character, and culture, the task is to set in place a structure that will lead to a flourishing of this people rather than to its decline and degeneration.

Today one can make only tentative pronouncements about the future; we must leave maneuvering space to take into account our unfolding experience and any further thoughts on the matter. The ultimate form of government (if indeed there were such a thing) for a given nation can only be the product of successive approximations and trials.

Plato, and Aristotle after him, identified three types of states. In the usual sequence, these are monarchy (the rule of one), aristocracy (the rule of the best ones or for the best purpose), and polity (the rule of the people in a small city-state, the polis, for the common good—which we call "democracy" today). The Greek philosophers went on to warn about the specific perversions of these categories into, respectively, tyranny, oligarchy, and mob rule.[514]

Each of these three primary forms of government can be beneficial if directed toward the public or common good, and all three become perverted when they serve private interests.

If we disregard the complete absence of rule (i.e., anarchy, or the rule of every strong individual over every weak one), and avoid falling once more into the trap of totalitarianism (that twentieth-century invention), then we do not have much choice. Either we choose polity (democracy) or the rule by the best (aristocracy).

The price of choosing democracy has already been demonstrated. The philosopher Karl Popper and Aleksandr Solzhenitsyn agreed that "one chooses democracy not because it abounds in virtues but only in order to avoid tyranny"—as some Western countries did following their painful experiences with totalitarianism.[515] Many states have suffered a fiasco after introducing democracy. Nevertheless, despite such evidence, the catastrophic twentieth century has seen the elevation of democracy into a sort of universal principle of human existence—almost a cult. The usually heard explanation is that we have already tried everything else and failed, and only democracy, in spite of its many weaknesses, can lead to a peaceful and fruitful society. These remarks may have been understandable after World War II, the

United States–led Western alliance having been twice victorious within thirty years, or even after winning the Cold War. However, is this logic not equivalent to saying that the end justifies the means? Moreover, even if it is accepted that democracies can defeat totalitarian regimes (by use of force), does it automatically follow that they must be the best possible systems everywhere, under all circumstances, for everyone, at all times?

This author has also explained the reasons for not choosing democracy as the ultimate form of government; therefore, he proposes embracing an aristocratic method (rule by the best)—in full awareness of its faults and with the intention of seeking ways to overcome them.

The proposal for a form of government that is adapted to preserve liberty in the West and steers clear of the catastrophic errors of the past (and present) is based on four premises—or, rather, postulates:

The maximum possible and reasonable liberty of the individual must be preserved and protected since freedom is the essence of the common good.

The political party system as an instrument of holding power in government must be abolished because of its inherent drive and disposition toward corruption and totalitarianism.

The ideological, philosophical, or theoretical conflicts that can neither be avoided nor be made an organic process of the governmental system have to be delegated to the private sphere.

The power of the majority gives it no right to overcome the reasonable and useful; the utilitarian and rational values, in turn, have to be subordinated to the commands of ethics.

From the first three premises, this author, therefore, proposes to establish a constitutional equality between a corporative popular representative body, or assembly, and the executive, administering the bureaucracy.

The delegates in the corporative legislative assembly are freely elected. The executive administration of the experts consists of officials coming from all layers of the population; they are employed by competitive examinations, plus at least a couple of probationary years after having thus demonstrated their knowledge and ability.

Neither the popular representation (assembly) nor the executive administration has an ideological pattern.

The popular representation expresses honestly and freely the wishes and demands of the various groups of public interest. In a sense, it consists of lobbies, if one can call even a single individual a lobby.

The executive administration, dominated by the expert ministries (departments), strives to attain the useful and the feasible.

The corporative legislative assembly of the people can reach decisions that have binding power if they are unopposed by the executive and receive the signature of the head of the state. Moreover, the ministries of the executive, the experts, also can issue regulations, which may become laws if the assembly or the head of state does not veto them.

Thus, we get a clear and unequivocal separation of the two things: those that are good and those the people want. We can dispense with the pretensions, make-believe, and dishonesties of mere politics.

In a democracy today, a president, prime minister, or public representative is the pawn of a party, and a party is, in turn, the pawn of those who pay for it. The power of private capital is forcing a unification of socialist and conservative principles.

Therefore, this author proposes an elected head of state to look over both the legislative assembly and the executive administration, ensuring their subordination to the commands of ethics—the fourth premise mentioned earlier. The head of state, or moral guardian, is a sovereign governor or guardian arbitrator, if you will, to represent the element of continuity and ultimate responsibility. This governor, the head of state, is the neutral and supreme element in the state. His state council (coordinating body) consists partly of his appointees, and partly of individuals delegated by the assembly, the executive, and the supreme court.

One of the governor's two main tasks is to act, together with his state council, as an umpire between the people and the experts. He can vote for the people (the legislative assembly) against the experts and bureaucrats (executive), or the latter against the representatives of the corporations. He can also act as an intermediary by helping to work out a compromise.

The governor's second main task is to use his right to initiate laws, edicts, ordinances, or proclamations—provided both the assembly and the executive approve them. However, each body would need at least 75 percent of the votes to be able to reject the governor's proposal.

The head of state or governor of a hierarchical state will obey the responsibility of his position and the philosophy of his calling. No matter what our opinion of this may be, it removes him from the political special interest of parties as we have them now. The governor is a government's primary protection against big business.

The fourth organ of government is the supreme court, which also has the right to propose motions through its representative in the assembly. The members of the supreme court are nominated by the governor (head of state) and by political, legal, and academic institutions but can be vetoed by a three-quarter majority of the assembly. The supreme court has to examine all laws and decide as to their compatibility with the constitution and the moral law and ethics.

However, we have already learned in a democracy that there is no supreme court that a political party, body, or system long enough in power cannot manipulate. This author's proposal, therefore, is to remove the supreme court altogether from the direct control of the three legislating, administrative, and coordinating bodies and give it only the indirect, legal counseling, interpreting, or consulting role. This new capacity would mean that even the decisions of the supreme court could be vetoed and rejected by a three-quarter majority of the assembly or the executive. Thereby, the supreme court would cease to be a government organ unaccountable to any other branch; its decisions could *not* become the law of the land unchallenged; its members could *not* serve lifelong terms and could be recalled by the assembly with the approval of the governor.

This whole system has to be based on a constitution that defines and limits the prerogatives and power of the state. The rights and liberties of man must be duly safeguarded in such a written document. This blueprint also rests on the oaths given to the constitution by all those serving it and that these solemn oaths are, in the last resort, subject to moral convictions and sanctions. Every other system of purely human checks and balances rests on sand.

The democratic principle could find a limited expression not only in the corporative legislative assembly but also in the administration of smaller units.

Political parties on an ideological basis will have the opportunity to organize strictly as private associations with the right to propagandize their ideas. Ideas and ideologies would probably make themselves felt in the assembly no less than in the executive, and even in the supreme court; but their strife, not being able to find full expression, will hardly assume that destructive character it has in the purely parliamentary state. This author's plan eliminates the necessity of a totalitarian society determined to preserve, whatever the cost may be, the common denominator, since it is not based on the existence of political parties. Diverging political views, different interests, and even opposing ideologies would manifest themselves in the legislative assembly and the executive administration without being able to tear the state asunder or, what is even worse, to enslave it.

Again, there is no inherent connection between the precepts of democracy and those of liberalism. The masses are the poorest guardians of liberty, which has its real guarantee not in scores of voters (who might prefer security to freedom) but in immutable laws. These laws curtail the prerogatives of the state and protect the rights and privileges of the individual, the family, and the smaller political (i.e., administrative) units.

This author also gives the executive administration the character of the elite, because if we cannot avoid having administrators, we should have and use the best ones available. The people may weigh and decide all of the critical issues, but they cannot be present daily to run the state. For this reason, the process of governing will inevitably entail an admixture of the aristocratic mode. The government must not rush to keep up with fluctuating and ever-changeable popular opinion to get reelected, and it must not cajole voters with tempting rhetoric. The goal of government should be to act in the way in which a rational majority of the people would respond if they had all the facts before them.

A centralized bureaucracy by its very nature tries to restrict the sphere of society's self-management—a bureaucrat being a person whose power is derived from the office he holds. This observation, however, is valid only for the bureaucracy itself; it is indeed not applicable to the people; nor is it necessary for the government.

In normal times, the public is hungry for action, and the broadest possible opportunities should be made available for this urge. Wherever the public is capable of maintaining necessary standards by itself, any action by state agencies is superfluous, and even harmful, to the extent that it needlessly weakens the people's habit of self-reliance. Public awareness, understanding, and cooperation are essential to help to control the central bureaucracy and to ensure that its officials will perform an honest and efficient service.

With this type of combined system, there is a working partnership between the state bureaucracy and the administration of local self-governing units.

A good government allows the better and more dynamic natures among the people to fulfill their promise while ensuring that these individuals shall not tyrannize over the masses. However, such a good government is also in accord with the traditions and prescriptive ways of its population. Beyond these two principles, there is no rule of politics that may be applied, uniformly and universally, with any success.

People are *not* created equal; they are created to be different. Any government that ignores this ineluctable law becomes an unjust government, for it sacrifices nobility to mediocrity; it pulls down the aspiring natures to satisfy the minor characters. This degradation hurts human happiness in two ways.

First, it frustrates the natural longings of talented and energetic persons to realize their potentialities. It leaves the better individuals dissatisfied with themselves and their nation, and makes them sink into boredom. It impedes, in terms of quality, any improvement of the moral, intellectual, and material condition of humanity.

Second, it adversely affects the happiness of the masses sooner or later, for deprived of talented leadership and the example of aspiring personalities, the countless men and women of all walks of life suffer not only the attitude of their civilization but also from their material condition. A government that makes a secular dogma of moral equality is, in short, hostile to human happiness.

A just government should recognize the rights of the more talented natures and understand the desire of the masses not to be abused and bullied by these aspiring talents. There have been ages in which the aristocracy—natural or hereditary—has usurped the entire governance of life, demanding of the average person a tribute and obedience that deprive the majority of their natural desire to live a regular, everyday life. Such a regime, ignorant of the happiness of the majority, is as bad a government as the one indifferent to the claims of the talented minority. Nowadays, however, the danger is not that the stronger natures—referring to moral and intellectual qualities, not merely to domineering and acquisitive abilities—will lord it over an abused majority. Instead the threat is that mediocrity may trample underfoot every just claim for the elevation of mind and character, every decent talent for leadership and tangible improvement. Therefore, the sagacious statesman of our age must be more acutely concerned with the preservation of the rights of the talented minority than with the extension of the rights of the crowd.

Democracy in the West has been associated with a kind of loose egalitarianism, a leveling of standards to the measure of the common man. This equalizing is a false premise, and it is connected with a great misunderstanding—namely with the notion that equality in citizenship implies equality in everything. Since the many never rule, and since any form of government may be in accord with the will of the majority, democracy cannot be identified along the line of equality. The distinctive feature of a democratic republic, at least in theory, is not the rule of the majority but the fundamental rights it assures to the minority.

Democracy, which identifies popular government with *equality* of moral worth, *equality* of intellect, and *equality* of condition, is a bad government. A good government respects the desire of extraordinary characters to find expression for their gifts, and it recognizes the right of the contemplative person to his solitude. A good government respects the power of the competent leader to take an honest initiative in the affairs of the country. It recognizes the right of the innovator to his ingenuity and of the manufacturer or merchant to the rewards of his industry. It respects the right of the thrifty man to retain his savings and bequeath them to his heirs. The good government respects all such desires and rights, because in the pleasure of enjoying them and in the carrying out of the duties to which these rights are linked, people find not only fulfillment but also that a considerable measure of justice—to each his own—is achieved.

It was not American democracy as such that stood at the antipodes from the Soviet undertaking; American moral and political tradition together with American constitutionalism was the force of resistance. It is entirely possible for political democracy to attain a sustainable balance between the demands of the talented personalities and the rights of the average types. However, it is also possible for a monarchy, an aristocracy, or some other form of government to achieve that balance. Respect for natural and customary rights is not specific to any single set of political institution. Nevertheless, it is true that the kind of government that seems most likely to appreciate and defend the claims of either interest in society is what Aristotle called a "polity"—the process of balancing and checking of the different classes. The United States remains, in a high degree, a polity; the founders of the American Republic did not intend pure democracy, and it has not yet triumphed among us. It should not triumph. For the good government does not grow from the simple protection of entrenched property or from the victory of the proletariat.

The good government must always safeguard the two elements of rights: the rights of the extraordinary characters and the rights of the settled citizenry.

No ideology will suffice to maintain this balance. Reflective conservatism is the renunciation of doctrine, for it settles for man as he is, substantially; it aspires only to reconcile for the common good the primary interests of a nation. If it can accomplish this reconciliation, a government has brought the people as close to human happiness as possible.

The good government helps people to find their own happiness. It permits the gifted individuals to discover their joy in putting their talents to work and allows the majority, who usually prefer security and typical everyday activities to the excitements of risk-taking and experimentation, to find their way to tranquility. This prudent government leaves every person to consult his or her own peculiarities, for one person's happiness, even among the talented natures, is another person's misery. By salutary neglect, this government allows private happiness to take care of itself. This government prefers principle to ideology, variety to uniformity, and balance to omnipotence.

The second principle of good government is that it accords with the traditions and customary ways of the people. A good government is not an artificial creation; it is not the invention of coffeehouse philosophers got up upon a priori abstractions to suit the mood of the hour. Governments hastily designed upon principles of pure reason ordinarily are wretched dominations.

No nation can detach itself from its past and still flourish, for the dead alone give us energy; a people are taught the lessons of politics through their historical experience. Whichever constitution has been long accepted by a nation, that constitution is the best its people can expect. A structure may be improved or restored, but if it is discarded like wastepaper, every order in society suffers terribly.

Although all people can learn something from the experience of other people, there is no single form of government calculated to work everywhere. The political institutions of a people develop from its religion, moral habits, economy, and even literature. The political institutions are merely part of an intricate structure of civilization, the roots of which, being ancient, go infinitely deep. Attempts to impose borrowed institutions upon an alien culture always end in disaster, though it may take decades, if not generations, for the experiment to run its unlucky course.

Still, Western political theory and foreign policy are plagued by the delusion of the coming universal ascendancy of Western institutions and manners. The West forever expects to find liberal, gradualist, middle-of-the-road, temperate, rational, parliamentary-minded political factions in China, Russia, Ukraine, Morocco, and Senegal, replete with people who will disavow either feudalism or Marxism, behaving as if they had gone at least to some American state college, if not to Princeton or Vassar.

Then they fail to find such people and grow vexed, but Western hopes, apparently, spring eternal. Lee Kuang Yew, Vladimir Putin, Hosni Mubarak, Viktor Orbán, Donald Trump, Recep Tayyip Erdoğan, Jarosław Kaczyński, and Narendra Modi fall from Western favor; they have deviated from the course of righteousness, they have not been "good Westerners," and they have not been good, preferably left-leaning, liberals. The Western elite is, accordingly, disappointed in them and calls them "illiberal," "populist," "national-conservative," or much worse.

The West is never, but always hopes to be, blessed with some political leader or party of the non-Western world with enough common sense to immediately install the infallible remedies of the American Way or European Values. This fond hope is the delusion of political universalism. As Chesterton once said of individuals, they are happy only when they are their own petty little selves. This finding is as true of nations as it is of individuals.[516] To impose the US Constitution upon all nations would not render the entire world happy; quite to the contrary, the US Constitution would work in few lands and would make most people miserable in short order. States, like people, must find their own private paths to order and justice and freedom, and usually those paths are old and twisting ways, and their signposts are tradition and prescription.

Ignoring history, the West tends to assume that the states it calls "less-developed countries" are mere primitive aggregations of people, lacking only Western political theories and practices for the triumph of domination of sweetness and light. Alas, the Western elites, and *not* the inhabitants of the underdeveloped regions, are the fools in this matter. The fact that many states of Asia, Africa, Latin America, and even Europe, suddenly exposed to the challenging influences of modern technology and increased population growth, now must do something more than just conform to old routine and custom, indeed cannot be denied. Nevertheless, all nations must work out their own reforms. These reforms, if they are to bear a satisfactory relation to the search for human happiness, must be in line with the prescriptive ways of the particular country.

Good government is not, and cannot be, of uniform design. Order, justice, and freedom can be found in diverse ways, and any government that is determined to look out for the happiness of its people must be founded upon the moral convictions, the cultural inheritance, and the historical experience of that people. Theory divorced from experience is infinitely dangerous—the plaything of the ideologue, the favorite weapon of the fanatic.

Governments are the offspring of religion, morals, philosophy, and social experience; they are neither the source of civilization nor the manufacturers of happiness. The various forms of government are best only under certain circumstances, at certain times, and in certain nations. Far from being right to revolt against small imperfections in government, people are fortunate if their political order maintains a tolerable degree of freedom and justice for the various interests in society. Humans are not made for perfect things, and if ever they found themselves under the domination of the ideal government, they would make mincemeat of it, from pure boredom.

Ronald Reagan famously called the Soviet Union "an evil empire," and he was undoubtedly right. The Soviet Union was an empire indeed, and it was evil. So must an empire always be evil?

By all accounts, the first Roman emperor, Caesar Augustus, was a hardworking, well-educated, intelligent, and noble idealist. His reign initiated the Pax Romana, in which the world was mostly free from large-scale conflict for more than two centuries. He enlarged the empire and secured the borders. He reformed the tax system, developed an infrastructure of roads, developed a courier system, maintained an effective standing army, organized official police and firefighting services for Rome, and rebuilt much of the city.

Furthermore, Augustus—Rome's "first citizen," as he called himself—was intent on encouraging personal virtue. He lived in noble simplicity and instituted generous plans to help the ordinary people. He supported marriage and family life through grants of land for those who got married and had children. He wanted employment, security, peace, prosperity, and enjoyment for all. That is to say, he wanted Rome to be great again.

That puts a slick and quick gloss on Caesar Augustus to make a more fundamental point—that a republic is not necessarily superior to an empire. Common sense reminds us that any form of government is only as good as the individuals in it. A virtuous emperor would be better than venal senators. A pious monarch is preferable to an oligarch, and a self-sacrificial dictator would be better than a self-serving president.

Furthermore, the real happiness of a population has little to do with the form of government. The most virtuous leader—whether he is an emperor, a senator, a dictator, a monarch or a judge—cannot rule virtuously over a vile people. For real prosperity and peace to prevail, the people, as well as the ruler, must seek true virtue.

If the people themselves are virtuous, any system of government can be virtuous. However, the people cannot be virtuous without an order of virtue, and order of virtue cannot be established without a higher authority than government to establish it. For if only government authority determines the order of virtue, then this system will inevitably support, maintain, and defend the government and those individuals in government. Therefore, the system of virtue that does not transcend the government itself will be and must be governed by the government.

For any government to be good and virtuous, the people must be good and virtuous, and the people can be good and virtuous only as long as they believe in something. Therefore, philosophy is more important than politics, because one cannot have good politics without good politicians, and one cannot have good politicians without goodness. However, there cannot be goodness without truth, and one cannot know the truth unless he or she has embarked on a philosophical quest, for that is where truth, prudence, and goodness are hidden.

Russia and Western Europe: Proposal for Eastern Europe

The author would like to elaborate separately upon the most important aspects of Western foreign policy toward the onetime enemy and current nemesis. In no other area of Western politics is there a higher threat of committing blunders as in this one.

The political, economic, financial, and military conditions in Russia have undergone significant transformations, no less in its interior than in its exterior aspects. The world's view of Russia will no doubt continue to change, possibly heading in an altogether opposite direction as what we are witnessing today. Unless the West finally recognizes the essence of these changes, it will pay very dearly for them.

Given both the geographic location and history of Eastern Europe, its peoples and nations should know and understand Russia's emerging essence better than the citizens of Western Europe. If they do not, they will fail to determine the correct path in their relations with Russia and become a mere tool again, easily manipulated for the benefit of foreign, primarily Western, political interests.

The peoples of Eastern Europe must learn how to think about Russia vis-à-vis the West—something they have never really been capable of doing. They have taken the burden of conflicts and wars upon themselves while "defending the West," "protecting Christianity" or apologizing for "Western values" many times in the past, yet for most of them the Russians have remained a distant people, unknown and incomprehensible. Then, whenever Eastern Europe directly encountered Russia, the encounters were always too close for comfort. Moreover, these close encounters were all the more unfortunate because they made it impossible for the Eastern Europeans to look at the Russians from a proper perspective—to understand what Russia and her role were in the world and what their own positions were or should have been vis-à-vis that nation.

The last three centuries of Russian history are the most important to Eastern Europe, from the times of Peter the Great to the present. During this period, the lack of effectiveness, unity, and clarity in their politics and the corresponding prevalence of disorder have caused the nations of Eastern Europe to be capable only of reactive politics toward both Russia and the West. These were always instinctive reactions that—if they served any interests at all—certainly did not serve any Eastern European interests.

The Eastern European struggle against Russia is a history littered with sacrifice and martyrdom. The longer they fought, the more their thinking became clouded and childish, a caricature of thought; their comportment toward Russia became more and more thoughtless and pitiful. In several, mostly confused, unrealistic and idealistic uprisings against Russia (or the Soviet Union), the nations of Eastern Europe repeatedly ended up serving as tools or marionettes of Western interests, mere instruments of their very enemies—who were, in fact, their exploiters and abusers. Then, finally, there came, or should have come, the breakthrough in Eastern European national psychology with the collapse of the Soviet Union—yet this breakthrough has not yet made their comportment to Russia any wiser, let alone worthy of sovereign nations.

Some people in Eastern Europe, seeing the prospect of economic development and trade with Russia arising from energy supplies and compensating for the hitherto one-sided trade with Western Europe, began to take up the banner of abandoning all political aspirations; they ceased to think about politics.

Others, primarily members of the traditionally extreme right, speak of the historical uprisings with such menace as to make the people ready to give up all hope for their respective countries and prepare for foreign occupation again—either by Russia or by the West.

The hardest for all of them is to think objectively and realistically about Russia. The lesser minds, who are always in the majority, hold fast to patriotic orthodoxy rooted in a tradition of armed uprisings and romanticism while at the same time forgetting their real history and experience. Regardless of whether it is czarist Russia, the Soviet Union, or the new Russia, Russia is and remains Russia, and as such, it remains a constant and principal factor in the political calculus of any Eastern European state. Consequently, Russia should become the primary focus of Eastern European political thought; they must understand the essence, the meaning, and the mindset of Russia, her geopolitics, and, finally, her politics. They must realize this because the conditions of their statehood demand it.

Simultaneously, one must be also conscious of the humiliation in the form of the Eastern Europeans' passively offering themselves to the West as eternal slaves. There is a one-thousand-year-old conflict in which the only side with any brains has been the Western European side that kept losing all respect for the inhabitants of Eastern Europe because, in their estimation, those people could not think—and therefore could not help themselves. The Western Europeans feel superior to Eastern Europeans only because the Eastern Europeans think of themselves as inferior.

This author therefore respectfully proposes a new politics for Eastern Europe to follow concerning both Russia and Western Europe—a real politics. This is not a politics calculated to extract some short-term benefit, but a politics that would weigh down and change the future course of the national history of both Russia and Eastern Europe.

Russia exists today as the neighbor of the Eastern European nations, and the future will inevitably show her to be their most important neighbor, for despite all the work the Americans, Germans, and the European Union now undertake to gain the ears of Eastern Europe, it appears that their role and power, still gigantic today, will recede with time—not to mention their marginal credibility. The new and modern Russia is slowly becoming a world power again, in conjunction with her ascending Asian neighbors. All Eastern European nations must recognize what the location of Russia means and what her role in the world will be; they must have a clear understanding of what it is they wish to achieve concerning Russia—and beyond. This challenge is not only the hardest one to befall Eastern European political thought, but it is also the most important task for future generations.

This area requires careful work not only because the mentality of Eastern Europe is what it is up to this point but also because a variety of interests clash with one another—interests that are foreign, Western, superficially friendly, or outright hostile. These interests, for their own benefit, will attempt to exploit Eastern Europe again. Therefore, Eastern Europeans must bring clarity to their thinking and weed out what is unreasonable, which is what remains from earlier, sadder times.

The Russian question, independent of the political forms governing modern Russia, is so grand that it obliges not only the peoples of Eastern Europe but also the entire civilized world to contemplate it.

Mikhail Gorbachev recalled talking to Ronald Reagan, who almost singlehandedly convinced him that rapprochement was no greedy trick and the West welcomed a real partner. Then what happened? A continuing rush of slick Ivy League ideologues urged massive Russian privatization under the guise of developing a market economy, creating billionaires for a corrupt plutocracy without advancing stability from the bottom up by letting families buy their plots of land or small businesses open bank accounts. Wittingly or not, the United States and the West proved to be false friends—again.

The West, meaning America and its cronies, stands to lose the most from Russia, China, and Iran developing their Central Asian backyard, connecting Eurasia with railways, roads, and pipelines, and replacing petrodollar hegemony with currencies of their own. No wonder it is an attractive proposition to India, Turkey, South America, and many others weary of Western manipulation; theirs is an honest and sensible response to Western greed and wanton bullying. How ironic it would be if the powers that defeated Marx's dialectical materialism were to be slain by the materialism of their own.

Meanwhile, there are quite valuable lessons to be drawn from the strategy employed by Lenin in 1917—and the right dismisses them, a hundred years later, at its peril.

Just as the case was one hundred years ago, a corrupt, arrogant, and hideously out-of-touch Western establishment lies teetering on the brink today. Just as the case was one hundred years ago, the gap between rich and poor is genuinely staggering.

Fortunately, and unlike one hundred years ago, it is the populist right—and not the left—that is making all the headway today. Instead of embracing working-class populism and positioning themselves at the forefront of antiestablishment protests as Lenin and the Bolsheviks did in 1917, the liberal-dominated Western left of today seems to be scared of proletarian rebelliousness and has instead sided on issue after issue with the political, financial, and business establishment. The Western left is the Western elite of today.

We see this in their left-liberal attachment to parliamentarianism, and the failure to promote more democratic ways of organizing society. We see this in the way that bread-and-butter issues that affect the everyday lives of ordinary people are mostly ignored, with the focus instead on fighting culture wars at home and promoting wars of humanitarian intervention abroad.

The fact is that the socialist-liberal left is as detached from working-class concerns today as were the reformist left opponents of the Russian Bolsheviks in 1917. The reformist left could only say, "Please wait for the constituent assembly elections" when millions of Russians were starving. However, Lenin was under no illusions about liberal democracy and whom it benefited. "Democracy for an insignificant minority, democracy for the rich – that is the democracy of capitalist society," he wrote in 1917. He knew that Russian involvement in the war had to end, that land had to be given to the peasants without delay, and that Russia's economy had to be radically restructured. His slogan of "Peace! Bread! Land!" resonated throughout the country.

Now, one does not have to be a Bolshevik, or even a socialist, to acknowledge Lenin's clarity and his sense of purpose. The lessons learned from the 1917 October revolution and the "Ten Days That Shook the World"[517] should galvanize the right into action once again to forge ahead, with working-class, populist, and illiberal support, in 2017.

THE COMING OF THE POSTSECULAR AGE

We are now entering the age of postsecular society. As the name implies, a postsecular society is one that no longer subscribes to the two fundamental commitments of secularism: scientific rationalism and personal autonomy or lifestyle values. At a basic level, postsecular society is about the return of religion and religious values in the public square.

We have recognized the advent of sharia councils that arbitrate between conflicts among Muslims in the United Kingdom and the resurgence of the Russian Orthodox Church as a significant political, moral, and cultural force in the Russian Federation. We have seen the revival of Shintoism at the highest levels of the Japanese government, the revitalization of Confucian philosophy among Chinese officials, Hindu nationalism in India, Islam in Turkey, and on and on.

Like developments are evident in the increasing collapse of multiculturalism and political correctness, which together represent the value system of secularization in the West today. Multiculturalism is the idea that Western society is to be made up of a plurality of cultural identities, with no single culture being dominant or superior. Political correctness is multiculturalism married to the state, whereby government policies favor some cultural or ethnic groups at the expense of others. Hence, on the night of Mr. Trump's victory, CNN could spout that white people voting their interests amounts to racist and nativist bigotry while black people voting their interests equals liberation and justice.

The politically correct, multicultural vision of life is about to collapse. While a hardline anti-immigration policy is bound to win at the ballot box, multiculturalism is morphing into tribalization and balkanization on the political left. The Black Lives Matter movement, for example, is nothing less than an ethnonationalist movement, a kind of absolutist tribalization that rejects secular notions of tolerance and inclusivity. Secular multicultural and tolerance norms are collapsing everywhere; there is not only a wave of national patriotic populist sentiments on the right but also split allegiances that occur as the result of multiculturalism.

Moreover, the turn toward national patriotic sentiments all around the globe entails a resurgence of religious identities and moral commitments, mostly as a consequence of the interrelationship between nationalism, patriotism, and revived traditions. In the face of threats to local or national identity by global secular processes, people reassert the symbols of their cultural identity, such as language, custom, tradition, and religion, as mechanisms of protest.

In one of his campaign speeches, Mr. Trump said, "Imagine what our country could accomplish if we started working together as one people, under one God, saluting one American flag." This cry became a refrain in his campaign speeches: "One people under one God." While some cannot get past the potential threat to religious freedom that such a conditional statement symbolizes, it is just the kind of revitalization of public religion—or ideology, if you will—that explains the ascendancy of national patriotic sentiments.

Thus it seems that the waning of multiculturalism and the rise of a patriotic populism indicate the dawning of a postsecular age. Despite the sporadic protests to the contrary, a Trump presidency signals to the global culture that it is now acceptable to denounce political correctness.

Ars Politica

This author came to the West in 1972 with only one desire: to leave his past behind the Iron Curtain and live his life sensibly, usefully, hopefully, and happily in a free world.

Nevertheless, only a few years later, he was like an aircraft lying on the bottom of the ocean: perhaps good at something somewhere but useless in its current environment. One can recognize, of course, that the oceans cover our planet entirely, and there are many, many aircraft lying on the bottom. This author was not the only one feeling like an airplane lost and sunk in the water while yearning to fly freely in the vastness of the air; in reality, the oceans of our society are filled with people who feel displaced and displeased but who are, at the same time, hopeful.

Modern Western society, not unlike the one this author escaped from, is designed to make any thinking person feel like a prison inmate, serf, or slave. We all know that casting votes is a useless farce, that our invisible rulers neither know nor care about us, and that political dissent is frowned upon when it is real. We are all aware that any credible opposition or disobedience is crushed in violence, that the prevailing ideology viciously represses pluralism, and that our schools brainwash and stupefy our kids. We all know that the domestic indoctrinating appliances, such as television, radio, and the newspapers, do only three things: entertain us, get our money, and make senseless robots out of us.

We know all that but feel powerless to do anything about it.

Today, not only is the Cold War over, but the post–Cold War is already over as well. We are living in a changed and forever-changing world with regimes falling, old parties dying, and new parties rising, where old allegiances are fraying and quasiallies are drifting away. The forces of national patriotism and populism have been unleashed all over the West and across the globe. There is no going back.

The entire West is at such a plastic moment in history, when it needs nothing so much as reflective thought about a quarter century of failures—and fresh thinking about its future.

All through his adult life, this author has been opposed to socialism and centralism and remained suspicious even of federalism that might lead to the first two; he has always preferred national independence and an effective, vigorous, but limited state, and considered socialism and conciliatory federalist policies as prioritizing an international idea to the national one.

Still, to quote Eric Voegelin: "Just because I am not stupid enough to be a liberal does not mean I am stupid enough to be a conservative."[518]

Over the years, this author has become a national patriotic thinker seeing life as a fierce and merciless struggle between strong, arrogant, methodical, and piously righteous nations that dominate and weak, bewildered, intimidated, and awed nations that are being dominated. National sovereignty is more important than ever in resisting the wriggling movement of left-liberal socialism hiding behind the names of "globalization," "progress," and "social justice"—and every nation must campaign against this creeping power.

There is democracy in the West today, but modern democracy, or liberal democracy, certainly cannot be called a priori the very best possible of all conceivable political systems.

This author is less concerned about the form of government that administers the laws of society, so long as it does so fairly. Society must balance its demands for liberty with the need for strong authority without sacrificing either.

This author is somewhat sympathetic to a suitably constrained and stratified quasidemocracy. He is for a political system like stratified democracy (as opposed to "one man, one vote") and a mixed economy.

This author believes that a bottom-up social order overseen by a hierarchical state enforcing the principle of subsidiarity is superior to democracy. Globalization is working against Röpke's "true home," the bottom-up social order, just as the externalization of costs is causing a reversed social market. Therefore, the hierarchical state must provide incentives to the community to do work on the local level.

This author believes that social and political order determine economic progress and *not the other way around*.

The essential option must work with the proletariat for lifting it up; it must support the working class for it to become petit bourgeois, it must facilitate the social surge, and it must be a supporter of welfare—just like the Bismarck conservatives were.

This author has no problem accepting the argument that by his polemics against the direction the West is taking, particularly its acceptance of socialism, he would gain the reputation of a conservative ideologist seeking to uphold the importance of tradition and being skeptical about rationalism and fixed ideologies.

According to Michael Oakeshott, "To be conservative is to prefer the familiar to the unknown, to prefer the tried to the untried, fact to mystery, the actual to the possible, the limited to the unbounded, the near to the distant, the sufficient to the superabundant, the convenient to the perfect, present laughter to utopian bliss."[519]

Yes, realism is preferable to idealism.

Because presuppositions condition every action, any attempt to change the world is reliant upon a scale of values that themselves presuppose a context of experience. Even the conservative disposition to maintain the status quo relies upon managing inevitable change.

In the classical conservative view, individual liberty is cherished, ennobled, and ordered within social institutions, such as families, voluntary associations, religious communities, neighborhoods, local governments, and nations. Individual success depends on the health of these institutions, which prepare people for the responsible exercise of freedom and the duties of citizenship.

However, while higher levels of government should always yield or show courteous regard to private associations and local institutions wherever these exhibit their competency, there is also a criterion for appropriate governmental action. Such a step is needed when local and private institutions are enervated or insufficient in scale to act in support of the common good.

The obvious question immediately arises: How is it determined what appropriate governmental action can achieve a public good?

Since we are in an era when social institutions are in decline, partially owing to the ruling elite and its governments, but owing as much also to culture, what limits, if any, should expansionists recognize concerning the size and scope of government? This question is the equivalent of the general welfare clause: Isn't it good for people to be healthier, even if it is the result of the nanny state? Would local and private institutions in truth deal with the problems of the consumption of too much fat, soda, and salt?

Conservatives like to say they believe in limited government. Very good, but can anyone tell what kind of limiting principle one would have in mind—as the definition of "minimal provision" could vary widely? One of the main problems with an unremittingly hostile view of government—held by many associated with conservatism, libertarianism, and constitutionalism—is that it obscures and undermines the social contributions of a truly conservative vision of government.

This author considers himself a quasiconservative Western renewer, emphasizing that modern conservatism has no relation to true or traditional conservatism. He is also elitist, in the sense of "elite based on merit," realizing that the ruling modern Western elite has sold out to liberalism and socialism.

This author also regards himself as a quasi-irrationalist, believing that human experience can see things that are invisible to science. He does not repudiate reason itself but argues that it has lost its dominant role, as personal insights are impervious to testing.

This author also shares Spengler's opinion on history, which he viewed as an irrational process of organic growth and decay.

This author thinks of himself as a quasianarchist of the nonviolent variety. His quasianarchism is neither the modern anarchocapitalism nor anarchosocialism; it only means that he genuinely believes in subsidiarity, which is the principle that power should reside at the most immediate level possible.

While being a quasianarchist, philosophically understood, this author would also support a semiconstitutional sovereign authority. By this, it is meant that the head of state, the governor, should be bound *primarily* by his oath to his people and ideology, and only *secondarily* to the constitution. The only true leader is the guardian leader, who is willing to sacrifice himself for the common good. This ruler is restrained first by tradition, custom, and common law as opposed to a constitution. This author is not against a constitution per se; he only believes that a real ruler should stand by his word, his oath, his conscience, and his beliefs.

If this author had to be pegged as anything, he would feel least insulted to be pegged as a conscientious dissenter. He rejects imperialism in any form, together with racism and tribalism. When he speaks of patriotism, he speaks of a nation, not a supranational entity of any kind. He has learned to shun the West mostly for its disingenuous and hypocritical character. He sees the tribal minorities living as parallel communities in the diaspora as a direct threat to the cultural identity, integrity, and ethnic cohesion of distinct nations.

Today it seems we live again in a world dominated by the forces of falsehood, duplicity, and ugliness. One needs only to read the mendacious propagandistic media or to hear lies told by corrupt politicians and their cronies by turning on the television. One needs only to see atrocities committed by criminals on our neighborhood streets and by fanatics in faraway places, or to view the latest salacious performances by famous and wealthy entertainers or the newest monstrosities created by our postmodern artists.

The Western renewer must seek to preserve the true, the good, and the beautiful in the face of this onslaught and decay. The essential option offers the best of current conservative thought on issues of culture, liberal learning, and politics. It strives to preserve the best of what Western civilization has produced concerning man's thinking and artistic achievement.

However, in the end, there appears the ever-present yin-yang principle again. This author has written that liberalism is the shameless changing from one principle to another—the backbone philosophy or hypocritical underpinning of the West. But how else could otherwise a small country—say the Netherlands, stuck between Germany, Britain, and France—not only survive but also prosper? How else could such a country have endured as a normal, healthy, and wealthy nation after being born from seventeen provinces only in 1579, during the Eighty Years' War against Spain? How else could such a small nation then come out victorious from the Napoleonic Wars only to lose Belgium and Luxemburg a few years later? The Netherlands remained neutral in WWI, was defeated and occupied by Germany at the outset of WWII, but reemerged victorious again on the side of the Allies at the end. The liberal Netherlands lost most of its overseas colonies in Asia and South America but absorbed a significant portion of their colonial population within the home country and then became one of the founding nations of the European Union.

This kind of cunning liberalism, social flexibility, and tolerance based on utilitarianism are the driving principles of the Western nations' progress. Never having all eggs in one single basket, never being on one side only, never fully trusting any friend or neighbor but offering instead multiple sacrifices and considered options, and always walking on both sides of the aisle, is the essence of liberalism—the liberal principle of all Western nations and all merchant nations. No moral questions and no conservative principles, but only ruthless utilitarianism and sophisticated rationalism mixed with liberal values progress through perfidy—the essential elements of Western hypocrisy.

It is a very complex three-dimensional worldview that this author can offer. On one axis, the cyclical development of civilizations (the Sprenglerian cycle) can be depicted; on the second axis, the oscillating yin-and-yang state of civilizations between amoral liberalism and illiberal conservatism; and on the third axis, the ranking of the political systems from totalitarian through authoritative to democracy.

In the resulting maelstrom of permanent civilizational changes, it is easy to lose orientation and, like the drowning man desperately trying to grab even the last straw, define any fleeting system as "optimal," "ultimate," or "irrefutable." Such efforts are utterly futile; there is no best political system, no best government, and no best solution. We humans literally live in a maelstrom, be it galactic or spiritual, philosophical or political, absolute or relative.

The present Western culture of collapse is doomed to self-destruct. The only pertinent question is whether it will explode or implode—whether it will explode in revolutionary violence or whether it will wither in the decadence of its corruption, the victim of its own excesses. Briefly, whether it will end with a blast or a whimper, one way or the other, it is doomed to self-destruct. Regardless, we need to understand that the present culture of collapse will be replaced by something that, if not worse, could hardly be described as being much better.

The Politics of Richard Nixon

Talking about absolute and relative concepts in politics, this author would like to discuss the person and politics of Richard M. Nixon, the thirty-seventh president of the United States of America and the only president to resign from his office, which occurred after the 1970s Watergate scandal. Some readers might think this is pointless because the media, Nixon's sworn enemy, will always ignore and trivialize as gossip the scandals of the left-liberal elite while relentlessly blaming anyone who takes up the mantle of Richard Nixon. In that case, they have already given up on fighting the elite media that Nixon struggled against on behalf of the silent majority. With this in mind, this author asks for the indulgent reader's kind permission to offer up some reflections for the consideration of the Western renewer trying to find his way in the twenty-first century as to why he might be wise to look deep into the darkness of the spirit of President Richard Nixon.

Most people, including many conservative Republicans, tend to regard Nixon's abandonment of the gold standard established in Bretton Woods, his wage and price controls, and his infamous proclamation that "we're all Keynesians now" as his most grievous failures.[520] It is not this author's place to defend Nixon's errors in economic thinking.

However, this author will support Nixon's sense of priorities. Richard Milhous Nixon might have been the last American president who felt a grave concern for the direction of national culture that tended away from the American traditions of self-restraint, local government, and the work ethic and toward self-indulgence, big centralized government, and the entitlement ethic.

We see all around us a culture that screams for the right of same-sex couples to get married just as loudly as it screams for the right of married couples to get divorced, while remaining oblivious to the children's right to a mother and a father.

Those who lament the demise of the free market in America ought to note that Richard Nixon did not cause it by not reading Friedrich Hayek or Ludwig von Mises; it was caused by the American liberal elite that rose to prominence during the New Deal putting more faith in economic policy than in culture. The programs and projects of the New Deal followed by the politics of the Great Society bred a culture that was accustomed to the idea that experts, embedded in governmental institutions, would solve America's ills and perhaps the evils of the world as well.

The proud American worker, who was still around in Nixon's day, was methodically replaced with the proud American consumer by cultural changes no less than by economic policy. Bretton Woods was a symptom of the coming culture of consumerism—a culture that decided to produce paper money instead of real things.

Nixon did not start the trend toward laxity in work ethic. He had to tolerate it and do what he could to remind people that they still had duties; that the university was where one went to study, not protest; that the factory was where one went to work, not to strike; and that citizenship consisted in silent and moral duty, not loud demonstration. The old New Deal generation, having matured in a culture that still honored work, demanded it from their government when it was not to be had on the market. By Nixon's day, the culture did not demand work but only social justice. In our day, the citizens demand everything from everyone but themselves and are ready to push, kick, threaten, and beat anyone who stands in the way of their handout. Nixon saw the tide of popular entitlement growing, blessed by wild new ideas spewing forth from the universities, and saw it, instead of economic policy, as the most dangerous challenge to the nation.

No amount of economic growth or liberty will convince an entitlement culture that work is preferable to demanding things to be received. Cutting taxes or applying the gold standard or even abolishing the welfare state will not change this, because such people will not respond with greater thrift and enterprise but with revolution. If the culture is convinced that entitlements are people's birthright, the people will not respond to economic stimulus, such as lower taxes or higher government spending, by becoming more productive; they will instead continue to demand angrily that the state gives them their perceived due.

The content of culture is what the people perceive as their due. When Americans perceived liberty as their due, they demanded the present Constitution. When they perceived security as their due, they demanded the current warfare and welfare state. President Nixon understood this, and he exhorted the American people to stop grumbling about problems and start doing their duties—alas, to no avail.

Nixon also knew that it was the universities, the institutes of higher education, from where these destructive tendencies in the culture came. He recognized the culprits for the malaise afflicting the American body politic as the intelligentsia and the university administrations who had surrendered the campuses to leftist radicals and activists rather than protecting them as places of liberal learning. Nixon was not an anti-intellectual or a hick. He recognized the benefits resulting from the pathos of distance from present concerns for intellectual adventure that the liberal university had to offer to a young person. He knew what a terrible waste of an excellent opportunity it was when the young students were recruited into dubious ideological movements instead of being sheltered from the world and surrounded by books in an environment of liberal learning. There they spent their precious student days learning to hate America rather than reading, writing, and listening to the wisdom of wise teachers. Nixon realized that the universities that failed to serve the scholar in favor of the activist were failing the nation.

Nixon did not necessarily have any immediate antidotes for this cultural disease. His call for a new federalism, which envisioned the reinvigoration of self-government at the local level, was an outstanding idea because it aimed to get Americans to revive their political and civic associations.[521] This kind of thinking, rejected by economists who believe it would be enough to restore economic growth through the right fiscal or monetary policies, is more important than ever today.

How much more economic growth does the world need before we realize it does not solve our problems as humans? The generation that burned down America with righteous anger in the 1960s was the beneficiary of postwar growth that saw the United States become the wealthiest nation on earth. Growth did not stop American decline. Nixon saw this and worked to find other means of addressing the problems of culture.

The media have always portrayed Nixon as a man of deep inferiority complexes, a nonintellectual who was jealous of the cosmopolitan sophistication of those who were of better stock. That was, of course, total nonsense. Nixon was the epitome of American middle-class intelligence and style. The media denigrated his image because it represented what the anti-American left bitterly resented: a no-nonsense, self-made, and independent man who successfully worked his way up, provided for his family, and adopted the gentleman's ethos despite not having been born into the company of gentlemen. In other words, Nixon was the quintessential middle-class American democratic-republican man. The left-liberal media wanted Americans to worship their elite and depend on their noblesse oblige, just as they do today. Nixon wanted Americans to cultivate democratic-republican nobility rather than a starry-eyed admiration for the American elite.

Of course, this same media made sure to juxtapose the elegance of the Kennedys with the common crassness of the Nixons. Nixon himself was serious, uptight, and businesslike compared to the punchy Irish chops of President Kennedy. Nixon's style as a gentleman was brought to life by his intelligence. People often tend to see him as bitter, unhappy, and cold. He could not smile like an attractive and trendy politician even if he tried; he always looked as though the effort caused him physical pain. Nixon grave and gruff was Nixon at his best. He smiled with his intellect; he was happiest when engaged in the delicate tasks of statesmanship.

The people respond only to appeals to emotion—be they idealistic or angry, the people crave Neronic politics (see the modern-day Trump method), not the diplomacy of reflection that Nixon tried to offer them at every step. A culture that is dead to politics and believes that feel-good citizenship occurs only every so often at the ballot box would, of course, hate Nixon. It would be responsive to dumber and dumber slogans; not least of which is "It's the economy stupid." Nixon recognized, however, that the slogan should be "It is, in reality, the culture, stupid."

It has gone mostly unnoticed that President Barack Obama presided over the erasure of Richard Nixon's crowning foreign policy achievement, which made the end of the Cold War possible—namely Nixon's trip to China in 1972. The significance of that journey was not only that it established the economic and political relations between the United States and China, but also that it put an end to the close economic and political ties between the Soviet Union and China. Nowadays, American foreign policy is supposedly reorienting toward the Far East. It is too bad that the West has not taken the time to learn from Richard Nixon on this note. After all, the West has stupidly supported a coup d'état in Ukraine, thereby threatening, or preventing, Russia's economic and political integration with its Western partners. As a consequence, Vladimir Putin was compelled to agree to the strict terms that Beijing demanded of the Russian–Chinese energy deal, which is the single biggest contract between China and Russia since the Nixon days.

The Sino-Russian energy deal had been negotiated for about twenty years, with both sides wanting to iron out its details. Then, suddenly exposed and feeling threatened by the recent debacle in Ukraine, the Russians consented to a pricing structure for natural gas far below what they had initially hoped to obtain, most likely calculating that in light of the American and European sanctions confronting them, an immediate reorientation of Russian energy toward the East was necessary. The effect of the deal is that Russia, which had tried to integrate with the West for the last twenty-five years and been caught between a liberal West and an illiberal China, has been forced to respond to the Western sanctions by reviving its special relationship with the "middle people's republic." The price of the West's shortsighted, mischievous, and deceptive Russian and Ukraine policies is the reunification of Crimea with Russia and a renewed Russian–Chinese alliance.

Meanwhile, the righteous West, rather than clobber its political elite for abandoning the Nixonian diplomacy, has helped all of this to come to pass by clobbering Russia—as if geopolitics did not exist.

For President Nixon, geopolitics certainly did exist, and the application of wise international statesmanship, as opposed to the dangerous alternatives of exclusion, ostracism and messianic ideology, was a top priority. To do what Nixon did required exceptional intelligence, clear vision, patience, experience in international relations, and in-depth knowledge and understanding of history. It was not enough to just read the Declaration of Independence and hope for the best, or unreflectively lob bombs into foreign countries for short-term political gains. In Richard Nixon, the Western elites have an example of the international statesmanship of the highest order, and were they to emulate him, they could find themselves once again seen as responsible leaders. Nixon, an enemy of both interventionism and isolationism, offered an alternative that was, albeit difficult to explain and implement, very effective—creative, patient, and realistic statesmanship that understood that morality was best served in politics when this was expertly executed.

Still, the Republicans in the United States tend to focus more on President Reagan as exemplifying the best in foreign policy. That is understandable; Reagan evokes memories of a robust and free America that was respected abroad, triumphing over a Soviet tyranny that was hated by even its own people. Nixon evokes memories of an America that was undergoing internal disintegration and losing its first foreign war. However, and with all due respect to President Reagan, the main reason he could restore American political and military prestige and successfully counter the weakened Soviets was that Richard Nixon had disentangled America from Vietnam *and* detached Russia from China.

Nixon's Vietnam policy itself, culminating in the abandonment of Vietnam to the Vietnamese (not an unjust thing) for a broader geopolitical focus, was the foundation of Nixon's attempt to lay the groundwork for the post-Yalta international order that came to fruition under President Reagan's watch.

It was Nixon who did the ugly, hard work that brought peace in our time and avoided nuclear war with the Soviets. His statesmanship is also the reason China is today a vibrant market economy rather than a billion-man-strong carbon copy of North Korea. As is often the case, the fruits of Nixon's work came decades after he had left office. People like to think that Ronald Reagan spoke some harsh words, rattled some sabers, flexed some muscles, and financed some mujahideen in addition to a few Polish labor leaders and, voilà, the Soviet Union collapsed. We then make the ominous blunder of believing that the Reagan Doctrine can be repackaged as a one-size-fits-all ideology that is applicable in Iraq or Ukraine, requiring no thought and presenting no problems that a lower tax rate or a cruise missile cannot solve. Again, without meaning any disrespect to Ronald Reagan, this kind of thinking ignores, at our peril, the far more complicated and intellectually demanding details of the Nixon presidency. Nixon is not remembered for a clever slogan or a patriotic sentiment, a catchy campaign or an idyllic effect. Nevertheless, it would be necessary to become educated about the world if one were to emulate Richard Nixon.

Most importantly, Richard Nixon was the last president to argue forcefully for executive leadership when the ability to lead was slowly giving way to celebrity seeking as the defining factor in presidential politics. Television and the intrusion of the boob tube into practical politics had become a frustrating occurrence by the time Nixon ran against Kennedy. This fact had nearly catastrophic consequences when, during the Tet Offensive in Vietnam, Americans suddenly realized, thanks to their television sets, that people indeed die in war and that war is hideous and ugly.

The penchant of the press to poison rather than elevate public discourse, to play on emotion rather than appeal to reason, was still in its infancy while Nixon was president. However, the emotional appeals of the media concerning Vietnam did nothing useful to end the war but wreaked havoc with controlling it and frustrated President Nixon's attempts to use diplomacy and military means to achieve a decent peace in Southeast Asia.

Only the destructive impact of modern media communications on American political life could make it possible that millions of people could love John F. Kennedy. The media loved Kennedy, who bumbled the United States into a full-scale war by killing Ngo Dinh Diem and sending US soldiers to Vietnam, and it hated Richard Nixon, who did the hard work of getting them out of that awful quagmire without sacrificing America's international standing. Nowadays, Americans—and, it is to be hoped, all Westerners—are finally more aware that the press does not conduct foreign and domestic policy but profits from the injection of emotion and sensationalism into the political organism of a nation. Sadly, we no longer have presidents or politicians willing to stand up to the media for the good of the country—with the exception of Donald Trump, perhaps. Instead we have a generation of leaders who, having learned from Nixon's futile fighting of the all-powerful elite and their news doctors, crave media attention above everything else.

Nixon, as president, did not behave like a movie star. He was dark and brooding and too aware of the heavy weight of presidential politics to suffer the fluffiness of being necessary to act the celebrity. Nixon's delight was apparently in the act of political existence, work, and reflection; nowhere is this more evident, paradoxically, than in the Nixon tapes.

The publication of the tapes was designed to destroy him, but they instead clear his name and view of the presidency in the eyes of honest and responsible citizens. On the tapes, Nixon is a patriot, contemptuous of intellectuals who forget that their intellects should serve the nation, suspicious of unusual social arrangements, and, above all, always worried about America rather than about himself. When he is self-centered, he is focused on the presidency, not on the person of Richard Nixon. His desire to safeguard the presidency and its capacity for independent reflection, independent utilization of counsel, and independent action is going to be seen in the future as some of the most exceptional efforts in pursuit of constitutionalism.

Those who deliberately misidentify Nixon's view of his office as being the basis for the growth of the "imperial presidency" misunderstand the difference between a strong executive within a republic and the lawlessness of an empire. By abandoning the democratic messianism that had marked American foreign policy from Woodrow Wilson through Harry Truman, and working for peace instead while looking through the lens of realism, Nixon did more to restore American constitutionalism than any president since Warren G. Harding's "Return to Normalcy."[522] The Founders designed the Constitution for self-government, not for an imperial top-level government of shadowy elites. The executive branch is to be strong when necessary for the protection of the republic. If the mechanisms of constitutional republicanism find themselves being used for imperious ends, the outcome will not serve the public good.

Empires require the means that America's Constitution was *not designed* to provide. That is the reason why, as it has slid more and more into an imperial role, America has been such an incompetent imperial actor. Americans as a people and their institutions are suited poorly if at all for "playing empire."

Empires conquer and exact retribution; they do not do nation-building, and they do not spread democracy. They kill their enemies on a mass scale and enslave the survivors. The idea of liberal imperialism or liberal democracy is futile, and Richard Nixon did not make any attempt to implement it. He accepted the geopolitical realities of his presidency and used the executive office to maximum effect to extract America from regional war and craft a more peaceful geopolitical order with the only strategic partners he had at his disposal: the Soviet Union and the People's Republic of China. Peace and diplomacy between America and its ideological adversaries did more to move the Communist world toward collapse than Kennedy and Johnson's wars.

Nixon's presidency was strong, constitutional, and republican—not an imperial presidency. Nixon, who has been one of the few American presidents effectively to accomplish the task of ending instead of starting a war and bringing about peace while not only maintaining national security but also assuring the future, successful conclusion of the Cold War, should be looked to as an example for all future presidents.

Epilogue

The materialist view of history that postulates economic conditions as cause (in the physical sense) and religion, laws, customs, arts, and science as effect doubtless has its compelling aspects in this late period of Western culture, for it appeals to the mentality of irreligious and traditionless urban people. This is not because economic conditions are in fact a cause, but because art and religion have become empty, lifeless, and external as they now linger on as the pale shadow of the only strongly developed form that identifies our age.

The nineteenth century was the century of natural science; the twentieth century belonged to psychology. We have lost our optimism and become skeptics. What concerns us is not what ought to be but what *shall* be. Rather than be slaves of ideals, we want to be able to control reality.

Our task is to give the modern Man a new perspective that will necessarily produce an original image. Life has no goal. Humanity has no goal. The existence of this universe, in which we humans play off a little episode on our little planet, is much too majestic a thing to be simply explained by such puny slogans as "Happiness for the largest number." The greatness of the universal drama lies in its aimlessness. Goethe was aware of this. What we are called on to do is to render the greatest possible meaning to the life that has been granted us, to the reality that surrounds us, and into which destiny has placed us. We must live so that we can be proud of ourselves. We must act in such a way that some part of us will live on in the process of reality that is heading toward eventual completion.

People are not human beings per se, and "cosmopolitanism" is an awful word. We are people of a particular century, a particular nation, a particular circle, and a particular type. These are the necessary conditions under which we can give meaning and depth to existence by being doers, even if we do with words. The more we fill out the area within these given boundaries, the greater will be our effect. Plato was an Athenian, Caesar a Roman, Goethe a German, Franklin an American. That they were so first and foremost is the reason for their universal and timeless importance.

Life is of first and last importance, and life has no system, no program, and no reason. It exists for and by itself, and the profound orderliness with which it manifests itself can only be felt or envisioned—and then perhaps described but not thoroughly analyzed.

Man is yearning for safety and security, stability and permanence, finality and finding solutions. To achieve them, he will not flinch from any danger or hardship. (Here it is again—the ever-recurring struggle of dichotomy). Realizing all that, this author finds it appropriate for a quasianarchist dissenter to close his discourse with the words of Joseph Conrad:

"Faith is a myth and beliefs shift like mists on the shore; thoughts vanish; words, once pronounced, die; and the memory of yesterday is as shadowy as the hope of to-morrow … In this world – as I have known it – we are made to suffer without the shadow of a reason, of a cause or of guilt … There is no morality, no knowledge and no hope; there is only the consciousness of ourselves which drives us about a world that … is always but a vain and floating appearance … A moment, a twinkling of an eye and nothing remains – but a clot of mud, of cold mud, of dead mud cast into black space, rolling around an extinguished sun. Nothing. Neither thought, nor sound, nor soul. Nothing."[523]

Appendix A

Major US military interventions since WWII

Korean War: 1950–54
Lebanon Crisis: 1958
Vietnam War: 1959–75
Thailand Crisis: 1962
Dominican Civil War: 1965
Libya (First Gulf of Sidra Incident): 1981
Lebanon War: 1982–83
Grenada Invasion: 1983
Libya (Gulf of Sidra): 1986
Persian Gulf (Iran–Iraq War): 1986–88
Panama Invasion: 1988–90
Libya (Second Gulf of Sidra Incident): 1989
Iraq-Kuwait (Gulf War): 1990–91
Bosnian War: 1992–96
The bombing of Iraq (Operation Desert Fox): 1998
Afghanistan and Sudan (Operation Infinite Reach): 1998
The bombing of Serbia: 1999
Afghanistan War: 2001–present
Iraq War: 2003–present
Libya Military Intervention: 2011
Syria War: 2011–present

Appendix B

Summary of the Essential Option

The essential option is the philosophy of Western renewal: new conservatism and subsidiarity.

New Conservatism

New conservatism is an opposition to breaking with the past concerning government and social institutions. It is anti-ideological insofar as it emphasizes means (slow change) over ends (any particular form of government).

Whether one decides on a right- or left-wing government is less important than whether a change is effected through the rule of law rather than through revolution and sudden innovation.

Family values and tradition are of primary importance to society; the institution of marriage should be recognized as a legal contract between members of the opposite sex and not between two members of the same sex. Profanity, sexuality, and extreme violence in the media and movies must be avoided.

The role of the federal government must be limited; the teachings of Thomas Jefferson and James Madison in their suspicion of a powerful federal (meaning central) government must be supported and followed.

The modern form of conservatism, or neoconservatism, supporting a more assertive, interventionist foreign policy aimed at promoting democracy abroad must be rejected. The aims of international affairs shall support the domestic policy of the government at home and not any other disaffected groups.

Multiracial, multiethnic, and egalitarian states are inherently unstable. The policy of the Western renewal is more isolationist and suspicious of foreign influence.

While the military strength of the nation is paramount, foreign militarily intervention must be forbidden.

Work must be the universal duty and the meaning of life itself.

There will be a controlled aristocracy that is subject to the principle of subsidiarity without the right to supersede the power invested in legitimately elected local, regional, or state government. That means there must be a hierarchical and aristocratic political system (representative hierarchy) with limited control that serves the people and is answerable to the moral law.

A national-conservative ideology will promote national conservatism for the preservation of the nation's political sovereignty and right to self-determination. This ideology will also support the principle of individual responsibility while being skeptical of the uncontrolled expansion of governmental services or military involvement abroad.

There will be neither organized political parties nor career party leaders nor periodic elections.

Widespread ownership of productive assets must be encouraged and nurtured; the deproletarianization of society must be carried out through gaining possession of profit-producing properties by the masses.

A new tax policy based entirely on incentives must be implemented. These incentives must take into account whether the particular expenditure draws money from the state (that expenditure will have to be more highly taxed) or reduces the demand for current or future financial assistance by the state. When expenditures that currently require state or public funds are financed with more private funds, the burden on the state will *decrease*, and public participation and support will significantly *increase*. Private financing of the welfare state must be encouraged; it is the only way the eventual bankruptcy of the state can be avoided and the national debt reduced.

A foreign policy based on national interest, sovereignty, and self-determination must be pursued instead of globalizing adventures, nation-building, and the spreading of democracy abroad based on moralizing sentiments.

A leadership principle based on proven merit, and not on electioneering, must be followed. Leaders will rise higher in the structures by virtue of character, competency, and efficiency, as displayed by their track records.

Forgiveness is essential and fundamental to healthy social order. People can live in peace with each other in a sound, robust, and thriving society only if they are ready to forgive others' faults and to confess to their own shortcomings. The collective consciousness must be open to the ideas of achievement, aspirations, and ideals.

Liberty and peace begin with morals and nothing else; society must be taught to understand the superiority of morality and virtue over human wisdom in order to overcome anger and evil with grace, integrity, honesty, and decency.

The political leadership must remake the social bonds and rebuild society and its structures based on trust. The political elite must unite and reorganize the nation around those permanent virtues of courage, duty, courtesy, justice, and charity, which encourage moderation and build strong social bonds.

Education must return to the humanities and recognize the individual.

A strictly controlled immigration and naturalization process based on national interest, merit, and employment opportunities must be introduced and enforced. Economic refugees and guest workers cannot become citizens and must return to their home countries after reaching retirement age.

The judiciary must stand *for* the national law but is *not above* that law and the state. The national public law must be agreed to by the national high courts. International law must therefore always remain subordinate to the national law. The courts must *not* have the power to bring decisions against the will of the people and in the interest of the political elite.

In the context of reducing CO_2 emissions, the essential option supports only globally and legally binding agreements while demanding, as a prerequisite to any environmental understanding, controlled and enforced population growth.

In social welfare policy, any further expansion of the welfare state and governmental support of an "identicalization" of both genders must be prevented. The strengthening of crime prevention measures against social crimes and—especially in the areas of social welfare and education policy—a return to meritocracy must be implemented.

A stable society is achieved by the principle that we are always duty-bound to defer to the sense of moral justice or conscious self-limitation. The essential option is guided by the conviction that freedom is linked to our various responsibilities and our self-restraint, emphasizing moral justice instead of social justice. There is no freedom for either the individual or the state without discipline and honesty.

The essential option holds that a high or noble culture over a popular or mass culture must be supported and maintained. Since all high culture is aristocratic culture, it follows that a hierarchical political system is better at promoting high culture than purely democratic or republican systems.

SUBSIDIARITY

Although the essential option stands for a limited but explicitly professional role of the government, it is against laissez-faire economics and rejects the power of large corporations and lobbies.

Most political and social problems that are currently being addressed by supranational organizations on international levels must be dealt with by newly empowered or re-empowered national, local, and regional governments. Subsidiarity is consonant with localism and the decentralization of political power.

The subsidiarist view of multiculturalism calls for the thriving of independent national, regional, and local cultures.

The problems caused by globalization, centralization, and uniformization are to be solved by the empowerment of local and regional governments and the devolution of power away from macro-oriented central government.

Bibliography

Adorno, Theodor W. *Philosophy of Modern Music*. The Continuum International Publishing Group, 2004.

Agence France-Presse in Moscow. "China, Russia proclaim unity ahead of Xi visit." *South China Morning Post*, February 23, 2013. http://www.scmp.com/news/china/article/1156659/china-russia-proclaim-unity-ahead-xi-visit.

Alinsky, Saul D. *Rules for Radicals: A Pragmatic Primer for Realistic Radicals*. New York: Random House, 1971.

Ames, Fisher. Letter of October 26, 1803. In Kirk, Russell. *The Conservative Mind: From Burke to Eliot*. Washington DC: Regnery Publishing, Inc., 2001.

———. *Works of Fisher Ames, compiled by a number of his friends*. Oxford University, 1809.

Amnesty International. "Amnesty International Submission for the Universal Periodic Review of Libya," October 2014. http://www.refworld.org/docid/553a024f4.html.

Ancil, Ralph. "The Legacy of Wilhelm Roepke: Essays in Political Economy." *The Imaginative Conservative*, 1998.

Antonio, Robert J. and Alessandro Bonanno. "Periodizing Globalization: From Cold War Modernization to the Bush Doctrine." *Current Perspectives on Social Theory* 24, special volume edition (2006).

Aquinas, Thomas, *De Regno* [On Kingship]. Translated by Gerald B. Phelan. Divine Providence Press, 2014.

Arendt, Hannah. *The Human Condition*. University of Chicago Press, 1998.

Aristotle. *Nicomachean Ethics*. Cambridge University Press, March 2000.

Ashton, Catherine. Remarks by EU High Representative Catherine Ashton upon arrival at the Foreign Affairs Council, Brussels, March 17, 2014. http://europa.ba/?p=11827.

Atanassova-Cornelis, Elena and Frans-Paul van der Putten. *Changing Security Dynamics in East Asia: A Post-US Regional Order in the Making?* Palgrave Macmillan, November 2014.

Babbitt, Irving. *Character and Culture: Essays on East and West*. Transaction Publishers, 1995.

Baehr, Stephen Lessing. *The Paradise Myth in Eighteenth-century Russia: Utopian Patterns in Early Secular Russian Literature and Culture*. Stanford University Press, 1991.

Bærentzen, Lars and John O. Iatrides. *Studies in the History of the Greek Civil War, 1945-1949*. Copenhagen: Museum Tusculanum Press, 1987.

Baker, Peter. "Pressure Rising as Obama Works to Rein In Russia." *New York Times*, March 2, 2014. https://www.nytimes.com/2014/03/03/world/europe/pressure-rising-as-obama-works-to-rein-in-russia.html.

Balfour, Arthur James. "The Balfour Declaration." British Foreign Office, November 2, 1917.

Bandow, Doug. "Nationalism: Back with a Vengeance." *Intercollegiate Review* (September 22, 2014).

Bardos, Gordon N. "Spectre of Separatism Haunts Europe." *The National Interest*, January 17, 2013.

Barron, Zackary D. "General Electric: Is It Worth Being a Ubiquitous Conglomerate?" The *Cheat Sheet*, February 23, 2011.

Barsam, Ara Paul. *Reverence for Life: Albert Schweitzer's Great Contribution to Ethical Thought*. Oxford University Press, 2008.

Bastiat, Frédéric. *The Law*. Ludwig von Mises Institute, 2007.

Bayor, Ronald H. *The Oxford Handbook of American Immigration and Ethnicity*. Oxford University Press, 2016.

Beck, Ulrich. *German Europe*. Cambridge/Oxford: Polity Press, April 2013.

Belloc, Hilaire. *The Servile State*. 1912. Reprint, Indianapolis: Liberty Classics, 1980.

Bentham, Jeremy. *An Introduction to the Principles of Morals and Legislation*. Batoche Books: Kitchener, Ontario, Canada, 2000. http://www.efm.bris.ac.uk/het/bentham/morals.pdf.

Berdiaev, Nikolai, Sergei Bulgakov, Mikhail Gershenzon, A. S. Izgoev, Bogdan Kistiakovskii, Petr Struve, Semen Frank, Marshall S. Shatz, and Judith E. Zimmerman. *Landmarks*. M. E. Sharpe, 1994.

Berlin, Isaiah. *Four Essays on Liberty.* Oxford University Press, 1990.

Bernstein, Leonard. *The Infinite Variety of Music.* New York: Simon & Schuster, 1966.

Best, James D. "A Republic, if You Can Keep It . . . ." What Would The Founders Think? (blog). 2010–2014, August 21, 2016. http://www.whatwouldthefoundersthink.com/a-republic-if-you-can-keep-it.

Binder, David. "Erich Mielke, Powerful Head of Stasi, East Germany's Vast Spy Network, Dies at 92." *New York Times,* May 26, 2000.

Blagoy, D. D.: *История русской литературы XVIII века* [Istoriya russkoy literatury XVIII veka / History of Russian literature of the eighteenth century]. Moscow, Uchpedgiz Publ., 1955.

Boas, Taylor C. and Jordan Gans-Morse. *Neoliberalism: From New Liberal Philosophy to Anti-Liberal Slogan.* In German. *Studies in Comparative International Development* (2009).

Boese, Wade. "Bush Approves Major Arms Deal To Taiwan, Defers Aegis Sale." Arms Control Association, May 1, 2001. https://www.armscontrol.org/act/2001_05/taiwan.

Bojanowska, Edyta M. *Nikolai Gogol: Between Ukrainian and Russian Nationalism.* Harvard University Press, 2007.

Booth, T. Y. "The Supreme Organ of the Mind's Self-Ordering Growth." Utah State University. DigitalCommons@USU. USU Faculty Honor Lectures, April 1, 1973. https://digitalcommons.usu.edu/cgi/viewcontent.cgi?referer=&httpsredir=1&article=1015&context=honor_lectures.

Bradlaugh, Charles and John Saville. *A Selection of the Political Pamphlets of Charles Bradlaugh.* A. M. Kelley, 1970.

Bremer, Francis J. *John Winthrop: America's Forgotten Founding Father.* Oxford University Press, 2003.

Brookings Institution. *Beyond Preemption—Force and Legitimacy in a Changing World.* Washington, DC: Brookings Institution Press, 2007.

Broome, John. *Rationality Through Reasoning.* John Wiley & Sons, August 2013.

Brown Jr., J. Robert. "Order from Disorder: The Development of theRussian Securities Markets." *University of Pennsylvania Journal of International Law* 15, no. 4 (1995).

Brown, Stephen and Gareth Jones. "German Faith in Euro and EU Lags Behind French—Poll." Reuters. September 17, 2012. https://uk.reuters.com/article/uk-eurozone-germany-poll/german-faith-in-euro-and-eu-lags-behind-french-poll-idUKBRE88G08W20120917.

Buccola, Nicholas. *The Tyranny of the Least and the Dumbest: Nietzsche's Critique of Socialism. Quarterly Journal of Ideology* 31 (2009).

Buffett, Warren E. and Lawrence A. Cunningham. *The Essays of Warren Buffett: Lessons for Corporate America.* 1997.

Burke, Ciarán J. "'Like the Roman': Enoch Powell and English Immigration Law." Amsterdam Law Forum. VU University Amsterdam 1, no. 1, 2008. http://amsterdamlawforum.org/article/view/50/65.

Burke, Edmund. "A Letter from Mr. Burke to a Member of the National Assembly; In Answer to Some Objections to his Book on French Affairs." 3rd Edition (printed in Paris and London; reprinted for J. Dodsley, 1791). http://metaphors.iath.virginia.edu/metaphors/20164.

———. *The Works of the Right Honourable Edmund Burke.* Vols. 3–5 and 8. F. & C. Rivington, 1803.

———. *The Portable Edmund Burke.* Edited by Isaac Kramnick. Penguin, 1999.

———. *Reflections on the Revolution in France.* Vols. 1–2. Palladium Press, 2003.

Burtless, Gary, Robert Z. Lawrence, Robert E. Litan, and Robert J. Shapiro. *Globaphobia—Confronting Fears About Open Trade.* Washington: Brookings Institution / Progressive Policy Institute / Twentieth Century Fund, 1998.

Busygina, Irina. "Political Crisis in Russia: The Regional Dimension." Bonn: Friedrich-Ebert-Stiftung, Abteilung Außenpolitikforschung, December 1993.

Catechism of the Catholic Church, part three, "Life in Christ," section one, "Man's Vocation Life in the Spirit," chapter two, "The Human Communion," article 1, "The Person and Society," I. The Communal Character of the Human Vocation, #1883. CA 48 § 4; cf. Pope Pius XI, "Quadragesimo Anno" I, 184–86. http://www.vatican.va/archive/ccc_css/archive/catechism/p3s1c2a1.htm.

Cecil, Hugh. *Conservatism.* Williams and Norgate, 1912. https://archive.org/details/conservatism00ceciuoft.

Chamberlain, Houston Stewart. *The Foundations of the Nineteenth Century.* Vols. 1 and 2. New York: John Lane Co., 1912.

Chazan, Robert. *Church, State, and Jew in the Middle Ages*. Behrman House, Inc., 1980.

Chernow, Ron. *The House of Morgan: An American Banking Dynasty and the Rise of Modern Finance*. Grove Press, New York, 1990.

Chesterton, Gilbert Keith. *The Collected Works of G.K. Chesterton*. Vol. XXXIII, *The Illustrated London News 1923-1925*. Ignatius Press, 1990.

———. "The Unfinished Temple." Part I, chapter 5 in *What's Wrong with the World*. http://www.online-literature.com/chesterton/wrong-with-the-world/5/, January 21, 2017.

———. *Utopia of Usurers*. New York: Boni and Liveright, 1917.

———. *The Outline of Sanity*. New York: Dodd, Mead, and Co., 1927.

———. "The Case for the Ephemeral." In *The Complete Works of G. K. Chesterton*. Delphi Classics, 2014.

Christianson, Scott. *The Origins of the World War I—Agreement That Carved Up the Middle East. Smithsonian*, November 16, 2015.

Cicero, Marcus Tullius. *Republic*. G. & C. Carvill, 1829.

Clinton, Bill. "Speech on Diversity." Commencement address delivered at Portland (Oregon) State University. The Social Contract Press, Summer 1998. http://www.thesocialcontract.com/artman2/publish/tsc0804/article_755.shtml.

Cohen, Ariel. "The Russia-China Axis Grows." *Frontpage Mag*, March 13, 2013.

Cohen, Michael A. *Live from the Campaign Trail: The Greatest Presidential Campaign Speeches of the Twentieth Century and How They Shaped Modern America*." Walker & Company, 2008.

Collier, Paul. *Exodus: How Migration is Changing Our World*. Oxford University Press. 1st edition. September 1, 2013.

Conant, James Bryant. *General Education In A Free Society*. Report of the Harvard Committee, Harvard University Press, 1945.

Corey, David D. "George Santayana on Liberalism and the Spiritual Life." *Modern Age: A Quarterly Review* 45, no. 4 (2003).

Corfe, Robert. *The Spirit of New Socialism and the End of Class-Based Politics*. Arena Books, 2005.

Courtois, Stéphane, Nicolas Werth, Jean-Louis Panné, Andrzej Paczkowski, Karel Bartošek, and Jean-Louis Margolin. *The Black Book of Communism—Crimes, Terror, Repression*. Harvard University Press, 1999.

Cox, Christopher. "Russia's Road to Corruption: How the Clinton Administration Exported Government Instead of Free Enterprise and Failed the Russian People." Speaker's Advisory Group on Russia. United States House of Representatives, 106th Congress, Hon. Christopher Cox, Chairman. September 19, 2000. https://fas.org/irp/congress/2000_rpt/russias-road.pdf.

Coyle, John Kevin. *Manichaeism and Its Legacy*. Leiden, The Netherlands: Koninklijke Brill NV, 2009.

Crocker, Richard L. *A History of Musical Style*. Dover Publications, 1986.

Curtis, Eugene Newton. *Saint-Just, Colleague of Robespierre*. Octagon Books, June 1973.

Daly, Herman E. *Ecological Economics and Sustainable Development—Selected Essays*. Edward Elgar Publishing Limited, 2007.

Davis, Robert C. *Christian Slaves, Muslim Masters: White Slavery in the Mediterranean, the Barbary Coast, and Italy, 1500-1800*. London: Palgrave Macmillan, December 2003.

Dawson, Christopher. "The Left-Right Fallacy." The *Catholic Mind*, April 1946.

———. *Medieval Essays (The Works of Christopher Dawson)*. The Catholic University of America Press, 1954.

Defotis, Dimitra. "Will US Manufacturing Go to Zero?" *Barron's*, June 23, 2003. https://www.barrons.com/articles/SB105638264848535500.

Descartes, René. *Principia Philosophiae* [Principles of Philosophy]. 1644. Reprinted with translation and explanatory notes by Valentine Rodger and Reese P. Miller. Dordrecht: Reidel, 1983.

Dimitrovova, Bohdana. "Bosniak or Muslim? Dilemma of One Nation with Two Names." *Southeast European Politics* 2, no. 2 (2001). http://www.seep.ceu.hu/issue22/dimitrovova.pdf.

Dionne, E. J. Jr. "Two Politicians with Bluntness in Common." *Washington Post*, November 30, 2011.

Deng Xiaoping. "Building Socialism with a Specifically Chinese Character." Excerpt from a talk with the Japanese delegation to the second session of the Council of Sino-Japanese Non-Governmental Persons. June 30, 1984. http://www.china.org.cn/english/features/dengxiaoping/103371.htm.

———. *Selected Works*. Vol. 3. Beijing: Foreign Languages Press, November 1, 1984. https://archive.org/details/SelectedWorksOfDengXiaopingVol.3.

Deng Yong. *China's Struggle for Status: The Realignment of International Relations.* Cambridge University Press, April 2008.

Dickens, Charles. *A Christmas Carol.* Unabridged edition. Dover Publications, 1991.

Domhoff, G. William. *Wealth, Income, and Power.* University of California at Santa Cruz, Sociology Department, 2013.

Dostoyevsky, Fyodor. *The Brothers Karamazov.* Farrar, Straus & Giroux, 2002.

Draper, Hal. "The Concept of the 'Lumpenproletariat' in Marx and Engels." *Institut de science économique appliquée* 15, Série S (1972).

Duchhardt, Heinz. *Freiherr vom Stein: Preussens Reformer und seine Zeit."* C. H. Beck, 2010.

Economist Leaders. "The Future of the European Union: The Choice," May 26, 2012. http://www.economist.com/node/21555916.

Egan, David R. and Melinda A. Egan. *Joseph Stalin: An Annotated Bibliography of English-Language Periodical Literature to 2005.* Scarecrow Press, July 25, 2007.

Einstein, Albert. "Autobiographical Notes." In Albert Einstein. *Philosopher-Scientist.* Edited by Paul Arthur Schilpp. New York: Harper & Row, 1959.

Eisel, Stephan. "Between Ideologies: The Social Market Economy." Study paper. Konrad Adenauer Stiftung, January 2012.

Embassy of France in Washington, DC. "Liberty, Equality, Fraternity." November 30, 2007. https://franceintheus.org/spip.php?article620.

Emerson, Donald Eugene. *Metternich and the Political Police: Security and Subversion in the Hapsburg Monarchy, 1815-1830.* Springer-Science+Business Media, B.V., 1968.

Engelstein, Laura. *Slavophile Empire: Imperial Russia's Illiberal Path.* 1st edition. Cornell University Press, October 2009.

Evans, Alfred, Jr. "The Public Chamber and Social Conflicts in Russia." Western Political Science Association 2010 annual meeting paper. Social Science Research Network, April 2010.

Fang, Lee. "Where Have All the Lobbyists Gone?", The *Nation*, March 10–17, 2014. https://www.thenation.com/article/shadow-lobbying-complex/.

Fantini, Bernardino, Dolores Martin Moruno, and Javier Moscoso. *On Resentment: Past and Present.* Cambridge Scholars Publishing, 2013.

Fischer, Joschka. "The Erosion of Europe." Project Syndicate, April 30, 2013.

Freud, Sigmund. *Civilization and Its Discontents.* New York: W. W. Norton, 1961.

Fried, Daniel. "Current Policy Toward Russia, Serbia, and Kosovo." Interview With Ivana Kuhar, VOA Eurasia Division, January 16, 2007. US Department of State. https://2001-2009.state.gov/p/eur/rls/rm/78973.htm.

Friedman, George. "The State of the World: Germany's Strategy." *Geopolitical Weekly*, March 12, 2012.

Fukuyama, Francis. *The End of History and the Last Man.* Free Press, 2006.

Galsworthy, John. *The Forsyte Saga.* Start Publishing LLC, 2017.

Gibbon, Edward. *The History of the Decline and Fall of the Roman Empire.* Reprint edition. Penguin Classics, 1996.

Gill, Graeme and James Young. *Routledge Handbook of Russian Politics and Society.* Routledge, March 2013.

Gintis, Herbert. "Review of Milton Friedman, Capitalism and Freedom." http://people.umass.edu/~gintis/papers_index.html.

Girard, René. *The Scapegoat.* Johns Hopkins University Press, 1989.

Glossner, Christian L. *60 Years of Social Market Economy - Formation, Development and Perspectives of a Peacemaking Formula.* Konrad-Adenauer-Stiftung e.V., 2009. http://www.kas.de/wf/doc/kas_20040-544-2-30.pdf?100630164654.

Goethe, Johann Wolfgang von. *Zahme Xenien: Den Vereinigten Staaten.* Stuttgart und Tübingen: Cotta, 1842.

———. *Sprüche in Prosa, Maximen und Reflexionen* [Proverbs in Prose; What, then, is your duty? What the day demands]. Leipzig: Insel, 1908. https://archive.org/details/sprcheinprosam00goetuoft.

Goldberg, Jonah. *Liberal Fascism: The Secret History of the American Left, From Mussolini to the Politics of Meaning.* Doubleday, January 8, 2008.

Golder, Frank Alfred. *Documents of Russian History 1914-1917.* Read Books, 2008.

Golding, William. *Lord of the Flies.* Aoenian Press, 1975.

Goldirova, Renata. "France Muddies Waters with 'Mediterranean Union' Idea." *EUobserver*, October 25, 2007.

Goodhart, David. *The British Dream: Successes and Failures of Post-war Immigration.* Atlantic Books, 2013.

Graham, Thomas, Jr. "World Without Russia?" Jamestown Foundation Conference. Washington, DC. Carnegie Endowment for International Peace. June 9, 1999.

Greenstein, Tracey. "The Fed's $16 Trillion Bailouts Under-Reported." *Forbes*, September 20, 2011.

Gregory, Frederick. *Scientific Materialism in Nineteenth Century Germany*. Springer Science & Business Media, 2012.

Grayson, Richard S. *Liberals, International Relations and Appeasement: The Liberal Party, 1919-1939*. Routledge, 2013.

Groves, Jason. "Britons 'too ignorant' for EU referendum." *Daily Mail*, February 11, 2014. http://www.dailymail.co.uk/news/article-2556397/Britons-ignorant-EU-referendum-Top-official-says-debate-Europe-distorted-people-not-make-informed-decision.html.

Haas, Ernst B. *The Uniting of Europe, 1950-1957*. Stanford University Press, 1968.

Hamilton, Alexander. "Federal Convention, 18 June 1787." Farrand 1 in *The Records of the Federal Convention of 1787*. Revised edition. New Haven and London: Yale University Press, 1937.

———. *The Papers of Alexander Hamilton*. Vol. 9. New York: Columbia University Press, 1962.

Hamilton, Alexander, James Madison, John Jay, and Michael A. Genovese. *The Federalist Papers: Alexander Hamilton, James Madison and John Jay*. Palgrave Macmillan, 2009.

Hamilton, Lawrence. *Freedom is Power*. Cambridge University Press, 2014.

Harnsberger, Caroline Thomas. *Mark Twain at Your Fingertips: A Book of Quotations*." Dover Publications, Inc., 2009.

Hayek, Friedrich A. *The Road to Serfdom*. George Routledge & Sons, 1944.

———. *The Constitution of Liberty*. University of Chicago Press, 1960.

———. *Law, Legislation, and Liberty*. Vol. II. 1976.

Hemingway, Ernest. *A Farewell to Arms*. Scribner, 2012.

Herbert, Auberon E. W. M. *The Right and Wrong of Compulsion by the State*. Williams and Norgate, 1885. https://archive.org/details/rightandwrongco01herbgoog.

Hicks, L. Edward. *Sometimes in the Wrong, But Never in Doubt: George S. Benson and the Education of the New Religious Right*. University of Tennessee Press, 1994.

Hicks, Stephen. "Why Art Became Ugly." *Navigator Magazine*, September 2004.

Higonnet, Patrice. *Goodness beyond Virtue: Jacobins during the French Revolution*. Harvard University Press, 1998.

Hill, Fiona, and Clifford G. Gaddy. *Mr. Putin: Operative in the Kremlin*. Brookings Institution Press, February 2015.

Hill, Lisa. *The Passionate Society: The Social, Political and Moral Thought of Adam Ferguson*. Springer Netherlands, 2006.

Hirsch, Mark D. "William C. Whitney, Modern Warwick." Columbia University dissertation. New York: Dodd, Mead, 1948.

Hobbes, Thomas. *Leviathan*. Oxford University Press, May 2012.

Höffe, Otfried. *Kant's Critique of Pure Reason: The Foundation of Modern Philosophy*. Springer Science & Business Media, January 2010.

Hotelling, Harold. "Stability in Competition." The *Economic Journal*, 1929.

Hughes, Philip. *History of the Church*. Sheed & Ward, 1934–1947.

Hülsmann, Jörg Guido. *Mises, The Last Knight of Liberalism*. Ludwig von Mises Institute, 2007.

Huszka, Beata. "The Presevo Valley of Southern Serbia alongside Kosovo: The Case for Decentralization and Minority Protection." CEPS Policy Brief No. 120, Centre for European Policy Studies, January 2007.

Hutchings, Robert L. *American Diplomacy and the End of the Cold War: An Insider's Account of US Diplomacy in Europe, 1989-1992*. Woodrow Wilson Center Press, 1997.

International Coalition for the Responsibility to Protect (ICRtoP). "The Crisis in Syria." Retrieved January 13, 2017. http://www.responsibilitytoprotect.org/index.php/crises/crisis-in-syria.

International Progress Organization. *The Principles of Non-Alignment: The Non-Aligned Countries in the Eighties: Results and Perspectives*. Edited by Hans Köchler. Vienna: International Progress Organization, 1982.

Jackson, John H. *Sovereignty, the WTO, and Changing Fundamentals of International Law*. Cambridge University Press, 2006.

Jefferson, Thomas. *Notes on the State of Virginia*. Query 13, 120–21. Edited by William Peden. Chapel Hill: University of North Carolina Press, 1954.

Johansson, Goeran B. *Vladimir Putin: A Geostrategic Russian Icon*. Lulu.com, 2013. (Original Title. "Vladimir Putin: En geostrategisk rysk ikon." Published in Sweden by BoD in 2012).

John Paul II. "Centesimus Annus." Encyclical letter on the hundredth anniversary of "Rerum Novarum." May 1, 1991.

Jones, James H. *Alfred Kinsey: A Public/Private Life."* New York: Norton, 1997.

Joyce, James. A Portrait of the Artist as a Young Man. 1st edition. Penguin Classics, March 25, 2003.

Juergensmeyer, Mark. *Thinking Globally: A Global Studies Reader.* University of California Press, 2014.

Kant, Immanuel. *Grundlegung zur Metaphysik der Sitten* [Groundwork of the Metaphysics of Morals]. 1785.

———. *On the Old Saw: That May be Right in Theory But It Won't Work in Practice.* University of Pennsylvania Press, July 2013.

Kaufmann, Franz-Xaver. *Variations of the Welfare State: Great Britain, Sweden, France and Germany Between Capitalism and Socialism.* Springer Science & Business Media, November 2012.

Kennedy, Anthony M., Sandra Day O'Connor, and David Hackett Souter. "Planned Parenthood of Southeastern Pennsylvania versus Casey." In *Constitutional Law: 1995 Supplement.* Edited by Geoffrey R. Stone, et al. Boston: Little, Brown & Co., 1995.

Kennan, George F. "The Sources of Soviet Conduct." February 22, 1946. Published in *Foreign Affairs*, July 1947..

Kershaw, Ian. *Hitler: A Biography.* W. W. Norton & Company, 2008.

Kesselman, Mark, Joel Krieger, and William Joseph. *Introduction to Comparative Politics.* Boston: Cengage Learning, 2012.

Khalifa, Sherif. *Egypt's Lost Spring: Causes and Consequences.* ABC-CLIO, LLC, 2015.

Kierkegaard, Søren. *Kierkegaard's Writings, XII.* Vol. II, *Concluding Unscientific Postscript to Philosophical Fragments.* Princeton University Press, 2013.

King, John E. *David Ricardo.* Palgrave Macmillan, 2013.

King, Martin Luther. "How My Mind Has Changed." *Christian Century*, 1960. http://okra.stanford.edu/transcription/document_images/Vol05Scans/13Apr1960_PilgrimagetoNonviolence.pdf.

Kinsey, Alfred C., Wardell B. Pomeroy, and Clyde E. Martin. *Sexual Behavior in the Human Male.* Philadelphia: W. B. Saunders and Co., 1948.

———, Wardell B. Pomeroy, Clyde E. Martin, and Paul H. Gebhard, *Sexual Behavior in the Human Female.* Philadelphia: W. B. Saunders and Co., 1953.

Kirchhoff, Gerhard. *Views of Berlin: From a Boston Symposium*. Springer Science+Business Media, LLC, 1989.

Kirk, Russell. *Enemies of the Permanent Things: Observations of Abnormity in Literature and Politics*. Open Court, November 24, 1999.

Kizilov, Mikhail. *Slave Trade in the Early Modern Crimea from the Perspective of Christian, Muslim, and Jewish Sources*. Leiden: Koninklijke Brill N.V., 2007.

Klaus, Václav. *Renaissance: The Rebirth of Liberty in the Heart of Europe*. Cato Institute, 1997.

———. "Europe and America: Our Common Crisis." Speech at Hillsdale College, Hillsdale, Michigan, October 10, 2013. https://www.klaus.cz/clanky/3456.

Kluth, Andreas. *The Dilemma at the Heart of Europe: Germany and the German Question*. The Institute for Public Policy Research, September 2013.

Korybko, Andrew. "Destabilization and the Geopolitics of NATO's Black Sea Bloc, Part II." Global Research. Centre for Research on Globalization, June 2015. https://www.globalresearch.ca/destabilization-and-the-geopolitics-of-natos-black-sea-bloc/5453717.

Kraynak, Robert. "Conservative Critics of Modernity." *Intercollegiate Review* 37, no. 1 (fall 2001).

Krier, Léon. "The Fear of Backwardness." Future Symphony Institute. Edited transcription of the lecture delivered by Léon Krier at the inaugural Future of the Symphony Conference in September 2014.

Kuehnelt-Leddihn, Erik von. *Leftism: From de Sade and Marx to Hitler and Marcuse*. Arlington House, 1974. https://mises.org/system/tdf/Leftism%20From%20de%20Sade%20and%20Marx%20to%20Hitler%20and%20Marcuse_5.pdf?file=1&type=document.

———. *Liberty or Equality—The Challenge of Our Times*. Angelico Press, 2013.

Kymlicka, Will. *Multicultural Citizenship: A Liberal Theory of Minority Rights*. Oxford: Oxford University Press, 1995.

Lasch, Christopher. "The Corruption of Sports." The *New York Review of Books*, April 28, 1977.

Lawler, Peter Augustine, and Robert Martin Schaefer. *American Political Rhetoric: Essential Speeches and Writings*. Rowman & Littlefield, 2015.

Lawrence, Robert Z. and Matthew J. Slaughter. "International Trade and American Wages in the 1980s: Giant Sucking Sound or Small Hiccup?" Brookings paper on economic activity. *Microeconomics* 2 (1993). https://www.brookings.edu/wp-content/uploads/1993/01/1993b_bpeamicro_lawrence.pdf.

Lecky, William E. H. *Democracy and Liberty.* Vol. II. Indianapolis: Liberty Classics, 1980.

Lee Kuan Yew. *The Grand Master's Insights on China, the United States, and the World.* Interviews and selections by Graham Allison and Robert D. Blackwill. 2013.

Lenin, Vladimir I. *Lenin on the Dictatorship of the Proletariat.* Progress Publishers, Moscow, 1976.

Lensch, Paul. *Drei Jahre Weltrevolution.* Berlin: S. Fischer, 1918.

Leo XIII. "Rerum Novarum." Encyclical of Pope Leo XIII on capital and labor. May 15, 1891.

Leontief, Wassily. *Input-Output Economics.* 2nd Edition. Oxford University Press, 1986.

Lessig, Lawrence. *Republic, Lost: Version 2.0.* Hachette UK, 2015.

Levine, George, et al. "Speaking for the Humanities." American Council of Learned Societies occasional paper no. 7. New York: ACLS, 1989. http://archives.acls.org/op/7_Speaking_for_Humanities.htm.

Lewes, George Henry. *The Life and Works of Goethe: With Sketches of His Age and Contemporaries.* Cambridge University Press, 2010.

Lewis, C. S. "The Problem of Pain." 1940.

———. "The Screwtape Letters." 1942.

———. "The Great Divorce." 1945.

———. "Miracles." 1947.

———. "Mere Christianity." 1952.

Lewis, Paul. "US attack on Syria delayed after surprise U-turn from Obama." The *Guardian*, September 1, 2013.

Lewis, Timothy B. "The Meaning of Equality - Constitution and Law Series." *Meridian Magazine*, June 18, 2004. https://ldsmag.com/article-1-4360/.

Lincoln, Abraham. *Abraham Lincoln: Selected Speeches and Writings.* Library of America, July 2009.

Lippman, Thomas W. "The Day FDR Met Saudi Arabia's Ibn Saud." The *Link* 38, no. 2 (April–May 2005).

List, Friedrich. *The National System of Political Economy* [1841]. Fourth Book: The Politics, Chapter XXXIII. London: Longmans, Green, and Co., 1909.

Locke, John. *The works of John Locke, Esq; in Three Volumes*. Vol. 2, book 2. (Printed for John Churchill and Sam. Manship.) 1714. https://babel.hathitrust.org/cgi/pt?id=nyp.33433006428431;view=1up;seq=12.

———, John. *Second Treatise of Government.* Hackett Publishing Company, Inc., June 1980.

———. *Essays on the Law of Nature.* Oxford University Press, December 2002.

———. *An Essay Concerning Human Understanding.* New York: Barnes & Noble Books, 2004.

Lovejoy, Paul E. "The Impact of the Atlantic Slave Trade on Africa: A Review of the Literature." *Journal of African History* (1989).

Lukic, Renéo, and Lynch, Allen. *Europe From the Balkans to the Urals: The Disintegration of Yugoslavia and the Soviet Union.* Oxford University Press, 1996.

Lynch, Matthew. "Examining the Democratic Mechanisms of Political Parties." The Huffington Post, January 11, 2012.

Lynn, Robert Athan. *Basic Economic Principles.* McGraw-Hill, 1965.

Lyon, Aisling. *Decentralization and the Management of Ethnic Conflict: Lessons from the Republic of Macedonia.* Routledge, October 2015.

MacArthur, John R. "Remember Nayira, Witness for Kuwait?" *New York Times*, January 6, 1992. http://sites.suffolk.edu/fs183a/files/2009/08/macarthur-remember-nayirah-the-new-york-times-op.doc.

Maccoby, Michael. *Narcissistic Leaders: Who Succeeds and Who Fails.* Crown Publishing Group, April 2012.

Machiavelli, Niccolò. *Discourses on Livy.* University of Chicago, 1996.

Machlup, Fritz. *Essays on Hayek.* Routledge Library Editions, 2010.

Mahoney, Daniel J. *Aleksandr Solzhenitsyn: The Ascent from Ideology."* Rowman & Littlefield Publishers, 2001.

Malatesta, Errico. *Life and Ideas—The Anarchist Writings of Errico Malatesta.* Translated and edited by Vernon Richards. PM Press, 2015.

Malthus, Thomas. *An Essay on the Principle of Population.* Oxford University Press, 2008.

Marietta Jr., Don E. *Introduction to Ancient Philosophy.* M. E. Sharpe, Inc., 1998.

Marrison, Andrew. *Free Trade and Its Reception 1815-1960: Freedom and Trade*. Vol. I. Routledge, 1998.

Martel, Gordon. *A Companion to Europe 1900-1945*." Blackwell Publishing Ltd, 2011.

Marx, Anthony W. *Faith in Nation: Exclusionary Origins of Nationalism*. Oxford University Press, May 2003.

Marx, Karl. *Critique of the Gotha Program*. Part I. 1875.

Marx, Karl and Friedrich Engels. *Manifesto of the Communist Party*. 1848.

Mattern, Frank, Eckart Windhagen, Markus Habbel, Jörg Mußhoff, Hans-Helmut Kotz, and Wilhelm Rall. *The Future of the Euro*. McKinsey & Co. Inc., January 2012. https://www.mckinsey.de/files/The%20future%20of%20the%20euro_McKinsey%20report.pdf.

Matviyenko, Valentina. "Russian-Chinese trade to hit record $90 billion in 2014." TASS Russian News Agency. Business & Economy. September 23, 2014. http://tass.ru/en/economy/750855.

Mazzini, Giuseppe. "The Economic Question," chapter XI in *The Duties of Man and Other Essays*. J. M. Dent & Sons, Ltd., London, 1907.

McClanahan, Brion and Clyde N. Wilson. *Forgotten Conservatives in American History*. Pelican Publishing Company, Inc., 2012.

McClellan, James. *Liberty, Order, and Justice: An Introduction to the Constitutional Principles of American Government*. Liberty Fund, 1989.

McConnell, Scott. "A Coup in Crimea—or in Russia?" The *American Conservative*, March 19, 2014.

McKeever, Porter. *Adlai Stevenson: His Life and Legacy*. Quill, 1991.

McLellan, David, and Karl Marx. *The thought of Karl Marx: An Introduction*. Harper & Row, 1972.

McMahon–Hussein Correspondence, July 14, 1915–March 10, 1916. Published by George Antonius in *The Arab Awakening*. London, 1938.

McMillan, John. *Reinventing the Bazaar: A Natural History of Markets*. W. W. Norton & Company, 2002.

Merk, Frederick. *Manifest Destiny and Mission in American History*. Harvard University Press, 1963.

Merk, Frederick and Lois Bannister Merk. *Manifest Destiny and Mission in American History: A Reinterpretation*. Harvard University Press, 1963.

Merry, Wayne. *Yeltsin Under Siege: The October 1993 Constitutional Crisis*. Interview by Charles Stuart Kennedy. Moments in US Diplomatic History. Association for Diplomatic Studies and Training, February 2010. http://adst.org/2014/10/yeltsin-under-siege-the-october-1993-constitutional-crisis/#.Wk-WRxM-cqw.

Meyer, Frank S., ed. *What Is Conservatism?—A New Edition of the Classic by 12 Leading Conservatives*. 1st edition. Intercollegiate Studies Institute, September 15, 2015.

Meyers, Jeffrey. *Joseph Conrad: A Biography.* Letter to Robert Bontine Cunninghame Graham. Cooper Square Press, 2001.

M'Gregor, John James. *History of the French Revolution, and of the wars resulting from that memorable event.* Vol. II, book II, chapter IV. Waterford: Printed by John Bull, Oxford University, 1817.

Mierzejewski, Alfred C. *Ludwig Erhard: A Biography.* The University of North Carolina Press, 2004.

Millar, Simon. *Rossbach and Leuthen 1757*. Osprey Publishing, 2002.

Miller, Fred. "Aristotle's Political Theory." In *The Stanford Encyclopedia of Philosophy*. 1998. Substantive revision November 7, 2017. https://plato.stanford.edu/entries/aristotle-politics/.

Mill, John Stuart. *On Liberty*. J. W. Parker and Son, 1859.

Mises, Ludwig von. *Omnipotent Government: The Rise of the Total State and Total War*. Yale University Press, 1944.

———. "Planned Chaos." Excerpt from *Socialism: An Economic and Sociological Analysis*. Ludwig von Mises Institute, 2009. https://liberty.me/wp-content/uploads/2014/12/Mises-PlannedChaos.pdf.

Mishin, Dmitrij. *The Saqaliba Slaves in the Aghlabid State*. Central European University. 2008. http://www.columbia.edu/itc/history/conant/mushin1998.pdf.

Moeller van den Bruck, Arthur. *Germany's Third Empire*. Arktos Media Ltd., 2012.

Mommsen, Theodor. *The History of Rome*. [Römische Geschichte]. Vol. 4. Translated by William P. Dickson. London: Richard Bentley Publisher, 1867. https://archive.org/details/historyofrom04momm.

Montesquieu, Charles-Louis de Secondat. *The Spirit of Laws: A Compendium of the First English Edition*. University of California Press, 1977.

Morris, Charles. *Twentieth Century Encyclopædia: A Library of Universal Knowledge*. Vol. 5. Syndicate Publishing Company, 1912.

Moseley, Alexander. *An Introduction to Political Philosophy.* Continuum International Publishing Group, 2007.

Münchau, Wolfgang. *Das Ende der Sozialen Marktwirtschaft.* Hanser, 2006.

Mussolini, Benito. "Capitalism and the Corporate State." Speech, November 1933. https://archive.org/details/CapitalismAndTheCorporateState.

———. "Capitalism and the Corporate State." Address to the National Corporative Council on November 14, 1933 in Rome. In *Fascism: Doctrine and Institutions.* Ardita, 1935.

Nathan, Andrew J. and Andrew Scobell, "How China Sees America: The Sum of Beijing's Fears." *Foreign Affairs* 91, no. 5 (September/October 2012).

National Assembly of France. *Declaration of the Rights of Man and Citizen.* Charles River Editors, August 2011.

Naughton, Barry. *The Chinese Economy, Transitions and Growth.* The MIT Press, 2007.

Nebelin, Manfred. *Ludendorff: Diktator im Ersten Weltkrieg.* Siedler, 2010.

Nell-Breuning, Oswald von. *Reorganization of Social Economy: The Social Encyclical Developed and Explained.* Bruce Publishing Company, 1936.

New York Times. The New York Times Guide to the Arts of the 20th Century. Vol. 4, *1980-1999.* Fitzroy Dearborn Publishers, 2002.

Nietzsche, Friedrich. *The Will to Power.* Translated by Walter Kaufmann and R. J. Hollingdale. New York: Vintage, 1968.

———. *The Gay Science.* New York: Vintage, 1974.

———. *Ecce Homo.* New York: Penguin Classics, 1992.

———. *Twilight of the Idols.* New York: Oxford University Press, 1998.

———. *Also sprach Zarathustra: Ein Buch für Alle und Keinen.* [Thus Spake Zarathustra: A Book for All and None]. Unabridged edition. Dover Publications, January 5, 1999.

———. *On the Genealogy of Morals.* New York: Oxford University Press, 1999.

———. *The Antichrist.* Amherst: Prometheus Books, 2000.

———. *Beyond Good and Evil.* New York: Penguin Classics, 2003.

Nigro, Samuel A. *Everybody for Everybody: Truth, Oneness, Good, and Beauty for Everyone's Life, Liberty, and Pursuit of Happiness.* Vol. 1. Xlibris Corporation, 2012.

Nisbet, Robert. *The Quest for Community: A Study in the Ethics of Order and Freedom.* 1st edition. Intercollegiate Studies Institute, July 5, 2010.

Nola, Robert. *Rescuing Reason: A Critique of Anti-Rationalist Views of Science and Knowledge.* Springer Science & Business Media, 2012.

Norris, Frank. *The Pit: A Story of Chicago.* New York: Penguin Books, 1994.

Nozick, Robert. *Anarchy, State, and Utopia.* Basic Books, 1974.

O'Donnell, James J. "A Common Quotation from 'Augustine'?" Georgetown University, 2010. https://web.archive.org/web/20140912032329/http://faculty.georgetown.edu/jod/augustine/quote.html.

Oakeshott, Michael. "On Being Conservative." In *Rationalism in Politics and Other Essays.* Liberty Fund, 1991.

Odoyevsky, Vladimir Fyodorovich. *Russian Nights.* Northwestern University Press, September 1997.

Oettingen, Alexander von. *Die Moralstatistik und die christliche Sittenlehre. Versuch einer Socialethik auf empirischer Grundlage.* Vol. 1. Erlangen: Deichert, 1868.

Office of the Coordinator for Counterterrorism. "Foreign Terrorist Organizations." US State Department. https://www.state.gov/j/ct/rls/other/des/123085.htm.

Officer, Lawrence H. *Two Centuries of Compensation for US Production Workers in Manufacturing.* Palgrave Macmillan, 2009.

Orwell, George. *1984.* Penguin Publishing Group, 1950.

———. *The Road to Wigan Pier.* New York: Harcourt Brace Jovanovich, 1958.

Oswald Spengler. *The Decline of the West* [Der Untergang des Abendlandes]. Alfred A. Knopf, 1939.

Oswalt, Walter. *Liberale Opposition gegen den NS-Staat. Zur Entwicklung von Walter Euckens Sozialtheorie.* 2005.

Overy, Richard. *The Dictators: Hitler's Germany and Stalin's Russia.* Penguin Books, 2005.

Owen, Robert. "Address to the Inhabitants of New Lanark." Longman, London, 1817. http://www.infed.org/archives/e-texts/owen_new_lanark.htm.

Pack, Spencer J. "Paul Krugman and the Illusion of the Illusion of Conflict in International Trade." *Peace Economics, Peace Science and Public Policy* 2, no. 4 (1995). http://digitalcommons.conncoll.edu/cgi/viewcontent.cgi?article=1021&context=econfacpub.

Partlett, William. "Vladimir Putin and the Law." The Brookings Institution. February 28, 2012. https://www.brookings.edu/opinions/vladimir-putin-and-the-law/.

Pashukanis, Evgeny Bronislavovich. *The General Theory of Law & Marxism*. Transaction Publishers, 2001.

Paulino, Jose M. *The Fraud of the Fraud*. Facts Movement, 2008.

Perkins, Mark. "On Difference and Equality." The *Imaginative Conservative*, December 20, 2014.

Pew Forum, "The Future of the Global Muslim Population." January 2011. http://www.pewforum.org/2011/01/27/future-of-the-global-muslim-population-regional-europe/.

Pipes, Richard. *Russian Conservatism and Its Critics: A Study in Political Culture*. Yale University Press, 2005.

Pippin, Robert B. *The Persistence of Subjectivity: On the Kantian Aftermath*. Cambridge University Press, 2005.

Pius XI. "Quadragessimo Anno." Encyclical of Pope Pius XI on reconstruction of the social order. May 15, 1931.

Plato. *Laws*. Translated by Thomas L. Pangle. The University of Chicago Press, 1988.

———. *The Republic*. Translated and edited by Allan Bloom. New York: Basic Books, 1991.

Politkovskaya, Anna. *Putin's Russia*. Random House, December 2012.

Popper, Karl. *The Logic of Scientific Discovery*. Routledge Classics, 1959.

———. *The Open Society and Its Enemies*. Princeton University Press, April 2013.

Porkert, Manfred. *The Theoretical Foundations of Chinese Medicine: Systems of Correspondence (East Asian Science)*. MIT Press, July 1974.

Portland Independent Media Center. "*Der Markt hat kein Herz.*" Interview with Paul A. Samuelson. Der Spiegel 38 (2005). http://www.spiegel.de/spiegel/print/d-41834764.html.

Powell, Enoch. Speech delivered to a conservative association meeting in Birmingham on April 20, 1968. The *Telegraph*, November 6, 2007. http://www.telegraph.co.uk/comment/3643823/Enoch-Powells-Rivers-of-Blood-speech.html.

Pozsgai, Joseph. *Der Preis der Wende: Gorbatschows Masterplan für den Systemwechsel*. München: Olzog Verlag GmbH, 2006.

Правительство Российской Федерации. "Prime Minister Vladimir Putin Chairs a Meeting of the Organizing Committee for the Celebration of Pyotr Stolypin's 150th Birthday Anniversary." 2010. http://archive.government.ru/eng/docs/15878/.

Przeworski, Adam and Fernando Limongi. *Modernization: Theories and Facts.* Cambridge University Press, 2010. https://www.cambridge.org/core/journals/world-politics/article/modernization-theories-and-facts/24CC3E289332FF2D39B5FACEAD75C408.

Putin, Vladimir. "Annual Address to the Federal Assembly of the Russian Federation." The Kremlin. Moscow, April 25, 2005. http://en.kremlin.ru/events/president/transcripts/22931.

Quigley, Carroll. *Tragedy and Hope: A History of the World in Our Time.* Macmillan, 1966.

Raspail, Jean and Norman R. Shapiro. "The Camp of the Saints." Social Contract Press, 1994.

Ratzinger, Joseph. "Pro Eligendo Romano Pontifice." Homily of His Eminence Cardinal Joseph Ratzinger, dean of the College of Cardinals. Vatican Basilica. Monday April 18, 2005. http://www.vatican.va/gpII/documents/homily-pro-eligendo-pontifice_20050418_en.html.

Rawls, John. *A Theory of Justice.* Revised edition. Belknap Press, September 1999.

Reagan, Michael D. *The New Federalism.* Oxford University Press, 1977.

Reagan, Ronald. "Public Papers of the Presidents of the United States: Ronald Reagan." Remarks at the Annual Washington Conference of the American Legion, February 22, 1983. https://www.reaganlibrary.gov/sites/default/files/archives/speeches/1983/22283b.htm.

———. "Public Papers of the Presidents of the United States: Ronald Reagan, 1983." Remarks at a Flag Day ceremony in Baltimore, Maryland, June 14, 1985. https://www.reaganlibrary.gov/sites/default/files/archives/speeches/1985/61485f.htm.

———. "Public Papers of the Presidents of the United States: Ronald Reagan, 1988." Remarks and a question-and-answer session with the students and faculty at Moscow State University, May 31. 1988, https://www.reaganlibrary.gov/sites/default/files/archives/speeches/1988/053188b.htm.

———. *An American Life.* New York: Simon and Schuster, 1990.

Reed, John. *Ten Days that Shook the World.* 1st edition. New York: Boni & Liveright, 1919.

Richardson, G. B. *The Economics of Imperfect Knowledge—Collected Papers of G.B. Richardson.* Edward Elgar Publishing Limited, 1998.

Rich, Arthur. "Business and Economic Ethics: The Ethics of Economic Systems." Peeters, 2006.

Richters, Katja. *The Post-Soviet Russian Orthodox Church: Politics, Culture and Greater Russia*. Routledge, 2012.

Rieth, Peter S. "Russia & Foreign Policy: The Forgotten Teachings of Henryk Krzeczkowski." The *Imaginative Conservative*, June 27, 2014.

———. "The Russian 'Conservative Mind,'" The *Imaginative Conservative*, February 28, 2015.

Roberts, Paul Craig. *A World Overwhelmed By Western Hypocrisy*. Information Clearing House, June 29, 2011.

Robinson, Paul. "Putin's Philosophy." The *American Conservative*, March 28, 2012.

———. "Putin's Philosopher." Irrusianality (blog). December 22, 2014. https://irrussianality.wordpress.com/2014/12/22/putins-philosopher/.

Roosevelt, Theodore. Letter to the American Defense Society, 1919. "Broken Borders: Teddy Roosevelt's words to live by." CNN International, Monday, March 27, 2006. http://edition.cnn.com/2006/US/03/27/quote.roosevelt/.

Röpke, Wilhelm. *Mass und Mitte*. Erlenbach-Zürich: Eugen Rentsch Verlag, 1950.

———. *A Humane Economy - The Social Framework of the Free Market*. South Bend, Indiana: Gateway Editions, 1960.

Rosen, Michael. *On Voluntary Servitude: False Consciousness and the Theory of Ideology*. Harvard University Press, 1996.

Ross, Alex. "Why do we hate modern classical music?" The *Guardian*, November 28, 2010.

Rousseau, Jean-Jacques. *The Social Contract or Principles of Political Right*. Translated by G. D. H. Cole. 1762. https://www.ucc.ie/archive/hdsp/Rousseau_contrat-social.pdf.

———. *Emile*. New York: Basic Books, 1979.

———. *Discourse on the Origin and Foundations of Inequality among Men*. Bedford/St. Martin's, 2010.

Rucker, Philip. "Hillary Clinton says Putin's actions are like 'what Hitler did back in the '30s'." The *Washington Post*, March 5, 2014. https://www.washingtonpost.com/news/post-politics/wp/2014/03/05/hillary-clinton-says-putins-action-are-like-what-hitler-did-back-in-the-30s/?utm_term=.c10495809803.

Rummel, R. J. *Death by Government*. Transaction Publishers, 1997.

Russell, Bertrand. *Freedom Versus Organization, 1814-1914: The Pattern of Political Changes in 19th Century European History.* W. W. Norton & Company, April 1, 1962.

Ryn, Claes G. "Leo Strauss and History: The Philosopher as Conspirator," in *Humanitas.* Vol. XVIII, nos. 1 & 2. National Humanities Institute. 2005. http://www.nhinet.org/ryn18-1&2.pdf.

———. "The Decline of American Intellectual Conservatism." *Modern Age*, fall 2007.

Saez, Emmanuel. "Income and Wealth Inequality: Evidence and Policy Implications." Neubauer Collegium lecture. University of Chicago, October 2014. https://eml.berkeley.edu/~saez/lecture_saez_chicago14.pdf.

Sage, Alexandria. "Swiss immigration vote 'worrying': French foreign minister." Reuters, February 10, 2014. https://www.reuters.com/article/us-swiss-vote-immigration/swiss-immigration-vote-worrying-french-foreign-minister-idUSBREA180H220140210.

Sartre, Jean-Paul. *Being and Nothingness: An Essay on Phenomenological Ontology.* Translated by Hazel E. Barnes. New York: Washington Square Press, 1984.

———. *Being and Nothingness.* Open Road Media, January 2012.

Sattler, Columban. *A Critique of Contemporary Art.* Catholic Culture, 1952.

Schnapp, Jeffrey Thompson, Olivia E. Sears, and Maria G. Stampino. *A Primer of Italian Fascism.* University of Nebraska Press, 2000.

Schneider, Friedrich. "Size and Development of the Shadow Economy of 31 European and 5 other OECD Countries from 2003 to 2015: Different Developments." January 20, 2015. http://www.econ.jku.at/members/Schneider/files/publications/2015/ShadEcEurope31.pdf.

Schoen, Douglas and Melik Kaylan, *The Russia-China Axis: The New Cold War and America's Crisis of Leadership.* Encounter Books, September 2014.

Scruton, Roger. "The Journey Home." Essay in *Intercollegiate Review* 44, no. 1 (Spring 2009).

———. *Renewing and Rejecting.* Future Symphony Institute, 2015.

Second Continental Congress, United States. *Declaration of Independence.* Manuscript. August 2, 1776. US National Archives and Records Administration. https://www.loc.gov/rr/program/bib/ourdocs/DeclarInd.html.

Segal, Ronald. *The Black Diaspora: Five Centuries of the Black Experience Outside Africa*. New York: Farrar, Straus and Giroux, 1995.

Shakespeare, William. "The Merchant of Venice." In *The Oxford Shakespeare—The Complete Works*. 2nd edition. Edited by Stanley Wells and Gary Taylor. Oxford University Press, 2005.

Shalhope, Robert E. *The Roots of Democracy: American Thought and Culture, 1760-1800*. Rowman & Littlefield, 2004.

Shanker, Thomas, C. J. Chivers, and Michael R. Gordon. "Obama Weighs 'Limited' Strikes Against Syrian Forces." The *New York Times*, August 27, 2013.

Shirer, William L. *The Rise and Fall of the Third Reich*. London: Secker & Warburg, 1960.

Simmons, Christine. "Bill Clinton: Be Proud US is More Diverse." NBC Miami, July 14, 2009.

Sinclair, Upton. *The Jungle*. Barnes & Noble, 1995.

Sindelar, Daisy. "Was Yanukovych's Ouster Constitutional?" Radio Free Europe—Radio Liberty. February 23, 2014. https://www.rferl.org/a/was-yanukovychs-ouster-constitutional/25274346.html.

Smith, Adam. *An Inquiry into the Nature and Causes of the Wealth of Nations*. 1776. http://files.libertyfund.org/files/220/0141-02_Bk.pdf.

Smith, Christian, Kari, Christoffersen, Hilary Davidson, and Patricia Snell Herzog. *Lost in Transition: The Dark Side of Emerging Adulthood*. New York: Oxford University Press, 2011.

Smith, Marion. "What Is America's Role in the World?" The Heritage Foundation. Research report. November 16, 2010. https://www.heritage.org/global-politics/report/what-americas-role-the-world.

Solash, Richard. "Despite Wariness, China-Russia Relations Warming." Radio Free Europe—Radio Liberty. August 9, 2013.

Solzhenitsyn, Aleksandr. *The Voice of Freedom*. 1975. https://archive.org/details/SolzhenitsynTheVoiceOfFreedom.

———. *Warning to the Western World*. The Bodley Head Ltd., May 1976.

———. "A World Split Apart." Commencement address delivered at Harvard University. June 8, 1978.

———. *Rebuilding Russia: Reflections and Tentative Proposals*. First edition. Farrar, Straus and Giroux, September 1, 1991.

Soyfer, Valery N. *Lysenko and the Tragedy of Soviet Science*. 1st edition. Rutgers University Press, June 1, 1994.

Spencer, Herbert. *The Man versus the State*. New York: M. Kennerley, 1916. https://archive.org/details/manversusstatea01spengoog.

Spengler, Oswald. "Prussians and Englishmen," Chapter III in *Prussianism and Socialism*. 1920. https://archive.org/details/PrussianismAndSocialism.

———. *The Decline of the West* [Der Untergang des Abendlandes]. Alfred A. Knopf, 1939.

Stachura, Peter D. *Gregor Strasser and the Rise of Nazism*. Routledge, 2014.

Stavrianos, Leften Stavros. *The Balkans Since 1453*. New York University Press, May 2000.

Stegherr, Marc. *The Social Market Economy in Eastern Europe—An Underestimated Option?* Konrad-Adenauer-Stiftung e.V., 2010. http://www.kas.de/upload/dokumente/2010/06/60_Years_SME/stegherr.pdf.

Steinbeck, John. *Tortilla Flat*. Penguin Publishing Group, 1997.

———. *Cannery Row*. Penguin Classics, 2011.

Steinberg, James B. "Administration's Vision of the US-China Relationship." Keynote address at the Center for a New American Security, Washington, DC, September 24, 2009. US Department of State. https://www.state.gov/s/d/former/steinberg/remarks/2009/169332.htm.

Stiglitz, Joseph. *Globalization and Its Discontents*. W. W. Norton & Company, 2002.

Stipp, John L., Charles Warren Hollister, and Allen Wendell Dirrim. *The Rise and Development of Western Civilization*. Band 2, 1972.

Stoddard, Lothrop. *The Revolt Against Civilization: The Menace of the Under Man*. New York: Charles Scribner's Sons, 1922.

Strauss, Leo. *Natural Right and History*. University of Chicago Press, 1953.

Szamuely, Tibor. *The Russian Tradition*. London: Secker & Warburg, 1974.

———. *Socialism and Liberty*. London: Aims for Freedom and Enterprise, 1977.

Talbott, Strobe. "America Abroad." *Time*, June 24, 2001.

———. *The Russia Hand: A Memoir of Presidential Diplomacy*. Random House, 2002.

Tax Policy Center. "The Numbers: What Are the Federal Government's Sources of Revenue?" The Tax Policy Center's Briefing Book. 2015. http://www.taxpolicycenter.org/briefing-book/what-are-sources-revenue-federal-government.

Tiky, Narcisse. "The African Origins of the Athenian Democracy." *SSRN*, October 28, 2011.

Tocqueville, Alexis de. *Democracy in America*. Translated by George Lawrence. New York: Harper & Row, 1966.

———. *Democracy in America: Historical-Critical Edition*. Vol. IV. Edited by Eduardo Nolla. Translated by James T. Schleifer. Indianapolis: Liberty Fund, 2010.

———. *The Old Regime and the Revolution: The Controversial Bestselling Guide to the Origins of the French Revolution*. New York, Harriman House Ltd, 2013.

Tomaszewski, Fiona K. *A Great Russia: Russia and the Triple Entente, 1905-1914*. Greenwood Publishing Group, 2002.

Tonelson, Alan. "Anti-Globalization and the US Middle Class." The *Globalist*, September 1, 2003. https://www.theglobalist.com/anti-globalization-and-the-u-s-middle-class/.

Traynor, Ian. "Switzerland faces 'difficult talks' with EU after immigration referendum." The *Guardian*, February 10, 2014. https://www.theguardian.com/world/2014/feb/10/switzerland-talks-eu-immigration-referendum.

Treitschke, Heinrich von. *Deutsche Geschichte im neunzehnten Jahrhundert* [History of Germany in the Nineteenth Century]. Hirzel, Leipzig, 1894.

Trilling, Lionel and Leon Wieseltier. *The Moral Obligation to Be Intelligent: Selected Essays*. Northwestern University Press, 2008.

Tseng, Roy: "Conservatism, Romanticism, and the Understanding of Modernity." In Abel, Corey. *The Meanings of Michael Oakeshott's Conservatism*. Andrews UK Limited, October 2015.

Turner, William. "History of Philosophy." HardPress Publishing. 2012.

Twitchell, Evelyn Ellison. "Will The Great Shakeout Take Its Toll?" *Barron's*, June 26, 2003. https://www.barrons.com/articles/SB105663319289188500.

United Nations Office on Drugs and Crime (UNODC). *Global Study on Homicide 2013*. April 2014. https://www.unodc.org/documents/gsh/pdfs/2014_GLOBAL_HOMICIDE_BOOK_web.pdf.

United Nations Security Council, Counter-Terrorism Committee. "Counter-Terrorism Committee Welcomes Close Cooperation with the Regional Anti-Terrorist Structure of the Shanghai Cooperation Organization." October 23, 2014. http://www.un.org/en/sc/ctc/news/2014-10-24_cted_shanghaicoop.html.

Unz, Ron. "Immigration, the Republicans, and the End of White America." *The American Conservative*, September 19, 2011.

US Department of Health & Human Services, CDC / National Center for Health Statistics. "Births: Final Data for 2013." https://www.cdc.gov/nchs/data/nvsr/nvsr64/nvsr64_01.pdf.

US Department of State. *Foreign Relations of the United States, 1969–1976*, volume XVII, *China, 1969–1972*. Document 203. "Joint Statement Following Discussions With Leaders of the People's Republic of China." Shanghai, February 27, 1972. United States Department of State, Office of the Historian, Bureau of Public Affairs.
https://history.state.gov/historicaldocuments/frus1969-76v17/d203.

———. "Milestones: 1977–1980, China Policy." United States Department of State, Office of the Historian, Bureau of Public Affairs. https://history.state.gov/milestones/1977-1980/china-policy.

———. "Milestones: 1981–1988, The August 17, 1982 US-China Communiqué on Arms Sales to Taiwan," United States Department of State, Office of the Historian, Bureau of Public Affairs. https://history.state.gov/milestones/1981-1988/china-communique.

Ustryalov, Nikolay V. *From NEP to Soviet Socialism*. Shanghai, 1934. http://www.magister.msk.ru/library/philos/ustryalov/ustry035.htm.

Vanberg, Viktor J. "The Freiburg School: Walter Eucken and Ordoliberalism." Freiburg discussion papers on constitutional economics. Walter Eucken Institut, Freiburg, 2004.

Vander Elst, Philip. *Idealism Without Illusions: A Foreign Policy for Freedom*. The Freedom Association, 1989.

Vazsonyi, Balint. *America's Thirty Year War—Who is Winning?* Regnery Publishing, Inc., 1998.

Viereck, Peter. *Conservatism Revisited: The Revolt Against Ideology*. Transaction Publishers, January 2005.

Voegelin, Eric. *Modernity Without Restraint—The Political Religions, The New Science of Politics, and Science, Politics, and Gnosticism (Collected Works of Eric Voegelin)*. Vol. 5. University of Missouri, November 1, 1999.

Voltaire. *Dictionnaire philosophique portatif* [A Philosophical Dictionary], 1764.

Wacquant, Loïc. *Punishing the Poor: The Neoliberal Government of Social Insecurity.* Duke University Press, 2009.

Walicki, Andrzej. *The Slavophile Controversy: History of a Conservative Utopia in Nineteenth-Century Russian Thought.* Oxford: Clarendon Press, 1975.

Wallace, David Foster. Kenyon College commencement address. 2005.

Wall Street Journal. "The Great Misallocators - What Barack Obama and General Electric Have in Common." Review & Outlook. January 26, 2011.

Walsh, Lynn. "China's Hybrid Economy." *Socialism Today* 122, October 2008.

Ward, Bruce K. *Dostoyevsky's Critique of the West: The Quest for the Earthly Paradise.* Wilfrid Laurier University Press, 1986.

Ward, Lee. *Modern Democracy and the Theological-Political Problem in Spinoza, Rousseau, and Jefferson.* Palgrave Macmillan, 2014.

Warren, Mark. *Nietzsche and Political Philosophy.* Political Theory, 1985.

Watts, John and Anthony Collins. *Half-hours with the Freethinkers.* Edited by J. Watts, and A. Collins. Oxford University, 1857.

Weart, Spencer R. *Never at War: Why Democracies Will Not Fight One Another.* Yale University Press, 1998.

Weaver, Richard M. *Reclaiming Liberal Education.* Intercollegiate Studies Institute, December 2014.

Wee, H. van der. *The Great Depression Revisited: Essays on the Economics of the Thirties.* Springer Netherlands, 1972.

West, Nigel and Oleg Czarev. *Triplex: Secrets from the Cambridge Spies.* Yale University Press, 2009.

Whyte, William H. *The Organization Man.* Simon & Schuster, 1956.

World Bank Group. "Population density (people per sq. km of land area)." Data Bank. 2015. https://data.worldbank.org/indicator/EN.POP.DNST.

Worldometers (data from two major sources: United Nations Population Division of the Department of Economic and Social Affairs and the US Census Bureau). "Population Growth Rate." http://www.worldometers.info/world-population/.

Yale Law School. *Nuremberg Trial Proceedings*, vol. 22. September 30, 1946. http://avalon.law.yale.edu/imt/09-30-46.asp.

Yao Xinzhong and Yanxia Zhao. *Chinese Religion: A Contextual Approach.* Continuum International Publishing Group, 2010.

Zhong, Raymond. "Gerhard Schröder: The Man Who Rescued the German Economy." *The Wall Street Journal*, The Weekend Interview, July 6, 2012.

Zinoviev, Alexander. *Homo Sovieticus*. The Atlantic Monthly Press, 1985.

Zoellick, Robert B. "Whither China: From Membership to Responsibility?" Remarks to National Committee on US-China Relations. New York City, September 21, 2005. US Department of State. http://2001-2009.state.gov/s/d/former/zoellick/rem/53682.htm.

Endnotes

1 Hans Köchler, *The Principles of Non-alignment: The Non-Aligned Countries in the Eighties: Results and Perspectives* (International Progress Organization, 1982).

2 Eventually it was East Germany that constituted the only exception; whatever the original plan might have been, the fact of the reunification with the western part of Germany rendered it impossible to sweep the awkward questions entirely under the rug. However, even here there has not been a thorough survey carried out concerning the many forms of political crimes committed, although West Germany alone would have had the means and legitimacy to do that.

The situation in East Germany was different; on the one hand, the final criminal showdown with the dictatorship could not happen, because the political transition, unlike that with the Nuremberg trials, amazingly did not bring about any new legal order. The German Democratic Republic's leaders could only be held liable by the legislation in force. The Stasi, officially the Ministry of State Security, was one of the most repressive intelligence and secret police agencies in the world. Its boss, Stasi Minister Erich Mielke could be sentenced not for the murders committed in the service of the Communist state but for manslaughter perpetrated against two police officers during the days of the Weimar Republic in 1931. Had the legal rules of the Nuremberg trials been applied, Erich Mielke could have received the capital punishment. With a few tort cases involving individual offenders followed by mild sentencing, the issue of retribution was checked off on the agenda. The victims had practically no chance to press charges against their wrongdoers.

Furthermore, the showdown with the old Communist system could not happen, because the Communist parties (which had insisted on keeping the party assets to themselves) have never been dissolved; they were able to live on and function under other names. While the Nazi party and its offspring organizations were banned, the East German communist party SED was only renamed first to PDS then later to Die Linke (Left).

This author would like to recall that only the total collapse of Germany ended the Nazi regime for good—that is, a defeat caused by external powers. It was the responsibility of the occupiers to educate and teach democracy to German society. The Nuremberg trials were meant to be the ultimate showdown with the old Nazi system; this was necessary for political hygiene. Without the active collaboration of the victorious powers, it is hard to imagine that Germany would have done this on its own.

3   David Binder, "Erich Mielke, Powerful Head of Stasi, East Germany's Vast Spy Network, Dies at 92," the *New York Times*, May 26, 2000.

4   Mark Kesselman, Joel Krieger, and William Joseph, *Introduction to Comparative Politics* (Boston: Cengage Learning, 2012).

5   József Mindszenty was the prince primate, archbishop of Esztergom, cardinal, and leader of the Catholic Church in Hungary from October 1945 to December 1973. For five decades, he personified uncompromising opposition to both fascism and communism in support of religious freedom in Hungary. During World War II, the pro-Nazi authorities imprisoned him; after the war, the pro-Soviet regime did the same. Since Cardinal Mindszenty opposed communism and resisted the Communist oppression in his country, he was arrested and tried, and he received a life sentence in a 1949 show trial. The case generated worldwide attention and condemnation, including a United Nations resolution. After eight years in prison, Mindszenty was freed during the Hungarian Revolt of 1956 and, after the defeat of the uprising by the Soviet troops, fled to the United States Embassy in Budapest, where he was confined to live for the next fifteen years.

Eventually Pope Paul VI offered a compromise to the Communist rulers of Hungary by ambiguously declaring Mindszenty a "victim of history" (instead of Communism) and annulling the excommunication imposed on his political opponents. The Hungarian Communist government allowed Mindszenty to leave the country in September 1971. Pope Paul VI welcomed him reassuringly: "You are and remain Archbishop of Esztergom and Primate of Hungary. Continue working, and if you have difficulties, always turn trustfully to us."

Beginning of October 1971, Mindszenty lived in Vienna, Austria, as he was offended by Rome's condition that he resign from the primacy of the Hungarian Catholic Church in exchange for a Vatican-approved publication of his memoirs. Although most bishops retire at or near age seventy-five, Mindszenty continuously denied rumors of his resignation, and he was not canonically required to step down at the time. After settling in Vienna, Cardinal Mindszenty had to endure another humiliation when, to improve church relations with Hungary, Pope Paul VI removed him as primate of that country and announced his removal from the see of Esztergom. In December of 1973, at the age of eighty-one, and only two years after the assurances by the Vatican, Mindszenty was stripped of his titles by the pope (an unprecedented act in modern history), who declared the Archdiocese of Esztergom officially vacated—although he refused to fill the seat while Mindszenty was still alive.

Mindszenty died in exile in Vienna in May 1975, at the age of eighty-three. In early 1976, the pope made Bishop László Lékai the primate of Hungary, ending a long struggle with the Communist government. Lékai turned out to be quite cordial toward the Kádár regime. Some questioned the pope's *Ostpolitik* and contacts with Communism and the deals he engaged in for the faithful. Cardinal Mindszenty felt betrayed by the Vatican policy of rapprochement with Communism led by Pope Paul VI.

6   Joschka Fischer, "The Erosion of Europe," Project Syndicate, April 30, 2013, https://www.project-syndicate.org/commentary/the-european-union-s-crumbling-foundations-by-joschka-fischer?barrier=accesspaylog.

7   Ernst B. Haas, *The Uniting of Europe, 1950–1957* (Stanford, CA: Stanford University Press, 1958), 16.

8   Leften Stavros Stavrianos, *The Balkans Since 1453* (New York: New York University Press, 2000).

9   ordon N. Bardos, "Spectre of Separatism Haunts Europe," *The National Interest*, January 17, 2013.

10 Renéo Lukic and Allen Lynch, *Europe From the Balkans to the Urals: The Disintegration of Yugoslavia and the Soviet Union*" (Oxford: Oxford University Press, 1996).

11 Bohdana Dimitrovova, "Bosniak or Muslim? Dilemma of One Nation with Two Names," *Southeast European Politics* 2, no. 2 (2001), http://www.seep.ceu.hu/issue22/dimitrovova.pdf.

12 Beata Huszka, "The Presevo Valley of Southern Serbia alongside Kosovo: The Case for Decentralization and Minority Protection," CEPS Policy Brief No. 120, Centre for European Policy Studies, January 2007.

13 Aisling Lyon: *Decentralisation and the Management of Ethnic Conflict: Lessons from the Republic of Macedonia* (Routledge, 2015).

14 Andrew Korybko, "Destabilization and the Geopolitics of NATO's Black Sea Bloc, Part II," Global Research, Centre for Research on Globalization, June 2015, https://www.globalresearch.ca/destabilization-and-the-geopolitics-of-natos-black-sea-bloc/5453717.

15 Stephen Brown and Gareth Jones, "German Faith in Euro and EU Lags Behind French—Poll," Reuters, September 17, 2012, https://uk.reuters.com/article/uk-eurozone-germany-poll/german-faith-in-euro-and-eu-lags-behind-french-poll-idUKBRE88G08W20120917.

16 Carroll Quigley, *Tragedy and Hope: A History of the World in Our Time* (Macmillan, 1966).

17 Robert L. Hutchings, *American Diplomacy and the End of the Cold War: An Insider's Account of US Diplomacy in Europe, 1989–1992* (Woodrow Wilson Center Press, 1997).

18 Ulrich Beck, *German Europe* (Cambridge: Polity Press, 2013).

19 Andreas Kluth, *The Dilemma at the Heart of Europe: Germany and the German Question* (The Institute for Public Policy Research, 2013).

20 Renata Goldirova, "France Muddies Waters with 'Mediterranean Union' Idea," EUobserver, October 25, 2007

21 George Friedman, "The State of the World: Germany's Strategy," *Geopolitical Weekly*, Stratfor, March 12, 2012.

22 Raymond Zhong, "Gerhard Schröder: The Man Who Rescued the German Economy," The Weekend Interview, *Wall Street Journal*, July 6, 2012.

23 Frank Mattern, Eckart Windhagen, Markus Habbel, Jörg Mußhoff, Hans-Helmut Kotz, and Wilhelm Rall, *The Future of the Euro* (McKinsey & Co. Inc., 2012). https://www.mckinsey.de/files/The%20future%20of%20the%20euro_McKinsey%20report.pdf.

24 The Economist, "The Future of the European Union: The Choice", Leaders, May 26, 2012, http://www.economist.com/node/21555916.

25 Narcisse Tiky, "The African Origins of the Athenian Democracy," SSRN, Elsevier, October 28, 2011.

26 Lillian Goldman Law Library, *The Judgment of the International Military Tribunal, Nuremberg Trial Proceedings*, vol. 22 (New Haven, CT: Lillian Goldman Law Library, 1946) http://avalon.law.yale.edu/imt/09-30-46.asp.

27 Robert Chazan, *Church, State, and Jew in the Middle Ages* (New York: Behrman House, Inc., 1980).

28 Anthony W. Marx, *Faith in Nation: Exclusionary Origins of Nationalism* (Oxford: Oxford University Press, 2003).

29 Amnesty International, *Amnesty International Submission for the Universal Periodic Review of Libya, 22nd Session of the UPR Working Group* (Amnesty International, 2014) http://www.refworld.org/docid/553a024f4.html.

30 Tracey Greenstein, "The Fed's $16 Trillion Bailouts Under-Reported," Forbes, Business, September 20, 2011.

31 Alexis de Tocqueville, *Democracy in America: Historical-Critical Edition*, vol. IV, ed. Eduardo Nolla, trans. James T. Schleifer (Indianapolis: Liberty Fund, 2010).

32 Peter S. Rieth, "Russia & Foreign Policy: The Forgotten Teachings of Henryk Krzeczkowski," *The Imaginative Conservative*, June 27, 2014, https://theimaginativeconservative.org/2014/06/russia-foreign-policy-forgotten-teachings-henryk-krzeczkowski.html

33 eter Viereck, *Conservatism Revisited: The Revolt Against Ideology* (Transaction Publishers, 2005).

34 Bertrand Russell, *Freedom Versus Organization, 1814–1914: The Pattern of Political Changes in 19th Century European History* (W. W. Norton & Company, 1962).

35 David R. Egan and Melinda A. Egan: *Joseph Stalin: An Annotated Bibliography of English-Language Periodical Literature to 2005* (Scarecrow Press, 2007); Ian Kershaw, *Hitler: A Biography* (W. W. Norton & Company, 2008).

36 Tibor Szamuely, *Socialism and Liberty* (London: Aims for Freedom and Enterprise, 1977); Tibor Szamuely, *The Russian Tradition* (London: Secker & Warburg, 1974).

37 Aleksandr I. Solzhenitsyn, *The Voice of Freedom* (Washington: American Federation of Labor and Congress of Industrial Organizations, 1975), https://archive.org/details/SolzhenitsynTheVoiceOfFreedom.

38 Wayne Merry, "Yeltsin Under Siege—The October 1993 Constitutional Crisis," Moments in US Diplomatic History, Association for Diplomatic Studies and Training, February 2010, http://adst.org/2014/10/yeltsin-under-siege-the-october-1993-constitutional-crisis/#.Wk-WRxM-cqw.

39 Irina Busygina, *Political Crisis in Russia: The Regional Dimension* (Bonn: FES, 1993).

40 Members of the Speaker's Advisory Group on Russia, United States House of Representatives, *Russia's Road to Corruption: How the Clinton Administration Exported Government Instead of Free Enterprise and Failed the Russian People*, September 19, 2000, https://fas.org/irp/congress/2000_rpt/russias-road.pdf.

41 Thomas Graham Jr., "World Without Russia?" Jamestown Foundation Conference, Washington, DC, Carnegie Endowment for International Peace, June 9, 1999.

42 Thomas Graham Jr., "World Without Russia?" Jamestown Foundation Conference, Washington, DC, Carnegie Endowment for International Peace, June 9, 1999.

43 Graeme Gill and James Young: *Routledge Handbook of Russian Politics and Society* (Routledge, March 2013).

44 Katja Richters, *The Post-Soviet Russian Orthodox Church: Politics, Culture and Greater Russia* (Routledge, 2012).

45 Anna Politkovskaya, *Putin's Russia* (Random House, December 2012).

46 Richard Pipes, *Russian Conservatism and Its Critics: A Study in Political Culture* (New Haven, CT: Yale University Press, 2005).

47 Paul Robinson, *Putin's Philosophy*, the *American Conservative*, March 28, 2012.

48 Nikolai Berdiaev et al., *Landmarks* (Armonk, NY: M.E. Sharpe, 1994).

49 Fiona K. Tomaszewski, *A Great Russia: Russia and the Triple Entente, 1905-1914* (Greenwood Publishing Group, 2002).

50 Правительство Российской Федерации, "Prime Minister Vladimir Putin Chairs a Meeting of the Organizing Committee for the Celebration of Pyotr Stolypin's 150th Birthday Anniversary," Правительство Российской Федерации, 2010, http://archive.government.ru/eng/docs/15878/.

51 Paul Robinson, "Putin's Philosopher," *Irrussianality* (blog), December 22, 2014, https://irrussianality.wordpress.com/2014/12/22/putins-philosopher/.

52 William Partlett, "Vladimir Putin and the Law," The Brookings Institution, February 28, 2012, https://www.brookings.edu/opinions/vladimir-putin-and-the-law/.

53 Fiona Hill, and Clifford G. Gaddy, *Mr. Putin: Operative in the Kremlin* (Washington, DC: Brookings Institution Press, February 2015).

54 Alfred Evans Jr., *The Public Chamber and Social Conflicts in Russia*, Western Political Science Association 2010 Annual Meeting Paper, Social Science Research Network, April 2010.

55 Lee Kuan Yew: *The Grand Master's Insights on China, the United States, and the World* (2013).

56 Laura Engelstein, *Slavophile Empire: Imperial Russia's Illiberal Path*, 1st edition (Cornell University Press, October 2009).

57 Oswald Spengler, *The Decline of the West* [Der Untergang des Abendlandes] (New York: Alfred A. Knopf, 1939).

58 Ibid.

59 D. D. Blagoy, "*История русской литературы XVIII века*" [Istoriya russkoy literatury XVIII veka / History of Russian literature of the eighteenth century] (Moscow, Uchpedgiz Publ., 1955).

60 Stephen Lessing Baehr, *The Paradise Myth in Eighteenth-century Russia: Utopian Patterns in Early Secular Russian Literature and Culture* (Stanford University Press, 1991).

61 Edyta M. Bojanowska, *Nikolai Gogol: Between Ukrainian and Russian Nationalism* (Harvard University Press, 2007).

62 Andrzej Walicki, *The Slavophile Controversy: History of a Conservative Utopia in Nineteenth-Century Russian Thought*, (Oxford: Clarendon Press, 1975).

63 Charles-Louis de Secondat Montesquieu, *The Spirit of Laws: A Compendium of the First English Edition* (University of California Press, 1977).

64 The story of Benthamia is a story about men who emigrate from the old world, break all of their bonds to all traditions, and come to inhabit a deserted island. They decide to enact the Benthamite, utilitarian system on the island. Their God is profit. The word "Profit" momentarily cures all ills, and the Benthamite colony prospers. A giant statue of Jeremy Bentham is built in the center of the capital city with a plaque reading "Profit."

Then some of the citizens would like to build a church. When asked, "What is the usefulness of a church?" they defend their request by explaining that a church can forever remind people that profit is not only the basis for morality but also the only law governing human action. Everyone agrees, and the church is built.

Some artists propose that the colony should build a theater. Others argue that theaters are useless. In the end, the theater is constructed to strengthen the idea that profit is the source of all virtues and action without any interest is the primary source of all human miseries.

A prophet comes and foretells that the Benthamite colony will collapse and calls the people to repent. He is ignored and shut up in a home for the mentally insane. However, his prophecy comes true; the dictatorship of the moneychangers is overthrown, and thereupon begins a time of upheaval, during which various groups on the island fight for power. Each of the classes, whether the farmers or the artisans, take control and make use of the state for their profit. The Benthamite colony collapses into chaos and ruin; the people are pauperized and starved. They murder one another when it is useful or profitable to do so. Thus in the end there stood only an island and a nameless city with a plaque reading "Profit."

Odoyevsky's 1844 characterization of the Benthamite economic life appears to be an early exaggeration of *The Protestant Ethic and the Spirit of Capitalism*, the first major work written by Max Weber and published in 1905. It is presented in the spirit of exploitative economic rationality that subsumes all areas of individual life under the dictate of systematic planning and precise calculation.

65 Vladimir Fyodorovich Odoyevsky, *Russian Nights* (Northwestern University Press, 1997).

66 Peter S. Rieth, "The Russian 'Conservative Mind,'" the *Imaginative Conservative*, February 28, 2015.

67 Richard Pipes, *Russian Conservatism and its Critics: A Study in Political Culture* (Yale University Press, 2005).

68 Ibid.

69 Thomas Shanker, C. J. Chivers, and, Michael R. Gordon, "Obama Weighs 'Limited' Strikes Against Syrian Forces," the *New York Times*, August 27, 2013.

Paul Lewis, "US attack on Syria delayed after surprise U-turn from Obama," the *Guardian*, September 1, 2013.

70 Remarks by EU High Representative Catherine Ashton upon arrival at the Foreign Affairs Council, Brussels, March 17, 2014, http://europa.ba/?p=11827.

71 "Annual Address to the Federal Assembly of the Russian Federation," the Kremlin, Moscow, April 25, 2005, http://en.kremlin.ru/events/president/transcripts/22931.

72 Philip Rucker, "Hillary Clinton says Putin's actions are like 'what Hitler did back in the '30s,'" the *Washington Post*, March 5, 2014, https://www.washingtonpost.com/news/post-politics/

wp/2014/03/05/hillary-clinton-says-putins-action-are-like-what-hitler-did-back-in-the-30s/?utm_term=.c10495809803.

73 Daisy Sindelar, "Was Yanukovych's Ouster Constitutional?" Radio Free Europe—Radio Liberty, February 23, 2014, https://www.rferl.org/a/was-yanukovychs-ouster-constitutional/25274346.html.

74 Scott McConnell, "A Coup in Crimea—or in Russia?," the *American Conservative*, March 19, 2014.

75 Strobe Talbott, *The Russia Hand: A Memoir of Presidential Diplomacy* (New York: Random House, 2002).

76 Frederick Merk, *Manifest Destiny and Mission in American History* (Cambridge, MA: Harvard University Press, 1963).

77 Lee, *The Grand Master's Insights*.

78 Deng Xiaoping, "Building Socialism with a Specifically Chinese Character," Excerpt from a talk with the Japanese delegation to the second session of the Council of Sino-Japanese Non-Governmental Persons, June 30, 1984, http://www.china.org.cn/english/features/dengxiaoping/103371.htm.

79 Deng Xiaoping, *Selected Works*, vol. 3 (Beijing: Foreign Languages Press, November 1, 1984), https://archive.org/details/SelectedWorksOfDengXiaopingVol.3.

80 The "Critique of the Gotha Program" (German: Kritik des Gothaer Programms) is a document based on a letter by Karl Marx written in early May 1875 to the Social Democratic Workers' Party of Germany (SDAP). It is notable for elucidating the principles of "To each according to his contribution" as the basis for a "lower phase" of communist society directly following the transition from capitalism and "From each according to his ability, to each according to his needs" as the basis for a future "higher phase" of communist society (New York: International Publishers Co.,1938).

81 Deng Xiaoping, "Building Socialism."

82 Deng Xiaoping, *Selected Works*.

83 Lynn Walsh, "China's Hybrid Economy," Socialism Today, Issue 122, October 2008.

84 Barry Naughton, *The Chinese Economy, Transitions and Growth* (The MIT Press, 2007).

85 Andrew J. Nathan, and Andrew Scobell, "How China Sees America: The Sum of Beijing's Fears," *Foreign Affairs* 91, no. 5 (September/October 2012).

86 Ibid.

87 Ibid.

88 United States Department of State, *Foreign Relations of the United States, 1969–1976*, volume XVII, *China, 1969–1972*, Document 203: "Joint Statement Following Discussions With Leaders of the People's Republic of China," Shanghai, February 27, 1972, United States Department of State, Office of the Historian, Bureau of Public Affairs, https://history.state.gov/historicaldocuments/frus1969-76v17/d203.

89 United States Department of State, "Milestones: 1977–1980: China Policy," United States Department of State, Office of the Historian, Bureau of Public Affairs, https://history.state.gov/milestones/1977-1980/china-policy.

90. Taiwan Relations Act, Public Law 96-8, 96th Congress, Effective as of January 1, 1979, Approved April 10, 1979, http://photos.state.gov/libraries/ait-taiwan/171414/ait-pages/tra_e.pdf.
91. United States Department of State, "Milestones: 1981–1988, The August 17, 1982 US-China Communiqué on Arms Sales to Taiwan," United States Department of State, Office of the Historian, Bureau of Public Affairs, https://history.state.gov/milestones/1981-1988/china-communique.
92. Nathan, "How China Sees America."
93. Wade Boese, "Bush Approves Major Arms Deal To Taiwan, Defers Aegis Sale," Arms Control Association, May 1, 2001, https://www.armscontrol.org/act/2001_05/taiwan.
94. Elena Atanassova-Cornelis and Frans-Paul van der Putten, *Changing Security Dynamics in East Asia: A Post-US Regional Order in the Making?* (Palgrave Macmillan, November 2014).
95. Robert B. Zoellick, "Whither China: From Membership to Responsibility?," remarks to National Committee on US–China Relations, New York City, September 21, 2005, US Department of State, https://2001-2009.state.gov/s/d/former/zoellick/rem/53682.htm.
96. James B. Steinberg, "Administration's Vision of the US-China Relationship," keynote address at the Center for a New American Security, Washington, DC, September 24, 2009, US Department of State, https://www.state.gov/s/d/former/steinberg/remarks/2009/169332.htm.
97. Nathan, "How China Sees America."
98. Yong Deng, *China's Struggle for Status: The Realignment of International Relations*, (Cambridge University Press, April 2008)
99. Valentina Matviyenko, "Russian-Chinese trade to hit record $90 billion in 2014," TASS Russian News Agency, Business & Economy, September 23, 2014, http://tass.ru/en/economy/750855.
100. Ariel Cohen, "The Russia-China Axis Grows," *Frontpage Mag*, March 13, 2013.
101. Agence France-Presse in Moscow, "China, Russia proclaim unity ahead of Xi visit," *South China Morning Post*, February 23, 2013, http://www.scmp.com/news/china/article/1156659/china-russia-proclaim-unity-ahead-xi-visit.
102. United Nations Security Council, Counter-Terrorism Committee, "Counter-Terrorism Committee Welcomes Close Cooperation with the Regional Anti-Terrorist Structure of the Shanghai Cooperation Organization," October 23, 2014, http://www.un.org/en/sc/ctc/news/2014-10-24_cted_shanghaicoop.html.
103. Douglas Schoen and Melik Kaylan, *The Russia-China Axis: The New Cold War and America's Crisis of Leadership* (Encounter Books, September 2014).
104. Solash, Richard: "Despite Wariness, China-Russia Relations Warming," Radio Free Europe—Radio Liberty, August 9, 2013.
105. Alexander Moseley, *An Introduction to Political Philosophy* (Continuum International Publishing Group, 2007).
106. James McClellan, *Liberty, Order, and Justice: An Introduction to the Constitutional Principles of American Government* (Liberty Fund, 1989).
107. Balint Vazsonyi, *America's Thirty Years War—Who is Winning?* (Regnery Publishing, Inc., 1998).

108 Timothy B. Lewis, "The Meaning of Equality," June 18, 2004, *Meridian Magazine*, https://ldsmag.com/article-1-4360/.

109 Theodore Roosevelt, letter to the American Defense Society, 1919; CNN, "Broken Borders: Teddy Roosevelt's words to live by," CNN International, Monday, March 27, 2006, http://edition.cnn.com/2006/US/03/27/quote.roosevelt/.

110 Mark Perkins, "On Difference and Equality," the *Imaginative Conservative*, December 20, 2014.

111 Karl R. Popper, *The Open Society and Its Enemies* (Princeton University Press, April 2013).

112 Jean-Jacques Rousseau, *The Social Contract or Principles of Political Right*, trans. G. D. H. Cole (1762) https://www.ucc.ie/archive/hdsp/Rousseau_contrat-social.pdf.

113 Stephan Eisel, "Between Ideologies: The Social Market Economy," study paper, Konrad Adenauer Stiftung, January 2012.

114 John Locke, *Second Treatise of Government* (Hackett Publishing Company, Inc., June 1980).

115 Immanuel Kant, *On the Old Saw: That May be Right in Theory But It Won't Work in Practice* (University of Pennsylvania Press, July 2013).

116 Abraham Lincoln, *Abraham Lincoln: Selected Speeches and Writings* (Library of America, July 2009).

117 John Locke, *Essays on the Law of Nature* (Oxford University Press, December 2002).

118 Søren Kierkegaard, *Kierkegaard's Writings XII*, volume II, *Concluding Unscientific Postscript to Philosophical Fragments* (Princeton University Press, 2013).

119 Jean-Paul Sartre, *Being and Nothingness* (Open Road Media, January 2012).

120 Christopher Dawson, "The Left-Right Fallacy," the *Catholic Mind*, April 1946.

121 Aristotle, *Nicomachean Ethics* (Cambridge University Press, March 2000).

122 John Stuart Mill, *On Liberty* (J. W. Parker and Son, 1859).

123 Ibid.

124 Ibid.

125 Ibid.

126 Ibid.

127 Popper, *The Open Society*.

128 George Levine, et al., "Speaking for the Humanities," American Council of Learned Societies, occasional paper no. 7, New York: ACLS, 1989, http://archives.acls.org/op/7_Speaking_for_Humanities.htm.

129 Christian Smith, Kari Christoffersen, Hilary Davidson, and Patricia Snell Herzog, *Lost in Transition: The Dark Side of Emerging Adulthood* (New York: Oxford University Press, 2011), 27.

130 Alexis de Tocqueville, *Democracy in America*, trans. George Lawrence (New York: Harper & Row, 1966), 430.

131 Isaiah Berlin, *Four Essays on Liberty* (Oxford University Press, 1990).

132 Anthony M. Kennedy, Sandra Day O'Connor, and David Hackett Souter, "Planned Parenthood of Southeastern Pennsylvania versus Casey" in *Constitutional Law: 1995 Supplement*, ed. Geoffrey R. Stone et al. (Boston: Little, Brown & Co., 1995), 955.

133 Friedrich Nietzsche, *The Will to Power*, trans. Walter Kaufmann and R. J. Hollingdale (New York: Vintage, 1968), 3.
134 David Foster Wallace, Kenyon College Commencement Address, 2005.
135 Aristotle, "Nicomachean Ethics"
136 Plato, "The Republic," trans. And ed. Allan Bloom (New York: Basic Books, 1991), 557b.
137 Fisher Ames, *Works of Fisher Ames, compiled by a number of his friends* (Oxford University, 1809).
138 James J. O'Donnell, "A Common Quotation from 'Augustine'?" Georgetown University, 2010, https://web.archive.org/web/20140912032329/http://faculty.georgetown.edu/jod/augustine/quote.html.
139 Erik von Kuehnelt-Leddihn, *Liberty or Equality—The Challenge of Our Times* (Angelico Press, 2013)
140 Arthur Moeller van den Bruck, *Germany's Third Empire* (Arktos Media Ltd., 2012).
141 Franz-Xaver Kaufmann, *Variations of the Welfare State: Great Britain, Sweden, France, and Germany Between Capitalism and Socialism* (Springer Science & Business Media, November 2012).
142 Charles-Louis de Secondat Montesquieu, *The Spirit of Laws: A Compendium of the First English Edition* (University of California Press, 1977).
143 Rousseau, *The Social Contract*
144 Theodor Mommsen, *The History of Rome* [Römische Geschichte], vol. 4, trans. William P. Dickson (London: Richard Bentley Publisher, 1867), https://archive.org/details/historyofrom04momm.
145 Errico Malatesta, *Life and Ideas—The Anarchist Writings of Errico Malatesta*, trans. and ed. Vernon Richards (PM Press, 2015).
146 Ian Traynor, "Switzerland faces 'difficult talks' with EU after immigration referendum," the *Guardian*, February 10, 2014, https://www.theguardian.com/world/2014/feb/10/switzerland-talks-eu-immigration-referendum.
147 Alexandria Sage, "Swiss immigration vote 'worrying': French foreign minister," Reuters, February 10, 2014, https://www.reuters.com/article/us-swiss-vote-immigration/swiss-immigration-vote-worrying-french-foreign-minister-idUSBREA180H220140210.
148 Jason Groves, "Britons 'too ignorant' for EU referendum," *Daily Mail*, February 11, 2014, http://www.dailymail.co.uk/news/article-2556397/Britons-ignorant-EU-referendum-Top-official-says-debate-Europe-distorted-people-not-make-informed-decision.html.
149 Matthew Lynch, "Examining the Democratic Mechanisms of Political Parties," The Huffington Post, January 11, 2012, https://www.huffingtonpost.com/matthew-lynch-edd/political-parties_b_1164310.html, December 18, 2016.
150 Oswald Spengler, "Prussians and Englishmen," chapter III in *Prussianism and Socialism* (1920), https://archive.org/details/PrussianismAndSocialism.
151 Harold Hotelling, "Stability in Competition," The *Economic Journal*, Vol. 39, No. 153 (March 1929), http://www.math.toronto.edu/mccann/assignments/477/Hotelling29.pdf,
152 Niccolò Machiavelli, *Discourses on Livy* (University of Chicago Press, 1996).

153 Lawrence Lessig, *Republic, Lost: Version 2.0* (Hachette UK, 2015),
154 Alexander Hamilton, James Madison, John Jay, and Michael A. Genovese, *The Federalist Papers: Alexander Hamilton, James Madison and John Jay* (Palgrave Macmillan, 2009).
155 Plato, *The Republic*
156 Ames, *Works of Fisher Ames.*
157 Erik von Kuehnelt-Leddihn, *Liberty or Equality.*
158 Ibid.
159 Daniel Fried, "Current Policy Toward Russia, Serbia, and Kosovo," Interview With Ivana Kuhar, VOA Eurasia Division, January 16, 2007, US Department of State, https://2001-2009.state.gov/p/eur/rls/rm/78973.htm.
160 Martin Luther King, "How My Mind Has Changed," *Christian Century*, 1960, http://okra.stanford.edu/transcription/document_images/Vol05Scans/13Apr1960_PilgrimagetoNonviolence.pdf.
161 Aristotle, *Nicomachean Ethics.*
162 Thomas Hobbes, *Leviathan* (Oxford University Press, May 2012).
163 John Rawls, *A Theory of Justice*, revised edition (Belknap Press, September 1999).
164 John Locke, *An Essay Concerning Human Understanding* (New York: Barnes & Noble Books, 2004).
165 William Turner, *History of Philosophy* (HardPress Publishing, 2012), 83.
166 Lawrence Hamilton, *Freedom is Power* (Cambridge University Press, 2014).
167 John Watts and Anthony Collins, *Half-hours with the Freethinkers*, ed. J. Watts and A. Collins (Oxford University, 1857), 2006 digitized e-book.
168 John L. Stipp, Charles Warren Hollister, and Allen Wendell Dirrim, *The Rise and Development of Western Civilization* (Band 2, 1972).
169 Richard S. Grayson, *Liberals, International Relations and Appeasement: The Liberal Party, 1919-1939* (Routledge, 2013).
170 Voltaire, *Dictionnaire philosophique portatif* [A philosophical dictionary] (1764).
171 Simon Millar, *Rossbach and Leuthen 1757* (Osprey Publishing, 2002).
172 National Assembly of France, *Declaration of the Rights of Man and Citizen* (Charles River Editors, August 2011).
173 John James M'Gregor, *History of the French Revolution, and of the Wars Resulting from That Memorable Event*, vol. II, book II (1817, repr., BiblioBazaar, 2011), 65.
174 Samuel A. Nigro, *Everybody for Everybody: Truth, Oneness, Good, and Beauty for Everyone's Life, Liberty, and Pursuit of Happiness*, vol. 1 (Xlibris Corporation, 2012).
175 George Henry Lewes, *The Life and Works of Goethe: With Sketches of His Age and Contemporaries* (Cambridge University Press, 2010).
176 Karl Marx and Friedrich Engels, *Manifesto of the Communist Party*, 1848.
177 George F. Kennan, "The Sources of Soviet Conduct," February 22, 1946, published in *Foreign Affairs* in July 1947.
178 Quigley, *Tragedy and Hope.*
179 Lord Hugh Cecil, *Conservatism* (Williams and Norgate, 1912), https://archive.org/details/conservatism00ceciuoft.

180 Taylor C. Boas and Jordan Gans-Morse, "Neoliberalism: From New Liberal Philosophy to Anti-Liberal Slogan," (in German) *Studies in Comparative International Development*, 2009.

181 Walter Oswalt, "Liberale Opposition gegen den NS-Staat. Zur Entwicklung von Walter Euckens Sozialtheorie," in *Wirtschaft, Politik und Freiheit*, ed. Nils Goldschmidt (Tübingen: Mohr Siebeck, 2005).

182 Jörg Guido Hülsmann, *Mises, The Last Knight of Liberalism* (Ludwig von Mises Institute, 2007).

183 Friedrich A. Hayek, *The Constitution of Liberty* (University of Chicago Press, 1960).

184 Friedrich A. Hayek, *Law, Legislation, and Liberty*, volume II (1976).

185 Warren E. Buffett and Lawrence A. Cunningham, *The Essays of Warren Buffett: Lessons for Corporate America* (1997).

186 Joseph Stiglitz, *Globalization and Its Discontents* (W. W. Norton & Company, 2002).

187 Robert J. Antonio and Alessandro Bonanno, "Periodizing Globalization: From Cold War Modernization to the Bush Doctrine," *Current Perspectives on Social Theory* 24, special volume edition, 2006.

188 Loïc Wacquant, *Punishing the Poor: The Neoliberal Government of Social Insecurity* (Duke University Press, 2009).

189 Paul Craig Roberts, *A World Overwhelmed By Western Hypocrisy* (Information Clearing House, June 29, 2011).

190 Scott Christianson, "The Origins of the World War I—Agreement That Carved Up the Middle East," *Smithsonian*, November 16, 2015; excerpted from *100 Documents That Changed the World: From the Magna Carta to Wikileaks* (Pavilion Books, 2015).

191 Lord Arthur James Balfour, "The Balfour Declaration," British Foreign Office, November 2, 1917.

192 Thomas W. Lippman, "The Day FDR Met Saudi Arabia's Ibn Saud," the *Link* 38, no. 2, April–May 2005.

193 McMahon–Hussein Correspondence, July 14, 1915–March 10, 1916, published by George Antonius in *The Arab Awakening* (London, 1938).

194 International Coalition for the Responsibility to Protect (ICRtoP): "The Crisis in Syria," http://www.responsibilitytoprotect.org/index.php/crises/crisis-in-syria.

195 Brookings Institution, *Beyond Preemption—Force and Legitimacy in a Changing World*, Washington, DC: Brookings Institution Press, 2007.

196 Wassily Leontief, *Input-Output Economics*, 2nd edition (Oxford University Press, 1986).

197 Robert Nozick, *Anarchy, State, and Utopia* (Basic Books, 1974).

198 Embassy of France in Washington, DC, "Liberty, Equality, Fraternity," November 30, 2007, https://franceintheus.org/spip.php?article620.

199 Stéphane Courtois et. al, *The Black Book of Communism: Crimes, Terror, Repression* (Harvard University Press, 1999).

200 R. J. Rummel, *Death by Government* (Transaction Publishers, 1997).

201 Philip Vander Elst, *Idealism Without Illusions: A Foreign Policy for Freedom* (The Freedom Association, London, 1989).

202 Aleksandr Solzhenitsyn, *Warning to the Western World* (The Bodley Head Ltd., May 1976).
203 Mill, *On Liberty*.
204 Giuseppe Mazzini, "The Economic Question," chapter XI in *The Duties of Man and Other Essays* (1907; repr. Cosimo Classics, 2005).
205 Frédéric Bastiat, *The Law* (Ludwig von Mises Institute, 2007).
206 William E. H. Lecky, *Democracy and Liberty*, volume II (Indianapolis: Liberty Classics, 1980).
207 Charles Bradlaugh and John Saville, *A Selection of the Political Pamphlets of Charles Bradlaugh* (A. M. Kelley, 1970).
208 Auberon E. W. M. Herbert, *The Right and Wrong of Compulsion by the State* (Williams and Norgate, 1885).
209 Herbert Spencer, *The Man versus the State* (1884, repr., New York: M. Kennerley, 1916), https://archive.org/details/manversusstatea01spengoog.
210 Nicholas Buccola, "The Tyranny of the Least and the Dumbest: Nietzsche's Critique of Socialism," *Quarterly Journal of Ideology* 31, 2009.
211 Friedrich Nietzsche, *Will to Power* (New York: Random House, Inc., Vintage Books Edition, 1968).
212 Friedrich Nietzsche, *The Antichrist* (Amherst: Prometheus Books, 2000).
213 Buccola, Nicholas: "The Tyranny of the Least and the Dumbest: Nietzsche's Critique of Socialism," Quarterly Journal of Ideology 31, 2009
214 Nietzsche, *Will to Power*.
215 Friedrich Nietzsche, *Ecce Homo* (New York: Penguin Classics, 1992).
216 Nietzsche, *Will to Power*.
217 Ibid.
218 Ibid.
219 Nietzsche, *The Antichrist*.
220 Nietzsche, *Will to Power*.
221 Ibid.
222 Ibid.
223 Friedrich Nietzsche, *Beyond Good and Evil* (New York: Penguin Classics, 2003).
224 Nietzsche, *The Antichrist*.
225 Ibid.
226 Ibid.
227 Nietzsche, *Beyond Good and Evil*
228 Nietzsche, *The Antichrist*.
229 Friedrich Nietzsche, *The Gay Science* (New York: Vintage, 1974).
230 Ibid.
231 Ibid.
232 Nietzsche, *Will to Power*.
233 Friedrich Nietzsche, *Twilight of the Idols* (New York: Oxford University Press, 1998).
234 Nietzsche, *Will to Power*.
235 Ibid.

236 Ibid.
237 Ibid.
238 Ibid.
239 Ibid.
240 Nietzsche, *Twilight of the Idols*
241 Nietzsche, *Will to Power.*
242 Ibid.
243 Friedrich Nietzsche, *On the Genealogy of Morals* (New York: Oxford University Press, 1999).
244 Nietzsche, *Will to Power.*
245 Ibid.
246 Ibid.
247 Ibid.
248 Ibid.
249 Friedrich Nietzsche, *Beyond Good and Evil* (New York: Penguin Classics, 2003).
250 Nietzsche, *Will to Power.*
251 Nietzsche, *The Antichrist.*
252 Ibid.
253 Nietzsche, *Will to Power.*
254 Ibid.
255 (Mussolini: "The Doctrine of Fascism," 1932)
256 Nietzsche, *Will to Power.*
257 Ibid.
258 Ibid.
259 Sigmund Freud, *Civilization and Its Discontents* (New York: W.W. Norton, 1961).
260 Robert Owen, "Address to the Inhabitants of New Lanark," Longman, London, 1817, http://www.infed.org/archives/e-texts/owen_new_lanark.htm.
261 Freud, *Civilization and Its Discontents.*
262 Nietzsche, *Will to Power.*
263 Ibid.
264 Michael Oakeshott, "On Being Conservative," in *Rationalism in Politics and Other Essays* (Liberty Fund, 1991).
265 Nietzsche, *Will to Power.*
266 Arthur Moeller van den Bruck, *Germany's Third Empire* [Das Dritte Reich] (1923, repr. London: Arktos Media Ltd., 2012.)
267 Marx and Engels, "Manifesto."
268 Jean-Jacques Rousseau, *Discourse on the Origin and Foundations of Inequality among Men* (Bedford/St. Martin's, 2010).
269 Christopher Dawson, *Medieval Essays (The Works of Christopher Dawson)* (The Catholic University of America Press, 1954).
270 Robert Nola, *Rescuing Reason: A Critique of Anti-Rationalist Views of Science and Knowledge* (Springer Science & Business Media, 2012).

271 Claes G. Ryn, "The Decline of American Intellectual Conservatism," *Modern Age*, fall 2007.
272 Herbert Gintis, "Review of Milton Friedman, Capitalism and Freedom," http://people.umass.edu/~gintis/papers_index.html.
273 Patrice Higonnet, *Goodness beyond Virtue: Jacobins during the French Revolution* (Harvard University Press, 1998).
274 Marion Smith, "What Is America's Role in the World?" The Heritage Foundation, research report, November 16, 2010, https://www.heritage.org/global-politics/report/what-americas-role-the-world.
275 Hobbes, *Leviathan*.
276 Lisa Hill, *The Passionate Society: The Social, Political and Moral Thought of Adam Ferguson* (Springer Netherlands, 2006).
277 Edmund Burke, *Reflections*.
278 Robert Corfe, *The Spirit of New Socialism and the End of Class-Based Politics* (Arena Books, 2005).
279 Claes G. Ryn, "Leo Strauss and History: The Philosopher as Conspirator," in *Humanitas* XVIII, nos. 1 and 2, 2005, http://www.nhinet.org/ryn18-1&2.pdf.
280 Burke, *Reflections*.
281 Robert Nisbet, *The Quest for Community: A Study in the Ethics of Order and Freedom*, 1st edition (Intercollegiate Studies Institute, July 5, 2010).
282 Leo Strauss, *Natural Right and History* (University of Chicago Press, 1953).
283 Babbitt, Irving: *Character and Culture: Essays on East and West* (Transaction Publishers, 1995).
284 Andrew Marrison, *Free Trade and Its Reception 1815-1960: Freedom and Trade*, volume I (Routledge, 1998).
285 Porter McKeever, *Adlai Stevenson: His Life and Legacy* (Quill, 1991).
286 Edmund Burke, *The Works of the Right Honourable Edmund Burke*, volume 4 (F. & C. Rivington, 1803).
287 Edmund Burke, *The Works of the Right Honourable Edmund Burke*, volume 8 (F. & C. Rivington, 1803).
288 Ibid.
289 Edmund Burke, *The Works of the Right Honourable Edmund Burke*, volume 5 (F. & C. Rivington, 1803).
290 Fisher Ames, Letter of October 26, 1803, in Russell Kirk, *The Conservative Mind: From Burke to Eliot* (Washington D.C.: Regnery Publishing, Inc., 2001), 483.
291 James D. Best, "A Republic, if You Can Keep It …," What Would The Founders Think? (blog), http://www.whatwouldthefoundersthink.com/a-republic-if-you-can-keep-it.
292 Edmund Burke, *A Letter from Mr. Burke to a Member of the National Assembly; In Answer to Some Objections to his Book on French Affairs*, 3rd Edition (printed in Paris and London; reprinted for J. Dodsley, 1791), http://metaphors.iath.virginia.edu/metaphors/20164.
293 John Locke, *The works of John Locke, Esq; in Three Volumes*, volume 2, book 2 (printed for John Churchill and Sam. Manship, 1714), https://babel.hathitrust.org/cgi/pt?id=nyp.33433006428431;view=1up;seq=12.

294 Ronald Reagan, "Public Papers of the Presidents of the United States: Ronald Reagan," remarks at the Annual Washington Conference of the American Legion, February 22, 1983, https://www.reaganlibrary.gov/research/speeches/22283b.

295 Ronald Reagan, "Public Papers of the Presidents of the United States: Ronald Reagan, 1985," remarks at a Flag Day ceremony in Baltimore, Maryland, June 14, 1985, https://www.reaganlibrary.gov/research/speeches/61485f.

296 Ronald Reagan, "Public Papers of the Presidents of the United States: Ronald Reagan, 1988," remarks and a question-and-answer session with the students and faculty at Moscow State University, May 31, 1988, https://www.reaganlibrary.gov/research/speeches/053188b.

297 Oswald Spengler, *The Decline of the West* [Der Untergang des Abendlandes] (Alfred A. Knopf, 1939).

298 Johann Wolfgang von Goethe, *Zahme Xenien: Den Vereinigten Staaten* (Stuttgart und Tübingen: Cotta, 1842).

299 Immanuel Kant, *Grundlegung zur Metaphysik der Sitten* [Groundwork of the metaphysics of morals] (1785).

300 Jeremy Bentham, *An Introduction to the Principles of Morals and Legislation* (Ontario, Canada: Batoche Books, 2000), http://www.efm.bris.ac.uk/het/bentham/morals.pdf.

301 Oswald Spengler, "Prussians and Englishmen," chapter III in *Prussianism and Socialism* (1920), https://archive.org/details/PrussianismAndSocialism.

302 Adam Smith, *An Inquiry into the Nature and Causes of the Wealth of Nations* (1776), http://files.libertyfund.org/files/220/0141-02_Bk.pdf.

303 Paul Lensch, *Drei Jahre Weltrevolution* (Berlin: S. Fischer, 1918).

304 Johann Wolfgang von Goethe, *Sprüche in Prosa, Maximen und Reflexionen* [Proverbs in prose; What, then, is your duty? What the day demands] (Leipzig: Insel, 1908), https://archive.org/details/sprcheinprosam00goetuoft.

305 Heinrich von Treitschke, *Deutsche Geschichte im neunzehnten Jahrhundert* [History of Germany in the Nineteenth Century] (Leipzig: Hirzel, 1894).

306 Houston Stewart Chamberlain, *The Foundations of the Nineteenth Century*, volumes 1 and 2 (New York: John Lane Co., 1912).

307 Ludwig von Mises, *Omnipotent Government: The Rise of the Total State and Total War* (Yale University Press, 1944).

308 Friedrich A. Hayek, *The Road to Serfdom* (George Routledge & Sons, 1944).

309 Ludwig von Mises, "Planned Chaos," an excerpt from *Socialism: An Economic and Sociological Analysis*, Ludwig von Mises Institute, 2009, https://liberty.me/wp-content/uploads/2014/12/Mises-PlannedChaos.pdf.

310 Russell Kirk, *Enemies of the Permanent Things: Observations of Abnormity in Literature and Politics* (Open Court, November 24, 1999).

311 William L. Shirer, *The Rise and Fall of the Third Reich* (London: Secker & Warburg, 1960).

312 Jonah Goldberg, *Liberal Fascism: The Secret History of the American left, From Mussolini to the Politics of Meaning* (Doubleday, January 8, 2008).

313 Erik von Kuehnelt-Leddihn, *Leftism: From de Sade and Marx to Hitler and Marcuse* (Arlington House, 1974), https://mises.org/system/tdf/Leftism%20From%20de%20Sade%20and%20Marx%20to%20Hitler%20and%20Marcuse_5.pdf?file=1&type=document.

314 Peter D. Stachura, *Gregor Strasser and the Rise of Nazism* (Routledge, 2014).

315 Richard Overy, *The Dictators: Hitler's Germany and Stalin's Russia* (Penguin Books, 2005).

316 E. J. Dionne Jr., "Two Politicians with Bluntness in Common," *Washington Post*, November 30, 2011.

317 Balint Vazsonyi, *America's Thirty Years War—Who is Winning?* (Regnery Publishing, Inc., 1998).

318 Ronald H. Bayor, *The Oxford Handbook of American Immigration and Ethnicity* (Oxford University Press, 2016).

319 Friedrich List, *The National System of Political Economy* [1841], J. Shield Nicholson, ed. Sampson S. Lloyd, trans., Fourth Book: The Politics, Chapter XXXIII (London: Longmans, Green, and Co., 1909).

320 Jeffrey Thompson Schnapp, Olivia E. Sears, and Maria G. Stampino, *A Primer of Italian Fascism* (University of Nebraska Press, 2000).

321 Benito Mussolini, "Capitalism and the Corporate State," address to the National Corporative Council on November 14, 1933 in Rome, from *Fascism: Doctrine and Institutions* (Ardita, 1935).

322 Benito Mussolini, "Capitalism and the Corporate State," speech, November 1933, https://archive.org/details/CapitalismAndTheCorporateState.

323 Karl Popper, *The Logic of Scientific Discovery* (Routledge Classics, 1959).

324 "Der Markt hat kein Herz," interview with Paul A. Samuelson, Portland Independent Media Center, *Der Spiegel* 38, 2005, http://www.spiegel.de/spiegel/print/d-41834764.html.

325 Stephan Eisel, "Between Ideologies: The Social Market Economy," study paper, Konrad Adenauer Stiftung, January 2012.

326 Viktor J. Vanberg, "The Freiburg School: Walter Eucken and Ordoliberalism," Freiburg discussion papers on constitutional economics. Walter Eucken Institut, Freiburg, 2004.

327 Röpke, Wilhelm: *A Humane Economy: The Social Framework of the Free Market* (South Bend, Indiana: Gateway Editions, 1960).

328 Bundesministerium der Justiz und für Verbraucherschutz, Basic Law for the Federal Republic of Germany, Article 14, trans. Christian Tomuschat, David P. Currie, and Donald P. Kommers in cooperation with the Language Service of the German Bundestag, https://www.gesetze-im-internet.de/englisch_gg/englisch_gg.html#p0090.

329 Alexander von Oettingen, *Die Moralstatistik und die christliche Sittenlehre. Versuch einer Socialethik auf empirischer Grundlage*, vol. 1 (Erlangen: Deichert, 1868).

330 Pope Leo XIII, "Rerum Novarum," encyclical of Pope Leo XIII on capital and labor, May 15, 1891.

331 Pope Pius XI, "Quadragessimo Anno," encyclical of Pope Pius XI on reconstruction of the social order, May 15, 1931.

332 Wilhelm Röpke, *Mass und Mitte* (Erlenbach-Zürich: Eugen Rentsch Verlag, 1950).

333 Oswald von Nell-Breuning, *Reorganization of Social Economy: The Social Encyclical Developed and Explained* (Bruce Publishing Company, 1936).

334 Friedrich Schneider, "Size and Development of the Shadow Economy of 31 European and 5 other OECD Countries from 2003 to 2015: Different Developments," January 20, 2015, http://www.econ.jku.at/members/Schneider/files/publications/2015/ShadEcEurope31.pdf.

335 Pope John Paul II, "Centesimus Annus," encyclical letter on the hundredth anniversary of "Rerum Novarum," May 1, 1991.

336 Ibid.

337 Wilhelm Röpke: "A Humane Economy," affirming, in opposition to the Eurocrats, that "'decentrism' is the essence of the spirit of Europe," p. 242-244.

338 Roger Scruton, "The Journey Home," essay in *Intercollegiate Review* 44. No. 1, Spring 2009.

339 Deutsche Sozialversicherung (German Social Insurance), http://www.deutsche-rentenversicherung.de/Allgemein/de/Inhalt/5_Services/03_broschueren_und_mehr/01_broschueren/01_national/unsere_sozialversicherung.pdf?_blob=publicationFile&v=31.

340 Václav Klaus, "Europe and America: Our Common Crisis," speech at Hillsdale College, Hillsdale, Michigan, October 10, 2013, https://www.klaus.cz/clanky/3456.

341 John McMillan, *Reinventing the Bazaar: A Natural History of Markets* (W. W. Norton & Company, 2002).

342 Wolfgang Münchau, *Das Ende der Sozialen Marktwirtschaft*, (Hanser, 2006).

343 Václav Klaus, *Renaissance: The Rebirth of Liberty in the Heart of Europe*, Cato Institute, 1997.

344 J. Robert Brown Jr., "Order from Disorder: The Development of the Russian Securities Markets," *University of Pennsylvania Journal of International Law* 15, no. 4, 1995.

345 Marc Stegherr, "The Social Market Economy in Eastern Europe—An Underestimated Option?," Konrad-Adenauer-Stiftung e.V., 2010, http://www.kas.de/upload/dokumente/2010/06/60_Years_SME/stegherr.pdf.

346 Christian L. Glossner, "60 Years of Social Market Economy: Formation, Development and Perspectives of a Peacemaking Formula," Konrad-Adenauer-Stiftung e.V., 2009, http://www.kas.de/wf/doc/kas_20040-544-2-30.pdf?100630164654.

347 Arthur Rich, *Business and Economic Ethics: The Ethics of Economic Systems* (Peeters, 2006).

348 Friedrich A. Hayek, *The Road to Serfdom: A Classic Warning Against the Dangers to Freedom Inherent in Social Planning* (George Routledge & Sons, 1944).

349 Friedrich A. Hayek, *The Constitution of Liberty* (University of Chicago Press, 1960).

350 Fritz Machlup, *Essays on Hayek* (Routledge Library Editions, 2010).

351 G. B. Richardson, *The Economics of Imperfect Knowledge—Collected Papers of G.B. Richardson* (Edward Elgar Publishing Limited, 1998).

352 Alfred C. Mierzejewski, *Ludwig Erhard: A Biography* (University of North Carolina Press, 2004).

353 Thomas Malthus, *An Essay on the Principle of Population* (Oxford University Press, 2008).

354 John E. King, *David Ricardo* (Palgrave Macmillan, 2013).

355 Hobbes, *Leviathan*.

356 Alan Tonelson, "Anti-Globalization and the US Middle Class," the *Globalist*, September 1, 2003, https://www.theglobalist.com/anti-globalization-and-the-u-s-middle-class/.

357 Evelyn Ellison Twitchell, "Will The Great Shakeout Take Its Toll?" *Barron's*, June 26, 2003, https://www.barrons.com/articles/SB105663319289188500.

358 Dimitra Defotis, "Will US Manufacturing Go to Zero?" *Barron's*, June 23, 2003, https://www.barrons.com/articles/SB105638264848535500.

359 Spencer J. Pack, "Paul Krugman and the Illusion of the Illusion of Conflict in International Trade," *Peace Economics, Peace Science and Public Policy* 2, no. 4, Walter de Gruyter GmbH, 1995, http://digitalcommons.conncoll.edu/cgi/viewcontent.cgi?article=1021&context=econfacpub.

360 Robert Z. Lawrence and Matthew J. Slaughter, "International Trade and American Wages in the 1980s: Giant Sucking Sound or Small Hiccup?" Brookings paper on economic activity, *Microeconomics* 2, 1993, https://www.brookings.edu/wp-content/uploads/1993/01/1993b_bpeamicro_lawrence.pdf.

361 Gary Burtless, Robert Z. Lawrence, Robert E. Litan, and Robert J. Shapiro, *Globaphobia—Confronting Fears About Open Trade* (Washington: Brookings Institution / Progressive Policy Institute / Twentieth Century Fund, 1998.)

362 John H. Jackson, *Sovereignty, the WTO, and Changing Fundamentals of International Law* (Cambridge University Press, 2006).

363 Spencer R. Weart, *Never at War: Why Democracies Will Not Fight One Another* (Yale University Press, 1998).

364 Aleksandr Solzhenitsyn, "A World Split Apart," commencement address delivered at Harvard University, June 8, 1978.

365 Peter Baker, "Pressure Rising as Obama Works to Rein In Russia," *New York Times*, March 2, 2014, https://www.nytimes.com/2014/03/03/world/europe/pressure-rising-as-obama-works-to-rein-in-russia.html.

366 Herman E. Daly, *Ecological Economics and Sustainable Development: Selected Essays* (Edward Elgar Publishing Limited, 2007).

367 Marx and Engels, *Manifesto*.

368 Zackary D. Barron, "General Electric: Is It Worth Being a Ubiquitous Conglomerate?" the *Cheat Sheet*, February 23, 2011.

369 The *Wall Street Journal*, "The Great Misallocators - What Barack Obama and General Electric Have in Common," Review & Outlook, Jan. 26, 2011.

370 Ralph Ancil, "The Legacy of Wilhelm Roepke: Essays in Political Economy," the *Imaginative Conservative*, 1998.

371 William Shakespeare, "The Merchant of Venice," in *The Oxford Shakespeare—The Complete Works*, 2nd edition, ed. Stanley Wells and Gary Taylor (Oxford University Press, 2005).

372 Robert B. Pippin, *The Persistence of Subjectivity: On the Kantian Aftermath* (Cambridge University Press, 2005).

373 William Golding, *Lord of the Flies* (Aoenian Press, 1975).

374 Frederick Gregory, *Scientific Materialism in Nineteenth Century Germany* (Springer Science & Business Media, 2012).

375 Hal Draper, "The Concept of the 'Lumpenproletariat' in Marx and Engels," *Institut de science économique appliquée* 15, Série S, 1972.

376 Quigley, *Tragedy and Hope*.

377 Mark D. Hirsch, *William C. Whitney: Modern Warwick*, Columbia University dissertation (New York: Dodd, Mead, 1948); Ron Chernow, *The House of Morgan: An American Banking Dynasty and the Rise of Modern Finance* (New York: Grove Press, 1990).

378 Upton Sinclair, *The Jungle* (Barnes & Noble, 1995); Frank Norris, *The Pit: A Story of Chicago* (New York: Penguin Books, 1994).

379 Quigley, *Tragedy and Hope*.

380 Charles Dickens, *A Christmas Carol*, unabridged edition (Dover Publications, 1991).

381 Ernest Hemingway, *A Farewell to Arms* (Scribner, 2012); John Steinbeck, *Cannery Row* (Penguin Classics, 2011); John Steinbeck, *Tortilla Flat* (Penguin Publishing Group, 1997).

382 George Orwell, *1984* (Penguin Publishing Group, 1950).

383 Jean-Jacques Rousseau, *Emile* (New York: Basic Books, 1979).

384 Don E. Marietta, Jr., *Introduction to Ancient Philosophy* (M. E. Sharpe, Inc., 1998).

385 John Kevin Coyle, *Manichaeism and Its Legacy* (Leiden, The Netherlands: Koninklijke Brill NV, 2009).

386 John Galsworthy, *The Forsyte Saga* (Start Publishing LLC, 2017).

387 Quigley, *Tragedy and Hope*.

388 James Bryant Conant, *General Education in a Free Society*, report of the Harvard Committee (Harvard University Press, 1945).

389 Nikolay V. Ustryalov, *From NEP to Soviet Socialism* (Shanghai, 1934), http://www.magister.msk.ru/library/philos/ustryalov/ustry035.htm.

390 Alexander Zinoviev, *Homo Sovieticus* (The Atlantic Monthly Press, 1985).

391 William H. Whyte, *The Organization Man* (Simon & Schuster, 1956).

392 Friedrich Nietzsche, *Thus Spake Zarathustra: A Book for All and None* [Also sprach Zarathustra: Ein Buch für Alle und Keinen], unabridged edition (Dover Publications, January 5, 1999).

393 C. S. Lewis, *The Problem of Pain* (1940); *The Screwtape Letters* (1942); *The Great Divorce* (1945); *Miracles* (1947); *Mere Christianity* (1952).

394 Alfred C. Kinsey, Wardell B. Pomeroy, and Clyde E. Martin, *Sexual Behavior in the Human Male* (Philadelphia: W. B. Saunders and Co., 1948); Alfred C. Kinsey et al., *Sexual Behavior in the Human Female* (Philadelphia: W. B. Saunders and Co., 1953).

395 James H. Jones, *Alfred Kinsey: A Public/Private Life* (New York: Norton, 1997).

396 Caroline Thomas Harnsberger, *Mark Twain at Your Fingertips: A Book of Quotations* (Dover Publications, Inc., 2009).

397 Ara Paul Barsam, *Reverence for Life: Albert Schweitzer's Great Contribution to Ethical Thought* (Oxford University Press, 2008).

398 Aleksandr Solzhenitsyn, "A World Split Apart," commencement address, Harvard University, June 8, 1978.

399 Fyodor Dostoyevsky, *The Brothers Karamazov*, trans. Richard Pevear and Larissa Volokhonsky (Farrar, Straus & Giroux, 2002).

400 David Goodhart, *The British Dream: Successes and Failures of Post-war Immigration* (Atlantic Books, 2013).
401 Pew Forum, "The Future of the Global Muslim Population," January 2011, http://www.pewforum.org/2011/01/27/future-of-the-global-muslim-population-regional-europe/.
402 Case of Hirsi Jamaa and Others v. Italy, 27765/09, Hudoc, Europ. CHR, https://hudoc.echr.coe.int/eng - {"itemid":["001-109231"]}.
403 Saul D. Alinsky, *Rules for Radicals: A Pragmatic Primer for Realistic Radicals* (New York: Random House, 1971).
404 Paul Collier, *Exodus: How Migration is Changing Our World*, 1st edition (Oxford University Press, September 1, 2013).
405 United Nations Office on Drugs and Crime (UNODC), *Global Study on Homicide 2013* (April 2014), https://www.unodc.org/documents/gsh/pdfs/2014_GLOBAL_HOMICIDE_BOOK_web.pdf.
406 The World Bank Group, "Population density (people per sq. km of land area)," Data Bank, 2015, https://data.worldbank.org/indicator/EN.POP.DNST.
407 Wilhelm Röpke, *A Humane Economy: The Social Framework of the Free Market* (South Bend, Indiana: Gateway Editions, 1960).
408 Alexis de Tocqueville, *Democracy in America: Historical-Critical Edition*, vol. IV, ed. Eduardo Nolla, trans. James T. Schleifer (Indianapolis: Liberty Fund, 2010).
409 George Orwell, *The Road to Wigan Pier* (New York: Harcourt Brace Jovanovich, 1958).
410 Brion McClanahan and Clyde N. Wilson, *Forgotten Conservatives in American History* (Pelican Publishing Company, Inc., 2012).
411 US Department of Health & Human Services, CDC / National Center for Health Statistics, "Births: Final Data for 2013," https://www.cdc.gov/nchs/data/nvsr64/nvsr64_01.pdf.
412 Donald Eugene Emerson, *Metternich and the Political Police: Security and Subversion in the Hapsburg Monarchy, 1815-1830* (Springer-Science+Business Media, B.V., 1968).
413 Dmitrij Mishin, "The Saqaliba Slaves in the Aghlabid State," Central European University, 2008. Retrieved May 14, 2015, from http://www.columbia.edu/itc/history/conant/mushin1998.pdf.
414 Robert C. Davis, *Christian Slaves, Muslim Masters: White Slavery in the Mediterranean, the Barbary Coast, and Italy, 1500-1800* (London: Palgrave Macmillan, December 2003).
415 Mikhail Kizilov, *Slave Trade in the Early Modern Crimea from the Perspective of Christian, Muslim, and Jewish Sources* (Leiden: Koninklijke Brill N.V., 2007).
416 Ronald Segal, *The Black Diaspora: Five Centuries of the Black Experience Outside Africa* (New York: Farrar, Straus and Giroux, 1995).
417 Paul E. Lovejoy, "The Impact of the Atlantic Slave Trade on Africa: A Review of the Literature" *Journal of African History* (1989).
418 Davis, *Christian Slaves*.
419 Roger Scruton, *Renewing and Rejecting* (Future Symphony Institute, 2015).
420 Columban Sattler, *A Critique of Contemporary Art* (Catholic Culture, 1952).

421 The *New York Times, The New York Times Guide to the Arts of the 20th Century*, volume 4, *1980-1999* (Fitzroy Dearborn Publishers, 2002).

422 Hannah Arendt, *The Human Condition* (University of Chicago Press, 1998).

423 Gerhard Kirchhoff, *Views of Berlin: From a Boston Symposium* (Springer Science+Business Media, LLC, 1989).

424 Stephen Hicks, "Why Art Became Ugly," *Navigator Magazine*, September 2004.

425 Robert Kraynak, "Conservative Critics of Modernity," *Intercollegiate Review 37*, no. 1, fall 2001.

426 Albert Einstein, "Autobiographical Notes," in Albert Einstein, *Philosopher-Scientist*, ed. Paul Arthur Schilpp (New York: Harper & Row, 1959), 33.

427 James Joyce, *A Portrait of the Artist as a Young Man* (Penguin Classics, 1st edition, March 25, 2003). Stephen Dedalus, the protagonist in the book, argues that the three universal qualities of beauty in the arts are wholeness, harmony, and radiance—his translation of Aquinas's integritas, consonantia, and claritas.

428 Leonard Bernstein, *The Infinite Variety of Music* (New York: Simon & Schuster, 1966), 198.

429 Alex Ross, "Why do we hate modern classical music?," the *Guardian*, November 28, 2010.

430 Richard L. Crocker, *A History of Musical Style* (Dover Publications, 1986).

431 Theodor W. Adorno, *Philosophy of Modern Music* (The Continuum International Publishing Group, 2004).

432 Léon Krier, "The Fear of Backwardness," Future Symphony Institute, edited transcription of the lecture delivered by Léon Krier at the inaugural Future of the Symphony Conference in September 2014.

433 Christopher Lasch, "The Corruption of Sports," the *New York Review of Books*, April 28, 1977.

434 Worldometers (data from two major sources: United Nations Population Division of the Department of Economic and Social Affairs and the US Census Bureau), "Population Growth Rate," http://www.worldometers.info/world-population/.

435 Ibid.

436 Jose M. Paulino, *The Fraud of the Fraud* (Facts Movement, 2008).

437 Sherif Khalifa, *Egypt's Lost Spring: Causes and Consequences* (ABC-CLIO, LLC, 2015).

438 William Clinton, "Speech on Diversity" commencement address delivered at Portland (Oregon) State University, The Social Contract Press, Summer 1998, http://www.thesocialcontract.com/artman2/publish/tsc0804/article_755.shtml.

439 Christine Simmons, "Bill Clinton: Be Proud US is More Diverse," NBC Miami, July 14, 2009.

440 Ron Unz, "Immigration, the Republicans, and the End of White America," the *American Conservative*, September 19, 2011.

441 Valery N. Soyfer, *Lysenko and the Tragedy of Soviet Science*, 1st edition (Rutgers University Press, June 1, 1994).

442 Will Kymlicka, *Multicultural Citizenship: A Liberal Theory of Minority Rights* (Oxford: Oxford University Press, 1995).

443 Strobe Talbott, "America Abroad," *Time*, June 24, 2001; Mark Juergensmeyer, *Thinking Globally: A Global Studies Reader* (University of California Press, 2014).

444 Jean Raspail and Norman R. Shapiro, *The Camp of the Saints* (Social Contract Press, 1994).

445 Edward Gibbon, *The History of the Decline and Fall of the Roman Empire*, reprint edition (Penguin Classics, 1996).

446 Adam Przeworski, and Fernando Limongi, *Modernization: Theories and Facts*, Cambridge University Press, 2010, https://www.cambridge.org/core/journals/world-politics/article/modernization-theories-and-facts/24CC3E289332FF2D39B5FACEAD75C408

447 Gordon Martel, *A Companion to Europe 1900-1945* (Blackwell Publishing Ltd, 2011).

448 Francis Fukuyama, *The End of History and the Last Man* (Free Press, 2006).

449 Goeran B. Johansson, *Vladimir Putin: A Geostrategic Russian Icon*, Lulu.com, 2013 (original title "Vladimir Putin: En geostrategisk rysk ikon," published in Sweden by BoD in 2012).

450 Doug Bandow, "Nationalism: Back with a Vengeance," *Intercollegiate Review*, September 22, 2014.

451 Enoch Powell. Speech delivered to a conservative association meeting in Birmingham on April 20, 1968, the *Telegraph*, November 6, 2007, http://www.telegraph.co.uk/comment/3643823/Enoch-Powells-Rivers-of-Blood-speech.html.

452 Ciarán J. Burke, "'Like the Roman': Enoch Powell and English Immigration Law," Amsterdam Law Forum, VU University Amsterdam 1, no. 1, 2008, http://amsterdamlawforum.org/article/view/50/65.

453 Lionel Trilling and Leon Wieseltier, *The Moral Obligation to Be Intelligent: Selected Essays* (Northwestern University Press, 2008).

454 Nigel West, and Oleg Czarev, *Triplex: Secrets from the Cambridge Spies* (Yale University Press, 2009).

455 Jean-Paul Sartre, *Being and Nothingness: An Essay on Phenomenological Ontology*, trans. Hazel E. Barnes (New York: Washington Square Press, 1984).

456 Tax Policy Center, "The Numbers: What Are the Federal Government's Sources of Revenue?" The Tax Policy Center's Briefing Book, http://www.taxpolicycenter.org/briefing-book/what-are-sources-revenue-federal-government; Lee Fang, "Where Have All the Lobbyists Gone?," the *Nation*, March 10–17, 2014, https://www.thenation.com/article/shadow-lobbying-complex/.

457 Emmanuel Saez, "Income and Wealth Inequality: Evidence and Policy Implications," Neubauer Collegium lecture, University of Chicago, October 2014, https://eml.berkeley.edu/~saez/lecture_saez_chicago14.pdf.

458 Office of the Coordinator for Counterterrorism, "Foreign Terrorist Organizations," US State Department, https://www.state.gov/j/ct/rls/other/des/123085.htm.

459 Philip Hughes, *A History of the Church* (Sheed & Ward, 1934–1947).

460 Second Continental Congress, United States, *Declaration of Independence*, manuscript, August 2, 1776, US National Archives and Records Administration, https://www.loc.gov/rr/program/bib/ourdocs/DeclarInd.html.

461 Eugene Newton Curtis, *Saint-Just, Colleague of Robespierre* (Octagon Books, June 1973).

462 Michael Maccoby, *Narcissistic Leaders: Who Succeeds and Who Fails* (Crown Publishing Group, April 2012).

463 G. K. Chesterton, "The Case for the Ephemeral," from *The Complete Works of G. K. Chesterton* (Delphi Classics, 2014).

464 Joseph Ratzinger, "Pro Eligendo Romano Pontifice," Homily of His Eminence Cardinal Joseph Ratzinger, dean of the College of Cardinals, Vatican Basilica, Monday April 18, 2005, http://www.vatican.va/gpII/documents/homily-pro-eligendo-pontifice_20050418_en.html.

465 Alexis de Tocqueville, *The Old Regime and the Revolution: The Controversial Bestselling Guide to the Origins of the French Revolution* (New York: Harriman House Ltd, 2013).

466 Eric Voegelin, *Modernity Without Restraint—The Political Religions, The New Science of Politics, and Science, Politics, and Gnosticism (Collected Works of Eric Voegelin, Volume 5)*, University of Missouri, November 1, 1999.

467 Planned Parenthood of Southeastern Pennsylvania v. Casey, 947 F.2d 682, 505 US 833 (Nos. 91–744, 91–902), https://www.law.cornell.edu/supremecourt/text/505/833.

468 Lothrop Stoddard, *The Revolt Against Civilization: The Menace of the Under Man* (New York: Charles Scribner's Sons, 1922).

469 René Descartes, *Principia Philosophiae* [Principles of Philosophy] (1644, repr. Dordrecht: Reidel, 1983).

470 John Broome, *Rationality Through Reasoning* (John Wiley & Sons, Aug 2013).

471 Michael Rosen, *On Voluntary Servitude: False Consciousness and the Theory of Ideology* (Harvard University Press, 1996).

472 Otfried Höffe, *Kant's Critique of Pure Reason: The Foundation of Modern Philosophy* (Springer Science & Business Media, January 2010).

473 Heinz Duchhardt, *Freiherr vom Stein: Preussens Reformer und seine Zeit* (C. H.Beck, 2010).

474 Charles Morris, *Twentieth Century Encyclopædia: A Library of Universal Knowledge*, volume 5 (Syndicate Publishing Company, 1912).

475 David McLellan and Karl Marx, *The thought of Karl Marx: An Introduction* (Harper & Row, 1972); Karl Marx, part I of *Critique of the Gotha Program* (1875).

476 Evgeny Bronislavovich Pashukanis, *The General Theory of Law & Marxism* (Transaction Publishers, 2001).

477 Vladimir I. Lenin, *On the Dictatorship of the Proletariat* (Moscow: Progress Publishers, 1976).

478 Edmund Burke, *The Works of the Right Honourable Edmund Burke*, volume 3 (F. & C. Rivington, 1803).

479 Gilbert Keith Chesterton, *The Collected Works of G. K. Chesterton*, Volume XXXIII, *The Illustrated London News 1923-1925* (Ignatius Press, 1990).

480 G. K. Chesterton, *Utopia of Usurers* (New York: Boni and Liveright, 1917); *The Outline of Sanity* (New York: Dodd, Mead, and Co., 1927); Hilaire Belloc, *The Servile State* (1912, repr., Indianapolis: Liberty Classics, 1980).

481 Gilbert Keith Chesterton, "*The Unfinished Temple*," part I, chapter 5 of *What's Wrong with the World*, https://www.gutenberg.org/files/1717/1717-h/1717-h.htm.

482 Pope Leo XIII, "Rerum Novarum."

483 Pope Pius XI, "Quadragessimo Anno"; Pope John Paul II, "Centesimus Annus."

484 Catechism of the Catholic Church, part three, "Life in Christ," section one, "Man's Vocation Life in the Spirit," chapter two, "The Human Communion," article 1, "The Person and Society," I. The Communal Character of the Human Vocation, #1883, CA 48 § 4; cf. Pope Pius XI, "Quadragesimo Anno" I, 184–86, http://www.vatican.va/archive/ccc_css/archive/catechism/p3s1c2a1.htm.

485 Manfred Porkert, *The Theoretical Foundations of Chinese Medicine: Systems of Correspondence (East Asian Science)* (MIT Press, July 1974).

486 Xinzhong Yao and Yanxia Zhao, *Chinese Religion: A Contextual Approach* (Continuum International Publishing Group, 2010).

487 Francis J. Bremer, *John Winthrop: America's Forgotten Founding Father* (Oxford University Press, 2003).

488 Peter Augustine Lawler and Robert Martin Schaefer, *American Political Rhetoric: Essential Speeches and Writings* (Rowman & Littlefield, 2015).

489 Lee Ward, *Modern Democracy and the Theological-Political Problem in Spinoza, Rousseau, and Jefferson* (Palgrave Macmillan, 2014).

490 Alexander Hamilton, James Madison, John Jay, and Michael A. Genovese, *The Federalist Papers: Alexander Hamilton, James Madison and John Jay* (Palgrave Macmillan, 2009).

491 Robert E. Shalhope, *The Roots of Democracy: American Thought and Culture, 1760-1800* (Rowman & Littlefield, 2004).

492 Thomas Jefferson, "Notes on the State of Virginia," query 13, 120–21, ed. William Peden (Chapel Hill: University of North Carolina Press, 1954).

493 John R. MacArthur, "Remember Nayira, Witness for Kuwait?" *New York Times*, January 6, 1992, http://sites.suffolk.edu/fs183a/files/2009/08/macarthur-remember-nayirah-the-new-york-times-op.doc.

494 Bruce K. Ward, *Dostoyevsky's Critique of the West: The Quest for the Earthly Paradise* (Wilfrid Laurier University Press, 1986).

495 Alexander Hamilton, *The Papers of Alexander Hamilton,* volume 9 (New York: Columbia University Press, 1962); Alexander Hamilton, "Federal Convention, 18 June 1787," Farrand 1, from *The Records of the Federal Convention of 1787*, revised edition (New Haven and London: Yale University Press, 1937) 282–93.

496 Thomas Aquinas, *De Regno* [On kingship], trans. Gerald B. Phelan (Divine Providence Press, 2014).

497 Edmund Burke, *The Portable Edmund Burke*, ed. Isaac Kramnick (Penguin, 1999); Plato, *Laws,* trans. Thomas L. Pangle (The University of Chicago Press, 1988); Marcus Tullius Cicero, *Republic* (G. & C. Carvill, 1829).

498 G. William Domhoff, *Wealth, Income, and Power* (University of California at Santa Cruz, Sociology Department, 2013).

499 H. van der Wee, The *Great Depression Revisited: Essays on the Economics of the Thirties* (Springer Netherlands, 1972).

500 Robert Athan Lynn, *Basic Economic Principles* (McGraw-Hill, 1965).

501 Lawrence H. Officer, *Two Centuries of Compensation for US Production Workers in Manufacturing* (Palgrave Macmillan, 2009).

502 Lars Bærentzen and John O. Iatrides, *Studies in the History of the Greek Civil War, 1945-1949* (Copenhagen: Museum Tusculanum Press, 1987).

503 Frederick Merk and Lois Bannister Merk, *Manifest Destiny and Mission in American History: A Reinterpretation* (Harvard University Press, 1963).

504 Manfred Nebelin, *Ludendorff: Diktator im Ersten Weltkrieg* (Siedler, 2010).

505 Fiona K. Tomaszewski, *A Great Russia: Russia and the Triple Entente, 1905-1914* (Greenwood Publishing Group, 2002).

506 Frank Alfred Golder, *Documents of Russian History 1914-1917* (Read Books, 2008).

507 Bernardino Fantini, Dolores Martin Moruno, and Javier Moscoso, *On Resentment: Past and Present* (Cambridge Scholars Publishing, 2013).

508 Mill, *On Liberty*.

509 René Girard, *The Scapegoat* (Johns Hopkins University Press, 1989).

510 Richard M. Weaver, *Reclaiming Liberal Education* (Intercollegiate Studies Institute, December 2014).

511 T. Y. Booth, "The Supreme Organ of the Mind's Self-Ordering Growth," Utah State University, DigitalCommons@USU, USU Faculty Honor Lectures, April 1, 1973, https://digitalcommons.usu.edu/cgi/viewcontent.cgi?referer=&httpsredir=1&article=1015&context=honor_lectures.

512 Worldometers (data from two major sources: United Nations Population Division of the Department of Economic and Social Affairs and the US Census Bureau), "Growth Rate as of 2015–2016," accessed on January 9, 2017, http://www.worldometers.info/world-population/.

513 Aleksandr Solzhenitsyn, *Rebuilding Russia: Reflections and Tentative Proposals*, 1st edition (Farrar, Straus and Giroux, September 1, 1991), 60–61.

514 Fred Miller, "Aristotle's Political Theory," in *The Stanford Encyclopedia of Philosophy*, 1998, substantive revision November 7, 2017, https://plato.stanford.edu/entries/aristotle-politics/

515 Daniel J. Mahoney, *Aleksandr Solzhenitsyn: The Ascent from Ideology* (Rowman & Littlefield Publishers, 2001).

516 Frank S. Meyer, ed., *"What Is Conservatism?—A New Edition of the Classic by 12 Leading Conservatives,"* 1st edition (Intercollegiate Studies Institute, September 15, 2015).

517 John Reed, *Ten Days that Shook the World*, 1st edition (New York: Boni & Liveright, 1919).

518 David D. Corey, "George Santayana on Liberalism and the Spiritual Life" *Modern Age: A Quarterly Review* 45, no. 4, 2003.

519 Roy Tseng: "Conservatism, Romanticism, and the Understanding of Modernity," in Corey Abel, ed. "The Meanings of Michael Oakeshott's Conservatism" (Andrews UK Limited, October 2015).

520 L. Edward Hicks, *Sometimes in the Wrong, but Never in Doubt: George S. Benson and the Education of the New Religious Right* (University of Tennessee Press, 1994).

521 Michael D. Reagan, *The New Federalism* (Oxford University Press, 1977).

522 Michael A. Cohen, *Live from the Campaign Trail: The Greatest Presidential Campaign Speeches of the Twentieth Century and How They Shaped Modern America* (Walker & Company, 2008).

523 Jeffrey Meyers, *Joseph Conrad: A Biography*, Letter to Robert Bontine Cunninghame Graham (Cooper Square Press, 2001), 166.